A
HISTORY OF
THE WAR
between Great Britain and
the United States of America
DURING THE YEARS
1812, 1813 & 1814

Lieutenant General

SIR JOHN COPE SHERBROOKE.

Maclear & Cᵒ Lith. Toronto.

A
HISTORY OF
THE WAR
between Great Britain and
the United States of America
DURING THE YEARS
1812, 1813 & 1814

G. AUCHINLECK

with an Introduction by

H.C.CAMPBELL

Chief Librarian, Toronto Public Libraries

ARMS AND ARMOUR PRESS
in association with
PENDRAGON HOUSE

Published in Great Britain by
Arms and Armour Press,
Lionel Leventhal Limited,
2-6 Hampstead High Street,
London N.W.3

*Published in Canada and the
United States of America by*
Pendragon House Limited,
71, Bathurst Street,
Toronto 135,
Ontario

and

Pendragon House Inc.,
899 Broadway Avenue,
Redwood City,
California 94063

85368 088 4

NOTE ON THIS EDITION
The publishers gratefully acknowledge the help of the
Canadian History and Manuscript Section of the Metropolitan Toronto
Central Library in making possible this facsimile
edition. The quality of some of the pages in the
original book fall short of the high standard of reproduction
normally expected in modern publications: they have of
necessity been reproduced to complete this facsimile edition.

Printed and bound in Great Britain

Introduction

This book has become a basic addition to our knowledge of the events that took place during the 'late' war between the United States and Great Britain.

Very little is known about the writer whose name appears on the title page. Gilbert Auchinleck has left no easily discernable trace of his whereabouts in Toronto or Upper Canada. It is presumed that he had arrived in Canada shortly before 1853 and that he left the country shortly after 1855. The *History of the War between Great Britain and the United States of America* was written to provide a documentary history of the war which would have popular appeal. Today it can be seen as a useful source of eye witness accounts, as well as the source of a good deal of valuable secondary information. The story of the death of General Brock, for example, by a contemporary eye witness is a useful account that has been preserved through the appearance of this work.

The War itself, which was of dubious purpose, had received uncertain support in the United States. Shortly after President Madison had announced the declaration of hostilities against the British in June 1812, delegates from several counties in New York State met in Albany to speak out against the war. They felt that it was of an arbitrary character and had plunged the nation into an unjust and unnecessary struggle. As true Americans they felt it their duty to pronounce it 'a most rash, unwise and inexpedient measure'. On 5th August 1812 the House of Assembly of Upper Canada had stated that war against Great Britain by the United States appeared to be an act of folly and desperation that had excited the greatest surprise amongst the inhabitants of Upper Canada as well as the United States.

In spite of such statements, the War was to run for three years, to be filled with stirring adventures, bloody massacres, and the looting and pillaging of cities and towns by a foreign army on a scale neither hitherto witnessed in North America nor since seen. While the British stormed Baltimore and Washington, Detroit and New Orleans, the Americans invaded and burned Newark and York in Upper Canada, and bombarded the Atlantic coast, sinking and capturing ships.

The January 1853 issue of the *Anglo-American Magazine,* the first issue of which had – in June 1852 – been eulogized by the Toronto *Weekly Globe* as a welcome addition to the literary works then appearing, contained the first part of a 'History of the War between Great Britain and the United States of America', which was to run for the succeeding 25 numbers of the magazine. Each article covered approximately 16 pages and was illustrated with a variety of maps and drawings. The last of the 26 parts appeared in January 1855, and in December of the same year the magazine ceased publication.

The editors of the *Anglo-American Magazine*—published in Toronto by Thomas Maclear—had stated in the first issue that its purpose was to support monarchial principles, and to fight against the invasion of Canadian life by the influence of the United States or, as they christened it, invasion from 'Dollardom'. This thread also ran through the 'History of the War' and, although its introduction declares that it is an impartial examination, it turns out to be strongly favourable to the British side in the War of 1812–14 – understandably so, as even in 1852, (nearly 40 years after the war's end) feelings still ran strong in Toronto, which had been a victim of the Siege of 1813.

In 1855, Maclear republished the series of 26 articles in book form, without substantial change. It is from this book that the present volume is reproduced.

Gilbert Auchinleck's serial account for the magazine had been written in popular terms and was infused with some of the feelings of those who had seen the war at first hand. The author did, however, take pains to incorporate a good deal of the printed and manuscript sources available to him, all of which were fully acknowledged and organized on a chronological basis. The reader is taken from the early naval, engagements through to the final blockade of the United States' forces on the Great Lakes, and to the terms of the Ghent Treaty which settled the conflict in 1815.

H. C. Campbell
Chief Librarian,
Toronto Public Libraries

A

HISTORY OF THE WAR

BETWEEN

GREAT BRITAIN

AND THE

UNITED STATES OF AMERICA.

DURING THE YEARS 1812, 1813, AND 1814.

BY G. AUCHINLECK.

"FERRUM QUO GRAVES PERSÆ MELIUS PERIRENT."

TORONTO:
PUBLISHED BY MACLEAR AND CO., 16 KING STREET EAST.
1855.

TO

THE VETERANS OF 1812,

AND

THEIR DESCENDANTS,

THIS HISTORY

IS

RESPECTFULLY INSCRIBED

BY

THE AUTHOR.

CONTENTS.

A

HISTORY OF THE WAR

OF 1812, 1813, AND 1814.

CHAPTER I.

From the Berlin Decree to the close of Mr. Jefferson's Second Administration—21st Nov. 1806....
3rd March, 1809.

CONTENTS OF CHAPTER I.—Preliminary Remarks.—The Berlin Decree.—Rigorous execution of the Decree.—
British Order in Council, 7th Jan., 1807.—The Order in Council though strictly just, not perhaps the best
course open to the British Government.—The United States raise no voice against Buonaparte's Decree.—The
affair of the Chesapeake, 22nd June, 1807.—Right of Search.—Some merchant vessels of the United States
under British convoy.—British Order in Council, 11th Nov., 1807, and Milan Decree.—Distressing predicament
of the United States.—Plea advanced by France, and repeated by the United States.—Liberality of the British
Government before the Berlin and Milan Decrees.—Embargo Act of United States Congress, 25th Dec., 1807.
—Mr. Rose's Mission.—Public feeling in the United States unfriendly to Great Britain.—Additions to the U. S.
troops voted by Congress, with supplies.—Effect of the Embargo.—Non-intercourse Act, 1st March, 1808.

Preliminary remarks. AN historical narrative which wilfully offends against truth, or distorts it to serve party purposes, is an imposture ; and one that is devoid of feeling is a skeleton : the one, unprincipled ; the other, spiritless and forbidding. We, in the discharge of our humble office, will strive to eschew both ; keeping clear, to the best of our ability, of the lively, but prejudiced and disingenuous political pamphlet, on the one hand; and of the dry and meagre outline of the mere annalist, on the other. We write, jealously observant of truth, so far as we can discern it ; but, at the same time, we are not ashamed to confess that we write with emotion,—as from the heart,—and a heart too, which, to its last pulsation, will remain true, we hope, to the glorious British constitution. To tell of gradual estrangement and final collision, where nature herself, no less than interest, urged to close alliance ; to recite the afflicting details of war, where peace, to either side, was in an eminent degree prosperity, happiness, and wisdom; —this is our undertaking, and the occasion of it we well may, as we do, most conscientiously deplore. In such a strife of brothers, victory, even on our own side, is not recorded without pain,—the pain which a man feels when he discovers that the errors of human conduct have given him an enemy where, in the ties of common language and race, Divine Providence, he might argue, had designed that he should find a friend. The late war with the United States, is not the only contest in the world's history, which warns us that the permanent peace of nations, is not to be implicitly trusted to the mere physical circumstance of their being " *gentes unius labii* ; " yet the consciousness that we have fought, even in self-defence, with those who speak the same tongue and claim the same lineage with ourselves, will be felt to damp the ardor of triumph in the moment of victory, and to cloud its remembrance afterwards. To this feeling we are not insensible; yet, at the same time, it would be affectation in us to disguise the satisfaction we derive from the conviction that the War of 1812 was attended with, at least, one good result. It shewed that Canada, as to her deliberate preference of British connection, and her devotion to the British throne, was sound to the heart's core. By declaimers in Congress—who refused to hear the voice of reason from the just and sensible minority in that Legislature —the loyalty of Canada was impeached,— spoken of as a thing of nought, to be corrupted by the first offered bribe, detached from its hollow adherence to British rule by the first military proclamation, or daunted by the first gleam of the Republican bayonets. Transported with the genuine spirit of democratic inebriation, these Congress declaimers were never able, for a moment, to entertain the idea of loyalty, superior to all the arts and enchantments of democratic seduction, growing up to any extent under the mild and equitable and parental rule of Great Britain:—of filial love incorruptible, inseparably weaving itself round the time-honored institutions of a monarchy popular, free, and engrossing the hearts of its subjects. Disaffection, in their judgment, prevailed far and wide in Canada : disaffection, according to their confident but not very statesman-like vaticinations, was to afford them an easy conquest. The mass of our population were to rush into their arms : very different was the spirit which our invaders, when they crossed the line, found amongst us,—they found a spirit, not fondly anticipating their embrace, but sternly prepared to grapple with them in mortal conflict; not pliant for proselytism, but nerved for battle ; and they found that spirit (we say it not in bitterness, but we say it with honest pride), they found that spirit too much for them. Their invasion was repelled; and with it were repelled likewise their groundless imputations against the fidelity and attachment of the Canadas to the parent state.

Thus had Canada the credit of contributing her quota to the brilliant evidence which history supplies—in patriotic struggles and sacrifices such as the peasant-warfare of the Tyrol, and the conflagration of Moscow—that monarchy may evoke in its behalf a spirit of chivalrous devotion, and implant a depth of religious faith, equal even in the strength and vigor and courage of the moment, to democratic fervor, and infinitely superior to it in sustained effort and patient endurance.

As to the gallant spirit and the bold deeds of our adversaries, sorry should we be—with our eyes open to their merit—to depreciate them as they, in their imperfect knowledge of us, depreciated our loyalty. Whilst we frankly bear testimony to their skill and their valor, on the lakes and sea more especially ; whilst we confess that the energy and the success with which they worked their diminutive navy

commanded the respect, and even awakened the fears of Great Britain ; we do not forget that their enterprise by land ended in discomfiture, and that Canada was greatly instrumental to that discomfiture. It was by the side of a mere handful of British troops that our Canadian militia achieved the expulsion of the invading foe ; and, what is more, we do not regard it as an extravagant supposition that, had the Mother Country been unable to send them a single soldier, but regular officers only, to discipline and lead them, their own true hearts and strong arms—so thoroughly was their spirit roused—would, unaided, have won the day. Be this as it may ; Canada did her part, and nobly too. Far be it from us to think of casting away or of unworthily hiding the laurels which she has gained ; though most sincere is our desire to interweave with them for aye the. olive branch of peace. Many of her native sons who took up arms in her defence, are still living amongst us, honored as they deserve to be ; and so long as they shall be spared to us (and may Almighty God spare them long), we trust that political vicissitude will not bring them the mortification of seeing the great principle of British supremacy for which they bore the musket and drew the sword, falling into anything like general disrepute. And when, in obedience to the common destiny of men, they shall have been removed, may their spirit long survive them, animating the bosoms of an equally gallant and loyal race in generations yet unborn, and cherished as a pearl of great price by an affectionate mother country, in " the adoption and steady prosecution of a good system of colonial government."

We proceed now to take up, in the order of time, the causes of the war.

The Berlin Decree, 21st November, 1806. Placed in a position of power, apparently impregnable, by his recent victory of Jena (14th Oct., 1806), which left the Prussian monarchy prostrate at his feet : but smarting still with the galling memory of Trafalgar, the French Emperor deemed the opportunity afforded by the complete humiliation of Prussia favorable for returning, as fiercely and as fully as he could, the terrible blow inflicted by Great Britain in the annihilation of his navy. Disabled from attempting his revenge where the ruinous catastrophe had befallen him,—on the sea, from which his fleets had been swept by the skill and courage and maritime genius of his island-foe; he put forth the full strength of his passionate nature and his prodigious energies to accomplish on the land, where his arms had been hitherto irresistable, those plans for the destruction of British commerce, which —as Mr. Alison has described them—were owing to "no momentary burst of anger or sudden fit of exultation; but the result of much thought and anxious deliberation." These plans were embodied in the famous manifesto which is known by the name of "the Berlin Decree," having been issued on the 21st November, 1806, from the subjugated court of the unfortunate King of Prussia.

The Berlin Decree is an ordinance familiar to all, mainly through the medium of Mr. Alison's widely circulated history; but in order to make our present publication as complete in itself as we can, we will introduce the eleven articles of the Decree,* as they appear in that admirable work to which, no less than to its own extraordinary pretensions, the Berlin Decree is likely to be indebted for immortality.

Rigorous execution of the Decree. It is undoubtedly correct to consider Buonaparte's anathema against British commerce as being, in one sense, extravagant and frantic, for it introduced a system of warfare unparalleled in the annals of civilized nations, and the menaces it expressed very far exceeded the ability of its author to carry them out. It is, however, quite contrary to fact, to represent it as a mere ebullition of rage, and a proceeding utterly Quixotic and impracticable. It said, in effect, to Great Britain,—" The French Emperor declares that you shall have no trade ;" and, although the extinction of British trade was greatly beyond his power, there is no question that he was able to inflict upon it, and did inflict upon it, serious damage. The Berlin Decree was far from being a vapoury threat. It did not, by any means, resolve itself into empty air, but was rigorously executed ; and the losses known to have been suffered under its operation were in many instances extremely severe. In the Hans Towns, for example, the proprietors of English

* See Decree at end of chapter.

merchandise were glad to be allowed to compound for their valuable goods with the large payment of £800,000. The Berlin Decree obviously, then, was not—as politicians in the United States would have it—a dead letter.

British Order in Council: 7th Jan. 1807. Pressed by this unusual and threatening emergency, the British Ministry were evidently forced to adopt defensive measures. Accordingly, on the 7th January, 1807, the Order in Council, which will be found in the note below,* was issued,—being the first of those

---

* BRITISH ORDER OF COUNCIL.
At the Court at the Queen's Palace, January 7, 1807.
PRESENT
The King's Most Excellent Majesty in Council.

" Whereas the French Government has issued certain orders, which, in violation of the usages of war, purport to prohibit the commerce of all neutral nations with his majestys dominions ; and also to prevent such nations from trading with any other country in any articles the growth, produce, or manufacture of his majesty's dominions ; and whereas the said Government has also taken upon itself to declare all his Majesty's dominions to be in a state of blockade, at a time when the fleets of France and her allies are themselves confined within their own ports, by the superior valour and discipline of the British navy ; and whereas such attempts on the part of the enemy would give to his majesty an unquestionable right of retaliation, and would warrant his majesty in enforcing the same prohibition of all commerce with France, which that power vainly hopes to effect against the commerce of his majesty's subjects, a prohibition which the superiority of his majesty's naval forces might enable him to support, by actually investing the ports and coasts of the enemy with numerous squadrons and cruisers, so as to make the entrance or approach thereto manifestly dangerous ; and whereas his majesty, though unwilling to follow the example of his enemies, by proceeding to an extremity so distressing to all nations not engaged in the war, and carrying on their accustomed trade, yet feels himself bound by a due regard to the just defence of the rights and interests of his people, not to suffer such measures to be taken by the enemy, without taking some steps on his part to restrain this violence, and to return upon them the evils of their own injustice ; his majesty is thereupon pleased, by and with the advice of his privy council, to order, and it is hereby ordered, that no vessel shall be permitted to trade from one port to another, both which ports shall belong to, or be in the possession of France or her allies, or shall be so far under their control as that British vessels may not freely trade thereat ; and the commanders of his majesty's ships of war and privateers shall be, and are hereby instructed to warn every neutral vessel coming from any such port, and destined to another such port, to discontinue her voyage, and not to proceed to

two memorable Orders which, unhappily, contributed to aggravate the prejudices previously entertained against Great Britain by a large majority of the inhabitants of the United States, and supplied the ostensible, but—as circumstances, to be hereafter noticed, entitle us to argue—not the real ground for the War of 1812. It is well to bear in mind that this Order was not the production of a Tory Ministry; but of a Whig Cabinet, headed by Mr. Fox,—a man who will hardly be charged with any bias towards the arbitrary exercise of the influence and power of the British Crown. It is still more important to remark that, when Mr. Munroe, the United States Minister in London, communicated the Order to his government, he did so with comments expressive of concurrence and satisfaction. " The spirit of this Order," observes Mr. Alison, "was to deprive the French, and all the nations subject to their control, which had embraced the Continental system, of the advantages of the coasting trade in neutral bottoms : and, considering the much more violent and extensive character of the Berlin Decree, there can be no doubt that it was a very mild and lenient measure of retaliation."

The Order in Council though strictly just, not perhaps the best course open to the British Government. The issuing of the Order in Council, though just and defensible, was, perhaps, an infelicitous proceeding. The British Government might have tried instead one or other of two expedients, either of which, as matters turned out, would probably have answered better than that which was adopted. If they would not have been justified in treating the Emperor's fulmination with contempt ; they might—on the one hand—have paused, at least, to ascertain whether neutral powers would acquiesce in his furious enactment.

any such port ; and any vessel, after being so warned, or any vessel coming from any such port, after a reasonable time shall have been afforded for receiving information of this his majesty's orders which shall be found proceeding to another such port, shall be captured and brought in, and, together with her cargo, shall be condemned as lawful prize. And his majesty's principal secretaries of state, the lords commissioners of the admiralty, and the judges of the high court of admiralty, and courts of vice admiralty, are to take the necessary measures herein as to them shall respectively appertain.

                  W. FAWKENER.

This would have put the United States to the test. Had they acquiesced, their French sympathies would have stood confessed, and the pretext of a grievance—not discovered until an interval of some months had elapsed*—in the Order in Council, would have been completely shut out ; had they remonstrated ; that would have been taking part with justice, and Buonaparte might have given way. Or— on the other hand—the boldest course of all might have been pursued, and the whole strength of our irresistible navy sent to lay waste the French coast from Ostend to Bayonne, which would soon have brought Buonaparte to reason, and made him consider deliverance from such a scourge—the severity of which he had good cause to know and dread —cheaply purchased by the abrogation of his Decree. The British Government, however, resolved on a middle course ; and published the " Order in Council," which, whilst it was insufficient to repel the violence of the enemy, assisted afterwards to bring on collision with a neutral power. Still—as we have said. and will repeat—the Order in Council, if it were comparatively feeble and inefficient, stands nevertheless, as to justice, on a position perfectly unassailable.

The United States raise no voice against Buonaparte's Decree. The alternative of observant inactivity might have been tried at the outset ; but certainly could not have been long maintained ; and must have given place soon to energetic resistance. Whilst the Berlin Decree was being unsparingly executed, the neutral nations of Denmark, Portugal, and the United States— by abstaining from remonstrance—received it, as we are warranted in considering, with at least silent acquiescence. The silence of the United States is the more to be deplored, because that country—remote from the theatre of war, and completely secure from any attempt of Buonaparte to shut up its ports— might have spoken out in frank and honest terms with safety. It is to be regretted, however, that the current of public feeling had already begun to set the other way. When tidings of the first aggression on the part of the French Emperor reached them, no voice

* The first notice of it is to be found in the President's angry message of October 27, 1807.

of public indignation was raised; no authoritative document emanated from the government indicating, even indirectly and in the mildest terms, their sense of the outrage which had been committed by the oppressor and trampler of Europe. Not a word even of expostulation was breathed by the great North American republic—independent as it was of Napoleon's iron-handed despotism, and deeply interested in British commerce; until the arm of French violence fell heavily on the ships of its own citizens; and, even then,—although confiscation followed on confiscation, and millions of francs accruing from the sequestration of American property enriched the French treasury,—the tone adopted by the President of the United States towards the French government, though petulant enough, was gentle and plaintive and supplicatory, compared with the strong and angry language frequently addressed from Washington to ministers and plenipotentiaries of Great Britain.

The affair of the Chesapeake, 22d June, 1807. Whilst dissatisfaction was thus too evidently increasing on the part of the Government and inhabitants of the United States, an inauspicious enforcement of the right of search, by H. M. ship Leopard, against the American frigate, Chesapeake, contributed still further to agitate the public mind.

As it was known that several British seamen had deserted from different ships and vessels of H. M. navy, whilst lying at anchor in Hampton Roads, Va., and that, after the whole body of the deserters had openly paraded the streets of Norfolk, under the American flag, and protected by the Magistrates of the town, four of them, at least, had been received on board the U. S. frigate Chesapeake, Admiral Berkeley, then in command of the North American station, issued instructions for their requisition and removal,—the deserters having been previously demanded, but without effect, by the British Consul at Norfolk, as well as by the Captains of the ships from which they had deserted. About one month after the issuing of these instructions,—afterwards disavowed by the British Government, as an improper extension of the right of search to armed vessels,—Captain Humphries, of H. M. ship Leopard, 74 guns, on the 22nd June, followed the Chesapeake

to sea, off Cape Henry, and in a few hours came up with her. On being hailed by the Leopard, and receiving an intimation that the Captain of that ship desired to send a message on board the Chesapeake, the commander of the latter vessel, Commodore Barron, hove to; whereupon a letter was sent by Captain Humphries, covering an order from Admiral Berkeley, in which the men known to have been received into the American frigate, and alleged to be deserters from the Melampus, were designated by name and claimed. Compliance with the order was refused by Commodore Barron, who replied by letter to Captain Humphries, denying that he had the men, intimating his unwillingness to permit the search, and adding that his crew could not be mustered for examination by any other officers than his own. Captain Humphries, on receiving this reply, fired a broadside into the Chesapeake, to which the latter vessel returned a few shots, in a confused manner; the Leopard then repeating her fire, the American frigate struck her colors. A boat was then put off from the Leopard; and the men were discovered and removed. In this affair the Chesapeake had three men killed and eighteen wounded, amongst the latter of whom was Commodore Barron; besides which the damage done to her hull and masts was considerable. The captured deserters were taken to Halifax and tried; and one of them, being found guilty of piracy and mutiny, was hanged. It is a circumstance worthy of notice,—as evincing on the part of the U. S. navy at the time a spirit gallant and resolute enough, though too irascible,—that Commodore Barron was censured and suspended soon afterwards by a naval court, for not preparing his vessel more fully for action, when there was sufficient time to do so, and thus incapacitating himself from making more than the slight and very ineffective resistance which he offered

This collision between the two vessels was specially unfortunate at such a juncture; but the hasty proceeding of the President of the United States served to make matters vastly worse. On the 2nd July following, he set forth precipitately an angry proclamation, in which, after reciting the transaction, in language calculated to inflame the public mind in a very high degree, he peremptorily " required all armed vessels bearing commissions under the Government of Great Britain, then within the harbors or waters of the United States, immediately and without any delay to depart from the same, and interdicted the entrance of all the said harbors and waters to the said armed vessels, and to all others bearing commissions under the authority of the British Government."* This, in its bearing, was a hostile measure; for, at the same time that this interdiction of British vessels was proclaimed, the fleets of France had free access to the ports from which their enemies were thus imperiously excluded. And this step was taken, before the President knew in what light the British Government would view the act of its officer. The proclamation was, to a considerable extent, a retaliation of the violence complained of, for, by the sudden stoppage of supplies, it caused no small inconvenience and privation to many of H. M. vessels at that time in the harbours of the United States; whilst at the very moment when this method of self-redress was put in execution, a demand for satisfaction and reparation had been despatched to the British Government. That Government, before any suit for satisfaction had reached it, disavowed the act on the ground that "the right of search, when applied to vessels of *war*, extended only to a *requisition*, but could not be carried into effect by actual force." Captain Humphries was recalled and Admiral Berkeley suffered the severe disgrace of being superseded. In this frank and honorable spirit did the British Government,—before one word of complaint or expostulation had been borne across the Atlantic,—promptly and spontaneously testify their concern at the mistaken proceedings of their officer, and their cordial desire to make reparation. It will be apparent, we think, to every one that their treatment of the affair exhibits, in a very strong light, the President's proclamation as a measure premature and unjustifiable.

Right of Search,†   In the American mer-

chant service, about the time of the war, there were between *thirty* and *fifty* thousand of our seamen employed, many of them deserters, and liable to be reclaimed as such; and, as to the rest, their impressment was just as lawful from a merchant vessel of the United States as an English vessel; for surely their having sought the service of the United States,—probably for the very purpose of evading that of their own country in the hour of peril—did not absolve them from their allegiance, nor render nugatory the established law of nations, that "every State has a right to the services of its subjects, and especially in time of war." On the trial of the men taken from the Chesapeake, it was shown that three of them were unquestionably American citizens, but that they had entered the service of Great Britain voluntarily: the fourth, who was convicted of piracy and mutiny, and for these crimes hanged, was a native British subject.

We can readily understand that American seamen, whether native or naturalized—language, garb, appearance, and other characteristic peculiarities being the same in both cases, —may have been now and then mistaken for British seamen, and, as such, impressed into the service of Great Britain; but there is positively no proof, either that the impressment was made with wilful disregard of ascertained origin, or that the mistake

---

pendence of the country was achieved. It was enough to protect them while they remain within our territories. Within these we had a right to make regulations. But we had no right to make regulations on the ocean, which would conflict with the pretensions of all civilized nations, who claimed the allegiance of their native born subjects either by the divine right of the governors, or by implied compact. He should not inquire whether these claims were compatible with the rights of man. It was sufficient that they grew out of the established usages and principles of civilized kingdoms, which we had no right to controvert out of our own limits. He would therefore not protect any other than natural American citizens on the ocean. We did not deny the right of England to search for property; she went further, and claimed the privilege of searching for her seamen. The similarity of our manners and language occasioned her to abuse the privilege in some cases by the impressment of our seamen. This was not an abuse of principle but of honor. And before we go to war with her for impressment he would make her this offer: he would agree not to let any man enter our merchant vessels but a natural citizen of these United States."

---

* American *Weekly Register*, 28th Sept., 1811.

† Extract from Mr. Sheffey's speech in the House of Representatives, on the bill to raise an additional military force—January, 3, 1812 :— "He protested against waging a war for the protection of any other than native born American seamen, or those who were citizens when the inde-

occurred so frequently as to involve anything like the wrong and the suffering depicted in a proclamation of the President of the United States,—in which document it is stated, that "under pretext of searching for her seamen, thousands of American citizens under the safeguard of public laws, and of their national flag, have been torn from their country and from everything dear to them." The question, as it happens, was discussed, soon after the declaration of war, by an "AMERICAN CITIZEN," a member of the local legislature in one of the New England States, and evidently a man of talent and education. From a vigorous and lucid pamphlet, published by this writer, in opposition to the intemperate policy of his government, we borrow the following extract bearing on the "right of search:"—

"The whole number of sailors pretended to have been impressed from our ships, for fifteen years past, was 6258, out of 70,000, and of which, all but 1500 have been restored. Of this remainder, at least one half are probably British seamen, and of the residue it is probable that at least another moiety *entered voluntarily*. The whole number of British seamen in their marine, *or public ships only*, is 150,000, and in their merchant ships, over whom they have a perfect control, 240,000. Is it probable, we ask, that for the sake of gaining 1500 seamen, they would hazard the peace of their country."*

What the United States should have done, is simply this:—they should have taken effectual steps to prevent the entrance into their service of British seamen, during the war with France. This would have put a stop at once to the grievance. Instead of doing this, the merchant service of the United States offered them double the pay given to a seaman in a British ship of war, besides not disdaining to use other more direct allurements; so that, whilst Great Britain was striving to rally round her standard all the stout hearts and stalwart arms she could bring together *of her own sons* in a struggle for existence, the States of Maryland, North Carolina, South Carolina, and Georgia were employing—for lucre's sake—three foreign seamen to one native American.

Some merchant vessels of the U. S. under British convoy.   It is a curious and significant circumstance that,

whilst this exciting topic was in debate, instances were occurring of merchant vessels of the United States placing themselves under British convoy. Cases such as these, however, were no doubt rare; for, to say nothing of the hostile interpretation likely to be put upon them by France had they been numerous, there was, we fear, but little inclination on the part of citizens of the United States, to seek protection under the guns of a British ship of war. Still, few as they were, they may serve to suggest the reflection, how readily the national feeling on both sides might have been conciliated into firm and mutually profitable friendship, had the United States been able to perceive at once—as Washington had striven that they should perceive—that their interest, no less than their origin, bound them to Great Britain; and had they sincerely and strenuously labored, under that persuasion, to suppress their strangely misplaced and deeply prejudicial sympathy with France; a country, at that time the very antithesis of a popular State; ambitious, merciless, despotizing; seeking to enslave the rest of Europe, and herself virtually enslaved by as thoroughpaced a tyrant as the world has ever seen.

British Order in Council, 11th Nov., 1807, and Milan Decree.   The Treaty of Tilsit (7th July, 1807) having secured the adhesion of Russia to the Continental league, and established Buonaparte in his coveted position of supreme arbiter, of the destinies of the Continent, it became imperative on the British Government to enact a more effectual measure than the Order of the 7th January, which not only was, in its actual bearing, comparatively lenient and mild; but had been very generally evaded, and afforded to Great Britain little or no protection against the extreme and unscrupulous proceedings of her adversary. In this condition of affairs, on the 11th November, 1807, the Order which we give below was issued* To this Order

* The Government on this occasion were well supported by Parliament—in the Upper House by a majority of 127 to 61; in the Lower by 214 to 94.—Alison, vol. 3, p. 559.

ORDER IN COUNCIL

At the Court at the Queen's Palace, the 11th of November, 1807, present, the king's most Excellent Majesty in Council.

"Whereas certain orders, establishing an un-

* Mr. Madison's War, by a New England Citizen.

Buonaparte, on the 17th December of the same year, replied by his Milan Decree, which put the finishing stroke to his excommunication of Great Britain.*

---

precedented system of warfare against this kingdom, and aimed especially at the destruction of its commerce and resources, were some time since issued by the government of France, by which " the British Islands were declared to be in a state of blockade," thereby subjecting to capture and condemnation all vessels, with their cargoes, which should continue to trade with his majesty's dominions :

And whereas by the same order, " all trading in English merchandize is prohibited, and every article of merchandize belonging to England, or coming from her colonies, or of her manufacture, is declared lawful prize :"

And whereas the nations in alliance with France and under her controul, were required to give, and have given, and do give, effect to such orders :

And whereas his majesty's order of the 7th of January last has not answered the desired purpose, either of compelling the enemy to recall those orders, or of inducing neutral nations to interpose, with effect, to obtain their revocation ; but, on the contrary, the same have been recently enforced with increased rigour :

And whereas his majesty, under these circumstances, finds himself compelled to take further measures for asserting and vindicating his just rights, and for supporting that maritime power which the exertions and valour of his people have, under the blessing of Providence, enabled him to establish and maintain ; and the maintenance of which is not more essential to the safety and prosperity of his majesty's dominions, than it is to the protection of such states as still retain their independence, and to the general intercourse and happiness of mankind :

His majesty is therefore pleased, by and with the advice of his privy council, to order, and it is hereby ordered, that all the ports and places of France and her allies. or of any other country at war with his majesty, and all other ports or places in Europe, from, which. although not at war with his majesty, the British flag is excluded, and all ports or places in the colonies belonging to his majesty's enemies, shall, from henceforth be subject to the same restrictions in point of trade and navigation, with the exceptions hereinafter-mentioned, as if the same were actually blockaded by his majesty's naval forces, in the most strict and rigorous manner:—And it is hereby further ordered and declared, that all trade in articles which are of the produce or manufacture of the said countries or colonies, shall be deemed and considered to be unlawful ; and that every vessel trading from or to the said countries or colonies, together with all goods and merchandize on board, and all articles of the produce or manufacture of the said countries or colonies, shall be captured, and condemned as prize to the captors.

But although his majesty would be fully justified, by the circumstances and considerations above recited, in establishing such system of restrictions wish respect to all the countries and colonies of his enemies, without exception or qualification ; yet his majesty, being nevertheless desirous not to subject neutrals to any greater inconvenience than is absolutely inseparable from the carrying into effect his majesty's just determination to counteract the designs of his enemies, and to retort upon his enemies themselves the consequences of their own violence and injustice ; and being yet willing to hope that it may be possible (consistently with that object) still to allow to neutrals the opportunity of furnishing themselves with colonial produce for their own consumption and supply ; and even to leave open, for the present, such trade with his majesty's enemies as shall be carried on directly with the ports of his majesty's dominions, or of his allies, in the manner hereinafter mentioned :

His majesty is therefore pleased further to order that nothing herein contained shall extend to subject to capture or condemnation any vessel, or the cargo of any vessel, belonging to any country not declared by this order to be subjected to the restrictions incident to a state of blockade, which shall have cleared out with such cargo from some port or place of the country to which she belongs, either in Europe or America, or from some free port in his majesty's colonies, under circumstances in which such free trade from such free ports is permitted, direct to some port or place in the colonies of his majesty's enemies, or from those colonies direct to the country to which such vessel belongs, or to some free port in his majesty's colonies, in such cases, and with such articles, as it may be lawful to import into such free port ;—nor to any vessel, or the cargo of any vessel, belonging to any country not at war with his majesty, which shall have cleared out under such regulations as his majesty may think fit to prescribe, and shall be proceeding direct from some port or place in this kingdom, or from Gibraltar or Malta, or from any port belonging to his majesty's allies, to the port specified in her clearance :—nor to any vessel or the cargo of any vessel, belonging to any country not at war with his majesty, which shall be coming from any port or place in Europe which is declared by this order to be subject to the restrictions incident to a state of blockade, destined to some port or place in Europe belonging to his majesty, and which shall be on her voyage direct thereto ; but these execeptions are not to be understood as exempting from capture or confiscation any vessel or goods which shall be liable thereto in respect of having entered or departed from any port or place actually blockaded by his majesty's squadrons or ships of war, or for being enemies' property, or for any other cause. than the contravention of this present order.

And the commanders of his majesty's ships of war and privateers, and other vessels acting under his majesty's commission, shall be, and are hereby instructed to warn every vessel which shall have

---

* IMPERIAL DECREE.

Rejoinder to his Britannic Majesty's Order, in Council, Nov. 11, 1807.—At our Royal Palace, at Milan. Dec. 17, 1807.

Napoleon, emperor of the French, king of Italy, and protector of the Rhenish Confederation :—

Observing the measures adopted by the British

Distressing predicament of the United States. We can sympathise in the distress to which the United States, the only neutral power, were now exposed. The ocean, whose waves had borne for years vast wealth to their shores, whilst it was strewn with the wreck of Europ-

commenced her voyage prior to any notice of this order, and shall be destined to any port of France, or of her allies, or of any other country at war with his majesty, or to any port or place from which the British flag as aforesaid is excluded, or to any colony belonging to his majesty's enemies, and which shall not have cleared out as is here-before allowed, to discontinue her voyage, and to proceed to some port or place in this kingdom, or to Gibraltar or Malta ; and any vessel, which after having been so warned, or after a reasonable time shall have been afforded for the arrival of information of this his majesty's order at any port or place from which she sailed, or which, after having notice of this order, shall be found in the prosecution of any voyage, contrary to the restrictions contained in this order, shall be captured, and together with her cargo, condemned as lawful prize to the captors.

And whereas countries, not engaged in the war, have acquiesced in these orders of France, prohibiting all trade in any articles the produce or manufacture of his majesty's dominions ; and the merchants of those countries have given countenance and effect to those prohibitions, by accepting from persons styling themselves commercial agents of the enemy, resident at neutral ports, certain documents, termed, " certificates of origin," being certificates obtained at the ports of shipment, declaring that the articles of the cargo are not of the produce or manufacture of his majesty's dominions, or to that effect :

And whereas this expedient has been directed by France, and submitted to by such merchants, as part of the new system of warfare directed against the trade of this kingdom, and as the most effectual instrument of accomplishing the same, and it is therefore essentially necessary to resist it :

His majesty is therefore pleased, by and with the advice of his privy council, to order, and it is hereby ordered that if any vessel, after reasonable time shall have been afforded for receiving notice of this his majesty's order at the port or place from which such vessel cleared out, shall be found carrying any such certificate or document as aforesaid, or any document referring to, or authenticating the same, such vessel shall be adjudged lawful prize to the captor, together with the goods laden therein, belonging to the person or persons by whom, or on whose behalf, any such document was put on board.

And the right honorable the lords commissioners, &c. are to take the necessary measures herein as to them shall respectively appertain.

W. FAWKENER.

Government, on the 11th of November last, by which vessels belonging to neutral, friendly, or even powers the allies of England, are made liable not only to be searched by English cruisers, but to be compulsorily detained in England, and to have a tax laid on them of so much per cent. on the cargo, to be regulated by the British legislature :

Observing that by these acts the British government *denationalizes* ships of every nation in Europe; that it is not competent for any government to detract from its own independence and rights, all the sovereigns of Europe having in trust the sovereignties and independence of their flag ; that if, by an unpardonable weakness, and which, in the eyes of posterity, would be an indelible stain, such a tyranny was allowed to be established into principles, and consecrated by usage, the English would avail themselves of it to assert it as a right; as they have availed themselves of the intolerance of governments to establish the infamous principle, that the flag of a nation does not cover goods, and to give to their right of blockade an arbitrary extension, and which infringes on the sovereignty of every state ; we have decreed, and do decree, as follows :

" ART. I. Every ship, to whatever nation it may belong, that shall have submitted to be searched by an English ship, or to a voyage to England, or shall have paid any tax whatsoever to the English government, is thereby, and for that alone, declared to be *denationalized*, to have forfeited the protection of its king, and to have become English property.

" II. Whether the ships thus *denationalized* by the arbitrary measures of the English government, enter into our ports, or those of our allies, or whether they fall into the hands of our ships of war, or of our privateers, they are declared to be good and lawful prizes.

" III. The British islands are declared to be in a state of blockade, both by land and sea. Every ship, of whatever nation, or whatsoever the nature of its cargo may be, that sails from the ports of England, of those of the English colonies, and of the countries occupied by English troops, is good and lawful prize, as contrary to the present decree; and may be captured by our ships of war or our privateers, and adjudged to the captor.

" IV. These measures, which are resorted to only in just retaliation of the barbarous system adopted by England, which assimilates its legislation to that of Algiers, shall cease to have any effect with respect to all nations who shall have the firmness to compel the English government to respect their flag. They shall continue to be rigorously in force as long as that government does not return to the principle of the law of nations, which regulates the relations of civilized states in a state of war. The provisions of the present decree shall be abrogated and null ; in fact as soon as the English abide again by the principles of the law of nations, which are also the principles of justice and of honour.

" All our ministers are charged with the execution of the present decree, which shall be inserted in the bulletin of the laws.

(Signed) " NAPOLEON.

" By order of the Emperor, the Secretary of State.

(Signed) " H. B. MARET."

ean navies, had ceased to be to them a safe highway to commercial affluence. Their ships, liable to be captured by one or other of the belligerents, could only at great risk carry on their commercial intercourse with either. But it must be remembered that the United States, not having interfered when their interposition might possibly have checked Bonaparte, and perhaps recalled him within the limits of international law, made no effort to arrest and remove at once the original cause of their subsequent misfortunes; so that it is impossible to say how far they had themselves to blame for those misfortunes. That the attitude which they might have assumed, had they chosen, was likely to have some influence on Bonaparte, can hardly be doubted. He thought it worth his while to manœuvre in various ways—at one time pillaging, at another flattering them—in the hope of either driving or coaxing them into a war with Great Britain. Their policy, therefore, was not a matter of indifference to him; so that we may not venture to say with what effect remonstrance from that quarter might not have been attended. As to the eminently characteristic avowal of attachment,—"His Majesty loves the Americans,"—which, after a while, he thought might answer his purpose better than spoliation, the people of the United States have no doubt made up their minds by this time as to what interpretation they ought to put on that declaration—as to whether it be genuine regard or shameless effrontery. His protestation of love may be accepted for what it was worth; but the fear of compelling the United States to throw themselves eventually into the arms of Great Britain might have-induced him to treat a remonstrance from that republic with at least some respect.

Plea advanced by France and repeated by the United States. It was pleaded by France, and the plea was echoed by the United States, that the British blockade of May, 1806, as constituting the first aggression, justified the Berlin decree; but the two cases were, in principle, widely different. The blockade declared by Great Britain embraced no greater extent of coast than the immense strength of the British Navy supplied the means of adequately watching; and special pains were taken beforehand, by communication with the Admiralty, to ascer-

tain whether the coast from the Elbe to Brest could be guarded, and the blockade effectually enforced. The French Emperor, on the other hand, proclaimed the blockade of the entire coast of the British Isles,—no half-dozen ports of which could he have actually invested with his navy, shattered and almost extinguished as that had been, by the gigantic victories of Great Britain at sea. Thus to attempt, by means of a wrathful manifesto what the law of nations recognizes as the function only of a sufficient naval force—which naval force he had not—was an outrage on international law, not surprising in the man to whom the rights of nations were a fiction, and treaties meditated treachery and violence in masquerade; but it is incongruous and startling that such an outbreak of lawless and anti-commercial rage—such a mercantile excommunication of England, as we may call it,—should have ever found apologists on this side of the Atlantic, amongst a people, like the inhabitants of the United States, animated by an ardent spirit of commercial enterprise, and claiming, even in advance of Great Britain herself, the possession of free institutions.*

Liberality of the British Government before the Berlin and Milan Decrees. The perfect honesty of the plea of absolute necessity, advanced by the British Government, agrees with their liberal and even munificent treatment of the United States, in regard to the commerce of that country, as a neutral State, prior to the Berlin Manifesto. In 1803, when hostilities with France were renewed, the commanders of His Britannic Majesty's ships of war and privateers, were instructed "not to seize any neutral vessels which should be found carrying on trade directly between the colonies of the enemy and the neutral country; provided

---

* Nine-tenths of the revenue of the United States was at this time derived from commerce; yet their bias lay with a man who was a downright hater of commerce; who evinced a sort of fanatical malice against commerce. His policy was to make France independent of commerce (a scheme wilder than the Crusades!); and in his efforts to realize this, he literally attempted to force nature herself into subservience to him:—"Enacting penal statutes to force the cultivator of the soil to employ his land in endeavouring to raise certain products in a climate ungenial to their growth: to plant beet instead of corn; and cotton and tobacco and indigo, where nature never intended them to grow."

that such neutral vessel should not be supplying, nor should, on the outer voyage, have supplied the enemy with any articles contraband of war, and should not be trading with any blockaded, (that is, *actually* blockaded,) ports." The generosity, and the value of this indulgence,—for indulgence it literally was, are to be appreciated from the fact, that it had been a law generally understood and acted upon for a century, at least, that " a neutral has no right to carry on a trade with the colonies of one of two, or more, belligerent powers in time of war." Great Britain, however, during her contest with revolutionary France, relaxed this rule in 1794, and still further in 1798, when permission was granted to neutrals to carry the produce of the French West Indian colonies, either to a British port, or to any one of their own ports. This relaxation had the effect of throwing the French carrying trade almost wholly into the hands of the United States, and from it the commerce of that country prospered amazingly,—great wealth being realised by American merchants, who were able to make a lucrative profit out of British munificence, and, as it was shown, to the detriment of British commerce. Even so late as 1806, when, to arrest the farther introduction of supplies into France from the United States, the blockade from the Elbe to Brest was declared, the interests of the American Republic were specially consulted, in an explanation communicated by Mr. Fox to Mr. Monroe, that "such blockade should not extend to prevent neutral ships and vessels laden with goods, not being the property of His Majesty's enemies, and not being contraband of war, from approaching the said coasts, and entering into and sailing from the said rivers and ports." We dwell complacently upon these concessions; we regard them with national pride; for they shew conclusively that the disposition of our Government towards the American Union was the very reverse of arbitrary, selfish, or oppressive. Now, if subsequently to the publication of the French decrees, Great Britain was compelled to adopt a different course, who, with a knowledge of her previous liberality, will suspect that any desire to impair the trade of the United States, entered into her motives, or that the step was other than, as the British Ministry represented it to be, an equitable " retorting of his own violence on its author's head," and as such, a measure of just retaliation.

Embargo Act of U. S. Congress, 25th Dec. 1807. Despatches from the United States Minister at Paris—General Armstrong—were received at Washington on the 16th December, 1807, from which it appeared plainly that the confiscation of the American ship *Horizon** was merely the first enforcement of a *rule* which the French government intended to pursue; and that, consequently, it was no part of the Emperor's policy to exempt the United States from the operation of the Berlin Decree. Intelligence was brought at the same time, through London papers of the 12th November, to the effect " that orders in council were about to be issued, declaring France and the countries under her control in a state of blockade, a reference no doubt to the orders dated the day before, but which had not then been published, and were not until a week afterward."† At this period it was that the first step in the way of commercial restriction was taken by the United States. An embargo was laid on all the shipping in their ports, the measure being recommended to Congress, on the mere responsibility of the executive,‡ and passed with the utmost precipitation. " It prohibited the departure, unless by special direction of the President, of any vessel from any port of the United States bound to any foreign country, except foreign armed vessels possessing public commissions, and foreign merchant ships in ballast, or with such cargo as they might have on board when notified of the act. All registered or sea-letter vessels—the latter denomination including fo-

---

* This was the first confiscation of American property under the Berlin decree, and occurred on the 10th November, 1807. The Horizon had accidentally been stranded on the French coast; and the ground of confiscation was that the cargo consisted of merchandise of British origin.—*Hildreth.*

† *Hildreth.*

‡ On this occasion John Quincy Adams, who had recently abandoned the federal party and, unhappily, had lent the aid of his remarkable powers to the democrats, supported the government with vehement zeal. " The President, he urged, has recommended this measure on his high responsibility. I would not consider. I would not deliberate, I would act. Doubtless the President possesses such further information as will justify the measure."

reign-built vessels owned by Americans—
which, during this restriction from foreign
voyages, might engage in the coasting trade,
were to give bonds, in double the value of the
cargo, to re-land the same within the United
States. "Thus"—Mr. Hildreth forcibly remarks
in regard to the legislative proceedings of his
own countrymen on this occasion—" on the
mere recommendation of the executive, almost
without debate, with closed doors, without
any previous intimation to the public, or opportunity for advice from those most able to
give it, was forced through, by night sessions,
and the overbearing determination of a majority at once pliable and obstinate, an act
striking a deadly blow at the national industry, and at the means of livelihood of great
numbers ; the real nature and inevitable operation of which seem to have been equally
misapprehended by the cabinet which recommended, and by the supple majority which
conceded it." The embargo thus imposed was
afterwards made still more stringent by supplementary measures denouncing severe penalties, and excluding foreign vessels from the
coasting trade altogether.

Mr. Rose's Mission.   On the 25th December Mr. Rose, envoy extraordinary of Great
Britain, arrived in the United States, with instructions from our government to offer repa-

* " In whatever spirit that instrument was issued, it is sufficiently obvious, that it has been
productive of considerable prejudice to his majesty's interests, as considered to his military and
other servants in the United States, to the honor
of his flag, and to the privileges of his ministers
accredited to the American government. From
the operation of this proclamation have unavoidably resulted effects of retaliation, and self-assumed
redress, which might be held to affect materially
the question of the reparation due to the United
States, especially inasmuch as its execution has
been persevered in after the knowledge of his
Majesty's early, unequivocal, and unsolicited disavowal of the unauthorized act of Admiral Berkeley—his disclaimer of the pretensions exhibited
by that officer to search the national ships of a
friendly power for deserters, and the assurances
of prompt and effectual reparation, all communicated without loss of time, to the minister of the
United States in London, so as not to leave a
doubt as to his Majesty's just and amicable intentions. But his Majesty, making every allowance
for the irritation which was excited, and the mis-
apprehensions which existed, has authorized me
to proceed in the negotiation upon the sole discontinuance of measures of so inimical a tendency."—Mr. Rose to Mr. Madison.

ration for the affair of the Chesapeake. There
was an indispensable preliminary, however,
that the President's proclamation* of the 2d
July should be previously withdrawn. Before
this should have been done, he stated that he
had no authority to enter on any negotiation,
and even declined to specify the reparation
which he was empowered to offer. As the
President declined recalling the proclamation
Mr. Rose returned home, and the settlement
of the difficulty was postponed.

Public feeling in   Throughout the irrita-
the States unfriendly
to Great Britain.   ing discussion which ensued, the disposition of the American Republic is to be taken into account, as evidently
operating to protract and embarrass negotiation.—That disposition was unquestionably
the reverse of amicable towards Great Britain.
Whilst the effort was made to remain strictly
neutral, the heart of the nation was not in its
profession of neutrality. Ever since the accession of the Democratic party to power under
Mr. Jefferson—who was inaugurated into his
first Presidency on the 4th March, 1801—the
war spirit against Great Britain was steadily
growing up, with some few exceptions, amongst
the inhabitants of the United States. Under
the administration of that rigid republican and
philosopher of the Rousseau school, the idea
of quarrelling with Great Britain seems to have
become, by degrees, palatable rather than
otherwise to the party who raised him to the
chief Magistracy, and these formed a large
majority. We do not forget, however, that
in the very respectable minority, chiefly in the
Eastern States, who participated not in the
defiant spirit so widely cherished and exhibited towards Great Britain, were to be found
that sterling part of the nation who, in point
of fortune, talent, education, moral and religious principles, have always compared most
favorably with the rest of their countrymen.

It is evident that the well known prevalence
of a predilection for France and antipathy
towards her adversary, must have materially
influenced, in a manner injurious on either
side to just and reasonable and advantageous
policy, the controversy which preceded the
declaration of war.

Whilst Great Britain had reason to be extremely cautious in negotiation, for, as we shall
see hereafter, France had laid a deep plot

against her through the United States!—the latter country, on the other hand, would jealously, but most unworthily, guard against conceding, except for its own obvious benefit, and not always even then, anything likely to strengthen the hands of the British Government in the terrible contest it was waging with that colossal despotism which threatened to bear down and obliterate, beneath its withering tread, the last vestige of free institutions in Europe.*

Additions to the U. S. troops voted by Congress, with supplies. On the application of the President at this time, an addition was made to the army of 6,000 men, to be enlisted for five years unless sooner discharged. Authority was likewise given to him to raise 100,000 troops; whilst a subsidy of five millions of dollars was voted for the establishment of the arsenals, and for other military supplies.

Effect of the Embargo. The effect of the embargo and its supplementary exacerbations—as we may style the rigorous enforcement-acts which followed it—

---

* In his message to Congress of 5th November, 1811, Mr. Madison, at that time president, spoke thus with reference to what he termed "the hostile inflexibility" of Great Britain— "Congress will feel the duty of putting the United States into an armour and an attitude demanded by the crisis, and corresponding with the national spirit and expectations." But four years before, upon the passing of the embargo act, *The Intelligencer*, an official journal, did not hesitate to write in this inflammatory strain :— "The national spirit is up. That spirit is invaluable. In case of war it is to lead us to conquest. In such event, *there must cease to be an inch of British ground on this Continent.*" And this was when the second Order in Council had only been heard of, but not yet made public. With a government, so fiercely thirsting for strife with Britain, was friendly negotiation likely to be successful? Was an amicable adjustment of difficulties possible with the spirit which possessed them? Hildreth cites a remarkable incident which exhibits, in a strong light, the unhappy hostility to England at this period (1807-8). How strong and prevalent this antipathy to England was, fully appeared on the floor of Congress. A suggestion by Livermore, of Massachussetts, that, since the United States were driven by invincible necessity to choose between the belligerents, a regard as well for commercial interests as for the independence of nations, ought to induce them to side with Great Britain, was received with marked indignation, almost as if there had been something treasonable in it."

was highly prejudicial to the United States. Their commerce had received the severest blow it had yet suffered, from the hands of their own rulers. Despair settled on the minds of all who depended for their livelihood on the sea. Merchants gloomily anticipated the time when their ships should sink beside their wharves, and grass grow in their streets. The British Order in Council—they said—had left them some traffic, but the acts of their own legislature had cut every thing off. By men who were never tired of asserting their free and inalienable right to the highways of the ocean, the ocean had been treacherously abandoned.

Non-intercourse Act, 1st March, 1808. For the embargo was substituted, on the 1st March, 1808, a non-intercourse act, whereby all commercial transactions with either of the belligerent powers was absolutely prohibited, but the embargo was taken off as to the rest of the world. This act, however, contained a clause (§ 11.) authorizing the President, by proclamation, to renew the intercourse between America and either of the belligerent powers who should first repeal their obnoxious orders in council or decrees. "This non-intercourse act"—observes Mr. Alison— had the effect of totally suspending the trade between America and Great Britain, and inflicting upon both these countries a loss tenfold greater than that suffered by France, with which the commercial intercourse of the United States was altogether inconsiderable."

3d March, 1809. Nothing of note occurred between the passing of the non-intercourse act and Mr. Jefferson's retirement from his second term of office on the 3d of March, 1809. He declined presenting himself for election a third time, both because—as he stated—he considered a third tenure of office would be alien from the spirit of the constitution, and because, as it seems, he was thoroughly weary of the cares and distractions of public life. On the eve of his retirement into private life his language was this —"never did prisoner released from his chains feel such relief as I shall on shaking off power." He was a man of great ability; but, unfortunately, both for Great Britain and his own country, his strong anti-British prejudices stood very much in his way in administering, with impartiality and wisdom, the government with which during eight years he was entrusted. We can make allowance for the perplexities and annoyances of the time during which he held the reins of power; but, had Washington been in his place, with his dignified and sagacious views of relations with Great Britain, we have little doubt that he would have brought his country through the dark and trying time, not by nourishing the war-spirit as Jefferson did, but by firmly facing and repressing it. It was an inauspicious circumstance that, just at that critical time, the chief magistracy of the United States should have been vested in a man whose heart was filled with hatred of Great Britain; and who had more than once patronized and placed in positions of authority disaffected subjects of the British Crown.* Liberally endowed, as he unquestionably was, with natural talent, this was greatly recommended and rendered in a very considerable degree practically influential, by agreeable manners and plausible address. As to his religious opinions, we believe that all that can be said in their favor is this—that he admired the morality of the Gospel. His belief in any of the articles of the Christian faith whatsoever would seem equivocal, if on no other account, from his letter to the notorious Thomas Paine, in which he invited that avowed and immoral enemy of divine revelation to the bosom of his country, with "prayers for the success of his *useful* labors." A disciple—as he was—of that philosophy which overthrew the throne of the French monarch, and brought its unhappy occupant to the guillotine, his sympathies were thoroughly with France and against Great Britain Nurtured under the congenial associations of French republicanism,† his sympathies—as with many others of his countrymen—were

not stifled when republicanism in France had been fairly shackled and put under-foot by military and imperial despotism ; so that his heart, it seems, still went lovingly with the ruthless soldiers of France, even when the "sacred" flame of republicanism had long vanished from the points of their swords. But, if Mr. Jefferson's administration, in point of French predilections, was bad, that of Mr. Madison, his successor, was vastly worse. Both were decided in their bias towards Napoleon Buonaparte ; but whilst the former was too dextrous and wary to be made the tool of French intrigue, the latter—there is too much reason for believing—was completely entangled in its toils.

(To be continued.)

BERLIN DECREE.

" 1. The British islands are placed in a state of blockade. 2. Every species of commerce and communication with them is prohibited ; all letters or packets addressed in English, or in the English characters, shall be seized at the post-office, and interdicted all circulation. 3. Every British subject, of what rank or condition whatever, who shall be found in the countries occupied by our troops, or those of our allies, shall be made prisoners of war. 4. Every warehouse, merchandise, or property of any sort, belonging to a subject of Great Britain, or coming from its manufactories or colonies, is declared good prize. 5. Commerce of every kind in English goods is prohibited ; and every species of merchandise belonging to England, or emanating from its workshops or colonies, is declared good prize. 6. The half of the confiscated value shall be devoted to indemnifying those merchants whose vessels have been seized by the English cruizers, for the losses which they have sustained. 7. No vessel coming directly from England, or any of its colonies, or having touched there since the publications of the present decree, shall be received into any harbour. 8. Every vessel which, by means of a false declaration, shall have effected such entry, shall be liable to seizure, and the ship and cargo shall be confiscated, as if they had also belonged to England. 9. The prize court of Paris is intrusted with the determination of all questions arising out of this decree in France, or the countries occupied by our armies ; that of Milan, with the decision of all similar questions in the kingdom of Italy. 10. This decree shall be communicated to the kings of Spain, Naples, Holland, and Etruria, and to our other allies, whose subjects have been the victims, like our own, of the injustice and barbarity of English legislation. 11. The ministers of foreign affairs, of war, of marine, of finance, and of justice, of police, and all postmasters, are charged, each in his own department, with the execution of the present decree."

---

* Duane, for example, to whom Mr. Jefferson gave a colonel's commission in the U. S. militia, and the editorial charge of the Aurora newspaper, had been shipped off just before from Calcutta—having been detected in attempts to excite disturbance and insurrection in that city.

† We do not mean to say he approved of its bloody atrocities : perhaps the wildest democrat in the United States would have hesitated there.

CHAPTER II.

From the commencement of Mr. Madison's Administration to preparations for War.

4th March, 1811. .... *12th January,* 1812.

CONTENTS.

stimulated by the complete cessation of commercial intercourse produced by the war, has rendered the market which Great Britain now finds in the United States for her manufactures, greatly inferior to what it ought to have been, considering the rapid increase in the population of the neighbouring republic, and to what it certainly would have been' but for the war. At the time of Mr. Madison's accession, the Non-intercourse Act of the 1st March 1809 was, of course, in operation, which, it will be remembered, bore equally upon both of the belligerent powers; and contained a clause giving to the President the power of renewing trade with that one of the two contending nations which should first revoke its hostile edicts, so far as these affected the United States.

Mr. Madison's Inauguration, 4th March, 1809. Mr. Jefferson, with whose retirement from office we closed our last chapter, was succeeded by Mr. Madison, who, on the 4th March 1809, took the oath of office, with the ceremony usual on such occasions. It may be taken as a hint of what was to be the future policy of his country, in their efforts to make themselves as independent as possible of British manufactures, that he was dressed at his inauguration " in a full suit of cloth of American manufacture." The circumstance was significant; and sufficiently evinced the determination of the United States to continue indebted to Great Britain for no more than was imperatively necessary. The President's attire indicated the spirit of the nation; and that spirit, still further

Negotiation of Mr. Erskine with Mr. Madison. Mr. Rose, the British Envoy before mentioned, who returned home, *re infecta*, in the spring of 1808, was succeeded by Mr. Erskine. He was the son of the celebrated Judge Erskine, and a man of talent; but of a sanguine temperament; very favourably disposed towards the United States, partly, no doubt, from his having resided there; and too readily confiding in the fair professions of those old tacticians—Messrs. Madison, Gallatin, and Smith, with whom, during his negotiation, he had to deal. When we make the remark that these last named gentlemen had the advantage of Mr. Erskine in the way of experience and ingenuity, we do not wish it to be understood that we consider them as having made promises to the British minister which

2

they had no intention of performing. On the contrary, the embarrassments of Mr. Madison's administration, in consequence of the non-intercourse act which he inherited from his predecessor, were so vexatious at the time that Mr. Erskine entered on the negotiation, that the President was in the humour of making concessions; and if he did make very material concessions to Great Britain, during that negotiation, we must regard them as extorted by his difficulties, without considering that he had it in view afterwards to evade them. Messrs. Smith and Gallatin, with apparent frankness and great freedom, spoke to Mr. Erskine of the favourable views and intentions of their government; Mr. Madison with greater caution; but all with an air and manner of sincere friendship, of the genuineness of which Mr. Erskine appears to have been fully convinced; in which Mr. Canning, on the other hand, at that time British Secretary for Foreign Affairs, seems to have put little or no faith at all. Mr. Canning, we feel convinced, was not very far wrong in his low estimate of the alleged friendliness of Mr. Madison's administration generally; but in this particular instance we could have wished that the secretary's sagacious scepticism had yielded to the confidence so generously reposed by the young envoy in the protestations he received. In consequence of Mr. Erskine's representations of what he believed to be an improved temper and tone of feeling in the United States, Mr. Canning—though he stated that he could see no symptoms of the satisfactory change suggested by Mr. Erskine—sent him new instructions, in two separate dispatches of the same date, (Jan. 23); one relating to the affair of the Chesapeake, the other to the Orders in Council.

In the former of these two dispatches, ample reparation for the attack on the Chesapeake was offered, in a promise that the men taken from that vessel should be restored; whilst it was added, His Majesty would be willing, " as an act of spontaneous generosity," to make a provision for the widows and orphans of the men who had been killed in the action. The proffered reparation was accepted; but the official note, intimating the President's acceptance of it, closed with the rude and most un-gracious clause,—inserted, as Mr. Smith afterwards alleged, against his remonstrances, and by Mr. Madison's express direction:—" I have it in express charge from the President to state, that while he forbears to insist on a further punishment of the offending officer, he is not the less sensible of the justice and utility of such an example, nor the less persuaded that it would best comport with what is due from His Britannic Majesty to his own honour." This impertinent lecture on the principles of honor, addressed by Mr. Madison to His Britannic Majesty, was so deeply resented by the British Cabinet, that the negotiation relative to the Chesapeake was immediately broken off in consequence, and Mr. Erskine was severely censured for transmitting a note, containing language so discourteous and unbecoming. Offensive as this breach of propriety was, the British Cabinet, it must be confessed, carried their resentment of it too far, when they made it a reason for withholding reparation for an acknowledged wrong.

In regard to the Orders in Council, which were the subject of Mr. Canning's other dispatch, the correspondence between Mr. Erskine and Mr. Smith ended in an assurance given by the former, that " His Majesty's Orders in Council of January and November 1807, will have been withdrawn, as respected the United States, on the 10th June next. " To which Mr. Smith rejoined, that the non-intercourse act would be withdrawn, in virtue of the powers conferred on the President by the act establishing it, from and after the 10th of June;" and a proclamation, to that effect, from him appeared the same day.

Rejoicing in the United States. The utmost satisfaction was felt in the United States by the Federal party, and by the moderate men at this favourable change. On the 24th of April, five days after the issuing of the President's proclamation declaring the resumption of commercial intercourse with Great Britain, the auspicious event was celebrated in New York by salutes of guns, ringing of church-bells, splendid illuminations, and other demonstrations of public rejoicing. The sentiments of the Federal Press appeared in articles preceded by headings such as these:—"Triumph of Federal policy—No embargo—No French party—A return of peace, prosperity, and commerce."

Mr. Erskine's arrangement disavowed by the British Government. In proportion to this enthusiastic joy were the depression in some quarters, and the indignation in others, when, on the 20th July, three weeks after the adjournment of Congress, information reached the United States that Mr. Canning had declared in the House of Commons, that the arrangement made by Mr. Erskine was wholly unauthorised by his instructions, and that the government could not ratify it. A very grave charge against the good faith of the government was advanced by the opposition in both Houses of Parliament; and, in order to rebut this, the instructions were eventually printed and laid open to public inspection. The correctness of Mr. Canning's statement was then apparent, viz.: that Mr. Erskine had acted not only inconsistently with, but in contradiction to his orders; and the opposition were silenced. A comparison of the correspondence between Mr. Erskine and the American government with Mr. Canning's despatch to the former, does indeed exhibit the alleged contradiction in a very strong light; for, whilst in the correspondence no mention is made of any condition besides the withdrawal of the Non-intercourse Act, Mr. Canning in his despatch specifies *three* conditions on which the recall of the Orders was to be contingent. · "First—the repealing as to Great Britain, but the keeping in force as to France, and all countries adopting her decrees, so long as those decrees were continued, all existing American non-importation and non-intercourse acts, and acts excluding foreign ships of war. Second—the renunciation by the United States, during the present war, of any pretensions to carry on any trade with the colonies of belligerents, not allowed in time of peace; and, third—the allowing British ships of war to enforce by capture the American non-intercourse with France and her allies." With terms so express and positive as these before him, it seems amazing that Mr. Erskine should have ventured to conclude even a "conditional agreement" as he described that into which he entered,

merely on the single condition of the withdrawal of the Non-intercourse Act as regarded Great Britain. But the British Envoy, though ready to put a liberal interpretation on his instructions, was not so venturous as might at first sight appear. Mr. Madison—so uneasy was he under his political dilemma, and so anxious to extricate himself from it even with humiliation—had, in words, conceded substantially all the demands of the British Government; to make those concessions definitive was beyond his power, as it was indispensable to refer them to Congress, which was not at that time in session. His perplexities lead us to the conviction that he would have kept his word, and done his best to obtain from Congress its sanction of his verbally expressed understanding with Mr. Erskine. That gentleman trusted to Mr. Madison's good faith: Mr. Canning, we suspect, did not. "The refusal of the English Ministry to ratify Mr. Erskine's arrangement," writes Mr. Alison, "although justified in point of right by Napoleon's violence, and Mr. Erskine's deviation from his instructions, may now well be characterized as one of the most unfortunate resolutions, in point of expediency, ever adopted by the British Government; for it at once led to the renewal of the Non-intercourse Act of the United States: put an entire stop for the next two years to all commerce with that country; reduced the exports of Great Britain fully a third during the most critical and important year of the war; and, in its ultimate results, contributed to produce that unhappy irritation between the two countries, which has never yet, notwithstanding the strong bonds of natural interest by which they are connected, been allayed." On the 9th August, in consequence of the non-fulfilment of the Erskine arrangement, the President issued a proclamation withdrawing the proclamation previously issued; thereby leaving in full effect the Non-intercourse Act both against Great Britain and France.

Mission and Recall of Mr. Jackson. Mr. Erskine was recalled, and succeeded by Mr. Francis James Jackson, who arrived at Washington in the month of October He had done his country service at Copenhagen, in the negotiation which preceded the seizure of the Danish fleet, a circumstance not likely to recommend him to the government of the United States. From the moment of his landing to his departure in about a month's time, he was subject to galling insults in different degrees, from the President, the populace, and the press. His recall, at last, was requested by the United States government, and, of course, granted by the British Cabinet; though without any mark of disapprobation on the part of his sovereign.

Decree of Rambouillet: May 18th, 1810. The forbearance of the United States with France was tried to the uttermost, and stood the shock, in the Decree of Rambouillet—the climax of French rapacity—issued on the 18th May, 1810. By this all vessels sailing under the flag of the United States, or owned wholly or in part by any American citizen, which, since the 20th May, 1809, had entered, or which should thereafter enter, any of the ports of France or her colonies, or countries occupied by French armies should be seized. This act was carried into immediate execution ; the number of sequestered ships amounted to one hundred and sixty, the value of which was calculated at one million of francs. Yet even this devastating sweep excited no war-spirit in the United States; there was, to be sure, sharp and vehement remonstrance about it; but the spoliation was never resented as the grievances laid to the charge of Great Britain were resented ; and the French Emperor never atoned, nor even evinced the slightest disposition to atone, for it.

Pretended Revocation of the French Decrees: 1st November, 1810. The Emperor of France, growing impatient under his ineffectual attempt to drive the United States into war with Great Britain, thought proper at last to affect a conciliatory policy towards the North American republic, and to try what fair and plausible professions could accomplish. Without any intention, as his subsequent proceedings shewed, of keeping his hands off their vessels, the confiscation of which had all along furnished so convenient a tribute to his impoverished exchequer, Buonaparte determined, at least, to change his tone. The disappointment and dissatis-

faction prevailing in the United States in consequence of the disallowance of the Erskine arrangement gave him pleasure ; and, more particularly, the act against Great Britain with which the session of Congress had terminated was altogether to his taste. The Duke of Cadore—his minister—was accordingly instructed to make to the American minister, Mr. Armstrong, the following declaration, which was communicated in a note dated 5th August:—" At present Congress retraces its steps. The act of the 1st March, 1809 (the Non-intercourse act as regards France) is revoked: the ports of America are open to French trade ; and France is no longer shut to America. Congress, in short, engages to declare against the belligerent which shall refuse to recognise the rights of neutrals. In this new state of things, I am authorised to declare to you that the decrees of Berlin and Milan are revoked ; and that from the 1st November they shall cease to be executed, it *being well understood*, that in consequence of this declaration, the English shall revoke their Orders in Council, and renounce the new principles of blockade, which they have attempted to establish, or that the United States shall cause the right to be respected by the British." The President of the United States with eager delight laid hold of this *conditional* revocation ; dependent though it was on a condition which Buonaparte knew very well, and Mr. Madison might have known, too, was on the part of Great Britain wholly inadmissable. On the very next day after that on which it was conditionally promised they should be revoked, Madison issued a proclamation asserting that "the said edicts *have been* revoked ;" and that "the enemy *ceased* on the first day of that month to violate the neutral commerce of the United States." But the President's gratification was unwarranted, and his proclamation premature. There had been—as we shall see hereafter—no revocation.

Intelligence of this prospective revocation of the French decress was communicated at once to Mr. Pinckney, the United States Minister at London, who, without delay proceeded on the 25th August following to make a formal call on the British Government to repeal their Orders in Council. Lord Wellesley, very naturally, replied that it would be necessary to wait to see whether the French decrees would be actually repealed. Subsequently, when a temporary intermission of French violence, together with the release of some detained American vessels, afforded color for the government of the United States asserting, and probably at the time hoping, that the French decrees had been virtually repealed, though no authentic document beyond the Duke of Cadore's note had appeared to that effect; Mr. Pinckney laboured strenuously and repeatedly to prove to the British Cabinet that those decrees had actually been repealed, and reiterated his demands, that the Orders in Council should be annulled. Lord Wellesley replied that, "admitting the Duke of Cadore's letter to be correctly interpreted by Pinckney, as announcing a repeal of the French decrees to commence absolutely on the first of November, but conditional as to its continuance, or the recall, within a reasonable time, of the British Orders, he should not hesitate to concede such a recall, *had that been the only thing required.* But there was another condition mentioned in that letter wholly inadmissable—the renouncing what were called " the new British principles of blockade."

What France required was the relinquishment by England of " her new principles of blockade;" an expression which unquestionably implied much more than a mere declaration by the British Cabinet that, as a matter of fact, the blockade of 1806 had, as an actual blockade, ceased to exist. We do not see how the British Government could have disputed that point, seeing it was a thing obvious to the eyes of any man, that Lord Keith's ships no longer watched the coast between Brest and the Elbe; Lord Wellesley, we consider, admitted as much, when he told Mr. Pinckney that the blockade of 1806 was included in the more extensive Orders in Council; that is, he admitted, we take it, that the line of coast originally confined by actual blockade was no longer in that predicament; but, in common with the rest of France, affected by the retaliation of Buonaparte's own paper blockades. But this admission, expressed or implied, was not what France wanted. Her view of the case was

this:—" Granting that Britain had 160 vessels* to blockade thirty ports and harbours of ours; she did not invest those ports and harbours by land as well as by sea; and, therefore, in our estimation, it was no actual blockade. It was Great Britain's new principles of blockade. She must, notwithstanding her immense naval force, put that blockade virtually on the same footing with the Berlin and Milan Decrees; she must deny its existence, and—what we are especially aiming at—she must acknowledge its insufficiency. She must do this before our promised repeal of our decrees in favour of the United States is to take effect; and, in doing so, it is to be distinctly understood that in future, unless she can beleaguer our seaport towns by land as well as by sea, there will be no actual blockade." That is, Great Britain was not to shut up the French ports from foreign intercourse, and debar them from foreign supplies—how effectually soever she might be able to do it with her powerful navy—until her Peninsular heroes should have crossed the Pyrenees. Then, if she chose, she might use her fleets to co-operate with her troops on land. The transcendent insolence of such terms is equalled only by their prodigious absurdity; and yet this was what France meant by Great Britain " renouncing her new principles of blockade." These, or a declaration of war by the United States against Great Britain, were the conditions on which the Berlin and Milan Decrees were, by an anticipation, repealed as regarded the United States. The French government, in short, revoked, or more strictly promised to revoke, their decrees in favour of the United States, on the understanding that one of two things was to follow: either that Great Britain should be entrapped into the surrender of her maritime superiority; of which being in itself flagrantly absurd, France, we must believe, entertained no expectation,—or that the United States would go to war with Great Britain: this latter alternative being, as they no doubt imagined, the more probable of the two; and which, within less than two years, was the actual issue of French stratagem and American irascibility.

* This was the force actually watching the French coast in 1806.

This revocation, then, which was so paraded in public documents of Mr. Madison's Administration, and triumphantly quoted both in those documents and in Congress, as creating an irresistible claim on Great Britain for the repeal of her Orders, was nothing more than a revocation contingent on impossible conditions, and was, therefore, no revocation at all. It was simply a piece of French intrigue, seen through without difficulty by the British Cabinet, as a transparent fraud, and failing, therefore, to draw Great Britain into the snare; but ultimately successful in the other quarter; that is, in aggravating the discontent felt by the United States towards Great Britain, and contributing to bring on hostilities between those two countries. Still, it might be asked,— " Did this French stratagem preclude Great Britain from making a relaxation of her Orders in favour of the United States, supposing that good policy dictated such a step?" Pledged to such a concession she certainly was not, for her pledge—as we have seen— was based on nothing short of an absolute and unconditional repeal on the part of France, which was never made. But was she not at liberty to make the concession of her own accord? We think she was. We cannot see that she was in the slightest degree bound by any interpretation which France might put upon; by any extravagant conditions which her furious adversary, in her own distempered imagination and inflated pretensions, might gratuitously attach to such a concession. She was, it appears to us, altogether in a position to take, and to maintain her own view of her own policy, and to say to the United States :—" It will be mutually advantageous that we should discontinue the restraints which French violence at the first compelled us to put on your commerce; and we do so: we strike off the trammels we imposed; you, of course, abrogating your retaliatory enactments. It is true, the violence of France continues; for, as she has relaxed her Decrees with an understanding utterly ridiculous,—on conditions surpassingly inequitable and absurd,—which can never be fulfilled, she has, in point of fact, not relaxed those Decrees at all. But your Non-Intercourse Act, and our Orders in

Council, hurt both you and ourselves, infinitely more than they annoy or injure France, and this we judge to be a sufficient reason for rescinding the Orders. This we are ready to do, without compromising our right, which is sanctioned by all national law and precedent, to close where we can the ports of France with our fleets, which are quite adequate to the maintenance of any actual blockade we have as yet attempted. This relief we are ready to afford you, without for one moment debarring ourselves from turning against our enemy, as God shall give us ability, that maritime superiority, whose crowning honours and strength were bought with the blood of Aboukir and Trafalgar." This, we conceive, would have been good and safe policy on the part of Great Britain. It would have conciliated the United States, and miserably disappointed France, without involving, so far as we can see, any concession detrimental to our maritime superiority, or discreditable to the nation at large. The persistence of the British Cabinet in their original policy at this period, and subsequently, when the Erskine arrangement was disallowed, may be pronounced, we think, unfortunate, and seems, indeed, unaccountable, when we consider how loudly the increasing commercial distress in the British Isles cried out for relief. During the year 1810, two thousand bankruptcies were announced; whilst the elements of the riots which in 1812 broke out in the manufacturing districts were visibly fermenting. We do not mean to attribute the whole of this commercial distress to the Orders in Council and the retaliatory acts of Congress; but we are aware that a great deal of it arose from that source; whilst it may be acknowledged that the chief cause of such a depression was Buonaparte's Continental system,—the confiscation of British merchandise with which it commenced, and the subsequent exclusion of that merchandise from all the Continental ports under his control. The re-establishment of satisfactory relations with the United States would certainly have been, under these circumstances, a measure of relief; and it was simply as a measure of relief to suffering and complaining multitudes that the Orders in Council were, in the end, rescinded. How much is it to be regretted, we are ready to say, that they had not been rescinded before, when the grounds for revocation were the same, and the revocation would not have come, as it did at last, too late ! Menaced with augmented embarrassments; surrounded by affecting evidences of public suffering, and symptoms by no means dubious of an outbreak amongst the lower classes of the people ; with the prospect of a diminished revenue at a time when its burthens, entailed by the war with Napoleon, were enormous,—the British Cabinet, unhappily, thought it their duty to hold on their course.

French Seizures and Burnings still continued.

Nothing can show more conclusively the justice of styling Buonaparte's conditional revocation of his Decrees "a pretended revocation," than the fact, that the French still persisted in capturing vessels belonging to the United States, seizing their cargoes, and, in many instances, burning the ships after the cargo had been removed. Buonaparte, it is true, to save appearances, did release by his special license, and not on the ground of the alleged revocation, some United States' merchant-ships which had been detained in French ports ; but this was all he did. During the summer of 1811, French privateers in the Baltic and Mediterranean took every American vessel they fell in with, and carried them for condemnation into the ports of Italy, Dantzic, and Copenhagen. At the very moment when the Congress Committee of November, 1811, were making their report, in which they called their countrymen to arms, and spared no force of language to rouse the deadliest resentment against " British injustice and outrage,"—at that very moment —when France seemed to be as effectually forgotten as though it had formed a part of some distant planet,—a small squadron of French frigates, evading the British surveillance, which might have done the United States some service, had escaped from the Loire, and were pillaging and plundering American vessels in the Atlantic. Great reason, then, had Lloyd for expressing himself as he did, in the Senate, on the 27th June, 1812,—after the declaration of war :

" Did the justification of the British Orders in Council depend merely on the non-repeal of the French Decrees, they might then, indeed, well enough stand, since every arrival from Europe brought news of fresh seizures and condemnation of American vessels, under cover of those very edicts of which the repeal was so boldly alleged." With Mr. Hildreth's testimony we leave this topic : " As to the alleged repeal, by France, and the refusal of Great Britain to repeal her orders, which had been made the occasion, first of the revival of non-importation from Great Britain, and now of war ; not only had no decree of repeal been produced ; not only had no captured American vessel ever been released by any French prize court on the ground of such repeal, but all the public documents of France ; the Duke of Cadore, in his report to the Emperor, of December 3, 1810 ; the Emperor himself, in his address to the Council of Commerce, of March 31, 1811 ; and the Duke of Bassano, in his recent report of March 10, 1812 ; all spoke of the Berlin and Milan Decrees as subsisting in full force, the cherished policy of the Empire." Here surely, is ample evidence to show how unmerited was the imputation attempted to be fixed upon Great Britain, of having falsified her pledge.

Mr. Pinckney's departure from London : 1st March, 1811.

After ineffectual efforts to carry out his views and wishes, Mr. Pinckney requested, and, on the 1st March, 1811, obtained his audience of leave from the Prince Regent. In his letter to Mr. Smith, the United States Secretary for Foreign Affairs, describing the interview at Carlton House, he informed his government that the Prince Regent had conveyed to him " explicit declarations of the most amicable views and feelings towards the United States." The business of the legation was left in the hands of a Chargé d'Affaires. From this time the government of the United States acted as if the French edicts were revoked ; though, as we have shown, captures and seizures were still going on; whence French ships were admitted into the ports of the United States, whilst those of Great Britain were excluded.

Engagement between
the United States frigate
President, and His Bri-
tannic Majesty's sloop
of war Little Belt: 16th
May, 1811.
Whilst the diplomatic relations of the two countries exhibited this state of growing alienation, an incident occurred at sea, which threatened to precipitate the rupture which the discussion about the Orders in Council was steadily bringing on. On the 16th May, about 14 or 15 leagues from Cape Charles, Captain Bingham, of the British sloop of war Little Belt, at that time looking for her consort, the Guerriere, for which she had dispatches, came in sight of a frigate, with which, on the supposition that she might be the Guerriere, Captain Bingham endeavoured to close. When he had approached sufficiently near, he displayed his private signals; and on these not being answered, he took it for granted that the frigate was an American, abandoned the pursuit, and steered to the south. The frigate in question was the President, Commodore Rogers, which was cruizing in those waters, as one of the home squadron, for the protection of the commerce of the United States. The President, from some motive on the part of her commander which it seems hard to reconcile with amicable intentions, gave chase to the other vessel, so soon as the latter had changed her course. The pursuit of the Little Belt, in the first instance, was afterwards accounted for in the manner we have already stated; but, even at the time, it would naturally have occurred to the Commander of the President that his ship must have been mistaken by the other for either a British or French vessel, and whether that other was British or French could have made no difference to him, as his nation was not at war with either Great Britain or France. Why, then, should he have given chase? He had no antagonist at sea. But, to proceed. As the President was evidently gaining, Captain Bingham, deeming it advisable to speak the stranger before dark, lay to at half-past six o'clock,—having by that time discerned the stars in the President's broad pennant,—and, to guard against surprise, prepared his ship for action. The other approached slowly, with a light breeze, and, as if with hostile intentions, made several efforts to secure the weatherly gage, which, after having been frustrated in some three or four times, by Captain Bingham's manœuvres, she at length succeeded obtaining. At about a quarter past eight, the vessels were within hail, the distance between them being less than a hundred yards. Up to this hour the accounts on both sides agree; but here we meet with most perplexing discrepancy in the narratives of the two commanders. Captain Bingham thus states the matter: "I hailed, and asked what ship it was? He repeated my question. I again hailed, and asked what ship it was? He again repeated my words, and fired a broadside, which I immediately returned." Commodore Rogers, on the other hand, gave in this statement: "I hailed, What ship is that? To this inquiry no answer was given; but I was hailed by her commander, What ship is that? After a pause of fifteen or twenty seconds, I reiterated my first inquiry; and before I had time to take the trumpet from my mouth was answered by a shot, that went into our mainmast." The action, however brought on, became general, and lasted for about three-quarters of an hour, at the end of which time the fire of the Little Belt was silenced, as she was reduced almost to a wreck, and none of her guns could be brought to bear. Commodore Rogers stated, that, after four or five minutes he desisted from firing, as he perceived that his adversary was very inferior: but the officers of the Little Belt made no mention of this pause. After the action, Commodore Rogers hailed again, and ascertained the name and character of his small,[*] but spirited antagonist. He then gave his own, after which the two vessels separated for the night. In the morning, the Commander of the President sent a boat on board the Little Belt, with a message, expressing his regret that the unfortunate collision had taken place, and tendering assistance to his crippled adversary, —an offer which Captain Bingham declined. The Little Belt then made the best of her way to Halifax, severely damaged, with eleven

---

[*] A glance at the plate will show the reader the vast difference in size between the vessels. We may take this opportunity of remarking, that, with but two or three exceptions, there was a disparity of force, in favor of the enemy, in every naval action throughout the war.

ENGAGEMENT BETWEEN THE U. S. 44 GUN FRIGATE "PRESIDENT," AND H. B. M.'s 18 GUN SLOOP "LITTLE BELT."

men dead and twenty-one wounded.   The President suffered but trifling damage, and lost none of her crew—one only being wounded, and that slightly.   No censure was passed on either of the Commanders by their respective Governments.   Captain Bingham was deservedly applauded, for so bravely fighting a vessel of 18 guns against one of 44 ; whilst Commodore Rogers, after having been brought to an open court-martial, at the request of the British minister at Washington, was honourably acquitted. During this inquiry, several of his officers and crew were examined, who bore out his statement, that the Little Belt fired the first shot.   To attempt a decision of the question, " Who fired the first shot?" seems a hopeless undertaking, where the evidence on either side is directly contradictory,— captain against captain, and ship against ship: yet it is but just to make the remark, that both the probability of the case, and other circumstances, distinct from the testimony given in, are greatly against the American.   It is not probable that a vessel of eighteen guns should have attacked another of forty-four.   No hostile design can be attributed to Captain Bingham ; for his orders, which were made public after the encounter, expressly cautioned him against giving any unnecessary offence to the government or the people of the United States ; and an attack of his on an American frigate would have been a flagrant violation of those orders, such as—we may conceive—no man in his senses, how daring and impetuous soever, would have attempted.   The orders, on the other hand, under which the President sailed, were never published, which is somewhat singular; but the United States government disavowed, to Mr. Foster, the British minister, the issuing of any orders of an unfriendly character.   In regard to the American orders, however, it is connected with our subject, though it may not be of much importance to state, that an opinion very generally prevailed in the United States, as Mr. Hildreth, the American historian, informs us, that "Rogers had pursued the Little Belt, with the very purpose of avenging on her the still unatoned-for attack on the Chesapeake."   In relation to this suspicion of a hostile purpose on the part of the

2*

Americans, we must attach great weight to a remark made by Captain Bingham :—" By the manner in which he (Commodore Rogers) apologized, it appeared evident to me that, had he fallen in with a British frigate, he would certainly have brought her to action. And what farther confirms me in that opinion is, that his guns were not only loaded with round and grape shot, but with every scrap of iron that could be collected."   As the British Government was satisfied with the disavowal of hostile orders on the part of the United States Government, the matter was allowed to drop: and the excitement arising from it at the moment soon died away.

The President's War Message, 4th November, 1811.   The President, at the close of the year, having called Congress together after a shorter recess than usual, communicated to them, on the 4th November, a message, in which, after enumerating the subjects of complaint against Britain (of which we have already said enough), he suggested the appeal to arms in these words,—" Congress will feel the duty of putting the United States into an armour and an attitude demanded by the crisis, and corresponding with the national expectations."

Nov. 29.   The Committee on Foreign Affairs recommended the raising of 10,000 regulars and 50,000 militia, with other preparations ; but, such was the passionate ardour of the Legislature, that the numbers voted were, by a majority of 109 to 22, increased to 25,000 regular troops, and a loan was agreed to of ten millions of dollars.

Was there, to any extent, a secret understanding between the United States and France?   At the very time that the angry majority in Congress were preparing the unhappy collision with Great Britain, the privateers and cruizers of France,, as we have said, under the professed revocation of the French decrees, were repeatedly making captures of American vessels, and seizing their cargoes.   It was less than one month prior to the declaration of war against Great Britain, that a correspondence was laid before Congress, by the President, between Mr. Barlow, the American minister at Paris, and the Secretary of State, in which the former communicated to his government the vexatious intelligence that his efforts to conclude a treaty with France had proved abortive, and that no redress had, as yet, been obtained for the seizures and confiscations either prior or subsequent to the relaxation of the French decrees. It is evident, then, that Buonaparte's relaxation of his decrees in favour of the United States, was not honestly carried out. The grievances of which they complained at the hands of France were, on their own showing, unredressed; and yet the President of the United States found himself unable to " recommend to the consideration of Congress definitive measures in respect to France," in that very message which called his countrymen to arms against Great Britain. In that message, every subject of discontent with the British Government was paraded in the manner, and with the embittering language, best calculated to inflame, to the highest degree, the rising passions of the nation. No peace; no breathing-time; no further waiting, for what the future might still bring forth as the foundation of pacification, was to be permitted. It is true, the United States had waited long,—had suffered long; and too long, also, had the British Ministry—as it proved—withheld the concession which, had it been made sooner, might not, perhaps, have wholly sweetened the bitter waters of strife, but would, at least, have strengthened the friends of peace in the American Congress, whilst, in corresponding measure, it would have embarrassed the fiery spirits in that body, and have prevented possibly, (though we do not feel sure of this,) the outbreak of war. But, if the patience of the United States had been tried by Great Britain, (which we do not deny,) it had been tried, perhaps with equal severity, by France too; and yet—so unequally did the spirit of retaliation work!—the wrongs charged upon Great Britain were to be fiercely and promptly effaced with blood; whilst those which had been suffered, and were still endured, from France, remained a matter for discussion; Congress, in regard to these, still taking time " to decide with greater advantage on the course due to

the rights, the interests, the honour of their country."* The contrast is too obvious to be overlooked ;—the temper of " sudden quarrel" towards Great Britain,—the long-suffering with France. The bias in Napoleon Buonaparte's favour appears in a still stronger light ; if it be truly alleged—as has been done—that there was a general impression in the United States that the repeal of the Orders could not be far distant; and that, acting under that impression, the democratic party did their utmost to press the declaration of war before intelligence of the expected repeal should have reached America. Be this as it may ; the small, but able minority expressed in energetic terms their sense of the inconsistency of declaring war with one adversary only, when two had given equal provocation. " As the injuries (said they) which we have received from France are at least equal in amount to those we have sustained from England, and have been attended with circumstances of still greater insult and aggravation; if war were necessary to vindicate the honour of the country, consistency and impartiality required that both nations should have been included in the declaration."† ‡ We have

---

* President's Message of 1st June, 1812.

† Other passages, besides the two we have incorporated with the text, are worthy of republication.

‡ " Resolutions passed at a Convention of Delegates from several Counties of the State of New York, held at the Capitol, in the City of Albany, on the 17th and 18th days of September, 1812."

" Resolved, that without insisting on the injustice of the present war, taking solely into consideration the time and circumstances of its declaration, the condition of the country, and state of the public mind, we are constrained to consider, and feel it our duty to pronounce it a most rash, unwise, and inexpedient measure ; the adoption of which ought for ever to deprive its authors of the esteem and confidence of an enlightened people—because, as the injuries we have received from France, are at least equal in amount to those we have sustained from England, and have been attended with circumstances of still greater insult and aggravation— if war were necessary to vindicate the honor of the country, consistency and impartiality required that both nations should have been included in the declaration. Because if it were deemed expedient to exercise our right of selecting our adversary, prudence and common

already recorded our persuasion, that Mr. Madison was entangled in the toils of French intrigue ; and we have not formed that opinion without, as we think, sufficient evidence. Still we do not desire to convey the impression, in itself preposterous, that either Mr. Madison or his coadjutors were so devoid of patriotism, as to be simply desirous of serving France, without a primary regard to what they considered would best conduce to the interests of their own country. It may be asked, however, how could it enter into their minds to suppose that the interests of the United States would be best promoted by selecting for their adversary the one of the two offending nations which, in peace, maintained with them the closest relations, founded on a commerce eminently prosperous and profitable; and, in war, had the means of giving them the heaviest blows? The force of this objection was felt by the minority, whose language we have already quoted: " If it were deemed expedient (they urged) to exercise our right of selecting our

sense dictated the choice of an enemy, from whose hostility we had nothing to dread. A war with France would equally have satisfied our insulted honour, and at the same time, instead of annihilating, would have revived and extended our commerce—and even the evils of such a contest would have been mitigated by the sublime consolation, that by our efforts we were contributing to arrest the progress of despotism in Europe, and essentially serving the great interests of freedom and humanity throughout the world. Because a republican government, depending solely for its support on the wishes and affections of the people, ought never to declare a war, into which the great body of the nation are not prepared to enter with zeal and alacrity ; as where the justice and necessity of the measure are not so apparent as to unite all parties in its support, its inevitable tendency is, to augment the dissentions that have before existed, and by exasperating party violence to its utmost height, prepare the way for civil war. Because, before a war was declared, it was perfectly well ascertained, that a vast majority of the people in the middle and northern states, by whom the burden and expenses of the contest must be borne almost exclusively, were strongly opposed to the measure. Because we see no rational prospect of attaining, by force of arms, the objects for which our rulers say we are contending—and because the evils and distresses which the war must of necessity occasion, far overbalance any advantages we can expect to derive from it. Because the great power of England on the ocean, and the amazing resources she derives from commerce and navigation, render it evident, that we cannot compel her to respect our rights and satisfy our demands, otherwise than by a successful maritime warfare ; the means of conducting which we not only do not possess, but our rulers have obstinately refused to provide. Because the exhausted state of the treasury, occasioned by the destruction of the revenue derived from commerce, should the war continue, will render necessary a resort to loans and taxes to a vast amount—measures by which the people will be greatly burthened, and oppressed, and the influence and patronage of the executive alarmingly increased. And, finally,

because of a war begun with such means as our rulers had prepared, and conducted in the mode they seem resolved to pursue, we see no grounds to hope the honourable and successful termination."

"Whereas the late revocation of the British Orders in Council, has removed the great and ostensible cause of the present war, and prepared the way for an immediate accommodation of all existing differences, inasmuch as, by the confession of the present secretary of state, satisfactory and honourable arrangements might easily be made, by which the abuses resulting from the impressment of our seamen, might, in future, be effectually prevented—Therefore,

Resolved, That we shall be constrained to consider the determination on the part of our rulers to continue the present war, after official notice of the revocation of the British Orders in Council, as affording conclusive evidence, that the war has been undertaken from motives entirely distinct from those which have been hitherto avowed, and for the promotion of objects wholly unconnected with the interest and honour of the American nation.

Resolved, That we contemplate with abhorrence, even the possibility of an alliance with the present Emperor of France, every action of whose life has demonstrated, that the attainment, by any means, of universal empire, and the consequent extinction of every vestige of freedom, are the sole objects of his incessant, unbounded, and remorseless ambition. His arms, with the spirit of freemen, we might openly and fearlessly encounter ; but, of his secret arts, his corrupting influence, we entertain a dread we can neither conquer nor conceal. It is therefore with the utmost distrust and alarm, that we regard his late professions of attachment and love to the American people, fully recollecting, that his invariable course has been, by perfidious offers of protection, by deceitful professions of friendship, to lull his intended victims into the fatal sleep of confidence and security, during which, the chains of despotism are silently wound round and rivetted on them."

In the same strain, during the debate on

adversary, prudence and common sense dictated the choice of an enemy, from whose hostility we had nothing to dread. A war with France would equally have satisfied our insulted honour, and, at the same time, instead of annihilating, would have revived and extended our commerce."* But there were countervailing considerations falling in with, whilst, on the other hand, every cause of complaint against France was borne along and overwhelmed by the current of the popular antipathy to Great Britain.

" Everything in the United States," says James, in his Naval History, " was to be settled by a calculation of profit and loss. France had numerous allies,—England scarcely any. France had no contiguous territory; England had the Canadas ready to be marched into at a moment's notice. France had no commerce; England had richly-laden merchantmen traversing every sea. England, therefore, it was against whom the death-blows of America were to be levelled."*   These considerations, no

the War-Report, did Mr. Randolph speak in Congress :—

This war of conquest (he said), a war for the acquisition of territory and subjects, is to be a new commentary on the doctrine that republics are destitute of ambition—that they are addicted to peace, wedded to the happiness and safety of the great body of their people. But it seems this is to be a holiday campaign—there is to be no expense of blood, or treasure, on our part—Canada is to conquer herself—she is to be subdued by the principles of fraternity. The people of that country are first to be seduced from their allegiance, and converted into traitors, as preparatory to the making them good citizens. Although he must acknowledge that some of our flaming patriots were thus manufactured, he did not think the process would hold good with a whole community. It was a dangerous experiment. We were to succeed in the French mode, by the system of fraternization—all is French!—but how dreadfully it might be retorted on the southern and western slaveholding states. He detested this subornation of treason. No—if he must have them, let them fall by the valor of our arms, by fair legitimate conquest; not become the victims of treacherous seduction.

*   *   *   *   *   *   *

He was gratified to find gentlemen acknowledging the demoralizing and destructive consequences of the non-importation law—confessing the truth of all that its opponents foretold when it was enacted—and will you plunge yourselves in war, because you have passed a foolish and ruinous law, and are ashamed to repeal it? " But our good friend the French emperor stands in the way of its repeal," and as we cannot go too far in making sacrifices to him, who has given such demonstration of his *love for the Americans*, we must, in point of fact, become parties to his war. " Who can be so cruel as to refuse him this favour?"—His imagination shrunk from the miseries of such a connection. He called upon the house to reflect whether they were not about to abandon

all reclamation for the unparalleled outrages " insults and injuries" of the French government—to give up our claim for plundered millions, and asked what reparation or atonement they could expect to obtain in hours of future dalliance, after they should have made a tender of their persons to this great deflowerer of the virginity of republics. We had by our own wise (he would not say *wise-acre*) measures, so increased the trade and wealth of Montreal and Quebec, that at last we began to cast a wistful eye at Canada. Having done so much towards its improvement by the exercise of " our restrictive energies," we began to think the laborer worthy of his hire, and to put in claim for our portion. Suppose it ours—are we any nearer to our point? As his minister said to the king of Epirus, "may we not as well take our bottle of wine before as after this exploit?" Go! march to Canada!—leave the broad bosom of the Chesapeake, and her hundred tributary rivers—the whole line of sea-coast from Machias to St. Mary's, unprotected:—You have taken Quebec—have you *conquered England?* Will you seek for the deep foundations of her power in the frozen deserts of Labrador?"

*   *   *   *   *   *   *

Mr. Randolph then proceeded to notice the unjust and illiberal imputation of *British attachments*, against certain characters in this country, sometimes insinuated in that house, but openly avowed out of it. Against whom were these charges brought? Against men who in the war of the revolution were in the council of the nation, or fighting the battles of your country. And *by whom* were they made? *By run-aways* chiefly *from the British dominions*, since the breaking out of the French troubles. He indignantly said—it is insufferable. It cannot be borne. It must and ought, with severity, to be put down in this house—and out of it to meet the *lie direct*. We have no fellow feeling for the suffering and oppressed Spaniards! Yet even *them* we do not reprobate. Strange! that we should have no objection to any other people or government, civilized or savage, in the whole

* Resolutions of the New York Delegates.

* Life and Correspondence of Sir Isaac Brock.

doubt, powerfully contributed to attract the explosion and the shock of war on Britain; but, allowing to these their undeniable influence, we are perfectly satisfied, notwithstanding, that it was not merely the comparison of advantages or risks; it was not solely the answer returned by the oracle of republican shrewdness to the question,—" Whether more were to be gained from a war with Great Britain than with France?" which brought the controversy to its deplorable issue. There were other motives at work. The Government of the United States, and Mr. Madison's Administration more particularly, may not have had precisely " a secret understanding with France:" but there are circumstances, on that head, which—it must be owned—look extremely suspicious. It is curious, at least, to observe how exactly their proceedings contributed to aid the policy of Napoleon Buonaparte. Their embargo, non-intercourse, and non-importation acts were, in name, impartial, for they were avowedly directed against

world. The great autocrat of all the Russias receives the homage of our high consideration. The dey of Algiers and his divan of pirates are very civil good sort of people, with whom we find no difficulty in maintaining the relations of peace and amity—" Turks, Jews and infidels," *Melimeli*, or the *Little Turtle*, barbarians and savages of every clime and color, are welcome to our arms. With chiefs of banditti, negro or mulatto, we can *treat* and can *trade*. Name, however, but England, and all our antipathies are up in arms against her. Against whom? Against those whose blood runs in our own veins; in common with whom we can claim Shakspeare and Newton, and Chatham for our countrymen: whose form of government is the freest on earth, our own only excepted; from whom every valuable principle of our own institutions has been borrowed—representation—jury trial—voting the supplies—writs of habeas corpus—our whole civil and criminal jurisprudence—against our *fellow Protestants* identified in blood, in language, in religion with ourselves."

*   *   *   *   *   *   *

Mr. Sheffey, too, of Virginia, spoke, with equally moral courage, the language of truth, and justice, and common sense:—

You have been told that you could raise volunteers to atchieve the possession of Canada. Where are these volunteers? I have seen none of these patriotic men who were willing to go to Canada in the private rank; all of them want offices. You may raise a few miserable wretches for your army, who would disgrace the service, and only serve as unprincipled minions to their officers. Will your farmers' sons enlist in your army? They will not, sir. Look at the army of '98. It had twelve or fifteen regiments nominally. It was disbanded in eighteen months; when half the men had not been raised. Why, sir, you had more patriotism on paper then even than you have now; and yet you could not raise half the forces for your army. If you pass the bill, you will not raise twenty-five thousand men in three years. The object of the war may by that time vanish. The nation will be saddled with all the vast expenses of

these troops for nothing. No nation can safely engage in a foreign war without being prepared for it when they take the resolution. Are you prepared? Your secretary at war has told gentlemen that even blankets could not be procured; and you saw a letter from him yesterday, which informed you that the small supplies for the Indians could not be had without a relaxation of your commercial restrictions. Will you send your soldiers to Canada without blankets? Or do you calculate to take it by the end of the summer, and return home to a more genial clime by the next winter! This would be well enough; but I think it will require several compaigns to conquer Canada.

You will act absurdly if you expect the people of that country to join you. Upper Canada is inhabited by emigrants from the United States. They will not come back to you; they will not, without reason, desert the government, to whom they have gone for protection. No, sir, you must conquer it by force, not by sowing the seeds of sedition and treason among the people.

But, suppose you raise the men, what will Great Britain be doing in the mean time? Will she be asleep? You march to Canada: where will be your security at home? will you desert your own country; will you leave your cities to be sacrificed, plundered and sacked, for the sterile deserts of Canada, of Nova Scotia, and New-Brunswick, and all the frozen regions of the north? Sir, go to Canada, and you will soon have to recal your army to defend your southern soil; to rescue your people from rapine and destruction. You will have to employ your energies in protecting the south from British invasion. Sir, will the little force you leave at home, be able to oppose the power of British 74's? Look at Copenhagen. It is true, sir, as honourable gentlemen say, that I am secure beyond the Alleghany, after eastern states shall have fallen. Liberty is there secure! But as a member of this confederacy, I cannot consent to exchange my present situation for such a state of things."

*   *   *   *   *   *   *

" He knew gentlemen would stare at him, when he contended that they were going to

both of the belligerents ; but, in reality, they were far from pressing equally on both ; for, whilst they scarcely molested France, with her inconsiderable American commerce, they inflicted an injury that was felt, on Great Britain, accustomed, as she had been, to find, before the enactment of those measures, a large and profitable market in the United States. In the manufacturing towns of France no popular commotions were provoked by the commercial restrictions of the United States : those restrictions were the main agent in exciting the most alarming riots in Manchester, Sheffield, and other parts of England, where large numbers of operatives found themselves cut off from the ordinary sources of employment and subsistence. Little did France, in her mad immolation of her best and bravest to the phantom of military glory, appreciate or heed the loss of an extinguished commerce ; whilst Britain, dependent on her commerce for the means of protracted resistance, felt the wound,—her Parliament besieged with the petitions of suffering millions ; her towns distracted with violent mobs ; and the bankruptcies of her merchants year by year increasing. Mr. Jefferson's and Mr. Madison's measures were certainly impartial, in name ; far from impartial, in effect. In regard to Mr. Madison's personal feelings, there is nothing to make it improbable, but much to the contrary, that they were identical with those of Mr. Jefferson, to whose school in politics he belonged, whose Secretary of State he had been, and whose influence was exerted for his election to the Presidency. Mr. Madison was one of that party

---

war against Great Britain, while she was struggling for the liberties of the world. But this had great weight on his mind. She was the only power that stemmed the torrent of universal despotism. *He* had little experience in the human heart, *who* believed that there would remain any security for us after the maritime dominion, as well as the dominion of the land should be consecrated in the hands of the great Napoleon. These conquerors had always been the same. When they had subdued the world, they sat down and shed tears because they could find no other world to conquer. Our victory over Great Britain would be our defeat."

*　　*　　*　　*　　*　　*　　*

in the revolutionary Congress who set their faces against concluding peace with Great Britain on terms not sanctioned by France ; and who, in strict consistency with their vehement French predilections, attempted a censure on Mr. Jay and Mr. Adams, because they had negotiated a treaty of peace, without the consent of the French Government, though that treaty was honourable and advantageous to the United States. It is well known that Washington laboured, in every possible way, even to the length of risking his popularity, to maintain and perpetuate friendly relations with Great Britain ; but Mr. Madison opposed his pacific mission to that country in 1794 ; and, about the same time, whilst the revolutionary rulers of France were ferociously plunging through their dreadful career of massacre and confiscation, Mr. Madison, at that frightful epoch of human calamity, stepped forward in Congress to commence that warfare against British commerce, which he afterwards waged with so much determination,—introducing resolutions which, it is worth remarking, were the same in character with Buonaparte's continental system. We have styled that continental system, as embodied in the Berlin and Milan Decrees, a commercial excommunication of Great Britain,—a view which the American merchants did, in a body, take of Buonaparte's enormous pretensions ; but Mr. Madison represented acts, which virtually excluded Great Britain from the pale of civilized nations, and were devised with the avowed purpose of destroying her, as mere " municipal regulations." And, though the ships of his own nation, if detected in the " infamous guilt" of trading with, or through England, were by the Milan Decree, declared to be *denationalized,* and were, in fact, confiscated, with their cargoes, there was queralousness, it is true, in his communications with the French Government, but there was nothing that sounded of war. Our convictions, however, of the more than sympathy,—of the co-operation of Mr. Madison with France,—are founded chiefly on his secret manœuvering in connection with the blockade of 1806. The history of the thing is curious ; and, though it may not weigh with all of our readers as it has done with us, we fancy that those to whom it may be new, will be, equally with ourselves, interested in it. We give it, therefore, below, as we find it in the London Quarterly Review, of September, 1812; composed of extracts from the New England Farme's pamphlet previously noticed by us, together with the Reviewer's observations.* When our readers have sufficiently examined this curious case, they may attach what force they think is due to the only observation we intend to add to this head, viz., that Mr. Madison—it has been asserted—sent out a copy of his war message to France, in the *Wasp ;* and that this is not the only circumstance which affords reason for believing that France for some time be-

---

* What shall we say if it appear that this *first aggression of* 1806, which is now represented as the immediate cause of the Berlin Decree, was, *for the first time,* suggested by Mr. Madison, in 1806, (through General Armstrong to Buonaparte,) as a justifiable cause of the French decree ?—that this blockade of 1806, which was approved by Mr. Munroe,—was not objected against by Mr. Jefferson in 1808,—was not even mentioned by Mr. Madison in the arrangement made with Mr. Erskine in 1809—but that this great and atrocious injury done to France and America, forgotten, neglected, and not once adverted to in four years' negociation,—was brought forward, *for the first time,* to make a principal figure in 1810, for the express purpose, as it would seem, of throwing in the way invincible obstacles to any adjustment with Great Britain ? Let us hear the 'farmers' on the subject.

"The first notice of it, as far as we can find, is in a letter from General Armstrong to Mr. Smith, our secretary of state, of January 28th, 1810, in which he details a conversation which he had held with Count Champagny, the French minister. In that letter Mr. Armstrong refers to a letter of December 1st, 1809, from Mr. Smith to himself, *which has never been published,* in which he is directed to demand of France—*Whether, if Great Britain revoked her blockades of a date anterior to the decree commonly called the Berlin Decree, His Majesty the Emperor would consent to revoke that decree ?"* To which the Emperor, falling into the views of our government, and foreseeing the *snare* which would be laid for Great Britain, insomuch as, if she consented to repeal said orders, it would be an admission that she had been the aggressor upon neutral commerce, and further, it would be an admission that she had no right to exert her *only force,* her *maritime power,* for the coercion of her enemy, replied "*That the* ONLY *condition required for the revocation of the decree of Berlin, will be a previous revocation by Great Britain of her blockades of France, or ports of France, of a date anterior to the aforesaid decree.*"

"So far the plot went on prosperously; and if Great Britain had fallen into the project, it would have been made the pretext for preventing any future blockades of even single ports of France, in which armaments for her destruction, or the destruction of her commerce, should be formed; and she would have relinquished to an enemy, whom she cannot attack upon the continent on equal terms, the only weapons which God and her own valour had placed within her power."

The next step was to transmit this project for swindling Great Britain out of her maritime rights to Mr. Pinckney, the American minister in London, who accordingly demanded of Lord Wellesley 'whether Great Britain considered any, and if any, what blockades of the French coast, of a date anterior to the Berlin Decree, in force?' Lord Wellesley briefly answered, that 'the blockade of May, 1806, was comprehended in the Order of Council of January, 1807, which was yet in force.' A month afterwards, 7th March, 1810, Mr. Pinckney again asked 'whether the order of May, 1806, was merged in that of January, 1807 ?' to which Lord Wellesley replied 'that it was comprehended under the more extensive orders of January, 1807.'

Mr. Pinckney, though not quite satisfied with Lord Wellesley's answers, wrote to General Armstrong, 'that the inference from them was, that the blockade of May, 1806, *is virtually at an end,* being merged and comprehended in an Order of Council issued *after* the date of the Berlin Decree.' This inference, however, did not suit any of the intriguing parties; and General Armstrong does not seem to have thought it necessary to ruffle the repose of his Imperial Majesty, by submitting the point to M. Champagny; at least nothing farther appears till the extraordinary letter of the Duc de Cadore, in which the Berlin and Milan Decrees are premised to be repealed, provided Great Britain will repeal her orders, and 're-nounce her *principles of blockade* which she wishes to establish :'—' terms,' says the Farmer, 'which every man will perceive might be construed to amount to the surrender of *all* her maritime rights.'

"That there was a secret understanding between our cabinet and that of France, that Great Britain should be required to annul her blockades of a date anterior to the Berlin Decree, and that this suggestion *first* came from our cabinet, will appear from the two following extracts of letters from our secretary Smith, to Mr. Pinckney; the one is dated in July, 1810, in which he says, "you will let it be distinctly understood that the repeal must *necessarily include* an annulment of the blockade

fore knew that war would be declared, whilst Great Britain, the other belligerent, said to be impartially treated, never suspected such a thing, even at the moment of repealing her Orders in Council : for, although it evinced strange insensibility to the lowering portents of the future, that the possibility of a war with the United States, arising from those Orders, was never once alluded to by those members of the British Parliament who spoke against them in the debate of June, 1812 ; still, that very insensibility to transatlantic presages shows, in the strongest manner, how little the catastrophe of war* with the United States was anticipated

of May, 1806 ; this is the explanation which *will be given* by our minister at Paris to the French government, *in case it shall* then be required." It seems it *had not then* BEEN required by France.

" That this was a concerted thing is apparent, from another clause of the same letter, in which Mr. Smith says, that " should Great Britain not withdraw *all her previous partial* blockades, it is probable that France will draw Great Britain and the United States to issue on the legality of *such blockades* (that is, all partial blockades) by acceding to the act in Congress, *on condition* that the *repeal of the blockade shall accompany* that of the Orders in Council.

" Within one month after these despatches arrived in France, Buonaparte *did* bring us to issue with Great Britain on *this very point* ; and yet Mr. Madison was *no prophet*, because it was *he* who first suggested the thought to Armstrong, and Armstrong to the ingenious cabinet of St. Cloud. " In conformity to *your suggestions*, in your letter of December 1st, 1809," (says General Armstrong to Mr. Smith,) " I demanded whether, if Great Britain revoked her decrees of a date anterior to the Berlin decree, his Majesty would consent to revoke that decree."

After this clear exposition, we think that no reasonable being can entertain any doubts of Mr. Madison's intrigues with France.

———

* Whilst this political ferment was agitating the different parties of candidates for ministerial power, the examinations in reference to the effects of the Orders in Council upon the commercial and manufacturing interests in the kingdom were going on with little interruption in both houses of parliament. A vast mass of evidence being at length collected, Mr. Brougham, on

by Great Britain, five days after† Congress had signed and sealed the warrant for the unnatural strife.

———

June 16th, brought the matter for final decision before the House of Commons. He began his speech with observing, that the question, though of unexampled interest, was one of little intricacy. Its points were few in number, and involved in no obscurity or doubt. At a distance, indeed, there appeared a great mass of details, and the eight or nine hundred folios of evidence, together with the papers and petitions with which the table was covered, might cause the subjects to appear vast and complicated ; yet he did not doubt in a short time to convince his hearers that there has seldom been one of a public nature brought before that house through which the path was shorter, or led to a more obvious decision.

The hon. gentleman then took a general survey of the severe distress which was now pressing upon so many thousands of our industrious fellow-subjects, proved not only by their petitions, but by the numerous schemes and devices which had been resorted to as a remedy for the evils caused by the suppression of their accustomed sources of employment. He reminded the house of the general outline of the inquiry. Above a hundred witnesses had been examined from more than thirty of the great manufacturing and commercial districts. Among all these there was only one single witness who hesitated in admitting the dreadful amount of the present distresses ; Birmingham, Sheffield, the clothing trade of Yorkshire, the districts of the cotton trade, all deeply participated in them. He then adverted to the proofs by which this evidence was met on the other side of the house; and took into consideration the entries in the Custom-house books, and the substitutes and new channels of commerce said to compensate for those that are closed. He next touched upon the topic so often resorted to by the defenders of the Orders in Council, that of the dignity and honour of the nation, and the necessity of asserting our maritime rights ; and he maintained that every right may safely be waved or abandoned for reasons of expediency, to be resumed when those reasons cease. He lastly, dwelt upon the great importance of the American market to the goods produced in this country, and the danger of accustoming the Americans to rely on their own resources, and manufacture for themselves. After a long and eloquent harangue on these and other connected subjects, Mr. B. concluded with the following motion :—

———

† The debate in Parliament took place on the 23rd June ; the Declaration of War passed on the 18th.

February 6th, 1812. In addition to the regular troops, the President was authorised to employ 25,000 volunteers for twelve months, who were to form a body of men intermediate between the regulars and the militia, resembling the latter in most points, but differing from them in being liable to foreign service. Their clothing was to be provided by themselves; their arms were to be furnished by the government. Rapidly, however, as the forces of the United States, at this crisis, accumulated on paper, and ardent as the votes of Congress were for military preparation, the actual enlistment was anything but enthusiastic.

Recruits came in slowly—at the ratio of one thousand in six months—notwithstanding the liberal bounty which was offered. It is curious to observe the comparative coldness with which at this time Congress addressed themselves to promoting the efficiency of the navy,—that arm of the service which certainly did the republic most credit during the war. A subsidy of only $300,000 was voted for repairs; and a further sum of $200,000 annually, for rebuilding certain ships. What was proposed to be accomplished by this paltry sum, was to repair and fit out the Constellation, Chesapeake, and

March 28th.

"That an humble address be presented to his royal highness the Prince Regent, representing that this house has for some time past been engaged in an inquiry into the present distressed state of the commerce and manufactures of the country, and the effects of the Orders in Council issued by his Majesty in the years 1807 and 1809;* assuring his Royal Highness that this house will at all times support his Royal Highness to the utmost of its power in maintaining those just maritime rights which have essentially contributed to the prosperity and honour of the realm—but beseeching his Royal Highness that he would be graciously pleased to recall or suspend the said Orders, and adopt such measures, as may tend to conciliate neutral powers, without sacrificing the rights and dignity of his Majesty's crown."

Mr. Rose acknowledged that a very considerable degree of distress did exist among our manufactures, but would not admit that it was so much owing to the Orders in Council as the hon. gentleman had represented. He corrected several statements made by him, and showed that the commerce of France had suffered in much greater proportion from the effects of these Orders. Our shipping interest, he asserted, had been benefitted by them, and if they were repealed, the Americans would come in for a large share of our carrying trade, especially to South America. Upon the whole, he would not deny that our manufactures were likely to obtain some relief from the repeal, but government was placed between difficulties on both sides, and it was their duty to adopt the measures which would be least detrimental. In his opinion, the preponderance of argument led to the conclusion that the repeal of the Orders would be more prejudicial than their continu-

ance. The great body of merchants held the same opinion. Four-fifths of those of Glasgow had petitioned in support of the orders; those of Bristol were unanimous in their favour; and so were a majority of those of Liverpool: there was no petition from London against them, whilst a great number of London merchants had petitioned in their favour.

Mr. Baring, after a warm eulogy of the enlightened view of the subject taken by the honorable mover, said that the house had two questions to decide: 1. whether these distresses were attributable to the Orders in Council? 2. Whether any benefits had arisen from them in any other quarter to compensate for these calamities? Mr. B. made a number of particular observations relative to these two points; and concluded with giving it as his conviction, that by our Orders in Council we lost the most substantial commercial advantages for an object we could never obtain—that of forcing our trade with the continent.

Lord Castlereagh began with lamenting the precipitation of the hon. gentleman in bringing forward this motion, and pressing to hasty discussion a question than which none more vital ever came before the consideration of parliament. He deprecated any interference on the part of the house in a question in which commercial considerations were mixed with those of maritime right, and, pending a delicate negociation, dictating to the executive government the course it ought to pursue. After various observations in defence of the policy and justice of the Orders in Council, and in answer to some of the mover's statements, the noble lord came to the point by saying, that Great Britain would consent to suspend her Orders in Council, provided America would suspend her non-importation act. The experiment might then be tried of the practicability of restoring things to their ancient system. Under

---

* There was a modification of the Orders in April, 1809.

3

Adams frigates; and with the annual subsidy, to rebuild three other frigates of the old navy, too rotten to be repaired. The truth was, the war mania originated, mainly, with men who cared little or nothing about commerce—as they did not live by it,—and could contemplate its ruin without concern. The politlcians of the back-woods, who formed so strong and so stern a section of the violent faction seem to have hardly given a thought to the sufferings in store for the commercial cities on the sea-coast,—sufferings which, in any contest with a naval power like Great Britain, must always be terribly severe.

In this Congress (the twelfth) the celebrated Henry Clay, then a young and ardent man, made his first entrance on the great world of politics. He was a fervent advocate for war ; and his remarkable talents, combined with his sanguine and impetuous spirit, soon enabled him to outstrip the old champions of war, who raised him to the Speakership of the House of Representatives, and tacitly acknowledged him for their leader.

---

these circumstances he trusted that the house would not consent to the address—and he moved the order of the day.

Mr. Whitbread then begged the noble lord to say precisely what he proposed to do with respect to America.

Lord Castlereagh said, that he meant that a proposition should be made to the American government to suspend immediately the Orders in Council, on condition that they would suspend their non-importation act.

Mr. Whitbread was of opinion that if this proposition were to be sent out to America, and it was expected that the house and country should wait till they received an answer, it was the greatest delusion that had ever been attempted; and he proceeded to express in strong terms the urgency of the distress felt by the manufacturers, and the necessity of giving the intended relief without delay. Mr. Ponsonby also spoke against the measure proposed, as calculated to create delay.

Lord Castlereagh, in further explanation, said that it was never meant that there should be any delay in suspending the Orders in Council : the intention was that they should be suspended for a definite time, and that this circumstance should be communicated to the American government for the double purpose of ascertaining whether it would, in consequence, abrogate its non-importation act ; and also that it might apply to France to return to the ancient system of belligerents.

Mr. Wilberforce objected to the mode proposed by the noble lord, because it showed an unwillingness to do that which, in fact, he intended to do.

Mr. Canning, in giving a kind of middle opinion on the subject, contended that revocation was better than suspension.

Mr. Brougham, after congratulating the house on the prospect of speedily getting rid of these Orders, hoped that the noble lord would withdraw his motion for proceeding to the orders of the day, and explain more distinctly what was the exact intention of the government.

The final result was, that Mr. B. and Lord Castlereagh severally withdrew their motions on the understanding that an official instrument on the subject should appear in the next Gazette.

It was a remarkable circumstance in this debate, that Mr. Stephens, the most strenuous defender and promoter of the Orders in Council, was not present : a certain proof that ministers were already prepared to make the sacrifice which the voice of the country rendered inevitable.

On June 23rd, there appeared in the Gazette a declaration from the Prince Regent, absolutely and unequivocally revoking the Orders in Council as far as they regarded American vessels ; with the proviso, that if after the notification of this revocation by our minister in America, the government of the United States do not revoke their interdictory acts against British commerce, the same, after due notice, shall be null and of no effect.

Mr. Brougham, on this occurrence, declared the full satisfaction of himself and his friends with the frank and manly conduct of government in the mode it had adopted ; and both sides of the house seemed happy in the prospect of the amicable intercourse which this proceeding would restore between the two countries. We cannot, however, refrain from expressing our astonishment, that during the debates there appeared so little consciousness that the question of repealing or continuing the Orders in Council, was a real question of peace or war with America ; and that deferring the decision so long, was rendering it altogether unimportant. In fact, before the news of the repeal reached the United States, *they were actually at war with Great Britain.*

CHAPTER III.

—

Papers relating to Henry's Mission communicated to Congress by the President, on the 5th March.

In the year 1809, about the time of the first embargo, Mr. Madison told the British Minister at Washington that, in his estimation, such had been the conduct of Great Britain, that the United States would be justified in declaring war at any moment, and without further notice. The newspapers, at that time, were boiling over with invective against Great Britain, and the invasion of her North American Colonies was, even at that early period of the dispute, publicly talked of and discussed as a very feasible and very effectual measure of retaliation. Halifax and Quebec were both mentioned as points on which the attack might be advantageously commenced. As the President's language, taken in conjunction with the popular animosity, seemed to threaten an immediate assault, intelligence was despatched to Sir James Craig, the Governor of Canada, who, lest the Province under his command should be taken by surprise, sent an embassy into the Eastern States, for the purpose of procuring information. The instructions given to that agent were not inconsistent with the Governor's honourable character. All that he contemplated was,—to ascertain the real state of affairs in the United States; how far the war-spirit had spread; with what amount of success the resistance of the federal party would probably be attended; and, generally, to acquire such information as might assist him in putting the Province under his charge into a proper state of defence. Sir James Craig, however, was unfortunate, as it proved, in his choice of the person employed. This person was a Captain John Henry, a clever and active, but, as circumstances afterwards showed, a purely mercenary and unprincipled man. He was an Irishman by birth; had come to the United States as an adventurer; became a captain in the army of 1798; and ultimately settled on an estate in Vermont, close to the frontier. According to his own account, the attention of Sir James Craig was drawn to him by essays which he had written in newspapers against republican government, which he professed to hold in utter detestation. By some means or other, however, the Governor of Canada had heard of him, invited him to Montreal, and from thence despatched him to Boston early in 1809, for the purpose we have already described. After remaining in Boston about three months, during which period he wrote Sir James Craig's secretary fourteen letters, embodying information of no great value, as we think, he was recalled, on the apparent settlement produced by the Erskine arrangement. In 1811 he visited England, and applied at the Foreign Office for a reward for his services; but was referred back to Sir James Craig's successor in the government, " as better able to appreciate the ability and success with which his mission had been executed. Henry did not like this; and so, instead of returning to Canada, proceeded to the United States, where, in the genuine temper of an unfaithful hireling, he presented himself before Mr. Madison; told the tale of his mission; and offered to sell his papers. Mr. Madison closed with the profferred bargain, and paid him out of the secret service fund the large sum of $50,000 for the papers; apparently having only a general notion of their contents, and not imagining—as we must argue from the handsome price he paid for them—how little they contained. He expected, no doubt, when he made the liberal offer of $50,000, that the correspondence thus purchased would furnish disclosures highly serviceable to the Administration, both by blackening the character of the British government and by bringing suspicion and odium generally on the opposition in Congress,—perhaps by fixing a charge of treason on some. His disappointment, then, must have been extreme, on discovering that the British agent had received no authority or commission to offer bribes in any shape; that neither his letters nor the replies sketched out any plan of insurrection; and that the correspondence did not implicate, or even name a single citizen of the United States. Still, having got the papers into his hands, and paid dearly for his bargain, the President determined to make all the use of them that he could . He accordingly transmitted them to Congress, accompanied by a message, putting upon the whole affair the bitterest interpretation he could devise,—representing it as an effort, on the part of the British Government to foment disaffection in the United States, and to bring about the separation of the Eastern States from the Union. His end, however, was not answered. A momentary excitement, it is true, was produced; but, as he was unable to hold up to public indignation any of the "traitors" whom he may have hoped to detect in Congress, nothing material was effected in favour of the Administration. The opposition were not silenced; for not one of their number was caught in the trap. Had the result been different; had there been grounds for suspicion against them, it would assuredly have gone hard with them—as to their influence

at all events; for the minds of the multitude were in that heated state which renders the appeal of an unpopular minority to the bar of public opinion a perfectly hopeless affair. During the debate in Congress on the correspondence, a Mr. Johnson delivered himself of the sensible and elegant sentiment, that "he considered Canada as rogues' harbour, and saw in the correspondence additional reasons for attacking it." A vehement onset was made on the British Ministry in the House of Commons on this head; but, whilst they stated that Henry's mission was Sir James Craig's own act, unknown to them until all was over, they defended it on the ground that its object was nothing more than legitimate information, very desirable at so critical a time; though they admitted that the transaction was not in all its circumstances managed with perfect discretion. Poor Sir James was then in his grave; but, although his own voice was not raised in self-defence, we may venture to assert that his memory, which is that of a straightforward, honest, and fearless man, has not suffered even from the baseness of the agent whom it was his misfortune to employ. Alison's brief allusion to this transaction involves a slight error as to date, representing it as following the ninety days' embargo, of which we are about to speak. He uses, too, the words,—"certain documents *found* on a Captain Henry," from which the general inference would be, that Henry was detected, whereas he sold himself, as we have shown above, to Mr. Madison.

Ninety days' embargo, 4th April.

War having been determined upon by the Administration, the President sent a confidential message to Congress, recommending, "under existing circumstances and prospects," an embargo for sixty days. A bill to that effect passed the House of Representatives by 70 to 41; but the term was extended in the Senate to 90 days, with which extension it passed both branches of the Legislature. This was a committal of the Administration to war; for it was admitted by the Government party, that, as a peace-measure, the embargo could never have been entertained. Still the opposition—notwithstanding the serious alarm they felt—professing themselves unable to believe that the Government would commit so rash and so "treasonable" an action as that of plunging the nation, utterly unprepared, into war, suggested that the embargo was intended to serve the interests of Buonaparte, by stopping the export of provisions to Spain, where the British arms were beginning to be triumphant. The measure, however, was undoubtedly designed as preparatory to war, for the declaration of which, at the expiration of the ninety days, the Government had now made up their minds. Mr. Alison describes the object of the measure only in part, when he represents it as intended to "prevent intelligence of their preparations from reaching Great Britain, and to furnish them with the means, from their extensive commercial navy, of manning their vessels of war." Its main object was to remove from the ocean as many of their merchant-ships as possible, and thus place them out of the reach of British ships of war, when the proclamation of hostilities should become known. The passing of the embargo was conducted under an injunction of secrecy; but the secret was divulged; and the commercial cities which gained intelligence of it improved the few days allowed them in lading and despatching ships with extraordinary ardour and celerity. The Democratic journals were infuriated. Flour, by hundreds of thousands of barrels, they said, had been exported selfishly and unpatriotically, to feed the British troops in Spain. It was nothing to them that those troops were fighting in the noblest cause which God has ever blessed with success; fighting side by side with the soldiers of an oppressed people,—groaning beneath the exactions, the massacres, and the odious rule of a French usurper. These embargoes exhibited, in a remarkable manner, the blind rage of an irritated democracy, bent on inflicting vengeance on an enemy even at the certain risk of greater damage to themselves. "The direct national injury," says a writer in the American Review, of April, 1812, "caused by an embargo of twelve

months duration, would be, according to statistical calculation, as follows :—

Mercantile loss, ... $24,814,249
Deteriorated value of surplus
  produce and waste, ... 40,196,028
Loss sustained by the revenue, 9,000,000

Total direct national loss,..... $74,010,277
  Or, $6,167,523 per month.

The same moment, therefore, that the nation is called upon to aid their government with a loan of 11,000,000 dollars, this government, without any single openly avowed or obviously beneficial purpose, at the bare suggestion of expediency on the part of the Executive, destroys, by an embargo of three months, national wealth to the amount of $18,502,570, not to reckon the indirect and collateral mischief, of enormous magnitude, with which the same measure is pregnant."

President's Message, 1st June.

On the 1st June, "the President sent a confidential Message to Congress, in which he recapitulated all the causes of complaint against Great Britain;"

War declared on the 18th, and persisted in, although Intelligence subsequently arrives of the repeal of the Orders in Council.

and on the 18th a bill, declaring war against Great Britain, passed the House of Representatives, by a vote of 79 to 49; and the Senate, by 19 to 14. Hostilities were therefore immediately ordered to be commenced. "Nor did the American Government," writes Mr. Alison, "make any attempt to recede from these hostile acts, when intelligence arrived a few weeks after this resolution, and before war had commenced,* that, by an Order in Council,

---

* No blow had as yet been struck. "Mr. Madison," as the London Quarterly, of January, 1814, humourously observed, "had forged his thunderbolts; but held them yet unlaunched in his red right hand." The pleasure of hurling them, however, was not to be resisted; more especially as the British standard in Canada was to be utterly shivered and annihilated by them.

the British Government had actually *repealed the previous Orders*, so that the ostensible ground of complaint against this country was removed." The war—the grand provocation having been thus removed—was persisted in, for want of a better excuse, on the ground of the Impressment question. But the Impressment matter had actually been arranged in the Treaty of 1806,—a Treaty approved of to the fullest extent, and signed by the negotiators of the United States concerned in framing it, though Mr. Jefferson afterwards, for reasons best known to himself, refused to ratify it. Nobody, therefore, could pretend but that the question of Right of Search and Impressment, as it had once been settled, might be settled again, without recourse to arms, and was still open for amicable adjustment.

The War of 1812, 13, and 14, a War of Aggression, on the part of the United States.   Besides the moral obligation manifestly resting on the government of the United States to abandon, in common honesty and fairness, a war, the alleged provocation to which had been removed ; the American Congress were virtually pledged to such an abandonment, their own words witnessing against them. In the Report of the Committee (November 29th, 1811) urging preparation for war, it was stated that their intention was, " as soon as the forces contemplated to be raised should be in any tolerable state of preparation, to recommend the employment of them for the purpose for which they shall have been raised, *unless Great Britain shall, in the meantime, have done us justice.*"*

* The Committee, Mr. P. said, have not recommended this course of measures without a full sense of the high responsibility which they have taken upon themselves. They are aware that war, even in its best and fairest form, is an evil deeply to be deprecated : but it is sometimes, and on few occasions perhaps more than on this, a necessary evil. For myself, I confess I have approached the subject not only with diffidence, but with awe : but I will never shrink from my duty because it is arduous or unpleasant, and I can most religiously declare that I never acted under stronger or clearer convictions of duty than I do now in recommending these preparatory measures; or than

Thus, the course which they themselves acknowledged would be just, and gave implied promise of adopting, was not adopted when the condition had been fulfilled. The government of the United States stand, then, self-convicted of wanton aggression on the North American Colonies of Great Britain, and of prosecuting the war on grounds different from those which they were accustomed to assign. If to our mother-land there attach the reproach of impolitic pertinacity in maintaining, so long, a system prejudicial to her own commerce, and irritating to a neutral power, under an

I shall ultimately in recommending war, in case Great Britain shall not have rescinded her Orders in Council, and made some satisfactory arrangements in respect to the impressment of our seamen. If there should be any gentlemen in the house who were not satisfied that we ought to go to war for our maritime rights, Mr. P. earnestly entreated that they would not vote for the resolutions. Do not, said he, let us raise armies, unless we intend to employ them. If we do not mean to support the rights and honour of the country, let us not drain it of its resources.

Mr. P. said, he was aware that there were many gentlemen in the house who were dissatisfied that the committee had not gone further, and recommended an immediate declaration of war, or the adoption of some measures which would have instantly precipitated us into it. But he confessed such was not his opinion; he had no idea of plunging ourselves headlong into a war with a powerful nation, or even a respectable province, when we had not three regiments of men to spare for that service. He hoped that we should not be influenced by the howling of newspapers, nor by a fear that the spirit of the 12th Congress would be questioned, to abandon the plainest dictates of common sense and common discretion. He was sensible that there were many good men out of Congress, as well as many of his best friends in it, whose appetites were prepared for a *war feast*. He was not surprised at it, for he knew the provocatives had been sufficiently great. But he hoped they would not insist on calling in the guests, at least until the table should have been spread. When this was done, he pledged himself, in behalf of the Committee of Foreign Relations, that the gentleman should not be disappointed of the entertainment for the want of bidding; and he believed he might also pledge himself for many of the members of the Committee, that they would not be among the last to partake personally, not only in the pleasures, if any there should be, but in all the dangers of the revelry.—American **Weekly** Register, vol. 1, p. 268.

impression of necessary self-defence, right in the first instance, but subsequently, by the angry legislation of the United States, rendered delusive; there is, at least, no moral turpitude in such a charge. The lust of conquest, however, involving, as it does, moral guilt, provokes a censure and fixes a stain which the honour of a nation, and of a Christian nation especially, is deeply concerned in repelling, if it can. For this offence against national integrity and good faith the government of the United States are answerable, in prosecuting the war from motives clearly distinct from those which they avowed; motives not at all consistent with the position in which they desired to place themselves before the world,—that of an aggrieved people contending for rights which had been infringed; motives, in short, arising wholly from popular feelings at once covetous of the possessions of another nation, and exasperated for the time by passions beyond control. In a word, the war of 1812 was a war of AGGRESSION; and its fate was that with which it is the usual Providence of God to visit, sooner or later, all aggressive wars: it was a failure; and a failure, though brightened by occasional triumph, involving, on the whole, a large amount of retributive calamity. It is, too, a remarkable; we might say, providential circumstance, that the failure was mainly brought about through the gallant and the unexpected resistance of the very colony which was regarded by its invaders as likely to prove an easy conquest, in consequence, more particularly, of the disloyalty to the British Crown vainly imagined to lurk in its heart. That very colony which, to the war-party in Congress, was the object of cupidity, and by a "strong delusion" afforded them their highest hopes of success, became largely instrumental to their discomfiture. This looks like a judicial disappointment of schemes not merely visionary and inconsiderate; but—what is far worse—violent and unjust.

The War Declared simultaneously with the Invasion of Russia. Six days after the declaration of war by the United States, Buonaparte passed the Niemen, with the vast and brilliant armament which, in the purpose of its imperial leader, was to bring down Russia as low as the rest of the Continent; but was destined, in the designs of Providence, to afford in modern history, a parallel to Pharoah and Sennacherib. Had the United States awaited the issue of that expedition it is possible that their war against Great Britain would not have been declared. Even if the flames of Moscow had proved as ineffectual as the woes of Spain to exasperate them against the scourge and the oppressor of Europe, still destruction, in one campaign of half a million of his veterans, was too evident and too serious a blow to his military strength, not to impair the prestige of his alliance, and to shake that faith in his destiny which may have extended from Europe to his Transatlantic allies; for in that false position our Anglo-Saxon brethren had, on the 18th June, 1812, unhappily placed themselves. A little more patience on the part of the United States would have set all right, without war, which remedied nothing, and produced no settlement but what would have been made, had peace continued, two years before; and that on terms more explicit and more advantageous to the Republic than the treaty of Ghent, which closed the unprofitable contest. Their troubles were the troubles of the age; caused by the convulsion and the disorganization of the civilized world,· not by any ill will harboured by Great Britain against them. Tyrants aiming at universal dominion cannot send their whirlwinds of men and steel over the earth without causing general suffering—and the United States suffered. With the breaking of the oppressor's rod, their sufferings would have ceased. The tide of French invasion once driven back, the ancient landmarks would have reappeared; the rights of nations, the renewal of intercourse, the revival of commerce; everything, in short, worth contending for would have followed the fall of Buonaparte, since it was by his conquests and decrees alone that the order and the happiness of the world had been interrupted. The United States, by throwing themselves into the contest, only delayed that happy consummation.

The British North American Provinces, the main object of the War. There were many things which, in and out of Congress, were grievously misunderstood in the United States. The loyalty of the British North American Provinces was misunderstood when the political seers of Congress asserted, with that vehement asseveration and implicit faith which are often found to bear an inverse proportion to truth and information, that those Colonies were ripe for defection. The power of Great Britain, hampered as she was by the mortal struggle with her European foe, was greatly misunderstood, when a member in Congress expressed apparently the expectations of the majority in the utterance of the appalling prediction,— " We shall drive the British from our continent ;" and the ability of the United States to cope with such an adversary was considerably overrated by wiser heads than another Congress orator possessed who delivered himself of this truly magnificent bombast,—" The Falls of Niagara could be resisted with as much success as the American people, when they should be called into action !" But amid all this deplorable misapprehension, there was one point which was not misunderstood,—THE VALUE OF THE BRITISH NORTH AMERICAN PROVINCES TO THE BRITISH CROWN. That point, both inside Congress and outside, was fully comprehended ; and what was said in regard to it was no more than the truth. " These Provinces," said Mr. Porter, the Chairman of the Committee of Foreign Relations," " were not only immensely valuable in themselves, but almost indispensable to the existance of Great Britain, cut off as she now is, in a great measure, from the North of Europe. He had been credibly informed that the exports from Quebec, only, amounted during the last year (1810) to near six millions of dollars, and most of these, too, in articles of the first necessity,—in ship timber and in provisions for the support of her fleets and armies." " The conquest of Canada," wrote the Weekly Register, about the same time, " will be of the highest importance to us in distressing our enemy ; in cutting off his supplies of provisions and naval stores for his West India Colonies and home demand. There is no place from whence she

can supply the mighty void that would be occasioned by the loss of this country, as well in his exports as imports. It would operate upon him with a double force : it would deprive him of a vast quantity of indispensable materials, as well as of food, and close an extensive market for his manufactures. Canada and Nova Scotia, if not fully conquered immediately, may be rendered useless to him in a few weeks. Without them, and particularly the latter, he cannot maintain those terrible fleets on our coast that we are threatened with, or bridge our harbours with frigates, admitting he may have no use for them to defend his own shores ; for he will not have a dockyard, fitting the purposes of his navy, within 3,000 miles of us." The great worth of these possessions was, at the time of which we are writing, and is now, well known to politicians in the United States. Whilst the war-spirit was raging, the democrats thought it distressing, intolerable that the British flag should be proudly waving, on their very borders, over so choice a tract of territory ; the rescue from monarchical rule of such a land, by nature so favoured, in position so conveniently situated for annexation, was to be resolutely attempted,—it was like taking the Holy City out of the hands of the infidels, and was eminently worthy of all the exuberant patriotism, and the blind sacrifice, and the furious effort of a republican crusade. The British North American Provinces were coveted ; coveted most ardently, for their own sake, and for the anticipated gratification of extirpating from the continent every vestige of kingly government. The ardour of the cupidity can scarcely excite surprise, where the object was so valuable, and the appropriation deemed so easy,—everything having been previously settled by the democrats to their perfect satisfaction,—in a manner the most easy and comfortable that can be imagined,— as to the political purpose which the British Colonies were to serve, when blessed with the privilege of incorporation with the United States. " I am willing," was the magnanimous declaration of Mr. Grundy, of Tennessee, " to receive the Canadians as adopted brethren ; it will have beneficial political effects ; it will preserve the equilibrium of the government. When Louisiana shall be fully peopled, the Northern States will lose their power; they will be at the discretion of others; they can be depressed at pleasure, and then this union might be endangered. I therefore feel anxious not only to add the Floridas to the South, but the Canadas to the North of this empire." This is all very amusing; but, unhappily, it suggests the painful reflection, that should the same dishonest cupidity continue, it may, at a future period again embroil the two nations. That the United States would be glad to annex the British Provinces; that the acquisition of these truly valuable, if not fully valued Colonies, would be hailed and celebrated by them as an event second in interest and importance only to their Declaration of Independence ;—this we believe to be undeniable. But the follies and the losses, the sacrificed treasure and life of the last war have taught them, we trust, the salutary lesson that there is more of profit to be derived from commerce with Great Britain in peace, than of glory or of territory to be wrested from her in war; and that to alehouse politicians alone ought to be left the madness of proposing the sacrifice of that lucrative traffic which now employs about one-half of all their shipping, with the hope of tarnishing the renown, disgracing the flag, or subduing any of the dependencies of that Empire which is still— and long may it so continue!—the most powerful on the face of the earth. As to the jealousy they may feel in consequence of having a foreign power—so formidable as

Great Britain—on their frontier, the counsel may be fitly applied to their case which was honestly and wisely given to Louis XIV., who, had he been guided by that sage advice, would have spared himself a dishonourable peace and a dismembered empire: " It is useless to allege," urged this honest counsellor of an unscrupulous king, " that these towns of Holland were necessary to your state : the property of others is never necessary to us. That which is truly necessary to us, is to observe strict justice. You ought not even to pretend that you have a right to retain in perpetuity certain places, because they contribute to the security of your frontier. It is your wisdom to seek that security by good alliances, by your moderation, or by strongholds which you have it in your power to fortify in the rear. But, be this as it may, the necessity of watching over our own security can never give us the right of seizing our neighbour's territory." By this advice, republics as well as kings may be profited ; and the United States in particular, if chargeable at all with frontier-conquest ; of which let themselves be judges. As to annexing the British North American Colonies by force of arms, the time has not yet arrived when that would be an exploit easy of accomplishment, or likely to prove remunerative, if we consider the sufferings and the disasters which must precede. The alternative of " peaceful cession" we will leave our posterity to discuss in the last days of Britain's decrepitude.

WHICH MAY ALMIGHTY GOD LONG FOREFEND !

CHAPTER IV.

" War is declared,"— " Great Britain is the enemy,"—"Our ancient and inveterate foe has at length been proclaimed, by the constituted authorities in the United States,"—" In the valley of humiliation ; at the foot of the throne of her idiot monarch ; at the threshold of the palaces of the knaves who administer the government in his name, we sought justice, and begged for peace ; not because we feared war, but from that moderation which distinguishes the people, as well as the government of the United States." Such was the chord which was ever and anon struck by a very large body of the people throughout the United States, as if, by awakening discord, to drown the last faint harmonious notes of moderation breathed by the reflecting portion of the community. The effort, however, was a vain one—unless we record the outbreak at Baltimore as a first successful result of the war feeling. Very different were the popular sentiments in the Southern States, where swarms of privateers were preparing to reap the expected harvest of prizes among the West India islands. Of the towns in this interest, Baltimore stood foremost in violence and outrage. A newspaper published there, entitled 'The Federal Republican,' had rendered itself obnoxious, by its opposition to the measures of the war-party, and menaces had repeatedly been thrown out against the conductors. On the night of July 27th, a mob assembled before the house of the editor, for the purpose of destroying it. In expectation of this attack, he had collected a number of friends with fire-arms, to defend it from the inside, among whom were Generals Lee and Lingan. A furious affray arose, in which the mob were several times repulsed, with loss. At length a party of military were brought to the spot, by the Mayor and General Stricker, to whom those of the defenders who were left in the house, twenty-six in number, surrendered themselves, upon assurance of their safety, and were conducted to prison. On the next day, at the shameful instigation of a public journal, the mob re-assembled before the jail, with the intention of taking their revenge; and having broken open the door, after some of the prisoners had rushed through and made their escape, they fell upon the rest with clubs, and beat them till scarcely any signs of life remained. General Lingan, a man of seventy, and formerly a friend of Washington, was killed on the spot. General Lee, a distinguished partizan in the revolutionary war, had his skull fractured; and many others were severely injured. The militia refused to turn out while this massacre was perpetrating, and the Mayor is said to have absented himself. It must be added, that this atrocity was regarded with horror and indignation in all the other parts of the United States.

At Boston, on the day of the declaration of war, all the ships in the port displayed flags half mast high, the usual token of mourning ; and a town meeting was held in that city, at which a number of resolutions were passed, stigmatizing the war as unnecessary and ruinous, and leading to a connexion with France, destructive to American liberty and independence. In several of the minor eastern cities, and in New York, similar, though not quite so broadly manifested, demonstrations occurred. At a convention of delegates from the several counties of the State of New York, held at the capital, in Albany, on the 17th and 18th of September, 1812, the spirit of the resolutions passed was :—

First, that the attempt, amongst a free people, to stifle enquiry, as to the arbitrary and despotic measures adopted by government, in plunging the country into an unjust war, is essentially hostile to republican institutions, and one of the worst species of tyranny which the ingenuity of the foes of freedom has yet contrived.

Secondly, that the declaration of war was a most rash, unwise, and inexpedient measure ; and, considering the time and circumstances of its declaration, the condition of the country, and state of the public mind, one which ought forever to deprive its authors of the esteem and confidence of an enlightened people.

With regard to the proposed descent on Canada, the convention decided, also, that " the creation of New States, out of territories not within the ancient limits of the United States, is inconsistent with the spirit of the federal compact, and calculated to destroy the weight which the old, great, and populous States ought to have in the Union." A most emphatic protest against prosecuting the war, on the grounds officially noted, was also entered, with a declaration, that *even the possibility of an alliance* with France should be regarded with abhorrence. All these attempts, however, of the moderate party were unsuccessful, as we have shown, and but resulted in the final declaration of hostilities, in June, 1812.

Declaration of Hostilities. We introduce here both the acts declaratory of hostilities on both sides,* although one preceded the other nearly four months ; but it may be interesting to the reader to mark the spirit of the two declarations— the one, short, uncompromising, and leaving no choice whatever to the British Go-

vernment, appeared as if it had been dictated by the parties, who for six months before had been equipping their fastest vessels as privateers, and who well knew that their best chance of securing easy and rich prizes lay in intercepting the last of the homeward bound West India men for that year ; as, when once the declaration of war should be fully made known, no vessels would be permitted to run without convoy ; and thus the chances of the smaller class of privateers securing prizes would be mate-

---

* An Act declaring War between the United Kingdom of Great Britain and Ireland, and the Dependencies thereof, and the United States of America, and their Territories.

Be it enacted, by the Senate and House of Representatives of the United States of America, in Congress assembled, that war be, and the same is hereby declared to exist, between the United Kingdom of Great Britain and Ireland, and the Dependencies thereof, and the United States of America and their Territories ; and that the President of the United States be, and is hereby authorised, to use the whole land and naval force of the United States, to carry the same into effect ; and to issue to private armed vessels of the United States commissions or letters of marque and general reprisal, in such form as he shall think proper, and under the seal of the United States, against the vessels, goods, and effects of the government of the said United Kingdom of Great Britain and Ireland, and the subjects thereof.

JAMES MADISON.

June 18, 1812.—Approved.

—

Declaration of War against America—at the Court of Carlton-House, October 13, 1812— present, His Royal Highness the Prince Regent in Council.

Whereas, in consequence of information having been received of a declaration of war by the United States government against His Majesty, and of the issue of letters of marque and reprisal by the said government, against His Majesty and his subjects, an Order in Council, bearing date the 31st of July last, was issued, directing that American ships and goods should be brought in and detained till further orders ; and whereas His Royal Highness the Prince Regent, acting in the name and on the behalf of His Majesty, forbore at that time to direct

letters of marque and reprisal to be issued against the ships, goods, and citizens of the said United States of America, under the expectation that the said government would, upon the notification of the Order in Council, of the 23rd of June last, forthwith recall and annul the said declaration of war against His Majesty, and also annul the said letters of marque and reprisal.

And whereas the said government of the United States of America, upon due notification to them of the said Order in Council, of the 23rd of June last, did not think fit to recall the said declaration of war and letters of marque and reprisal, but have proceeded to condemn, and persisted in condemning the ships and property of his Majesty's subjects, as prize of war, and have refused to ratify a suspension of arms agreed upon between Lieutenant-General Sir George Prevost, His Majesty's Governor-General of Canada, and General Dearborn, commanding the American forces in the northern provinces of the United States, and have directed hostilities to be recommenced in that quarter.

His Royal Highness the Prince Regent, acting in the name and on the behalf of His Majesty, and with the advice of His Majesty's Privy Council, is hereby pleased to order, and it is hereby ordered, that general reprisals be granted against the ships, goods, and citizens of the United States of America, and others inhabiting within the territories thereof (save and except any vessels to which His Majesty's license has been granted, or which have been directed to be released from the embargo, and have not terminated the original voyage on which they were detained or released,) so that as well His Majesty's fleets and ships, as also all other ships and vessels that shall be commissioned by letters of marque or general reprisals, or otherwise by His Majesty's commissioners for executing the office of Lord High Admiral of Great Britain, shall or may lawfully seize all ships, vessels, and goods belonging to the government of the United States of America, or the citizens thereof, or others

rially lessened. East Indiamen, it was well known, were beyond the mark of any cruisers but those of considerable force, and subsequent events showed that the harvest of prizes in this field was but inconsiderable. The declaration of the British Government is noteworthy, for the moderation which even at that last stage it evinced, nothing can more clearly mark the spirit which then actuated the British Council, or more satisfactorily demonstrate their unwillingness to precipitate hostilities. Having, however, fairly disposed of the question, we will now turn to Canada, and take up, in order, the events which then shook to its core that, as yet, infant state.

Before, however, commencing our account of the various warlike proceedings which almost immediately commenced, it would be as well for us to take a brief review of the actual position in which Canada stood at the breaking out of the war,—to examine into her means of defence, and to endeavour to ascertain, if possible, the causes which could have led to the belief, so universally held by their neighbours, that Canadians, as a body, might be considered as disaffected ; and Canada as not unwilling to assist in the cause of annexation.

inhabiting within the Territories thereof, and bring the same to judgment in any of the Courts of Admiralty within His Majesty's dominions; and to that end His Majesty's Advocate-General, with the Advocate of the Admiralty, are forthwith to prepare the draught of a commission, and present the same to His Royal Highness the Prince Regent, at this board, authorising the Commissioners for executing the office of Lord High Admiral, or any person or persons by them empowered and appointed, to issue forth and grant letters of marque and reprisals to any of His Majesty's subjects, or others whom the said Commissioners shall deem fitly qualified in that behalf for the apprehending, seizing, and taking the ships, vessels, and goods belonging to the United States of America, or the citizens thereof, or others inhabiting within the countries, territories, or dominions thereof, (except as aforesaid,) and that such powers and clauses be inserted in the said commission as have been usual, and are according to former precedents ; and His Majesty's Advocate-General, with the Advocate of the Admiralty, are also forthwith to prepare the draft of a commission, and present the same to His Royal Highness the Prince Regent, at this board, authorising the said Commissioners for executing the office of Lord High Admiral to will and require the High Court of Admiralty of Great Britain, and the Lieutenant and Judge of the said Court, his Surrogate or Surrogates, as also the several Courts of Admiralty within His Majesty's dominions, to take cognizance of, and judicially proceed upon all and all manner of captures, seizures, prizes, and reprisals of all ships and goods that are or shall be taken, and to hear and determine the same, and, according to the course of Admiralty and the laws of nations, to adjudge and condemn all such ships, vessels, and goods as shall belong to the government of the United States of America, or the citizens thereof, or to others

inhabiting within the countries, territories, and dominions thereof (except as aforesaid(; and that such powers and clauses be inserted in the said commission as have been usual, and are according to former precedents ; and they are likewise to prepare and lay before His Royal Highness the Prince Regent, at this board, a draught of such instructions as may be proper to be sent to the Courts of Admiralty in His Majesty's Foreign Governments and Plantations, for their guidance herein ; as also another draught of instructions for such ships as shall be commissioned for the purpose above-mentioned.

His Royal Highness the Prince Regent is nevertheless pleased hereby to declare, in the name and on the behalf of His Majesty, that nothing in this order contained shall be understood to recall or affect the declaration which His Majesty's Naval Commander on the American station has been authorised to make to the United States of America—namely, that His Royal Highness, animated by a sincere desire to arrest the calamities of war, has authorised the said Commander to sign a convention, recalling and annulling, from a day to be named, all hostile orders issued by the respective governments, with a view of restoring, without delay, the relations of amity and commerce between His Majesty and the United States of America.

From the Court of Carlton-House, the 13th of October, 1812.

(Signed) CASTLEREAGH.
N. VANSITTART.
CHARLES LONG.
LIVERPOOL.
BATHURST.
MELVILLE.
SIDMOUTH.

Canadians were not disloyal at that period.

We may fairly deduce this fact, as far as Upper Canada is concerned, from the tenor of General Brock's despatches. Even so far back as 12th February, 1812, we find him writing to Colonel Baynes, the Adjutant-General,— " I have reason to look for the acquiescence of the two Houses to every measure I may think necessary to recommend, for the peace and defence of the country. A spirit has manifested itself little expected by those who conceived themselves the best qualified to judge." Even in speaking of those who were considered, if not hostile, to be, at least, indifferent to British interests, the Lieutenant-Governor remarks : " I do not, of course, think it expedient to damp the ardour displayed by those once doubtful characters. The most powerful opponents to Governor Gore's Administration take the lead on the present occasion. Some opposed Mr. Gore evidently from personal motives, but *never forfeited* the right of being numbered among the loyal. Few, very few are actuated by base or unworthy considerations; their character will very soon, however, be put to a severe test. The measures which I intend to propose are—1. ' A Militia Supplementary Act ;' 2. ' The Suspension of the Habeas Corpus ;' 3. ' An Alien Law ;' 4. ' An Act for the better apprehension of deserters.' "

Now, although General Brock found himself beaten, in the House of Assembly, on both the Militia and Habeas Corpus Acts, yet we find, in the reasons he assigns, no ground to change our opinion. On the contrary, he distinctly attributes the miscarriage of these two measures—the first was lost by the casting-vote of the chairman, and the second by an almost equally trifling majority—to the strong sentiment that prevailed, that war was not likely to occur with the United States ; an opinion which was carefully disseminated by the numerous settlers from that country, and which tended materially to influence the votes of the members, or of such of them at least as, by their ignorance of the real position of

affairs, were easily betrayed into error. That General Brock, at all events, saw no reason to induce a change of opinion, is pretty evident, if we may judge from the tone of his despatch, of 16th May, to Sir George Prevost, the Governor-General :— " Every one with whom I have had an opportunity of conversing, assures me that an exceedingly good disposition prevails among the people." The soundness of this opinion was most triumphantly established by subsequent events,—not the least important of which was, that as soon the Militia Bill, but slightly modified, was passed, although a clause had been introduced, authorizing the raising of flank companies, to be trained at least six times in each month, and although the inhabitants knew that they would have to go to a great distance to attend parade, would be liable to heavy expense, and be subject to no inconsiderable privations, the flank companies, in the districts in which they were established, were instantly completed with volunteers ; and, indeed, an almost unanimous disposition to serve was evinced. Now, this feeling was manifested at a time when the prospects of the Colony were most gloomy, and when the almost defenceless condition of the Province was but too apparent,—at a time when the Governor, on whose judgment so much depended, was forced to acknowledge, that although every man capable of carrying a musket, along the whole of the line, should be prepared to act, he " had not a musket more than would suffice to arm part of the militia from Kingston westward."

The advices from England at this juncture were also equally dispiriting, so much so, that, about this time, Col. Baynes is found expressing himself, " Sir Geo. Prevost has directed me to inform you, that unless reinforcements arrive from England, (of which his Excellency is not sanguine, as the prevailing apprehension in England seems to be, that hostilities would not ensue on this continent; and as, moreover, the pledge held out in the Prince Regent's speech, of supporting with energy the contest in Portugal and Spain, renders it little likely that troops will be sent to this quarter,) although he may be very desirous to render you any assistance to strengthen the Upper Province, his means of doing so will be but very limited. When we remember, besides all these dispiriting influences, that a numerous body of settlers from the United States were everywhere disseminating their evil counsels, and that well-founded fears were entertained that the American intrigues among the different Indian tribes, which had been openly carried on, and in the conducting of which no expence had been spared, had not failed of success, but that divisions had been sown among our Indian allies, and the minds of many altogether estranged, have we not ample grounds on which to base our assertions that the Canadas were sound to the core, and that all the rash and flatulent speeches made in the American houses of Legislature were but occasioned by the knowledge of their own weakness and divided state? Is it possible for any sane person to credit that the Americans were so totally led away by overweening vanity as to suppose that, when Great Britain should arise in her might, it would be possible for them to hope for success in a war of aggression? Is it not much more likely that French gold it was which originated the idle speculations respecting the Canadas, and not any evidences of discontent or disaffection in those Provinces? The following extracts, however, from an address of the assembly of Upper Canada, to their constituents, put the matters beyond the possibility of doubt and prove to demonstration the loyalty of the Province.

Remarks on the Address of the Assembly of Upper Canada, on the Declaration of War. It happened, most opportunely, that the House of Assembly had so nearly completed the business before them, that they were at liberty to take all the steps necessary at this crisis, without neglecting any other important measures.

"The declaration of war issued against Great Britain by the United States, when first announced, appeared to be an act of such astonishing folly and desperation, as to be altogether incredible, and not only excited the greatest surprise among the inhabitants of this Province, but among the great majority of our enemies themselves. So many

cogent reasons from interest, affection, and virtue, pleaded for an opposite policy, that the most intelligent became the most credulous. That a government professing to be the friend of man and the great supporter of his liberty and independence, should light up the torch of war against the only nation that stands between itself and destruction, exhibited a degree of infatuation or madness altogether incomprehensible — "it cannot be," said the wiser part of our inhabitants —"the United States will never declare war against a nation which has uniformly treated them with kindness and respect, whose fleets protect their commerce, and whose armies support their freedom and independence." But the men at present ruling the states, infatuated, or, as their more enlightened countrymen say, "bribed by the tyrant of France," regardless of the best interests of their country and the feelings and affections of a great majority of their own people, have commenced hostilities against our mother country while treating their vessels with hospitality, and instead of threatening their liberties, offering the most equitable terms of accommodation."

Here follows a long and spirited appeal to the descendants of the U.E. loyalists, who had been driven from the land of their adoption ; and there is very little doubt but that the spirit which was roused amongst Canadians was attributable, in a great measure, to the unshaken fidelity of these settlers.

"Already have we the joy to remark, that the spirit of loyalty has burst forth in all its ancient splendor. The militia in all parts of the Province have volunteered their services with acclamation, and displayed a degree of energy worthy of the British name. They do not forget the blessings and privileges which they enjoy under the protection and fostering care of the British Empire, whose government is only felt in this country by acts of the purest justice, and most pleasing and efficacious benevolence. When men are called upon to defend every thing they call precious, their wives and children, their friends and possessions, they ought to be inspired with the noblest resolutions, and they will not be easily frightened by menaces, or conquered by force. And beholding as we do, the flame of patriotism burning from one end of the Canadas to the other, we cannot but entertain the most pleasing anticipations. Our enemies have indeed said, that they can subdue this country by a proclamation; but it is our parts to prove to them that they are sadly mistaken; that the population is determinately hostile, and that the few who might be otherwise inclined, will find it their safety to be faithful."

That this part of the address produced the most beneficial results, was pretty clearly proved by the timid and vacillating measures adopted by General Hull; the more so, as every day afforded fresh proof to that General, after he was fairly on British ground, that he had been grossly deceived by the representations which had induced him to believe that Canada was ripe for a revolt.

" Innumerable attempts will be made by falsehood, to detach you from your allegiance; for our enemies, in imitation of their European master, trust more to treachery than to force; and they will, no doubt, make use of many of those lies, which unfortunately for the virtuous part of these states, and the peace and happiness of the world, had too much success during the American rebellion: they will tell you that they are come to give freedom—yes, the base slaves of the most contemptible faction that ever distracted the affairs of any nation—the minions of the very sycophants who lick the dust from the feet of Buonaparte, will tell you, that they are come to communicate the blessing of liberty to this Province; but you have only to look at your situation to put such hypocrites to confusion."

"Trusting more to treachery than open hostility, our enemies have already spread their emissaries through the country to seduce our fellow subjects from their allegiance, by promises as false as the principles on which they are founded. A law has therefore been enacted for the speedy detection of such emissaries, and for their condign punishment on conviction—a law which it will not be easy to escape."

The moderation of the different acts which were then passed, for the preservation and defence of the Province, is an additional proof that internal treachery was not one of the causes which were feared. The exigency of the time would have warranted the adoption of much more stringent measures ; and had there been any real grounds to fear the settlers from the United States, whose inclinations, though in the main good, would be naturally with the interests of their native country, could have caused any danger, doubtless effective measures would have been adopted. The Legislature, however, knew their men, and trusted to Canadian loyalty. We shall shortly see the proofs that their confidence was not misplaced.

"Remember, when you go forth to the combat, that you fight not for yourselves alone, but for the whole world. You are defeating the most formidable conspiracy against the civilization of man that ever was contrived; a conspiracy threatening greater barbarism and misery than followed the downfall of the Roman Empire—that now you have an opportunity of proving your attachment to the parent state which contends for the relief of oppressed nations, the last pillar of true liberty, and the last refuge of oppressed humanity.

"Persevere as you have begun, in your strict obedience to the laws and your attention to military discipline; deem no sacrifice too costly which secures the enjoyment of our happy constitution; follow, with your countrymen in Britain, the paths of virtue, and, like them, you shall triumph over all your unprincipled foes."

State of feeling in Lower Canada. Having, we think, satisfactorily, though briefly, disposed of any question that may have arisen with respect to the loyalty of Upper Canadians, we will take a glance at the state of parties in Lower Canada, and examine into the reasons why the stain of disaffection should be supposed to rest any more on them, than on their brethren in the Upper Province.

If there were grounds for apprehending that a feeling of disloyalty existed at all in Canada, reason would have at once suggested that in Lower Canada was the evil to be sought. Yet, on examination into this part of our subject, we find, that although Sir George Prevost had at this time a very delicate card to play with his House of Assembly, he succeeded in obtaining from them a Militia Act, which, though not affording all that was required, was still a material point gained. 2,000 men were to be balloted, to serve for three months, in two successive summers. One reason why more was not gained was, that an apprehension existed that Canadians might contract military habits, and enlist into the service. This feeling, however, did not prevent the establishment of the Glengarry Light Infantry,* who numbered, by the 1st May, 1812, four hundred rank and file; and we find, farther, that on Sir George Prevost's issuing orders to recruit for a still higher establishment, the officers engaged to double the number, and did it. This does not look like disaffection; and, whether we go still further east, or south, we trace the same spirit. We find two officers dividing Nova Scotia and New Brunswick, and enlisting Acadians, while Lieutenant McDonell is reported as making great progress among the Highland settlers on the coast and gulf. When we take all these circumstances, then, into consideration, we confess that we are at a loss to find any sounder reasons for imputing disaffection to Lower Canadians, than we have found to exist among their brethren of the Upper Province; and although they were not called on, in the course of the events which followed, to make such sacrifices, or give such unequivocal proofs of their loyalty, as Upper Canadians; yet, we venture to assert, that the animus was there which would have proved that in both Provinces alike the same pure spirit of patriotism burned.

We cannot well see what reasons the rulers of the United States could have adduced for arriving at a different conclusion. So far back as that momentous period, when their fellow colonists threw off their allegiance to the mother country, the French Canadians, though pressingly invited to assist, refused. They were, even then, aware of the blessings which they enjoyed under British Government, and willingly submitted to the Stamp Act, which caused so great a revolt amongst

their neighbours. On the 31st December, 1775, at the siege of Quebec, we find that almost to Lower Canadians alone was the successful resistance against the combined attack of Generals Arnold and Montgomery, attributable. "The party who defended the principal battery, consisted of CANADIAN MILITIA, with nine British seamen to work the guns." On no one occasion, in point of fact, can we detect the slightest trace of a hostile feeling towards the British Government amongst Lower Canadians: in the present instance what is the result of our examination? we find that "four battalions of militia were instantly raised, and the voltigeurs were organised and equipped in the short space of six weeks by the liberality of the young Canadians: we find the Legislature issuing government papers, bearing interest and payable in bills of Exchange in England, to prevent specie from going to the United States; and again, are our old friends, the inhabitants of Quebec, found at their post, guarding the citadel, proud of the duty, and of the consequence reposed on them. We think we need say no more on the head of the loyalty of Lower Canada.

On the 12th July, 1812, the American General Hull, with a force of twenty-five hundred men crossed over to Sandwich from Detroit and planted the American standard on Canadian soil, where he issued a proclamation,* inviting the inhabitants to join his standard.

First Hostile Demonstration; 12th July, 1812.

---

* PROCLAMATION.

Head Quarters, Sandwich,
12th July, 1812.

Inhabitants of Canada—

After thirty years of peace and prosperity, the United States have been driven to arms. The injuries and aggressions, the insults and indignities of Great Britain, have once more left them no alternative but manly resistance, or unconditional submission. The army under my command has invaded your country. The standard of the Union now waves over the territory of Canada. To the peaceable, unoffending inhabitants it brings neither danger nor difficulty. I come to find enemies, not to make them. I come to protect, not to injure you.

Separated by an immense ocean and an extensive wilderness from Great Britain, you have no participation in her councils, no interest in her conduct. You have felt her tyranny; you have seen her injustice; but I do not ask you to avenge the one, or to redress the other.

---

* Although the levies raised for the corps belonged generally to the Lower Province, yet strict geographical justice would assign these troops to the Upper Province.

As a foil to General Hull's vaporing gasconade, General Brock's proclamation, which

The United States are sufficiently powerful to afford every security consistent with their rights and your expectations. I tender you the invaluable blessing of civil, political, and religious liberty, and their necessary result, individual and general prosperity. That liberty which gave decision to our councils and energy to our conduct, in a struggle for independence, and which conducted us safe and triumphantly through the stormy period of the revolution. That liberty which has raised us to an elevated rank among the nations of the world, and which afforded us a greater measure of peace and security, of wealth and improvement, than ever fell to the lot of any country.

In the name of my country, and by the authority of government, I promise you protection to your persons, property and rights; remain at your homes, pursue your peaceful and customary avocations, raise not your hand against your brethren. Many of your fathers fought for the freedom and independence we now enjoy. Being children, therefore, of the same family with us, and heirs to the same heritage, the arrival of an army of friends must be hailed by you with a cordial welcome. You will be emancipated from tyranny and oppression, and restored to the dignified station of freemen. Had I any doubt of eventual success, I might ask your assistance, but I do not. I come prepared for every contingency —I have a force which will look down all opposition. And that force is but the vanguard of a much greater. If, contrary to your own interest and the just expectation of my country, you should take part in the approaching contest, you will be considered and treated as enemies, and the horrors and calamities of war will stalk before you. If the barbarous and savage policy of Great Britain be pursued, and the savages be let loose to murder our citizens, and butcher our women and children, this war will be a war of extermination. The first stroke of the tomahawk, the first attempt with the scalping knife, will be the signal for one indiscriminate scene of desolation. No white man found fighting by the side of an Indian will be taken prisoner; instant destruction will be his lot. If the dictates of reason, duty, justice, and humanity, cannot prevent the employment of a force which respects no rights, and knows no wrong, it will be prevented by a severe and relentless system of retaliation. I doubt not your courage and firmness—I will not doubt your attachment to liberty. The United States offer you peace, liberty, and security— your choice lies between these and war, slavery, and destruction. Choose, then, but choose wisely; and may He who knows the justice of our cause, and who holds in his hands the fate of nations, guide you to a result the most compatible with your rights and interests, your peace and happiness.

By the General. A. P. HULL,
Capt. of the 13th Regt. of U. S. Infantry, and Aide de Camp, &c.
Head Quarters, Sandwich,
July 12, 1812.

will be found at length in our notes, may appropriately be placed, the one as remarkable for firmness and dignity of tone, as the other was noteworthy for presumption and bombast. The artful and threatening language, in which Gen. Hull's proclamation was couched, failed, however, in producing the anticipated effect, and seemed but to nerve, still more keenly for the contest, the gallant few on whom the successful defence of the province depended—even then, in fact, had the foresight and energy of the British General prepared the first of those disasters which were so shortly to overwhelm the unfortunate Hull.* Early in the spring,

*The unprovoked declaration of war by the United States of America against the United Kingdom of Great Britain and Ireland, and its dependencies, has been followed by the actual invasion of this Province, in a remote frontier of the western district, by a detachment of the armed force of the United States.

The officer commanding that detachment has thought proper to invite his Majesty's subjects, not merely to a quiet and unresisting submission, but insults them with a call to seek voluntarily the protection of his government.

Without condescending to notice the epithets bestowed, in this appeal of the American commander to the people of Upper Canada, on the administration of his Majesty, every inhabitant of the Province is desired to seek the confutation of such indecent slander in the review of his own particular circumstances. Where is the Canadian subject who can truly affirm to himself that he has been injured by the government, in his person, his property, or his liberty? Where is to be found, in any part of the world, a growth so rapid in prosperity and wealth, as this colony exhibits? Settled, not thirty years, by a band of veterans, exiled from their former possessions on account of their loyalty, not a descendant of these brave people is to be found, who, under the fostering liberality of their sovereign, has not acquired a property and means of enjoyment superior to what were possessed by their ancestors.

This unequalled prosperity would not have been attained by the utmost liberality of the government, or the persevering industry of the people, had not the maritime power of the mother country secured to its colonists a safe access to every market, where the produce of their labour was in request.

The unavoidable and immediate consequences of a separation from Great Britain must be the loss of this inestimable advantage; and what is offered you in exchange? To become a territory of the United States, and share with them that exclusion from the ocean which the policy of their government enforces; you are not even flattered with a participation of their boasted independence: and it is but too obvious that, once estranged from the powerful protection of the United Kingdom, you must be re-annexed to the dominion of France, from which the provinces of Canada were wrested

ere events had assumed a decidedly hostile aspect, General Brock had provided for the protection of Fort St. Joseph, a small post to the north-east of the American island of Michilimacinac, and one of his first acts, on hearing of the declaration of war, was to send a notification of it to Captain Roberts, then in command at St. Joseph's, with instructions to make, if practicable, an immediate attack upon Michilimacinac. This order was acted upon by Captain Roberts with singular promptitude and decision, and on the 16th July he embarked with forty-five men of the 10th Royal Veteran Battalion, two hundred Militia under the command of Mr. Crawford, and two hundred and fifty Indians, composed principally of Sioux, Ottawas, and Chippewas. This force on the morning of the 17th effected a landing, and, without opposition, this vital post, with a garrison of some sixty regulars, was

surrendered.—Lieutenant Hancks, the officer in command of the Americans, has officially stated that the summons to surrender the fort was the first information he had of the declaration of war. This, however, appears but little probable, when we remember that the Americans had been making preparations* for a decisive attack in this very quarter for nearly six months, and that General Hull's army alone, the fruit of this preparation, exceeded the whole available force in Upper Canada.

---

by the arms of Great Britain, at a vast expense of blood and treasure, from no other motive than to relieve her ungrateful children from the oppression of a cruel neighbour. This restitution of Canada to the empire of France, was the stipulated reward for the aid afforded to the revolted colonies, now the United States; the debt is still due, and there can be no doubt but the pledge has been renewed as a consideration for commercial advantages, or rather for an expected relaxation in the tyranny of France over the commercial world. Are you prepared, inhabitants of Canada, to become willing subjects, or rather slaves, to the despot who rules the nations of continental Europe with a rod of iron? If not, arise in a body, exert your energies, co-operate cordially with the king's regular forces to repel the invader, and do not give cause to your children, when groaning under the oppression of a foreign master, to reproach you with having so easily parted with the richest inheritance of this earth—a participation in the name, character, and freedom of Britons!

The same spirit of justice, which will make every reasonable allowance for the unsuccessful efforts of zeal and loyalty, will not fail to punish the defalcation of principle. Every Canadian freeholder is, by deliberate choice, bound by the most solemn oaths to defend the monarchy, as well as his own property; to shrink from that engagement is a treason not to be forgiven. Let no man suppose that if, in this unexpected struggle, his Majesty's arms should be compelled to yield to an overwhelming force, the province will be eventually abandoned; the endeared relations of the first settlers, the intrinsic value of its commerce, and the pretensions of its powerful rival to repossess the Canadas, are pledges that no peace will be established between the United States and Great Britain and Ireland, of which the restoration of these provinces does not make the most prominent condition.

Be not dismayed at the unjustifiable threat of

the commander of the enemy's forces to refuse quarter, should an Indian appear in the ranks. The brave bands of Aborigines which inhabit this colony were, like his Majesty's other subjects, punished for their zeal and fidelity, by the loss of their possessions in the late colonies, and rewarded by his Majesty with lands of superior value in this Province. The faith of the British Government has never yet been violated—the Indians feel that the soil they inherit is to them and their posterity protected from the base arts so frequently devised to over-reach their simplicity. By what new principle are they to be prohibited from defending their property? If their warfare, from being different to that of the white people, be more terrific to the enemy, let him retrace his steps—they seek him not—and cannot expect to find women and children in an invading army.— But they are men, and have equal rights with all other men to defend themselves and their property when invaded, more especially when they find in the enemy's camp a ferocious and mortal foe, using the same warfare which the American commander affects to reprobate.

This inconsistent and unjustifiable threat of refusing quarter, for such a cause as being found in arms with a brother sufferer, in defence of invaded rights, must be exercised with the certain assurance of retaliation, not only in the limited operations of war in this part of the King's dominions, but in every quarter of the globe; for the national character of Britain is not less distinguished for humanity than strict retributive justice, which will consider the execution of this inhuman threat as deliberate murder, for which every subject of the offending power must make expiation.

                              ISAAC BROCK,
                        Major-Gen. and President.
Head Quarters,
    Fort-George, July 22, 1812.
By order of his honor the President.
                        J. B. GLEGG, Capt. & A.D C.

* We learn from General Armstrong, (Secretary at War at that period,) that preparations had been made along the whole Canadian frontier, in the fall of 1811, and that warlike stores had been sent to Burlington, on Lake Champlain. From the same authority we also learn, that General Hull began his march from Drayton, a frontier town in the State of Ohio, on the 1ST DAY OF JUNE, 1812, twelve days before the declaration of war, to coöperate with such other corps as might be destined to the invasion of Canada.— ED. A. A. M.

Be this,however, as it may—with Michilimacinac fell at once General Hull's hopes of an easy and bloodless conquest of Canada,—spirit and confidence were thereby infused into the Indian tribes, and the poor old General—already familiarized with Indian warfare, finding them less inclined for neutrality, and the Canadian Militia less favorable than he anticipated—even at this time began to discover the fallacy of the expectations he had so prematurely formed. Michilimacinac, (or Mackinaw, as it is now more commonly called,) is an island in the Straits between the Lakes Michigan and Huron, about four miles from land at the nearest point—its name is derived from a fancied resemblance to a turtle's back. The fort, on the south-east side, was situated on a rock, almost perpendicular in some places, extending nearly half round the island, and rising some two hundred feet from the water. It overlooked, and, of course, commanded the harbor, a beautiful basin of about a mile in extent, sheltered from Lake Huron by two islands stretching across its mouth, and leaving only a narrow ship channel by which to enter the harbor. This position was a most valuable one, as it commanded the passage by which, if necessary, Hull might expect his supplies or reinforcements. In the fort were a quantity of military stores and seven hundred packs of fur, the first fruits of the war.

While these scenes, so important in their effects, were being transacted in his rear, Gen. Hull commenced an advance on Fort Malden, or Amherstburg. At this time the British force on the frontier was nearly nominal, and could scarcely have been expected to offer much resistance, the garrison at Amherstburg, consisting of but about two hundred men of the 1st Battalion of the 41st Regiment, commanded by Captain Muir, a very weak detachment of the Royal Newfoundland Fencibles, and a subaltern's (Lieutenant Troughton's) command of Artillery—such was the material on which Canadians had to trust for a defence of one of the most important points along their frontier. This point was, indeed, of the most vital importance to the British, as it formed the key to their relations with the Indians of the West, and was, naturally, an object of very great interest to the enemy. General Hull had experienced no difficulty in ascertaining the weakness of its defences, and judging from the

almost utter impossibility of its obtaining supplies, he looked forward to the fate of Amherstburg as an event which did not admit of a doubt—with this view, therefore, he laid his plans, and against this point was the thunder of the American artillery to be first directed. The fort at Amherstburg could not have sustained a seige of long duration, four bastions flanking a dry ditch, with a single interior defence of picketing, perforated with loop-holes for musketry, offering but little obstacle to an enterprising enemy; a few shells, indeed, would have sufficed to destroy all the defences, as, with the exception of the magazine, all the buildings were of wood, and covered with pine shingles unfit for resisting any missile. The disadvantage of remaining in this position, Col. St. George, the commanding officer, well knew—orders were therefore given to the garrison to be ready at a moment's notice, as Col. St. George preferred giving battle, even with his inferior force, to remaining cooped up without the means of offering any resistence whatever.

The want of decision and energy* on the part of General Hull became at this time very apparent to his more enterprising opponents, indeed, the American General seemed to have forgotten altogether the intended objects of his invasion and to have confined his efforts to levying provisions and forage from the inhabitants towards whom the troops behaved with great severity, as if to avenge their disappointed hopes at meeting enemies where they expected to find friends.

This state of inaction was only interrupted by some desultory attempts to cross the river Canard, but the daily skirmishes which ensued led to no action of a decisive character. Here,

* The following extract, from General Armstrong's work, will show how eager the Americans were to find any excuse, at whatever sacrifice of previously well established reputation and character, for want of success:—" The General's conduct on this occasion could not escape animadversion. His more severe critics,—combining his uniform indifference to the state of his communications, the presure necessary to induce him to take any means for re-opening them, and the perverse preference given to those of the most inefficient, shapeless character,—did not scruple to impute to him a secret and systematic cooperation with the enemy; while others, less prone to suspicion, and *f more charitable* temperament, ascribe it to an honorable but false estimate of the value of the objects to be attained, and of the degree of danger

however, was shed the first blood,* and the gallant behaviour of the troops is apparent from the following extract from a general order dated August 6th :—"The Commandant of the Forces takes great pleasure in announcing to the troops, that the enemy under Brigadier-General Hull have been repelled in three attacks made on the 18th, 19th and 20th of last month, upon part of the garrison of Amherstburg, on the river Canard," particular mention is here made of the heroism and devotion displayed by two privates (Hancock and Dean, the former kil'ed, the latter taken prisoner,) of the 41st, and the general order goes on " Instances of such firmness and intrepidity deserve to be thus publicly recorded, and his Excellency thinks that it will not fail to animate the troops under his command with an ardent desire to follow so noble an example, whenever an opportunity shall hereafter be offered to them."

Amongst the records of gallant deeds we must not omit to mention the bravery of twenty-two warriors of the Minoumim tribe of In-

---

to be incurred in attaining them, and, lastly, to a persuasion that the safety of his own position required cautious measures."

* The first blood was shed here, but the first hostile act was the capture of a merchant vessel in Lake Ontario, by the brig Oneida, commanded by Capt. Woolsey. This vessel was a fast sailer, and, while beating up the Lake from Prescott, in company with serveral others, was considerably a-head. The Oneida made for her first, intending to take those to leeward afterwards, but night coming on, they fortunately escaped. The object of the American Government in thus attacking, *in time of peace,* the vessel of a friendly nation, was to secure as many of the vessels on the Lake as they could, to assist any future contemplated attacks against Canada. One of the owners proceeded immediately to Sackett's Harbor, and reclaimed his property—war not having been declared at the time, nor was it till a fortnight afterwards that it was declared—his remonstrance and claims were, however, disregarded, and the vessel was immediately armed and manned. This same vessel was, the next year, upset in a squall on Lake Ontario, during a night action with the British fleet under Sir James Yeo, and went to the bottom, very few of her crew escaping.—Strange to say, the owners of the vessel have never been indemnified for their loss, by either their own or the American Government, although repeated applications have been urged on both, and even a joint address to the Crown voted by both branches of the Legislature of Upper Canada,— although more recently we have seen a British fleet sent to Athens, to compel payment of a few hundred pounds to Don Pacifico.—ED. A. A. M.

dians, who repelled the attack of a body of Americans ten times their number, who, under the command of Major Denny had advanced with a view of crossing the river Canard, here not more than a few yards wide—a timber bridge crossed the river at this point, but Col. St. George seeing the importance of the position, and anxious to retard the advance of the enemy had caused it to be destroyed, and had placed, in ambush among the grass and weeds which lined the banks, a picked body of marksmen for the purpose of preventing its reconstruction.

The Queen Charlotte, a vessel of some size and force, was also mounted with twenty guns and anchored across the mouth of the river to keep the enemy more effectually in check.

While Col. St. George was thus engaged in keeping the enemy in check, Gen. Brock was anxiously expecting the time when, having disposed of the business for which the Legislature were about to assemble, he might be at liberty to repair in person to the scene of action—in the meantime he despatched Col. Proctor of the 41st Regiment, with such reinforcements as he could spare, to assume the command at Amherstburg. Immediately on his arrival he learned the fate of a detachment of the enemy, two hundred strong, under the command of Major Van Horne, which, sent as a convoy to guard the mail, and open a communication by which provisions could be obtained, had been intercepted at the river Raisin, thirty-six miles from Detroit, and cut to pieces by Tecumseh with a small party of his Indians ; and having been informed that a second convoy with provisions was then on its march to Detroit, Col. Proctor ordered Captain Muir with about one hundred of the 41st, the same number of militia, and about two hundred and fifty Indians to cross the river and occupy Brownstown, a small village on the American side, through which the convoy was expected to pass. The expedition did not, however, prove as successful as former attempts, as the following account given by Major Richardson fully proves :—

"On the morning of Sunday the 9th, the wild and distant cry of our Indian scouts gave us to understand that the enemy were advancing. In the course of ten minutes afterwards

(marginal note: Movements of Col. St. George.)

they appeared issuing from the wood, bounding like wild deer chased by the huntsman, and uttering that peculiar shout which is known among themselves as the *news-cry.*— From them we ascertained that a strong column of the enemy, cavalry and infantry, were on their march to attack us, but that the difficulty of transporting their guns rendered it improbable they could reach our position before night, although then only at a distance of eight miles. It being instantly decided on to meet them, the detachment was speedily under arms, and on its march for Maguaga, a small Indian village distant about a league.— The road along which we advanced was ankledeep with mud, and the dark forest waving its close branches over our heads, left no egress to the pestilential exhalations arising from the naked and putrid bodies of horses and men of Major Horne's detachment, which had been suffered to lie unburied beneath our feet. No other sound than the measured step of the troops interrupted the solitude of the scene, rendered more imposing by the wild appearance of the warriors, whose bodies, stained and painted in the most frightful manner for the occasion, glided by us with almost noiseless velocity, without order, and without a a Chief; some painted white, some black, others half black, half red, half black, half white; all with their hair plaistered in such a way as to resemble the bristling quills of the porcupine, with no other covering then a cloth around their loins, yet armed to the teeth with rifles, tomahawks, war clubs, spears, bows, arrows, and scalping-knives. Uttering no sound, and intent only on reaching the enemy unperceived, they might have passed for the spectres of those wilds, the ruthless demons which war had unchained for the punishment and oppression of man.

" Having taken up a position about a quarter of a mile beyond Maguaga, our dispositions for defence were speedily made, the rustling of the leaves alone breaking on the silence which reigned throughout our line. Following the example of the Indians, we lay reclined on the ground in order to avoid being perceived, until within a few yards of the enemy.— While awaiting, in this manner, the approach of the column, which we knew to be, at no great distance, advancing upon us, our little force was increased by the arrival of Lieut.

Bullock of the 41st Grenadiers, who, with a small detachment of twenty men of his own company, twenty Light Infantry, and twenty Battalion men had been urged forward by Gen. Brock, from the head quarters of the Regiment, then stationed at Fort George, for the purpose of reinforcing the little garrison of Amherstburg, and who, having reached their destination the preceding day, had been despatched by Col. Proctor, (lately arrived to assume the command) to strengthen us. Shortly the report of a single shot echoed through the wood; and the instant afterwards the loud and terrific yells of the Indians, followed by a heavy and desultory fire, apprised us that they were engaged. The action then became general along our line, and continued for half an hour, without producing any material advantage; when unluckily, a body of Indians that had been detached to a small wood about five hundred yards distant from our right, were taken by the troops for a corps of the enemy endeavouring to turn their flank. In vain we called out to them that they were our Indians. The fire which should have been reserved for their foes, was turned upon their friends, who, falling into the same error, returned it with equal spirit. The fact was, they had been compelled to retire before a superior force, and the movement made by them, had given rise to the error of the troops. That order and discipline which would have marked their conduct as a body in a plain, was lost sight of, in a great measure, while fighting independently and singly in a wood, where every man, following the example of the enemy, was compelled to shelter his person behind the trees as he could. Closely pressed in front by an almost invisible foe, and on the point of being taken in the rear, as was falsely imagined, the troops were at length compelled to yield to circumstance and numbers.

" Although our retreat, in consequence of this unfortunate misapprehension, commenced in some disorder, this was soon restored, when Major Muir, who had been wounded early in the engagement, succeeded in rallying his men, and forming them on the brow of a hill which commanded a short and narrow bridge intersecting the high road, and crossing a morass over which the enemy's guns must necessarily pass. This was about a quarter of a mile in rear of the position we had previously occupied. Here we remained at least fifteen minutes, when finding that the Americans did not make their appearance as expected, Major Muir, whose communication with Tecumseh had been cut off, and who now heard some smart firing in the woods beyond his left, naturally inferred that the enemy were pushing the Indians in that quarter, with a view of turning his flank, gaining the high road in our rear, and thus cutting off our retreat. The order was then given to retire, which we certainly did at the double quick, yet without being followed by the enemy, who suffered us to gain our boats without further molestation.

"In this affair, which we never then regarded as anything more than a sharp skirmish, yet to which the Americans have since attached an undue importance, their loss was eighteen killed and sixty-three wounded ; ours, one rank and file killed, two Officers, two Sergeants, nineteen rank and file wounded, and two rank and file missing, but afterwards recaptured by the Indians. The wounded officers were, Major Muir, and Lieutenant Sutherland. They were near each other when the attack commenced, and Major Muir having observed an American taking a deliberate aim at them, hastily placed a short rifle, which he usually carried with him on these occasions, on the shoulder of his companion, and levelled it at his enemy. Both fired at the same instant. The ball of the American, entering Lieut. Sutherland's cheek, came out at the back of his neck, and passed through one of Major Muir's wings (he commanded the Light Company of the 41st,) while the rifleman himself fell dead on the spot, from his adversary's bullet. Major Muir soon afterwards received another ball in the leg, yet without being disabled. Severe as proved the wound of Lieut. Sutherland, (who was borne off the field when the retreat commenced, on the back, if I do not greatly mistake, of one of the Messrs. Caldwell of Amherstburg) he would have recovered had he not imprudently, some ten days afterwards, made premature use of his tooth-brush. This opened the wound, brought on hemorrhage, and before medical assistance could be procured, (the main body of the force being then in occupation of Detroit) he bled to death.—Tecumseh was also slightly wounded, by a buck-shot, on this occasion."

Here it was that an opportunity was first

afforded of proving the extreme disadvantage of opposing regular troops to the enemy in the woods. Accustomed to the use of the rifle from his infancy—dwelling in a measure amid forests with the intricacies of which he was wholly acquainted, and possessing the advantage of a dress which rendered him almost undistinguishable to the eye of an European, the American marksman entered with comparative security into a contest with the English soldier, whose glaring habiliment and accoutrements were objects too conspicuous to be missed, while his utter ignorance of a mode of warfare, in which courage and discipline were of no avail, rendered the struggle for mastery even more unequal. The principal armies to which the British troops were opposed during the war, consisted not of regular and well-disciplined troops only, but of levies taken from the forests of Ohio and Kentucky, scarcely inferior as riflemen to the Indians. Dressed in woollen frocks of a gray color, and trained to cover their bodies behind the trees from which they fired, without exposing more of their persons than was absolutely necessary for their aim, they afforded, on more than one occasion, the most convincing proofs that without the assistance of the Indian Warriors, the defence of so great a portion of Western Canada, as was entrusted to the charge of the few regulars and militia, would have proved a duty of great difficulty and doubt.

The Americans attached an undue* importance to this affair—and when the disparity of the forces engaged is considered, it will be seen that there was in reality but little to boast of. By Col. Miller's admission the forces under his command consisted of the whole of the 4th Regiment of United States Infantry, except one company left at Sandwich to garrison a fort, built by order of General Hull : a small detachment of the 1st Infantry, and Artillerists enough to man the guns,—this composed the regular force, there was besides about four hundred militia, making in all about seven hundred men : the total force opposed to them, was, as we have shewn, not more than four

---

* This is pretty evident from General Hull's remarks. His official letter giving an account of it, laments "that nothing was gained by it but honor ; and that the blood of seventy-five men had been shed in vain ; as it but opened his communications as far as their bayonets had extended.'

hundred and fifty men, two hundred and fifty of whom were Indians.

Great stress has been laid on the cruel policy
Conduct of our Indian militia. of the English for acting in concert with allies so little disposed to deal mercifully with the captives placed by the chances of war in their hands, and the Americans in particular have been loud in their condemnation of a measure to the adoption of which the safety of the Western Province was in a great measure to be attributed. These writers are however forgetful that every possible exertion was employed by the agents of the United States Government to detach the Indians from us and to effect an alliance with them on the part of the States.

"Besides," as Major Richardson observes,— "The natives must have been our friends or our foes; had we not employed them the Americans would, and although humanity must deplore the necessity, imposed by the very invader himself, of counting them among our allies, and combating at their side, the law of self-preservation was our guide, and scrupulous indeed must be the power that would have hesitated at such a moment in its choice." On the other hand too the Indians had always been our allies. No faithless dealing nor treachery on our parts had alienated their trust and confidence from a Government which had heaped bounties on them with no sparing hand. We were not the aggressors, we did not, for the purpose of adding to our territorial boundaries, carry ruin and desolation among an almost defenceless population, we only availed ourselves of the right, common to every one, of repelling invasion by every means possible, and while we admit that our allies were in some instances guilty of the excesses peculiar to every savage nation, it cannot be supposed that these acts were sanctioned by the Government, or that, so far as it was possible, principles of toleration and mercy were not inculcated by us amongst our red allies.

In justice, too, to the Indians, we must remark, that acts of barbarous cruelty were not confined to them. The American backwoodsmen were in the habit of scalping also, and, indeed, it is singular enough that, although General Hull's famous, or rather infamous,

proclamation awarded death to any one of the subjects of Great Britain, found combating at the side of, and therefore assumed to be a participator in the barbarities attributed to the Indians, the very first scalp should have been taken by an officer of his own army, and that within a few days after the proclamation was issued.*

On the 6th of August, General Brock had
General Brock, with a body of volunteers, leaves York for the scene of action, and arrives on the 13th of August. the satisfaction of finding that he could be spared from the seat of Government for, at least, a short time. He had divided the small force at his disposal for the defence of the Province, in the various quarters most likely to be attacked; but still he was without a military chest, without money enough at his command to buy provisions, blankets, or even shoes for the militia. Under these circumstances, he made his wants known to a number of gentlemen of credit, who formed themselves into what was called "the Niagara and Queenston Association," the late Mr. Robert Grant of Queenston being manager, and several thousand pounds were issued in the shape of bank notes, which were currently received throughout the country, and afterwards redeemed with army bills. Having thus disposed of his difficulties, General Brock found himself at liberty to

---

* James, in his History of the War, writes :—At the action fought at Brownstown, where Major Van Horne was defeated, a letter was found in the pocket of Captain McCulloch (who was among the slain on that occasion) addressed to his wife, and stating that he had shot an Indian near the Canard Bridge, on the 15th of July, and had the pleasure of *tearing off his scalp with his teeth.* Now of the fact itself there can be very little doubt, for we had one Indian (and one only) killed and scalped at the Canard. But, although Captain McCulloch is entitled to all the credit of this feat, there is reason to infer that James is incorrect in stating this information was obtained from a letter found in his pocket. In the first instance, it is extremely unlikely that the Indians, in rifling and stripping the body, would have brought off anything so valueless to them as a letter, and secondly, it is much more probable that such communication from McCulloch to his wife had been placed in the mail, which the party to which he belonged, were escorting from Detroit, with the correspondence of General Hull's army, and which, it will be recollected, was captured by the Indians. The whole of the letters passed through our hands, and it is highly probable the disclosure was made in this manner.

repair in person to the scene of hostilities, and he accordingly embarked for Burlington Bay, whence he proceeded by land to Long Point on Lake Erie. General Brock's force, on leaving York, amounted to two hundred volunteers,—forty men of the 41st regiment had been, some time previously, despatched to Long Point, for the purpose of collecting the Militia in that neighbourhood, and fifty men of the same regiment had been sent into the interior, with a view of encouraging and being joined by the Indians,—part of these troops would, the English General anticipated, be ready to join his force on the shores of Lake Erie.

It may not be uninteresting to give a short extract from the note book of one of those veteran militia men who so distinguished themselves during this and subsequent campaigns. It will shew the spirit which actuated Canadians:—

"After having been a few weeks in garrison, and made as much progress in the duties of a soldier's life as was possible, I and several others, having volunteered, in addition to the ordinary duties, to make ourselves acquainted with the great gun exercise, began to be very anxious for the more active duties of a soldier's life, it was with no little excitement, then, we heard that General Hull, with a strong force, had crossed into Canada from Detroit—a proposition was then made to me by two persons much older than myself to aid them in forming a company of volunteers, in which I was to hold the rank of Ensign, to march to the west to meet Gen. Hull. This scheme, however, was put an end to by General Brock's proclamation calling for volunteers of which the York Garrison was to furnish one hundred. When the proclamation or general order was read on parade by Major Alton, most gladly did I avail myself of my position, as right hand man of the Grenadier company, to shoulder my musket and step to the front as the first volunteer for that service. I was followed in a few minutes by the necessary number, we were then allowed three days to visit our friends and make the necessary preparations for our first campaign. Many were the predictions made that we should never return, and that we should be overpowered by the immense force of Gen. Hull, but, with two exceptions, every man was ready at the appointed time. As far as I was myself concerned, had I even been disposed to hang back, (though such a thought never entered into my head, I was too much elated at the prospect before me,) it would have been at the risk of suffering the most severe reproaches from my mother—who, at parting, as she clasped me in her arms and then tore herself from my embrace, exclaimed—Go, my son, and let me hear of your death rather than your disgrace. I marched off with a full heart but a buoyant spirit."

With such volunteers as these fighting for the protection of their homes and the sanctity of their native land, General Brock had not much reason to shun an encounter as far as the spirit of his troops was in question.

When passing the Mohawk settlement on the Grand River, General Brock held, on the 7th, a council of war for the purpose of ascertaining how far their professions of friendship could be trusted, and from them he received the assurance that sixty of their braves would on the 10th of the same month follow him.— At Long Point, on Lake Erie, he embarked his few regulars and three hundred militia in boats of every description, collected amongst the neighbouring farmers, who usually employed them for the transportation of their corn and flour, but now cheerfully and willingly urged on the General his making use of them as a means of transportation. The distance from Long Point to Amherstburg is somewhat under two hundred miles, with scarcely a bay for shelter, and this want the little flotilla suffered materially from, as they encountered much rough weather on their passage along the Lake. The spirit, however, of the volunteers was sustained by the hope of ere long finding themselves in presence of the enemy, and they felt each day increased confidence, as the varied resources of their gallant and indefatigable leader were developed. After four days and nights of incessant exertion the little squadron reached Amherstburg shortly before midnight on the 13th, and in a rough memo taken from General Brock's note book the following entry is penned: "In no instance have I seen troops who would have endured the fatigues of a long journey in boats, during extremely bad weather, with greater cheerfulness and constancy; and it is but justice to this little band to add, that their conduct throughout excited my admiration."

Shortly after landing at Amherstburg, Gen. Brock was first brought into actual communication with the Shawanee Chief, the celebrated Tecumseh, and the manner of their introduction was so interesting, that we quote the passage from "Sir Isaac Brock's Life":—

"The attention of the troops was suddenly roused by a straggling fire of musketry, which, in a few minutes, became general, and appeared to proceed from an island in the Detroit river. Colonel Elliott, the superintendent of the Indians, quickly explained that the firing arose from the Indians attached to the British cause, who thus expressed their joy at the arrival of the reinforcement under their white father. Major General Brock, aware of the scarcity of the munitions of war, sent Col. Elliott to stop this waste of powder, saying: "Do, pray, Elliott, fully explain my wishes and motives, and tell the Indians that I will speak to them to-morrow on this subject. His request was promptly attended to, and Colonel Elliott returned in about half an hour with the Shawanee chief, Tecumseh, or Tecumpthé, already mentioned. Capt. Glegg, the aide-de-camp, being present, had an opportunity of closely observing the traits of that extraordinary man, and we are indebted to him for the following graphic particulars:—'Tecumseh's appearance was very prepossessing; his figure light and finely proportioned; his age I imagined to be about five and thirty; his height, five feet nine or ten inches; his complexion, light copper; countenance, oval, bright hazle eyes, beaming with cheerfulness, energy, and decision. Three small silver crowns, or coronets, were suspended from the lower cartilage of his aquiline nose; and a large silver medallion of George the Third, which I believe his ancestor had received from Lord Dorchester, when Governor General of Canada, was attached to a mixed coloured wampum string, and hung round his neck. His dress consisted of a plain, neat uniform, tanned deer skin jacket, with long trowsers of the same material, the seams of both being covered with neatly cut fringe; and he had on his feet leather mocassins, much ornamented with work made from the dyed quills of the porcupine.'

"The first and usual salutations of shaking hands being over, an allusion was made to the late firing of musketry, and Tecumseh at once approved of the reason given by Major-General Brock for its discontinuance. It being late, the parties soon separated, with an understanding that a council would be held the following morning. This accordingly took place, and was attended by about a thousand Indians, whose equipment generally might be considered very imposing. The council was opened by General Brock, who informed the Indians that he was ordered by their great father to come to their assistance, and, with their aid, to drive the Americans from Fort Detroit.— His speech was highly applauded, and Tecumseh was unanimously called upon to speak in reply. He commenced with expressions of joy, that their father beyond the great salt lake (meaning the king of England) had at length awoke from his long sleep, and permitted his warriors to come to the assistance of his red children, who had never ceased to remain steady in their friendship, and were now all ready to shed their last drop of blood in their great father's service. After some speeches from other chiefs, and replies thereto, the council broke up. General Brock, having quickly discovered the superior sagacity and intrepidity of Tecumseh, and his influence over the Indians, and not deeming it prudent to develop before so mixed an assemblage the views which were at that moment uppermost in his thoughts, and intended to be carried so quickly into execution, directed Col. Elliott to inform the Shawanee chief that he wished to see him, accompanied by a few of the oldest chiefs, at Colonel Elliott's quarters. There the General, through the medium of interpreters, communicated his views, and explained the manner in which he intended to carry into execution his operations against Fort Detroit. The chiefs listened with the utmost apparent eagerness, and expressed their unanimous assent to the proposed plan, assuring General Brock that their co-operation, as pointed out, might be depended on. On General Brock asking whether the Shawanee Indians could be induced to refrain from drinking spirits, Tecumseh assured him that his warriors might be relied on, adding, that before leaving their country on the Wabash river, they had promised him not to taste that pernicious liquor until they had humbled the 'big knives,' meaning the Americans. In reply to this assurance, General Brock briefly said: ' If this resolution be persevered in, you must conquer.'"

Previous to General Brock's arrival, General Hull had, on the 7th

Offensive and retaliatory measures at once adopted by Gen. Brock. and 8th, recrossed the river with the whole of his army, abandoning at once all his visionary schemes for the conquest of the western district of Canada, if indeed he cherished the hope of effecting any movement of importance after the fall of Michilimacinac.

The day after his arrival, General Brock

resolved on, and began to prepare in his turn for, offensive operations. Batteries had already been erected under the superintendence of Capt. Dixon of the Engineers, and Capt. Hall of the Provincial Navy, on an elevated part of the bank of the Detroit, here about a mile across, and directly opposite the American fort of that name, and Brock resolved to strike a decisive blow ere his opponent should be strengthened by reinforcements.

General Brock despatched a flag to the American Commander, with the following summons, having previously arranged for the concentration of all his available force on the spot :—

"Head Quarters, Sandwich, August 15th, 1812.

"SIR.—The force at my disposal authorizes me to require of you, the immediate surrender of Fort Detroit.—It is far from my inclination to join in a war of extermination, but you must be aware that the numerous body of Indians, who have attached themselves to my troops, will be beyond my control the moment the contest commences. You will find me disposed to enter into such conditions as will satisfy the most scrupulous sense of honor. Lieut. Colonel McDonnell, and Major Glegg, are fully authorised to conclude any arrangement that may tend to prevent the unnecessary effusion of blood.

"I have the honor to be,
"Sir, your most obdt. Servant,
"(Signed,)   ISAAC BROCK, Major Gen.
"His Excellency,
"Brigadier Gen. Hull,
"Commanding at Fort Detroit."

"To which the subjoined answer was returned :
Head Quarters, Detroit, Aug. 15, 1812.

"SIR,—I have received your letter of this date. I have no other reply to make, than to inform you that I am prepared to meet any force which may be at your disposal, and any consequences which may result from any exertion of it you may think proper to make.

"I avail myself of this opportunity to inform you that the flag of truce, under the direction of Captain Brown, proceeded contrary to the orders, and without the knowledge of Col. Cass, who commanded the troops which attacked your picket, near the river Canard bridge.

"I likewise take this occasion to inform you that Gowie's house was set on fire contrary to my orders, and it did not take place until after the evacuation of the Fort. From the best information I have been able to obtain on the subject, it was set on fire by some of the inhabitants on the other side of the river.

"I am, very respectfully,
"Your Excellency's most obt. Servant,
"(Signed,)   W. HULL, Brig. Gen.
"Commg. the N. W. Army.
"His Excy. Major Gen. Brock,
"Comm'g. His Britannic Majesty's Forces,
"Sandwich, Upper Canada."

A requisition of this kind, alike so important and unexpected, coming from an enemy, too, so inferior in force, could meet with but one response, and accordingly, as we have seen, the American General rejected the demand, and to God and his sword committed the issue. Fortunately, however, the defiance was addressed to one who did not for a moment suffer it to abate his diligence or lessen his hopes, and the return of his messenger was but the signal of attack, and a galling fire was immediately opened on the town and fort of Detroit.

On the court-martial held on General Hull for cowardice, the strength of the respective forces was pretty clearly ascertained. In speaking of General Brock's army, it is stated —" The force at his disposal did not exceed seven hundred combatants, and of this number *four hundred were Canadian militia, disguised in red coats ;* with this small corps, preceded by five pieces of light artillery, six and three-pounders, he began his operations." Respecting the Americans, the following admissions were made on the same occasion :—"The strength, position, and supplies of the American army have been frequently stated, and even judicially established. The morning reports to the Adjutant General made its effective force one thousand and sixty, exclusive of three hundred Michigan militia, and as many Ohio volunteers, detached under M'Arthur. Of this force, four hundred effectives (native and artillerists of the line) occupied the fort—a work of regular form and of great solidity ; surrounded by a wide and deep ditch, strongly fraised and palisadoed, and sustained by an exterior battery of twenty-four pounders. Three hundred Michigan militia held the town, which in itself formed a respectable defence against the troops. Flanking the approach to the fort, and covered by a high and heavy picket fence, were stationed four hundred Ohio volunteers, while a mile and a half on the right, and advancing rapidly, was M'Arthur's detachment. Of provisions and ammunition the supply was abundant ; in fine, everything was then sufficient for the trial of strength and courage which impended."

The following extract from General Brock's official communication to Sir George Prevost will place all the events of the memorable 16th

August clearly and succinctly before the reader :—

"The force at my disposal being collected in the course of the 15th, in the neighborhood of Sandwich, the embarkation took place a little after daylight on the following morning, and under the able arrangements of Lieut. Dewar, of the Quarter-Master General's department, the whole was in a short time landed without the slightest confusion at Springwell —a good position, three miles west of Detroit. The Indian, who had in the meantime effected their landing two miles below, moved forward and occupied the woods, about a mile and a half on our left.

I crossed the river, with an intention of waiting in a strong position the effect of our force upon the enemy's camp, and in hopes of compelling him to meet us in the field; but receiving information upon landing, that Col. M'Arthur, an officer of high reputation, had left the garrison three days before with a detachment of five hundred men, and hearing, soon afterwards, that his cavalry had been seen that morning three miles in our rear, I decided on an immediate attack. Accordingly, the troops advanced to within one mile of the fort, and having ascertained that the enemy had taken little or no precaution towards the land side, I resolved on an assault, whilst the Indians penetrated his camp. Brigadier General Hull, however, prevented this movement, by proposing a cessation of hostilities, for the purpose of preparing terms of capitulation. Lieutenant-Colonel John Macdonell and Captain Glegg were accordingly deputed by me on this mission, and returned within an hour with the conditions, which I have the honor herewith to transmit. Certain considerations afterwards induced me to agree to the two supplementary articles.

"The force thus surrendered to his Majesty's arms cannot be estimated at less than 2500 men. In this estimate, Col. M'Arthur's detachment is included, as he surrendered, agreeably to the terms of capitulation, in the course of the evening, with the exception of two hundred men, whom he left escorting a valuable convoy at some little distance in his rear; but there can be no doubt the officer commanding will consider himself equally bound by the capitulation.

"The enemy's aggregate force was divided into two troops of cavalry; one company of artillery engineers; the 4th United States regiment; detachments of the 1st and 3d United States regiments, volunteers; three regiments of the Ohio Militia; one regiment of the Michigan territory.

"Thirty pieces of brass and iron ordnance have already been secured."

Besides the cannon four hundred rounds of twenty-four pound shot fixed, one hundred thousand cartridges, forty barrels of powder, and two thousand five hundred stand of arms fell into the hands of the conquerors. The articles of capitulation* will excite in the

*Camp at Detroit, Aug. 16, 1812,

Capitulation for the surrender of Fort Detroit, entered into between Major General Brock, commanding his Britannic Majesty's forces, on the one part, and Brigadier Gen. Hull, commanding the north-western army of the United States, on the other part.

Article I. Fort Detroit, with all the troops, regulars as well as militia, will be immediately surrendered to the British forces under the command of Maj. Gen. Brock, and will be considered as prisoners of war, with the exception of such of the militia of the Michigan territory, who have not joined the army.

Art. II. All public stores, arms, and all public documents, including everything else of a public nature, will be immediately given up.

Art. III. Private persons, and property of every description will be respected.

Art. IV. His Excellency, Brigadier. General Hull, having expressed a desire that a detachment from the state of Ohio, on its way to join his army, as well as one sent from Fort Detroit, under the command of Col. McArthur, should be included in the capitulation, it is accordingly agreed to. It is, however, to be understood, that such part of the Ohio militia as have not joined the army, will be permitted to return to their homes, on condition that they will not serve during the war, their arms will be delivered, up if belonging to the public.

Art. V. The garrison will march out at the hour of 12 this day, and the British will take immediate possession of the fort.

J. Macdonell,
Lieut. Col. militia, P. A. D. C.,
J. B. Glegg,
Major, A. D. C.
James Miet r,
Lieut. Col. 5th U. S. Infantry,
E. Brush,
Col. commanding 1st regt. of Michigan Militia,

Approved, { W. Hull,
Brig. Gen. com'g. N. W. Army.
Isaac Brock, Major General.

An article supplementary to the articles of cap-

reader's breast some surprise—some curiosity will be awakened, to ascertain the reasons why to so small a body of regulars and a few DISAFFECTED Militia, *disguised in red-coats,* (Vide Armstrong,) such abject submission should have been manifested, or why, without one blow being struck, or one sign (except of extreme trepidation) exhibited, so powerful a force,—"in sure anticipation of victory, awaiting anxiously the approach of the enemy; each individual at his post, expecting a proud day for his country and himself,"*—should so tamely consent to stack their arms and hoist a white flag, in token of submission to an enemy so vastly inferior in numbers and only with difficulty re-trained from deserting. The only solution of the question is to be found in the following position :—That it required all the exaggerated statements, which could be brought to bear on the subject, to induce the citizens of the United States to enter on the service at all, and that, on finding how grossly they had been deceived with respect to Canadian loyalty, and the numbers flocking to their standard, and that the bayonet's point, not the warm grasp of friendship, was the reception awaiting them, they were dismayed at the

---

itulation, concluded at Detroit, the 16th of Aug. 1812 :—

It is agreed that the Officers and soldiers of the Ohio militia and volunteers shall be permitted to proceed to their respective homes, on this condition, that they do not serve during the present war, unless they are exchanged.

W. HULL,
Brig. Gen. commanding U. S. N. W. Army.
ISAAC BROCK,
Maj. Gen.

An article in addition to the supplementary article of capitulation, concluded at Detroit, the 16th of August, 1812 :—

It is further agreed that the officers and soldiers of the Michigan militia and volunteers, under the command of Major Wetherall, shall be placed on the same principles as the Ohio militia and volunteers are placed by the supplementary article of the 16th instant.

W. HULL,
Brig. Gen. commanding N. W. Army U. S.
ISAAC BROCK,
Maj. Gen.

Return of the Ordnance taken in the fort and batteries at Detroit, August 16th, 1852.

Iron Ordnance—nine 24 pounders, eight 12 pounders, five 9 pounders. Brass Ordnance—three 6 pounders, two 4 pounders, one 3 pounder, one 8 inch howitzer, one 3¼ inch ditto.

* Vide Armstrong, page 27.

---

bold front, and energetic measures of the British commander.

Another solution is, that Gen. Hull lacked confidence in his troops—he knew what fighting was, they did not. National vanity has endeavored to find a salve for the disgrace, in aspersions on General Hull. Imbecility, treachery, and cowardice,* were the charges brought

* We felt it due to truth—to Government—to General Hull, and to all persons directly or indirectly concerned with the facts or circumstances leading to the shameful capitulation of Detroit, to suspend our opinion until a sufficiency of light was afforded to chase away the doubts and shadows that rested on the strange transaction. But doubt has resolved itself into certainty—we no longer hesitate to join in opinion with the whole people of the west, " of every sect or persuasion, religious or political," that the army at Detroit was treacherously surrendered ; and that General Brock instead of General Hull ought to have been the prisoner. This idea is powerfully enforced by many private letters from gentlemen of the first respectability in the State of Ohio, who had opportunity to know the verity and strength of the opinion advanced ; but the detail by Colonel Cass is conclusive—it is, besides, supported by a host of testimony in all the substantial facts it exposes. —*Niles' Register, Baltimore.*

Extracts from Col. Cass' Letter, with reference to the same subject, to the Secretary at War :

Letter of Colonel Cass, of the Army late under the Command of Brigadier General William Hull, to the Secretary of War.

WASHINGTON, September 10th, 1812.

"When the forces landed in Canada, they landed with an ardent zeal and stimulated with the hope of conquest. No enemy appeared within view of us, and had an immediate and vigorous attack been made upon Malden, it would doubtless have fallen an easy victory. I knew General Hull afterwards declared he regretted this attack had not been made, and he had every reason to believe success would have crowned his efforts. The reason given for delaying our operations was to mount our heavy cannon, and afford to the Canadian militia time and opportunity to quit an obnoxious service. In the course of two weeks, the number of their militia who were embodied had decreased by desertion from one thousand to six hundred men : and, in the course of three weeks, the cannon were mounted, the ammunition fixed, and every preparation made for an immediate investment of the fort. At a council, at which were present all the field officers, and which was held two days before our preparations were completed, it was unanimously agreed to make an immediate attempt to accomplish the object of the expedition. If by waiting two days we could have the service of our artillery, it was agreed to wait ; if not, it was determined to go without it and attempt the place by storm. This opinion appeared to correspond with the views of the general, and the day was appointed for commencing our march.

against him, throughout the length and breadth of the country ; and errors fairly attributable to the Administration at Washington, were all imputed to the poor old General. The senti-

---

He declared to me that he considered himself pledged to lead the army to Malden. The ammunition was placed in the waggons, the cannon were embarked on board the floating batteries, and every requisite was prepared. The spirit and zeal, the ardor and animation displayed by the officers and men on learning the near accomplishment of their wishes, was a sure and sacred pledge, that in the hour of trial they would not be wanting in duty to their country and themselves. The plan of attacking Malden was abandoned, and instead of acting offensively, we broke up our camp, evacuated Canada, and re-crossed the river in the night, without even the shadow of an enemy to injure us. We left to the tender mercy of the enemy the miserable Canadians who had joined us, and the *protection* we afforded them was but a passport to vengeance. This fatal and unaccountable step dispirited the troops, and destroyed the little confidence which a series of timid, irresolute, and indecisive measures had left in the commanding officer.

" On the 13th, the British took a position opposite to Detroit, and began to throw up works. During that and the two following days, they pursued their object without interruption and established a battery for two eighteen pounders and an eight inch howitzer. About sunset on the 14th, a detachment of 350 men from the regiments commanded by Colonel M'Arthur and myself was ordered to march to the river Raisin, to escort the provisions, which had some time remained there protected by a company under the command of Captain Brush.

" On Saturday, the 15th, about one o'clock, a flag of truce arrived from Sandwich, bearing a summons from General Brock, for the surrender of the town and fort of Detroit, stating he could no longer restrain the fury of the savages. To this a immediate and spirited refusal was returned. About four o'clock their batteries began to play upon the town. The fire was returned and continued without interruption and with little effect till dark. Their shells were thrown till eleven o'clock.

" I have been informed by Colonel Findlay, who saw the return of the Quarter-Master-General the day after the surrender, that their whole force, of every description, white, red, and black, was one thousand and thirty. They had twenty-nine platoons, twelve in a platoon, of men dressed in uniform. Many of these were evidently Canadian militia. The rest of their militia increased their white force to about seven hundred men. The number of the Indians could not be ascertained with any degree of precision—not many were visible. And in the event of an attack upon the town and fort, it was a species of force which could have afforded no material advantage to the enemy.

" In endeavoring to appreciate the motives and to investigate the causes which led to an event so unexpected and dishonorable, it is impossible to find any solution in the relative strength of the contending parties, or in the measures of resistance in our power. That we were far superior to

the enemy, that upon any ordinary principle of calculation we would have defeated them—the wounded and indignant feelings of every man there will testify.

" A few days before the surrender, I was informed by Gen. Hull, we had four hundred rounds of twenty-four pound shot fixed, and about one hundred thousand cartridges made. We surrendered with the fort forty barrels of powder and two thousand five hundred stand of arms.

" The state of our provisions has not been generally understood. On the day of the surrender we had fifteen days' provisions of every kind on hand. Of meat there was plenty in the country, and arrangements had been made for purchasing and grinding the flour. It was calculated we could readily procure three months' provisions, independent of one hundred and fifty barrels of flour, and one thousand three hundred head of cattle which had been forwarded from the state of Ohio, which remained at the river Raisin under Captain Brush, within reach of the army.

" But had we been totally destitute of provisions, our duty and our interest, undoubtedly, was to fight. The enemy invited us to meet him in the field. By defeating him the whole country would have been open to us, and the object of our expedition gloriously and successfully obtained. If we had been defeated, we had nothing to do but to retreat to the fort, and make the best defence which circumstances and our situation rendered practicable. But basely to surrender without firing a gun—tamely to submit without raising a bayonet—disgracefully to pass in review before an enemy as inferior in the quality as in the number of his forces, were circumstances which excited feelings more easily felt than described. To see the whole of our men flushed with the hope of victory, eagerly awaiting the approaching contest, to see them afterwards dispirited, hopeless, and desponding, at least five hundred shedding tears because they were not allowed to meet their country's foe, and to fight their country's battles, excited sensations which no American has ever before had cause to feel, and which, I trust in God, will never again be felt, while one man remains to defend the standard of the Union.

" I was informed by General Hull, the morning after the capitulation, that the British forces consisted of one thousand eight hundred regulars, and that he surrendered to prevent the effusion of human blood. That he magnified their regular force nearly five-fold, there can be no doubt. Whether the philanthropic reason assigned by him is a sufficient justification for surrendering a fortified town, an army and a territory, is for the Government to determine. Confident I am, that had the courage and conduct of the general been equal to the spirit and zeal of the troops, the event would have been as brilliant and successful as it now is disastrous and dishonorable.

" Very respectfully, sir, I have the honor to be, your most obedient servant,   LEWIS CASS,
     " Col. 3rd Regt. Ohio Volunteers.
" The Hon. WM. EUSTIS,
     " Secretary of War."

ments and feelings expressed by General Arm
strong, in his history of the war, may be
fairly taken as a sample of the exertions which
were made at the time to find a victim, somewhere, on which to wreak the vengeance of
mortified national vanity. In order to make
the case still more strong against Gen. Hull,
rashness and ignorance are qualities freely
bestowed on the English General,—a short
extract will, however, enable the reader to
judge for himself:—" Notwithstanding the
repeated blunders of the American General,
fortune did not yet entirely abandon him; and
on the 16th August, presented a new occasion,
requiring on his part only the vulgar quality
of defensive courage, to have completely baffled the designs of Brock, and re-established
his own ascendancy on the Detroit. This
occasion was found in the *indiscretion* of his
adversary; who on crossing the river with a
force smaller than that it was his purpose to
assail, had hastily determined to risk the storming of a fortification, strong in itself, abundantly supplied and sufficiently garrisoned.
If it be thought extraordinary, that under
these circumstances, General Brock *should
have forgotten* all the dissuasions from attack
furnished by history, it was certainly still less
to be expected that General Hull should have
forgotten all the motives for defence furnished
by the same source. Such, however, was the
fact: the *timidity* of the one kept pace with
the *temerity* of the other; and at last, in an
agony of terror, which cunning could no longer
dissemble, and which history is ashamed to
describe, the fort, army, and territory were
surrendered without pulling a trigger." We
have been thus particular in exposing the
attempt of Americans to bolster up their
wounded honor, because every attempt to
attach imbecility or cowardice to the American General, tarnishes directly the lustre shed
on the British arms on that occasion.

Immediately after the surrender of Detroit,
General Brock issued his proclamation* to the

inhabitants of the Michigan territory, and took
such precautionary measures as he deemed
necessary for the protection of the inhabitants
of the conquered territory. To the honor of
the Indians, however, be it said, that although
many enemies fell into their hands, no loss of
life was sustained, beyond that caused by the
British batteries. Faithfully did they obey
the injunctions of Tecumseh and the other
chiefs, who had impressed on them that in
nothing could they testify more strongly their
love to the king, their great father, than in
following the dictates of honor and humanity
which he, through his General, had inculcated. This behavior on the part of our
Indian allies did not, however, prevent General
Hull from basely aspersing them in his attempt
to vindicate his conduct. "The bands of
savages," wrote the General, "which had then
joined the British force, were numerous beyond any former example. Their numbers
have since increased, and the history of the
barbarians of the north of Europe does not
furnish examples of more greedy violence than
these savages have exhibited." This passage
must always reflect everlasting disgrace on
him who penned it, as in no one American
work on the war have we been able to discover
an authenticated statement of the excesses
imputed to the Indians by General Hull.
There is very little doubt but that the fear of
them, however, operated effectually on Gen.

of his Majesty's government, I do hereby announce
to all the inhabitants of the said territory, that
the laws heretofore in existence shall continue in
force until his Majesty's pleasure be known, or so
long as the peace and safety of the said territory
will admit thereof; and I do hereby also declare
and make known to the said inhabitants, that they
shall be protected in the full exercise and employment of their religion, of which all persons,
both civil and military, will take notice, and govern themselves accordingly.

All persons having in their possession, or having
any knowledge of, any public property, shall
forthwith deliver in the same, or give notice
thereof, to the officer commanding, or to Lieut.-
Colonel Nichol, who are duly authorized to receive
and give proper receipts for the same.

Officers of militia will be held responsible, that
all arms in the possession of militia-men be immediately given up, and all individuals whatever
who have in their possession arms of any kind,
will give them up without delay.

Given under my hand at Detroit, this 16th day
of August, 1812, and in the 52d year of his Majesty's reign.

        ISAAC BROCK, Major-General.

---

*Proclamation by Isaac Brock, Esq., Major-Gene-
ral, commanding his Majesty's forces in the
Province of Upper Canada, &c.

Whereas the territory of Michigan was this day,
by capitulation, ceded to the arms of his Britannic
Majesty, without any other condition than the
protection of private property, and wishing to
give an early proof of the moderation and justice

Hull, and produced in a great measure the surrender of Detroit, as in another part of his official despatch he thus expresses himself:—" It was impossible, in the nature of things, that an army could have been furnished with the necessary supplies of provisions, military stores, clothing, and comfort for the sick, on pack-horses through a wilderness of two hundred miles, filled with hostile savages " The General's fears for the safety of his troops certainly here got the better of his judgment, as he goes on. " It was impossible, Sir, that this little army, worn down by fatigue and sickness, by wounds and deaths, could have supported itself against not only the collected force of all the Northern Nations of Indians, but against (save the mark !) THE UNITED FORCE of Upper Canada, whose population consists of more than twenty times the number contained in the territory of Michigan, (as if the General had depended for his defence on the Michigan Militia) aided by the principal part of the regular forces of the Province."

Our readers are in a position to judge of the truth of this part of the statement. The General by way of climax arrays also against him and his devoted army " the whole influence of the north-west and other trading establishments among the Indians, which have in their employment and under their control MORE THAN TWO THOUSAND WHITE MEN. We will close this portion of our subject with an extract from one of General Brock's letters to his brothers, which shows pretty clearly the real secret of his success :—" Some say nothing could be more desperate than the measure ; but I answer that the state of the Province admitted of nothing but desperate remedies. —I got possession of the letters my antagonist addressed to the Secretary at War, and also of the SENTIMENTS WHICH HUNDREDS OF HIS ARMY uttered to their friends,—evident despondency prevailed THROUGHOUT. I crossed the river contrary to the opinion of Colonel Proctor ; it is, therefore, no wonder that envy should attribute to good fortune what, in justice to my own discernment, I must say proceeded from a cool calculation of the *pours et contres.*"

The first and greatest effect was at once to
Effect produced on Canadians by these unhoped for successes.
release Canadians of all fears of invasion, and to

suggest to them that the frontiers of Ohio, Pennsylvania, and Kentucky were now open to a retaliatory invasion, either by themselves or their Indian allies. They were now taught how a conjunction of incidents, under Providence, had occurred, which shortsighted man could not provide for or foresee. The boasted prospects of acquiring Canada, at least as far as the Niagara, had been frustrated and overturned, and the whole Union as much astonished at the failure of their long-cherished plans, as if the mighty Niagara had changed its current and been thrown from Lake Ontario to Erie upwards, by earthquakes or other convulsive phenomena. Such was the revulsion from overweening confidence to utter amazement. The effect, indeed, produced throughout the Canadas by the fall of Detroit was as electrical as it was unexpected. It was the first enterprise in which the militia had been engaged, and its complete success not only imparted confidence to that body, but it inspired the timid, fixed the waverers, and awed the few disaffected who might have been inhabitants of the Province. This victory, too, at the very commencement of the campaign, produced the most beneficial results in attaching yet more strongly to the British cause, the Indians of the west—many of whom, had reverses overtaken the British arms, would have seceded from a cause which they conceived us too helpless to defend, or joined the American standard. The tribes, also, and numerous they were, who were undecided which party to join, would have thrown their influence and numbers into the opposite scale.

Fortunate, indeed, was it for Canada, that to a General of such energy and decision as Brock, had been entrusted the defence of the Province, and by the capture of Detroit he may fairly and deservedly be called the saviour of Canada. Had this decisive blow not been struck, both the Canadas must have passed under the yoke of the United States, and cut off, as they were, during six months of the year by ice, from all European assistance, they would, in all probability, have become integral portions of that country. To General Brock it may be ascribed that Canada was not only not conquered, but not even injured, and that a delay of nearly a year was, at least, ensured ere another invading force could be organised from the same quarter. The effect produced in the lower Province, also, was not less marked, and the arrival at Montreal of General Hull and the regulars of the American regular army, as prisoners of war, did not fail to produce a marked and beneficial result. We subjoin a short account of the event :—

"Montreal, September 12.

"Last Sunday evening the inhabitants of this city were gratified with an exhibition equally novel and interesting.

"That Gen. Hull should have entered into our city so soon, at the head of his troops, rather exceeded our expectations. We were, however, very happy to see him, and received him with all the honors due to his high rank and importance as a public character. The following particulars, relative to his journey and reception at Montreal, may not be uninteresting to our readers :—

"It appears that General Hull and suite, accompanied by about 25 officers and 350 soldiers, left Kingston, under an escort of 130 men, commanded by Major Heathcote, of the Newfoundland regiment. At Cornwall, the escort was met by Capt. Gray, of the Quartermaster-General's department, who took charge of the prisoners of war, and from thence proceeded with them to La Chine, where they arrived about two o'clock on Sunday afternoon. At La Chine, Captains Richardson and Ogilvie, with their companies of Montreal militia, and a company of the King's from Lower Chine, commanded by Captain Blackmore, formed the escort till they were met by Colonel Auldjo, with the remainder of the flank companies of the militia, upon which Captain Blackmore's company fell out and presented aims as the General and line

passed, and then returned to La Chine, leaving the prisoners of war to be guarded by the militia alone. The line of march then proceeded to the town in the following order, viz :

"1. Band of the King's regiment.

"2. The first division of the escort.

"3. General Hull in a carriage, accompanied by Captain Gray. Captain Hull and Major Shekleton followed in the second, and some wounded officers occupied four others.

"4. The American officers.

"5. The non-commissioned officers and soldiers.

"6. The second division of the escort.

"It unfortunately proved rather late in the evening for the vast concourse of spectators assembled to experience the gratification they so anxiously looked for. This inconvenience was, however, in a great measure remedied by the illuminations of the streets through which the line of march passed. When they arrived at the General's house, the General was conducted in, and presented to his Excellency Sir George Prevost, and was received with the greatest politeness, and invited to take up his residence there during his stay at Montreal. The General appears to be about sixty years of age, and is a good looking man, and we are informed by his friends that he is a man of general information. He is communicative, and seems to bear his misfortunes with a degree of philosophical resignation that but few men in similar circumstances are gifted with. On Thursday last General Hull, with eight American officers, left this city for the United States, on their parole."

CHAPTER V.

The failure of all the military movements Naval encounters at undertaken, so far, by the sea,general remarks on. Americans was, in some degree, balanced by the unexpected success which attended their operations on an element which had long been the scene of triumph to their opponents—we may advisedly use the expression ' scene,' as the sea had hitherto been the stage on which the triumphs of British prowess had been most brilliantly represented. In entering, however, on a contest with American sailors, bone of their bone and sinew of their sinew, the British Government appear to have lost sight of the fact, that the strength of the United States navy consisted of a few frigates, of scantling and armament corresponding to their own seventy-fours, and that, by their own well understood regulations, every single-decked vessel was bound to engage any single-decked vessel of the enemy, nominally of her own class, however superior, in reality, in tonnage, guns and crew;—another important fact also, must not be lost sight of, that the American vessels were manned by sailors, many of whom, unfortunately, were British, while many more had been trained in the British service. For many years previous to

the declaration of war, America had been decoying men from British vessels by every artful scheme, so that the captains of American vessels had to pick their complement not only from amongst men of their own nation, but from a numerous body also of foreign seamen. The constitution also of the body of American marines was wholly different from the British.

In the United States every man may learn to shoot, every man may be a marksman. To collect these expert marksmen officers were sent into the western parts of the Union, and to complete still farther their efficiency, a marine barrack was established near Washington, from which depôt the American ships were regularly supplied. There was another point in which the British were found, as compared with their opponents, very deficient— gunnery,—nor was this entirely the fault of the commanders of H. M. ships, as the Admiralty instructions, which they were bound to obey, restricted them, during the first six months after the ship received her armament, from expending more shots per month* than amounted to one-third in number of her upper-deck guns, and after these six months had expired, they were to use only half the quantity. The disastrous consequences of this discouragement of the expenditure of powder and shot will be apparent, as we shall have to bring forward in quick succession, instances that will show how much the British navy suffered by inattention to this most essential point in war, the proper handling of the weapons by which it was to be waged.

We have boldly made the assertion that the American frigates were of the scantling of seventy-fours, and a few explanatory remarks will show the correctness of the statement.

---

* Vide James' Naval History, part 8.

5

In 1794, an English shipwright,* Mr. Joshua Humphreys, resident at Philadelphia, gave in estimates of the cost of building three seventy four gun ships, to measure sixteen hundred and twenty tons, American measurement, about seventeen hundred and fifty English. Before, however, the keels of these vessels had been much more than laid, Mr. Jay's treaty restored the amicable relations between England and America, and it was resolved to convert the vessels, begun as seventy-fours, into frigates. This was done by contracting the breadth about three feet and a half, and not connecting the quarter-deck and forecastle, so as to give in reality only one continuous tier of guns,—thus were these seventy-fours converted into enormous sixty-two gun frigates. A frigate, the Constellation, begun at the same time, and originally intended to class as a forty-four, was in a *similar manner* reduced to the rate of a thirty-six. It appears from the estimates rendered to Congress that the original intention had been to construct two forty-fours and a thirty-six; but, by the new arrangement it was confidently expected that the sphere of utility of these vessels would be widely extended "It was expected (vide estimates) from this alteration, that they would possess in an eminent degree, the advantages of sailing, that separately they would be superior to any single European frigate of the same rate and of the usual dimensions; that if assailed by superior force, they would be always able to lead a-head; that they could never be obliged to go into action but on their own terms, except in a calm; and that in heavy weather they would be capable of engaging double-decked ships." These were the principal advantages contemplated in thus rating vessels of this heavy scantling as forty-four gun frigates. Having thus shown that in designating these "line of battle ships in disguise" by their true titles we have not greatly erred, we shall add a few remarks on the Constellation, nominally a thirty-six gun frigate. "Even here (says James) was a frigate more than equal to any French or English frigate of the largest class, carrying long eighteen-pounders, and, be it remembered, in the year 1811, France did not own any, and England only three frigates (Cornwallis, Indefatigable, and Endymion) that carried long twenty-four-pounders." The Constellation was a sister frigate to the Chesapeake, and "had ports for mounting on her two broadsides (vide James) fifty-four guns." Had the Americans, possessed no stronger frigates than the heaviest of these, Europeans would not have been so surfeited with tales of American naval prowess.

First objects of the War, chase of Belvidera—Escape of English homeward bound fleet of West Indiamen.

An object of paramount importance to the Americans was, the capture of the homeward bound West India fleet, supposed to be on the coast, and known to be under the convoy of but one thirty-six gun frigate, and a sloop of war. This fleet had left Jamaica on the 20th May, and had passed Havanna on the 4th June, at 3, a. m.: on the 23rd (*five days after the declaration of war*) the American Commodore spoke a brig, and ascertained that, four days previous, in lat. 36° long. 67°, the Jamaica fleet had been seen, steering to the eastward. In that direction he immediately proceeded, and, at 6, a. m., that day made out a large sail to the northward and eastward, standing directly towards them. This was the British thirty-six gun frigate, Belvidera, Capt. Byron, then on the look-out to intercept a French privateer schooner, hourly expected from New London. Capt. Byron having a few days before, spoken a New York pilot boat, and ascertained what was likely to happen, finding his private signals unanswered, and coupling this circumstance with the efforts of the Americans to close, was no longer in doubt as to the hostile intentions of the approaching squadron, and immediately tacked and made all sail, hoisting his colors. The American squadron did the same, the two commanders displaying their broad pennants; and, by signal, the frigates and the sloops hauled to the wind in chase. For twelve hours the chase was continued, during which time the Belvidera kept up a steady stern fire, firing upwards of three hundred round shot from her two cabin eighteen pounders. Commodore Rodgers, in the President, the leading frigate of the squadron, finding himself by this time three miles astern, shortened sail. The Belvidera suffered only from the fire of the President, (as the shot of the Congress, the only other vessel that got up, all fell short,) and her loss amounted to two killed, and twenty

* Vide James, part 8, page 2.

two wounded, the greater part slightly. According to the American official account, the President lost altogether, two midshipmen and one marine killed, the commodore, one lieutenant, one lieutenant of marines, three midshipmen, and twelve seamen wounded. This alone was a high price to pay for the day's amusement, but this was not all, as the homeward bound fleet, through Capt. Byron's judgment in leading the American squadron, so long a dance, arrived safely on the 23rd August, in the Downs, Com. Rodgers only falling in with a fleet, not of ships, but, of cocoa nuts, orange peel, &c. To complete his misfortunes, the scurvy broke out among the men, and thus conferred an additional value on the oranges and lemons that were known to be in such profusion in the much coveted vessels.

It had been intended that the frigate Essex
Manning of American fleet as compared with that of the British. should have formed part of Commodore Rodgers' squadron, but she could not be got ready in time ; the complement of this vessel, as acknowledged by Capt. Porter, was three hundred and twenty-eight men. Another confession was also made by Capt. Porter, (one for which his government did not thank him), that, out of his three hundred and twenty-eight men, there were but eleven landsmen. To those cognizant of the material from which the complement of a British ship is made up, this admission must appear most extraordinary, and establishes the very important fact that, no pains were spared by the Americans to send their vessels to sea equipped and manned in the most complete way. We will now show the importance that was attached to the retention of British seamen on board the American ships of war, and this should be held in remembrance by all who desire to judge fairly of those encounters between British and American ships, of which we are now about to begin the account.

We give, on the authority of Mr. James,
Captain Porter's inhuman treatment of an English sailor. the following statement which shows, if true, and we would hardly suppose that Mr. James would lightly advance so grave a charge ; the barbarous means to which an American officer could resort, to punish a native of England for refusing to become a traitor to his country :— " A New York newspaper, of June 27th, 1812, contains the following as the substance of the formal deposition of the victim of Capt. Porter's unmanly treatment.   The deposition states,that John Erving was born in Newcastle-upon-Tyne, England ; that he has resided within the United States, but has never been naturalized ; that, on the 14th October, 1811, he entered on board the Essex, and joined her at Norfolk ; that Captain Porter, on the 25th June, 1812, caused all hands to be piped on deck, to take the oath of allegiance to the United States, and gave them to understand, that any man who did not choose to do so should be discharged ; that, when deponent heard his name called, he told the Captain that, being a British subject, he must refuse taking the oath ; on which the captain spoke to the petty officers, and told them they must pass sentence upon him ; that they then put him into the launch which lay alongside the frigate, and there poured a bucket of tar over him, and then laid on a quantity of feathers having first stripped him naked from the waist ; that they then rowed him ashore, stern foremost, and landed him ; that he wandered about, from street to street, in this condition, until a Mr. Ford took him into his shop, to save him from the crowd then beginning to gather ; that he staid there until the police magistrate took him away, and put him into the city prison for protection, where he was cleansed and clothed.   None of the citizens molested him or insulted him." He says he gave as an additional reason to the Captain why he did not choose to fight against his country, that, if he should be taken prisoner, he would certainly be hung.   This, as we remarked above, if true, is a significant fact, and shows the importance attached to the retention of a good seaman. So much has been already written on the way in which British vessels are manned, that it is almost unnecessary to remark, that there was no great cause for wonder that, seduced by promises of high pay, good seamen should enter the American service, and fight desperately ; especially with a noose dangling from the foreyard arm ever before their eye when in sight of a British man-of-war.

The first fatal consequence of the disregard

First consequences of the meeting of unequal forces. Loss of the Guerrière.

of the difference of size and armament of American vessels, and of undervaluing their opponents' strength, was experienced by the frigate Guerrière, commanded by Captain Dacres, which, on August 19th, lat. 40° 20' N. and long. 53° W., was brought to action by the American frigate Constitution, Captain Hull.

The respective force is thus officially stated,—Guerrière forty-eight guns, throwing one thousand and thirty-four pounds of shot: crew, two hundred and forty four: tons, one thousand and ninety-two;—Constitution fifty-six guns, throwing fifteen hundred and thirty-six pounds of shot: crew, four hundred and sixty: tons, fifteen hundred and thirty-eight. Even this statement will fail to convey an adequate idea of the real inequality that existed between the vessels, as it should be also borne in mind that the Guerrière was on her return from a long cruise with foremast and bowsprit sprung, and in absolute need of the refit for which she was then hastening to Halifax.*

The Constitution was seventeen days from port, and in all respects as well prepared for an engagement as the greatest care could make her. At half-past four the frigates came to close quarters, and by half-past six the unequal contest was ended by Capt. Dacres lowering his flag, the Guerrière being, by this time, an unmanageable wreck, rolling her main deck guns under, with her three masts gone by the board.

No imputation can be attached to Capt. Dacres on this occasion, he fought and handled his ship well, and he with his crew yielded only to the irresistible superiority of physical

strength. So heavy indeed had been the fire* that after removing the officers and crew it

* Sir,—I am sorry to inform you of the capture of His Majesty's late ship Guerrière, by the American frigate Constitution, after a severe action on the 19th August, in lat. 40 deg. 20 minutes N. and long. 55 deg. W. At 2 P. M. being by the wind on the star-board tack, we saw a sail on our weather beam, bearing down on us. At 3, made her out to be a man-of-war, beat to quarters and prepared for action. At 4, she closing fast, wore to prevent her raking us. At ten minutes past 4, hoisted our colors and fired several shot at her: at twenty minutes past 4, she hoisted her colors and returned our fire, wore several times to avoid being raked, exchanging broadsides. At 5, she closed on our starboard beam, both keeping up a heavy fire and steering free, his intention being evidently to cross our bow. At 20 minutes past 5, our mizen-mast went over the star-board quarter, and brought the ship up in the wind; the enemy then placed himself on our larboard bow, raking us, a few only of our bow guns bearing, and his grape and riflemen sweeping our deck. At forty minutes past 5, the ship not answering her helm, he attempted to lay us on board; at this time Mr. Grant, who commanded the forecastle, was carried below badly wounded. I immediately ordered the marines and boarders from the main deck; the master was at this time shot through the knee, and I received a severe wound in the back. Lieut. King was leading the boarders, when the ship coming too, we brought some of our bow guns to bear on her, and had got clear of our opponent, when at twenty minutes past 6, our fore and mainmast went over the side, leaving the ship a perfect unmanageable wreck, The frigate shooting ahead I was in hopes to clear the wreck, and get the ship under command to renew the action, but just as we had cleared the wreck, our sprit sail yard went, and the enemy having rove new braces, &c., wore round within pistol shot, to rake us, the ship lying in the trough of the sea, and rolling her main deck guns under water, and all attempts to get her before the wind being fruitless, when calling my few remaining officers together, they were all of opinion that any further resistance would only be a needless waste of lives, I ordered, though reluctantly, the colors to be struck.

The loss of the ship is to be ascribed to the early fall of her main-mast, which enabled our opponent to choose his position. I am sorry to say, we suffered considerably in killed and wounded, and mostly while she lay on our bow, from her grape and musquetry; in all, fifteen killed and sixty-three wounded, many of them severely; none of the wounded officers quitted the deck until the firing ceased.

The frigate proved to be the United States' ship Constitution, of thirty 24-pounders on her main deck and twenty-four 32-pounders, and two 18's on her upper deck, and 476 men: her loss in comparison with ours is trifling, about twenty: the first lieutenant of marines and eight killed; the first lieutenant and master of the ship, and eleven men wounded; her lower masts badly wounded, and stern much shattered, and very much cut up about the rigging,

* "The Guerrière had nearly expended, not only her water and provisions, but her boatswain's and carpenter's stores; her gunner's stores were also deficient; what remained of her powder, from damp and long keeping, was greatly reduced in strength; her bowsprit was badly sprung, her mainmast, from having been struck by lightning, in a tottering state, and her hull, from age and length of service, scarcely seaworthy. No one hen will deny that this rencontre was rather unfortunate; in fact, such was the state of general decay in which the Guerrière, at this time, was, that, had the frigate gone into Portsmouth or Plymouth, she would, in all probability, have been disarmed and broken up."

was found by the captors impossible to keep this, their first naval trophy, afloat, and the Guerrière was accordingly set on fire and blown up. This must have been the more mortifying, as this ship had been made particularly obnoxious to the Americans, although the causes of quarrel arose before Capt. Dacres joined and while Capt. Pechell commanded her, still it was the same ship, and most acceptable would her acquisition as a trophy have been. It is not unworthy of remark, that on board of the Guerrière, at the time of this engagement, there were ten American seamen who had for a number of years belonged to her; but as the declaration of war by the United States was not known at the

---

The Guerrière was so cut up, that all attempts to get her in would have been useless. As soon as the wounded were got out of her, they set her on fire; and I feel it my duty to state, that the conduct of Captain Hull and his officers to our men, has been that of a brave enemy, the greatest care being taken to prevent our men losing the smallest trifle, and the greatest attention being paid to the wounded, who, through the attention and skill of Mr. Irvine, the surgeon, I hope will do well.

I hope, though success has not crowned our efforts, you will not think it presumptuous in me to say, the greatest credit is due to the officers and ship's company for their exertions, particularly when exposed to the heavy raking fire of the enemy. I feel particularly obliged for the exertions of lieut. Kent, who, though wounded early by a splinter, continued to assist me; in the second lieutenant the service has suffered a severe loss; Mr. Scott, the master, though wounded, was particularly attentive, and used every exertion in clearing the wreck, as did the warrant officers.— lieutenant Nicholl of the royal marines, and his party, supported the honorable character of their corps, and they suffered severely. I must recommend Mr. Shaw, master's mate, who commanded the foremast main deck guns in the absence of lieutenant Pullman, and the whole after the fall of lieutenant Ready, to your protection, he having received a severe contusion from a splinter. I must point out Mr. Garby, acting purser, to your notice, who volunteered his services on deck, and commanded the after quarter-deck guns, and was particularly active, as well as Mr. Bannister, midshipman. I hope, in considering the circumstances you will think the ship entrusted to my charge, properly defended—the unfortunate loss of our masts, the absence of the third lieutenant, second lieutenant of marines, three midshipmen and twenty-four men, considerably weakened our crew, and we only mustered at quarters two hundred and forty-four men, on coming into action; the enemy had such an advantage from his marines and riflemen, when close, and his superior sailing enabled him to choose his distance.

I enclose herewith a list of killed and wounded on board the Guerrière.

---

time of her sailing, no opportunity of course had since that period offered itself for discharging them. Capt. Dacres, however, conceiving it to be unjust in the extreme, to compel them to fight against their countrymen, ordered them to quit their quarters and go below. This conduct contrasts most favorably with the attempts made by Capt. Hull and his officers to inveigle the crew of the Guerrière and induce them to turn traitors. One of the means resorted to was to keep his prisoners manacled and chained to the deck during the night and the greater part of the day.

The reason assigned by Capt. Hull for this unusual severity was, that there were so many of his own crew who considered the Guerrière's men as their countrymen, (and who felt, as well they might, some degree of shame at their own fallen state), he was apprehensive the two bodies united would overpower him and the Americans, and carry the Constitution to Halifax. The more probable reason seems to have been to render the prospect of liberty the more alluring to those who would turn traitors. Capt. Hull calculated, it may be supposed, that any whom he could persuade to enter, would fight in the most desperate manner, rather than be taken and turned over to their former commanders, from whom they could only expect to receive a certain and well merited fate. Capt. Dacres bears testimony, in other respects, to Capt. Hull's treatment of himself and crew, and the care that was taken to prevent their losing the smallest trifle.

The author of the American "Naval History," Mr. Clark, remarks thus upon the Guerrière's capture:—"It appeared in evidence on the court martial, that many Englishmen were on board the Constitution, and that many of these were leading men, or captains of guns." The officers of the Guerrière knew some of them personally. One had been captain of the forecastle in the Eurydice, another had been in the Achille at Trafalgar, and the third lieutenant was an Irishman, named Read. In the latter end of 1816, a register of officers and others, military and naval, in the service of the United States, was issued from the Washington press, prepared by a resolution of Congress. Affixed to the list of names in this official document, is one column headed "State or country where born." Turning to this column, in the naval department, we find, as we descend in the list, the blanks in the column of "where born" increase amazingly. Of the superior officers, only three captains— Shaw, Patterson, and Crichton—were ashamed to name their birth-place. Of one hundred and sixty lieutenants, five appear to have been British; but seventeen, all English or Irish names have blanks after them. Of twenty boatswains, four were born in the United States; the rest nowhere. Of eighty-three sailing-masters, fifteen had no birthplace; and eight appear to be British. Of twenty-five gunners, three appear to have been born in the United States; and out of thirty-three carpenters and master-mates, five only could be found to fill up the blank with the term "American." The blanks in the list of able seamen increase surprisingly. This, however, is not to be wondered at, when we consider Captain Brenton's statement:—"It was said, and there is no reason to doubt the fact, that there were two hundred British seamen on board the Constitution."

After this analysis, Mr. Clark's remarks on the capture of the Guerrière can be taken at their value—"It has manifested the genuine worth of the American tar, which has enabled him to meet under DISADVANTAGEOUS CIRCUMSTANCES (save the mark), and to derive glory from the encounter, the naval heroes of a nation which has so long ruled the waves."

We have been thus particular in dwelling on all the circumstances connected with the capture of the Guerrière, as with few exceptions the same disparity of force prevailed and the same remarks apply. That the American successes were unexpected, is apparent from the instructions given to the officers in command of the vessels about to leave port, and, in fact, the first capture of an English by an American vessel was made, if not in direct breach of orders, at least contrary to the calculations of the Navy Department, and had not Hull put to sea before his countermand reached Boston, he certainly would not have made his capture of the Guerrière, nor is it probable that any capture would have been made at all, if we may judge from the tone of the following communications:—

"Naval Department, Washington,
18th June, 1812.

"SIR,—This day war has been declared between the United Empire of Great Britain, Ireland, and their dependencies, and the United States of America, and their territories, and you are, with the force under your command, entitled to every belligerent right to atttack and capture, and to defend. You will use the utmost despatch to reach New York, after you have made up your complement of men, &c., at Annapolis. In your way from thence, you will not fail to notice the British flag, should it present itself. I am informed that the Belvidera is on our coast, but you will not understand *me as impelling you* to battle previously to your having confidence in your crew, unless attacked, or with a reasonable prospect of success, of which you are to be, at your discretion, the judge. You are to reply to this, and inform me of your progress.

"P. HAMILTON.

"Capt. Hull, U. S. Frigate Constitution."

This discouraging and, considered with immediate results, somewhat pusillanimous order, was soon followed by another of the same tenor, as follows:—

"Navy Department, 3rd July, 1812.

"SIR,—As soon as the Constitution is ready for sea, you will weigh anchor and proceed to New York.

"If, on your way thither, you should fall in with an enemy's vessel, you will be guided in your proceeding by your own judgment, bearing in mind, however, that you are not voluntarily to encounter a force superior to your own. On your arrival at New York, you will report yourself to Commodore Rodgers. If he should not be in that port, you will remain there untill further orders.

"P. HAMILTON."

The Constitution, on her way to New York was chased by a British squadron and prevented from getting into that port, so that her stealing to sea from Boston, into which she had been driven, and her encounter with the Guerrière was purely accidental and in contravention of orders, for even after his escape into Boston, a new order was despatched.—

"Navy Department, 29th July, 1812.

"SIR,—Your letter of the 20th instant, just received, has relieved me from much anxiety. "I am truly happy to hear of your safety. Remain at Boston until further orders.

"P. HAMILTON."

Before receiving this order Capt. Hull had put to sea and escaped the doom, which his affrighted Government had prepared for him—to be laid up in port.

A second action, tending to augment the confidence of Americans in themselves, took place on the 18th October, between H. M. brig Frolic, Captain Whinyates, and the United S ates sloop of war Wasp, Captain Jones.

The Frolic was the convoy of the homeward bound fleet from the Bay of Honduras, and was repairing the damages her masts and sails received in a violent gale on the night of the 16th, in lat. 36° north, lon. 64°, in which she had carried away her main-yard, sprung her main-topmast, and lost both her topsails, when a vessel was made out which immediately gave chace to the convoy.

Although in the crippled state above mentioned, Captain Whinyates determined to save his convoy, and a close and spirited action ensued, which was maintained until the brig became, from her previous shattered condition, unmanageable. The Wasp taking advantage of this shot ahead, and raked the Frolic, which was unable to bring a gun to bear. She now fell with her bowsprit between the main and mizen rigging of the enemy, and was then immediately carried by boarding, after an action of an hour's duration. Such was the obstinacy with which she had been defended that, on the Americans taking possession of their prize, but three officers and the man at the wheel were found alive on the deck. In this dreadful conflict the British loss was thirty killed, and between forty and fifty wounded. The vessels were nearly equal in point of strength, both as regarded guns and men, and her previous crippled state alone brought on this disastrous and speedy issue. On the afternoon of the same day H.M. ship Poictiers, seventy-four guns, fell in with and captured both vessels, sending them into Bermuda. Congress awarded to Captain Jones a gold medal, to his officers a silver one, and to the crew generally, twenty-four thousand dollars, in testimony of their gallantry in capturing a British vessel of superior force. This may be accounted for, as Captain Jones in his official despatch, gave the Frolic two extra guns, and judiciously said nothing of her previous disabled state. The reader may, however, judge in what the superior force consisted from the statement here given :—Frolic, broadside guns,

nine, throwing two hundred and sixty-two pounds of shot, with two twelve-pounder carronades,—crew, ninety-two,—size, three hundred and eighty-four tons. Wasp, broadside, nine guns, throwing two hundred and sixty-eight pounds of shot, with two brass four-pounders,—crew, one hundred and thirty-five,—size, four hundred and thirty-four tons. Nearly matched as these vessels were, the superiority if anything leaning towards the side of Wasp, yet the usual exaggerations of American officers made it a victory over a superior force.

Seven days after this affair, on the 25th of October, in lat. 29° north, lon. 29° 30' west, the thirty-eight gun frigate Macedonian, Captain Carden, fell in with and brought to action the U. S. frigate, United States, Commodore Decatur. The action lasted for upwards of two hours, when, with one hundred shot in her hull, several of them between wind and water, her mizen mast gone by the board, main and fore topmasts shot away by the cap, her main yard in the slings, two remaining lower masts badly injured, and but few guns effective, the Macedonian surrendered. Of her complement of two hundred and fifty-four men, deducting eight foreigners who refused to fight, thirty-six were killed and sixty-eight wounded.

Commodore Decatur, in his official despatches, makes very light of the damage done to his vessel ; either in loss of men or injuries to hull or rigging, reporting only five killed and six wounded. Captain Carden, however, represents that the United States "was pumped out every watch till her arrival in port, from the effects of shot received between wind and water, and that two eighteen pounders had passed through her mainmast in a horizontal line." There is very little doubt, also, from what may be gathered from his account, but that these numbers were very far from representing the actual loss in killed and wounded.

The comparative force of the two combatants may be with correctness stated as follows:—Macedonian—weight of broadside, five hundred and twenty-eight pounds; crew, two hundred and fifty-four ; size, one thousand and eighty-one tons. United States—broadside, weight of metal, eight hundred and sixty-four pounds; crew, four hundred and seventy-four; size, fifteen hundred and thirty-three tons. James mentions, among other proofs, that a large proportion of the United States' crew were British; the following fact,—"One of the officers' servants, a young lad from London, named William Hearne, actually found among the hostile crew his own brother! This hardened traitor, after reviling the British, and applauding the American service, used the influence of seniority in trying to persuade his brother to enter the latter. The honorable youth, with tears in his eyes, replied: 'If you are a —— rascal, that's no reason I should be one.'" Mr. James alleges that several of the Macedonian's men recognized their old shipmates; and " Captain Carden," says Marshall, "observing 'Victory' painted on the ship's side over one part, and 'Nelson' over another, asked Commodore Decatur the reason of so strange an anomaly; he answered, 'the men belonging to those guns served many years with Lord Nelson, and in the Victory, and they claim the privilege of using the illustrious names in the way you have seen.'" The Commodore also declared, according to the same authority, publicly, that there were but few seamen in his ship, who had not served from twelve to fifteen years in a British man-of-war. After reading this, the reader will naturally like to know what the register, which has been already so useful to us, says of the birthplace of Commodore Decatur. This authority assigns, as might be expected, a birthplace, not quite so far north as Captain Hull's, to the Commodore—Maryland.

On the arrival of Decatur, with his prize, at New York, the Macedonian was purchased by the American Government, and was rated as a thirty-six gun frigate, of which class she was the smallest ship. The same ungenerous system of tampering with the prisoners, that prevailed in the case of the Guerriere, was carried on by the Commodore and officers of the United States, and in order that his attempts might be unrestricted by the presence of the Macedonian's officers, they were sent on shore on parole. The officers, however, becoming acquainted with the honorable schemes of the American officer, returned on board.

We look in vain in Commodore Decatur's official communications for any admission that he had conquered a vessel of inferior force. This confession would certainly have been honest, but, then, it would have interfered with the Act of Congress of 28th June 1798, which provided that, "if a vessel of superior or equal force shall be captured by a public armed vessel of the United States, the forfeiture shall accrue wholly to the captors." Two hundred thousand dollars, the valuation of the prizes, was accordingly paid over to the American commander and his crew. The verdict of the court-marshall, puts the conduct of Captain Carden and his crew, beyond question—the substance of the sentence is as follows:—"Having most strictly investigated every circumstance, and examined the different officers, and ship's company; and having very deliberately and maturely weighed and considered the whole, and every part thereof, the Court does most honorably acquit Capt. Carden, the officers and crew."

Great were the rejoicings throughout the Union, at their third naval victory, especially as it was the first of which the fruits had been secured,—and the arrival of the colors of the Macedonian at Washington was attended with illuminations and a public and most brilliant fête. The press, too, teemed with such rhapsodies as the one of which we give a specimen.* Had a faithful statement of the com-

---

* With unutterable pleasure we record another most gallant naval achievement—a thing without precedent or parallel—an action *sui generis*, unique, incomparable—a *British* frigate dismasted and compelled to surrender in *seventeen minutes*, with 106 of her crew, one-third of her number, killed and wounded, by a vessel but little her superior in force—by a new people, unused to the horrid business of war; by strangers to the thunder of cannon.

We are lost in astonishment at the *effect* of *Decatur's* fire—-no wonder that the *Britons* thought he was enveloped in flames, and rejoiced, giving three cheers. Weak mortals!—they had yet to learn the great activity of *Decatur's* youthful crew, and feel the power of the *vengeance-charged* guns of the *United States*.

Thus it was with *Hull*, with *Porter*, with *Jones*, and with *Chauncey*, on the lake. Every shot had its private commission to revenge a private wrong—some lashing at the gang-way of a *British* vessel of war—some privation of food for refusing to labor for " his Majesty "—some personal indignity which imperious *Britons* know so well to give to " Yankee rascals."

The gallant *Rodgers*, unsuccessful, vexes the deep. Like the bold bald eagle of his country, he darts over the region of waters in search of his enemy: groaning in spirit that the foe is not nigh.

parative force of the two vessels, been blazoned on the walls of that festive hall, we scarcely think that there would have been found cause for such extravagant demonstrations of joy, or room, on the part of the press, for such vainglorious paragraphs. Justice and truth would rather have awakened a feeling of admiration, at the bravery with which British sailors had contended against such unequal and fearful odds.

Another action, the result of which was

Java and Constitution, December 29th. even more disastrous to the British, yet remains to be chronicled, before closing the list of naval battles, for the year, on the ocean.

The Java, Captain Lambert, on her outward-bound voyage to the East Indies, with a number of passengers on board, besides a large body of recruits, on the 29th December, some forty miles from St. Salvador, in lat. 13° N. and long. 36° W., encountered, and was captured by, the American frigate Constitution. "The Java," according to Commodore Bainbridge's testimony, in a letter to a friend, bearing date January 29th, 1813, "was exceedingly well fought. Poor Lambert, who died, six days after the action, was a distinguished and gallant officer."

One can hardly credit that so much indifference could have been manifested by Government, as was shown in the case of preparing the Java for a voyage, in which the chances were so great that an enemy's vessel would be encountered. A little of the previous history of the Java will, however, place

But the time will come when he shall reap a rich harvest of glory.

Bainbridge, in the *Constitution,* with the sloop *Hornet,* commanded by the excellent *Lawrence,* was near the middle of the Atlantic, *hunting* British frigates, at the date of our last accounts from him.

Porter, in the little frigate *Essex* is,—we know not where; but doubtless desirous of paying his respects to Sir *James Yeo.* of the *Southampton;* who, *dubbed* a knight by a king, wants to be *drubbed* into a gentleman by a *Porter;* and we venture to say that if they meet, the knight will get a lesson on good manners.

The *Constellation,* Captain *Stewart,* will soon be at sea, to claim her portion of the laurels; and the *Adams* frigate, nearly fitted out at Washington city, will bring to the recollection of our aged patriots the ardent zeal that distinguished her *namesake* in "the times that tried men's souls." —*Niles' Weekly Register.*

the affair pretty clearly before the reader. The late French frigate Renommeé, newly christened the Java, was under orders to carry out to Bombay the newly appointed Governor, Lieutenant-General Hislop, and suite, with a number of supernumeraries,—Marine Society boys. Finding, on joining, that out of a complement of two hundred and ninety-two, the whole number of petty officers and men, who had ever trod a deck or been present at an action, amounted to less than fifty, Captain Lambert loudly remonstrated against the inefficiency of such a ship's company. The only reply was, that a voyage to the East Indies and back would make sailors of them. It was in vain to urge the matter further, but as some slight amendment to the Java's crew, eight men were allowed to volunteer. Manned in this way, with sixty Irishmen, who had never smelt salt water, except in crossing the channel—the rest of her complement made up from prison ships, Captain Lambert was despatched to sea. Is there room for wonder that with such a crew he and his vessel should have succumbed to a superior, unprepared as he was for a contest even with an equal, force? The great cause for astonishment is that, with such a crew, the Java should have maintained a fight from a little past two till six, and that the colors should have been lowered from the stump of the mizen mast only when the Constitution had taken up a raking position athwart the bows of her then defenceless antagonist. The Java lost her masts and bowsprit, had upwards of twenty guns disabled, her boats shot to pieces, and her hull so shattered, that it was found necessary to burn her. Twenty-two were killed, and ninety-two wounded on board the Java, in this murderous conflict; and the American loss, though trifling in comparison, was yet severe—ten killed and forty-eight wounded. This victory added no glory to the American flag, as, with the same difference of force as in the instance of the Guerrière, the crew, although nominally stronger, was in reality not half as effective; indeed, Mr. James remarks on this head: "The Constitution captured the Java certainly, but in so discreditable a manner that, had the latter been manned with a well-trained crew of three hundred and twenty men, no doubt remains in our mind, and we have considered the subject seriously, that, notwithstanding her vast superiority of force, the American frigate must either have succumbed or have fled." According to the same author, "the manner in which the Java's men were treated by the American officers, reflects upon the latter the greatest disgrace." One object, however, the Constitution's officers missed by their cruelty in manacling and pillaging their poor captives—three only of the Java's crew entered, while the remainder, jail birds though many of them were, treated with contempt their reiterated promises of high pay, rich land, and liberty.

The verdict of the court martial held on the surviving officers and crew of the Java was, that "the action was maintained with zeal, ability, and bravery," and the compliment paid to Lieut. Chads, who commanded after Captain Lambert's fall, a very high one. Rear Admiral Thorn was the president, and, returning Lieutenant Chads his sword, he thus addressed him—"I have much satisfaction in returning you your sword. Had you been an officer who had served in comparative obscurity all your life, and never before heard of, your conduct on the present occasion has been sufficient to establish your character as a brave, skilful, and attentive officer." We think it but justice to bring these facts forward, to enable those who may have seen only American accounts of the war, to come to a more correct conclusion respecting the events we have been just detailing. We cannot forbear quoting from James a short account of the reception of Commodore Bainbridge by the citizens of Boston :—

"At this moment our eyes light upon a passage in a book before us, giving an account of the reception of Commodore Bainbridge by the citizens of Boston, and we cannot resist the temptation of placing it before the British public. 'On the following Thursday (that succeeding the frigate's arrival,) Commodore Bainbridge landed at the long wharf from the frigate Constitution, amidst acclamations, and roaring of cannon from the shore. All the way from the end of the pier to the Exchange coffee-house, was decorated with colours and streamers. In State street they were strung across from the opposite buildings, while the windows and balconies of the houses were filled with ladies, and the tops of the houses

were covered with spectators, and an immense crowd filled the streets, so as to render it difficult for the military escort to march. The commodore was distinguished by his noble figure, and his walking uncovered. On his right hand was the veteran Commodore Rodgers, and on his left Brigadier-general Welles ; then followed the brave Captain Hull, Colonel Blake, and a number of officers and citizens ; but the crowd was so immense that it was difficult to keep the order of procession. The band of music in the balcony of the State Bank and the music of the New-England guards, had a fine effect." Here was a compliment to the British navy !

There is very little doubt but that the effect of these four actions on the American mind was most important, as the successive triumphs gave a tone and character to a war hitherto decidedly unpopular with the moderate portion of the community, and imparted a still greater confidence to the war party, already far from deficient in the language of pretension and vain glorious boasting.

Effect of these successes on the American people.

The tone, even, of the *National Intelligencer*, previously moderate, if not pacific, was at once altered, and the repeal of the orders in Council, simple and unconditional as it was, now failed to satisfy American demagogues, "the American flag was now to secure all that sailed under it."

This was a bold attitude to assume towards a nation whose seamen had beaten, in succession, every power in Europe into a confession of their superiority, more especially when we reflect that the Americans were to the full as much astonished as were the English at the unexpected aspect which naval events had now assumed. The various orders from Washington to the Commanders make this sufficiently apparent, and supply a more correct index to the reality of American expectations than do the vapourings of a few individuals, who prepared a highly seasoned dish of self-glorification for a public by no means unwilling to swallow the regale seasoned for the national taste.

"No one" says one Historian* "can compare the official accounts without acknowledging that accident or fortune had little to do with these battles, which were like nearly all

* Ingersoll.

the other naval engagements throughout the war, AFTER England had time to recover from her surprise, and endeavour to imitate or excel her antagonist. More extensive or more numerous battles would add little to the credentials of the few gained."

This last paragraph is a fortunate admission, as but few laurels were added to the American naval wreath after the first year, and as the American Navy disappeared nearly altogether from the ocean when the British Government awoke, at length, from their delusion, and adopted such measures as they should have done at the beginning of the war.

We have just given a full account, not only Measures adopted by of the exploits, but of the the British Government. force in tons, men, and guns, of the American forty-fours, and we will now, as far as lies in our power, point out the steps that were taken by the British Admiralty, to put a stop to their further successes.

Three of the small class seventy-fours, the Majestic, Goliath, and Saturn, were cut down, and thus armed : The first deck battery of twenty-eight long thirty-two pounders was retained, but in lieu of twenty-eight long eighteens' on the second deck, an equal number of forty-two-pound carronades were carried, with two long twelve-pounders as chase guns ; this, with a complement of four hundred and ninety-four men and boys, was judged a fair match for the American, nominally, forty-fours ; as, however, no glory could have accrued from the capture of an American forty-four, by what would have been styled a seventy-four in disguise, the policy or utility of this measure may be, and has been, very much doubted.

Besides the completion of these three razees, two vessels were built to answer the same purposes. They also merit a few remarks which we will take from James :—

"The Leander was constructed of pitch-pine, from a draught prepared by Sir William Rule, the ingenious architect of the Caledonia, and many other fine ships in the British navy ; and the Newcastle was constructed of the same light wood, from the draught of M. Louis-Charles Barrallier, then an assistant surveyor under Sir William, but now the principal naval architect for the French at Toulon. The first of these ships measured

1572, the other 1556 tons ; and they were both constructed of very thin and inadequate scantling. The establishment of each ship was 30 long 24-pounders on the first or 'upper' deck, and 26 carronades 42-pounders, and two, afterwards increased to four, long 24-pounders on the second or 'spar' deck ; total, at first 58, then 60 guns, with a net complement of 480 men and boys. The Leander and Newcastle, therefore, in the disposition of their guns, perfectly agreed with the cut-down 74s ; and yet they were officially registered as 'frigates,' but, by way of salvo for their anomalous structure 'with spar decks,' was superadded. If, by 'frigate,' is meant a ship with a single battery-deck from stem to stern, is it not a sufficient stretch of the term, to apply it to a vessel that has two additional short decks, upon which are mounted nearly as many guns as she carries on her whole deck ? But must a ship, having two whole decks, upon each of which an equal number of guns is mounted, be called a single-decked vessel ? And yet, in official language, the Leander and Newcastle are not two-decked ships, otherwise their lower battery-deck would not be called their upper deck, nor their upper, their spar deck ; neither would their depth of hold be measured from the deck below the first battery-deck, nor the length of the same deck be registered as the 'length of gun-deck.' These are the only points, in which these frigates with spar decks differ from the cut-down 74s, and from the 56 and 54 gun ships already mentioned.

The command of the Leander was given to Captain Sir George Rolph Collier, and the command of the Newcastle, to Captain Lord George Stuart. Great difficulty was experienced in getting these two ships manned ; and certainly the crew of the Leander, after it was obtained, was a very indifferent one, containing, besides many old and weakly men, an unusually large proportion of boys. This ineffectiveness of the Leander's crew has recently been contradicted ; but we allude to the period of the ship's arrival at Halifax, Nova Scotia.

" We were then on board the Leander several times, and not only witnessed the quality of her crew, but heard the officers complain, as well they might, of their great inferiority in that respect to the ships against which they were expected to contend.

" When she quitted Spithead, for Halifax, the Leander was so lumbered with stores, that the ship would scarcely have made the voyage, had she not received a refit in Cork; and even then it was fortunate, much as was to be expected from her captain and officers, that the Leander did not encounter one of the American 44s.

" Another ship, of the same force in guns, and nearly so in men, as the Leander and Newcastle, was produced by raising upon the Akbar, formerly a teak-built Indiaman, and more recently known as the 44-gun frigate Cornwallis. The Akbar proved a very indifferent cruiser, sailing heavily, and rolling to such a degree, that she was constantly carrying away or springing her masts. The ship actually stowed 450 tons of water; while the Caledonia, a ship of double her measurement, could not stow more than 421 tons. The Akbar has since been converted to the only purpose for which, and carrying a cargo, she was ever adapted, a troop-ship.

" If it was deemed necessary to build or equip ships to oppose the large American frigates in fair combat, they should have been frigates, and two-decked ships like the Leander Newcastle, and Akbar. There was a frigate laid down in the year 1813, which would have answered every purpose; but, after the draught of the Java had been prepared as that of a regular frigate, to carry 52 guns, the pen of authority filled up the gangway with a barricade and a row of ports, and hence the Java was built as a 60-gun two-decked ship, similar to the Newcastle and Leander. If the American frigates, of 1533 tons, could not carry, with ease, their gangway guns, and the two last-named British 60-gun ships, averaging 1564 tons, found some inconvenience in carrying theirs, how could it be expected that the Java, of 1458 tons, could bear the eight additional guns ordered for her?"

Besides these two anomalous classes of frigates, the cut down seventy-fours, and the fifty; a few ships were constructed to which the name of frigates was really applicable. Two fine frigates were then afloat, but one carried a broadside of only twenty-six guns, while the forty-fours carried one of twenty-eight; the proverb of " L'an scottato ha paura de l'acqua calda"* is here applicable; the Admi-

ralty had not scrupled to send out thirty-sixes, with instructions compelling them to bring to action any single-decked enemy's vessel, however superior; but now they hesitated to send a fine vessel, nay two, for the Egyptienne was rejected also, though mounting the proper number of guns, because she was inferior to her expected adversary by one broadside gun. The Firth, Liffey, Severn, Glasgow, and Liverpool were accordingly built, manned with a complement of three hundred men and boys, and with an armament of fifty guns—twenty-eight long twenty-four pounders, twenty carronades, thirty-two pounders, with two long nines. A new gun was also tried, and found to answer expectations. Says James—" The six-and-half feet thirty-three cwt. twenty-four pounders not having been found heavy enough, some guns of the same calibre were constructed, from a foot to a foot-and-a-half longer, and weighing from forty to forty-three cwt."

It is singular, that although American sloops were hunting for British frigates all over the ocean, as soon as the intention of arming British frigates with such guns was promulgated, the Americans seem to have suddenly mislaid their orders for hunting down the British, and we accordingly find that the Java was the last British frigate they captured or brought to action, although not, as we shall hereafter see, the last they fell in with.

Some of the minor classes of ships, must now receive our attention, as we shall soon have several cases to record, proving that the Americans were as keenly awake to "outbuild the British in sloops," as they had outwitted them in their frigates.

To whatever is classed under one head, people are disposed, and not unnaturally, to attach the notion also, of equality, so that when there does exist any difference, the stronger is sure to triumph over the weaker party,—while there always will be found many, whom it will be hard to convince that any disparity of force really existed: such is the difficulty of removing an impression once conveyed, and of substituting for it another.

The Americans had built their new sloops, the Peacock, Wasp, and Frolic, and to meet these on anything like equal terms, it was deemed necessary to build new vessels. What were considered equal terms by the Admiralty,

* The burn child dreads the fire.

we shall now show. The English had in their possession, the late French corvette "Bonne Citoyenne,"—a very fine vessel. After placing the force of the Bonne Citoyenne in juxta position with that of the Frolic, the reader will be able to judge how far the action of Government was judicious: Bonne Citoyenne —length of main deck, one hundred and twenty feet; breadth, thirty-one feet; tons, five hundred and eleven; guns, twenty; men, one hundred and thirty-five. Frolic, length, one hundred and twenty feet: breadth, thirty-two feet; tons, five hundred and forty; guns, twenty-two; men, one hundred and seventy-five. Now, surely the easiest mode of encountering the Americans, would appear to have been, to have built vessels of some twenty-five tons burthen larger than the Bonne Citoyenne, and to have added thirty men, at least, to her complement. The Lords of the Admiralty thought otherwise, so, as the surest means of producing the effect they desired to bring about, the vessels, built from the lines of the Bonne Citoyenne, were shortened five feet, and instead of increasing, the burthen was decreased fifty-five tons,—two extra guns were put on board a smaller vessel, and to work the extra guns no extra men were considered necessary—the complement of one hundred and thirty-five being considered sufficient. Sir Jos. Yorke had the merit of sending his improved vessels to sea—the improvement consisting in diminishing a vessel's capacity to carry, and at the same time increasing her armament. Let us take Mr. James' testimony : "Scarcely were the twenty thirty-pounder carronades, and two long nines brought on board, than two of the carronades were sent on shore again, as having no proper ports fitted to receive them—already the remaining twenty guns were too close together, to render the quarters sufficiently roomy. With these, however, the ships went to sea; and they were soon found neither to sail well nor to work well. The utility of their stern chase ports, may be judged of when it is stated, that, owing to the narrowness of the ships at the stern, there was no room to work the tiller while the guns were pointed through the ports."

Of this last discreditable oversight and its attendant consequences, we shall have to give hereafter a practical illustration. Fortunately for the credit of the Brtiish navy, and for the individual honor of the captains and crews of the new twenty-gun vessels, the press gave rather an exaggerated account of their force and size, and held them up to view as much more formidable than they really were. The consequence was that the Wasp, Frolic, Peacock, and Hornet avoided every three-masted man-of-war they saw. Relative to the boasting that took place in the case of the Hornet and Bonne Citoyenne, we shall now speak, and shall establish, with Mr. James' help, the fact that the behavior of the Americans on the occasion was nothing but braggadocio of the most despicable character.*

* While in the early part of December, 1812, the United States' frigate Constitution, Commodore Bainbridge, and ship-sloop Hornet, of eighteen 32-pounder carronades and two long 12-pounders, Captain James Lawrence, were waiting at St. Salvador, to be joined by the Essex, an occurrence happened, which the characteristic cunning of Americans turned greatly to their advantage. In the middle of November the British 20-gun ship Bonne-Citoyenne, of eighteen 32-pounder carronades and two long 9-pounders, Captain Pitt Barnaby Greene, having, while coming from Rio-de-la-plate, with half a million sterling on board, damaged herself greatly by running on shore, entered the port of St. Salvador, to land her cargo and be hove down.

When the ship was keel-out, the two American ships arrived in the port. The American Consul and the two American commanders now laid their heads together to contrive something which, without any personal risk to any one of the three, should contribute to the renown of their common country. What so likely as a challenge to Capt. Greene? It could not be accepted; and then the refusal would be as good as a victory to Captain Lawrence. Accordingly, a challenge for the Hornet to meet the Bonne-Citoyenne was offered by Captain Lawrence, through the American Consul, to the British consul, Mr. Frederick Landeman; Commodore Bainbridge pledging his honour to be out of the way, or not to interfere.

Without making the unpleasant avowal, that his government upon this occasion, had reduced the vessel he commanded from a king's cruiser to a merchant-ship, Captain Greene transmitted, through the consular channel, an animated reply, refusing a meeting "upon terms so manifestly advantageous as those proposed by Commodore Bainbridge." Indeed, it would appear as if the commodore had purposely inserted the words, "or not interfering," lest Captain Greene, contrary to his expectation, should accept the challenge. For, had the two ships met by agreement, and engaged, the Constitution looked on without interfering, and the British ship been the conqueror, the pledge of honor, on the part of both American commanders, would have been fulfilled; and can any one for a moment imagine, that Commodore Bainbridge would have seen the Bonne-Citoyenne carry off a United States' ship of war, without attempting her rescue? It was more than

Before entering on the subject of the naval operations on the lakes, we shall proceed to give the American account of the havoc committed on British commerce, through the instrumentality of their cruisers, from the declaration of war to the end of the year 1812. It will be amusing, as the anxiety of the Americans to magnify every little coasting vessel, captured among the West India islands, into a sloop of war or armed vessel, will be thus shown.

According to the American account, from American list of captures made. the date of the declaration of war, 18th June, to the end of the year, three hundred and five prizes were taken by their privateers.

It appears that of this number, sixty-eight vessels mounted seven hundred and sixty-three guns, (nearly eleven guns each,) and that in specie alone, one million eight hundred and fifty thousand dollars was secured, in twenty-one vessels, independent of the value of the crafts and cargoes.

In looking over this long list, we find so many vessels of from four to eight hundred tons each, and described as laden with the most valuable cargoes, that we conceive we are very much under the mark in valuing the three hundred and five prizes, at ten thousand dollars each. This valuation, with the amount of specie and the value of the seven hundred and sixty-three guns, would thus give, even at our low estimate, a loss of over five millions of dollars. To those who may remember the facts as they occurred, or who are otherwise conversant with our mercantile marine, the absurdity of this statement speaks for itself. It may, however, be as well to explain, for the benefit of the uninitiated, that the richest of these prizes, those represented as carrying the largest number, and the heaviest guns, were West Indiamen, principally homeward bound, and that, with some few exceptions, this class of vessels could not carry on deck anything heavier than a four or six-pounder, and of guns even of this calibre, few could bear more than four, six, or eight. In the American account, the guns are nearly all put down as twelve or fourteen-pounders, some even as eighteen-pounders, which makes the exaggeration still more apparent. It was a common practice for these vessels to mount four or six guns, and to have a number of what were called "Quakers," that is wooden guns, and, no doubt, our Yankee brethren have, in their version, reckoned each one of these "Quakers" as a *bona fide* long twelve.

Not the least injury done was the depriving Great Britain of the services of so many sailors, for, according to this list, forty-five thousand seamen were captured during the first six months of the war.

A brief notice of a few of the most remarkable of the captures, as chronicled in the American papers, will be amusing :—

Louisa Ann, laden with molasses, captured by a boat from the Benjamin Franklin, privateer, with seven men, *under the guns* (and we presume, also under the fire,) *of a battery of twelve eighteen-pounders.*

Ship Grenada, seven hundred tons burthen, eleven guns and thirty men, with schooner Shaddock, also armed, (with a complement, it may be presumed, of at least twelve men,)

---

his head was worth. Where was the guarantee against re-capture, which always accompanies a serious proposal of this sort, when a stronger force, belonging to either party, is to preserve a temporary neutrality? The bait, therefore, did not take : the specie remained safe ; and the American officers were obliged to content themselves with all the benefit they could reap from making a boast of the circumstance. This they did ; and, to the present hour, the refusal of the Bonne-Citoyenne to meet the Hornet, stands recorded in the American naval archives, as a proof of the former's dread, although the " superior in force," of engaging the latter. The two ships, as has just been seen, were equal in guns, and not very unequal in crews ; the Hornet having 171 men and two boys, the Bonne-Citoyenne, including 21 supernumeraries, 141 men and nine boys. But this inferiority was in a great degree compensated, by the pains which Captain Greene had taken to teach his men the use of their guns. After the Constitution had sailed for Boston, the Hornet continued blockading the Bonne-Citoyenne and her dollars, until the arrival, on the 24th of January, of the British 74-gun ship Montagu, Captain Manley Hall Dixon, bearing the flag of Rear-Admiral Manley Dixon. The American sloop, on being chased, ran for the harbor ; but night coming on, the Hornet wore, and, by standing to the southward, dexterously evaded her pursuer. Escorted by the Montagu, the Bonne-Citoyenne, with her valuable cargo on board, put to sea on the 26th of January ; and on the 22nd of February, in latitude 5 ° 20' south, longitude 40 ° west, the rear-admiral left Captain Greene, to pursue his voyage alone. Sometime in the month of April, having stopped at Madeira by the way, the Bonne-Citoyenne arrived in safety at Portsmouth.

Could any scheme have been more cunningly devised for acquiring credit at a cheap rate ?—ED.

both captured at the same time, by the Young Eagle, of New York, *one* gun and forty-two men.

Ship Hassan, fourteen guns and twenty men, captured by the Tom Jones, three guns.

Ship Osborne, ten guns, long eighteen-pounders, twenty-six men, five hundred tons, captured by the Teazer, two guns, and *not* thirty men.

Brig Amelia, captured by the Mary Ann, one gun.

These are some of the more prominent exaggerations, but the list is filled with such, and, unfortunately for their credit, the cord has been too tightly drawn by these veracious chroniclers, and the arrow has, consequently, over-shot the mark.

In the case of the Hassan, for instance, who ever heard of a vessel carrying fourteen twelve-pounders intended to be used, and a complement of only twenty men! It would, however, be a waste of time to adduce further instances of the means resorted to, throughout the States, to blind the eyes of the public, and, under the smoke of the seven hundred and sixty-three guns, to conceal the real ruin that was fast approaching. A few individuals, like drawers of prizes in a lottery, were fortunate enough to realise large fortunes by a series of lucky captures at the very commencement of the war; but very soon these prizes were exhausted, as we find by the 1st of December the lamentation that "it has not been our good fortune, latterly, to record the capture of many prizes. This has not arisen from want of activity in our many privateers, but from the scarcity of the enemy's vessels. Several have cruised ten thousand miles without seeing an Englishman. Whether the British Government is unable to furnish the needful convoys, or whether the commercial mind of the nation is panic-struck by the hardy exploits of our tars, and will not venture forth, time will determine."

We are not at all astonished at the commercial panic which at that time pervaded the nation—the thought, that half a dozen frigates, and as many brigs and sloops of war aided by privateers, (some only open boats, and others mounting only one gun,) had in four months effected what the united navies of France and Spain had failed to do, must have been indeed a humiliating one to the Briton, and there is

not much cause for wonder that the commercial energies of Great Britain were paralyzed. Five millions of dollars abstracted in five months. We only wonder that a national bankruptcy did not ensue.

Before closing this history we trust we shall be able to make it apparent, on which nation the greater injury was wrought, and that, during the years 1813 and '14, while English vessels were in every sea, and while her flag waved triumphantly everywhere, the American Marine, whether naval or commercial, was as effectually swept from the ocean, as if the besom of destruction had passed over it.

Before closing the chapter a few short extracts from Mr. Madison's speech will throw some additional light on the motives which prompted the American Government to prefer a war with England to one with France, even supposing that equal causes of complaint had existed against both those nations. We give one very significant paragraph towards the end of the message :

American President's Message. Nov. 4.

"The receipts into the Treasury, during the year ending on the 30th Sept. last, have exceeded sixteen millions and a half of dollars, which have been sufficient to defray all the demands on the Treasury to that day, including a necessary reimbursement of near three millions of the principal of the public debt. In these receipts are included a loan of *near eight million eight hundred and fifty thousand dollars* received on account of the loans authorized by the acts of the last session. The whole sum actually obtained on *loan amounting to eleven milloins of dollars*, the residue of which being receivable subsequent to the 20th Sept., will, together with the current revenue, enable us to defray all the expenses of this year."

Here we have, at once, a very obvious reason for the choice made by the American Government. We do not imagine that it was ever seriously contemplated that any prizes, taken could be an equivalent to the people, generally, for the certain drain on their resources which a war must inevitably entail, a list however of three hundred and odd prizes, with a certain amount of national glory acquired, backed, too, by nearly two millions of dollars in specie looked well on paper, and would not only furnish the Government with a satisfactory answer to any outcry that might arise relative to increase of taxation, but would also render Mr. Madison's re-election to the Presidential chair pretty certain.

It is amusing to note how lightly Mr. Madison touches on the military events that had taken place in the west. The single sentence : "The expedition, nevertheless, terminated unfortunately," is deemed sufficient, and by way of accounting, we suppose, for the unfortunate failure, a long paragraph is introduced, relative to the British availing themselves of the aid of their Indian allies. We cannot forbear quoting the passage, as it will shew to what the chief magistrate of a powerful nation can ' stoop to serve a selfish end :—" A distinguished feature in the operations which preceded and followed this adverse event, is the use made by the enemy of the merciless savages under their influence. Whilst the benevolent feeling of the United States invariably recommended peace, and promoted civilization amongst that wretched portion of the human race, and was *making exertions to dissuade them from taking either side* in the war, the enemy has not scrupled to call to his aid their ruthless ferocity, armed with the instruments of carnage and torture, which are known to spare neither age nor sex. In this outrage against the laws of honorable war, and against the feelings sacred to humanity, the British commanders cannot resort to the plea of retaliation, for it is committed in the face of our example. They cannot mitigate it, by calling it a self-defence against men in arms, for it embraces the most shocking butcheries of defenceless families : nor can it be pretended that they are not answerable for the atrocities perpetrated, since the savages are employed with the knowledge, and even with menaces, that their fury could not be controlled. Such is the spectacle which the deputed authorities of a nation, boasting its religion and morality, have not been restrained from presenting to an enlightened age."

This reads well, and no doubt impressed the American mind with a very sufficient and wholesome indignation against a people who, if they did not themselves perpetrate atrocities, could at least countenance and encourage them in their allies. But what are the facts of the case :—That it was notorious that the Americans exhausted every possible means to induce

the Indians to act as their allies, and that it was only on finding, that the memories of injuries perpetrated and wrongs inflicted by the Americans, were too fresh in the recollection of the Indians and rankled too deeply for the wound to be easily forgotton, that the Americans began to inveigh against the British, for their deviation from the rules of "civilized warfare."

Besides, we fearlessly challenge Americans to adduce the flagrant instances " of butcheries against defenceless families," mentioned in the presidential address.

The speech furnishes, also, another very convincing proof, that, in spite of all efforts, the war had not, even then, become as popular as generally represented by the American press :—

"Among the incidents to the measures of the war, I am constrained to advert to the refusals of the governors of Massachusetts and Connecticut, to furnish the required detachments of militia towards the defence of the *maritime frontier*. The refusal was founded on a novel and unfortunate exposition of the provision of the constitution relating to the militia.

"It is obvious, that if the authority of the United States to call into service and command the militia for the public defence, can be thus frustrated, even in a case of declared war, and, of course, under apprehensions of invasion preceding war, they are not *one nation* for the purpose most of all requiring it, and that the public safety may have no other resources than those large and permanent military establishments which are forbidden by the principles of our free government, and against the necessity of which the militia were meant to be a constitutional bulwark."

It is apparent from the tenor of this, that fears were entertained, even after the publication of the list of three hundred and five prizes, nearly eight hundred guns, and a large amount of specie, with any quantity of national glory added, that the Northerners might be found too ready to weigh the real value of these advantages against the certain disbursements of dollars and cents.

In short, there were fears that the Northerners could not be easily blinded as to the certain ruin which awaited them commercially.

CHAPTER VI.

AFTER having regulated, as far as circumstances would admit, all matters, civil* and military, in the west, General Brock hastened his

General Brock returns to York.

return to the Niagara frontier, leaving all the force he could spare at Detroit, under General Proctor, and on his way thither, while on his voyage across Lake Erie, in the schooner Chippewa, he received the first intelligence of the armistice, which Sir George Prevost and General Dearborn, the American commander, had concluded. This intelligence occasioned the deepest regret to General Brock, as his foresight enabled him at once to perceive that the plans, which he had been maturing for an attack on Sackett's Harbor, must now necessarily be abandoned. His mortification must have been excessive at finding that the fruits of his successes in the west, which he was now prepared to gather, would be thus, in all probability, lost.

Without joining in the outcry raised against Sir George Prevost, this armistice deserves serious consideration, as its operations tended

---

NOTE.—Such was General Brock's anxiety to return to the Niagara frontier, that, though unwillingly, he was obliged to leave some affairs of importance unsettled, as the following shows :—

From Lieut. Col. Nichol, Quartermaster-General of Militia, to Major-General Brock.

* I have just been informed by Colonel Proctor that he intends sending an express to-morrow to Fort George, which gives me an opportunity to forward a few printed copies of your proclamation, and to inform you that in order to carry it into effect, it has been found absolutely necessary to organize the civil government. Under existing circumstances, I have advised Colonel Proctor to assume the administration until your pleasure is known, to which he has agreed, and the necessary arrangements consequent thereto have been adopted and promulgated. In Judge Woodward, who has been appointed secretary *pro tem*, he will find an able coadjutor ; and as your object undoubtedly was to tranquillize the public mind, and to give the inhabitants a proof of the moderation and benevolence of His Majesty's Government, as well as to ensure the due administration of the laws, I do not think a more judicious choice could have been made. In all the discus-

sions which took place on this subject, Colonel Proctor did me the honour to consult me ; and I have no hesitation in saying, that I urged him to the step he has taken, of which I hope you will, as it is only temporary, approve. It has not been in my power as yet to send a statement of all that we have captured, as the property is so scattered, but I hope to finish this week. We got upwards of £1,200 in money, and have sent down a hundred packs worth, I suppose, £1,500 more. I have reason to think the captured property will not be much under £40,000.

We have still 350 prisoners to ship off, but I hope to get rid of them in a few days. Public confidence seems to be partially restored ; business is again going on, and I hope that the country will become perfectly quiet.

It is impossible for me to say when I shall get done here. I hope, however, it will not be long. I regret that we are not able to send you complete returns of everything ; but the captured property is in so many different places, and so scattered, that it cannot be done.

materially to strengthen and favor the future movements of the enemy, whilst the opportunity of making a decisive attack on the American positions was thrown away. General Brock was most desirous, ere the enemy should recover from the panic into which General Hull's catastrophe had thrown them, to profit, to the utmost, by vigorous and active movements; but he now found himself compelled to remain inactive, whilst he felt that prompt measures alone could ensure ultimate success.

The transport of the American stores,* ordnance and provisions, of each of which they were much in want, not being prohibited by that armistice, was accordingly protected and facilitated by it on Lake Ontario, and along the Niagara frontier, beyond their most sanguine expectations.

"Most fortunately† Hull's business was settled by capitulation before the armistice was known to him or to General Brock, for had it reached him in time, he, of course, would gladly have accepted it, to *gain delay for the arrival of reinforcements, and a supply of provisions*, from which would have resulted the salvation of his army, the prejudicial consequences whereof are incalculable; for had a knowledge of it reached the Indian nations at that time, such a disgust and distrust must thereby have been excited, as could never have been removed; and the first effects of which would, probably, have appeared in the immediate dispersion of the Indians, whose powerful and indispensable aid, at that early period of the contest, would have been totally lost to us. To the facts above stated I must add the extraordinary circumstance, that a staff-officer was sent express from Montreal to Upper Canada, to prevent General Brock from proceeding to the Western District, but which most happily was prevented from taking effect, by the extraordinary rapidity of the movements of that zealous and gallant officer, who had proceeded thither before the officer so sent could reach him."

We are as little desirous of entering into a defence of Sir George Prevost, as of making a case against him, but the above strikes us as scarcely fair, either to General Brock or to Sir George Prevost. In the first place, Veritas makes use of the expression "to give delay for the arrival of reinforcements, and a supply of provisions," now we have already shewn in Col. Cass's letter to the Secretary at War, that General Hull's catastrophe was to be ascribed neither to the want of one nor the other,—"that we were far superior to the enemy, that upon any ordinary principle of calculation we would have defeated them, the wounded and indignant feelings of every man there will testify;" again, "the state of our provisons has not generally been understood. On the day of surrender we had fifteen days provisions of every kind on hand. Of meat there was plenty in the country, and arrangements had been made for purchasing and grinding the flour. It was calculated we could readily procure three months provisions, independent of one hundred and fifty barrels of flour, and one thousand three hurdred head of cattle which had been forwarded from the State of Ohio, and which remained at the river Raisin under Captain Brush, within reach of the army." Now, these passages prove distinctly that General Brock's success was in no way attributable to the destitute state of his opponents, but was solely to be ascribed to his own energy and tactics. We do not think that Veritas meant in any degree to lessen the credit due to General Brock, on the contrary, his letters have all a direct tendency the other way; but we do think that, in his anxiety to establish a strong case against Sir George Prevost, he has, inadvertently, strengthened the hands of General Hull's apologists. With respect to Sir George Prevost the case is still more unfair, he says, "In short, military foresight, anticipation, or counteraction of possible or probable movements or designs of the enemy, formed no part of Sir George's system of operations." Now, how was it possible for Sir George, hampered as he was by instructions from the English ministry, to run counter to the express orders he had received. What does Sir George say in his letter of August 30th to General Brock? "The king's government having most unequivocally expressed to me their desire to preserve peace with the United States, that they might, uninterrupted, pursue, with the whole disposable force of the country, the vast interests committed in Europe, I have endeavoured to be instrumental in the accomplishment of their

* Vide the letters of Veritas.
† Ibid.

views; but I consider it most fortunate that I have been enabled to do so without interfering with your operations on the Detroit. I am in hourly expectation of receiving from Gen. Dearborn intelligence respecting the reception of the proposed suspension of hostilities, in consequence of the revocation of the orders in Council, which are the plea for war on the part of the American Cabinet." * * * "I consider the arrangement entered into by General Dearborn, with Colonel Baynes, requiring the confirmation of the President, to establish its sacredness."

In his anxiety to criminate Sir George, Veritas is again unfair, for speaking of him, (page 20) he writes, "He was mainly a passive instrument at that time; neither did he give any orders or impulse." * * * * "In the whole of these events, all that he had to do was to reap the fruits of what others had done, and it would be supposed that all was owing to Sir George." When we come to consider the testimony of General Brook's biographer, his own nephew, we shall discover that whatever Sir George Prevost's immediate friends may have done, to Sir George himself, at all events, cannot be ascribed the desire of shining in borrowed plumage. Mr. F. Brock Tupper's evidence will prove this—"as we have already commented on Sir George Prevost's management of the war, and shall have occasionally to do so again, WE GLADLY GIVE HIM CREDIT FOR THE VERY HANDSOME manner in which he spoke of Major General Brock, in his despatch to Lord Bathurst, one of His Majesty's principal Secretaries of State, announcing the surrender of Detroit, and dated Montreal, 26th August, 1812."

The extracts from the despatch, however, will prove this still more effectually :—

"It was under these circumstances, at this critical period, and when the enemy were beginning to consult their security by entrenching themselves, that General Brock entered Amherstburg with a reinforcement, which he was fortunately enabled to do on the 13th instant, without the smallest molestation, in consequence of our decided naval superiority on the lakes. To his active and intelligent mind, the advantages which his enemys's situation afforded him over them, even with his very inferior force, were immediately apparent; and that he has not failed most effectually to

avail himself of those favorable circumstances, your lordship will, I trust, be satisfied, from the letter which I have the honor of transmitting.

"Having thus brought to your lordship's view the different circumstanses which have led to the successful termination of the campaign in the western frontier of Upper Canada, I cannot withhold from Major General Brock the tribute of applause so justly due to him for his distinguished conduct on this occasion; or omit to recommend him, through your lordship, to the favorable consideration of his Royal Highness the Prince Regent, for the great ability and judgment with which he planned, and the promptitude, energy, and fortitude with which he has effected, the preservation of Upper Canada, with the sacrifice of so little British blood in accomplishing so important a service."

This is scarcely the language which Sir George would have made use of had he been really desirous "to reap the fruits of what others had sown;" that it had not that effect, at all events, is pretty plain from Lord Bathurst's reply :—"I have had the honor of receiving your despatch, dated the 26th August, together with its enclosures from Major General Brock, and I lost no time in laying intelligence so important and satisfactory before his Royal Highness the Prince Regent.

"I am commanded by his Royal Highness to take the earliest opportunity of conveying his approbation of the ABLE, JUDICIOUS, and DECISIVE conduct of Major General Brock, of the zeal and spirit manifested by Col. Proctor and the other officers, as well as of the intrepidity of the troops under the command of Major General Brock.

"By the united exertions of this little army, the enterprise of the Americans has been defeated; the territories of his Majesty in Upper Canada have been secured; and on the enemy's fort of Detroit, so important to that security, the British standard has been happily placed.

"You will inform Major General Brock that his Royal Highness—taking into consideration all the difficulties by which he was surrounded, from the time of the invasion of the province by the American army, under the command of General Hull, and the singular judgment, skill, firmness, and courage with which he was enabled to surmount them so effectually—has been pleased to appoint him an extra Knight of the Most Honorable Order of the Bath."

This prompt action taken by the British Ministry in the recognition of what was due by a grateful country, to one who had so well and efficiently served her, should exonerate Sir George Prevost from the imputation of attempting to lessen General Brock's claims to distinction,—and with respect to "the vacillating measures pursued by him on all occasions," it should be borne in mind that it is a most hazardous thing for a commanding officer to run counter to instructions where the course of conduct to be pursued was so expressly defined. All that can be hoped for, at best, in case of success, is "not to be blamed," while, in the event of failure, sure and certain ruin must be the inevitable result.

It is more than probable that when we come to the consideration of the consequences of the policy pursued by Sir George Prevost, we shall find ample grounds for regret that a different course had not been adopted, but there is a wide difference between seeing that a measure has turned out a wrong one, and discovering the real parties to whom the blame should properly attach. The letters of Veritas should, therefore, be cautiously received, as, although, they are most valuable from the fund of information they contain; they are, nevertheless, tinctured with a spice of party feeling from which we are, at this latter time, perhaps more free.

The following note (see page 25) in reference to the Editor of the Quebec Gazette, will show this pretty clearly :—"This gentleman (the Editor of the Quebec Gazette) is now calling out for a truce or armistice, which would doubtless be very convenient for the purpose of his party, in order that the poison infused by his other false representations, might take full effect, by withholding the antidote of truth; but that cannot be, after such continued deceptions, and more especially after the most impudent and two-per-cent doctrine, promulgated by that editor, wherein he makes the approval of Sir George's measures, the criterion of loyalty; consequently, by that rule, those who stirred themselves most actively in the support of the Government during the war, and at its com-

mencement marched to suppress an insurrection striking at the vitals of our defence, are to be held as disloyal; and the insurgents with their abetters, at that time, good men and true—for true it is, that most of the former are non-addressees, whilst all the latter are addressees."

Amongst the various congratulatory letters *Complimentary and congratulatory letters received by General Brock. Col. Baynes' opinion of General Hull.* addressed to General Brock, on this occasion, we could select many that would tend to show how unfair it would be to assume that any attempt had been made by Sir George Prevost to profit by the deeds of another, or to deprive General Brock of any part of his fame. One, however, will suffice, from the Chief Justice of Lower Canada, where Sir George Prevost's popularity was deservedly very great, and where his influence was doubtless most felt.* From the whole tenor of these letters it is easy to perceive that credit was given where due, and that General Brock was not deprived of the glory he had so deservedly won.

From a letter of Col. Baynes to General Brock, it is apparent that General Hull inspired a very different sort of feeling amongst his captors. Col. Baynes says, " Sir George has consented to allow General Hull to return upon his parole, he is loud in his complaints against the Government at Washington, and the General thinks that his voice, in the general cry, may be attended with beneficial effects, and has allowed him to return and enter the lists. General Hull appears to possess less feeling and sense of shame than any man in his situation could be supposed to do. He seems to be perfectly satisfied with himself, is lavish of censure upon his Government, but appears to think that the most scrupulous cannot attach the slightest blame to his own immediate conduct at Detroit. The grounds upon which he rests his defence are not, I fancy, well founded, for he told us that he had not, at

---

*In your present situation, I am perfectly sensible of your occupations, and know that your time is precious. Yet I take the liberty to intrude upon you with my congratulations upon the brilliant success which has attended the measures which you have pursued with so much judgment in Upper Canada, and the thanks of an individual who feels the benefits which he, in common with every other subject of his majesty in British America, derives from your exertions.

Detroit, gunpowder for the service of one day. Sir George has since shewn him the return of the large supply found in the fort; it did not create a blush, but he made no reply. He professes great surprise and admiration at the zeal and military preparation that he has every where witnessed; that it was entirely unlooked for, and that he has no doubt that his friend, General Dearborn, will share his fate, if he has the imprudence to follow his example, Hull seems cunning and unprincipled: how much reliance is to be placed on his professions, time will shew."

Before entering on the consideration of the General situation of armistice, it will be expe- affairs. the effects of the armistice upon them. dient to cast a rapid glance at the general position of affairs in both Provinces, at that time, and to examine how far the enemy's plans were either promoted or impeded thereby.

On the confines of Lower Canada, large bodies of American troops were stationed, and each day was adding to their numbers, a descent upon Montreal by St. John's and Odelltown being evidently the object in contemplation. At Niagara, and along the whole of that frontier, General Van Ranselaer was indefatigable in his exertions and had already assembled so formidable a force as to afford serious grounds for apprehension; on the part of Gen. Brock, that an irruption, at no distant date, might be expected in that quarter. Furtherwestward General Harrison was actively employed in raising troops, and concentrating them about the river Raisin, near Detroit, with the intention of recapturing that position. According to some American accounts the hopes of this officer were sanguine. General Armstrong, after noticing several desultory attacks, by the Kentucky and Ohio militia, against some Indian settlements, observes " such was the state of things on the western frontier, when the Government, having decided the rival pretensions of Generals Winchester and Harrison, vested in the latter the command of the army and district : with orders sufficiently definite, as to the objects to be pursued, but entirely discretionary as to the time and mode of pursuing them." Availing himself of the latitude given by this new and increased authority, the General hastened to remodel his plan of campaigns and promptly rejecting his

first proposal of recapturing Detroit by a *coup de main*,* he planned a march by three separate and distinct routes across the swampy and uninhabited region in his front to the rapids of the Miami—whence, after accumulating one million of rations for the troops, and forage for two thousand horses and oxen, he proposed marching rapidly on Brownstown, crossing the river Detroit, and before the commencement of winter, taking Malden and recapturing the Michigan territory.

Such was the position of affairs along the whole frontier of both the Canadas; and we will now proceed to show what were the effects of (according to Veritas) the deadly armistice entered into by Sir George Prevost.

The American commander-in-chief, General Dearborn, a short time The Armistice, and the subsequent policy after the commencement pursued. of hostilities, fixed his quarters at Greenbush, near Albany, where he had formed a military dépôt, "with a view," says Christie, "of collecting an army to overawe Lower Canada, and, by preventing succours being sent to the upper province, afford General Hull every facility for the accomplishment of his designs in that quarter." About the commencement of August he received despatches from Sir George Prevost, by the Adjutant-General, Colonel Baynes, bearing a flag of truce notifying the repeal of the orders in Council, information whereof

* While acting in a subordinate capacity to Winchester, the General had no doubt of being able, with a few mounted men, to re-take Detroit by a *coup de main*, and was careful to inform the Government of his plans and their practicability. When, however, by means of this and other representations, having the same object, he became commanding officer of the army and district, his views suddenly changed; the rapid and certain process of a *coup de main* was abandoned as hopeless, and one more systematic and imposing substituted for it, requiring as a preliminary to any direct movement on Malden or Detroit, an accumulation of twelve months' provisions and forage, with carts, waggons, &c., to transport them from the place of deposit to the scene of action, or, in other words, the entire purchase of all surplus corn, flour or fodder, oxen, horses, carts, waggons, &c., to be found within the state of Ohio; and this at a time (22nd of October,) when he says of the roads, " to get supplies forward through a swampy wilderness of more than two hundred miles, in waggons, or on pack-horses, which are also to carry their own fodder, is absolutely impossible."—*McAffee's War, page* 167.

had been transmitted to his Excellency from Halifax, by Mr. Foster, the late Minister in America. A proposition accompanying these as to the propriety of suspending hostilities, until the pleasure of the President of the United States should be known, was submitted to the American General, in the hope that this conciliatory measure, removing the alleged principal ground of difference between the two nations, would be met by a corresponding disposition on the part of the American Government. General Dearborn readily consented to an armistice (except as to General Hull, who, he said, acted under the immediate commands of the secretary-at-war), and forwarded the despatches to his Government, which, misconstruing this friendly proffer into a sense of weakness and of danger on the part of the British commander, and probably flushed with the prospect of subjugating Upper Canada, refused to ratify the armistice.

We have already stated that the transport of American stores was much furthered by the operations of the armistice; but it should be remembered that it was equally in the power of the British to avail themselves of the time thus afforded them for preparation. Still it was clearly Sir George Prevost's duty to carry out by every means in his power the instructions he had received from the British Government, and we do not see what other course he could have adopted.

He availed himself of the very first opportunity that offered to re-establish amicable relations between the two countries. In short, he advised the American Government that they had now no cause to allege for a continuance of hostilities, inasmuch as all the grievances of which they complained had been removed. He, therefore, in furtherance of his instructions, proposed a temporary cessation of hostilities, in hopes of averting the miseries of a war between two kindred nations, and of affording time for the establishment of a permanent peace. As far as this proposal is in question, no other course was open to Sir George; he had not the power of choice. When, too, we consider the matter still further, it should be remembered that the armistice only lasted one month, although in force for a longer period on the western frontier, and on the 31st August Sir George despatched his instructions to the west, advising Gen. Brock

of the disallowance of the temporary truce. Besides if the Americans had availed themselves of it for one purpose, so also had the British for another. "A cordon was formed along the frontiers of Lower Canada, from Yamaska to St. Régis, where the line of separation between the United States and Lower Canada touches the St. Lawrence, consisting of Canadian voltigeurs and part of the embodied militia. A light brigade of the elite of the forces regular and militia, was formed at Blairfindie, under the command of Lieut.-Col. Young, of the 8th regiment, consisting of the flank companies of the 8th, 100th, and 103d regiments, with the Canadian Fencibles, the flank companies of the first battalion of embodied militia, and a small brigade of the royal artillery, with six field pieces.

"The road to the United States, from the camp at Blairfindie (or L'Acadie) through Burtonville and Odelltown, was cut up and rendered impracticable by abbatis, and every precaution taken to prevent a sudden irruption from that quarter. The voltigeurs, with extraordinary perseverance, effected this fatiguing duty in the course of a very short time, under the superintendence of their commanding officer, Major de Salaberry."

The enumeration of these various operations is a fair proof that, as the armistice benefitted the Americans, so did it, in like manner, operate beneficially on British interests. We will, however, to enable the reader to arrive at a just conclusion, make a few extracts from the narrative of S. Van Ranselaer, who acted as aide-de-camp to his relative, General Van Ranselaer, at that time commanding the troops on the Niagara frontier:—

"In this state of things, the armistice which had been concluded between General Dearborn and the Governor General of Canada, was announced to General Van Ranselaer, and it became necessary to settle with the commander of the British forces opposite to us, terms of an arrangement for the government of the armies on the Niagara, during the continuance of the armistice. The performance of this duty was assigned to me, and a suggestion having been made by me to that effect, I had the authority of General Van Ranselaer to attempt such an arrangement, as, besides securing the objects contemplated by General Dearborn, might enable us, pending the armistice, to use the waters of the Ontario, as a common and undisturbed highway for the purposes 'of transporation. My interview with General Sheaffe, in this mission, was one full of interest, as was anticipated. The terms proposed by me were met not only by objections, but at first by an unequivocal refusal to accede to them. The following clause, proposed and insisted on, on the part of the British General, will serve to show how wide of each other were our respective views and interests, 'It is moreover to be distinctly understood, that there is not anything in the foregoing articles, to be construed into granting facilities for the forwarding of troops, stores, &c. which did not exist before the declaration of the armistice, further than they are to pass unmolested as therein provided, in the mode and by the waters assigned to them prior to the cessation of hostilities.' The result of a protracted discussion, however, was an agreement which confined the restrictions to the movement of troops, stores, &c. to the country above Fort Erie, and left such movements elsewhere entirely unshackled and free.

" The importance of this arrangement has never been sufficiently appreciated. The immediate and pressing necessity for it on our part, was, that without it, the ordnance and supplies intended for the army, having been collected at Oswego, were not likely ever to reach us, the roads were impassable, especially for heavy cannon, and the highway of the lake was beset by a triumphant enemy. As soon as the negotiation was successfully completed, an express was dispatched to Col. Fenwick at Oswego, to move on with his supplies with all possible expedition. But General Van Ranselaer was enabled to use this advantage for another purpose of even greater importance to the service.—No sooner was the way open, than an express was sent to Ogdensburgh with an order for the removal of nine vessels from that place to Sackett's Harbor. To this movement was Commodore Chauncey indebted for the ascendancy which he, for a time, was enabled to maintain on the lake, and without which the subsequent descent on Little York could not have been attempted."

It is now for the reader to weigh well the position of Sir George Prevost. He had received certain instructions from home which he was bound to obey : a particular line of conduct presented itself which would confer certain advantages on the enemy, but which he saw that he could also turn to his own profit: forbearance towards America was the policy which he had been ordered to adopt : should he then be blamed because, in pursuance of his instructions, and in hopes of a speedy termination of the differences with America, he endeavored, by temporising, to avoid measures tending to widen the breach and give cause to the American people to embark heartily in the quarrel of their government.

In addition to the above reasons, it should also be borne in mind, that Sir George was conscious of his inferior strength, and was pretty well aware that at this juncture there was but little hope that such reinforcements could be expected, from any quarter, as would enable him to adopt any other than a defensive system. Whatever errors of judgment we may, at a later period of our narrative, find cause to attribute to Sir George Prevost, so far we can scarcely blame him for avoiding the risk of weakening his already small force in hazardous enterprises which, in case of failure, must end in certain ruin to the provinces committed to his charge.

A few extracts from the letters of Veritas will serve to prove how anxious Sir George's enemies were to find something to condemn in his measures. We have already, in former chapters, shewn how unexpected by Great Britain was a declaration of war on the part of the United States. We have shewn the forbearance and conciliatory attitude of the English ministry ;—we have brought before our readers proofs that the war was not popular with the majority of the inhabitants of the United States, certainly not with the reflecting part of the community ; in short, we have proved distinctly that the war was unexpected, and that, even at the eleventh hour, there were sound reasons for calculating that an amicable arrangement would be entered into. According to Veritas, soon after Sir George's arrival in Canada, "he made a rapid tour through the upper part of this province ; no doubt for the purpose of viewing it with a military eye, and thereby personally judging of the best positions for defence, in case of need. This was highly proper, but like many other excursions, no visible result followed.

"*The winter of* 1811 passed on without any preparations contemplative of war, (the before-mentioned militia act excepted,) notwithstanding the fulminations in Congress against us, during all that winter : the open avowel of their designs upon Canada, and the actual spreading of the cloth for Mr. Peter B. Porter's war feast, as announced in the committee of Congress, whereof he was the organ.

"The two internal keys of the province, viz.—Isle-aux-Noix and Coteau du Lac, were either despised or overlooked in that tour, notwithstanding the importance decidedly given to the former, especially by the French engineers, and by General Haldimand, who was an able judge of positions, and who had expended a large sum of money in fortifying it, in the former American war.

" The cause of the neglect I know not with certainty, but the fact is, that Isle-aux-Noix was not occupied until some time after the war, and might have been seized by the enemy, had he then possessed sufficient military capacity to estimate its value.   Coteau du Lac was not occupied until the summer of 1813.

"Not a gun-boat or vessel was built in the river Richelieu, at, or above St. John's, or even thought of, until the Almighty threw into the power of the brave 100th Regiment and a few artillery, in garrison at Isle-aux-Noix, two of the enemy's armed vessels, which were captured in a most gallant style, by the aid of a gun-boat or two, built, by order of Sir James Craig, at Quebec, which had been conveyed overland to St. John's; and which captures formed the basis of a flotilla for Lake Champlain, and first suggested the idea of endeavoring to command it.

" It has been matter of surprise to many, why a number of flat-boats, capable of carrying heavy guns, were never built at Lachine, to be stationed below the Cascades, at Isle Perrault, or wherever else on Lake St. Louis might have been considered most advisable and convenient, for a rapid movement to attack the enemy if they descended the St. Lawrence, immediately after passing the rapids of the Cedars, before they could collect together and form ; it being certain that their boats must necessarily sault or pass the rapids unconnected, and by comparison as it were, in

Indian-file, or in sections of a very small front ; consequently, their discomfiture would have been easy, had they been met immediately after by a respectable number of our armed boats, ready and fresh for the attack."

What is here complained of is, first, that no results followed Sir George's tour through the provinces on first assuming the government. We are rather at a loss to know what results were looked for, or could have been expected, to us it appears that all Sir George wanted was to make himself personally master of the different points most exposed to attack, and capable of being easily made defensible ; this he did by personal inspection, and having gained the information he required, he was prepared in case of necessity to make use of it.   We do not see that Sir George would have been warranted, in a young and poor colony, to waste its resources on works that it was very uncertain would be required.

The next complaint is, that the winter of 1811 was suffered to pass over without any preparation contemplative of war.   The passage, we presume, that is here alluded to in Mr. Porter's speech, and which we give at length below,* is as follows :—" In short, it

Mr. Porter said that the house were probably expecting from the committee on foreign relations some explanation of their views in reporting the resolutions now under consideration, in addition to the general exposition of them contained in the report itself.   The committee themselves felt that such explanations were due, inasmuch as they had only reported in part, and had intimated their intention to follow up those resolutions, should they be adopted, by the recommendation of ulterior measures.

The committee, Mr. P. said, after examining the various documents accompanying the president's message were satisfied, as he presumed every member of the house was, that all hopes of accomodation must be abandoned.   When they looked at the correspondence between the two governments ; when they observed the miserable shifts and evasions (for they were entitled to no better appelation) to which Great Britain resorted to excuse the violations of our maritime rights, it was impossible not to perceive that her conduct towards us was not regulated even by her own sense of justice, but solely by a regard to the probable extent of our forbearance.   The last six years have been marked by a series of progressive encroachments on our rights ; and the principles by which she publicly upheld her aggressions, were as mutable as her conduct.   We had seen her one year advancing doctrines which the year before she had reprobated.   We had seen her one day capturing our vessels under pretexts, which on the preceding day she would have been ashamed

was the determination of the committee to recommend open and decided war, a war as vigorous and effective as the resources of the country, and the relative situation of ourselves and our enemy would enable us to prosecute."

This we admit was pretty strong language, and was used on the 6th of December, 1811. On the 8th of December, however, we find Mr. Cheeves, from the committee appointed in that part of the President's message which relates to the naval force of the United States, and to the defence of the maritime frontier, making the following report, in part:—

"The committee to whom was referred so much of the President's message of the 5th of November, 1811, as relates to the defence of our maritime frontier, report, in part, that two communications from the Secretary at War,

or afraid to avow. Indeed, said Mr. P., she seems to have been constantly and carefully feeling our pulse, to ascertain what portions we would bear; and if we go on submitting to one indignity after another, it will not be long before we shall see British subjects, not only taking our property in our harbours, but trampling on our persons in the streets of our cities.

Having become convinced that all hopes, from further negociation were idle, the committee, Mr. P. said, were led to the consideration of another question which was—whether the maritime rights which Great Britain is violating were such as we ought to support at the hazard and expense of a war? And he believed he was correct in stating that the committee was unanimously of the opinion they were. The committee thought that the orders in council so far as they go to interrupt our *direct trade*, that is, the carrying the productions of this country to a market in the ports of friendly nations, and returning with the proceeds of them—ought to be resisted by war. How far we ought to go in support of what is commonly called the *carrying trade*, although the question was agitated in the committee, no definitive opinion was expressed. —It was not deemed necessary, at this time, to express such an opinion, inasmuch as the injury we sustain by the inhibition of this trade is merged in the greater one to our direct trade.

The orders in council, Mr. P. said, of which there seemed now to be no prospect of a speedy repeal, certainly none during the continuance of the present war, authorising the capture of our vessels bound to and from ports where British commerce is not favourably received; and as that nation is at war with most of the civilized world, the effect was (as he understood) from those who had much better information on the subject than he could pretend to, to cut up at once, about three fourths of our best and most profitable commerce. It was impossible that the mercantile or agricultural interests of the United States, which on the question of a right to the *direct trade* could never be separated, could submit to such impositions. It was his opinion that going upon the ground of a mere pecuniary calculation, a calculation of profit and loss, it would be for our interest to go to war to remove the orders in council, rather than to submit to them, even during the term of their probable continuance.

But there was another point of view in which the subject presented itself to the committee, and that was as regarded the character of the country. We were a young nation, and he hoped we cherished a little pride and spirit, as well as a great deal of justice and moderation. Our situation was not unlike that of a young man just entering into life, and who, if he tamely submitted to cool, deliberate, intentional indignity, might safely calculate to be kicked and cuffed for the whole remainder of his life; or, if he should afterwards undertake to retrieve his character, must do it at ten times the expense which it would have cost him at first to support it. We should clearly understand and define those rights which as a nation we ought to support, and we should support them at every hazard. If there be any such thing as rights between nations, surely the people of the *United States*, occupying the half of a continent, have a right to navigate the seas, without being molested by the inhabitants of the little island of Great Britain.

It was under these views of the subject that the committee did not hesitate to give it as their opinion, that we ought to go to war in opposition to the orders in council. But as to the extent of the war and the time when it should be commenced, there would be of course some diversity of sentiment, in the house, as there was at first in the committee.

That we can contend with Great Britain openly and even-handed on the element where she injures us, it would be folly to pretend. Were it even in our power to build a navy which should be able to cope with hers, no man who has any regard for the happiness of the people of this country, would venture to advise such a measure. All the fame and glory which the British navy has acquired at sea, have been dearly paid for in the sufferings and misery of that ill-fated people at home—sufferings occasioned in a great measure by the expense of that stupendous establishment. But without such a navy, the United States could make a serious impression upon Great Britain, even at sea. We could have, within six months after a declaration of war, hundreds of *privateers* in every part of the ocean. We could harrass, if not destroy, the vast and profitable commerce which she is constantly carrying on to every part of this continent. We could destroy her fisheries to the north; we could depredate upon her commerce to the West India islands which is passing by our doors; we could annoy her trade along the coast of South America; we could even carry the war to her own shores in Europe. But, Mr. P. said, there was another place where we could attack her, and where she would feel our power still more sensibly. We could deprive her of her extensive provinces lying along our borders to the north. These provinces were not only immensely valuable in themselves, but almost indispensable to the existence of Great Britain, cut off as she now is in a great measure from the north of Europe. He had been credibly informed that the exports from

—which accompany this report,—which were made in reply to queries propounded by the committee, contain the best information on the subject which they have been able to collect.

"That one of them contains an enumeration of the permanent fortifications which have been completed or commenced, with remarks on the troops necessary to garrison them, That for the completion of works already commenced, *no further appropriation is requisite.*

But that some additional works are deemed necessary, the precise extent of which *cannot at present be determined.*"

It is apparent from the tenor of this report, that with a great portion of the American people, the prospects of a war were by no means certain. We would also remind the reader of various extracts, we made in the introductory part of this narrative, of a decidedly pacific tone, (Mr. Sheffey's of Virginia,

---

Quebec alone amounted during the last year, to near six millions of dollars, and most of these too in articles of the first necessity—in ship timber and in provisions for the support of her fleets and armies. By carrying on such a war as he had described, at the public expense, on land, and by individual enterprise at sea, we should be able in a short time to remunerate ourselves tenfold for for all the spoliations she had committed on our commerce.

It was with a view to make preparations for such a war, that the committee had offered the resolutions on the table. Whether the means recommended were adequate to the object, or whether they were best adapted to the end, it would be for the house, when they came to discuss them separately, to determine. For himself, Mr. P. said, and he presumed such were the feelings of all the members of the committee, he should have no objections to any modifications of them which might be agreeable to the house, so that the great object was still retained. If these resolutions, or any other similar to them in object, should pass; it was then the intention of the committee, as soon as the forces contemplated to be raised should be in any tolerable state of preparation, to recommend the employment of them for the purpose for which they shall have been raised, unless Great Britain shall, in the mean time, have done us justice. In short, it was the determination of the committee to recommend open and decided war—a war as vigorous and effective as the resources of the country, and the relative situation of ourselves and our enemy would enable us to prosecute.

The committee, Mr. P. said, have not recommended this course of measures without a full sense of the high responsibility which they have taken upon themselves. They are aware that war, even in its best and fairest form, is an evil deeply to be deprecated : But it is sometimes, and on few occasions perhaps more than on this, a necessary evil. For myself, I confess I have approached the subject not only with diffidence but with awe : But I will not shrink from my duty because it is arduous or unpleasant, and I can most religiously declare that I never acted under stronger or clearer convictions of duty than I do now in recommending these preparatory measures ; or, than I shall ultimately in recommending war, in case Great Britain shall not have rescinded her orders in council, and made some satisfactory arrangements in respect to the impressment of of our seamen. If there should be any gentlemen in the house who were not satisfied that we ought

not to go to war for our maritime rights, Mr. P. earnestly desires them not to vote for the resolutions. Do not, said he, let us raise armies, unless we intend to employ them. If we do not mean to support the rights and honor of the country, let us not drain it of its resources.

Mr. P. said he was aware that there were many gentlemen in the house who were dissatisfied that the committee had not gone further and recommended an immediate declaration of war, or the adoption of some measures which would have instantly precipitated us into it. But he confessed such was not his opinion. He had no idea of plunging ourselves headlong into a war with a powerful nation, or even a respectable province, when we had not three regiments of men to spare for that service, He hoped that we should not be influenced by the howling of newspapers, nor by a fear that the spirit of the twelfth congress would be questioned, to abandon the plainest dictates of common sense and common discretion. He was sensible that there were many good men out of congress as well as many of his best friends in it, whose appetites were prepared for a *war feast.* He was not surprised at it for he knew the provocatives had been sufficiently great. But he hoped they would not insist on calling in guests, at least until the table should have been spread. When this was done, he pleged himself in behalf of the committee of foreign relations that the gentleman should not be disappointed of the entertainment for the want of bidding ; and he believed he might also pledge himself for many of the members of the committee, that they would not be among the last to partake personally. not only in the pleasures, if any there should be, but in all the dangers of the revelry.

M. P. said that this was the time and occasion on which, above all others, within his experience, we should act in concert. If the ultimate object of the great body of this house and of this nation was the same, and so far as he had been able to ascertain the sentiments of both, it was—there would be no difficulty in attaining it.. But we must yield something to the opinions and feelings of each other.—Instead of indulging in party reflections and recriminations in this house, he hoped that the whole house of the union would form but one party, and consider a foreign nation as the other.

Mr. P. said he had risen merely for the purpose of explaining to the house the opinions and views of the committe in relation to the resolutions now to be discussed. and he should be satisfied if he had been so fortunate as to succeed.

for instance.) Is there, then, any reason for astonishment, that Sir G. Prevost, combining his instructions from home with the strenuous efforts that were being made by the peace party in Congress, should have imagined that there might be a possibility of an amicable arrangement being finally entered into?

He naturally supposed that his Government, through their agents, must be more thoroughly masters of the intentions of the American Cabinet than he possibly could be. He was ordered to avoid all measures that could provoke hostile feelings, he obeyed his instructions, and is he open to blame for so doing, and should not rather the British Cabinet be blamed for fettering him with their instructions?

After the war was declared, (here the reader must not omit to bear in mind that the conclusion was so hastily come to, that five days after the declaration was signed and sealed in Congress, the cause, the obnoxious orders in Council, was removed by the repeal of the said orders,) and Sir George complained of the want of troops and every munition of war necessary for the defence of his government. Veritas observes, "It is the acme of assurance to insinuate, that Ministers were to blame for such insufficiency, especially as they could only have a knowledge of our wants through Sir George's information."— Now how in justice can Sir George be blamed for not informing ministers of his requirements for a war, which he was instructed by all the means in his power to avoid the promotion of.

In his anxiety to attack the movers of the address to Sir George Prevost, in reference to the war, Veritas has suffered himself to go to the verge of injustice towards the addressed. The following passage seems to have particu larly aroused his indignation, if we may judge from what follows: "'The smallness of the regular army with which your Excellency was left to withstand the whole efforts of the United States, for two years, and the insufficiency of the naval force on the lakes, have exposed his Majesty's arms to some reverses.' How came they to dare to venture upon such an imposture? Is it because they reckon upon the banishment of the use of memory, as is necessary in all the operations of the junto? or if not so, is it the idea that no person here durst attempt to expose it? or finally, is it, that at a distance, (as the addresses are manufactured for exportation), they counted upon no one finding it out, as they meant to keep their own counsel?

"However, I do entertain some hope that they have reckoned without their host; and that *le bon vieux temps* and myself, who are fellow-laborers in the same vineyard for the correction of falsehood and support of truth, without having any knowledge of, or communication with, each other, will open the eyes of many, if we cannot of all the blind; for of the cure of the honest really blind patriots I cannot doubt; but of the wilfully blind, they must be left to be cured by their own folly, and the contempt of all independent minds."

Referring to the charge of our losing the naval superiority of the lakes Veritas adds, "Upon the subject of the upper lakes, their neglect in 1812 cannot be excused, even upon the principle of ignorance or inadvertency; for the common table talk that summer at Montreal was the incompetency of the officers and men on board the King's ships on Lake Ontario (and that talk is supposed to have been always better known at head-quarters than the designs of the enemy), and that a strong remedy was necessary, or the command thereof would be lost. Of that incompetency there was furnished the most striking proof by Commodore Earle, when he went over in the Royal George to Sackett's Harbour, in 1812, to destroy the Oneida Brig; and on arriving there, finding her hauled into the inner harbour, and one or two of her guns landed and planted on the bluff point (for then there was no garrison), without cover, which fired at him—the gallant Commodore immediately turned his tail or stern to the enemy, and returned to Kingston, *re infectâ*, but with whole bones. Yet no notice was taken of this at head-quarters, nor any remedy attempted, and he remained in command of the Ontario squadron until the arrival of Sir James Yeo, and then, forsooth, was offended at being superseded. It is proper to remark that Commodore Earle does not belong to the Royal Navy."

We have now done with this head, on which we have dwelt, perhaps, at too great length; but if so, it must be ascribed to our desire to do justice to all, and to seek diligently, where a mistake has occurred, for the really culpable party. To the present period, therefore, have we desired to vindicate Sir George; the relation of subsequent events may, perhaps, compel us to exchange the language of apology for that of censure; if so, we shall endeavor to deal with his errors in the same spirit of fairness which has impelled us to the attempt to clear his memory from faults unjustly ascribed to him.

Before following General Brock to the Nia-
Arrival of Indians, as gara frontier, we must
a reinforcement, at De-
troit.   not omit to observe that
there was some shadow of truth in General Hull's statement respecting the force of our Indian allies, although the necessity of surrendering such a post as Detroit on that account may well be questioned. Besides Gen. Hull yielded, not to the actual strength of these allies, for he surrendered before their arrival, but to the apprehension of their arrival. Major Richardson observes, "Mr. Robert Dickson, a gentleman to whom long intercourse with the Indians had imparted a knowledge of their character, and influence over their minds, which proved highly beneficial to the British cause, was then actively engaged in collecting some of the most warlike tribes; while the present Col. Askin of London, at that time, in the Indian Department, was already within a few days journey of Detroit, with a body of two hundred and seventy warriors, under their Chief Big-gun. This little detachment had set out expressly for the relief of Amherstburg, and, in its passage down in bark canoes, encountered much peril and difficulty, having had to cross Saginaw bay, nearly fifty miles in extent, and for many hours in their frail barks, even out of sight of the land. Such was the celerity of their movements, that they reached Amherstburg in the remarkably short period of six days from their departure from Michilimacinac." Whether the fear of these allies was a sufficient excuse for General Hull's abandonment of a strong post we leave to the reader to decide.

In speaking of the capture of the Caledonia
Capture of the Detroit and Detroit by the Ame-
and Caledonia by the
Americans.   ricans, Major Richardson
remarks, "The two armed vessels already mentioned as having covered our landing, on the 16th, were put in requisition for this service (the transportation of the irregular forces of General Hull to Buffalo, there to be disembarked preparatory to their return to their native State, Ohio,) and to these were added the Detroit and the Caledonia, a fine merchant brig. I do not recollect who was appointed to the command of the Detroit, but the Caledonia had her own captain, Mr. Irvine, a young man of a peculiarly retiring and amiable disposition, yet endowed with great resolution and firmness of character. These two vessels, having reached their destination for landing the prisoners, were then lying wholly unprotected and unsuspicions of danger in the harbour of Erie when, one dark night, they were assailed by two large boats, filled with American sailors and troops, which had dropped along side without being perceived, until it was too late for anything like effectual resistance. The Detroit was almost immediately carried, but the young captain of the Caledonia, which lay a little below her, aroused by the confusion on board his consort, prepared for a vigorous, though almost entirely personal resistance. Hastily arming himself, and calling on his little and inexperienced crew (scarcely exceeding a dozen men) to do the same, he threw himself in the gangway, and discharged a loaded blunderbuss into the first advancing boat, now dropping from the Detroit to board the Caledonia."

After describing the gallant though unsuccessful defence made by Mr. Irvine, Major Richardson continues, "The intrepidity and self-devotion of Mr. Irvine, whose single arm had killed and wounded no less than seven of his assailants, met with that reward it so richly merited. The heads of the naval department anxious to secure so gallant an officer to the service, tendered to him, on his exchange, which took place shortly after, the commission of a lieutenant in the Provincial Navy, in which capacity he continued to serve during the whole of the subsequent naval operations."

The surprise of the Detroit and Caledonia was considered a very brilliant feat, but, without seeking to disparage the American character for bravery, we cannot look on the exploit in the same light in which they would have it considered. Both vessels having been simply employed in cartel service, were unprovided with other than the common means of defence peculiar to merchantmen, while their crews were not only weak in number, but composed of a class of men, French Canadian sailors and voyageurs, who were ill qualified to compete with two full boat loads of practiced and resolute American sailors and soldiers. Moreover, both vessels lay in a supposed perfect security, and in utter absence of any kind of preparation. It was not conceived necessary to be on the alert, as it was supposed that the pacific character in which they appeared, would have shielded them from all hostile attempts. At the moment of the surprise both vessels had on board the prisoners brought from Detroit for the purpose of being landed at Buffalo,—how, therefore, the Americans can be justified, in violating the sanctity of the flag which continued to float as long as there were American prisoners on board, we cannot perceive.

An accident,* at one time promising results

Escape of General Brock.

far more serious than any which could spring from the capture of the vessels just named, occurred about the same period.

Expedition against Fort Wayne, abandonment of enterprise.

Towards the latter end of August, Major Muir was despatched with a small force against Fort Wayne, which it was deemed expedient to attempt the destruction of.

The time selected for the attempt seemed most favorable, as the tranquillity of the Canadian frontier had been just secured by the surrender of Detroit, and the occupancy of the adjacent districts. According to reports also received, the garrison of this post consisted only of a hundred men or thereabouts, not

entirely out of the usual course of navigation. In this emergency, the officer commanding the watch (Lieut. Jarvis, now Superintendent of Indian affairs) hastened below to acquaint General Brock, who was lying on his bed, with the danger which threatened the vessel, which it was impossible, by reason of the calm, to get farther from the shore. General Brock immediately sprang to his feet, and rushing upon the deck, saw the situation of the vessel was precisely what has been described. He was extremely angry, and turning to the master of the schooner said, "you scoundrel you have betrayed me, let but one shot be fired from the shore and (pointing to it) I will run you up on the instant to that yard arm." The master, though innocent of all design, was greatly alarmed by the stern threat of the General, and as the only possible means of extricating the vessel from her perilous situation, ordered several of his crew into a small punt, attached to her stern, the only boat belonging to her. In this they attempted to tow her, but made so little progress that one of the guard asked permission of the General to discharge his rifle, in order to attract the attention of the Queen Charlotte, then lying at anchor between point Abino and Fort Erie, to a signal which had been previously hoisted. Apprehensive that the shot might not be heard by their friends, while it might be the means of informing the enemy of their true character, General Brock at first refused his sanction, but as the man seemed confident that the report of his rifle would reach the other shore he finally assented, and the shot was fired. Soon afterwards the answering signal was run up to the mast head of the Queen Charlotte and that vessel seeing the doubtful situation of the schooner, on board which however they were not aware the General had embarked, immediately weighed her anchor, and standing over to the American shore, under a slight breeze which was then beginning to rise hastened to cover the little bark with her battery. Taking her in tow she brought her safely into the harbour of Erie, greatly to the joy of those who, aware of the invaluable freight with which the schooner was charged, had, on the weighing of the Queen Charlotte's anchor entertained the utmost apprehension for the safety of the becalmed vessel, and watched with deep interest the vain attempts of her crew to bring her off."

* At this crisis General Brock, anxious to assume the offensive on the Niagara frontier, lost not a moment in returning across the Lake, ordering down at the same time, not only the Toronto Militia, but those troops of the 41st., who had preceded and accompanied him to Detroit. The Queen Charlotte, principally laden with the regulars of the captured army, had sailed on the very evening of the surrender, and General Brock the next day embarked in a very small trading schooner, on board which were about 70 Ohio Riflemen, guarded by a small party of militia rifles which composed a portion of the volunteers from Toronto. During the passage none of the guard were on any account permitted to go below, either by day or by night, and not more than half a dozen Americans were allowed to be upon deck at the same time—the hatches being secured above the remainder. It was a duty of some fatigue, and requiring the exercise of the utmost vigilance on the part of the little guard. One morning, about day break, when by their reckoning they judged they were close to the harbor of Fort Erie, they found themselves suddenly becalmed, and in the midst of a fog which had commenced during the night. As the sun rose the fog began to disperse but the calm prevailed, and gradually, as the wreathing mists rolled upwards, the guard discovered, to their dismay, that they were close upon the American shore near Buffalo. The danger was imminent, for a number of persons were already assembled, evidently at a loss to discover to what flag the vessel belonged, and wondering what had brought her into a position

very efficiently furnished with the means of defence, and hard pressed by the Indians, who had closely invested it. The reasons for attempting the destruction of this post were that it served as a dépôt for stores, from which the enemy's troops on the frontier could be supplied.

The force destined for this enterprise consisted of a small detachment of troops, a howitzer, and two field pieces, and was embarked in boats and proceeded to the Miami village, situated about fifteen miles beyond the entrance of the river of the same name. For the further progress of the expedition we will quote from Major Richardson, who was present:—

" Being there joined by the body of Indians destined to form a part of the expedition, the detachment continued its route by land, and along a track of country bearing no mark of civilization whatever. Our only covering was the canopy of Heaven, or rather the arches formed by the intermingling boughs of the forest through which we moved, and not even the wigwam of the savage arose to diversify the monotony of the scene. The difficulty of conveying the guns by land, caused their transportation to be a work of much time; and the river, from the point where we had disembarked, was so extremely low as to render the progress of the boats, following the sinuosities of its course, tedious to the last degree. Having at length, after much toil, gained that part of the Miami, where it was intended to disembark the stores, every obstacle appeared to be removed, and the capture of Fort Wayne, then at no great distance, an event looked forward to with confidence. Fate, however, had ordained otherwise. About nine o'clock on the evening of our arrival, the shrill cry of our scouts was heard echoing throughout the forest, and soon afterwards seven Indians issued from the wood on the opposite shore, and leaping through the river, reached us. The account they gave of their adventure was to the following effect: —At a distance of a few leagues, while advancing cautiously along the road, they observed a party, five in number, in a glen, and seated round a large fire, where they were busily occupied in preparing their food. After a slight consultation they proceeded towards the group, and had approached within a few paces before they were perceived by the

Americans, who instantly flew to their arms, and assumed a posture of defence. The Indians, however, held out their hands in token of amity, and were suffered to enter the circle. Here, pretending to be in the American interest, and describing themselves as hunters, on their way to one of their villages, they succeeded in lulling the suspicions of the officer, who in return, communicated to them that the party he commanded were scouts preceding the advanced guard of an army of 2,500 men, then on their march for the Miami village, and only distant a few miles."

In consequence of this intelligence, the expedition was forthwith abandoned, and a retreat determined on. On deliberation, however, Captain Muir decided on awaiting the approach of the enemy in order to gain a correct account of their force and destination.

The whole of one day was thus passed, and fears began at length to be entertained, that the Americans, apprised of the vicinity of an enemy's force, had taken a different route, with the intention of cutting of a retreat. This would have left the little detachment in the heart of the enemy's country, destitute of resources, with an overwhelming force before them, they were consequently ordered to retreat on the old fort of Defiance, situated about half way between the Miami village and the point from whence they had commenced their retrograde movement. Having crossed the river at this place, a position was again taken up at a point beyond which the enemy could not effect a passage unperceived. We again resume Major Richardson's narrative :

" Early on the morning after our arrival, a party of Indians appeared along our line, conducting a prisoner they had found straying in the woods, at a short distance from the enemy's camp. From his account it appeared that the information given by the American officer was perfectly correct. The force of the enemy consisted of 2,500 men, under the command of General Winchester ; and were destined for the Miami, where it was intended to construct a fortification. On arriving at the spot where their slaughtered scouts lay unburied along the road, an alarm was spread throughout their columns, and deeming a numerous enemy to be in their front, it was thought prudent to entrench themselves where they were. For this purpose trees were immediately felled, and in the course of a few hours, with that expedition for which the Western Americans, with whom the axe is almost as indispensible a weapon as the rifle, are remarkable, an enclosure with interstices for musquetry, and sufficiantly large to contain their whole force, together with their baggage and waggons, was completed. It being evident from this intelligence, that the object of our enterprise was entirely frustrated, and that an attack on the enemy's entrenchment with our feeble force, if unsuccessful, must necessarily compromise the safety of our own posts, Capt. Muir decided on returning to Amherstburg, which fortress the detachment at length reached after a fruitless absence of three weeks.

"Although little or no mention has ever been made of our retreat from Fort Wayne, before so overwhelming a force as that which we so unexpectedly encountered, and by which we ought to have been annihilated, the utmost praise is due to Captain Muir for having accomplished it, not only without the loss of a man of his detachment, but even without the abandonment of any of his guns or stores, which, as has already been stated, were being transported with great toil and difficulty. Every thing was brought off and, at no one moment, was our march precipitate. Indeed of the bold affront assumed by the detachment, some idea may be formed from the exaggerated accounts which appeared in the American papers, even during the time we were retiring upon Amherstburg."

Sir Isaac Brock, in speaking of this expedition, observes, "I am inclined to think Captain Muir acted judiciously;" and, with reference to the advance of the American party, states,* "It appears evident the enemy meditates a second attempt on Amherstburg. The greater part of the troops, which are advancing, marched from Kentucky, with an intention of joining General Hull. How they are to subsist, even for a short period, is no easy matter to conceive. This difficulty will probably decide them on some bold measure, in the hope of shortening the campaign. If successfully resisted, their fate is inevitable.

---

* Dispatch to Sir George Prevost, Sept. 9th, 1812.

"The Indians appear to be adverse to retreating, without first making a trial of their strength. Should they continue to afford a willing co-operation, I entertain not the smallest doubt of the result that awaits this second attempt to turn my right; but your Excellency will easily perceive that doubts and jealousies have already seized their minds. The officers of the Indian department will, I trust, be able to remove all such impressions.

"Although, from the daily observation of what is passing on the opposite shore, a single man can ill be spared from this line; I have, notwithstanding, determined to send the two flank companies of the Royal Newfoundland Regiment to Amherstburg. Fresh troops are daily arriving, supposed to belong to the Pennsylvania quota, of two thousand men, known to be intended for the frontier. After the whole arrives, an attack, I imagine, cannot be long delayed. The wretched state of these quotas, and the raggedness of the troops, will not allow them to brave the rain and cold, which, during the last week, have been so severely felt.

"Between two and three hundred Indians have joined and augmented the force on the other side. Their brethren here feel certain that they will not act with any spirit against us. So, I imagine, if we continue to show a bold front—but, in the event of a disaster, the love of plunder will prevail, and they may then act in a manner to be the most dreaded by the inhabitants of this country."

A despatch from Sir George Prevost to Sir Isaac Brock furnishes us with additional reasons for our assertion that, up to this period, Sir George Prevost is not as blameworthy as most writers of that day have described. We give the despatch at length :—

Despatch of Sir George Prevost to Sir I. Brock.

"Captain Fulton arrived, on the 11th inst., with your letter of the 7th : the intelligence you have communicated by it convinces me of the necessity of the evacuation of Fort Detroit, unless the operations of the enemy on the Niagara frontier bear a character less indicative of determined hostile measures against your line in their front than they did when you last reported to me. You will, therefore, be pleased, subject to the discretion I have given you under the circumstances to which I have alluded, to take immediate steps for evacuating that post, together with the territory of Michigan; by this measure you will be enabled to withdraw a greater number of the troops from Amherstburg, instead of taking them from Col. Vincent, whose regular force ought not on any account to be diminished.

"I have already afforded you reinforcements to the full extent of my ability; you must not, therefore, expect a further supply of men from hence, until I shall receive from England a considerable increase to the present regular force in this province; the posture of affairs, particularly on this frontier, requires every soldier who is in the country.

"In my last despatch from Lord Bathurst, he tells me 'that his Majesty's Government trusts I will be enabled to suspend, with perfect safety, all extraordinary preparations for defence which I have been induced to make, in consequence of the precarious state of the relations between this country and the United States; and that, as every specific requisition for warlike stores and accoutrements which had been received from me had been complied with, with the exception of the clothing of the of the corps proposed to be raised from the Glengarry emigrants, he had not thought it necessary to direct the preparation of any further supplies.'

"This will afford you a strong proof of the infatuation of his Majesty's Ministers upon the subject of American affairs, and show how entirely I have been left to my own resources in the events which have taken place."

With the various despatches containing full and particular accounts of the actual state of affairs in the Province, before us, we do not see how with justice it can be asserted, "that it is the acme of assurance to insinuate, that Ministers were to blame for any insufficiency." Yet this is the language too commonly held by Veritas and other writers of the day.

The latitude, also, allowed to Sir Isaac Brock, should not be lost sight of, and it is certain that he made use of the freedom of action thus permitted him. We have only to quote his despatch of September 20th, to prove this:—"I have been honored with your Excellency's despatch, dated the 14th instant. I shall suspend, under the latitude thus left by your Excellency to my discretion, the evacu-

ation of Fort Detroit. Such a measure would most probably be followed by the total extermination of the population on that side of the river, or the Indians, aware of our weakness and inability to carry on active warfare, would only think of entering into terms with the enemy. The Indians, since the Miami affair, in 1793, have been extremly suspicious of our conduct; but the violent wrongs committed by the Americans on their territory, have rendered it an act of policy with them to disguise their sentiments.

"Could they be persuaded that a peace between the belligerents would take place, without admitting their claim to the extensive tract of country, fraudulently usurped from them, and opposing a frontier to the present unbounded views of the Americans, I am satisfied in my own mind that they would immediately compromise with the enemy. I cannot conceive a coalition so likely to lead to more awful consequences.

"If we can maintain ourselves at Niagara, and keep the communication to Montreal open, the Americans can only subdue the Indians by craft, which we ought to be prepared to see exerted to the utmost. The enmity of the Indians is now at its height, and it will require much management and large bribes to effect a change in their policy; but the moment they are convinced that we either want the means to prosecute the war with spirit, or are negotiating a separate peace, they will begin to study in what manner they can most effectually deceive us.

"Should negotiations for peace be opened, I cannot be too earnest with your Excellency to represent to the King's ministers the expediency of including the Indians as allies, and not leave them exposed to the unrelenting fury of their enemies.

"The enemy has evidently assumed defensive measures along the strait of Niagara. His force, I apprehend, is not equal to attempt, with any probability of success, an expedition across the river. It is, however, currently reported that large reinforcements are on their march; should they arrive, an attack cannot be long delayed. The approach of the rainy season will increase the sickness with which their troops are already afflicted. Those under my command are in perfect health and spirits."

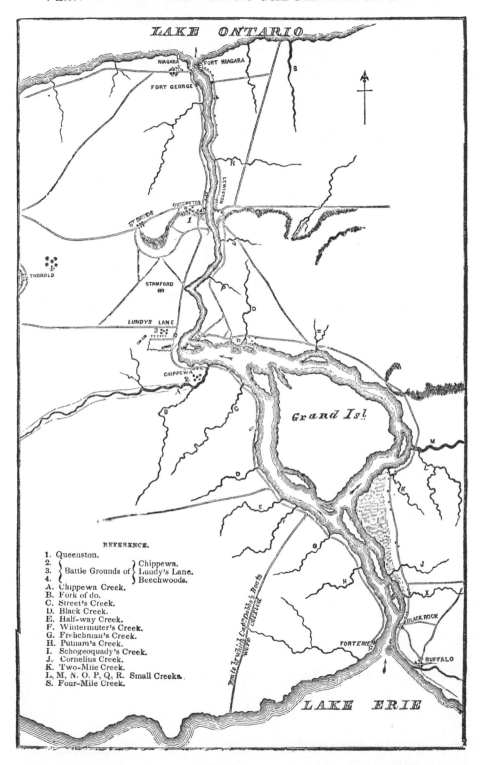

REFERENCE.

1. Queenston.
2. }
3. } Battle Grounds of { Chippewa.
4. } { Lundy's Lane.
   { Beechwoods.
A. Chippewa Creek.
B. Fork of do.
C. Street's Creek.
D. Black Creek.
E. Half-way Creek.
F. Wintermuter's Creek.
G. Frenchman's Creek.
H. Putnam's Creek.
I. Schogeoquady's Creek.
J. Cornelius Creek.
K. Two-Mile Creek.
L, M, N. O. P, Q, R. Small Creeks.
S. Four-Mile Creek.

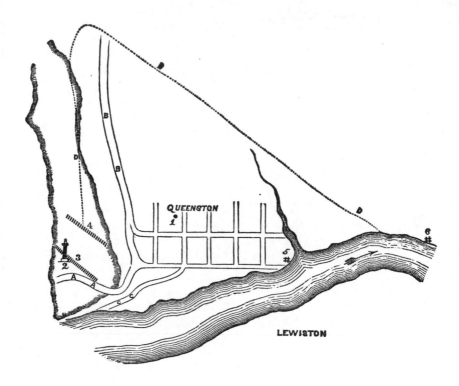

The spot where Queenston now stands, was then covered with trees.

A A—Road to the Falls.

B B—Road to St. David's and St. Catharine's.

C C—To Suspension Bridge.

D D—Road by which the reinforcements from Fort George gained the Heights in the afternoon.

No. 1. Spot where Brock fell.

 2. Brock's Monument.

 3. American line as drawn up in afternoon.

 4. English forces' do. do.

 5. Old Fort.

 6. Vromont's Battery.

CHAPTER VII.

Sir George Prevost, in his despatch to Gen.
Non-arrival of rein- Brock about the middle
forcements from Eu- of September, advised, it
rope, and movements
in Lower Province. may be remembered, that
officer of the impossibility of sending him any reinforcements, until there should be a "considerable increase to the regular force in the Province," as the presence of a large body of American regulars on the Lower Canadian frontier required every soldier who was in the country. A short extract from Christie will show how Sir George was situated, and how far any expectations of his being strengthened were realized. "The slender reinforcements that arrived were barely sufficient to relieve the citizens of Quebec for a short time from garrison duty. They consisted but of the 103rd regiment from England, with a few recruits from other regiments, and a battalion of the 1st (or Royal Scots) from the West Indies; and the three battalions of Quebec militia resumed garrison duty in the beginning of October, which they continued throughout the winter, each taking in turn its week." It is obvious, from this statement of

Christie, that Sir George Prevost was not, therefore, in a position which would warrant his weakening the force under his immediate command, and it will be further seen that the activity of the enemy at various points, kept him fully employed, and, indeed, compelled him to embody another battalion of militia, called the fifth battalion, afterwards "Canadian chasseurs." A corps of voyageurs was also raised by the North-West Company, which was disbanded in the spring, while the merchants and tradesmen of Montreal organized themselves into four companies of volunteers, for garrison duty and field service, in case of emergency. According to Christie, our troops, both regular and militia, seem, at this crisis, to have had their time fully occupied, for we find that a party of Americans, one hundred and fifty strong, under Captain Forsyth, crossed over from Gravelly Point to Gananoque, eighteen miles below Kingston, from whence they dislodged a party of fifty militia, and took possession of a quantity of arms and ammunition, which they carried away, after burning the store and a small quantity of provisions. Mr. Christie adds—"Their conduct is represented to have been disgraceful towards the defenceless inhabitants." We see also, from the same writer, that, "from the frequent interruptions of the convoys from Montreal, or rather Lachine, to Kingston, in Upper Canada, by the Americans at Ogdensburg, opposite Prescott, Col. Lethbridge, commanding at the latter place, formed the design of dislodging the enemy, and possessing himself of Ogdensburg. With a view of effecting this purpose, he assembled a force of some hundred and fifty men, regular and militia, and having collected a sufficient number of

7

batteaux, he pushed off on the forenoon of the 3rd October, under cover of a cannonnade from Prescott, with twenty-five batteaux escorted by two gun-boats. They advanced without opposition, until mid channel, when the enemy opened a tremendous discharge of artillery, which checked their progress. Confusion immediately ensued, and they were compelled to make a precipitate retreat, with the loss of three men killed and four wounded. The Americans were commanded by Brigadier General Brown, and behaved with much coolness and intrepidity." It may be as well to state that this enterprise, undertaken without the sanction of the commander of the forces, was censured by him ; and that public opinion condemned it also as rash. With this brief glance at the state of affairs in the Lower Province, we return to General Brock and the Niagara frontier.

As soon as it was ascertained that the General had reached Chippewa, it was suggested by Col. Holcroft, that a deputation of the principal residents in the district should wait on him, to congratulate his Excellency on the complete success which had attended his arms at Detroit. This deputation was accordingly organized, and the procession met their General at Queenston, as he was proceeding in an open carriage to Fort George. We have been assured by an eye-witness of the meeting, that General Brock was inexpressibly gratified at his enthusiastic reception, and the deep devotion testified by each member of the cortège to the cause, for which they were then in arms. So re-assured, indeed, was he, as to be enabled, with policy, to give but a cool reception to a party of Indians who had been playing fast and loose, and whose adherence to the British had been only secured by the intelligence, just received, of the successes at Detroit. It must have strengthened and cheered the General's heart to witness the enthusiasm with which, on that occasion, so many of Canada's best and bravest sons appeared to renew their pledge, that they were ready and willing to sacrifice their lives to prevent an invader's footstep polluting the soil of their native or adopted country. The procession, forming on both sides of the carriage, escorted General Brock in triumph to Niagara.

Gen. Brock's reception at Queenston.

It may, perhaps, enable the reader to comprehend the difficulties which attended any movement in force, and to perceive also the causes which left the troops, on both sides, in such apparent ignorance of each other's tactics, if we take a bird's-eye view of the general face and character of the country. Its appearance at the present day is thus described in " Canada ; Past, Present, and Future," before, however, quoting the passage, we will suppose the reader to be on the crest of the eminence immediately above Fonthill, just twelve miles west of Chippewa. A glance at the accompanying map will assist this.

Nature of the country along the Niagara frontier.

According to Mr. Smith, "The tourist after travelling for some miles along a road, where his view of the country on either side of him has seldom extended beyond two or three miles, on reaching this elevation, finds a most magnificent panorama, as it were by magic, displayed to his astonished vision. An immense plain, extending for many miles, lies before and below him, studded with towns, villages, groves and winding streams; before him lies the Welland Canal, crowded with vessels moving either way ; beyond it, the perpetually dashing, roaring cataract of Niagara, on one side, the waters of Lake Erie, and, on the other, those of Ontario. We know of no other spot from whence so extensive a view can be obtained. An observatory has been erected on the brow of the hill, and a telescope is kept for the accommodation of visitors."

We will now observe, that the hill here spoken of, is one of very inconsiderable elevation, consequently, the flatness of the surrounding district presenting such an extended view, may be easily imagined. When, therefore, the country was covered with dense forests, and it was impossible to gain, by observation, any insight into the marchings and countermarchings of either force, the difficulty of obtaining correct information may be easily understood, especially when we call to mind, that the various excellent roads which everywhere now open up the country, at that time existed only in the prophetic imaginings of some far seeker into the future destinies of this great Province.

We have said enough on the subject to assign at least one probable cause for the apparently contradictory orders, which, as our narrative will shew, were issued, and the consequent indecision which seemed to characterize many of the movements during the campaign of 1812 and '13.

The whole British force along a frontier of nearly thirty-six miles in extent, did not, at the date of General Brock's return from Detroit, amount to more than twelve hundred men, at least half of which were militia. These troops were disposed of in the following manner :—At Chippewa, a small detachment of the 41st, under Capt. Bullock, and the flank companies of the 2d Lincoln militia, under Capts. R. Hamilton and Rows ;—at Queenston, Capts. Dennis and Williams, with the flank companies of the 49th, with a small body of militia, were stationed; nearly all the remainder of the force was at Fort George, under General Sheaffe, with the exception of a few militia scattered here and there along the line. It will thus be seen how inadequately so extended a frontier was defended, and how the few troops scattered along the line were exposed to be cut off in detail by an energetic or enterprising enemy.

British force along the Niagara frontier at the time of General Brock's return from Detroit.

The American army, commanded by Major General Van Ranselaer consisted, according to their own official returns,* of five thousand two hundred and six men. This amount includes all the reinforcements which had arrived at the date of the battle of Queenston, but is exclusive of three hundred field and light artillery, with eight hundred of the 6th, 13th, and 23d regiments at Fort Niagara.—This gives a total of over six thousand three hundred men. James disposes of this force as follows:—" Of this powerful force, sixteen hundred and fifty regulars, under the command of Brigadier General Smith, were at Black Rock,†—three hundred and eighty-six militia, at the latter place and Buffalo,—nine hundred regulars and twenty-two hundred and seventy militia at Lewiston, distant from Black Rock, about twenty eight miles,—at Fort Niagara, were eleven hundred more, giving a force of six thousand three hundred

The American Army—force of.

men, of whom nearly two thirds were regular troops."*

Here was a force of regulars amounting to four thousand men, opposed to one of six hundred ; yet it will be shewn that various attempts have been made by American writers, to assign the inferiority of numbers, as the reason why the attack on Queenston so signally miscarried.

As it was quite out of the question for General Brock, in the presence of so superior a force, to adopt any other than precautionary and defensive measures, we will lay before the reader a sketch of what were really General Van Ranselaer's views. This we are enabled to do by means of a pamphlet published by Col. S. Van Ranselaer, his nephew and aide-de-camp.

General Van Ranselaer's plans.

The instructions from General Dearborn, on which General Van Ranselaer had to base his plan of operations, were as follows :—

" At all events, we must calculate on possessing Upper Canada before winter sets in. General Harrison will, I am assured, enter Canada by Detroit, with not less than from six to seven thousand men, exclusive of the troops necessary for guarding the frontier against Indian depredations.

" The force at Sackett's Harbour and that vicinity, is over two thousand, including an old company of regular artillery, and a large company of old riflemen.

" I have great confidence in the exertions now in operation in the navy department on Lake Ontario. In fact, we have *nothing to fear,* and much to hope as to the ultimate success of measures now in operation with a view to Upper Canada ; but much may immediately depend on what may happen at your post."

Such was the confident tone of General Dearborn's instructions, and that General Van Ranselear felt confidence also, may be assumed from the admission made by his nephew, Col. S. Van Ranselear. " He did not wish to be drawn from the object he had in view, by a controversy with General Smyth, *particularly so, as he knew that the forces which by this time had collected in his own immediate vicinity were amply sufficient for the purpose.*"

---

* Wilkinson's Memoris, Vol. 1, page 558.
† Wilkinson's Memoirs, Vol. 1, page 558.

* Vide Wilkinson.

This admission is of importance, as shewing what powerful reinforcements must have arrived between the middle of August, when Geo. Van Ranselaer arrived at the Niagara frontier on the 13th Oct. His situation in August is thus described :—" From the moment of his assuming the command, his position was one of the utmost exposure and danger. He lay within sight of a powerful enemy, separated from him only by a narrow river, for the crossing of which, that enemy possessed every facility. He had a line of thirty-six miles to guard, and his whole force was considerably less than one thousand men, many of them without shoes, and all of them clamorous for pay—of ammunition there were not ten rounds per man, and no lead. There was not one piece of heavy ordnance in the whole line, and there were no artillerists to man the few light pieces which we possessed. Add to this, that the troops could not take or keep the field for want of tents or covering; that the medical department, if one could be said to exist at all, was utterly destitute of everything necessary for the comfort of the sick or disabled ; and that there was among the men that entire want of subordination, to say nothing of discipline, which always characterizes raw militia, and some idea may be formed of the condition of our army."

Here was a lamentable condition for an amateur General to be placed in, especially when contrasted with the ease and comfort which pervaded the British frontier. "The condition of the forces on the opposite bank of the river was in contrast with ours in every particular. There was a *well-appointed* and *well-found* army, under the most exact discipline, and commanded by skilful and experienced officers. Every important post, from Fort Erie to Fort George, was in a defensible state, and the enemy had possessed himself of a very commanding position on the heights at Queenston, which he was rendering every day more secure and formidable. He had, moreover, the mastery of the lakes, and was at that moment industriously employed in using that advantage to increase his numbers, and add to his supplies at Niagara."

Let this statement be well considered, and the conclusion cannot fail to be arrived at, that General Van Ranselaer's reinforcements must have been very considerable, as we find the same writer, who in one case so touchingly depicted his helpless condition, in eight weeks asserting that " *he knew that the forces under his command were amply sufficient for his purpose.*"

As we have now established the fact that there was no lack of troops, we will proceed to enquire what was General Van Ranselaer's purpose. Fortunately, Ingersol's, Armstrong's, Wilkinson's, and Col. Van Ranselaer's works are sufficient to answer this question most satisfactorily.

In his letter of October 8th, to General Dearborn, General Van Ranselaer thus details his plans :—" Under these circumstances, and the impressions necessarily resulting from them, I am adopting decisive measures for closing the fall campaign. I have summoned Major-General Hall, Brigadier-General Smith, and the commandants of the United States regiments, to meet me in a consultation ; and I am well aware that some opinions, entitled to great respect, will be offered for crossing the Niagara, a little below Fort Erie, and pursuing the march down the river. I think this plan liable to many objections. The enemy have works at almost every point, and even an inferior force might hold us in check, and render our march slow ; by taking up the bridges at Chippewa, they might greatly embarrass us : the cleared country is but a mile or two wide, one flank would be constantly liable to be galled by Indians from the swamps ; for a considerable distance, the rapidity of the current, and the height of the banks render transportation across the river impracticable ; of course our supplies must follow the line of march, with the trouble and hazard of them every day increasing, and should the enemy retreat from General Harrison, they would have a double object in intercepting our supplies ; and by falling on our rear, and cutting off our communication, we might experience the fate of Hull's army. Besides these, and many other objections, there is no object on that side, until we should arrive at the commanding heights of Queenston, which are opposite my camp.

" The proposal, which I shall submit to the council, will be, that we immediately concentrate the regular force in the neighborhood of Niagara, and the militia here ; make the best possible dispositions, and, at the same time, that the regulars shall pass from the Four Mile Creek to a point in the rear of Fort George, and take it by storm ; I will pass the river here, and carry the heights of Queenston. Should we succeed, we shall effect a great discomfiture of the enemy, by breaking their line of communication, driving their shipping from the mouth of the river, leaving them no rallying point in this part of the country, appalling the minds of the Canadians, and opening a wide and safe communication for our supplies. We shall save our own land—wipe away part of the score of our past disgrace, get excellent barracks and winter quarters, and, at least, be prepared for an early campaign another year. As soon as the result of the council shall be known, I shall advise you of it."

This was a very feasible plan, and failed only, according to Colonel Van Ranselaer, through Brigadier-General Smyth's delay.

What says Ingersol on the subject :—" Gen. Alexander Smyth commanded at Buffalo, only a few miles from General Van Ranselaer, fifteen hundred men of the regular army ; but, as I was informed by a highly respectable officer still living, was not invited to take part in the projected descent upon Canada, lest the glory of the day should be taken from General Van Ranselaer's cousin, Colonel Solomon Van Ranselaer, an officer in the militia ; both of the Van Ranselaers being, perhaps laudably, though, as it turned out, unfortunately, bent on monopolizing the credit of this affair for the militia, if not exclusively, at any rate in preferance to the regular army."

General Armstrong's remarks are much to the same effect—"The troops employed, or intended to be employed in this service, were principally militia ; and, therefore, not better chosen than the object itself. Why this was so, is a problem not yet satisfactorily explained. If it originated in an *esprit de corps*, or belief of militia efficiency, there may be some color of excuse for the error; but if, as reported, the arrangement was made to gratify the ambition of an individual, the act was not merely injudicious but criminal. At the period, in question, there were at the General's disposal more than three thousand troops of the line ; from whom a corps might have been selected, which, well found, equipped, and commanded, would not have been either beaten or baffled."

We have been thus particular in making these extracts, as we are anxious to show that the failure of the attack on Queenston is not to be attributed to any want of troops, nor must it be considered as a hastily devised plan, as preparations had been making for it from the period when General Van Ranselaer first assumed the command of the army.

A few days before the battle of Queenston, Despatches of Gen. full instructions were Brock. forwarded by General Brock to the officers in command of the posts along the frontier, for their guidance in case of attack, and a despatch to Sir Geo. Prevost, dated 12th October, shows that he was fully aware of the impending storm, though uncertain of the direction in which it might break :

" Major-Gen. Brock to Sir Geo. Prevost,
October 12th.

" The vast number of troops which have been this day added to the strong force previously collected on the opposite side, convince me, with other indications, that an attack is not far distant. I have, in consequence, directed every exertion to be made to complete the militia to two thousand men, but fear I shall not be able to effect my object."

General Brock's letter of instructions to Col. Proctor shows that the situation of the British troops was far from being as comfortable as Col. S. Van Ranselaer's statement would induce one to suppose. "The unfortunate disaster which has befallen the Detroit and Caledonia will reduce us to great distress. They were boarded while at anchor at Fort Erie, and carried off; you will learn the particulars from others. A quantity of flour and a little pork were ready to be shipped for Amherstburg ; but as I send you the flank companies of the Newfoundland, no part of the provisions can go this trip in the Lady Prevost. It will be necessary to direct her to return with all possible speed, bringing the Mary under her convoy. You will husband your pork, for I sm sorry to say there is but little in the country.

" An interesting scene is going to commence with you. I am perfectly at ease as to the result, provided we can manage the Indians, and keep them attached to the cause, which, in fact, is theirs.

" The fate of the province is in your hands,

judging by every appearance; we are not to remain long idle in this quarter. Were it not for the positive injunctions of the commander of the forces, I should have acted with greater decision. This forbearance may be productive of ultimate good, but I doubt its policy, but perhaps we have not the means of judging correctly. You will, of course, adopt a very different line of conduct. The enemy must be kept in a state of continual ferment. If the Indians act as they did under Tecumseh, who probably might be induced to return to Amherstburg, that army will very soon dwindle to nothing. Your artillery must be more numerous and effective than any the enemy can bring,* and your store of ammunition will enable you to harass him continually, without leaving much to chance.

"I trust you will have destroyed every barrack and public building, and removed the pickets and other defences around the fort at Detroit.

"You will have the goodness to state the expedients you possess to enable you to replace, as far as possible, the heavy loss we have sustained in the Detroit. Should I hear of reinforcements coming up, you may rely on receiving your due proportion.   *   * May every possible success attend you."

These letters are interesting, from being the last ever written by General Brock, and from their showing, also, his energetic yet careful mind.

We have been most diligent in endeavoring
Battle of Queenston Heights.   to arrive at, as nearly as possible, a correct version of the events of the 13th October, and for that purpose have had many interviews with veterans in different parts of the country who were present on that occasion. Conflicting have been the statements, and it has been no easy task to reconcile all the discrepancies, should we therefore seem to err, the fault has arisen from no want of careful investigation, but from the multiplicity of accounts all differing from each other.

The morning of the 13th was of the the cold, stormy character, that marks so strongly the changeful climate of the Canadas. The alarm was given before daylight that the

enemy were in motion, and Captain Dennis of the 49th, who was in command at Queenston, immediately marched his company (grenadier) and the few militia who could be hastily assembled, to the landing place opposite Lewiston; this small force was soon followed by the light company of the 49th, and the remaining disposable militia force. Here the attempt of the enemy to effect a passage was, for some time, successfully resisted, and several boats were either disabled or sunk by the fire from the one-gun battery on Queenston Heights, and that from the masked battery about a mile below. Several boats were by the fire from this last battery so annoyed, that falling below the landing place, they were compelled to drop down with the current, and recross to the American side. A considerable force, however, had effected a landing, some distance above, by a path, which had been long considered impracticable, and was, therefore, unguarded, and succeeded in gaining the summit of the mountain. Had not this been done the Americans would have been defeated, by the force then present, as it was, the body, which had made good their ascent, far outnumbering the few troops opposed to them, carried the battery and turned the right of the British position, compelling them to retire with considerable loss. No resistance could now be offered to the crossing from Lewiston, except by the battery at Vromont's point, already spoken of, and from this a steady and harassing fire was kept up which did considerable execution. We give what now followed, on the authority of a volunteer who was attached to the light company of the 49th.

"On retiring to the north end of the village, on the Niagara road, our little band was met by General Brock, attended by his A.D.C., Major Glegg, and Colonel M'Donell." He was loudly cheered as he cried, "Follow me, Boys!" and led us at a pretty smart trot towards the mountain; checking his horse to a walk, he said, "Take breath, Boys!" we shall want it in a few minutes!" another cheer was the hearty response both from regulars and militia. At that time the top of the mountain and a great portion of its side was thickly covered with trees, and was now occupied by American riflemen. On arriving at the foot of the mountain, where the road diverges to St. David's, General Brock dis-

* The guns and ammunition captured at Detroit.

mounted, and, waving his sword, climbed over a high stone wall, followed by the troops; placing himself at the head of the light company of the 49th, he led the way up the mountain at double quick time, in the very teeth of a sharp fire from the enemy's riflemen—and, ere long, he was singled out by one of them, who, coming forward, took deliberate aim, and fired; several of the men noticed the action, and fired—but too late—and our gallant General fell on his left side, within a few feet of where I stood. Running up to him, I enquired, "Are you much hurt, sir?" He placed his hand on his breast, but made no reply—and slowly sunk down. The 49th now raised a shout, "Revenge the General!" and regulars and militia, led by Colonel McDonell, pressed forward, anxious to revenge the fall of their beloved leader, and literally drove a superior force up the mountain side, to a considerable distance beyond the summit. The flank companies of the York Militia, under Captains Cameron and Heward, and Lieutenants Robinson, McLean and Stanton, besides many others, whose names I forget, eminently distinguished themselves on this occasion.

"At this juncture the enemy were reinforced by fresh troops, and after a severe struggle, in which Colonel McDonell, Captains Dennis and Williams, and most of our officers, were either killed or wounded, we were overpowered by numbers, and forced to retreat, as the enemy had outflanked us, and had nearly succeeded in gaining our rear. Several of our men were thus cut off, and made prisoners—myself amongst the number."

So far, Mr. G. S. Jarvis' account agrees with those received from Captain Crooks, Colonel Clark, Colonel Kerby, and Captain John McMeekin—all of whom were present on this occasion. It agrees, also, strictly with James' statement. Up to the period of the engagement the numbers of the British regulars and militia had never reached three hundred, over two hundred of whom now retreated, and formed in front of Vromont's battery, there to await reinforcements—while Gen. Van Ranselaer, considering the victory as complete, crossed over in order to give directions about fortifying the camp which he intended to occupy in the British territory, and then recrossed to hasten the sending over reinforcements.

The position of the parties was now thus: The Americans occupied the heights at Queenston, with a force, certainly, exceeding eight hundred, and General Van Ranselaer admits, as will be seen in his letter to General Dearborn, that "a number of boats now crossed over, unannoyed, except by the one unsilenced gun," consequently more troops were hourly arriving.

Early in the afternoon, a body of about fifty Mohawks, under Norton and young Brant, advanced through the woods, took up a position in front, and a very sharp skirmish ensued, which ended in the Indians retiring on the reinforcements which had now begun to arrive from Fort George. This reinforcement consisted of three hundred and eighty rank and file of the 41st regiment, and Capts. James Crook's and McEwen's flank companies of the 1st Lincoln; Capts. Nellis' and W. Crook's flank companies of the 4th Lincoln; Hall's, Durand's and Applegarth's companies of the 5th Lincoln; (Cameron's, Heward's and Chisholm's flank companies of the York Militia;) Major Merritt's Yeomanry corps, and a body of Swayzee's Militia artillery, numbering in all between three and four hundred men. A short time afterwards, Col. Clark of the Militia, arrived from Chippewa, with Capt. Bullock's company of the 41st; Capts. R. Hamilton's and Row's flank companies of the 2nd Lincoln, and volunteer Sedentary Militia.

The whole British and Indian force thus assembled, did not amount to more than one thousand rank and file, of whom barely five hundred and sixty were regulars. The artillery consisted of two three-pounders, under the command of Lieutenant Crowther of the 41st. The Indians now mustered, perhaps, one hundred men.

After carefully reconnoitring, Gen. Sheaffe, who had now assumed the command, commenced the attack by an advance of his left flank, composed of the light company of the 41st, under Lieut. and Adjutant M'Intyre, supported by a body of militia and Indians, and a company of colored men under Capt. Runchey. After a volley, the bayonet was resorted to, and the Americans right driven in. The main body now advanced under cover of the fire from the two three-pounders, and after a short conflict forced the Americans over the first ridge of the heights to the road leading from Queenston to the Falls. Here, finding themselves unsupported from the opposite side, except by the fire from the American batteries, they surrendered, with the exception of a few who had thrown themselves down a steep ravine. James says " they threw themselves over the precipice, as if heedless of the danger, and many must have perished in the flood. Others, no doubt, swam across ; and some escaped in the few boats that remained entire, or whose crews could be persuaded to approach the Canadian shore." We have, however, a positive assurance from Capt. John MacMicking, that this was not the case, and that two only lost their lives by being forced over the cliffs ; the reports, also, that have been so industriously circulated, of the Indians lining the banks and firing on the fugitives, are, according to the same authority, equally unfounded. The numbers, according to James, under General Wadsworth, (who had been left in command by General Van Ranselaer, when he recrossed to hurry over reinforcements,) who now laid down their arms, amounted to seventy-two officers and eight hundred and fifty-eight rank and file, exlusive of two full boat loads previously taken. This account agrees with the statement of Mr. Hepburn, of Chippewa, who alleges that the return of prisoners given in by him was a trifle over nine hundred and fifty men.

The British loss amounted to sixteen killed, and about seventy wounded, making with the loss in the morning a sum total of about one hundred and fifty killed and wounded. The American loss, it is not so easy to arrive at ; one writer (Mr. Thompson), states the number as ninety killed and eighty-two wounded ; another, Dr. Smith, in his history of the United States* says, " in the course of the day eleven hundred troops, regulars and militia, passed into Canada from Lewiston, very few of whom returned." In the Albany Gazette, at the conclusion of a most accurate account of the battle, the number that crossed is fixed at sixteen hundred, of whom nine hundred were regulars. This last statement seems the more probable when we remember that General Van Ranselaer admits eight hundred as over, before he sent for the first reinforcements, and that the boats were crossing all the morning

almost undisturbed. This would give a loss of over six hundred killed and wounded, and the number seems by no means improbable when we remember that three boats were cut to pieces, and that the loss in crossing in the morning was very heavy.

The question now naturally arises, why did not General Van Ranselaer send over more troops, when he found General Sheaffe receiving reinforcements, so as to retain his superiority in numbers ? An answer to this will be found in his despatch to General Dearborn, in which a most ludicrous picture is drawn of the behaviour of the American militia at Lewiston, the more remarkable from the fact of these being the very men who, only two days previously, were determined. on an invasion of Canada, without waiting for orders from their commanding officer. "The ardor of the unengaged troops," says the General, " had entirely subsided." Why ? asks the reader ! Their wounded comrades had passed over, had described the charge of the " green-tigers " and militia in the morning, and had warned them what they might expect if they came in contact with troops infuriated at the loss of their beloved General. Ingersol says : " Riding among the miscreant militia, with some of their officers and Judge Peck to second him, the disheartened and disgusted General Van Ranselaer in vain tried to prevail on them to pass the river, and secure the victory won ; one-third would do it, he assured them. But neither reason, order, persuasion, nor shame had any effect." "Fifteen hundred able-bodied men," says Gen. Armstrong, " well armed and equipped, shortly before clamorous with prowess and untameable spirits, now put on the mask of lawfulness to hide their cowardice." Col Van Ranselaer observes :—" The panic had become so general that but a small portion of our army could be prevailed on to cross. The remainder, to their eternal shame, be it said, instead of lending their aid to sustain their gallant brethren in their victorious career, stood passively and saw them cut up, and captured in the end by a force amounting to about one-third of their united number."

These hard expressions, be it remembered, are none of our choosing ; they are the sentiments of American writers, and of writers, too, who were anxious to palliate the misdeeds of that day. It is not a little remarkable how

---

General Wilkinson, with the evidence of these passages before him, could pen the following:

" The names of the officers who accompanied Colonel Van Ranselaer in this hardy enterprise deserve to be engraved on the scroll of fame, for surmounting obstacles almost insuperable, in the face of a determined enemy, under a heavy fire, and dislodging and pursuing a superior force, consisting of two companies of the 49th British Regiment, advantageously posted, with an auxiliary body of militia and Indians. It was indeed a display of intrepidity rarely exhibited, in which the conduct and execution were equally conspicuous.

" Here true valour, so often mistaken for animal courage, was attested by an appeal to the bayonet, which decided the conflict without a shot. It must not be forgotten that two hundred and twenty-five men accomplished what six hundred were intended to achieve, and the reader will bear in mind, that with the single exception of Colonel Van Ranselaer, it was the first military combat in which either men or officers had been engaged. Under *all* the circumstances, and on the scale of the operations, the impartial soldier and competent judge will name this brilliant affair the *chef d'œuvre* of the war."

If this affair, resulting in unconditional surrender, is to be considered as the *chef d'œuvre* of the war, we are at a loss in what light the capitulation of Detroit is to be viewed. The passages following are still more remarkable. " Yet we heard of no mark of distinction, no honorary promotions on the occasion ;* the efficacy of brevets had not then been discovered, nor had it become necessary to cover the disgrace of the Cabinet, by raising up idols for the adoration of the people. It is true, complete success did not ultimately crown this enterprise, but two great ends were obtained for the country. It re established the character of the American army, and deprived the enemy, by the death of Brock, of the best officer that has headed their troops in Canada throughout the war, and with his loss put an end to their brilliant career,"—as was immediately exemplified by the still more unfortunate, because ridiculous attempt, by Gen. Smyth.

* Error ! General Van Ranselaer, who was only Brevet Major General was confirmed as Major General, for his distinguished gallantry and public spirit, in the military service of his country, especially during the late war on the Niagara frontier.—ED. A.A.M.

The absurdity into which General Wilkinson's patriotism has here hurried him, is on a par with that of some of the veracious histories put forth by sundry American authors.

One writer,(Thompson,) in his account of the affair in the morning, makes the Americans three hundred and twenty strong, "entirely routes the British 49th regiment of six hundred strong, and ursues them up the heights." Not satisfied with quadrupling the numbers of the 49th, he adds—" part of the 41st were acting with the 49th, both of which regiments distinguished themselves under the same commander in Europe ; and the latter had obtained the title of the Egyptian Invincibles, because they had never, ON ANY OCCASION BEFORE, been known to give ground."

One man of the 41st was present in the morning, Lieutenant Crowther—and he was the sole representative of the regiment on the occasion.

Another writer, Dr. Smith, like his friend Mr. Thompson, also introduces the "whole 49th regiment, six hundred strong," adding, "They mutually resorted to the bayonet ; and, after a bloody conflict, the famous Invincibles yielded to the superior energy of their antagonists, although so far inferior in numbers." We have, however, given extracts enough to show how entirely regardless of truth and facts the greater number of the American historians are, and how they have stooped, not only to distort, but actually to invent. "These," says James, " are the delusions so industriously practised upon the American people. No wonder then, that those among them who have never been beaten into a contrary opinion, still fancy they are possessed of the powess of demi-gods. What, by way of example, can show this more clearly than the letter from Lieut. Col. John Chrystie, of the 13th, to General Cushing, the Adjutant General. This letter begins, " In obedience to orders of the 8th inst., requiring from me a particular statement in relation to the affair at Queenston, I have the honor to transmit a journal of the incidents connected with that affair, which FELL UNDER MY OBSERVATION."

It is difficult to account for a man, holding high rank in the service, deliberately penning a falsehood, especially when its refutation was so easy, with so many actors on that bloody stage, at hand, and ready to note the untruth, we must therefore ascribe the following passage in his "particular statement," to a diseased imagination. "OUR WHOLE FORCE UNDER ARMS AT THE TIME, (*about two, P. M.*) WAS LESS THAN THREE HUNDRED, with but one piece of artillery, and not a dozen rounds for it; yet I am well persuaded a retreat much less a surrender, was not thought of; and that the troops were in fact in as high spirits as if we had been superior." The absurdity of this is too glaring, when we remember that half an hour after the exhibition of "high spirits," these very gallant soldiers broke and fled like so many sheep before a force slightly inferior.

We have now shewn the principal events of Despatches from the two commanding officers compared. the 13th, and propose to give and compare the despatches of the opposing Generals to their respective commanding officers. "From Major General Sheaffe to Sir George Prevost."*

---

* *From General Van Ranselaer, to the American Secretary of War.*

Head Quarters, Lewiston, Oct. 14th, 1812.

SIR,—As the movements of this Army under my command, since I had last the honor to address you on the 8th, have been of a very important character, producing consequences serious to many individuals; establishing facts actually connected with the interest of the service and the safety of the army; and as I stand prominently responsible for some of these consequences, I beg leave to explain to you, sir, and through you to my country, the situation and circumstances in which I have had to act, and .the reasons and motives which governed me, and if the result is not all that might have been wished, it is such that, when the whole ground shall be viewed, I shall cheerfully submit myself to the judgment of my country.

In my letter on the 8th instant, I apprised you that the crisis in this campaign was rapidly advancing; and that (to repel the same) "the blow must be soon struck, or all the toil and expense of the campaign will go for nothing, for the whole will be tinged with dishonor."

Under such impressions, I had, on the 5th instant, written to Brig. General Smyth, of the United States forces, requesting an interview with him, Major General Hall, and the commandants of regiments, for the purpose of conferring upon the subject of future operations. I wrote Major General Hall to the same purport. On the 11th I had received no answer from Gen. Smyth; but in a note to me of the 10th, General Hall mentioned that General Smyth had not yet then agreed upon any day for the consultation.

In the mean time, the partial success of Lieutenant Elliot at Black Rock (of which however, I have received no official information) began to

Fort George, Oct. 13, 1812.

SIR,—I have the honor of informing your Excellency, that the enemy made an attack with considerable force, this morning, before day light, on the position of Queenstown. On receiving intelligence of it, Major Gen. Brock immediately proceeded to that post, and I am excessively grieved in having to add, that he fell whilst gallantly cheering his troops to an exertion for maintaining it. With him the position was lost; but the enemy was not allowed to retain it long, reinforcements having been sent up from this post, composed of regular troops, militia, and Indians: a movement was made to turn his left, while some artillery, under the able direction of Capt. Holcroft, supported by a body of infantry, engaged his attention in front. This direction was aided, too, by the judicious position which Norton, and the Indians with him, had taken on the woody brow of the high ground above Queenston.

"A communication being thus opened with Chippewa, a junction was formed of succours

excite a strong disposition in the troops to act. This was expressed to me through various channels, in the shape of an alternative; that they must have orders to act, or at all hazards they would go home. I forbear here commenting upon the obvious consequences, to me personally, of longer withholding my orders under such circumstances.

I had a conference with ——, as to the possibility of getting some person to pass over into Canada. and obtain correct information. On the morning of the 4th, he wrote to me that he had procured the man, who bore his letter to go over. Instructions were given him: he passed over, and obtained such information as warranted an immediate attack. This was confidently communicated to several of my first officers, and produced great zeal to act; more especially as it might have a controlling effect upon the movement at Detroit, where it was supposed that General Brock had gone with all the force he dared to spare from the Niagara frontier. The best preparations in my power were, therefore, made to dislodge the enemy from the heights of Queenstown, and possess ourselves of the village, where the troops might be sheltered from the distressing inclemency of the weather.

Lieutenant Colonel Fleming's flying artillery, and a detachment of regular troops under his command, were ordered to be up in season from Fort Niagara. Orders were also sent General Smyth to send down from Buffalo such detachments of his brigade as existing circumstances in that vicinity might warrant. The attack was to be made at three o'clock on the morning of the 11th, by crossing over in boats from the old ferry opposite the heights. To avoid any embarrassment in crossing the river, (which is here a sheet of violent

that had been ordered from that post. The enemy was then attacked, and, after a short, but spirited conflict, was completely defeated. I had the satisfaction of receiving the sword ot their commander, Brigadier General Wadsworth, on the field of battle, and many officers, with nine hundred men, were made prisoners, and more may yet be expected. A stand of colors and one six-pounder, were also taken. The action did not terminate till nearly three o'clock in the afternoon, and their loss, in killed and wounded, must have been considerable. Ours I believe to have been comparatively small in numbers; no officers were killed besides Major-General Brock, one of the most gallant and zealous officers in his Majesty's service, whose loss cannot be too much deplored; and Lieut.-Col. M'Donell, provincial aide-de-camp, whose gallantry and merit render him worthy of his chief. Captains Dennis and Williams, commanding the flank companies of the 49th

regiment, who were stationed at Queenston, were wounded, bravely contending at the head of their men against superior numbers; but I am glad to have it in my power to add, that Captain Dennis was fortunately able to keep the field, though it was with pain and difficulty, and Captain Williams' wound is not likely long to deprive me of his service.

" I am particularly indebted to Capt. Holcroft, of the royal artillery, for his judicious and skilful co-operation with the guns and howitzers under his immediate superintendence; their well-directed fire contributed materially to the fortunate result of the day.

" Captain Derenzy, of the 41st regiment, brought up the reinforcements of that corps from Fort George, and Captain Bullock led that of the same regiment from Chippewa; and under their commands those detachments acquitted themselves in such a manner as to sustain the reputation which the 41st regiment had already acquired in the vicinity of Detroit.

---

eddies,) experienced boatmen were procured, to take the boats, from the landing below the place of embarkation. Lieutenant Sim was considered the man of the greatest skill for this service; he went ahead, and, in the extreme darkness, passed the intended place far up the river; and there, in the most extraordinary manner, fastened his boat to the shore, and abandoned the detachment. In this front boat he had carried nearly all the oars, which were prepared for the boats. In this agonizing dilemma stood officers and men, whose ardor had not cooled by exposure through the night, to one of the most tremendous north-cast storms, which continued unabated for twenty-eight hours, and deluged the whole camp. Colonel Van Ranselaer was to have commanded the detachment.

After this result I had hoped that the patience of the troops would have continued, until I could submit the plan suggested in my letter of the 8th, that I might act under, and in conformity to, the opinion which might be then expressed. But my hope was idle; the previously excited ardor seemed to have gained new heat from the late miscarriage; the brave men were mortified to stop short of their object, and the timid thought laurels half won by the attempt.

On the morning of the 12th, such was the pressure upon me from all quarters, that I became satisfied that my refusal to act might involve me in suspicion, and the service in disgrace.

Lieutenant-Colonel Christie, who had just arrived at the Four-Mile Creek, and had, late in the night of the 1st, contemplated an attack, gallantly offered me his own and his men's services: but he got my permission too late. He now again came forward, had a conference with Colonel Van Ranselaer, and begged that he might have the honor of a command in the expedition. The ar-

rangement was made, Colonel Van Ranselaer was to command one column of 300 militia; and Lieutenant-Colonel Christie a column of the same number of regular troops.

Every precaution was now adopted as to boats, and the most confidential and experienced men to manage them. At an early hour in the night, Lieutenant-Colonel Christie marched his detachment by the rear road from Niagara to the camp. At seven in the evening Lieut.-Colonel Stranahan's regiment moved from Niagara Falls; at eight o'clock Mead's, and at nine o'clock Lieutenant-Colonel Bland's regiment marched from the same place. All were in camp in good season. Agreeably to my orders, issued upon this occasion, the two columns were to pass over together; as soon as the heights should be carried, Lieutenant-Colonel Fenwick's flying artillery was to pass over; then Major Mullany's detachment of regulars; and the other troops to follow in order.

Colonel Van Ranselaer, with great presence of mind, ordered his officers to proceed with rapidity, and storm the fort. This service was gallantly performed, and the enemy driven down the hill in every direction. Soon after this, both parties were considerably reinforced, and the conflict was renewed in various places. Many of the enemy took shelter behind a stone guard-house, where a piece of ordnance was now briskly served. I ordered the fire of our battery to be directed upon the guard-house; and it was so effectually done, that with eight or ten shots the fire was silenced. The enemy then retreated behind a large stone house; but in a short time the route became general, and the enemy's fire was silenced, except from a one-gun battery, so far down the river as to be out of the reach of our heavy ordnance; and our light pieces could not silence it. A number of boats now passed over unannoyed,

" Major General Brock, soon after his arrival at Queenston, had sent down orders for battering the American fort at Niagara. Brigade-Major Evans, who was left in charge of Fort George, directed the operations against it with so much effect, as to silence its fire, and to force the troops to abandon it; and, by his prudent precautions, he prevented mischief of a most serious nature, which otherwise might have been effected—the enemy having u:ed heated shot in firing at Fort George.

" In these services he was most effectually aided by Colonel Claus, who remained in the fort at my desire, and by Captain Vigoureaux of the Royal Engineers. Brigade-Major Evans also mentions the conduct of Captains Powell and Cameron of the Militia Artillery, in terms of commendation.

" Lieut. Crowther, of the 41st Regiment, had charge of two three-pounders that had accompanied the movement of our little corps, and they were employed with good effect.

" Capt. Glegg, of the 49th Regiment, aide-de-camp to our lamented friend and General, afforded me most essential assistance ; and I found the services of Lieutenant Fowler, of the 41st Regiment, Assistant Deputy Quartermaster-General, very useful. I have derived much aid, too, from the activity and intelligence of Lieutenant Kerr, of the Glengarry Fencibles, whom I employed in communicating with the Indians and other flanking parties.

" I was unfortunately deprived of the aid of the experience and ability of Lieutenant-Colonel Myers, Deputy Quarter-Master General, who had been sent up to Fort Erie, a few days before, on duty, which detained him there.

" Lieutenant-Colonel Butler and Clark of the Militia, and Captains Hatt, Durand, Rowe, Applegarth, James, Crooks, Cooper, Robert Hamilton, McEwen, and Duncan Cameron ; and Lieutenants Robinson† and Butler, commanding flank companies of the Lincoln and York Militia, led their men into action with great spirit. Major Merritt, commanding the Niagara dragoons, accompanied me, and gave much assistance with part of his corps. Captain A. Hamilton, belonging to it, was disabled from riding, and attached himself to the guns, under Captain Holcroft, who speaks highly of his activity and usefulness. I beg leave to

except by the one unsilenced gun. For some time after I had passed over the victory appeared complete, but in expectation of further attacks, I was taking measures for fortifying my camp immediately ; the direction of this service I committed to Lieutenant Totten. of the engineers. But very soon the enemy were reinforced by a deatch-ment of several hundred Indians from Chippewa; they commenced a furious attack; but were promptly met and routed by the rifle and bayonet. By this time I perceived my troops were embarking very slowly. I passed immediately over to accelerate their movements; but, to my utter astonishment, I found that, at the very moment when complete victory was in our hands, the ardor of the unengaged troops had entirely subsided. I rode in all directions; urged the men by every consideration to pass over, but in vain Lieutenant-Colonel Bloom, who had been wounded in action, returned, mounted his horse and rode through the camp ; as did also Judge Peck, who happened to be here, exhorting the companies to proceed, but all in vain.

At this time a large reinforcement from Fort George was discovered coming up the river. As the battery on the hill was considered an important check against ascending the heights, measures were immediately taken to send them a fresh supply of amunition, as I learnt there were only left twenty shot for the eighteen-pounders. The reinforcements, however, obliqued to the right from the road, and formed a junction with the Indians in rear of the heights. Finding to my infinite mortification, that no reinforcements would pass over ; seeing that another severe conflict must soon commence ; and knowing that the brave men at the heights were quite exhausted, and nearly out of ammunition ; all I could do, was to send them a fresh supply of cartridges. At this critical moment I despatched a note to General Wadsworth acquainting him with our situation : leaving the course to be pursued much to his own judgment ; with the assurance that if he thought best to retreat, I would endeavor to send as many boats as I could command, and cover his retreat by every fire I could safely make. But the boats were dispersed ; many of the boatmen had fled, panic struck ; and but few got off. My note, however, could but little more than have reached General W., about four o'clock, when a most severe and obstinate conflict commenced, and continued for about half an hour, with a tremendous fire of cannon, flying artillery and musketry. The enemy succeeded in re-possessing their battery, and gaining advantage on every side ; the brave men who had gained the victory being exhausted of strength and ammunition, and grieved at the unpardonable neglect of their fellow soldiers, gave up the conflict.

I can only add, that the victory was really won; but lost for the want of a small reinforcement; one-third part of the idle men might have saved all.   I have the honor to be, &c.
                              STEPHEN VAN RANSELAER.
Hon. William Eustis.
    Secretary of War.

† Now Chief Justice of Upper Canada.

add, that volunteers Shaw, Thomson, and Jarvis, attached to the flank companies of the 49th Regiment, conducted themselves with great spirit; the first having been wounded, and the last having been taken prisoner.* I beg leave to recommend these young men to your Excellency's notice.

"Norton is wounded, but not badly; he and the Indians particularly distinguished themselves, and I have very great satisfaction in assuring your Excellency that the spirit and good conduct of His Majesty's troops, of the militia, and of the other provincial corps, were eminently conspicuous on this occasion.

"I have not been able to ascertain as yet the number of our troops, or of those of the enemy engaged; ours did not, I believe, exceed the number of the prisoners we have taken; and their advance, which effected a landing, probably amounted to thirteen or fourteen hundred men.

"I shall do myself the honor of transmitting to your Excellency further details, when I shall have received the several reports of the occurrences which did not pass under my own observation, with the return of the casualties, and those of the killed and wounded, and of the ordnance taken.

"I have the honor to be,

(Signed,)   R. H. SHEAFFE,

Major-General."

By comparing these two bulletins (General Sheaffe's and Van Ranselaer) with the text, the reader will be able to form a very fair judgment as to the parties who were really entitled to the honor of the day. Two passages in General Van Ranselaer's dispatch must not be overlooked: what he styles "the fort" that was stormed with such "presence of mind" by Col. Van Ranselaer, was in reality a one-gun battery, and was the only approach to a defence on the heights. In the afternoon there were two three pounders, but the eighteen-pounder had by that time been spiked. In another place General Van Ranselaer states, "The enemy were reinforced by a detachment of several hundreds of Indians from Chippewa." Now, after the most diligent enquiry into the Indian force, from various officers who distinguished themselves on this

occasion, we have not been able to make the numbers of the Indians anything approaching to one hundred, at any part of the day. Neither General Van Ransalaer, nor any of his officers, ever had an opportunity of knowing what the real number of the Indians were, for they were masked by trees; the several hundreds existed only in the imagination of the General and his troops.

Another dispatch* which we give below, is also very incorrect. Captain Wool gives the 49th regiment *four* flank companies, and stations General Brock at their head, thus giving the Americans credit for all the offensive operations in the early part of the day, when it is notorious that after compelling the two flank companies to retire, the Americans acted afterwards on the defensive.

---

* *From Captain Wool to Colonel Van Ranselaer.*

Buffalo Oct. 23, 1812.

DEAR SIR,

I have the honor to communicate to you the circumstances attending the storming of Queenston battery on the 13th inst; with those which happened previously you are already well acquainted.

In pursuance of your order, we proceeded round the point and ascended the rocks, which brought us partly in rear of the battery. We took it without much resistance. I immediately formed behind it, and fronting the village, when I observed Gen. Brock with his troops formed, consisting of four companies of the 49th regiment, and a few militia, marching for our left flank. I immediately detached a party of 150 men, to take possession of the heights above Queenston and to hold Gen. Brock in check; but, in consequence of his superior force, they retreated. I sent a reinforcement; notwithstanding which, the enemy drove us to the edge of the bank; when, with the greatest exertions, we brought the troops to a stand, and I ordered the officers to bring their men to a charge as soon as the ammunition was expended, which was executed with some confusion, and in a few moments the enemy retreated. We pursued them to the edge of the heights, when Col. M'Donald had his horse shot from under him, and was mortally wounded. In the interim, General Brock, in attempting to rally his forces, was killed, when the enemy dispersed in in every direction. As soon as it was practicable, I formed the troops in a line on the heights fronting the village, and immediately detached flanking parties, which consisted of Capt. Machesney, of the 6th regiment, Lieut. Smith, and Ensign Grosvenor, with a small detachment of riflemen, who had that moment arrived; at the same time, I ordered Lieut. Ganesvoort and Lieut. Randolph, with a detachment of artillery, to drill out an 18-pounder which had been previously spiked, and, if possible, to bring it to bear upon the village.

---

* A Captain of Militia was given in exchange for Mr. Jarvis a week after the battle.

Again, General Brock had not then arrived, and it was his arrival that led to the brilliant charge in which an inferior force compelled a superior force to retire UP HILL; one of the most brilliant and daring feats on record, and in which the militia distinguished themselves to the full as much as the regulars, fighting side by side, and animated with a burning desire to revenge the loss of a commander whose intercourse with them had inspired at once respect and affection. There is very little doubt that the death of the British General cost the life of many an invader on that day, which would otherwise have been spared.

As we are unacquainted with the preserva-

Personal appearance of Gen. Brock. tion of any portrait, public or private, of Gen. Brock in this country, it may not be uninteresting to give here a slight sketch. In person he was tall and stout, even inclining to corpulency; of fair and florid complexion, with a large forehead and full face, though the features were not prominent. His eyes were rather small, of a greyish blue, with a slight cast in one of them. His mouth was small, with fine teeth, and when his countenance was lighted by a smile the expression was particularly pleasing. In manner he was exceedingly affable and gentlemanlike, of a cheerful and social habit, partial to dancing, and, though never married, he was extremely partial to female society.

Of the soundness of his judgment and bravery we have already adduced sufficient

evidence to render any further comment superfluous, especially as our notes will show the sentiments of the Province on the occasion of his death.

The "Quebec Gazette" contained the notice

Public opinion of Gen. Brock's character and value. of his death which will be found below ;* and the sentiments of the British Government on the melancholy occasion, were thus expressed in a despatch from Earl Bathurst, Secretary of State for the Colonies, to Sir George Prevost: —

"His Royal Highness the Prince Regent is fully aware of the severe loss which His Majesty's service has experienced in the death of Major-General Sir Isaac Brock. This would have been sufficient to have clouded a victory of much greater importance. His Majesty has lost in him not only an able and meritorious officer, but one who, in the exercise of his functions of provisional Lieutenant-Governor of the Province, displayed qualities admirably adapted to dismay the disloyal, to reconcile the wavering, and to animate the great mass of the inhabitants against successive attempts of the enemy to invade the Province, in the last of which he fell, too prodigal of that life of which his eminent services had taught us to understand the value."

The wounded and prisoners I ordered to be collected. and sent to the guard-house. About this time, which was about three or four o'clock in the afternoon, Lieut.-Col. Christie arrived, and took the command. He ordered me across the river to get my wounds dressed. I remained a short time. Our flanking parties had been driven in by the Indians, but Gen. Wadsworth and other officers arriving, we had a short skirmish with them, and they retreated, and I crossed the river.

The officers engaged in storming the battery were Captains Wool and Ogilvie; Lieutenants Kearney, Hugouin, Carr, and Simmons, of the 43d regiment; Lieutenant Ganesvoort and Randolph, of the light artillery ; and Major Lush, of the militia.

I recommend to your particular notice Lieuts. Randolph, Carr, and Kearney, for their brave conduct exhibited during the whole of the action.

I have the honor to be,
Your most obedient humble Servant,
JOHN E. WOOL, Capt. 13th regt. inft.
Colonel Van Ranselaer.

* The news of the death of this excellent officer has been received here as a public calamity. The attendant circumstances of victory scarcely checked the painful sensation. His long residence in this province, and particularly in this place, had made him in habits and good offices almost a citizen ; and his frankness, conciliatory disposition and elevated demeanour, an estimable one. The expressions of regret as general as he was known, and not uttered by friends and acquaintance only, but by every gradation of class, not only by grown persons, but young children, are the test of his worth. Such too is the only eulogium worthy of the good and brave, and the citizens of Quebec have with solemn emotions, pronounced it to his memory. But at this anxious moment other feelings are excited by his loss. General Brock had acquired the confidence of the inhabitants within his own government. He had secured their attachment permanently by his own merits. They were one people animated by one disposition, and this he had gradually wound up to the crisis in which they were placed. Strange as it may seem, it is to be feared that he had become too important to them. The heroic militia of Upper Canada, more particularly, had knit themselves to his person ; and it is yet to be ascertained whether the desire to avenge his death can compensate the many embarrassments it will occasion..

CHAPTER VIII.

———

THE two notices, we have already given, might almost be considered sufficient evidence of the eminence to which Gen. Brock had raised himself by his civil and military talents, and of the correspondently deep grief with which his untimely fate was deplored throughout, not only these Provinces, but the Mother Country also. Yet we feel tempted to add one or two more tributes to his memory. The first is from a Montreal paper of the day;[*] the second from Howison's "Sketches of Upper Canada."[†] The most conclusive proof, however, of the general estimation in which Sir Isaac Brock was held, is, perhaps, to be found in General Van Ranselaer's letter of condolence to Gen. Sheaffe, on the occasion of his funeral, in which Gen. Van Ranselaer expresses his desire to pay " a just tribute of respect to the gallant dead," and informs Gen. Sheaffe, that " I shall order a salute for the funeral of General Brock to be fired here,[‡] and at Fort Niagara this afternoon.

This generous conduct of Gen. Van Ranselaer evinced feelings worthy of a soldier and a man.

The President, Mr. Madison, when alluding to the battle of Queenston in his message to Congress, observed, " Our loss has been considerable, and is deeply to be lamented. That of the enemy, less ascertained, will be the

Opinions of the Press, respecting Gen. Brock's character and value, continued.

———

[*] The private letters from Upper Canada, in giving the account of the late victory at Queenston, are partly taken up with encomiastic lamentations upon the never-to-be-forgotten General Brock, which do honor to the character and talents of the man they deplore. The enemy have nothing to hope from the loss they have inflicted; they have created a hatred which panteth for revenge. Although General Brock may be said to have fallen in the midst of his career, yet his previous services in Upper Canada will be lasting and highly beneficial. When he assumed the government of the province, he found a divided, disaffected, and, of course, a weak people. He has left them united and strong, and the universal sorrow of the province attends his fall. The father, to his children, will make known the mournful story. The veteran, who fought by his side in the heat and burthen of the day of our deliverance, will venerate his name.

[†] He was more popular, and more beloved by the inhabitants of Upper Canada, than any man they ever had among them, and with reason; for he possessed, in an eminent degree, those virtues which add lustre to bravery, and those talents that shine alike in the cabinet and in the field. His manners and dispositions were so conciliating as to gain the affection of all whom he commanded, while his innate nobleness and dignity of mind secured him a respect almost amounting to veneration. He is now styled the Hero of Upper Canada, and, had he lived, there is no doubt but the war would have terminated very differently from what it did. The Canadian farmers are not over-burthened with sensibility, yet I have seen several of them shed tears when an eulogium was pronounced upon the immortal and generous-minded deliverer of their country.

[‡] General Brock was killed close to the road that Lewiston.

8

more felt, as it includes amongst the killed the commanding general, who was also the Governor of the Province."

General Brock was interred on the 16th October, with his A.D.C., Col. McDonnell, at Fort George. Major Glegg says on the subject,—"Conceiving that an interment, in every respect military, would be the most appropriate, I made choice of a cavalier bastion which he had lately suggested, and which had just been finished under his daily superintendence."

On the morning after the battle, an armistice†
Armistice concluded the day after the battle. was concluded by Generals Van Ranselaer and Sheaffe. James, in reference to this proceeding, remarks,—"It is often said that we throw away with the pen, what we gain by the sword. Had General Brock survived the Queenston battle, he would have made the 13th October a still more memorable day by crossing the river and carrying Fort Niagara, which at that precise time was nearly stripped

of its garrison. Instead of doing this, and of putting an end to the campaign upon the Niagara frontier, General Sheaffe allowed himself to be persuaded to sign an armistice, the very thing General Van Ranselaer wanted. The latter, of course, assured his panic-struck militia, that the British General had sent to implore one of him; (rather a hasty conclusion this of James,) and that he, General Van Ranselaer, had consented, merely to gain time to make some necessary arrangements. Such of the militia as had not already scampered off, now agreed to suspend their journey homeward, and try another experiment at invasion."

When James penned the above, he did not take into consideration, that the number of American prisoners, then in General Sheaffe's charge, far exceeded the united strength of his whole army, when the Indian force was withdrawn; and, besides, that with his very limited means of defence, he had a frontier of forty miles to protect. He seems also to have lost sight of the fact that General Van Ranselaer retired from the command on the 18th

leads through Queenston village; this spot may be called classic ground, for a view of it must awaken in the minds of all those who duly appreciate the greatness of his character, and are acquainted with the nature of his resources and exertions, feelings as warm and enthusiastic as the contemplation of monuments consecrated by antiquity can ever do.

Nature had been very bountiful to Sir Isaac Brock in those personal gifts which appear to such peculiar advantage in the army, and at the first glance the soldier and the gentleman were seen. In stature he was tall, his fine and benevolent countenance was a perfect index of his mind, and his manners were courteous, frank, and engaging. Brave, liberal, and humane; devoted to his sovereign, and loving his country with romantic fondness; in command so gentle and persuasive, yet so firm, that he possessed the rare faculty of acquiring both the respect and the attachment of all who served under him. When urged by some friends, shortly before his death, to be more careful of his person, he replied: "How can I expect my men to go where I am afraid to lead them;" and although, perhaps, his anxiety ever to shew a good example, by being foremost in danger, induced him to expose himself more than strict prudence or formality warranted, yet, if he erred on this point, his error was that of a soldier. Elevated to the government of Upper Canada, he reclaimed many of the disaffected by mildness, and fixed the wavering by the argument of success; and having no national partialities to gratify, that rock on which so many provincial governors have split, he meted equal favor and justice to all.

† The armistice was to be in force only on the frontier between Lakes Ontario and Erie.

British-born subjects soon felt convinced that with him their religion or their birth-place was no obstacle in their advancement. Even over the minds of the Indians Sir Isaac Brock gained, at and after the capture of Detroit, an ascendency altogether unexampled, and which he judiciously exercised for purposes conducive equally to the cause of humanity and to the interests of his country. He engaged them to throw aside the scalping knife, implanted in their breasts the virtues of clemency and forbearance, and taught them to feel pleasure and pride in the compassion extended to a vanquished enemy. In return they revered him as their common father, and while under his command were guilty of no excesses. It is well known that this untutored people, the children of the forests, value personal much more highly than mental qualities, but the union of both in their leader was happily calculated to impress their haughty and masculine minds with respect and admiration; and the speech delivered by Tecumseh, after the capture of Detroit, is illustrative of the sentiments with which he had inspired these warlike tribes. "I have heard," observed that chief to him, "much of your fame, and am happy again to shake by the hand a brave brother warrior. The Americans endeavour to give us a mean opinion of British Generals, but we have been the witnesses of your valour. In crossing the river to attack the enemy, we observed you from a distance standing the whole time in an erect posture, and, when the boats reached the shore, you were among the first who jumped on land. Your bold and sudden movements frightened the enemy, and you compelled them to surrender to half their own force."

October. He (Gen. Van Ranselaer) seems indeed to have resolved on this course even two days before, for in his letter of the 16th, to General Sheaffe, he writes,—" As this is probably the last communication I shall have the honour to make to you," &c. This does not look much like entertaining hopes of a third descent on Canada. Christie's remarks are more deserving of consideration. In speaking of the armistice he writes:—" This and the former armistice, without affording any present advantage, proved of material prejudice to the British on Lake Erie. The Americans availed themselves of so favorable an occasion to forward their naval stores, unmolested, from Black Rock to Presque Isle, by water, which they could not otherwise have effected, but with immense trouble and expense, by land, and equipped at leisure the fleet which afterwards wrested from us the command of that lake." There is much force in these remarks, yet with a body of prisoners equalling in number his whole force, and with an enemy in front of double his strength, it is not to be wondered at, that General Sheaffe should have adopted prudent measures, so as to dispose, at least, of his prisoners.

Although it has been very generally acknowledged that the prisoners were treated with great kindness and consideration, yet a few misrepresentations have crept abroad on the subject. One writer (Author of Sketches of the War) says—" For want of will or power they put no restraint upon their Indian allies who were stripping and scalping not only the slain but the dying that remained on the field of battle," and in proof of his assertion he adduces the facts, that a Capt. Ogilvie recognised the corpse of an Ensign Morris, which had been stripped of its shirt, and a dead soldier whose scull had been cloven by a tomahawk; he forgets,however,or seems to consider it unnecessary, to enquire whether the ensign's shirt had not been stolen by one of his own men, or whether the soldier might not have received the fatal blow during the contest. We only bring these trifles forward to show how anxious to misrepresent some American writers have been, and how desirous to palliate the monstrous cruelties perpetrated by them

Treatment of the prisoners.

on the Indians during their long and numerous frontier wars.

Two days after the battle, the prisoners and wounded, both militia and regulars, were sent across the river, upon their parole, as were General Wadsworth, and (James says all, Christie some) the principal officers, the non-commissioned officers and privates of the regular army were sent to Montreal to await their exchange. Christie remarks on the subject,—" Among the American prisoners, twenty-three men were found, who, having declared themselves British-born subjects, were sent to England for trial as traitors."

Disposal of the prisoners.

This gave occasion to retaliate upon British prisoners in America, and a like number of the latter were put into close confinement as hostages for the safety of the traitors by order of the American government.

The attempts of the press to prevent the supporters of the now unpopular war from becoming disgusted with the manifold reverses which had, so far, attended all the military operations undertaken, would be amusing, were not a feeling, akin to contempt, excited. The Official Organ, corresponding to our Annual Register, or the Military and Naval Chronicle, appears at this time to have been " Nile's Weekly Register," and a few short exracts will show not only how, with General Van Ranselaer's dispatch before them, they misrepresented every occurrence, but how ignorant they actually were of the true position of the affairs on the frontier.

Attempts of the press to keep up the "war spirit" by misrepresentation.

In No. 9 of Vol. 3, we find the following particulars, page 140 :

" The landing appears to have been effected under a dreadful fire from the enemy. An instant appeal was made to the bayonet, and the British were soon dispossessed of all the advantages they had in the ground ;" no notice is taken of the manner in which Wool, " the hero of the day," as he is styled, ascended the heights without exposing himself or the troops under his command to a single shot. A little farther on, " three hundred and twenty men charged the famous 49th British Regiment, six hundred strong, and put them completely to flight," and as a crowning glory to the brilliant

achievements of the day, the afternoon occurrences are thus disposed of : " our men
though outflanked and *almost surrounded*,
fought for an hour and a half more; when,
worn down with eleven hours exertion, they
retreated without the loss of a man, to the
margin of the river, but to their extreme
mortification, not a boat was there to receive
them." Such gallantry deserved a better
fate, for after waiting in " this painful situation
for over a quarter of an hour, this GALLANT
little band surrendered to five times their
number." On page 141 we find that " the
position opposite Queenston *is Black Rock!*"
Enough, however, on this subject, although it
might have been expected that a paper,
almost bearing an official character, would
have scarcely dared to give publicity to such
ridiculous statements : statements which only
serve to show how strenuous were the efforts
made to prevent the refusal of the Militia to
cross at Lewiston, appearing in its true light,
viz. as a proof that the war was an unpopular
one.

We contend that the conduct of the greater
Refusal of the Militia to cross the Niagara River, another proof that the war was not as popular as represented. párt of the American
Militia on this occasion
may be fairly adduced
as an additional proof
that the war was far from being as popular as
one party in Congress would fain have represented it. It is notorious that many of the
Pennsylvania Militia refused to cross into
Canada, while others returned, after having
crossed the line, on constitutional pretexts.
An attempt has been made to excuse this, and
the argument has been brought forward that
the English Militia are not transported over
sea to Hanover, and that the French National
Guards and the German Landwehr are troops
appropriated to service within the country;
but on the other hand it should be borne in mind
that there are standing armies in these countries, and that there is none, or next to none,
in America, and that this doctrine is tantamount to a virtual renouncing of all offensive
operations in war, by that country where there
is but a regular standing force equal to
garrison duties, and destroys at once all
military operations.

The truth is, and American writers may
blink it or explain it as they please, that the

refusal to cross the border, on the plea of its
being unconstitutional, was one of the factious
dogmas of the war, preached by the disaffected
of Massachusetts, who imagined, doubtless,
that the doctrine might be very convenient
in the event of war in that region.

The Kentuckians marched anywhere, they
had no scruples; why ? Because the war was
popular with them, and they laughed at the
idea that it was unconstitutional to cross a
river or an ideal frontier, in the service of their
country.

Three or four days after the battle, General
Resignation of Gene-ral Van Ranselaer, and appointment of General Smyth. Van Ranselaer, disgusted
with the conduct of the
Militia, and, as he ex-
pressed it, with " being compelled to witness
the sacrifice of victory, so gallantly won, on the
shrine of doubt," received permission from
General Dearborn to retire, and the command
of the central or Niagara army devolved on
Brigadier General Smyth, an officer from
whose patriotic and professional pretensions,
the multitude had drawn many favorable conclusions. " Nor was," says General Armstrong,
" the estimate made of his military character by
the Government, more correct, as it took for
granted, a temperament, bold, ardent and
enterprising, and requiring only restriction to
render it useful." In the orders given for the
regulation of his conduct, he was accordingly
forbidden most emphatically by the minister
at war, " to make any new attempt at invasion with a force less than three thousand
combatants, or with means of transportation
(across the Niagara) insufficient to carry
over simultaneously the whole of that number."

Ingersol, in his notices of the war, observes,
" General Smyth closed the campaign of 1812,
in that quarter, by a failure much ridiculed,
and yet vindicated, at all events a miserable
abortion, which, in November, instead of
atoning for, much increased, our discredit of
October." Before, however, entering on the
subject of the invasion of Canada by General
Smyth, we must not omit two events which,
though not of importance, yet should not be
entirely lost sight of, as one especially was
made the subject of much boasting on the
part of the Americans.

The first of these events was the destruction

Destruction of part of the fortifications at Black Rock, and of the furs taken in the Caledonia.

of the east barracks at Black Rock, by the batteries at Fort Erie, under Lieut.-Col. Myers, and the burning of the furs which had formed part of the cargo of the Caledonia, the details of the capture of which we have already given. This was at least satisfactory, as the Americans had not failed in their accounts to give very magnificent estimates of the value of these same furs.

The second event was the capture on the

Capture of Canadian voyageurs.

21st October, of a body of forty-four Canadian voyageurs, who, under the command of Captain McDonnell, were surprised, and taken by the Americans under Major Young. Of this affair, James says, "The Major's force is not stated; but as the Americans proceeded to the attack in expectation of meeting from one to three hundred British, we may conjecture that their numbers fully equalled the latter amount. Forty prisoners, (one having escaped) along with their baggage and some immaterial despatches, fell into the hands of the Americans, who ingeniously enough converted a large pocket-handkerchief, which they found among the spoils, into a "stand of colours;" and Mr. O'Connor exultingly tells us, that "Major Young had the honor of taking the first standard from the enemy in the present war," following it up with, "the movements of the enemy, during these times, were not to them equally honorable or important."

We are without the means of ascertaining what was actually captured on this occasion by the enemy; the probability is, however, that some colours, a Union Jack perhaps, were captured. The handkerchief story is rather improbable even for American fertility of invention when national glory was at stake. One point we have ascertained, that whatever might have been captured, it certainly was not what is commonly termed "a stand of colours." Christie, in his notice of this affair, writes, "On the 23rd October, a party of nearly four hundred Americans from Plattsburgh, surprised the picquet at the Indian village of St. Regis. Twenty-three men, a lieutenant, a serjeant and six men were killed. The picquet consisted of Canadian voyageurs."

Christie's account bears out our statement respecting the colors. "In plundering the village they found a Union Jack or an Ensign, usually hoisted on Sundays or Holydays at the door of the Chief." "This occurrence," adds Christie, "was counterpoised by an attack upon a party of Americans near Salmon river, near St. Regis, on the 23rd November, by detachments of the Royal Artillery, 49th Regiment, and Glengarry Light Infantry, amounting to seventy men, with detachments from the Cornwall and Glengarry Militia, of near the same number, the whole under the command of Lieut.-Col. McMillan. In this affair the enemy took to a blockhouse, but finding themselves surrounded, surrendered prisoners of war. One captain, two subalterns, and forty-one men became prisoners on this occasion, and four batteaux, and fifty-seven stand of arms were taken." This was an affair so trifling that it would have been passed over did not the Americans make so much of the picquet affairs and the capture of the Detroit and Caledonia.

We find something quite Napoleonic in

General Smyth's proclamations.

the following proclamations of General Smyth —something deserving of the pen of an Abbott as the chronicler. Even the "audacious quackery" which dared to issue rescripts at St. Petersbourg for the management of the Opera in Paris, pales before General Smith's eloquent and spirited addresses. Fortunate, indeed, for the Canadas, that the General confined his operations to paper. The first of these productions was addressed "To the Men of New York," and revives the oft-repeated cry of oppression, &c.

"*To the Men of New York:*"

"For many years have you seen your country oppressed with numerous wrongs. Your Government, although above all others, devoted to peace, have been forced to draw the sword, and rely for redress of injuries on the valor of the American people.

"That valor has been conspicuous, but the nation has been unfortunate in the selection of some of those who directed it. One army has been disgracefully surrendered and lost. Another has been sacrificed by a precipitate attempt to pass it over at the strongest point of the enemy's lines, with most incompetent means. The cause of these miscarriages is apparent. The Commanders were popular men, "destitute alike of experience and theory," in the art of war.

"In a few days the troops under my command will plant the American standard in Canada. They are men accustomed to obedience,* steadiness and silence. They will conquer or die.

"Will you stand with your arms folded, and look on this interesting struggle? Are you not related to the men who fought at Bennington and Saratoga? Has the race degenerated? Or, have you, under the baneful influence of contending factions, forgotten your country? Must I turn from you, and ask the men of the Six Nations to support the Government of the United States? Shall I imitate the officers of the British King, and suffer our ungathered laurels to be tarnished with ruthless deeds? Shame, where is thy blush? No! Where I command, the vanquished and the peaceful man, the child, the maid, and the matron shall be secure from wrong. If we conquer, we conquer but to save."

"*Men of New York:*

"The present is the hour of renown. Have you not a wish for fame? Would you not choose to be named in future times, as one of those, who, imitating the heroes whom Montgomery led, have, in spite of the seasons, visited the tomb of the chief, and conquered the country where he lies? Yes! You desire your share of fame. Then seize the present moment: if you do not, you will regret it; and say ' the valiant have bled in vain; the friends of my country fell, and I was not there.'

"Advance, then, to our aid. I will wait for you a few days. I cannot give you the day of my departure. But come on. Come in companies, half companies, pairs or singly. I will organise you for a short tour. Ride to this place, if the distance is far, and send back your horses. But, remember, that every man

who accompanies us, places himself under my command, and shall submit to the salutary restraints of discipline." This proclamation was issued on the 17th; a second, which will be found below,* and was even more energetic than its predecessor, appeared, addressed "TO THE SOLDIERS OF THE ARMY OF THE CENTRE."

---

*"*Companions in arms!*—The time is at hand when you will cross the streams of Niagara to conquer Canada, and to secure the peace of the American frontier.

"You will enter a country that is to be one of the United States. You will arrive among a people who are to become your fellow citizens. It is not against them that we come to make war. It is against that government which holds them as vassals.

"You will make this war as little as possible distressful to the Canadian people. If they are peaceable, they are to be secure in their persons: and in their property, as far as our imperious necessities will allow.

"Private plundering is absolutely forbidden. Any soldier who quits his ranks to plunder on the field of battle, will be punished in the most exemplary manner.

"But your just rights as soldiers will be maintained; whatever is *booty* by the usages of war, you shall have. All horses belonging to the artillery and cavalry, all waggons and teams in public service, will be sold for the benefit of the captors. Public stores will be secured for the service of the U. States. The government will, with justice, pay you the value.

"The horses drawing the light artillery of the enemy are wanted for the service of the United States. I will order TWO HUNDRED DOLLARS for each to be paid the party who may take them. I will also order FORTY DOLLARS to be paid for the arms and spoils of each savage warrior, who shall be killed.

"*Soldiers!*—You are amply provided for war. You are superior in number to the enemy. Your personal strength and activity are greater. Your weapons are longer. The regular soldiers of the enemy are generally old men, whose best years have been spent in the sickly climate of the West Indies. They will not be able to stand before you, —you, who charge with the bayonet. You have seen Indians, such as those hired by the British to murder women and children, and kill and scalp the wounded. You have seen their dances and grimaces, and heard their yells. Can you fear them? No! you hold them in the utmost contempt.

Volunteers!—Disloyal and traitorous men have endeavoured to dissuade you from your duty. Sometimes they say, if you enter Canada, you will be held to service for five years. At others, they say, you will not be furnished with supplies. At other times, they say, that if you are wounded, the government will not provide for you by pensions. The just and generous course pursued by government towards the volunteers who fought at Tippecanoe, furnishes an answer to the last objection; the others are too absurd to deserve any.

---

* These very men accustomed to obedience, steadiness, and silence, formed a portion of the troops who had, that day four weeks, refused to cross, notwithstanding Judge Peck's and their general's intreaties, and this too, but a few days after using such threats against the general's life, if he refused to lead them over to Canada, and victory, as compelled him to adopt the measures which resulted in his defeat and their disgrace. Ed.

The very first step taken by General Smyth Invasion of Canada by General Smyth. in this operation was marked by a trick. It was necessary to give a thirty hours' notice of an intention to break off the armistice which had been concluded with General Sheaffe. This was accordingly done, but instead of the notice being given, as it ought, at head-quarters at Fort George, it was sent to the commanding officer at Fort Erie, on the extreme right of the British line. This was doubtless with a view of making the attack before succours could arrive from Fort George, which was thirty-six miles distant from Fort Erie.

No efforts had been left untried, not only to collect a large force, but to provide also the means of transportation. Six weeks had been consumed in these preparations, in drilling, equipping and organising, and the conditions imposed by Government as to numbers before an invasion should be attempted, had been strictly complied with, as a force, by his own admission, of two thousand three hundred and sixty men, FIT FOR DUTY, (exclusive of General Tannehill's brigade from Pennsylvania, of sixteen hundred and fifty strong,) now awaited General Smyth's orders : an engine of destruction, to be discharged (as will be seen with what terrible effect) against the devoted Canadians. To guard against the effects of such a "tornado bursting on Canadian shores, every provision had," according to Nile's Weekly Register, " been made by the British." These preparations, according to James, " consisted

" *Volunteers !*—I esteem your generous and patriotic motives. You have made sacrifices on the altar of your country. You will not suffer the enemies of your fame to mislead you from the path of duty and honor, and deprive you of the esteem of a grateful country. You will shun the *eternal infamy* that awaits the man, who having come within sight of the enemy, *basely* shrinks in the moment of trial.

" *Soldiers of every corps !*—It is in your power to retrieve the honor of your country and to cover yourselves with glory. Every man who performs a gallant action shall have his name made known to the nation. Rewards and honours await the brave. Infamy and contempt are reserved for cowards. Companions in arms ! You came to vanquish a valiant foe ; I know the choice you will make. Come on, my heroes ! And when you attack the enemy's batteries let your rallying word be, " *The Cannon lost at Detroit, or Death !*"
Alexander Smyth,
Brigadier-General Commanding.
Camp near Buffalo, 17th Nov., 1812.

of a detachment of eighty men of the 49th, under Major Ormsby, and about fifty of the Newfoundland regiment, under Capt. Whelan. The ferry, opposite Black Rock, was occupied by two companies of Militia, under Captain Bostwick." At a house on the Chippewa Road, distant about two and-a-half miles from Fort Erie, Lieut. Lamont of the 49th, with five-and-thirty rank and file, and Lieut. King R. A., with a three and six-pounder, and a few Militia artillerymen were stationed. There were also near the same spot two one-gun batteries, eighteen and twenty-four pounders, also under the command of Lieut. Lamont. A mile farther down the river, Lieut. Bartley, with two non-commissioned officers and thirty-five rank and file, occupied a post, and on Frenchman's Creek, Lieut. McIntyre commanded a party about seventy strong : this post was about four and-a-half miles from Fort Erie. Lieut. Col. Bishopp was at Chippewa, and under his immediate command were a battalion company of the 41st, a company of militia, and a small detachment of militia artillery ; Major Hate with a small detachment of militia, was stationed at no great distance. The whole force to guard a frontier of twenty miles, did not exceed, as will be seen from these figures, three hundred and sixty regulars, and two hundred and forty militia. This gives a force of but six hundred men, according to James, while Christie estimates the whole force as "nearly eleven hundred men." By what process Mr. Christie makes up his numbers we are rather at a loss to discover, as his account corresponds with James' in the enumeration of all the smaller detachments; and it is only by supposing that Col. Bishopp had a very large force at this time under his command, that his total can be arrived at, as certainly there was no time for the arrival of reinforcements from Fort George. Col. Kerby's and other veterans' statements, incline us to the belief that James' numbers are nearer the mark. This point is, however, unimportant, as not one half of even the troops mentioned by James were required on the occasion, or had any participation in the affair.

The demonstration was commenced by dispatching a marauding party on the night of the 27th, who succeeded in taking a few prisoners, destroying some public and private dwellings, and carrying and spiking four guns, viz., the two field-pieces, and two eighteen and twenty-four pounders.

The whole of this demonstration took place under cover of night, and the Americans had recrossed to the safe side of the river before daylight, and the arrival of Major Ormsby and Col. Bishopp with their several detachments, and the recrossing was effected so hastily that Captain King and some thirty-five men were left behind and became prisoners. Embold-ened by this negative success, General Smyth sent over in the afternoon of the 29th, a flag of truce to Col. Bishopp, with a summons to "pre-vent the unnecessary effusion of human blood by a surrender of Fort Erie, to a force so supe-rior as to render resistance hopeless." Col. Bishopp's answer to this was, " *Come, and take it !*" The answer was sent over by Capt. Fitz-gerald on whom the American General is said to have wasted both rhetoric and time, proving, doubtless very much to his own satisfaction, how plainly it was the British officer's duty to command a bloodless surrender of the post. There is every probability that Hull's sur-render of Detroit was quoted on this occasion, as a precedent, and a case strictly analogous.

The 28th closed with an order to the Ameri-can troops to disembark, with an assurance that "the expedition was only postponed until the boats should be put in a better state of prepa-ration." Much discussion now took place in the American camp, and on the 20th the troops were again ordered to hold themselves ready for crossing and conquest. This farce was repeated until the morning of the 1st, when it was de-cided by the American officers in council, that instead of conquering Canada, "an attempt which by precipitation might add to the list of defeats," it was advisable to disembark the troops and send them into winter quarters. Thus ended the third great invasion of Canada. The failure roused, as may be imagined, a per-fect storm of indignation against the poor Gen-eral, and this was the more violent as he had raised the nation's expectations to such a pitch by his manifestos, that failure was never con-templated. and the bitter pill was thus ren-dered still more unpalatable.

The official organ, already mentioned, of 19th December, thus notices the affair. " *Dis-aster upon disaster.* The old scenes of imbe-cility, treachery and cowardice, have been again displayed upon our frontier. With grief

and shame do we record that Smyth, who pro-mised so much, who centered in himself the generous confidence of strangers, of his friends, and government ; who was to convince the American people that all their Generals were not base, cowardly and treacherous ; even Smyth must be added to the catalogue of in-famy which began with the name of Hull. Our minds are depressed with shame, and our hands tremble with indignation, at this final prostration of all our dearest and fondest hopes. But we will endeavour to assume some calmness, while we state to our readers the disgraceful events that have occurred on the Niagara river."

Before quoting further, it may be well to re-mark, that this very journal in discussing the Queenston expedition, mentions it as "an affair to be classed with Bunker Hill," and gives a glowing account of General Van Ranselaer's reception at Albany after his retirement from the command. In the No. for Nov. 28th, page 202, we find the following : "There is a dis-position in many to attribute great blame to Major Gen. Van Ranselaer for the failure of his attack on Queenston on various grounds, but the General's official statement is before the public, and we shall not attempt to impeach it."

" *It is unpleasant to remark with what avi-dity some men, for mere party purposes, seize upon every little incident tending to throw discredit on the American army. Nay, not content with the naked facts as they are, they contrive to distort them into the most fright-ful shapes, and if the truth embellished will not make the story tell well, they curiously in-vent a few particulars to give it the needful graces.*"

It is not uninteresting to observe how entirely the writer of the above changed his opinion between Nov. 28th and Decr. 19th, and how an affair of which the General's account "was not to be impeached," at the former date, be-came by the latter an event to be "included in the catalogue of infamy which began with Hull."

It is ever thus, however, with distorted facts, and an indifference to truth, in preparing an historical narrative, is sure to end by the wri-ter's contradicting some statement previously laid down as incontrovertible.

A curious picture is given of Smyth's treat-ment by his "outraged countrymen." He was universally denounced as a coward and traitor; he was shot at several times, and was hooted through the streets of Buffalo. He was shifting his tent in every direction to avoid the indignation of the soldiers. Judge Grainger, MUCH TO HIS HONOR, refused to afford any shelter to Smyth, and every tavernkeeper declined the infamy of his company. Poor Smyth! —this treatment was experienced from the very men whom Judge Peck but six weeks before had upbraided for their cowardice. We suppose, however, that this behaviour of the populace is to be classed amongst the benefits resulting from a Democratical form of government. General Smyth's defence will be found below* with a few remarks on it by General Porter. These remarks led to a duel in which both parties behaved *most heroically.*

We suspect that the American people would have preferred a battle at Fort Erie to a private rencontre.

By an Act of Executive power, General Smyth was excluded from the regular army, and *deposed without a trial.* This proceeding was of course complained of, and a petition presented to the House of Representatives, who, however, referred it to the secretary at war, which was in fact delivering the lamb to the wolf, as the secretary was the arbitrary power complained of. This is a significant example of the mode in which justice is sometimes administered in free countries, and how the exe-

*GENTLEMEN,—Your letter of the 2d December is before me, and I answer it in the the the following manner:

On the 26th October, I ordered that 20 scows should be prepared for the transportation of artillery and cavalry, and put the carpenters of the army upon that duty.

By the 26th of November 10 scows were completed, and by bringing some boats from Lake Ontario, above the Falls of Niagara, the number was increased to 70.

I had, on the 12th Nov., issued an address to the men of New York, and perhaps 300 had arrived at Buffalo. I presumed that the regular troops, and the volunteers under Colonels Swift and McClure, would furnish 2350 men for duty; and of General Tannehill's brigade from Pennsylvania, reporting a total of 1650, as many as 412 had volunteered to cross into Canada. My orders were to "cross with 3000 men at once." I deemed myself ready to fulfil them.

Preparatory thereto, on the night of the 27th of November, I sent other two parties, one under Lieutenant-Colonel Bœrstler, the other under Captain King, with whom Lieutenant Angus, of the navy, at the head of a body of seamen, united. The first was to capture a guard and destroy a bridge about five miles below Fort Erie; the second party were to take and render useless the cannon of the enemy's batteries, and some pieces of light artillery. The first party failed to destroy the bridge—the second, after rendering unserviceable the light artillery, separated by misapprehension. Lieutenant Angus, the seamen, and a part of the troops, returned, with all the boats, while Captain King, Captain Morgan, Captain Sproul, Lieutenant Houston, and about 60 men remained. The party thus reduced, attacked, took, and rendered unserviceable two of the enemy's batteries, captured 34 prisoners, found two boats, in which Captain King sent the prisoners, and about half his party with the other officers; he himself remaining with thirty men, whom he would not abandon.

Orders had been given, that all the troops in the neighborhood should march, at reveillee, to the place of embarkation. A part of the detach-

ment sent in the night returned and excited apprehensions for the residue, about 250 men, under the command of Colonel Winder, suddenly put off in boats for the opposite shore; a part of this force had landed, when a force deemed superior, with one piece of artillery, was discovered; a retreat was ordered, and Colonel Winder's detachment suffered a loss of six killed and 18 wounded, besides some officers.

The general embarkation commenced as the troops arrived—but this being a first embarkation, the whole of the scows were occupied by about one third of the artillery, while about 800 regular infantry, about 200 twelve months' volunteers, under Colonel Swift, and about 200 of the militia who had volunteered for a few days, occupied all the boats that were ready. The troops then embarked, moved up the stream to Black Rock without loss, they were ordered to disembark and dine.

I had received from my commanding general an instruction in the following words—"In all important movements you will, I presume, consider it advisable to consult some of your principal officers." I deemed this equivalent to an order, and the movement important. I called for the field officers of the regulars, and twelve months' volunteers embarked. Colonel Porter was not found at the moment. These questions were put—Is it expedient NOW to cross? Is the force we have sufficient to conquer the opposite shore?

The first question was decided in the negative by Colonels Parker, Schuyler, Winder, Lieut.-Colonel Bœrstler, Coles, and Major Campbell; Colonel Swift alone gave an opinion for then crossing over.

The second question was not decided. Cols. Parker, Schuyler, Lieut.-Colonel Coles and Major Campbell were decidedly of opinion that the force was insufficient. Colonels Winder, Swift, Lieut.-Col. Bœrstler, and Captain Gilman deemed the force sufficient.

I determined to postpone crossing over until more complete preparation would enable me to embark the whole force at once, the counsel prescribed by my orders. The next day was spent in such preparation, and the troops were

cutive is often, that is, with popular opinion to back it, enabled to strike a blow and commit a wrong, which in a less free country would not be submitted to.

With respect to the behaviour of the British troops on this occasion, we would remark, that General Smyth's displays of force entirely failed to produce the effect he had desired, and that

it was unanimously decided at a council, held on the night of the 30th, composed of regular and militia officers, that "They did not consider a retreat at all necssary, nor a measure to be looked forward to, and that but a small reinforcement would enable them to repel any force which General Smyth might have it in his power to bring against their country.

---

ordered to be again at the place of embarkation at eight o'clock on the morning of the 30th of November. On their arrival they were sent into the adjacent woods, there to build fires and remain until three o'oclock A.M., of the 1st of Dec., when it was intended to put off two hours before day-light, so as to avoid the enemy's cannon in passing the position which it was believed they occupied below, to land above Chippewa, assault that place, and, if successful, march through Queenston for Fort George. For this expedition the contractor was called on to furnish rations for 2500 men for four days, when it was found he could furnish the pork, but not the flour; the deputy quarter-master called for 60 brrrels, and got but 35.

The embarkation commenced, but was delayed by circumstances, so as not to be completed until after daylight, when it was found the regular infantry, 688 men, the artillery, 177 men, Swift's volunteers, estimated at 236, companies of federal volunteers, under Captains Collins, Phillips, Allison, Moore, Maher, and Marshall, amounting to 276 men, commanded by Lieutenant-Colonel McClure, 100 men of Colonel Dobbin's militia, and a few men in a boat with General P. B. Porter, had embarked—the whole on board amounting, exclusive of officers, to 1465 men, or thereabouts; and it was two hours later than had been contemplated.

There were some groups of men not yot embarked; they were applied to, requested and ordered by the Brigade-Major to get into their boats —they did not. The number of these the Brigade Major estimated at about 150. It was probably greater.

It then became a question whether it was expedient to invade Canada in open daylight, with 1500 men, at a point where no reinforcement could be expected for some days. I saw that the number of the regular troops was declining rapidly—I knew that on them chiefly I was to depend.

I called together the officers commanding corps of the regular army, Colonel Parker being sick. Those present were Col. Porter of the artillery, Col. Schuyler, Col. Winder, and Lieut.-Col. Coles. I put to them this question—Shall we proceed ? They *unanimously* decided that we ought not.

I foresaw that the volunteers who had come out for a few days, would disperse—several of them on the evening of the 28th broke their muskets. I foresaw that the number of the regular troops would decrease; the measles and other diseases being amongst them; and they were now in tents in the month of December. I informed the officers that the attempt to invade Canada would not be made until the army was

reinforced; directed them to withdraw their troops, and cover their huts immediately.

You say that on Saturday every obstruction was removed, and that a landing might have been effected "without the loss of a single man." This proves you unacquainted with the occurrences of the day. Colonel Winder, in returning from the enemy's shore in the morning, lost a tenth part of his force, in killed and wounded. The enemy showed no more than 500 or 600 men, as estimated by Colonel Parker, and one piece of artillery, supposed a nine-pounder. That force we no doubt might have overcome, but not without loss; and that, from the great advantage the enemy would have had, might have been considerable.

To recapitulate—My orders were to pass into Canada with 3000 men *at once.* On the first day of embarkation, not more than 1100 men were embarked, of whom 400, that is, half the regular infantry, were exhausted with fatigue, and want of rest. On the second embarkation, only 1500 men were embarked, and these were to have put off immediately, and to have descended the river to a point where reinforcements were not to be expected. On both days, many of the regular troops were men in bad health, who could not have stood one day's march; who, although they were on the sick report, were turned out by their ardent officers.

The affair at Queenston is a caution against relying on crowds who go to the bank of Niagara to look on a battle as on a theatrical exhibition ; who, if they are disappointed of the sight, break their muskets; or, if they are without rations for a day, desert.

I have made you this frank disclosure without admitting your authority to require it, under the impression that you are patriotic and candid men; and that you will not censure me for following the cautious counsels of experience ; nor join in the senseless clamor excited against me by an interested man.

I have some reason to believe that the cautious counsel given by the superior officers of my command was good. From deserters, we learn that 2344 rations are issued daily on the frontiers, on the British side. Captain King, prisoner at Fort George, writes to an officer thus—"Tell our friends to take better care of themselves than it appears I have done."

I am, gentlemen, with great respect, your most obedient   ALEXANDER SMYTH,
                              Brigadier-General.

P.S.—It will be observed that the force *ready* could be no otherwise ascertained than by an *actual* embarkation—it being uncertain what portion of the volunteer force would embark.

The result of the attempt on Canada may be stated to have been, 1st. Grief and perplexity to the Washington Patriots, who were, with the exception of General Porter,† safe at home. 2ndly. The acquirement of the nickname of General Van Bladder by General Smyth, a token of remembrance of his brave efforts on paper, from his admiring and grateful countrymen. 3rdly. A lesson to admonish the American Government that the fidelity of Canadians towards the British Government and constitution was too deeply seated, founded on too immovable a basis to be shaken by any efforts of a foreign power, however popular. 4thly. Additional proofs, if such were required, to the American nation, that the war-feeling was popular only with a small portion of the Union.

Effects of this failure at invasion.

The first demonstration of this feeling occurred in the resolutions passed in the Legislature of Maryland, a short time after General Smyth's defeat.

In the preamble to these resolutions it is most emphatically laid down that " War resorted to without just cause must inevitably provoke the Almighty Arbitor of the universe; produce a boundless waste of blood and treasure ; demoralise the habits of the people ; give birth to standing armies, and clothe a dominant faction with power, in addition to to the inclination, to infringe the dearest privileges of freemen, to violate the constitution by implications and by new definitions of treason under the mask of law, and to subject to persecution, perhaps to punishment, citizens whose only crime was an opposition fairly, honestly, and constitutionally based on the system of the national administration."

In reference to the operations which had actually taken place, the preamble thus continues,—"To obviate the immediate and oppressive difficulties of the crisis thus induced, militia and volunteers are subjected to field and garrison duty, and called upon to supply the deficiency of regulars,—enormous sums are to be raised by loans and taxes, and a neighbouring colony of the enemy is invaded by detachments of undisciplined troops imperfectly supplied with necessaries. Under such circumstances, folly can only expect success; and should further defeat, disgrace and dismay, accompany our military operations the gloomy anticipations of an unnatural alliance with the conqueror of Continental Europe will inevitably be indulged. Thus embarked in a disastrous contest, the nation, harassed and debilitated by its continuance, will sigh for peace, and for its attainment the immediate and important object contended for must be abandoned." After this preamble, or rather this extract from it, for the original is too long for us to do more than give the sense of it. Several resolutions were passed, all reflecting strongly upon the injustice of the war, and the culpability of its supporters. It is unnecessary, however, for our purpose to do more than quote the following:—

"Influenced by these considerations, the constituents of Maryland, conceive it to be an imperious duty to express, through their representatives, their opinion relative to the present state of public affairs.

Resolution 2.—"That an offensive war is incompatible with the principles of republicanism, subversive to the ends of all just government, and repugnant to the best interests of the United States."

BUFFALO, Dec. 8.

A friend has just handed me the proof sheet of your paper of this morning, in which is contained what purports to be General Smyth's *official* account of the affairs of the 28th of November and 1st of December.

I beg you will suspend the publication so long as to assure the public that, in your next, I will give a *true* account of some of the most prominent transactions of those days.

When our lives, our property; when the precious and dear-bought gift of our ancestors—the sacred honour of our country; when everything

† No one would have imagined, after reading General Porter's war speech. that he intended really to expose himself to danger. Boasters rarely do.

that we prize as men, or ought to hold dear as patriots, are falling and fading before us, it is time to speak out, whatever be the hazard.

In ascribing, as I shall not hesitate to do, the late disgrace on this frontier, to the cowardice of General Smyth, I beg it to be understood as not intending to implicate the characters of the officers whose opinions he has brought forward to bolster up his conduct. *Several* of them I know to be as brave men as ever wielded a sword; and their advice, if indeed they gave the advice imputed to them, may be accounted for in the obvious consideration, with which every one who *saw* him must have been impressed, that any military attempt under such a commander, must, in all human probability, prove disgraceful.

PETER B. PORTER.

Resolution 3.—"That the declaration of war against Great Britain by a small majority of the Congress of the United States, was unwise and impolitic, and if unsuccessful, the grand object contended for must be abandoned."

Resolution 5.—"That the conduct of the Governors of Massachussetts, Connecticut and Rhode Island, respecting the quota of militia demanded from them, (*and refused*,) respectively, by the Secretary of War of the United States, was constitutional, and merits our decided approbation."

These resolutions passed on the 2nd January were strong, but are weak in comparison with Mr. Quincy's speech; in the House of Representatives, on the 15th. Mr. Quincy declares " that the invasion of Canada gave new strength to the British Ministers at the late elections," that " the British people were ready to meet Americans on principle, (here was an admission,) but when they saw that we grasped at the first opportunity to carry the war among their harmless colonists, sympathy enlisted them on the side of the latter, and produced an effect upon their temper, such as might readily be imagined."

That "even before war was declared, our armies were marching on Canada."

That "It was not owing to our Government, that the bones of the Canadians were not mixed with the ashes of their habitations," (another important admission,) that "since the invasion of the Buccaneers, there was nothing in history more disgraceful than this war."

After the assertion of these great facts which we have picked out from the speech, Mr. Quincy continues, "I have conversed on the subject with men of all ranks, conditions, and parties, men hanging from the plough and on the spade; the twenty, thirty, and fifty acre men, and their answers have uniformly been to the same effect. They have asked simply, what is the Invasion for? Is it for land? We have enough. Plunder? there is none there. New States? we have more than is good for us. Territory? if territory, there must be a standing army to keep it, and there must then be another standing army at home to watch that. These are judicious, honest, sober, patriotic men, who, if it were requisite,

and their sense of moral duty went along with the war, would fly to the standard of their country at the winding of a horn, but who heard it now with the same indifference as they would a Jew's harp or a Banjoe, because they were disgusted with the war, and the mode of carrying it on. In conclusion, that the invasion of Canada was cruel, as it brought fire and sword amongst an innocent, unoffending people—wanton because it could produce no imaginable good—senseless, as to this country, because it commences a system, which once begun, can never be closed, and the army of invasion will be the conquerors of home—and wicked because it is perverting the blessings and beneficence of God to the ruin of his creatures."

These extracts sufficiently establish our position, to ascertain that the war of 1812 was considered by the majority of the citizens of the Union as unnecessary, impolitic, and, with reference to the interests of the country, almost suicidal. These and subsequent debates almost justify the opinions entertained by some writers of that day, who did not hesitate to declare that a continuance of the war must lead to a disruption of the Union.

Although success had as yet attended the British arms, the aspect of affairs was still very threatening, both on the western frontier and in Lower Canada. Generals Harrison and Winchester, with a large force, overawed Detroit and the lately acquired Michigan territory, and General Dearborn, with ten thousand men, hovered on the confines of Lower Canada. A temporary check was given in the west by the defeat and capture of General Winchester at the River Raisin, and General Harrison's vigorous and spirited arrangements for the re-occupancy of the Michigan territory were somewhat disconcerted in consequence, but still Col. Proctor's situation was very critical, and the force under his command was wholly inadequate to the arduous and important duties which he was required to perform in the presence of an adversary triple his strength.

A short account of the engagements at the River Raisin and other points along that line, will not, perhaps, be found unnecessary or uninteresting, and we will continue to observe

Position of affairs on the Detroit and Lower Canadian frontiers.

the plan laid down, that is, to give first a short British account, and then to append the American version. The first movement in this quarter seems to have been directed against the Indians, and Mr. Thompson's (American) history shows a sickening detail of numerous Indian villages destroyed, and atrocities committed against the "wretched people whose civilization the United States Government was so anxious to promote." James has here a remarkable passage which we give entire.

"The spirit of party is often a valuable friend to the cause of truth. While the Democrats laboured at glossing over, the Federalists employed equal industry in rummaging every dusty corner for materials that might expose the odious measures of the Government. That they sometimes succeeded, appears from the following extract taken from an old newspaper, published at Pittsburgh, in the United States:—

"We, the subscribers, encouraged by a large subscription, do propose to pay one hundred dollars for every hostile Indian scalp, with both ears, if it be taken between this date and the 15th day of June next, by an inhabitant of Alleghanny County.

Signed,   G. WALLIS,
                   R. ELLIOTT,
                   W. AMBUSON,
                   A. TAUMHILL,
                   W. WILKINS. Junr.
                   J. IRVINE.

Mr. James continues, "A general officer of the United States, employed against the Indians, at the very outset of the war, inadvertently writes to a friend,—'The western militia always carry into battle a tomahawk and scalping knife, and are as dexterous in the use of them as any copper-colored warriors of the forest. Eight hundred tomahawks have been furnished by the war department to the north western army.' "

We know that these implements of civilised warfare were employed, for the American Government paper, the National Intelligencer, in reference to the Heroes of Brownstown states, "They bore triumphantly on the points of their bayonets, between thirty and forty fresch scalps, which they had taken on the field." We know farther that Logan and seven hundred warriors were in the pay of the United States, and we cannot help turning away with disgust and indignation at the cool impudence which characterizes nearly every American writer on this point. However, to return to our narrative. On the 17th Jan., General Winchester dispatched Col. Lewis with a considerable body against a party of British and Indians posted at Frenchtown. This party consisted of thirty of the Essex militia, and two hundred Pottawattamies. Major Reynolds, who commanded, after a sharp conflict, in which the Americans lost, by their own showing, twelve killed, and fifty-five wounded, retreated, and Col. Lewis, occupied the ground and maintained his position till he was joined on the 20th by General Winchester.

The United force now, according to Dr. Smith, another American writer, formed a division ONE THOUSAND STRONG, and consisted of the greater part of Col. Wells' regiment of United States Infantry—the 1st and 5th Kentucky regiments, and Col. Allen's rifle-regiment, forming the flower of the north-western army. We have here another proof of the advantage afforded to the British by the petty jealousy which exised between the American commanders, and which often compensated for inferiority of force. General Winchester piqued at General Harrison's promotion over him, and having ascertained the inferior number and motley character of Col Proctor's force, was anxious to engage before Gen. Harrison's joining, in order to monopolise the glory and honor to be acquired. Col. Proctor advanced on the 21st, and on the 22nd attacked General Winchester in his encampment. The British force, according to Christie, consisted of five hundred regulars, seamen, and militia, with about six hundred Indians. A severe contest now ensued, which resulted in the complete defeat and unconditional surrender of the Americans. The British loss may be estimated at twenty-four killed, and one hundred and fifty-eight wounded—that of the enemy at nearly four hundred killed and wounded, and the capture of the remainder.

The despatches of the respective commanding officers will follow in order. A vote of thanks was passed by the Assembly of Lower Canada to Col. Proctor and the troops, both regulars and militia, who had so gallantly conducted themselves. Col. Proctor was also promoted to the rank of Brigadier-General, by the commander of the forces, until the pleasure of the Prince-Regent should be known, who approved and confirmed the appointment.

From General Proctor to Major General Sheaffe.

Sandwich, January, 26th. 1813.

Sir,—In my last despatch I acquainted you that the enemy was in the Michigan Territory, marching upon Detroit, and that I therefore deemed it necessary that he should be attacked without delay, with all and every description of force within my reach. Early in the morning, on the 19th, I was informed of his being in possession of Frenchtown, on the River Raisin, twenty-six miles from Detroit, after experiencing every resistance that Maj Reynolds, of the Essex militia, had it in his power to make, with a three-pounder, well served and directed by bombardier Kitson of the royal artillery, and the militia, three of whom he had well trained to the use of it. The retreat of the gun was covered by a brave band of Indians, who made the enemy pay dear for what he had obtained. This party, composed of militia and Indians, with the gun, fell back, sixteen miles to Brown's Town, the settlement of the brave Wyandots, where I directed my force to assemble. On the 21st instant, I advanced twelve miles to Swan Creek, from whence we marched to the enemy, and attacked him at break of day on the 22nd instant, and after suffering, for our numbers, a considerable loss, the enemy's force, posted in houses and enclosures, and which, from dread of falling into the hands of the Indians, they most obstinately defended, at length surrendered at discretion; the other part of their force in attempting to retreat by the way they came, were, I believe, all or with very few exceptions, killed by the Indians. Brigadier General Winchester was taken in the pursuit, by the Wyandot Chief Roundhead, who afterwards surrendered him to me.

You will perceive that I have lost no time; indeed, it was necessary to be prompt in my movements, as the enemy would have been joined by Major-General Harrison in a few days. The troops, the marine, and the militia, displayed great bravery, and behaved uncommonly well. Where so much zeal and spirit were manifested, it would be unjust to attempt to particularize any: I cannot however refrain from mentioning Lieut. Colonel St. George, who received four wounds in a gallant attempt to occupy a building which was favorably situated to annoy the enemy; together with Ensign Carr, of the Newfoundland regiment, who, I fear, is very dangerously wounded. The zeal and courage of the Indian Department were never more conspicuous than on this occasion, and the Indian warriors fought with their usual bravery. I am much indebted to the different departments, the troops having been well and timely supplied with every requisite the district could afford.

I have fortunately not been deprived of the services of Lieutenant Troughton, of the royal artillery, and acting in the Quarter-Master-Generals department although he was wounded, to whose zealous and unwearied exertions I am greatly indebted, as to the whole of the royal artillery for their conduct in this affair.

I enclose a list of the killed and wounded, and cannot but lament that there are so many of both; but of the latter, I am happy to say, a large proportion of them will return to their duty, and most of them in a short time: I also enclose a return of the arms and ammunition which have been taken, as well as of the prisoners, whom you will perceive to be equal to my utmost force, exclusive of the Indians.

It is reported that a party, consisting of one hundred men, bringing five hundred hogs to General Winchester's force, has been completely cut off by the Indians, and the convoy taken. Lieutenant McLean, my acting Brigade-Major, whose gallantry and exertions were conspicuous on the 22nd instant, is the bearer of this despatch, and will be able to afford you every information respecting our situation.

I have the honor to be,
Yours,
H. Proctor.

The list of killed and wounded given by Colonel Proctor, corresponds with that we have given, although obtained from a different source, Major Richardsons work.—We now give General Winchester's letter to the American Minister at war :—

Sir,—A detachment of the left wing of the North-Western army, under my command, at Frenchtown, on the River Raisin, was attacked on the 23rd instant, by a force greatly superior in numbers, aided by several pieces of artillery.

The action commenced at the dawn of day : the picquet guards were driven in, and a heavy fire opened upon the whole line, by which part thereof was thrown into disorder; and being ordered to form on more advantageous ground, I found the enemy doubling our left flank with force and rapidity.

A destructive fire was sustained for some time ; at length borne down by numbers, the few of us that remained with the party retired from the lines, and submitted. The remainder of our force, in number about 400, continued to defend themselves with great gallantry, in an unequal contest against small arms and artillery, until I was brought in as a prisoner to that part of the field occupied by the enemy.

At this latter place, I understood that our troops were defending themselves in a state of desperation; and I was informed by the commanding officer of the enemy, that he would afford them an opportunity of surrendering themselves prisoners of war, to which I acceded. I was the more ready to make the surrender from being assured, that unless done quickly, the buildings adjacent would be immediately set on fire, and that no responsibility would be taken for the conduct of the savages, who were then assembled in great numbers.

In this critical situation, being desirous to preserve the lives of a number of our brave fellows who still held out, I sent a flag to them, and agreed with the commanding officer of the enemy, that they should be surrendered prisoners of war, on condition of their being protected from the savages, and being allowed to retain their private property, and having their side-arms returned to them. It is impossible for me to ascertain, with certainty, the loss we have sustained in this action, from the impracticability of knowing the number who have made their escape.

Thirty-five officers, and about four hundred and eighty-seven non-commissioned officers and privates, are prisoners of war. A list of the names of officers is herewith enclosed to you. Our loss in killed is considerable.

However unfortunate may seem the affair of yesterday, I am flattered by the belief that no material error is chargeable upon myself, and that still less censure is deserved by the troops I had the honor of commanding.

With the exception of that portion of our force which was thrown into disorder, no troops have ever behaved with more determined intrepidity.

I have the honor to be with high respect,

Your obedient Servant,

JAMES WINCHESTER,

Brig.-Gen. U. S. Army.

Hon. Secretary at War.

N. B. The Indians have still a few prisoners in their possession, who, I have reason to hope, will be given up to Colonel Proctor, at Sandwich.

James Winchester, Brig.-Gen.

From Major-General Harrison, to Governor Shelby.

Camp on Carrying Rock, 15 miles from the Rapids, January 24th, 1813.

MY DEAR SIR,—I send Colonel Wells to you, to communicate the particulars (as far as we are acquainted with them) of an event that will overwhelm your mind with grief, and fill your whole state with mourning.

The greater part of Colonel Wells's regiment, United States Infantry, and the 1st and 5th regiments Kentucky Infantry, and Allen's rifle regiment, under the immediate orders of General Winchester have been cut to pieces by the enemy, or taken prisoners. Great as the calamity is, I still hope that, as far as it relates to the objects of the campaign, it is not irreparable. As soon as I was informed of the attack upon General Winchester, about 12 o'clock on the 22nd instant, I set out to overtake the detachment of Kentucky troops, that I had sent that morning to reinforce him, and I directed the only regiment that I had with me to follow. I overtook Major Robb's detachment at the distance of six miles; but before the troops in the rear could get up, certain information was received of General Winchester's total defeat.

A council of war was called, and it was the unanimous opinion of the Generals Payne and Perkins, and all the field officers, that there was no motive that could authorize an advance but that of attacking the enemy, and that success was not to be expected after a forced march of forty miles against an enemy superior in number, and well provided with artillery. Strong detachments of the most active men were, however, sent forward on all the roads, to assist and bring in such of our men as had escaped. The whole number that reached our camp does not exceed thirty, amongst whom were Major M'Clannahan and Captain Claves.

Having a large train of heavy artillery, and stores coming on this road from W. Sandusky, under an escort of four companies, it was thought advisable to fall back to this place, for the purpose of securing them. A part of it arrived last evening, and the rest is within thirty miles. As soon as it arrives, and a rein-forcement of three regiments from the Virginia and Pennsylvania brigades, I shall again advance, and give the enemy an opportunity of measuring their strength with us once more.

Colonel Wells will communicate some circumstances, which, while they afflict and surprise, will convince you that Kentucky has lost none of her reputation for valor, for which she is famed. The detachment to the River Raisin was made without my knowledge or consent, and in direct opposition to my plans. Having been made, however, I did everything in my power to reinforce them, and a force exceeding by three hundred men that which General Winchester deemed necessary, was on its way to join him, and a fine battalion within fourteen miles of its destination.

After the success of Colonel Lewis, I was in great hopes that the post could be maintained. Colonel Wells will communicate my further views to you, much better than I can do in writing at this time.

I am, dear Sir, &c.

W. H. HARRISON,

His Excellency Governor Shelby.

The rapidity of Col. Proctor's movements, after the affair at Frenchtown, assisted, even more than the victory, to embarass and puzzle Gen. Harrison, and breathing space, a most desirable object, was gained by Gen. Proctor and his gallant little band, while the intention of the Americans, to throw the onus of their support during the winter on the Canadians, was completely defeated. Except one or two trifling demonstrations, scarcely amounting to a movement, nothing of importance occurred in this quarter until April. We will return, therefore, to the Lower Province and General Dearborn, whom we left threatening, with an army, ten thousand strong, our frontier. We

find, however, that, excepting two unim-portant affairs, there is nothing to record. Early in February, Capt. Forsythe with two companies of riflemen crossed from Ogdens-burg, and made a descent upon Gannanoque, and, according to the Americans, surprised the whole British force, killing a great many, cap-turing six officers, fifty-two men and immense* quantities of arms and ammunition, besides rescuing a good many prisoners. A few words will put the matter in its true light. The vil-lage consisted of one tavern and a saw-mill, with one small hut temporarily used by Col. Stone of the militia, on whom devolved the responsibility of guarding faithfully the immense military stores here deposited, which consisted of two kegs of powder and one chest containing thirty muskets. The killed amounted to one. The list of wounded to the same number. This unfortunate, ac-cording to James, was Mrs. Stone, who, while she lay in bed, was fired at, through a window, by some miscreant, and dangerously wounded.

It appears, doubtless, extraordinary, why Causes of General Dearborn's inaction. General Dearborn, who had full authority from the war department to employ troops of any or every sort, and to do whatever he thought necessary for action, and whose orders to act offensively as soon as possible, were positive, should have remained so long inactive, exhibiting even a torpor in his movements. Ingersol, on this subject has—"It was General Dearborn's misfortune to have an army to form, an inexperienced, not over ardent Exe-cutive, a secretary at war constrained to resign, a Senate inclined to distrust the Exe-cutive, Congress withholding taxes and sup-plies for nearly twelve months after war was declared, a country destitute of military means, and men unaccustomed to restraint, anx-ious for display—" All these causes com-bined, form no excuse for General Dear-born. We have seen how Sir George Prevost, who laboured under all these disadvantages, besides the still greater one of being pre-cluded, by the critical position in which Great Britain was then placed, from even a hope of being reinforced, has been con-demned. We cannot afford, then, any sym-pathy to Gen. Dearborn.

*Sketches of the war.

CHAPTER IX.

We concluded our last chapter with the observation that " we could find no grounds for sympathy with General Dearborn," and farther consideration of the subject induces us to bring forward additional reasons in support of that assertion.

<small>Causes of General Dearborn's and other failures considered further.</small>

We have already shown that General Dearborn was, (if we may so express it) his own master, and almost unfettered by instructions, during the entire autumn of 1812. He had ample time, with adequate means to prepare an army of five or six thousand strong, whom, if it had been only to keep them healthy, it would have been better to put in motion. The English Generals had many greater difficulties to contend with, in defending Canada, than the Americans to conquer it. Buonaparte's career in Italy, and Wellington's in Spain, began with, and overcame, much greater disadvantages, and so it ever will be, a true General must struggle against prejudices and hindrances, inflicted by his own constituents, and look on them as things to be overcome, and harder of achievement than the mere subduing the troops opposed to him. The American commanders were not men of this stamp, and, in consequence, the exfoliation of Generals during the first campaign was excessive, and allowing all indulgence for the novelty of their position, and perhaps the difficulty of sustaining themselves, it was right not only that they should be superseded, but it was also just that they should be censured. The campaign of 1812 ended in a total eclipse of American military pretensions, without leaving one lingering gleam of hope, and the commander-in-chief's inactivity, tantamount to miscarriage, afflicted the friends of the war with the conviction that they were doomed to defeat.

Some of Ingersol's conclusions on this subject are so remarkable as to claim notice, for the extreme ingenuity evinced in finding out good reasons for being beaten, and in showing that Americans were not vanquished by the prowess of their adversaries, but that, "encountering on the threshold of Canada only such insignificant obstacles as Voyageurs, traders, travellers and Indians, animated with but a faint spirit of resistance to invasion," they were conquered by the inactivity and poltroonery of their commanders alone. The same writer adds, "A man of talent leading our armies to Montreal, as might have been done in 1812, would have probably, brought the war to an end that year. England was completely surprised and unprepared for it. Such a General at Detroit, Niagara or Champlain as would have driven the English beyond Montreal, might have produced immediate peace. Hull and Dearborn, and executive inefficiency were answerable for prolonging the war, the vigorous and successful commencement of which might have creditably closed it soon

9

after it had begun. The feeling of haughty power did not then stimulate Great Britain, which followed the 'downfall of Napoleon. The time for war was fortunate for us, our chance of success was good, had either the Government or its agents in command made the most of the opportunity."

Ingersol winds up his lamentation by observing that Dearborn "discouraged *probably by militia disaffection*, (when he should with his regular forces have established himself at Isle aux Noix for the winter, at least threatening Montreal, if not making good his way there, and holding it, and such success would have rallied thousands to his standard), fell back after a failure—the climax of our military degradation."

These remarks are doubtless very satisfactory to subjects of the United States, but we question whether they will be found equally convincing by those who have enquired into the feelings which animated the Colonists at that time, or, from study of history, are enabled to judge of the determined resistance which a body of men, united, in heart and hand, can offer to an invading force. We, however, entered so fully, in a previous chapter, on this subject, that we think it unnecessary to dwell at greater length on it, or to do more than remind the reader that the failure of the attempts at invasion "were mainly brought about through the gallant resistance of the very colony which was regarded by its invaders as likely to prove an easy conquest, in consequence of the disloyalty vainly imagined to lurk in its heart." Ingersol justly observes, "England was completely unprepared for the war," but we deny the conclusion he arrives at from that circumstance, "that the conquest of Canada was therefore an easy one," and American failures only attributable to the want of capacity in the commanders. We contend that every incident of the war goes to disprove this, the numerical superiority of the Americans in point of numbers, was on all occasions so great as fully to compensate for any alleged inferiority of commanders. The solution of the question is to be found in the justice of their cause. This it was which nerved Canadian arms, and enabled them to overcome an invading force so immeasurably superior.

With the exception of a few hastily planned movements at Prescott, Ogdensburg and Elizabethtown (now Brockville,) no event of importance occurred during the first three months of 1813. There are, however, a few circumstances connected with these demonstrations with which the reader should not be left unacquainted, as one of them in particular was made the peg on which to hang the usual amount of misrepresentation to be found in most American despatches.

Demonstrations on St. Lawrence.

The River St. Lawrence affords, in its frozen state, during the early part of the year, an easy and safe mode of transit from the American to the Canadian shores, and advantage was taken of this by Capt. Forsythe, who commanded a detachment of United States riflemen at Ogdensburgh, to despatch marauding parties across who did not confine their operations to the destruction of public property, but exercised considerable severity towards the unarmed inhabitants.

A nocturnal predatory expedition, which has been thought worthy of being ranked amongst the "brilliant achievements" of American valour, took place on the 6th February. General Armstrong in his "notices of the war" says, "Forsythe, with two companies of rifle corps in sleighs, ascended the St. Lawrence from Ogdensburg to Elizabethtown on the Canada shore, surprised the British guard, made fifty-two prisoners, (among whom were the Major, three Captains and two Lieutenants), liberated sixteen deserters, and made prize of one hundred and forty muskets and a considerable quantity of ammunition without losing a man of his party." This statement, officially made, was of course highly gratifying and consolatory to the American public; in James' version, however, the affair assumes a different aspect. "After wounding a militia sentry, the houses in the village, the gaol not omitted, were ransacked and the male inhabitants to the number of fifty-two were carried off. Several of these, as in the United States, held commissions in the militia." This circumstance, according to James, was a fortunate one, and "the American public was, a few days afterwards, officially told of the capture, in a very gallant manner, of a British guard consisting of fifty-two men, including two Majors, three Captains, and two Lieutenants (*of militia not added.*) One circumstance, connected with this affair, will place it in its proper light.   Major McDonnell of the Glengarry fencibles was despatched with a flag of truce to remonstrate with the American commander about "the depredations committed by the parties under his command." This remonstrance, James adds, was met with "insolence, taunts and boastings," and a challenge to the British officers to meet the Americans on the ice. This challenge could not then be complied with, as Sir George Prevost declined to sanction the proceedings, assigning as his reason, "that he did not wish, by any offensive acts of the sort, to keep alive a spirit of hostility."

This predatory attack was, however, ere long, punished by the attack on Ogdensburgh, which was made on the 22nd, under the command of Major McDonnell, and resulted in the capture of a quantity of ordnance, marine and commercial stores, together with four officers and seventy privates. Two barracks, two armed schooners, and two gun boats were also destroyed. This attack was made under a heavy fire from the American batteries, at the cost of eight killed and fifty-two wounded. Major McDonnell's dispatch* clearly shows

the actual strength of the party under his command, yet, Mr. Thomson, in his sketches of the war, does not scruple to fix the British force at two columns "of six hundred men each," and to represent (without condescending to particulars) Forsythe's party as very inferior in point of numbers, omitting any mention of the prisoners, guns, stores and, destruction of barracks. We must here correct James, who says, "still the total silence of all the other American historians entitles Mr. Thomson to some credit for the account he has given of the attack on Ogdensburg." We deny that Mr. Thomson is entitled to any credit, even on this score, as General Armstrong in his notices has "the British commander retaliated, (for the Elizabeth affair,) by a visit on the 22nd to Ogdensburg, drove Forsythe out of the place, killing and wounding about twenty of his men, and capturing a quantity of provisions and stores, with six pieces of artillery." We doubt further whether Mr. Thomson would have alluded to the affair at all, had it not been so direct a sequence to the attack on Elizabethtown, to which he has attached so much importance. We may, perhaps, be unjust in denying even this credit to Mr. Thomson, but his whole work proves that, wherever he could, he has never hesitated to double the

---

* *From Major Macdonnell, to Sir G. Prevost.*
Prescott, February 23, 1813.

Sir,—I have the honour to acquaint you, for the information of his excellency the commander of the forces, that, in consequence of the commands of his excellency to retaliate, under favorable circumstances, upon the enemy, for his late wanton aggressions on this frontier, I this morning, about 7 o'clock, crossed the river St. Lawrence upon the ice, and attacked and carried, after a little more than an hour's action, his position in and near the opposite town of Ogdensburg, taking eleven pieces of cannon, and all his ordnance, marine, commissariat, and quarter-master-general's stores, four officers and 70 prisoners, and burning two armed schooners, and two large gun-boats, and both his barracks.

My force consisted of about 480 regulars and militia, and was divided into two columns: the right commanded by Captain Jenkins, of the Glengary light infantry fencibles, was composed of his own flank company, and about 70 militia; and, from the state of the ice, and the enemy's position in the old French fort, was directed to check his left, and interrupt his retreat, whilst I moved on with the left column, consisting of 120 of the king's regiment, 40 of the royal Newfoundland corps and about 200 militia, towards his position in the town, where he had posted his heavy field artillery.

The depth of the snow in some degree retarded the advance of both columns, and exposed them, particularly the right, to a heavy cross fire from the batteries of the enemy, for a longer period than I had expected ; but pushing on rapidly after the batteries began to open upon us, the left column soon gained the right bank of the river, under the direct fire of his artillery and line of musketry, posted on an eminence near the shore; moving on rapidly my advance, consisting of the royal Newfoundland and some select militia, I turned his right with the detachment of the king's regiment, and after a few discharges from his artillery, took them with the bayonet, and drove his infantry through the town ; some escaping across the Black river into the fort, but the majority fled to the woods, or sought refuge in the houses, from whence they kept such a galling fire, that it was necessary to dislodge them with our field-pieces, which now came up from the bank of the river, where they had stuck, on landing, in the deep snow.

Having gained the high ground on the brink of the Black river, opposite the fort, I prepared to carry it by storm ; but the men being quite exhausted, I procured time for them to recover breath, by sending in a summons, requiring an unconditional surrender. During these transactions, Captain Jenkins had gallantly led on his column, and had been exposed to a heavy fire of seven guns,

British, and represent the Americans as "whipping their enemies" under the most adverse circumstances that the creative mind of an American historian could conjure up.

Having disposed of these affairs we shall proceed to examine, before entering on the naval part of the history, into the position of both parties, their relative strength, and the plans formed by the American Government.

During the first quarter of the year 1813, the government at Washington had made the most strenuous efforts to prepare for opening, with vigor, the campaign. Ample reinforcements and supplies had been forwarded. To begin: we find, according to Armstrong, "that within district No. 9, commanded by General Dearborn, there were over thirteen thousand men of all arms. On the Niagara three thousand three hundred regulars, and three thousand volunteers and militia; at Sackett's Harbour, two hundred regulars, and two thousand militia; on Lake Champlain, three thousand regulars, and two thousand militia. In the West, although we are without the data which would enable us to give so detailed

American Force.

a statement of General Harrison's force, yet we are informed that while Proctor, after defeating and capturing Winchester, was hastening back to Malden, to escape the attacks of Harrison, this last mentioned officer, under similar apprehensions of his adversary, after setting fire to his stores, baggage and defences at the Rapids, retreated hastily to Portage River. The delusion, however,[†] under which this movement was made was not of long duration, and shortly afterwards, General Harrison announced to his government that "a few days would enable him to resume and defend the position he had left, against anything Proctor could bring against it, and advancing with a force of about two thousand men,[‡] on the eastern bank of the Miami, he began a fortified camp to cover his intended operations. Here, for the present, we will leave him with General Proctor watching him with five hundred and twenty regulars, four hundred and fifty militia and about twelve hundred Indians. We have already shown that the whole force along the Niagara frontier, thirty-six miles in length, exclusive of that stationed at Fort George, and which may be

Proctor's Force.

Sheaffe's Force.

---

which he bravely attempted to take with the bayonet, though covered with 200 of the enemy's best troops: advancing as rapidly as the deep snow, and the exhausted state (in consequence) of his men, would admit, he ordered a charge, and had not proceeded many paces, when his left arm was broken to pieces by a grape shot; but still undauntedly running on with his men, he almost immediately afterwards was deprived of the use of his right arm, by a discharge of a case-shot; still heroically disregarding all personal consideration, he nobly ran on, cheering his men, to the assault, till, exhausted by pain and loss of blood, he became unable to move; his company gallantly continued the charge under Lieutenant M'Auley; but the reserve of the militia not being able to keep up with them, they were compelled, by the great superiority of the enemy, to give way, leaving a few on a commanding position, and a few of the most advanced, in the enemy's possession, nearly about the time that I gained the height above mentioned. The enemy hesitating to surrender, I instantly carried his eastern battery, and by it silenced another, which now opened again; and ordering on the advance the detachment of the King's, and the Highland company of militia, under Captain Eustace, of the King's regiment, he gallantly rushed into the fort; but the enemy retreating by the opposite entrance, escaped into the woods, which I should have effectually prevented, if my Indian warriors had returned sooner from a detached service, on which they had that morning been employed.

I cannot close this statement without expressing my admiration of the gallantry and self-devotion of Captain Jenkins, who had lost one arm, and is in danger of losing the other. I must also report the intrepidity of Captain Lefevre, of the Newfoundland regiment, who had the immediate charge of the militia under Colonel Fraser; of Captain Eustace, and the other officers of the King's regiment; and particularly of Lieutenant Ridge, of that corps, who very gallantly led on the advance; and of Lieutenant M'Auley, and ensign M'Donnell, of the Glengarry regiment; as also Lieutenant Gangueben, of the royal engineers; and of Ensign M'Kay, of the Glengarry light-infantry; and of Ensign Kerr, of the militia, each of whom had charge of a field-peice; and of Lieutenant Impey, of the militia, who has lost a leg. I was also well supported by Colonel Fraser and the other officers and men of the militia, who emulated the conspicuous bravery of all the troops of the line. I inclose a list of killed and wounded. The enemy had 500 men under arms, and must have sustained a considerable loss.

I have the honor to be, &c.
G. MACDONNELL,
Major, Glengarry light infantry, Lieutenant-Colonel, commanding in the Eastern District of Upper Canada.

Sir G. Prevost. &c.

[†]Armstrong—page 121.
[‡]Ibid.

stated at fourteen hundred and forty regulars, and two hundred and sixty militia, amounted to but three hundred and sixty regulars, and two hundred and forty militia, in all twenty-three hundred men.

It is not so easy to get at the strength of the force at the disposal of Sir Geo. Prevost, but we can gather from " Veritas,"—who, in his anxiety to criminate Sir George, is not likely to have *understated* his means, whether for offence or defence—that it did not exceed three thousand regulars and militia at the outside.

Army in Lower Canada.

These numbers show fifteen thousand five hundred Americans to six thousand three hundred British and twelve hundred Indians.

The total numbers on both sides compared.

A glance at the state of affairs on Lake Ontario does not give a more satisfactory result, as we find a powerful American force, the united tonnage of which amounted to over nineteen hundred tons, besides boats, lying at Sackett's harbor. This fleet, mounting eighty-six heavy cannon, was in readiness to co-operate in the movements contemplated by the Cabinet at Washington. At this very time our vessels on Lake Ontario were lying unmanned and unfurnished in Kingston harbor and elsewhere, waiting for the arrival of seamen to enable them to be prepared for service!

Comparative naval strength.

Having shown the strength, we will now proceed to the plan of campaign proposed by General Dearborn and Commodore Chauncey, and, after some deliberation, agreed to by the American Government as certain of ultimate success. According to this plan, it was proposed that three simultaneous demonstrations should be made. At the west Harrison was to attack and drive back Proctor, compelling the surrender of Malden and the evacuation of the Michigan territory; Com. Chauncey and the fleet, with an army under Gen. Pike, were first to attack York, and from thence to proceed to the investment of Fort George by land and water ; a third force was to cross over from Buffalo, and, carrying the forts at

Plan of campaign.

Erie and Chippewa, to join that already assembled at Fort George. Canada West having been thus swept, the whole force was to proceed eastward to Kingston, to co-operate with General Dearborn in the reduction, first of that place, and afterwards of Quebec. This was a very well laid combination, and had Canadians been the disaffected body imagined by Americans, would in all probability have succeeded. As they, however, obstinately refused to believe themselves as enslaved and wronged as Hull and Smith represented, it did not realize all that had been expected.

About this time Sir James Yeo arrived to assume the naval command. This officer had formerly commanded the Southampton frigate, and immediately on his arrival he commenced with great energy the work of fitting, manning, and preparing for actual service. Before, however, entering with him on his labors, we must retrace our steps, and resume the narrative of naval events, which we closed with the capture of the Java by the Constitution. We must also remind the reader that, in the fifth chapter of this work, an act of great barbarity on the part of Captain Porter, of the Essex, towards a British seaman, was, on the authority of Mr. James, exposed. An account of this proceeding reaching Sir James Yeo, some natural expressions of indignation at the act, and of contempt for the perpetrator, escaped him ; and as these sentiments were uttered in the hearing of several American prisoners then on board the Southampton, they were soon made public, with appropriate emendations. Sir James Yeo's remarks were made to convey a challenge to Captain Porter, and this officer had now an opportunity of thrusting himself into more creditable notice than the inhuman tarring and feathering of poor John Ewing was calculated to gain for him. A formal acceptance by Captain Porter of this (we may call it pretended, as James declares there is no authority whatever for the sending) challenge afterwards went the round of the American papers. We have introduced this anecdote, as it is necessary for us, before resuming our narrative, at the date where we broke off, to accompany Capt. Porter on his first cruise in the Essex. The successful issue of this adventurous expedition did not fail to create

Arrival of Sir James Yeo.

great sensation throughout the United States, and we might expose ourselves to the charge of a *suppressio veri*, did we omit aught that might be supposed to bear on the subject.

We have, besides, an additional inducement to accompany Captain Porter, as we may be enabled to correct a few statements which, inadvertently of course, have been suffered to creep into his record.

The Essex had been prevented from forming part of Commodore Rodger's squadron, as she could not be fitted up in time, but on the 3rd July she sailed from New York, and on the 11th fell in with seven transports bound from Barbadoes, to Quebec, under the convoy of the Minerva, twelve pounder, thirty-two gun frigate. The Essex succeeded in cutting off the rearmost vessel with nearly two hundred soldiers on board, and Captain Hawkins wore in pursuit but, finding after a while, that by continuing in chase, he must run the risk of separating from, and perhaps losing the remaining six vessels of his convoy, he resumed his course.

James observes on this "Captain Porter was discreet, as well as shrewd enough to chuckle at this; and disarming and paroling the soldiers, and ransoming the vessel, he allowed the latter to proceed with the intelligence of the outrage she had suffered. He of course obtained from his prize, the name of the convoying frigate, whose protection had been of so much service, and by the first opportunity wrote an official account of his exploit, concluding with the, as applied to a British ship, galling words " we endeavored to bring the frigate to action, but did not succeed." Unfortunately for Captain Porter's declaration of inferiority, in point of sailing, of the Essex, this vessel was afterwards captured, and her sailing qualities so fully ascertained as to leave no doubt but that Captain Porter, had he really desired to bring the Minerva to action, could easily have come alongside of her. That no such thought, however, entered Captain Porter's head will be clear to all, as we proceed in our analysis of that Officer's claim to wear the laurel. A dispatch to the Navy Department, dated "At sea, August 17th," contains the next claim preferred by Captain Porter, " I have the honor to inform you that on the 13th His Britanic Majesty's

sloop of war, Alert, Captain T. L. R. Langharne, ran down on our weather quarter, gave three cheers, and commenced an action (if so trifling a skirmish deserves the name), and after eight minutes' firing, struck her colours, with seven feet of water in her hold, much cut to pieces, and with three men wounded. * * * * The Essex has not received the slightest injury. The Alert was out for the purpose of taking the Hornet."

Some credit is due for the modesty of this despatch, but when we state what the Alert really was, it will be seen that even Captain David Porter could scarcely have made more of the transaction. In the year 1804, twelve colliers were purchased by the British Government, and one of these, the Oxford, became the Alert sloop of war fitted with eighteen pound carronades, the highest calibre she could bear. By the end of the year 1811, ten of these choice vessels had either been broken up or converted into peaceable harbour ships. Two still remained, and, as if possessing in reality the qualities which their names implied, the Avenger and Alert were dispatched to the North American station a short time previous to the war. Had the Alert been rigged with two masts, Capt. Porter would only have had the glory of taking a small gun brig, but the unfortunate mizen mast classed her amongst vessels which were a full match for any two such craft. Captain Porter disarmed his prize and sent her, as a cartel, with the prisoners, eighty-six in number, to St. John's, Newfoundland, where Captain Langharne and his crew were tried for the loss of the ship. When we consider the verdict of the Court, however, we may be inclined to admire Captain Langharne's bravery, we cannot but condemn him somewhat for provoking, with such a crew, so unequal a contest. It was proved at the trial that the crew went aft to request the Captain to strike his colors, and the finding of the Court was " the honorable acquittal of Captain Langharne, the master and purser," while the first lieutenant was dismissed the service, and the marked disapprobation of the Court was expressed to the remaining officers and crew. On her return to the States, being found unfit for a cruiser, the Alert was first laid up in ordinary, and, after some time, then fitted up as a store ship; her creeping pace, however, betrayed her collier origin, and she was finally sent to New York, to be exhibited to the citizens as one of the national trophies of war.

Capt. Porter's next despatch must have carried with it a pleasing conviction that maritime supremacy had ceased to be "England's undoubted right," and must have inspired American sailors with a most contemptible opinion of their opponent's courage. We give the despatch entire.

"On the afternoon of the 30th August, I discovered one of the enemy's frigates standing forward, as under a press of sail, apparently with an intention of speaking us, stood for him under easy sail with the ship prepared for action, and, apprehensive that he might not find me during the night, I hoisted a light. At 9, he made a signal consisting of two flashes and a blue light, apparently about four miles distant from us. I continued to stand on for the point where they were seen until midnight, when not getting sight of the enemy, I concluded it would be best to heave to for him until daylight, presuming that he had done the same, or that he would at least have kept in our neigbourhood; but to my great surprise and the mortification of my officers and crew (whose zeal on every occasion excites my admiration,) we discovered in the morning that the bird had flown. From her fleetness which enabled her to disappear so soon, *I think it not unlikely that it was the Acasta, of fifty guns, and three hundred and fifty men sent out with the Ringdove of twenty-two guns to cruise for the Essex.*"

Ships usually carry logbooks, in which are entered every day's proceedings, with the latitude and longitude ; a reference to these, unfortunately for the correctness of Capt. Porter's assumption, shows that, on the day mentioned, the Acasta was in lat. 43° north, and long. 63° 16' west. The Essex being in 36° north and 62° west. The Ringdove (only of eighteen guns by the way) was on that day at anchor in the harbour of the island of St. Thomas. The ship that Capt. Porter fell in with, was the Ratler, eighteen gun sloop, Capt. Alexander Gordon, who knowing that it would be folly to engage in so unequal a contest, very wisely avoided an engagement.

On the 4th of September Capt. Porter was really gratified with a sight of a ship of war, as on that day, having in convoy the merchant ship Minerva, he fell in with (to use his own words) two ships of war. These two ships of war were the British thirty-eight gun frigate Shannon and the merchant ship Planter, recaptured from the Americans. The Essex, keeping the Minerva close astern of her, bore down as if to meet the Shannon, then in chase, but having closed to within ten miles, Capt. Porter's better judgment prevailed, and leaving the poor merchant ship to her fate, the Essex hauled to the wind and crowded all sail to get away. The Minerva was taken possession of and burnt, in hopes that the Essex might see the flames and clear down to avenge the indignity, but with no effect. This running away was the last exploit performed by Capt. Porter, who anchored, three days afterwards, in the Delaware, "crowned with glory."

We left, it may be remembered, the Hornet sloop of war off St. Salvador, where, with the Constitution, Capt. Lawrence had been blockading the Bonne Citoyenne, and whence she was chased by the Montague, seventy-four. After escaping from the line of battle ship, the Hornet stood to the westward, captured an English brig with some seven thousand pounds in specie on board, and then directed her course to the coast of Surinam and Demerara. While cruising on this station, the Hornet, when beating off the entrance to the Demerara river, discovered a sail bearing down on her, which proved to be the British brig sloop Peacock. The engagement commenced a little after five, and ten minutes before six, the Peacock, being in a sinking state from the heavy fire of the Hornet, hoisted an ensign, union down, from her fore rigging, as a signal of distress. Shortly afterwards her main mast went by the board. Every attempt was now made to save the crew, but all would not do, and a few minutes afterwards the Peacock went down in five and a half fathom water with thirteen of her men, four of whom only escaped by crawling into the fore rigging. An American Lieutenant, Midshipman, and three men with difficulty saved themselves by jumping, as the brig went down, into boats lying on the booms. Some of the men saved themselves in the stern boat, and, notwithstanding it was much damaged by shot, they arrived in safety at Demerara.

Of her hundred and ten men, the Peacock

lost her gallant commander and seven men, besides three officers and twenty-seven men wounded. The Americans state their loss at two killed and three wounded, out of a crew of one hundred and seventeen.

We give the comparative force of the combatants, before introducing James' remarks on the action.

Comparative force of the ships.

	Peacock.	Hornet.
Broadside guns....	9	10
No. of lbs.........	192	297
Crew	110	162
Size	386	460

The accuracy of this table has been proved, yet American writers have declared that the Hornet gained a victory over a "*superior British force.*" Now for James.—"If, in their encounter of British frigates the Americans were so lucky as to meet them with crippled masts, deteriorated powder, unskilful gunners, or worthless crews, they were not less fortunate in the brigs they fell in with. There was the Frolic, with her main-yard gone and topmasts sprung; and here is the Peacock, with twenty-four instead of thirty-two pound carronades, the establishment of her class, and with a crew that, owing to the nature of their employment ever since the brig had been commissioned, in August, 1807, must have almost forgotten that they belonged to a man-of-war. The Peacock had long been the admiration of her numerous visitors, for *the tasteful arrangement* of her deck, and had obtained, in consequence, *the name of the yacht. The breechings of the carronades were* lined with *white canvas*, the shot-lockers shifted from their usual places, and nothing could exceed in *brilliancy, the polish upon the traversing bars and elevating screws*." These remarks are deservedly severe, both on the commander of the Peacock and the authorities, whose duty it was to know that the Peacock was fitted in a manner suitable to her class. The brig was new, built of oak, and able to bear thirty-two pounders, and there could then have been no other cause for the change, but that the smaller guns took up less room, and gave a lighter appearance to the deck. It appears extraordinary that the British Government, after so many disasters, and the lapse of eight months from the declaration of war, should not have become alive to the importance of sending proper vessels to sea. The Peacock, Frolic and brigs of her class were mere shells, when compared with such ships as the Hornet and the Wasp, whose scantling was nearly as stout as a British twelve pounder frigate, but still they were entitled to be ranked in a certain class, and an extract from Lawrence's* official letter will show that he did not hesitate to claim for himself a very sufficient amount of credit. Captain Lawrence could have afforded to have dispensed with this, as we readily admit that he was really a gallant and truly brave officer; after all, we can hardly wonder at his becoming inoculated with the national disorder, especially as it was the policy of a government that has never yet been convinced of the inutility, even in a profit and loss point of view, of making a misstatement. The wreck of the Peacock was visible for a long time after the action, and this was a fortunate circumstance, as it gave an opportunity of ascertaining her relative positions and that of the Espiègle. This was necessary, as Captain Lawrence's statement makes the Espiègle "six miles in shore of me," and adds, "and could plainly see the

---

* "At the time I brought the Peacock to action, the Espiègle, (the brig mentioned as being at an anchor) mounting sixteen two and thirty pound carronades, and two long nines, lay about six miles in shore of me, and could plainly see the whole of the action. Apprehensive she would beat out to the assistance of her consort, such exertions were used by my officers and crew, in repairing damages, &c., that by nine o'clock our boats were stowed, a new set of sails bent, and the ship completely ready for action. At two, A.M., got under way and stood by the wind to the northward and westward under easy sail. On mustering next morning, found we had two hundred and seventy-seven souls on board (including the crew of the American brig, Hunter, of Portland, taken a few days before by the Peacock) and as we had been on two-thirds allowance of provisions for some time, and had but 3,400 gallons of water on board, I reduced the allowance to three pints a man, and determined to make the best of my way to the United States.

The Peacock was deservedly styled one of the finest vessels of her class in the British navy. I should judge her to be about the tonnage of the Hornet. Her beam was greater by five inches, but her extreme length not so great by four feet. She mounted sixteen four and twenty pound carronades, two long nines, one twelve pound carronade on her top-gallant forecastle as a shifting gun, and one four or six pounder, and two swivels mounted aft. I find by her quarter-bill that her crew consisted of one hundred and thirty-four men, four of whom were absent in a prize."

whole of the action." It has been proved that the actual distance between the vessels was twenty-four miles. Lieutenant Wright, senior, of the Peacock, has declared that the Espiègle " was not visible from the look-outs stationed at the Peacock's mast-heads, for some time previous to the commencement of the action," and if further information be wanted, it is to be found in the ignorance, of Captain Taylor, of the action, until informed of it the day after, by the Governor of Demerara. When the authorities awoke from their lethargy, some time afterwards, and began to examine somewhat into the real condition of ships, their efficiency of equipment, and their state of discipline, this same Captain Taylor was found guilty by a Court-Martial of having "neglected to exercise the ship's company at the great guns." It was therefore, perhaps, fortunate that the disordered state of her rigging prevented Capt. Taylor from engaging the Hornet. It was hard, at the same time, on Captain Taylor, that he should be punished for negligence, which was common to two-thirds of the navy, and to which the Admiralty, by their instructions, and their sparing allowance of powder and shot for practice at the guns, were in some degree instrumental.

Captain Philip Broke, of the Shannon frigate, was amongst that class of British officers, who mourned the imbecility of a Government, which saw the capture of vessel after vessel by the Americans, and yet could not be persuaded but that diplomacy and procrastination would convert small and inefficient, into large and well equipped vessels. This officer was determined to prove what an English thirty-eight could effect, when the ship and crew were properly fitted for battle.

The Chesapeake and the Shannon.

On the 21st March, 1813, the Shannon, in company with the Tenedos, same force, sailed from Halifax, and reconnoitred, on the 2nd of April, Boston Harbour, where they discovered the President and Congress, the latter quite, the former nearly ready for sea. According to James, the two British commanders determined to intercept and bring to action the two American vessels. It is rather hard to say how it happened, but, nevertheless, happen it did, that the American vessels got

to sea about the 1st of May, unperceived, leaving only the Chesapeake and Constitution in harbour. The Constitution was undergoing serious repair; the Chesapeake was expected to be ready for sea in a few days; Captain Lawrence therefore (as two frigates were not required to watch one,) despatched the Tenedos to sea with instructions to Captain Parkes not to join him before the 14th June, by which time Captain Broke trusted that his desire of meeting an enemy's vessel of equal force would be accomplished. While cruising off the harbour the Shannon captured several vessels, but destroyed them all that he might not weaken his crew. James states that "he sacrificed twenty-five sail of prizes to keep the Shannon in a state to meet one or the other of the American frigates." Our note* will show the comparative force of the two frigates. Captain Broke, on the 1st June, having received as yet no answer to the ver-

---

*On her main deck, the Shannon was armed the same as every other British frigate of her class, and her established guns on the quarter-deck and forecastle were 16 carronades, 32-pounders, and four long 9-pounders, total 48 guns. But Captain Broke had since mounted a 12-pounder boat carronade through a port purposely made on the starboard side of the quarter-deck, and a brass long 6-pounder, used generally as an exercise gun, through a similar port on the larboard side; besides which there were two 12-pounder carronades, mounted as standing stern-chasers through the quarter-deck stern-ports. For these last four guns, one 32-pounder carronade would have been more than an equivalent. However, as a 6-pounder counts as well as a 32-pounder, the Shannon certainly mounted 52 carriage-guns. The ship had also, to be in that respect upon a par with the American frigates, one swivel in the fore, and another in the main top.

The armament of the Chesapeake, we have already on more than one occasion described: she had at this time, as afterwards found on board of her, 28 long 18-pounders on the main deck, and 20 carronades, 32-pounders, and one long shifting 18-pounder, on the quarter-deck and forecastle, total 49 guns; exclusively of a 12-pounder boat-carronade, belonging to which there was a very simple and well-contrived elevating carriage for firing at the tops, but it is doubtful if the gun was used. Five guns, four 32-pounder carronades and one long 18-pounder, had, it was understood, been landed at Boston. Some have alleged, that this was done by Captain Lawrence, that he might not have a numerical superiority over his antagonists of the British 38-gun class: others say, and we incline to be of that opinion, that the reduction was ordered by the American government, to ease the ship, whose hull had already begun to hog, or to arch in the centre."

bal challenges which he had sent in, despatched by a Captain Slocum the following letter to Captain Lawrence, late captain of the Hornet, and now commanding the Chesapeake :—

"As the Chesapeake appears now ready for sea, I request you will do me the favour to meet the Shannon with her, ship to ship, to try the fortune of our respective flags." (Here follows the description of the Shannon's force.) "I entreat you, sir, not to imagine that I am urged by mere personal vanity to the wish of my meeting the Chesapeake, or that I depend only upon your personal ambition for your acceding to this invitation. We have both nobler motives. You will feel it as a compliment if I say that the result of our meeting may be the most grateful service I can render to my country ; and I doubt not that you, equally confident of success, will feel convinced that it is only by repeated triumphs in *even combats* that your little navy can hope to console your country, for the loss of that trade it can no longer protect. Favour me with a speedy reply. We are short of provisions and water, and cannot stay long here."

This letter did not reach Captain Lawrence in time to influence his proceedings, as it appears that he had already received permission from Commodore Bainbridge to capture or drive away a British ship that had repeatedly lain to off the port, and, in view of all the citizens, had used every endeavor to provoke the Chesapeake to come out and engage her. Captain Broke's anxiety as to the reply to his challenge induced him to mount the rigging himself, and while at the mast-head he perceived that, ere Capt. Slocum's boat reached the shore, the American frigate was under way, attended by numerous sailing pleasure-boats, and a large (schooner) gun-boat, with Commodores Bainbridge and Hull, besides several other American naval officers, on board. The Chesapeake got under weigh at half-past twelve, and at one rounded the lighthouse under all sail. The Shannon now filled and stood away from the land. At twenty minutes to four the Chesapeake hauled up and fired a gun, as James has it, "either in defiance, or perhaps to induce the Shannon to stop, so as to afford the gun-boat and pleasure seeking spectators the gratification of witnessing how speedily an American could 'whip'

a British frigate." The Shannon now hauled up and lay to. At half-past five the Chesapeake steered straight for the Shannon's starboard quarter, with a large white flag at the fore, on which was inscribed, as if to paralyze the efforts of the Shannon's sailors, the words "Sailors rights and free trade."

At ten minutes to six the Shannon fired the first gun, and between the period of its discharge and Captain Broke's boarding eleven minutes elapsed. In four minutes more the Chesapeake's flag was hauled down, and the vessel was completely his. Below* will be

---

*The following is the damage and loss of men sustained by the respective combatants. Five shots passed through the Shannon ; one, only, below the main deck. Of several round shot that struck her, the greater part lodged in the side, ranged in a line just above the copper. A bar-shot entered a little below the water-mark, leaving a foot or 18 inches of one end sticking out. Until her shot holes were stopped, the Shannon made a good deal of water upon the larboard tack ; but, upon the other, not more than usual. Her fore and main masts were slightly injured by shot ; and her bowsprit (previously sprung) and mizenmast were badly wounded. No other spar was damaged. Her shrouds on the starboard side were cut almost to pieces ; but, from her perfect state aloft, the Shannon, at a moderate distance, appeared to have suffered very little in the action.

Out of a crew, including eight recaptured seamen and 22 Irish labourers two days only in the ship, of 306 men and 24 boys, the Shannon lost, besides her first Lieutenant, her purser (George Aldham), captain's clerk (John Dunn), 13 seamen, four marines, three supernumeraries, and one boy killed, her Captain (severely), boatswain (William Stevens, mortally), one midshipman (John Samwell, mortally), and 56 seamen, marines, and supernumeraries wounded ; total, 24 killed and 59 wounded.

Out of a crew of at least 381 men and five boys or lads, the Chesapeake, as acknowledged by her surviving commanding officer, lost her fourth Lieutenant (Edward I. Ballard), master (William A. White), one Lieutenant of marines (James Broom), three midshipmen, and 41 petty officers. seamen, and marines killed, her gallant commander and first Lieutenant (both mortally), her second and third Lieutenants (George Budd and William L. Cox), acting chaplain (Samuel Livermore), five midshipmen, her boatswain (mortally), and 95 petty officers, seamen, and marines wounded ; total 47 killed and 99 wounded, 14 of the latter mortally. This is according to the American official account ; but, it must be added, that the total that reported themselves, including several slightly wounded, to the Shannon's surgeon, three days after the action, were 115 ; and the Chesapeake's surgeon wrote from Halifax, that he estimated the whole number of killed and wounded, at from 160 to 170.

found the English account and the American despatch, but a glance at the comparative force of the combatants will show that the superiority of force, though but trifling, was still on the 'side of the Chesapeake :—

	SHANNON.	CHESAPEAKE.
Broadside guns,	25	25
Weight of metal, lbs.	538	590
Number of crew,	306	376
Tonnage,	1066	1135

The capture of this vessel made public some of the extraordinary means of attack and de-fence adopted by the Americans in their naval engagements with the British. Among the Chesapeake's round and grape (Vide James, page 206) were found double-headed shot in abundance ; also bars of wrought iron, about a foot long, connected by links and folded together, so as, when discharged, to form an extended length of six feet. Other bars, of twice the length, and in number from three to six, were connected at the end by a ring ; these, as they flew from the gun, expanded at four points. The object of this novel artil-

Of the Chesapeake's guns we have already given a full account : it only remains to point out, that the ship had three spare ports of a side on the forecastle, through which to fight her shifting long 18-pounder and 12-pounder boat-carronade. The former is admitted to have been used in that way ; but, as there is some doubt whether the carronade was used, we shall reject it from the broadside force. This leaves 25 guns, precisely the number mounted by the Shannon on her broadside. The accuracy of Captain Broke's statement of his ship's force is, indeed, worthy of remark : he even slightly overrated it, because he represented all of his guns of a side on the upper deck, except the boat-gun, as 32-pounder carronades, when the number were long nines.

As a matter of course, a court of inquiry was held, to investigate the circumstances under which the Chesapeake had been captured. Commodore Bainbridge was the president of the court ; and the following is the first article of the very "lengthy" report published on the subject : "The court are unanimously of opinion, that the Chesapeake was gallantly carried into action by her late brave commander ; and no doubt rests with the court, from comparison of the injury respectively sustained by the frigates, that the fire of the Chesapeake was much superior to that of the Shannon. The Shannon, being much cut in her spars and rigging, and receiving many shot in and below the water line, was reduced almost to a sinking condition, after only a few minutes cannonading from the Chesapeake ; whilst the Chesapeake was comparatively uninjured. And the court have no doubt, if the Chesapeake had not accidentally fallen on board the Shannon, and the Shannon's anchor got foul in the after quarter-port of the Chesapeake, the Shannon must have very soon surrendered or sunk." Some very singular admissions of misconduct in the officers and crew follow ; and then the report proceeds as follows : "From this view of the engagement and a careful examination of the evidence, the court are unanimously of opinion, that the capture of the late United States' frigate Chesapeake was occasioned, by the following causes : the almost unexampled early fall of Captain Lawrence, and all the principal officers ; the bugleman's desertion of his quarters, and inability to sound his horn ; for the court are of opinion, if the horn had been sounded when first ordered, the men being then at their quarters, the boarders would have promptly re-paired to the spar deck, probably have prevented the enemy from boarding, certainly have repelled them, and might have returned the boarding with success ; and the failure of the boarders on both decks, to rally on the spar deck, after the enemy had boarded, which might have been done successfully, it is believed, from the cautious manner in which the enemy came on board."

It was certainly very " cautious" in Captain Broke, to lead 20 men on board an enemy's ship, supposed to be manned with a complement of 400 ; and which, at the very moment, had at least 270 men without a wound about them. The court of inquiry makes, also, a fine story of the firing down the hatchway. Not a word is there of the "magnanimous conquered foe" having fired from below, in the first instance, and killed a British marine. Captain Broke will long have cause to remember the treatment he experienced from this " magnanimous conquered foe." So far, indeed, from the conduct of the British being "a most unwarrantable abuse of power after success," Lieutenant Cox of the Chesapeake, in the hearing of several English gentlemen, subsequently admitted, that he owed his life to the forbearance of one of the Shannon's marines. When the American officers arrived on board the Shannon, and some of them were finding out reasons for being "taken so unaccountably," their first lieutenant, Mr. Ludlow, candidly acknowledged, that the Shannon had beaten them heartily and fairly.

SIR—The unfortunate death of Captain James Lawrence and Lieutenant C. Ludlow, has rendered it my duty to inform you of the capture of the late U. States frigate Chesapeake.

On Tuesday, June 1, at 8 A. M. we unmoored ship and at meridian got under way from President's Roads, with a light wind from the southward and westward, and proceeded on a cruise. A ship was then in sight in the offing which had the appearance of a ship of war, and which, from information received from pilot boats and craft, we believed to be the British frigate Shannon. We made sail in chase and cleared ship for action. At half past four P.M. she hove to, with her head to the southward and eastward. At 5 P. M. took in the royals and top-gallant-sails and at half past five hauled the courses up. About 15 minutes before 6 P. M. the action commenced within pistol shot. The first broadside did great execution on both sides, damaged our rigging, killed among others Mr. White, the sailing master, and wounded

lery was to dismantle the shrouds. The cannister shot, when opened, were found to contain in the centre angular and jagged pieces of iron and copper, broken bolts and nails. The musket cartridges, as we noticed before, each contained three buck shot, and rifle barreled pieces were amongst the small arms. Formidable preparations these !

The four victories gained by the Americans had exalted the national vanity to such a pitch

Remarks on the action.

that the disagreeable task of recording a defeat was somewhat puzzling to the caterers to public taste. It would not at all answer to "tell the story as it happened," consequently the various reasons assigned for the Chesapeake's mishap are not a little amusing. One officer says,† "had there been an officer on the quarter deck with twenty men the result of the action must have been different." Another, "it was with difficulty the Shannon was kept afloat the night after the action, the Chesapeake on the contrary, received scarcely any damage from the shot of his opponent. The English officers do not hesitate to say, they could not have withstood the fire of the Chesapeake ten minutes longer." In one place the public were informed that "the Chesapeake was greatly the inferior of her enemy in every respect, save the valor of her officers." In another, that "the officers and crew were strangers to each other, while the Shannon had a picked crew and was a MUCH STRONGER vessel than the Chesapeake, and had

greatly the odds in guns and men." The American purser declares that the Chesapeake "had the advantage, and that had Capt. Lawrence lived the Shannon must have been ours." Even Commander Bainbridge found in this engagement "the best evidence of the superiority of American over British frigates and demonstrated, much to his own satisfaction, doubtless from its result, that Americans must always conquer when they had an equal chance." We presume the Commodore alludes to the equal force and tonnage of the Guerière, Macedonian and Java. The Commodore was decidedly of opinion that "it is surely an evidence of our decided superiority that an American thirty-six gun frigate, five hours out of port, with an *undisciplined crew,* (we have merely the Commodore's *ipse dixit* for this assumption,) should put an English thirty-eight gun frigate, the best of her kind, in a *sinking state in fifteen minutes.*" The Commodore winds up with the declaration that the British victory "was certainly to be placed to the amount of good fortune on their side." These statements will suffice to shew the nature of the information supplied to the American public and how sedulously careful the journals and naval officers were not to awaken them from the dream of fancied invincibility. The atrocious calumnies invented and circulated throughout the Union, in reference to the treatment of prisoners are not worth the confuting, and do credit to American ideality. One startling fact must not be

Captain Lawrence. In about 12 minutes after the commencement of the action, we fell on board of the enemy, and immediately after one of our armchests on the quarter-deck was blown up by a hand grenade thrown from the enemy's ship. In a few minutes one of the captain's aids came on the gun deck to inform me that the boarders were called. I immediately called the boarders away and proceeded to the spar deck, where I found that the enemy had succeeded in boarding us and had gained possession of our quarter deck. I immediately gave orders to haul on board the fore tack, for the purpose of shooting the ship clear of the other, and then made an attempt to regain the quarter deck, I again made an effort to collect the boarders, but in the mean time the enemy had gained complete possession of the ship. On my being carried down to the cock-pit, I there found Captain Lawrence and Lieutenant Ludlow both mortally wounded ; the former had been carried below previously to the ship's being

† Niles Weekly Register, page 374.

boarded ; the latter was wounded in attempting to repel the boarders. Among those who fell early in the action was Mr. Edward J. Ballard, the 4th Lieutenant, and Lieutenant James Broom of marines.

I herein enclose to you a return of the killed and wounded, by which you will perceive that every officer, upon whom the charge of the ship would devolve, was either killed or wounded previously to her capture. The enemy report the loss of Mr. Watt, their first Lieutenant; the purser ; the captain's clerk, and 23 seamen killed ; and Captain Broke, a midshipman, and 56 seamen wounded.

The Shannon had, in addition to her full complement, an officer and 16 men belonging to the Belle Poule, and a part of the crew belonging to the Tenedos.

I have the honour to be, with very great respect, &c.

                                        GEORGE BUDD.
The Hon. William Jones,
        Secretary of the Navy, Washington.

omitted, before closing the account, THE CREW of the Chesapeake, *Proh pudor!* consisted, within about a twelfth part of NATIVE AMERICANS. Thus was the spell, cast by the incapacity of the Admiralty, over the British Navy, broken, and a salutary lesson taught to Americans, that they were not yet equal, much less superior, to British seamen.

One of the most favorite causes assigned for Want of discipline on board the Chesapeake. the loss of the Chesapeake was the rawness and want of discipline of the crew. A few facts connected with the manning of American ships in general, and of this vessel in particular, will serve to clear up this point. In order to fill up deficiencies, houses of rendezvous were opened, and as soon as a man declared himself a candidate, he received a dollar, and accompanied an officer to the ship. There he was examined as to his knowledge of seamanship, age, muscular strength, &c. by a board of officers, consisting of the surgeon, master, and others. If approved, the man signed the articles, and remained where he was; if rejected he returned to shore with a dollar in his pocket. So fastidious were the committees of inspection, that out of five boats loaded with men that would go off during the day, three would come back not eligible. The features of the engagements, we have already narrated, would have borne a very different aspect, could British ships have been manned in a similar manner. In reference to the crew of the Chesapeake in particular, we find in a letter from the secretary at war to Captain Evans (the former commander) instructions to complete the Chesapeake's armament, enumerating the classes at four hundred and forty-three. We also ascertain that the Chesapeake was re-manned in April, 1813, and that the greater part of the crew re-entered. In addition to this, several of the Chesapeake's petty officers, after their arrival at Melville prison, confessed that thirty or forty hands, *principally* from the Constitution, came on board, whose names, in the hurry and confusion, were not entered in the Purser's books. As a proof of the stoutness of the crew, it may be mentioned that the puncheon of handcuffs, *provided for the Shannon's crew,* and found on the half-deck, with the head ready knocked out, when put on the wrists of the Chesapeake's crew, were found

to be too small, and general complaints were made when it was found necessary to apply them, in consequence of an apparent inclination of the prisoners to mutiny. The best reply to the assertion that the Shannon was in a sinking state is the statement that she arrived at Halifax with her prize early on the 6th.

At the beginning of the war, Ontario was Naval events on Canadian lakes. the only lake on which floated a British armed vessel. The small fleet consisted of the Royal George, a ship of three hundred and fifty tons, mounting twenty guns, a brig of fourteen guns, and two or three smaller armed vessels, all under the command of Commodore Earle. We have already had occasion to touch on this Officer's incompetency or, as James terms it, "dastardly behaviour," we therefore allude to the failure in the plan for the destruction of the Oneida, merely to remark on James's sneer at Earle as "a Canadian, we will not call him a British Commander," as very uncalled for. We readily grant Earle's incompetency or want of courage, but we deny that this arose from his being a Canadian. General Brock was a Guernsey man yet he was generally considered an abler general than his chief, who was not a Colonist. We enter a protest against any similar impertinence on the part of any historian. Canada is in feeling an integral part of Britain, and the loyalty and bravery of the Canadian Militia throughout the war, entitle them to be classed as equal to any British subject, in every attribute of a man.

The American force on the lake at the commencement of the war, was a single brig of sixteen guns, and yet from the neglect or indifference of the British commanders (Sir George Prevost and Commodore Earle), by the end of the year, the Americans were masters of the lake and had afloat six fine schooners mounting forty-eight guns, besides the Madison, a fine ship of six hundred tons, pierced for twenty-four guns. In the meantime, the British were building two vessels, one at York, an unprotected port at one side of the lake, the other at Kingston, on the opposite shore.

The American Government had the good sense to despatch a competent person, with between four and five hundred prime sailors from the seaboard, to assume the direction of their naval affairs. This force was divided amongst the vessels, and, of course, assisted most materially in teaching the more undisciplined part of the crews their duty, and the Commodore was soon enabled to chase every British vessel into port, and thus become master of Lake Ontario. Between October 1812 and April 1813, Commodore Chauncey directed his attention and energies to prepare a fleet to co-operate with General Dearborn, in the combined attack we have already mentioned as in preparation, and by the 25th April, with a fleet of ten vessels, he announced his readiness for action. We will, however, leave him for the present, prepared for sea, and return to Colonel Proctor, whom we left in the west, watching General Harrison's movements.

After a brief glance at the operations in this quarter, we will proceed to take up in order the attack on York, that on Niagara, and follow, also, the fate of Sir George Prevost's expedition against Sackett's harbour. By this arrangement the reader will have placed before him, nearly in order of date, the various movements, military and naval, of the first six months of 1813, and will be enabled to judge of. the formidable difficulties against which the British commander had to contend.

After Gen. Winchester's defeat, and when sufficient time had been afforded to General Harrison to enable him to recover from his panic, he directed his attention to the construction of works, to serve as a sort of *point d'appui.* Gen. Proctor, anxious to frustrate his intentions, and desirous of striking a decisive blow in this quarter, prepared for an expedition to accomplish these designs.

Expedition to the Miami, and attack on the American defences.

He embarked, therefore, on the 23rd April, at Amherstburg, with five hundred and twenty regulars, four hundred and sixty militia, and about fifteen hundred Indians, accompanied by two gun-boats and some artillery. The season was wet, and, as is usually the case at this period, the heavy roads presented very formidable obstacles to the transportation of heavy artillery. By the first of May, however, his preparations were concluded, and a heavy fire was opened on the enemy's works. As to the effect of this fire there is a great discre-

pance in the various accounts. James, in describing it, relates : "No effect was produced, beyond killing one, and wounding seven of General Harrison's men." Major Richardson, who was present, says: "It was impossible to have artillery better served ; every ball that was fired sunk into the roof of the magazine, scattering the earth to a considerable distance, and burying many of the workmen in its bed, from whence we could distinctly perceive the survivors dragging forth the bodies of their slaughtered comrades."

Whatever the precise amount of loss experienced by the Americans, at all events General Harrison was desirous of ending it, and of dislodging a troublesome enemy, whose presence interfered most materially with his plans. He was the more inclined to this step as a reinforcement of twelve hundred Kentuckians under General Clay had just arrived. This body was ordered by Gen. Harrison to attack the British redoubts on one side of the river, while he should make a sortie from the fort on the other.

General Harrison's plan was a good one, had it been well carried out, and he had certainly troops enough to have executed any design he might have formed. The overwhelming force under General Clay easily succeeded in forcing the British line on one side, but advancing too far, and failing in forming a junction with the sallying party under Col. Miller, which had by this time carried the battery, they were attacked by Gen. Proctor, and nearly all captured or killed. Col. Miller's party were then in turn attacked by Proctor, and the battery retaken : the Americans making good their retreat to Fort Meigs. Ingersol observes, " thus another reverse was the result of rash confidence and discipline, and the insensibility of inexperienced troops to the vital importance of implicit obedience ; perhaps, too, on this, as on many other occasions, to the want of that energetic control by a commander, without which even discipline and obedience fail." Ingersol's concluding remark on this affair is too curious to be omitted. " HITHERTO WAR HAD BEEN CONFINED TO THE SORRY ENDEAVOUR TO DEFEND THE COUNTRY FROM INVASION, WHILE ITS NUMERICAL AND PHYSICAL POWER, IF WELL DIRECTED, WAS ABLE TO HAVE MADE ITSELF FELT IN LARGE CONQUESTS OF EXTENSIVE FOREIGN TERRITORIES."

There is something particularly absurd in this sentence : from the very commencement of the war, a series of aggressive demonstrations had been made by the Americans. Elizabeth, Queenston, Erie and Amherstburg had been successively the point of attack ; the main object of these movements had been the occupation of the rich peninsula which forms the western portion of Upper Canada, Gen. Harrison's present works were in furtherance of a combined attack to be made for the acquisition of this coveted territory ; yet forsooth we are told that hitherto with Americans the war had been defensive. This very war, denounced in Congress as an unjust attempt to acquire territory which the Union neither wanted, nor had the means to hold ; against the prosecution of which, the Eastern States had made so determined a stand as to refuse the quota of militia required from them. The repeated failures of this war we now find put forth as the struggle of a brave, but undisciplined militia, to repel invasion ! !

The facts of the war should have prevented Ingersol from setting up so very ridiculous and untenable a position.

The defeat of the Americans was very complete, but Richardson shows that scenes far less satisfactory now occurred. Major R. writes, "the victory obtained at the Miami was such as to reflect credit on every branch of the service ; but the satisfaction arising from the conviction was deeply embittered by an act of cruelty, which, as the writer of an impartial memoir, it becomes my painful duty to record. In the heat of the action a strong corps of the enemy, who had thrown down their arms, and surrendered themselves prisoners of war, were immediately despatched, under an escort of fifty men, for the purpose of being embarked in the gun-boats, where it was presumed they would be safe from the attacks of the Indians. This measure, however, although dictated by the purest humanity, and apparently offering the most probable means of security, proved one of fatal import to several of the prisoners. On gaining our encampment, then entirely deserted by the troops, they were assailed by a few cowardly and treacherous Indians, who had borne no share in the action, yet who now, guided by the savage instinct

of their nature, forced the British guard, and selecting their victims, commenced the work of blood. In vain did the harrassed and indignant escort attempt to save them from the fury of their destroyers ; the phrenzy of these wretches knew no bounds, and an old and excellent soldier of the name of Russell, of the 41st, was shot through the heart while endeavoring to wrest a victim from the grasp of his assailant. Forty of these unhappy men had already fallen beneath the steel of the infuriated party, when Tecumseh, apprised of what was doing, rode up at full speed, and raising his tomahawk, threatened to destroy the first man who resisted his injunction to desist. Even on those lawless people, to whom the language of coercion had hitherto been unknown, the threats and tone of the exasperated chieftain produced an instantaneous effect, and they retired at once humiliated and confounded."

"Never did Tecumseh shine more truly himself than on this occasion ; and nought of the savage could be distinguished save the color and the garb. Ever merciful and magnanimous as he was ardent and courageous, the voice of the suppliant seldom reached him in vain ; and although war was his idol, the element in which he lived, his heart was formed to glow with all the nobler and more generous impulses of the warrior ; nor was his high character less esteemed by ourselves than reverenced by the various tribes over which, in his quality of brother to the Prophet, he invariably presided. In any other country, and governing any other men, Tecumseh would have been a hero ; at the head of this uncivilized and untractable people he was a savage ; but a savage such as Civilization herself might not blush to acknowledge for her child. Constantly opposed to the encroachments of the Americans for a series of years previous to their rupture with England, he had combated their armies on the banks of the Wabash with success, and given their leaders proof of a skill and judgment in defence of his native soil which would not have disgraced the earlier stages of military science in Europe. General Harrison himself, a commander with whom he had often disputed the palm of victory, with the generous candor of the soldier, subsequently ascribed to him virtues as a man, and abilities as a warrior, commanding at once the attention and admiration of his enemies."

" The survivors of this melancholy catastrophe were immediately conveyed on board the gun boats moored in the river ; and every precaution having been taken to prevent a renewal of the scene, the escorting party proceeded to the interment of the victims, to whom the rites of sepulture were afforded even before those of our own men who had fallen in the action. Colonel Dudley, second in command of General Clay's division, was among the number of the slain."

Every one must deplore this transaction, and regret that proper measures had not been adopted to insure protection to the captives ; most unhappily, too, it afforded an opportunity to American writers to indulge still more freely in the strain of bitter invective already so common, and they were now enabled to color with some shadow of truth, the numerous appeals made against the British for acting in concert with the Indians. We do not pretend to palliate this inhuman massacre ; but still, it must be borne in mind that the Indians far outnumbered their allies, and that they were smarting under the sense of a long series of injuries inflicted on them by the Americans. They had never experienced mercy at the hand of their enemies, the lesson of moderation and mercy had never been taught them, and at this precise time, a reward had been offered by American officials for every Indian scalp. In place of so unjustly condemning the British as participators and instigators in such cruel scenes, Americans should have asked, have we not had meted to us the cup of tribulation and misery so unsparingly measured out by ourselves to our red brethren.

After the action General Proctor ascertained the impossibility of restraining the Indians from pursuing their established custom of returning home to secure the booty they had acquired. A great part of the militia also represented the absolute necessity that existed for them to return to their homes so as to take advantage of the short Canadian season for preparing their crops. General Proctor, therefore, found himself compelled to embark his guns and stores, raise the siege of Fort Meigs, and return to Amherstburg. We will begin our next chapter with the account of this embarkation to be found in General Proctor's letters to Sir G. Prevost.

General Proctor deserted by the Indians and part of the Militia.

Col. Proctor's embarkation return of the force, of all ranks and services, including Commissariat officers, &c., on this expedition, gives five hundred and twenty two regulars, and four hundred and sixty-one militia. His loss of killed, wounded and missing was estimated at one hundred and one.

BROCK'S MONUMENT, AS IT WAS—QUEENSTON.

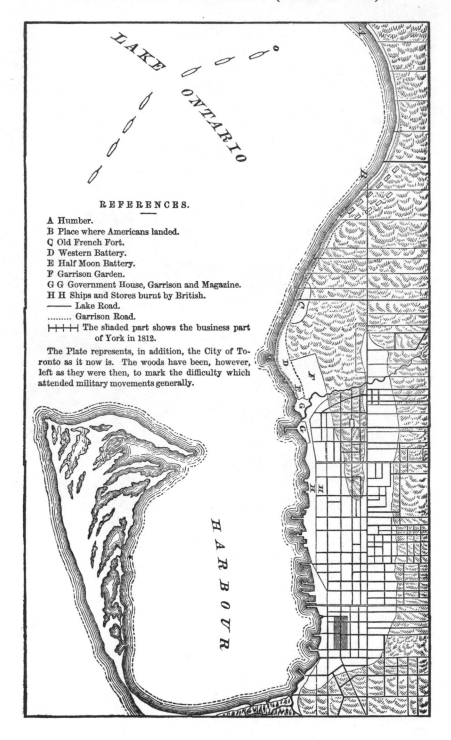

REFERENCES.

A Humber.
B Place where Americans landed.
C Old French Fort.
D Western Battery.
E Half Moon Battery.
F Garrison Garden.
G G Government House, Garrison and Magazine.
H H Ships and Stores burnt by British.
———— Lake Road.
········· Garrison Road.
⊢+++⊣ The shaded part shows the business part
        of York in 1812.

The Plate represents, in addition, the City of Toronto as it now is. The woods have been, however,
left as they were then, to mark the difficulty which
attended military movements generally.

CHAPTER X.

INGERSOL, in his historical sketch, touches

Fort Meigs.

but slightly on this affair, and appears indeed, to introduce it, only for the purpose of depreciating the regulars and militia. "Fort Meigs was besieged by Proctor and Tecumseh, with SEVERAL THOUSAND ENGLISH AND INDIANS,* who, after many days bombardment, were compelled to retire. Indians, even under so valiant a leader as Tecumseh, are of little use in besieging a fortified place ; and, WITHOUT THE INDIANS, the ENGLISH SOLDIERS SELDOM PERFORMED MUCH."

General Proctor's modest despatch will shew exactly what was effected.

Upper Canada, Sandwich, May 14th, 1813.

SIR,—From the circumstances of the war, I have judged it expedient to make a direct report to your Excellency of the operations and present state in this district.

In the expectation of being able to reach the enemy, who had taken post near the foot of the Rapids of the Miami, before the reinforcement and supplies could arrive, for which he only waited to commence active operations against us, I determined to attack him without delay, and with every means in my power ; but from the necessary preparations and some

untoward circumstances, it was not in my power to reach him within three weeks of the period I had proposed, and at which time he might have been captured or destroyed.

From the incessant and heavy rains we experienced, and during which our batteries were constructed, it was not until the morning of the 1st inst., the fifth day after our arrival at the mouth of the river, twelve miles from the enemy, that our batteries could be opened.

The enemy, who occupied several acres of commanding ground, strongly defended by block-houses, and the batteries well furnished with ordnance, had, during our approach, so completely entrenched and covered himself, as to render unavailing every effort of our artillery, though well served, and in batteries most judiciously placed and constructed, under the able direction of Captain Dixon, of the Royal Engineers, of whose ability and unwearied zeal, shown particularly on this occasion, I cannot speak too highly.

Though the attack has not answered fully the purpose intended, I have the satisfaction to inform your Excellency of the fortunate result of an attack of the enemy, aided by a sally of most of their garrison, made on the morning of the 5th inst., by a reinforcement which descended the river a considerable distance in a very short time, consisting of two corps, Dudley's and Rosswell's, amounting to thirteen hundred men, under the command of Brigadier-General Green Clay. The attack was very sudden, on both sides of the river.

* We gave, in our last chapter, the exact number of regulars, Militia and Indians.

The enemy were for a few minutes in possession of our batteries, and took some prisoners. After a severe contest, though not of long continuance, the enemy gave way, and except the body of those who sallied from the fort, must have been mostly killed or taken.

In this decisive affair, the officers and men of the 41st Regiment, who charged and routed the enemy near the batteries, well maintained the great reputation of the corps. Where all deserve praise, it is difficult to distinguish. Capt. Muir, an old officer, who has seen much service, had the good fortune to be in the immediate command of these brave men. Besides my obligations to Captain Chambers, for his unwearied exertions preparatory to, and on the expedition, as Deputy-Assistant Quarter-Master-General, I have to notice his gallant conduct in attacking the enemy near the batteries at the point of the bayonet; a service in which he was well supported by Lieuts. Bullock and Clements of the 41st regiment, and Lieut. Le Breton of the Royal Newfound land regiment. The courage and activity displayed through the whole scene of action by the Indian chiefs and warriors contributed largely to our success. I have not been able to ascertain the amount of the prisoners in possession of the Indians. I have sent off, according to agreement, near five hundred prisoners to the river Huron, near Sandusky.

I have proposed an exchange, which is referred to the American Government.

I could not ascertain the amount of the enemy's loss in killed, from the extent of the scene of action, and mostly in the woods. I conceive his loss, in killed and wounded, to have been between one thousand and one thousand two hundred men.

These unfortunate people were not volunteers, and complete Kentucky's quota. If the enemy had been permitted to receive his reinforcements and supplies undisturbed, I should have had at this critical juncture to contend with him for Detroit, or perhaps on this shore.

I had not the option of retaining my position on the Miami. Half of the militia had left us. I received a deputation from the chiefs, counselling me to return, as they could not prevent their people, as was their custom after any battle of consequence, returning to their villages with their wounded, their prisoners, and plunder, of which they had taken a considerable quantity in the boats of the enemy.

Before the ordnance could be withdrawn from the batteries, I was left with Tecumseh, and less than twenty chiefs and warriors, a circumstance which strongly proves that, *under present circumstances at least, our Indian force is not a disposable one, or permanent, though occasionally a most powerful aid.* I have, however, brought off all the ordnance ; and, indeed, have not left anything behind; part of the ordnance was embarked under the fire of the enemy.

The service on which we were employed has been, though short, a very severe one ; and too much praise cannot be given to both officers and men, for the cheerfulness with which, on every occasion, they met the service. To Lieut.-Colonel Warburton I feel many obligations, for the aid he zealously afforded me on every occasion. From my Brigade Major, Lieut. McLean, I received the same zealous assistance as on former occasions. To Captain Mockler, Royal Newfoundland Regt., who acted as my Aide-de-Camp, I am much indebted for the assistance afforded me.

Lieutenant Le Breton, of the Newfoundland Regiment, assistant engineer, by his unwearied exertions, rendered essential service, as did Lieutenant Gardiner, of the 41st Regiment, from his science in artillery. The Royal Artillery, in the laborious duties they performed, displayed their usual unwearied zeal, and were well assisted by the Royal Newfoundland (under Lieutenant Garden) as additional gunners. The laborious duties which the Marines, under Commodore Hall, were called upon to perform, have been most cheerfully met, and the most essential service performed.

I have the honor to send an embarkation return of the force that served under my command at the Miami, exclusive of the Indians, who may be stated at twelve hundred.

I also enclose a return of our killed, wounded, and prisoners, who have, however, been exchanged.

I have taken upon me to give the rank of Major to the six Captains of the line, as militia were employed on the same service with them ; some of them are old officers; all of them deserving; any mark of your Excellency's approbation of them would be extremely grateful to me.

I beg leave to mention the four volunteers of the 41st regiment, Wilkinson, Richardson, Laing, and Proctor, as worthy of promotion.

I have the honor to be, &c.

HENRY PROCTOR,

Brig.-Gen. Comg.

I beg to acknowledge the indefatigable exertions of the Commissariat.

(Signed,) HENRY PROCTOR.

To His Excellency Lieut.-Gen.
Sir G. Prevost, Bart., &c.

———

It will be perceived, by his dispatch, that General Proctor does

Slaughter of captives. not attach quite so much importance to the Indian force as Ingersol would fain make out. He and other American writers have always made this arm of the "allied force" a convenient excuse for any mistakes or failures, and we have, accordingly, already shewn that to the dread inspired by this force was "Hull's deplorable surrender" ascribed, while, in another instance, "to the vile use made by Proctor, with Elliot's aid, of the terror of the savages," all the disasters at the River Raisin were attributed.

The Elliot here spoken of has been frankly acknowledged by Thomson, in his sketches of the war, to have been "an American by birth, a native of Maryland." "The thrilling tales of cruelty and bloodshed," so liberally inter-woven into their narratives by most of the American chroniclers of these times, exhibit so much of the character of romance, that it were idle to attempt the refutation of the many and curious fictions ; we may, however, remark, en passant, that whilst we do not admit that cruelty was ever practiced, where the British could interfere, in the present instance the individual most obnoxious to censure was acknowledged to have been one of themselves. We close this part of our subject, by also reminding the readers of these "thrilling tales," that in General Winchester's official despatch, (as he wrote it) he expressed himself "highly gratified with the attention which had been paid to him, his officers, and the prisoners generally, by the British."

A signal proof of American disingenuousness is to be found in the suppression, or rather garbling of this document, and we can only account for this proceeding (the expunging from the despatch of that part of it we have just quoted) as ascribing it to the necessity which existed, that the war should, at all hazards, be rendered popular, and that it was, therefore, found expedient to keep alive the spirit of animosity which they had by this time partially succeeded in arousing, and which it had been their aim to establish, by circulating tales calculated to kindle a feeling of revenge throughout the length and breadth of the Union. It will be accordingly found that those tales are the most highly seasoned which were produced by the Government organs.

We left Commodore Chauncey with a large fleet at Sackett's Harbor,

Descent upon York. ready to co-operate in the meditated combined attack on Canada. It had been at one time proposed that this attack should have been commenced by a movement on Kingston, and that the two brigades wintering on Lake Champlain, and amounting to twenty-five hundred men, should be placed in sleighs, and transported under the command of General Pike, by the most eligible route, and with the greatest possible rapidity to Kingston: where (being joined by such force as could be brought from Sackett's Harbor) they should, by surprise or assault, carry that post, destroy the shipping wintering there, and subsequently be governed by circumstances, in either retaining the position or in withdrawing from it. This plan was, however, abandoned, probably from reports of the increased strength of the British, and the one detailed in our last chapter, substituted. The two letters from General Armstrong, Secretary at War, lay open the whole plan of operations, and prove most conclusively how well informed the American commanders were of Sir George Prevost's weakness at that time, although misled afterwards by the false reports which ultimately led to the change in plans.

(First Letter.)

February 10th.

"I have the President's orders to communicate to you, as expeditiously as possible, the outline of campaign which you will immediately institute and pursue against Upper Canada :—

1st. 4000 troops will be assembled at Sackett's Harbor.

2d. 3000 will be brought together at Buffalo and its vicinity.

3d. The former of these corps will be embarked and transported under convoy of the fleet to Kingston, where they will be landed. Kingston, its garrison, and the British ships wintering in the harbor of that place will be its first object. Its second object will be York, (the capital of Upper Canada) the stores collected, and the two frigates building there. Its third object, Forts George and Erie, and their dependencies. In the attainment of this last there will be a co-operation between the two corps. The composition of these will be as follows:

1st.	Bloomfield's Brigade	1,436
2d.	Chandler's do.	1,044
3d.	Philadelphia detachment	400
4th.	Baltimore do.	300
5th.	Carlisle do.	200
6th.	Greenbush do.	400
7th.	Sackett's Harbor do.	250
8th.	Several corps at Buffalo under the command of General Porter, and the recruits belonging thereto	3,000
	Total	7,030

The time for executing the enterprise will be governed by the opening of Lake Ontario, which usually takes place about the 1st of April.

The Adjutant-General has orders to put the more southern detachments in march as expeditiously as possible. The two brigades on Lake Champlain you will move so as to give them full time to reach their place of destination by the 25th of March. The route by Elizabeth will, I think, be the shortest and best. They will be replaced by some new raised regiments from the east.

You will put into your movements as much privacy as may be compatible with their execution. They may be masked by reports that Sackett's Harbor is in danger, and that their principal effort will be made on the Niagara, in co-operation with General Harrison. As the route to Sackett's Harbor and to Niagara is for a considerable distance the same, it may be well to intimate, even in orders, that the latter is the destination of the two brigades now at Lake Champlain."

(*Second Letter.*)

February 24th.

"Before I left New York, and, till very recently, since my arrival here, I was informed through various channels, that a winter or spring attack upon Kingston was not practicable, on account of the snow which generally lies to the depth of two, and sometimes of three feet, over all that northern region during those seasons. Hence it is that in the plan recently communicated, it was thought safest and best to make the attack by a combination of naval and military means, and to approach our object, not by directly crossing the St. Lawrence on the ice, but by setting out from Sackett's Harbor, in concert with, and under convoy of the fleet. Later information differs from that on which this plan was founded; and the fortunate issue of Major Forsyth's last expedition shews, that small enterprises, at least, may be successfully executed at the present season. The advices, given in your letter of the 14th instant, have a bearing also on the same point, and to the same effect. If the enemy be really weak at Kingston, and approachable by land and ice, Pike, (who will be a brigadier in a day or two,) may be put into motion from Lake Champlain by the Chateaugay route, (in sleighs) and, with the two brigades, cross the St. Lawrence where it may be thought best, destroy the armed ships, and seize and hold Kingston, until you can join him with the other corps destined for the future objects of the expedition; and, if pressed by Prevost before such junction can be effected, he may withdraw himself to Sackett's Harbor, or other place of security, on our side of the line. This would be much the shorter road to the object, and perhaps the safer one, as the St. Lawrence is now every where well bridged, and offers no obstruction to either attack or retreat. Such a movement, will, no doubt, be soon known to Prevost, and cannot but disquiet him. The dilemma it presents will be serious. Either he must give up his western posts, or, to save them, he must carry himself in force, and promptly, to Upper Canada. In the latter case he will be embarrassed for subsistence. His convoys of provision will be open to our attacks, on a line of nearly one hundred miles, and his position at Montreal much weakened. Another decided advantage will be, to let us into the secret of his real strength. If he be able to make heavy detachments to cover, or to recover Kingston, and to protect his supplies, and after all maintain himself at Montreal and on Lake Champlain, he is stronger than I imagined, or than any well-authenticated reports make him to be.

With regard to our magazines, my belief is, that we have nothing to fear; because, as stated above, Prevost's attention must be given to the western posts, and to our movements against them. He will not dare to advance southwardly, while a heavy corps is operating on his flank, and menacing his line of communication. But on the other sup_position, they (the magazines) may be easily secured; 1st, by taking them to Willsborough; or, 2d, to Burlington; or, 3d, by a militia call, to protect them where they are. Orders are given for the march of the eastern volunteers, excepting Ulmer's regiment, and two companies of axe-men, sent to open the route to the Chaudière.

The southern detachment will be much stronger than I had supposed. That from Philadelphia will amount to nearly one thousand effectives."

Although we are enabled from these letters to make out what was the original plan, we are left without much information as to the real reason why it was abandoned. Even Armstrong, although Secretary at War, and commenting on this particular enterprise at considerable length, is comparatively silent on ·this point, we may, therefore, with some degree of confidence, ascribe it to General Dearborn's and Commodore Chauncey's representations, influenced doubtless by private information gained through their spies.

Be this matter, however, as it may, on the 25th April, 1813, Commodore Chauncey's fleet sailed from Sackett's Harbor for York, having on board General Dearborn, as General-in-chief, and a considerable force. It is not easy to get at the exact number of troops sent on this enterprise, nor to ascertain the *materiel* of which it was composed. General Dearborn does not enumerate them, and most American historians have taken the number mentioned by Chauncey, who says that "he took on board the General and suite, and about seventeen hundred men." Ingersol reduces, on what authority we are ignorant,

this number to sixteen hundred, but an Albany paper, says James, actually states the number at "about five thousand." This is an evident exaggeration, but we think we may safely put the numbers down, after comparing the various accounts, including the crews of the armed vessels, at between two thousand five hundred and three thousand men.

This force reached its destination on the 27th, and preparations were immediately made for landing the troops. York seems at this time to have been in an almost defenceless condition, and a very reprehensible apathy appears to have prevailed. James represents that "the guns upon the batteries, being without trunnions, were mounted upon wooden sticks, with iron hoops, and, therefore, became of very little use. Others of the guns belonged to the ship that was building, and lay on the ground, partly covered with snow and frozen mud," James also mentions that the accidental circumstance of the Duke of Gloucester brig being in the port, undergoing some repairs, enabled the garrison to mount, on temporary field works, a few six-pounders. Still the defences were of the most insignificant character, and we are at a loss to account for the undertaking the building of vessels in a place so open to, and unprepared for, an attack.

Their various positions having been taken up by the armed vessels destined to cover the landing, and take part in the attack on the batteries, the debarkation of the troops began about eight o'clock in the morning, and Forsyth with his rifle corps were the first who attempted to make good a landing.

The spot at which the landing was intended to have been made was close to the site of an old French fort, and will be found on reference to the plan at the head of the chapter; the boats were, however, carried by a strong breeze and heavy sea, considerably to leeward of the intended point, and nearly half a mile to the westward the landing was effected. Armstrong says this spot was "thickly covered with brushwood, and already occupied by British and Indian marksmen." Had the spot been occupied as thus represented, the chances are, when we consider with what difficulty they overcame a mere handful of men, that the Americans would never have landed on that day; in reality it was occupied by Major Givens, with about five-and-twenty Indians, and a company (about sixty) of Glengarry Fencibles. Armstrong adds; "in the contest that followed, Forsyth lost some men, but no credit." We grant the former, as the defence made by the handful of men, then on the ground, was so determined that Forsyth would have found it difficult to effect a landing had he not been speedily reinforced by Major King and a battalion of infantry. The landing of the main body under General Pike now enabled the enemy to advance more boldly, and to drive back the British, (whose numbers had been in the meantime increased by the arrival of some two hundred and twenty militia, and fifty of the Newfoundland regiment,) from one position to another. The stand made at some of these positions was very gallant, as two companies of the 8th regiment (about two hundred strong) had now joined. James says, "the whole of the American troops, at this time on shore, amounted, by their own accounts, to upwards of one thousand. These were met by two hundred and ten men of the 8th, and Newfoundland, regiments, and about two hundred and twenty militia, who made a formidable charge upon the American column, and partially compelled it to retire." Reinforced, however, by the fresh troops that were continually being landed, the Americans rallied and compelled the British to retire, partially covered in their retreat by the batteries which, insignificant as they were, had still done good service, by partially occupying the attention of the enemy's vessels, which had by this time, from their light draught of water, approached within gun-shot. The companies of the 8th regiment suffered materially from their ignorance of the roads, the grenadiers being nearly annihilated, and this was the more to be regretted, as their gallantry was without any beneficial results, the main landing having been effected before their arrival. General Sheaffe appears to have laid his plans very badly; by early dawn the alarm of the enemies' approach was given; yet so confused does every movement appear to have been, that we find only a few Indians and a handful of militia on the spot to oppose a landing, while the two companies of the 8th were left to find their way through woods and cover without proper direction or guides. We find, in addition, Adjutant Gen. Shaw, with a body of men and a brass six-pounder, taking up a position on the line of Dundas street, where he remained, taking no part in the action. We do not blame Adjutant Gen. Shaw for this, as we presume he had his orders, but we question the judgment which placed him in such a position, as it was not probable that the Americans would advance by that route, leaving in the rear, a force which, small as it was, had kept them in check for six hours. On the retreat of the British, a movement effected through the woods, the Americans advanced and carried, without much resistance, the first defence: advancing towards the second, and observing the fire cease suddenly, Pike concluded, and not unreasonably, that it was for the purpose of making proposals for a surrender, and unfortunately halted his troops while yet at a distance of two hundred yards from the main battery. We say, unfortunately, as, had they advanced, the major part of them must have perished in the explosion which took place on the firing of the magazine, which had been just blown up by Sergeant Marshall to prevent the enemy gaining possession of a large quantity of powder deposited there. Ingersol styles the blowing up of the magazine "a vile stratagem;" and Thomson accuses General Sheaffe of treacherously ordering the train to be laid, and of artfully placing several cart loads of stones to increase the effect. This is quite incorrect, as we do not think Sheaffe clever enough to have suggested such a plan; besides, Marshall distinctly stated that had he known General Sheaffe wished it, or had it occurred to himself, he could easily have blown up the enemy by giving ten minutes more port fire. Had he done so, the destruction of the whole column would have been the natural consequence. A vast amount of nonsense, relative to this affair, has been penned by American historians, who do not seem to reflect that this was an invading force, and that the mine has always been a legitimate mode either of attack or defence. In the present instance, the only object in blowing up the magazine was to prevent General Pike getting possession of the powder; it was, therefore, blown up, and very clumsily too, it was done, as several of the British troops were killed or wounded by the explosion. We heartily agree with James, "that even had the whole column been destroyed, the Americans would but have met their deserts;" and if disposed to commiserate the poor soldiers, at least, we wish, with him, "that their places had been filled by the American President, and the ninety-eight members of the Legislature who voted for the war." The explosion, partial as were its effects, killed and wounded more than two hundred Americans, spreading its mischief far and wide, and creating in the remainder much temporary alarm and confusion. The stones and rubbish were thrown as far as the decks of the vessels near the shore, and, according to Ingersol, "the water shocked as with an earthquake."

General Pike was literally stoned to death, his breast and sides were crushed, and he lingered in great agony till he expired. Gen. Pike was a native of New Jersey, and is represented to have been a gallant and thorough-bred soldier, and one of the best commanders the Americans had. His death was a glorious one. Through motives of humanity he halted to prevent unnecessary effusion of blood, and paltry as was the victory gained with such overwhelming odds, still he had the satisfaction of knowing that he had gained a victory, such as it was. Thompson and Ingersol are very eloquent on his death; "carried on board the Commodore's ship, General Pike was laid on a mattress, and asking for the British captured flag to be laid under his head, in a few hours he nobly breathed his last upon it, without a sigh."

All honor we are ready to pay to the brave man who dies a sacrifice for his country, but considering the immense superiority of numbers, by which, after a long and desperate struggle, the feat of supplanting the flag was achieved, the officiousness of the American historians has conferred more of ridicule than of honor upon the last moments of their hero.

General Sheaffe was careful to avail himself of the temporary panic into which the enemy had been thrown, and collecting what regular force he could, and leaving to their own resources the civil authorities and embodied militia, he made a hasty retreat in the direction of Kingston, destroying, as he passed along, two ships on the stocks, and a magazine of military and naval stores in the harbour. The defence of the town being no longer practicable, a surrender necessarily followed, by which it was stipulated, that the militia and others at-tached to the British military and naval service, *who had been captured*, should be paroled; that private property of every kind should be respected, and that all public stores should be given up to the captors. We have italicised the words "who had been captured," as the Americans got possession of the militia rolls and included amongst the list of prisoners on parole, many who had never laid down their arms, and whom it was never contemplated to include in the list. We give Sheaffe's dispatch, with his list of killed and wounded:

Kingston, May 5th, 1813.

Sir,—I did myself the honor of writing to your Excellency, on my route from York, to communicate the mortifying intelligence that the enemy had obtained possession of that place on the 27th of April. I shall now give your Excellency a further detail of that event.

In the evening of the 26th, information was received that many vessels had been seen to the eastward. Very early the next morning, they were discovered lying-to, not far from the harbor; after some time had elapsed, they made sail, and to the number of sixteen, of various descriptions, anchored off the shore, some distance to the westward. Boats full of troops were immediately seen assembling near the commodore's ship, under cover of whose fire, and that of other vessels, and aided by the wind, they soon effected a landing, in spite of a spirited opposition from Major Givens and about forty Indians. A company of Glengarry light infantry, which had been ordered to support them, had, by some mistake (not in the smallest degree imputable to its commander,) been led in another direction, and came late into action. The other troops, consisting of two companies of the 8th (or King's regiment), and about a company of the royal Newfoundland regiment, with some militia, encountered the enemy in a thick wood. Captain M'Neal, of the King's regiment, was killed, while gallantly leading his company, which suffered severely. The troops at length fell back; they rallied several times, but could not maintain the contest against the greatly superior and increasing numbers of the enemy. They retired under cover of our batteries, which were engaged with some of the enemy's vessels that had moved nigher to the harbour. By some unfortunate accident the magazine at the western battery blew up, and killed and wounded a considerable number of men, and crippled the battery. It became too evident that our numbers and means of defence were inadequate to the task of maintaining possession of

York against the vast superiority of force brought against it. The troops were withdrawn towards the town, and were finally ordered to retreat on the road to Kingston ; the powder magazine was blown up, and the new ship and naval stores destroyed. Lieutenant-Colonel Chewett and Major Allen of the militia, residents in the town, were instructed to treat with the American commanders for terms ; a statement of those agreed on with Major-General Dearborn and Commodore Chauncey, is transmitted to your Excellency, with returns of the killed and wounded, &c. The accounts of the number of the enemy vary from eighteen hundred and ninety to three thousand. We had about six hundred, including militia and dock-yardmen. The quality of these troops was of so superior a description, and their general disposition so good, that, under less unfavourable circumstances, I should have felt confident of success, in spite of the disparity of numbers. As it was, the contest, which commenced between six and seven o'clock, was maintained for nearly eight hours.

When we had proceeded some miles from York, we met the light infantry of the King's rement, on its route for Fort George ; it retired with us and covered the retreat, which was effected without molestation from the enemy.

I have the honor to be, &c.,

R. H. SHEAFFE, Major-General.

His Excellency Sir George Prevost, &c.

Return of killed, wounded, prisoners, and missing, of the troops engaged at York, under the command of Sir Roger Hall Sheaffe, on the 27th ultimo :—

Kingston, May 10th, 1813.

Total—One captain, one sergeant-major, four serjeants, one drummer, fifty-two rank and file, three gunners, killed : one ensign, two serjeants, one drummer, thirty rank and file, wounded ; one lieutenant, four serjeants, one drummer, thirty-six rank and ffle, one driver, wounded and prisoners ; six rank and file, one bombardier, three gunners, prisoners ; six rank and file, one gunner, missing.

Names of officers killed and wounded.

Killed—8th (or King's regiment) — Captain M'Neal, volunteer D. Maclean, clerk of the House of Assembly.

Wounded—Royal Newfoundland Regiment— Lieutenant D. Keven, prisoner.

Glengarry Light Infantry— Ensign Robins, slightly.

General Staff —Captain Loring, 104th regiment, slightly.

Incorporated Militia—Capt. Jarvis, volunteer, —— Hartney, barrack-master.

RICHARD LEONARD,
Acting deputy-assistant-adjutant-general.

EDWD. BAYNES,
Adjutant-general, North America.

Terms of capitulation entered into on the 27th April, 1813, for the surrender of the town of York, in Upper Canada, to the army and navy of the United States, under the command of Major-General Dearborn and Commodore Chauncey :

That the troops, regular and militia, at this post, and the naval officers and seamen, shall be surrendered prisoners of war. The troops, regular and militia, to ground their arms immediately on parade, and the naval officers and seamen be immediately surrendered.

That all public stores, naval and military, shall be immediately given up to the commanding officers of the army and navy of the United States— that all private property shall be guaranteed to the citizens of the town of York.

That all papers belonging to the civil officers shall be retained by them—that such surgeons as may be procured to attend the wounded of the British regulars and Canadian militia shall not be considered prisoners of war.

That one lieutenant-colonel, one major, thirteen captains, nine lieutenants, eleven ensigns, one quarter-master, one deputy adjutant-general of the militia, namely—

Lieut.-Col. Chewett,	George Mustard,
Major Allen.	Barnet Vanderburch,
CAPTAINS.	Robert Stanton,
John Wilson,	George Ridout,
John Button,	Wm. Jarvis,
Peter Robinson,	Edward M'Mahon,
Reuben Richardson,	John Wilson,
John Arnold,	Ely Playter.
James Fenwick,	ENSIGNS.
James Mustard,	Andrew Thompson,
Duncan Cameron,	Alfred Senally,
David Thompson,	Donald M'Arthur,
John Robinson,	William Smith,
Samuel Ridout,	Andrew Mercer,
Thomas Hamilton,	James Chewett,
John Burn,	George Kink,
William Jarvis.	Edward Thompson,
QUARTER-MASTER.	Charles Denison,
Charles Baynes.	George Denison,
LIEUTENANTS.	Darcey Boulton.
John H. Shultz,	

Nineteen serjeants, four corporals, and two hundred and four rank and file.

Of the field train department, Wm. Dunbar ; of the provincial navy, Captain Frs. Góvereaux, Lieutenant Green, Midshipmen John Ridout, Louis Baupré, Clerk, James Langsdon, one boatswain, fifteen naval artificers ; of His Majesty's regular troops, Lieutenant De Keven, one serjeant-major ; and of the royal artillery, one bombardier and three gunners, shall be surrendered prisoners of war, and accounted for in the exchange of prisoners between the United States and Great Britain.

(Signed)   G. E. MITCHELL, Lieut.-Col.
3rd A. U. S.
SAMUEL S. CONNOR, Major and
A. D. C. to Maj.-Gen. Dearborn.
WILLIAM KING, Major.
15th U. S. Infantry.
JESSE D. ELLIOTT, Lieut.
U. S. Navy.
W. CHEWETT, Lieut.-Col. Com.
3rd Regt. York Militia.
W. ALLEN, Major 3rd Regt.
York Militia.
F. GAURREAU, Lieut. M. Dpt.

According to the capitulation the total of pri-soners amounted to two hundred and ninety-three, yet some American accounts swelled this number, one, to seven hundred and fifty, another, to nine hundred and thirty. These assertions, too, were made in the face of Gen. Dearborn's official letter, in whichi t will have been seen he does not, including Indians, rate the British force at more than eight hundred. Small as this force was, had it not been for the unfortunate (as we deem it) halt of the 8th on their way from Kingston to Fort George, the Americans would have had a still smaller force to contend with. Sir George Prevost and General Sheaffe deserve great censure for this affair of York—the one for allowing mil-itary and naval stores to be deposited, and a comparatively large sloop of war to be built, in an exposed situation—the other for gross negligence in not ordering the fortifications to be put in order, and neglecting to take proper measures for concentrating his troops and en-suring something like order and regularity. General Sheaffe was shortly afterwards super-seded in the command, in Upper Canada, by Major General De Rottenburg, and, returning toMontreal, he took the command of the troops in that district.

The Americans gained possession of a great quantity of naval stores, of which the destruc-tion had been neglected. The greatest loss, however, was that of the ships—one of which had been nearly planked. Fortunately the brig Prince Regent had left the harbor some three days before the attack, thereby escap-ing capture. The stores taken at York, writes Ingersol, " by another mistake, were burnt at Sackett's Harbour," so that the Americans had not even this to boast of as a recompense for the loss of so many men. James evidently seems disposed to accuse the Americans of dealing harshly with the town, and states that

"they set fire, not only to the public build-ings, civil as well as military, but to a tavern some distance from York; and were proceed-ing upon the same charitable errand to Hatt's Mills, had they not been deterred by informa-tion of Indians being in the neighbourhood." Christie is, however, silent on this point, and we are induced from the circumstance, as well as from information gained from the actors in the scene to consider James' statement as rather highly coloured. Ingersol does not rank the advantage that occurred by the cap-ture of York, at a very high rate, "with the exception," he says, " of the English General's musical snuff box, which was an object of much interest to some of our officers, and a scalp which Major Forsyth found suspended over the speaker's chair, we gained but barren honor by the capture of York, of which no permanent possession was taken."

Touching the scalp here mentioned, Inger-sol pretends to give an official letter from Commodore Chauncey to the Hon. William Jones, Secretary of the Navy, in which the Commodore is made to write:

Sir,—I have the honor to present you, by the hands of Lieut. Dudley, the British stand-ard taken at York, on the 27th April last, accompanied by the mace, *over which hung a human scalp.*

"This atrocious ornament," continues In-gersol, " was sent to the Secretary of War, General Armstrong, who refused to receive or suffer it to remain in his cabinet." Armstrong in relation to this affair, writes, " our trophies were fewer but better taken care of. One human scalp, a prize made, as we understand, by the *Commodore,* was offered, but not ac-cepted, as a *decoration* to the walls of the war office." It will be observed that Armstrong does not say how, or where, Commodore Chauncey acquired this valuable trophy, but from the expertness of the backwoodsmen in scalping, (we have already given one or two instances of this,) it is not at all unlikely, but that the scalp in question was that of an un-fortunate Indian who was shot while in a tree, by the Americans, in their advance on the town, on the other hand, it may be gathered from Armstrong's words, that Chauncey him-self took the scalp, which he afterwards offered as a prize to decorate the walls of the war office. Ingersol devotes six and a half pages to this one scalp, raking up all the horrors of the revolutionary war, and proving most distinctly how safe he, in common with other American writers, were to make up a case of cruelty, even by implication, against the British.

Sheaffe was superseded, as it is supposed, **Errors of the Commanders.** for his blunders in the defence of York, and certainly not without cause, as he appears on the occasion to have acted without judgment or any fixed plan. Numerous as his mistakes were, they still sink into insignificance, when we compare them with those of the American commanders, who failed in two great points, the capture of the frigate, and the prevention of Sheaffe's escape. Had General Dearborn been on the field, instead of being in safety three miles from the shore, on Pike's death, he might have prevented the escape of Sheaffe with the main body of the regulars; as it was, Col. Pierce, who succeeded to the command, was totally without orders, and knew not what to do. This would have been most important, for situated as Great Britain, at that time, was, she could have ill afforded to send more men to this country, and, scanty as were the means of defence, the capture of Sheaffe's force, small as it was, would have been a fatal blow. General Armstrong, in his letter to Dearborn, dwells particularly on this point, and writes, "I am assured that the regular force in both the Canadas has at no time since the declaration of war, exceeded three thousand men; and at the present time, by casualties, this force has been reduced *at least* one-fifth. Taking then this fact for granted, we cannot doubt but that in all cases in which a British commander is constrained to act defensively, his policy will be that adopted by Sheaffe, to prefer the preservation of his troops to that of his post, and thus carrying off the kernel, leave us only the shell. In your late affair, it appears to me that had the descent been made between the town and the barracks, things would have turned out better. On that plan, the two batteries you had to encounter, would have been left out of the combat, and Sheaffe, instead of retreating to Kingston, must have retreated to Fort George." General Armstrong's ignorance of the nature of the ground has led him to make some remarks not quite deserved:

nor did he make allowances for the strong east wind; yet there is very little doubt but that, had General Dearborn been a man of energy, much more might have been effected. A still more glaring instance of want of judgment occurred, however, in the next movement we have to touch upon; the descent upon Fort George, at the mouth of the Niagara River.

One object of the expedition against York; **Descent upon Fort George.** the capture of the stores, having been accomplished, the troops were re-embarked, in the hope that they would be able to proceed to the second and more important movement, without loss of time. Baffled, however, by light and adverse winds, it was not till the sixth day (8th of May) after leaving York, that they arrived off Fort George. It now cost General Dearborn three weeks to dispatch his wounded to Sackett's Harbor, and bring thence reinforcements; as Ingersol says, "a month of precious time was consumed before the attack on Fort George, and then again the commander-in-chief remained on board a vessel; while his army, six thousand strong, attacked and carried the place."

The British force on the Niagara line amounted, at that time, to about eighteen hundred regulars, and five hundred militia. The regular force consisted of the 49th Regt. and of detachments from the 8th, 41st, Glengarry and Newfoundland corps, with a small body of artillery, the whole commanded by Brigadier General Vincent. Eight companies of the 49th, five companies of the 8th, three companies of the Glengarry, two of the Newfoundland regiment, and a portion of the artillery, were stationed at Fort George, "amounting," says James, "to less than one thousand rank and file." About three hundred militia and some fifty Indians were also stationed at this post. We have seen on Armstrong's authority, that the Americans numbered, with the reinforcements drawn from Sackett's Harbor, six thousand men. A sufficient superiority (six to one) having been secured, the American general considered himself prepared for the attack on the post, before which he had spent three weeks, and on the 27th May, the batteries on the American side of the Niagara being ready for action, and means necessary for transportation provided, the combatants began their movement in boats, along the lake shore, to Two-mile Creek, the point designated for a general landing.

When Hull's surrender had put the British in possession of the artillery they so much required, five of the twenty-four pounders had been brought from Detroit, four of which had been mounted at Fort George, and the fifth on a battery, *en barbette*, about half a mile below Newark, now Niagara. A fire from some field pieces had been opened on the American boats, when proceeding, on the 26th, to the rendezvous. This had provoked a return from Fort Niagara, by which the block houses, some scattered dwellings near the fort, and the fort itself were considerably damaged. On the morning of the 27th a heavy cannonade was again commenced from fort Niagara to cover the attacking party, and " in addition," (says James,) " two schooners, by the use of their sweeps, had reached their stations at the mouth of the river, in order to silence the twenty-four pounder and the nine-pounder, also planted *en barbette* close to Newark. Another schooner stationed herself to the northward of the light house, and so close to the shore as to enfilade the first named battery, and cross the fire of the remaining two schooners." The remaining five schooners anchored so as to cover the landing of the troops. The frigate Madison, Oneida brig, and a schooner, took up also advantageous positions. The united broadside of these vessels was fifty-one guns, many of them thirty-two and eighteen-pounders. Against this formidable array what had the British ?—a weak position entirely exposed to a cross fire of shot and shells, and a scarcity of powder—incredible as this last assertion may appear, we are, nevertheless, borne out in making it by James, who asserts, in speaking of the events of the 26th, that " the guns at Fort George were compelled, owing to a scarcity of powder, to remain silent, while Commodore Chauncey, on that evening, was sounding the shore within half gunshot." The Americans, in speaking of this circumstance, and looking at the impunity with which Fort Niagara kept up, almost unanswered, its fire, may well boast that they received comparatively little injury from the British cannon. It would excite astonishment that

James should chronicle so extraordinary a circumstance as the want of powder in the principal British fort in Western Canada, had we not so recently seen that a frigate was built, and a quantity of provisions and stores deposited in so exposed and indefensible a position as York. Whoever was the culpable party, whether Sir George Prevost or General Sheaffe, there is very little doubt but that to this circumstance may be attributed much of the impunity with which the Americans made their preliminary movements on this occasion. The British force was posted as advantageously as circumstances would admit by General Vincent, and they made a most gallant resistance, being overpowered only by the numerical strength of the assailants, and the fire from the American shipping, which committed dreadful havoc, and rendered their efforts to oppose the landing of so immeasurably superior a force altogether ineffectual. Three times, under cover of the heavy fire from the fort and the shipping, the Americans attempted to land, and were repulsed, by the persevering courage of their opponents ; and it was only at last, when considerably reduced in numbers, that General Vincent, who saw the inutility of persevering in so unequal a contest, retired, blowing up, before his retreat, the small quantity of powder which yet remained in the magazine at Fort George.

The heavy fire had rendered the fort altogether untenable ; General Vincent had, therefore, no alternative left but to retreat in the direction of Queenston, first despatching orders to Col. Bishopp at Fort Erie, and to Major Ormsby at Chippewa, to evacuate their respective posts, and to move with as little delay as possible, by Lundy's Lane, to the Beaver-dam. In the retreat about fifty of the regulars unfortunately were made prisoners. The remainder, both regular and militia, made an undisturbed retreat, and were joined at the place of rendezvous, by the garrisons of Fort Erie and Chippewa. In General Vincent's dispatch* full particulars of this action will be

---

From Brigadier-General Vincent to Sir George Prevost.

FORTY-MILE CREEK, May 28, 1813.

SIR,—I have the honor to inform your Excellency, that yesterday morning, about day-break, the enemy again opened his batteries upon Fort George : the fire not being immediately returned,

found, we must not, however, omit to notice one exaggeration contained in it, relative to the American struggle. We allude to the passage "His whole force is stated to amount to nearly ten thousand men." This, in all probability, unintentional overstatement was quite unnecessary, as General Vincent made a very gallant resistance, and, when he was overpowered by numbers, he made a very able retreat—collecting by the next morning nearly sixteen hundred men, with a position, Burlington heights, to fall back on, which, according to Dearborn, while it remained in the power of the British, rendered the successful occupation by the Americans of the Western peninsula impracticable. As at York, Gen. Vincent again saved the kernel, and left, as the fruits of victory, to the Americans, the shell, consisting of a few ruined houses and untenable fort.

The British loss in killed and wounded was very heavy. The 8th, Glengarry and Newfoundland detachments lost full one-half of their united force, and the militia appear to have also suffered severely, at least eighty-five having been either killed or wounded. The total British loss was estimated at four hundred and forty-five. Thomson, in his "Sketches of the War," makes up a very imposing total of prisoners ; like most of his statements, however, his account is grossly exaggerated. He counts the wounded regulars twice over ; once as wounded, and a second time as prisoners—he adds further, "the militia prisoners who were paroled to the number of five hundred and seven," &c. Now, in the first place, no unwounded regulars fell into the hands of the Americans, except the fifty who were captured at the fort. Again, Mr. Thomson forgets to inform us how the

---

it ceased for some time. About 4 o'clock, A. M. a combination of circumstances led to a belief that an invasion was meditated. The morning being exceeding hazy, neither his means nor his intention could be ascertained, until, the mist clearing away at intervals, the enemy's fleet, consisting of fourteen or fifteen vessels, was discovered under way, standing towards the light-house, in an extended line of more than two miles, covering from ninety to one hundred large boats and scows, each containing an average of fifty to sixty men. Though at this time no doubt could be entertained of the enemy's intention, his points of attack could only be conjectured. Having again commenced a heavy fire from his fort, line of batteries, and shipping, it became necessary to withdraw all the guards and piquets stationed along the coast, between the fort and light-house, and a landing was effected at the Two-mile Creek, about half a mile below the latter place. The party of troops and Indians stationed at this point, after opposing the enemy, and annoying him as long as possible, were obliged to fall back, and the fire from the shipping so completely enfiladed and scoured the plains, that it became impossible to approach the beach. As the day dawned, the enemy's plan was clearly developed, and every effort to oppose his landing having failed, I lost not a moment in concentrating my force between the town of Fort George and the enemy, there awaiting his approach. This movement was admirably covered by the Glengarry light infantry, joined by a detachment of the royal Newfoundland regiment and militia, which commenced skirmishing with the enemy's riflemen, who were advancing through the brushwood. The enemy having perfect command of the beach, he quickly landed from three to four hundred men, with several pieces of artillery, and this force was instantly seen advancing in three solid columns, along the lake bank, his right covered by a large body of riflemen, and his left and front by the fire of the shipping, and bat-

teries in the fort. As our light troops fell back upon the main body, which was moved forwards to their support, they were gallantly sustained by the 8th (king's) regiment, commanded by Major Ogilvie, the whole being under the immediate direction of Colonel Myers, acting Quarter-mastergeneral, who had charge of the right wing. In the execution of this important duty, gallantry, zeal, and decision, were eminently conspicuous; and I lament to report that I was deprived of the services of Colonel Myers, who, having received three wounds, was obliged to quit the field. Lieutenant-Colonel Harvey, the deputy Adjutant-General, whose activity and gallantry had been displayed the whole morning, succeeded Colonel Myers, and brought up the right division, consisting of the 49th regiment, and some militia. The light artillery under Major Holcroft were already in position, awaiting the enemy's advance on the plain. At this moment the very inferior force under my command had experienced a severe loss in officers and men ; yet nothing could exceed the ardor and gallantry of the troops, who shewed the most marked devotion in the service of their king and country, and appeared regardless of the consequence of the unequal contest. Being on the spot, and seeing that the force under my command was opposed to ten-fold numbers, who were rapidly advancing under cover of their shipping and batteries, from which our positions were immediately seen, and exposed to a tremendous fire of shot and shells, I decided on retiring my little force to a position which I hoped might be less assailable by the heavy ordnance of the enemy, and from which a retreat would be left open, in the event of that measure becoming necessary. Here, after awaiting the approach of the enemy for about half an hour, I received authentic information, that his force, consisting of from four to five thousand men, had re-formed his columns, and was making an effort to turn my right flank. At this critical juncture not a mo-

five hundred and seven paroled militia prisoners were obtained—as he has failed in this, we must refer to James. " No sooner had the American army got possession of the Niagara frontier, than officers with parties were sent to every farm-house and hovel in the neighbourhood, to exact a parole from the male inhabitants of almost every age. Some were glad of this excuse for remaining peaceably at their houses; and those who made any opposition were threatened to be sent across the river, and thrown into a noisome prison. We cannot wonder, then, that by these industrious, though certainly unauthorized means, the names of as many as five hundred and seven Canadians were got ready to be forwarded to the Secretary at War, so as, not only to swell the amount of the loss sustained, but by a fair inference of the force employed,

on the part of the British, in resisting the attack."

Our loss was very great, but that of the enemy was quite as great in proportion—that is, the number that fell in the hand-to-hand conflict would be about equal, were we to make an allowance for the terrible execution done by the fifty-one gun broadside of the vessels. The Americans themselves state their loss at thirty-nine killed and one hundred and eleven wounded, which is very satisfactory; and, as James has it, not a little creditable to the few regular troops and Canadians by whom the fort was defended. One extraordinary bit of modesty is observable in Dearborn's official letter on this occasion. He does not state that the British were superior in force— this is particularly striking in an American— he, however, hints at "the advantage the enemy's position afforded him." We have

ment was to be lost, and sensible that every effort had been made, by the officers and men under my command, to maintain the post of Fort George, I could not consider myself justified in continuing so unequal a contest, the issue of which promised no advantage to the interests of his Majesty's service. Having given orders for the fort to be evacuated, the guns to be spiked, and the ammunition destroyed, the troops under my command were put in motion, and marched across the country in a line parallel to the Niagara river, towards the position near the Beaver Dam, beyond Queenstown Mountain, at which place I had the honor of reporting to your Excellency that a depôt of provisions and ammunition had been formed some time since. The rear-guard of the army reached that position during the night, and we were soon afterwards joined by Lieutenant-Colonel Bisshopp, with all the detachments from Chippewa to Fort Erie. The light, and one battalion company of the 8th, (king's,) joined us about the same time, as did Captain Barclay, with a detachment of the royal navy.

Having assembled my whole force the following morning, which did not exceed sixteen hundred men, I continued my march towards the head of the lake, where it is my intention to take up a position, and shall endeavour to maintain it, until I may be honored with your Excellency's instructions, which I shall feel most anxious to receive. I beg leave to suggest the great importance that exists for a communication being opened with me, through the medium of the fleet. The anchorage under Mr. Brandt's house is perfectly good and safe. I believe your Excellency need not be informed, that in the event of it becoming necessary that I should fall back upon York, the assistance of shipping would be requisite for the transport of my artillery. I cannot conclude this long communication, without expressing a well merited tribute of approbation to the gallantry and assiduity of every officer of the staff, and indeed of every individual composing

my little army;—every one most zealously discharged the duties of his respective station. The struggle on the 27th continued from three to four hours; and, I lament to add, it was attended with very severe loss.

I have the honor to enclose a list of the killed, wounded, and missing, with as much accuracy as the nature of existing circumstances will admit. Many of the missing, I hope, will be found to be only stragglers, and will soon rejoin their corps. I shall reach the head of the lake to-morrow evening. Hitherto the enemy has not attempted to interrupt my movements. Information reached me this morning, through an authentic channel, that he had pushed on three thousand infantry, and a considerable body of cavalry, towards Queenston. His whole force is stated to amount to nearly ten thousand men.

I send this despatch by Mr. Mathison, who acted as a volunteer on the 27th; and I am happy to inform your Excellency, that his conduct was very honorable to his character, and merits my marked approbation. Ammunition will be wanting by the first vessel. Captain Milnes has been kind enough to remain with me until my next despatch.

I have the honor to be, &c.
JOHN VINCENT, Brig. Gen.

His Excellency Lieutenant-General
Sir George Prevost, &c. &c. &c.

Return of killed, wounded, and missing, of His Majesty's troops in action with the enemy at Fort George, May the 27th, 1813.

One captain, one lieutenant, one ensign, one serjeant, forty-eight rank and file, killed; one general-staff, one major, two captains, five lieutenants, two ensigns, four serjeants, twenty-nine rank and file, wounded; one lieutenant, thirteen serjeants, eight drummers, two hundred and forty rank and file, wounded and missing.

already stated the exposed position of the British; our readers may, therefore, take this insinuation at its proper value. O'Connor in his account, reversing the real state of things, makes the British "five to one." Thomson, more modestly, says, "the action was fought by inferior numbers on the American side," and Dr. Smith, giving no numbers, dwells only on "the firmness and gallantry of the American troops."

The escape of General Vincent and his troops left the Americans as far as ever from the desired undisturbed occupancy of the western peninsula. Ingersol observes, "Vincent, the British General, effected his retreat (probably without *Dearborn's even knowing it*, for he stayed on shipboard), to the mountain passes, where he employed his troops in attacking, defeating, and capturing ours during all the rest of that year of discomfitures." Armstrong, in his remarks, has, "if, instead of concentrating his whole force, naval and military, on the water side of the enemy's defences, he had divided the attack, and, crossing the Niagara below Lewiston, advanced on Fort George by the Queenston road, the investment of that place would have been complete, and a retreat of the garrison impracticable."

It was certainly fortunate for the British that the Americans had generals who were not tacticians enough to profit by their superiority in numbers. Had Brock commanded the Americans, the campaign of 1813 might have had a more fortunate issue for our enemies.

Although the disasters at York and Niagara were disheartening in some degree, yet the descendants of the brave men who composed the militia at that time have cause to look on both these events with much pride and satisfaction. It is clear, from the conduct of the militia on each of these occasions, that they had attained a high degree of military discipline, and, as a contemporary justly observes, "the marked coolness and fearless intrepidity with which the York and Lincoln militia resisted the approach of the enemy towards their shores,

would have reflected honor on a band of veterans long accustomed to 'the din of arms.'"

We left General Vincent at the Beaver Dam, where he had been joined not only by the detachment from Fort Erie and Chippewa, but by one flank and one battalion company of the 8th, and Captain Barclay, R.N., with a small body of seamen on their way to Lake Erie. To cut off this force, Dearborn, who seems never to have been in a hurry, despatched, on the 28th, a considerable body; but, luckily, he sent them in the wrong direction, for had he chosen the Lake road, there would have been a probability of cutting off General Vincent. Two days were occupied in this fruitless pursuit, and, on the recall of the troops, two days more were passed in a consideration of how the lost time was to be made up. Dearborn's idea was to use the fleet as a means of transportation to Burlington Bay: but, fortunately for the British, the Cabinet at Washington gave this arm of the expedition a different direction. No alternative, therefore, remained to Dearborn but the pursuit by the Lake shore, which should have begun, had Dearborn possessed any energy, on the morning of the 28th.

Before, however, following the fortunes of the brigade despatched in pursuit, we will turn to Sackett's Harbor, and the fate of the expedition prepared against it by Sir George Prevost, and a considerable body of troops destined to act in concert with the fleet under Commodore Yeo.

After disposing of this subject, we will return to Gen. Vincent and his fortunes, taking, while in the west, a glance at Proctor, whom we left just after his return from Fort Meigs. Another chapter will, however, be required for a consideration of all these subjects; we will, therefore, conclude the present one with Ingersol's testimony as to the defence of Canada:—"On the land the defence of Canada was conducted with much more energy, enterprise and spirit, than the American attempts at invasion, which failed, after a long series of delays and reverses, and proved abortions as discreditable as Hull's."

CHAPTER XI.

Before entering on the subject of the expedition against Sackett's
Harbor, we would pre-
mise that we have hither-
to endeavoured to do full justice to Sir George
Prevost, wherever it appeared that blame had
been unjustly imputed to him, and to point
out the real quarter to which discredit should
attach, whether the causes of his failure
might be attributable to the orders from the
Home Government, by which he was in a
great degree fettered, or arose from the insufficient force under his command, and the
extended frontier which he was called upon
to defend. We can scarcely, then, be accused
of blindly or capriciously joining in a crusade
against this officer's memory in the present
instance, the more especially as we have
diligently sought to discover, in the American
accounts of the descent on Sackett's Harbor,
some extenuating causes for the failure of a
movement, on which the ultimate success of
the war seemed so mainly to depend, to which

*Expedition against
Sackett's Harbor, 27th
May.*

the attention of the entire Province was
directed, which, in consequence of the presence and co-operation of the two commanders-
in-chief, the inhabitants had flattered themselves would have a very different result, and
the failure of which inflicted a blow on the
military character of Sir George Prevost from
which it never recovered.

Prone to exaggeration as we have in most
cases found American historians, it is a
singular feature in the present instance, that
they seem to have laid aside their natural
characteristic, and to have modestly set forth,
with but little coloring of misrepresentation,
the facts as they really occurred. This moderation bears the harder on Sir George Prevost,
as it would almost seem as if his discomfiture
appeared in their eyes something scarcely
worth boasting of, ready as they always were
to lay hold of every circumstance, however
trivial, (and of this we have already adduced
several striking proofs,) that they could in any
manner distort, or magnify into a victory.

Without farther preamble, then, we would
remind the reader, that Commodore (Sir
James) Yeo's arrival from England, with a
party of officers and seamen, had given an
impetus to the naval preparations at Kingston,
and that the vessels there had been manned
and equipped in a manner sufficient to warrant
the expectation, that the fleet, under so able
a commander, might once more boldly appear
on the lake. Great, therefore, was the delight
of all, when it was ascertained that Sir George
Prevost's consent had been obtained for employing, this acquisition of naval strength, in a
combined attack, on the important post of
Sackett's Harbor, now considerably weakened
in its defences, by the absence of Commodore
Chauncey's fleet, and of the numerous army
which had recently been stationed there.

11

All preparations having been made, the fleet, having on board the troops for the expedition, under the command (most unfortunately says Veritas) of Sir George Prevost, set sail. The force embarked, consisted of the grenadier company of the 100th regiment, a section of the Royal Scots, two companies of the 8th, four companies of the 104th, one company of the Glengarry's, two companies of the Canadian volunteers, a small detachment of the Newfoundland regiment, and two six-pounders with the gunners, making in all a body of something less than seven hundred rank and file. The weather was extremely fine; and the fleet arrived off Sackett's Harbor at about noon of the same day (the 27th) it sailed. As a short description of Sackett's Harbor will not be irrelevant, we will here introduce James' account of it. "Sackett's Harbor bears from Kingston, on Lake Ontario, south by east; distant in a straight course, twenty-five, but, by a ship's course, thirty-five miles. It stands on the south-east side of an expansion of the Black River, near to where it flows into Hungry Bay. The harbor is small, but well sheltered. From the north-west runs out a low point of land, upon which is the dock-yard, with large stone houses, and all the buildings requisite for such an establishment. Upon this point there is a strong work called Fort Tomkins ; having within a block-house, two stories high : on the land side it is covered by a strong picketing, in which there are embrasures. At the bottom of the harbor is the village, consisting of sixty or seventy houses : to the southward of it is a barrack, capable of containing two thousand men, and generally used for the marines belonging to the fleet. On a point eastward of the harbor, stands Fort Pike, surrounded by a ditch, in advance of which there is a strong line of picketing. About one hundred yards from the village, and a little to the westward of Fort Tomkins, is Smith's cantonment, or barracks, capable of containing two thousand five hundred strong ; it is strongly built of logs, forming a square, with a block-house at each corner, and is loop-holed on every side." This was the state of Sackett's Harbor at the date of the attack, at which time also many of the guns belonging to the works had been conveyed to the other end of the lake. The wind was now light and favorable, enabling the vessels either to stand in for the shore or from it ; the squadron, therefore, with the *Wolfe* as the leading vessel, having on board Sir George himself, stood in towards the shore, to within about two miles, to reconnoitre the enemys' position. This having been effected, the ships were hove to, the troops were embarked in the boats, and every one anxiously awaited the signal to land. There is here some difference in the British accounts of the affair. After mentioning the embarkation of the troops in the boats, James says, "They waited in this state of suspense for about half an hour, when orders were given for the troops to return on board the fleet. This done, the fleet wore, and with a light wind stood out on its return to Kingston.

" About forty Indians, in their canoes, had accompanied the expedition. Dissatisfied at being called back without effecting anything, particularly as their unsophisticated minds could devise no reason for abandoning the enterprise, they steered round Stony Point, and discovering a party of troops on the American shore, fearlessly paddled in to attack them. These consisted of about seventy dismounted dragoons, who had just been landed from twelve boats, which, along with seven others that had pulled past the point and escaped, were on their way to Sackett's Harbor. As soon as the American troops saw the Indians advancing, they hoisted a white flag, as a signal to the British vessels for protection. The latter immediately hove to, and Lieutenant Dobbs, first of the *Wolfe*, stood in with the ship's boats, and brought off the American dragoons, along with their twelve batteaux. *This fortuitous capture was deemed an auspicious omen ; and Sir George Prevost determined to stand back to Sackett's Harbor.*"

It is clear from this account that James desires it to be understood that, in all probability, no attack would have been made, had it not been for what he terms the fortuitous capture, and on another point—the delay—he is equally explicit. This is of importance, as Christie also mentions it, only accounting for it in a different manner, and making it a shade less discreditable to the commander. In speaking of the events of the first day, Christie writes, "the weather was propitious, and the troops were transferred to the batteaux, to make their landing, under an escort of two gun-boats, commanded by Captain Mulcaster, the whole under the immediate direction of the land and naval commanders-in-chief. They had proceeded but a short distance, when a convoy of American boats, loaded with troops were descried doubling Stony Point, on their way from Oswego, to Sackett's Harbour. The Indians who had previously landed upon an island fired upon them as they passed, and threw them into confusion, when the boats and batteaux bore down and captured twelve of them, with about one hundred and fifty men: the remainder escaped into Sackett's Harbour. *The landing was then deferred until the next morning,* while the Americans raised the alarm and withdrew a detachment of their troops posted upon Horse Island, at the mouth of the harbour, and assumed a position on the Main, opposite a ford, leading from the island to the mainland, where they were reinforced by a body of militia, under General Brown, and prepared for a vigorous defence." This is additional testimony as to the delay, and we must further remark that, all the American accounts concur in stating that the British appeared off the port on two successive days. One, indeed, writes, "the delay and indecision on the part of the British brought in from the neighbouring counties a considerable number of militia, who, naturally thinking the enemy were afraid, betrayed great eagerness to join the contest." All these proofs are necessary, as none of the statements we have given are contained in Col. Bayne's letter,* from which it can only be

gathered that the attack failed in consequence of the ships not being able to near the shore. Nor is a syllable to be found relative to waste of time through which the opportunity, afforded by the previous fair wind, had been lost, but only an allusion to *the continuation of the light and adverse winds,* and the insufficiency of the gun-boats to accomplish what the larger vessels, "*still far off*" might have done. It is not often that we have occasion to complain of a "muddled dispatch," but assuredly the one in question seems written for the express purpose of making the best out of what was a very discreditable affair to Sir George Prevost. A shade of excuse for the loss of time is to be found in Christie as he represents the attack as begun on the first day, and only interrupted by the capture of prisoners, to secure whom it was perhaps necessary to return to the ship, rendering it thus too late for further operation on that day; but even this is a poor excuse, and the trifling delay, had an energetic officer been in command, would have been soon repaired, the fair wind profited by, and the attack of the troops covered by the fire from the large vessels of the squadron.

To return, however, to the attack which was finally made early on the morning of the 29th. It began by a mistake, and the troops were landed on Horse Island, "where," (according to James,) "the grenadier company of the 100th, which formed the advance, meeting with some slight opposition from a six-pounder mounted *en barbette,* as well as from three or four hundred militia, stationed

*From Adjutant-General Baynes to Sir George Prevost.

Kingston, May 30th, 1813.

Sir,—I have the honour to report to your Excellency, that in conformity to an arranged plan of operations with Commodore Sir James Yeo, the fleet of boats assembled a-stern of his ship, at 10 o'clock on the night of the 28th instant, with the troops placed under my command, and, led by a gun-boat, under Captain Mulcaster, royal navy, proceeded towards Sackett's Harbour, in the order prescribed to the troops, in case the detachment was obliged to march in column, viz :—the grenadier company, 100th, with one section of the royal Scots, two companies of the 8th, (or King's,) four of the 104th, two of the Canadian voltigeurs, two six pounders, with their gunners, and a company of Glengarry light infantry, were embarked on board a light schooner, which was proposed to be towed, under the

directions of officers of the navy, so as to insure the guns being landed in time to support the advance of the troops. Although the night was dark, with rain, the boats assembled in the vicinity of Sackett's Harbour, by one o'clock, in compact and regular order; and in this position it was intended to remain until the day broke, in the hope of effecting a landing before the enemy could be prepared to line the woods with troops, which surrounded the coast; but, unfortunately, a strong current drifted the boats considerably, while the darkness of the night, and ignorance of the coast, prevented them from recovering their proper station until the day dawned, when the whole pulled for the point of debarkation.

It was my intention to have landed in the cove formed by Horse Island, but, on approaching it, we discovered that the enemy were fully prepared, by a very heavy fire of musketry from the surrounding woods, which were filled with

at that point, carried the six-pounder before a second discharge could be fired from it, and drove the American militia with precipitation into the woods." Christie's account of this is different, he says, "they" (the British) "first attempted to land on the Main, in a cove formed by Horse Island, but on approaching it, they found the enemy prepared for them, by a heavy fire of musketry, from the surrounding woods, supported by a field-piece. *They then pulled round and landed on the outside of the island."*

After the troops were fairly landed it does not appear that they had any very obstinate resistance to encounter, and it is plain from both Christie's and James' account, that there was nothing to have prevented Sir George Prevost from accomplishing all that he desired. Thompson† is particularly severe on his countrymen, and his account by no means bears out Col. Bayne's assertion of the great resistance offered. "Though," says he, "they were well protected by the breast-work they rose from behind it, and abandoning the honorable promises of noble daring, which they had made but a little while before, fled with equal precipitation and disorder. A strange and unaccountable panic seized the whole line; and with the exception of a very few, terror and dismay were depicted on every countenance." Any remarks on Sir

George from Veritas must be taken with due allowance for the animus which marks everything he wrote respecting that commander. His version runs thus : "The troops were disembarked, but without artillery, and advanced with their usual spirit, when the enemy in dismay fled, whilst our men coming to a block-house, which made some resistance, were checked. During this advance so hopeless did the enemy consider their situation, that they burnt a barrack or store, spiked the guns of a battery, and began their retreat through the villages, setting fire to their new frigate, the *Pyke,* then on the stocks, and General Brown, who commanded, had actually written a letter of capitulation, which he had appointed a flag of truce to carry to the commander, whilst a few men were kept in the block-house, to give an appearance of resistance, so as to obtain better terms. At this period, in an evil hour, Sir George Prevost, mistaking the enemy in running away, with the dust thereby thrown up, for a column of reinforcements arriving, immediately gave orders for a re-embarkation, and then was exhibited the extraordinary military spectacle of a retreat, I will not say a flight back to back." This picture is highly colored, but there is still much truth in it, and when Colonel Bayne's letter is stripped of its apologetic character, it will not be found to differ materi-

infantry supported by a field-piece. I directed the boats to pull round to the other side of the island, where a landing was effected in good order and with little loss, although executed in the face of a corps, formed with a field-piece in the wood, and under the enfilade of a heavy gun from the enemy's principal battery. The advance was led by the grenadiers of the 100th regiment, with undaunted gallantry, which no obstacle could arrest. A narrow causeway, in many places under water, not more than four feet wide, and about four hundred paces in length, which connected the island with the mainland, was occupied by the enemy, in great force, with a six-pounder. It was forced, and carried in the most spirited manner, and the gun taken before a second discharge could be made from it; a tumbril, with a few rounds of ammunition, was found; but, unfortunately, the artillerymen were still behind, the schooner not having been able to get up in time, and the troops were exposed to so heavy and galling a fire from a numerous, but almost invisible foe, as to render it impossible to halt for the artillery to come up. At this spot two paths led in opposite directions round the hill; I directed Colonel Young, of the King's

† Sketches of the War, page 143

regiment, with half of the detachment, to penetrate by the left; and Major Drummond, of the 104th, to force the path by the right, which proved to be more open, and was less occupied by the enemy. On the left the wood was very thick, and was most obstinately maintained by the enemy.

The gun-boats which had covered our landing, afforded material aid, by firing into the woods; but the American soldier, behind a tree, was only to be dislodged by the bayonet. The spirited advance of a section produced the flight of hundreds. From this observation all firing was directed to cease, and the detachment being formed in as regular order as the nature of the ground would admit, pushed forward through the wood upon the enemy, who, although greatly superior in numbers, and supported by field-pieces, and a heavy fire from their fort, fled with precipitation to their block-house, and fort, abandoning one of their guns. The division under Colonel Young was joined in the charge, by that under Major Drummond, which was executed with such spirit and promptness, that many of the enemy fell in their enclosed barracks, which were set on fire by our troops;—at this point the further energies of the troops became

ally in substance. James adds his testimony on this point, and after describing the British advance, goes on : " so hopeless did the Americans consider their case, that Lieutenant Chauncey set fire to the Navy barracks, the prize schooner *Duke of Gloucester*, the ship *General Pyke*, and completely destroyed the naval stores and provisions, which had been captured at York." The whole affair of "Sackett's Harbour may be thus summed up. Sir George Prevost, with an adequate force, made his appearance before it, with the intention of striking a blow at the seat of American naval operations on Lake Ontario, and of establishing British supremacy in that quarter. Indecision, we will not call it timidity, prevented his striking the blow, while the weather was yet favorable, and the enemy unprepared. When he did attempt to carry his plans into execution, a change of wind prevented the co-operation of the fleet, on board of which

was also the artillery ; and this circumstance, joined to the show of resistance, which the enemy, through the time afforded, were enabled to offer, would appear to have completely overthrown what little energy or decision of character he might have possessed. The result, as shown in Colonel Bayne's dispatch, was a retreat which blasted forever his reputation as a military commander. An aggravation of the mistake committed, is also to be found in the want of necessity for the retreat. The testimony of James, Christie, and of American writers also, proves that it was perfectly practicable for Sir George to have made good his position until the ships could have come to his assistance, and even one passage of Col. Bayne's letter would go to establish the same fact. " But one sentiment of regret and mortification prevailed, on being obliged to quit a beaten enemy, whom a small band had driven before them for three hours."

---

unavailing. Their block-house and stockaded battery could not be carried by assault, nor reduced by field-pieces, had we been provided with them ; the fire of the gun-boats proved insufficient to attain that end : light and adverse winds continued, and our larger vessels were still far off. The enemy turned the heavy ordnance of the battery to the interior defence of his post. He had set fire to the store-houses in the vicinity of the fort.

Seeing no object within our reach to attain, that could compensate for the loss we were momentarily sustaining from the heavy fire of the enemy's cannon, I directed the troops to take up their position on the crest of the hill we had charged from. From this position we were ordered to re-embark, which was performed at our leisure, and in perfect order, the enemy not presuming to show a single soldier without the limits of his fortress. Your Excellency having been a witness of the zeal and ardent courage of every soldier in the field, it is unnecessary for me to assure your Excellency, that but one sentiment animated every breast, that of discharging to the utmost of their power their duty to their king and country. But one sentiment of regret and mortification prevailed, on being obliged to quit a beaten enemy, whom a small band of British soldiers had driven before them for three hours through a country abounding in strong positions of defence, but not offering a single spot of cleared ground favourable for the operations of disciplined troops, without having fully accomplished the duty we were ordered to perform.

The two divisions of the detachment were ably commanded by Colonel Young, of the King's, and Major Drummond, of the 104th. The detachment of the King's under Major Evans, nobly sustained the high and established character of that distinguished corps; and Captain Burke

availed himself of the ample field afforded him in leading the advance, to display the intrepidity of British grenadiers.

The detachment of the 104th regiment, under Major Moodie, Captain M'Pherson's company of Glengarry light infantry, and two companies of Canadian voltigeurs, commanded by Major Hammot, all of them levies in the British Province of North America, evinced most striking proofs of their loyalty, steadiness and courage. The detachment of the royal Newfoundland regiment behaved with great gallantry. Your Excellency will lament the loss of that active and intelligent officer, Captain Gray, acting as deputy quartermaster-general, who fell close to the enemy's work, while reconnoitring it, in the hope to discover some opening to favour an assault. Commodore Sir James Yeo conducted the fleet of boats in the attack, and, accompanying the advance of the troops, directed the co-operation of the gun-boats. I feel most grateful for your Excellency's kind consideration, in allowing your aide-de-camps, Majors Coote and Fulton, to accompany me in the field, and to these officers for the able assistance they afforded me.

I have the honor to be, &c.
EDWARD BAYNES,
Col. Glengarry Light Infantry commanding.
To His Excellency Lieut.-Gen.
Sir George Prevost, Bart., &c.

Return of the killed, wounded, and missing, in an attack on Sackett's Harbour, on the 29th of May, 1813.

1 general staff, 3 sergeants, 44 rank and file, killed ; 3 majors, 3 captains, 5 lieutenants, 1 ensign, 7 sergeants, 2 drummers, 172 rank and file, 2 gunners, wounded; 2 captains, 1 ensign, 13 rank and file, wounded and missing.

Had Sir George Prevost not proved his bravery in more than one field, his excess of prudence on this occasion, would almost warrant our giving a harsher appellation to his conduct, when we consider the insufficient causes which led to the precipitate abandonment of an enterprise which had cost so much preparation and loss of life. Besides, what were the causes for a retreat? Sir George assigned as his reason, the want of co-operation between the fleet and army. The Americans ascribe it to fear of being surrounded by General Brown, who, they allege, adopted the following stratagem to deceive the British General. Silently passing through the wood which led towards the point of landing, he evinced an intention to gain the rear of the British force, to take possession of the boats, and effectually to cut off his retreat. This convinced Sir George Prevost of the vast superiority of the American force, and induced him to give the order to retreat. There is some probability in this, although Sir George does not assign it as one of his motives, for if with the enemy in flight before him, he thought the absence of the ships a sufficient reason for his retreating in an opposite direction, the fear of being surrounded would have naturally added to his perplexity. Sir George's whole conduct in this affair, resembles that of a school-boy who has committed an inroad on an orchard, and half-frightened at his temerity, and scared at the sound of his own footsteps, runs away without securing the fruit which he had gathered. Sir James Yeo was quite opposed to the abandonment of the enterprise, and Sir George's conduct on the occasion gave rise to the animosity which afterwards existed between those officers.

What say American historians on this subject?* "He relinquished the further prosecution of an expedition, having for its primary object the capture and destruction of a post, the permanent possession of which only could give to the Americans any hope of a superiority on Lake Ontario; after having succeeded in his enterprise, in a degree which scarcely admits of being termed partial, and, through the predominance of his apprehension over his bravery and foresight, retired from the assault." The consequence which would have

resulted had Sir George been bolder are thus set forth : "Its effects would have been long and deplorably felt by the American Government. Immense quantities of naval and military stores, which had been from time to time collected at that depôt, the frames and timbers which had been prepared for the construction of vessels of war, and the rigging and armaments which had been forwarded hither for their final equipment, as well as all the army clothing, camp equipage, provisions, ammunition, and implements of war, which had been previously captured from the enemy, would have fallen into his hands. The destruction of the batteries, the ships then on the stocks, the extensive cantonments, and the public arsenal, would have retarded the building of another naval force; and that which was already in the Lake in separate detachments, could have been intercepted in its attempt to return, and might have been captured in detail. The prize vessel which was then lying in harbor, and which had been taken by the Americans, and the two United States schooners, would have been certainly taken, and the whole energies of the American Government, added to their most vigorous and unwearied struggles, might never again have attained any prospect of an ascendancy on the Lake."

After reading this, and reflecting on what was lost, an inquiry into the number of killed and wounded only places matters in, if possible, a worse position. "The loss," says James, "on this unfortunate expedition was fifty men killed and two hundred and eleven wounded." The Americans acknowledge to have had a loss of one hundred and fifty-seven.

Great was the mortification of the people of Kingston, when, on the morning of the 30th, they saw the return of the fleet, with, instead of the whole garrison of Sackett's Harbor and an immense amount of military and naval stores, about one hundred prisoners. Loud were the animadversions and most bitter the strictures. It must not, however, be lost sight of that not the slightest attempt was made, during the investigation of the disgraceful failure, to throw the faintest imputation on the behaviour of the troops concerned in it. We will conclude this part of our subject by an extract from James, which, though perhaps

---

* Sketches of the war.

rather fanciful, is yet worthy of consideration. "What should we have gained by even a temporary possession of Sackett's Harbor. The American fleet, having no port to which it could retire, would have been compelled to fight, and Sir James Yeo, having the *Pyke* to add to his squadron, or even without her assistance, would have conquered with ease. The British Ontario fleet no longer wanted; its officers, seamen, and stores would have passed over to Lake Erie, and averted the calamities there; that done, they would have re-passed to Champlain, and prevented the Saranac, that flows into it, from becoming so famous. The least benefit of all would have been the saving to the nation of the incalculable sums expended in the building of ships, and the transportation of ordnance stores. Some will feel that the national pride would have been no loser, and able politicians could, perhaps, expatiate upon fifty other advantages that would have accrued had we retained possession, even for a few days, of Sackett's Harbor."

Speculations of this kind are generally of very little use; still, when we look at the complaints that were then being loudly made, throughout the United States, of the enormous drain on the country's resources, and the squandering of the thewes and sinews of the population, it adds to the regret that a general's timid and wavering conduct should have omitted to inflict a blow, which must have considerably increased the financial embarrassments so complained of. Ingersol, on this subject writes—"The British repulse at Sackett's Harbor was the last American success in 1813 on Lake Ontario or the St. Lawrence, where the enemy's good fortune never afterwards failed, except in Chauncey's partial success on the Lake." After this admission, he proceeds: "Border warfare, the worst of all, the most wasteful of men, money, and character, was our resort during two, for the most part disastrous, years. Nowhere in the world were such costly and fruitless hostilities as those carried on, over many hundreds of miles, from the swamps and wildernesses of Michigan to the mountain gorges of Canada. We recruited armies to be wasted on the borders of the Lakes, built and equipped fleets upon them, at monstrous expense, to wage small border wars. The sum expended on building vessels for Lake Ontario was nearly two millions of dollars, that expended on Lakes Erie and Champlain four hundred thousand more. The waste of money was enormous; it was estimated that it cost a thousand dollars for every cannon conveyed to Sackett's Harbor! The flour for Harrison's army cost one hundred dollars per barrel. The multiplied incidental but inevitable charges of travel over wild regions without roads required, amongst other things, thousands of pack horses, each of which could only carry half a barrel of provisions, and required to be attended by trains of other horses, with forage for those laden with provisions. The distances were hundreds of miles over trackless deserts. Few horses survived more than one trip; many sunk under one. Of four thousand post-horses to supply Harrison's small army, but eight hundred were alive after the winter of 1812-13. Large quantities of flour were buried in mud and snow, from inability to carry it any further; large quantities damaged when arrived at the place of destination.

"Two-thirds of that deposited at Fort Meigs was spoiled and unfit for use. Fluctuations and increases of price were so great that many contractors were ruined, and it became necessary to purchase of other persons, when disappointed of regular supplies by the contractors. The waste of life in the American armies was also great from want of competent surgeons, instruments and medicines, and from the diseases caused by privations in insalubrious regions."

When we remember how prone our neighbors were to look at the £ s. d. view of matters, and how ill a young country could afford to support an expensive war, we find fresh cause for regret in Sir George Prevost's failure. Nothing would more surely have brought about a peace than the state of affairs recorded by Ingersol, a check had even been given to the national vanity by the capture of the *Chesapeake*, and the salutary lesson taught that they were not yet masters of the sea, and had vigorous measures been taken in the present instance, the movements on the frontiers of Canada, would in all probability, have dwindled down to mere petty skirmishes, until the Americans, wearied of hostilities resulting in nothing but loss of time and money, would have gladly made overtures for peace, even at the risk of compromising their new-fledged importance. We are the more inclined to hazard this assertion, from what appears to have been the state of the American army at that time. Stagnation in camps and garrisons on frontiers, bred disease; discontent and desertions, thinned the numbers and soured the tempers, and demoralized both men and officers. In one place we find as many as six soldiers shot for desertion, and such difficulties existed in procuring recruits, that "inveigling dissatisfied, worthless or intoxicated men to enlist, and then disciplining them by cruel and degrading corporal punishment, lashing them into good behaviour, was the only method of marshalling and replenishing our continually wasting armies."* Were our observations merely gleaned from the writings of one party, and that party opposed to the war, they would be as little worthy of attention as the mendacious columns put forth by the Government organ (Nile's Weekly Register), but they are not taken from the mere ebullitions of party feeling, but are the result of examination into Armstrong, the Secretary at War; Ingersol, who does not condemn the war, but only the mode in which it was carried on; and many others. The discussions in some of the State legislatures furnish additional proof that the American nation was beginning by this time to get heartily sick of the war. In short the more closely we examine the position of affairs, the deeper cause of regret do we find that General Brock's valuable life had not been spared, or that at least his mantle had not fallen on the shoulders of either Sir George Prevost or Sir Roger Sheaffe, to whose irresolution it may be ascribed, that a war begun with such vigour by General Brock should not have been checked more speedily. When it was possible to act vigorously without departing from the spirit of the instructions emanating from the Home Government.

We left General Dearborn, in our last chapter, just as he had dispatched Generals Chandler and Winder, with two brigades of infantry, a considerable body of cavalry, and a strong detachment of artillery in pursuit of General Vincent, who

Proceedings at west end of Lake Ontario: surprise at Stony Creek.

had by that time received his reinforcements, and was now encamped on Burlington Heights. Determined as was the attitude assumed by General Vincent, his situation was, in reality, extremely critical. York on one side and Fort George on the other had fallen, and with a powerful hostile fleet on the lake, he was left without resources should the enemy approach with such a superior force as not to warrant his risking a battle. Again, did even a favorable opportunity for risking a contest present itself, he had but ninety rounds of ammunition per man, a quantity too small to admit of any very steady or prolonged course of action.

On the evening of the 5th June, the American army had reached Stony Creek, a point but a few miles from the position held by General Vincent, and as it was sunset, the Generals found it necessary to halt, and they proceeded to make the necessary disposition of the troops, so as to pass the night in safety. The proper arrangements were accordingly made, and the camp secured. Vincent, whose critical situation we have just noticed, now saw that to retain his present position, on which all his hopes of eventual success depended, he must, even with his small quantity of ammunition, risk another battle. While still uncertain as to the best course to be adopted, he received intimation of his advanced pickets having been driven in, and he dispatched Lieutenant Colonel Harvey* to reconnoitre and take an accurate view of the enemy's position. Harvey soon ascertained that the enemy's camp guards were few and negligent, that his line of encampment was long and broken; that his artillery was feebly supported, and several of the corps placed too far in the rear to aid in repelling a blow, rapidly and vigorously struck at their front, and reported the result of his observations to General Vincent, accompanied with a proposal to hazard a night attack. This General Vincent consented to, hoping to effect by surprise, what the small number of his force and want of ammunition forbade him to accomplish in the open field. In pursuance of his, or rather, Col. Harvey's plan, he commenced his march about midnight of the 5th June, with a force of seven hundred and four

---

* Ingersol'

* Afterwards Sir John Harvey, and Governor of New Brunswick.

rank and file. We will now enquire into the strength of the force that lay encamped at Stony Creek, under Generals Chandler and Winder.

When General Dearborn first determined on the pursuit of General Vincent, he had dispatched General Winder with a single brigade. This officer, in the progress of his march, was not long in discovering that the enemy's force would require greater odds to overcome, and he accordingly decided on awaiting, at Forty-mile Creek, the arrival of such reinforcements as, on a representation of the circumstances of the case, the general might think proper to send to his aid. On the 3rd June, Brigadier General Chandler brought up a second brigade, thus accounting for the two brigades we have already mentioned. We will now pause to examine into the numerical strength of these two bodies.

They consisted, according to James (who, however, confesses that the only assistance he could procure from the American accounts was the name of the regiments and corps), of the 5th, 13th, 14th, 16th, 22d, and 23d regiments of infantry, divided into two brigades. The strength of these brigades, if we take the lowest returns in an American work, was fourteen hundred and fifty each. Admitting that only half the artillery force from Fort George was despatched, that would give four hundred more, (and this calculation is not unlikely, when we remember that General Winder had sent for reinforcements, on the plea of his weakness.) Col. Burns' cavalry force was ascertained to be two hundred and fifty. We have now two brigades of fourteen hundred and fifty each, with artillery and the cavalry, making in all, thirty-four hundred and fifty. Armstrong, in noticing Winder's pursuit, speaks of, first, one brigade eight hundred strong, and then mentions the second, but without condescending to numbers, or taking notice of the artillery or cavalry; even this, allowing the strength of the second brigade to have equalled the first, would give, including the cavalry and artillery, twenty-two hundred men. Ingersol states the force at thirteen hundred, but in such a confused manner as to render it difficult to determine whether the thirteen hundred men mentioned formed the whole body, or only the whole of Chandler's reinforcement. Be it as it may, there is every

ground for assuming, even from these statements, imperfect as they are, that the American force encamped at Stony Creek, on the night of the 5th June, was not less than twenty-two hundred to twenty-five hundred strong.

To return, however, to the attack which was led by Colonel Harvey in person. The first thing accomplished was the surprise and capture of every man of the American pickets, without giving the slightest alarm to the main body. This effected, the centre of the encampment was attacked. We prefer, however, giving General Vincent's official account, as it is modestly written, although differing somewhat from Ingersol's account, which unblushingly states — "The encampment was confounded by a surprise, which, nevertheless, the officers beat off, all behaving well, and many of the young officers displaying an ardor which only wanted occasion and good commanders." Armstrong, on this subject, writes: "But little more mismanagement was now wanting, to make the campaign of 1813, as much a subject of ridicule at home, and contempt abroad, as that of the preceding year, on the 6th of June, *the day on which Burns was flying when none pursued*, an order was received from the commander-in-chief, recalling, without loss of time, the whole army to Fort George, and virtually abandoning all the objects of the campaign; nor was even this ill-judged movement executed, without a disorder which entailed upon it the loss of twelve boats, principally laden with the baggage of the army." The Burns here mentioned is the officer on whom devolved the command of the American army after the capture of the two Generals, Winder and Chandler.

Is it probable that the Secretary at War would have expressed himself in such strong terms of condemnation had the " surprise " at Stony Creek been as trifling as Ingersol represents? To return, however, to Gen. Vincent's official account :—

Burlington-heights, head of Lake Ontario,
June 6th, 1813.

Sir,—Having yesterday received information of the enemy having advanced from the Forty-mile Creek, with a force consisting of 3500, eight or nine field-pieces, and 250 cavalry, for the avowed purpose of attacking the division under my command in this position, and having soon afterwards received a report that he had passed the swamp, and driven in my advanced posts from Stony Creek and Brady's, lieutenant-col. Harvey, deputy-adjutant-general, immediately went forward with the light companies of the king's, and 49th regiments; and having advanced close to, and accurately ascertained, the enemy's position, sent back to propose to me a night attack on the camp.

The enemy's camp was distant about seven miles. About half-past eleven I moved forward with five companies of the 8th (or King's), and the 49th regiments, amounting together to seven hundred and four firelocks; lieutenant-colonel Harvey who conducted it with great regularity and judgement, gallantly led on the attack. The enemy was completely surprised, and driven from his camp, after having repeatedly formed into different bodies, and been as often charged by our brave troops, whose conduct, throughout this brilliant enterprise, was above all praise. The action terminated before day light, when three guns and one brass howitzer, with three tumbrils; two brigadier-generals, Chandler and Winder, first and second in command, and upwards of 100 officers, non-commissioned officers, and privates, remained in our hands.

Not conceiving it prudent to expose our small force to the view of the enemy, who, though routed, and dispersed, was still formidable as to numbers and position, he having fled to the surrounding heights, and having still four or five guns, the troops were put in motion at day-break and marched back to their cantonments. After we had retired and it became broad day, the enemy ventured to re-occupy his camp, only, however, for the purpose of destroying his incumbrances, such as blankets, carriages, provisions, spare arms, ammunition, &c; after which, he commenced a precipitate retreat towards the Forty-mile Creek, where he effected a junction with a body of 2000 men, who were on their march from Niagara to reinforce him.

I cannot conclude this despatch without calling your excellency's attention to the following officers :—

To lieutenant-col. Harvey, the deputy-adjutant general, my obligations are particularly due. From the first moment the enemy's approach was known, he watched his movements, and afforded me the earliest information. To him, indeed, I am indebted for the suggestion and plan of operation; nothing could be more clear than his arrangements, nor more completely successful in the result. The conduct of major Plenderleath, who commanded the 49th regiment was very conspicuous. By his decision and prompt efforts, the surprize of the enemy's camp was completed, and all his efforts to make a stand were rendered ineffectual by the bayonet, which. overthrew all opposition. A party of the 49th, with major Plenderleath at their head, gallantly charged some of the enemy's field-pieces, and brought off two six-pounders.

Major Ogilvie led on, in the most gallant manner, the five companies of the King's regiment; and whilst one-half of that highly disciplined and distinguished corps supported the 49th regiment, the other part moved to the right, and attacked the enemy's left flank, which decided our midnight contest.

I have also received the greatest assistance from major Glegg, brigade-major to the forces, and beg leave to mention the names of captains M'Dowal and Milnes, your excellency's aides-de-camp, who accompanied me to the attack, and upon all occasions have volunteered their services. I have likewise to acknowledge the assistance of captain Chambers, of the 41st regiment, who had arrived some days before from Amherstburgh; and Mr. Brook, pay-master of the 49th, who assisted me as acting aide-de-camp.

To Mr. Hackett, acting-staff-surgeon to this army, I feel particularly indebted, for his judicious arrangements, by which the wounded have received every attention, and are most of them likely to be restored to the service.

It would be an act of injustice, were I to admit assuring your excellency, that gallantry and discipline were never more conspicuous than during our late short service; and I feel the greatest satisfaction in assuring you, that every officer and individual seemed anxious to rival each other in his efforts to support the honor of His Majesty's arms, and to maintain the high character of British troops.

I beg leave to refer your excellency to the

inclosed reports for particulars respecting our loss, which, I regret, has been very severe.

I have the honor to be, &c.

JOHN VINCENT,

Brigadier-gen'l.

General return of killed, wounded, and missing, in action with the enemy near the head of Lake Ontario, June 6th, 1813.

Total; 1 lieutenant, 3 serjeants, 19 rank and file, killed; 2 majors, 5 captains, 2 lieutenants, 1 ensign, 1 adjutant, 1 fort-major, 9 serjeants, 2 drummers, 113 rank and file, wounded; 3 serjeants, 52 rank and file missing.

General Dearborn's official letter is even more absurd than Ingersol's remarks; and it is impossible to reconcile the policy he adopted immediately afterwards with the contents of his despatch. It will be seen by this document, which follows, that he almost claims a victory:

"I have received an express from the head of the Lake this evening, with intelligence that our troops, commanded by Brigadier-General Chandler, were attacked at two o'clock this morning by the whole of the British and Indian force; and by some strange fatality, though our loss was but small (not exceeding thirty), and the enemy completely routed and driven from the field, both Brigadiers Chandler and Winder were taken prisoners. They had advanced to ascertain the position of a company of artillery, when the attack commenced. General Vincent is reported to be amongst the killed of the enemy. Col. Clarke was mortally wounded, and fell into our hands, with fifty prisoners of the 49th British regiment. The whole loss of the enemy is two hundred and fifty. They sent in a flag, with a request to bury their dead. General Lewis, accompanied by Brigadier-General Boyd, goes on to take command of the advanced troops."

An analysis of this letter will be interesting, and really so curious a document deserves the trouble, as it is but seldom that an official paper, written with such an utter disregard of truth, can be found. "The whole of the British and Indian force." The Secretary at War, at least, was not deceived by General Dearborn's letter, for, in his remarks, he speaks of the British force as "seven hundred combatants."

In the next place, as to the Indians, there

were not altogether more than thirty, and these were at Burlington Heights, where they remained. General Dearborn's allusion to them was, however, a sufficient foundation on which Mr. O'Connor, in his history, has constructed a very imposing passage. "The army, on this occasion, has proved its firmness and bravery, by keeping its position in a night attack, in which the yells of the Indians mingled with the roaring of the cannon and musketry, were calculated to intimidate." To resume our analysis, General Dearborn pronounces "the enemy completely routed and driven from the field," and yet practically contradicts his own statements by immediately after retiring from before a "routed enemy" again—so far from the British sending in a flag of truce "to bury the dead," the Americans retired,* and *left their own dead to be buried by the British.* Lastly, although General Vincent was killed by Dearborn over night, he had sufficiently recovered from the shock which he must have experienced at hearing of his own death, to entertain the two American generals, at dinner, next day, and to inform them of the capture of four of their guns and one hundred and twenty men, a point on which General Dearborn and others

* One of the American accounts of the Stony Creek business contains the following statement: "Captain Manners, of that regiment, (the 49th) was taken in his bed by lieutenant Riddle; who, from a principle of humanity, put him on his parole, on condition of his not serving the enemy, until he should be exchanged. An engagement which that officer violated, by appearing in arms against the American troops, immediately after the recovery of his health." This is a serious charge against a brave officer, now living. Thus it is answered. Close to captain Manners, on the field, lay a captain Mills, of the American army, still more severely wounded. The two officers agreed, and mutually pledged their honors, that, no matter by which party captured, they should be considered as exchanged and at liberty to serve again. Lieutenant Riddle soon afterwards came up; and, although he could not stay to bring away even his friend, exacted a parole from captain Manners. When the American army subsequently fled, the two officers were found by the British. The instant captain Mills recovered from his wounds, he was sent by a flag to the American lines; and captain Manners became of course, exonerated from his parole. That an American editor should give insertion to any story, reflecting upon a British officer, is not at all strange. But it is so, that an American officer should have allowed three editions of Mr. Thompson's book to pass, every one containing so scandalous a paragraph.

have thought it proper to observe a judicious silence.

Armstrong, in his strictures on this affair, declares that the position of the American army, on the morning of the 6th, was not such as to render a retreat, either necessary or expedient, and blames General Dearborn very severely for withdrawing the troops to Fort George. Could any credit be attached to the American accounts of the events that transpired between the 5th and 10th of June? this condemnation could not be wondered at, but there is such a discrepancy between their narrations and the British versions, as almost to induce the belief of his having been in some measure misled by the garbled accounts transmitted to him, and that, in consequence, he condemned the American general for retiring without sufficient cause.

Now, when we consult Christie and James, it will be seen that, to a man of General Dearborn's habits, there was really one, though an insufficient cause for his prudence. It was the appearance of the British fleet, off the coast, that induced Dearborn, under the apprehension that a serious attack was meditated on Fort George, to direct the immediate return of his troops to that point. James says, "On the 3rd of June, Sir James Yeo, with his squadron, on board of which he had some clothing and provisions, and about two hundred and eighty of the 8th regiment, for Major-General Vincent, sailed from Kingston to co-operate with that officer, as well as, by intercepting the enemy's supplies, and otherwise annoying him, to provoke Commodore Chauncey to reappear on the lake." At daylight, on the morning of the 8th, Sir James found himself close to General Lewis' camp, at the Forty-mile Creek. It being calm, the larger vessels could not get in, but the Beresford and Sidney Smith schooners, and one or two gun-boats, succeeded in approaching within range of the American batteries. Four pieces of artillery were brought down to the beach; and in less than half an hour a temporary furnace for heating shot was in operation."* Whatever effect the American guns, with their heated shot might have had on the

British fleet, it did not prevent General Lewis from breaking up his camp and retreating to Fort George, despatching his camp, equipage and baggage in batteaux to the fort. The fate of these batteaux was soon decided; twelve of them, with their contents, were captured by the Beresford, and the remaining five were driven on shore, where they were abandoned by their crews. Sir James Yeo, in order to carry out the instructions he had, by this time, received from General Vincent, landed the detachment of the 8th, under Major Evans, and this corps, joined by the flank companies of the 49th and one battalion company of the 41st, which had arrived from the Heights, now mustering four hundred and fifty rank and file, entered the deserted American camp, where they found five hundred tents, one hundred stand of arms, one hundred and forty barrels of flour, and about seventy wounded, whom they made prisoners. Not one syallable of all this appears in any of the American accounts. It is not, therefore, to be wondered at, that General Armstrong was at a loss to account for Dearborn's precipitate withdrawal of his troops.

If the hopes and expectations of the cabinet at Washington had been raised, to any very high pitch by anticipatory sketches of what was to be effected, by the combined attacks of the army and fleet, the actual results fell very far short of the promises held out by the general and the naval commander. The western peninsula, it was confidently anticipated, was to have been occupied, leaving the troops time and opportunity to attack in detail Kingston, Montreal, and Quebec. Instead of this state of affairs, what was the actual position of the American troops and fleet at this time?

Two demonstrations had been made, one at York, the other at Fort George: in the first instance, some munitions of war had been captured, but then, this had just been destroyed at Sackett's Harbour—so nothing had been gained there; in the second instance an untenable fort had been taken possession of. These exploits had cost, besides, much time and men, and money, but had not, in reality, advanced the plan of the campaign one iota. Chauncey had accomplished nothing, and was now at Sackett's Harbour, and Dearborn

Result of the Dearborn and Chauncey expedition.

---

*Sketches of the War. Notices of the War in which it is stated—"But a few discharges of hot shot soon convinced the British commanders, that the experiment was not likely to turn out advantageously."

himself was, through the tactics of Colonel Bisshopp and Gen. Vincent, confined to the precincts of Fort George, which, from a fortress, had been now virtually reduced to a prison, with limits, little, if at all exceeding the range of its cannon. To account for a state of things so unexpected, and, considering the slender means of defence possessed by the British, so unhoped for, we must look for other causes than the mere valour of the British regulars or Canadian militia, as however gallant their conduct might have been in the field, however patient their behaviour during the hardships and privations of the campaign, still the odds brought against them had been so overwhelming as properly directed to have swept away all opposition. We do not, by any means, desire to deprive the British or Canadian soldier of one particle of honor and praise to which he is so justly entitled; we only desire to observe that it was a most fortunate train of events that gave to the Americans a succession of leaders whose incapacity neutralized, in a great measure, their numerical superiority. Whatever Gen. Dearborn might have been, it is very evident that he was at this time quite unfit for the harrassing duties which had devolved upon him. A few extracts will shew this. In a letter of the 4th June, he says, "I am still very feeble, and gain strength very slowly." June 8th. "My ill-state of health rendes it extremely painful to attend to current duties, and unless it improves soon, I fear I shall be compelled to retire to some place where my mind may be more at ease." This state of health will account satisfactorily for the desponding tone of his despatch of 20th June, a short time before his recall from the command of the district. "From resignations, sicknesss, and other causes, the number of regimental officers present and fit for duty is far below what the service requires. A considerable portion of the army being new recruits, and the weather being unfavourable to health, the sick have become so numerous, in addition to the wounded, as to reduce the effective force far below what could have been contemplated. The enemy have been reinforced with about five hundred men of the 104th regiment, whence I conclude that he will endeavour to keep up such a plan, at, and near the head of the lake, as will prevent any part of our force

in this quarter from joining, or *proceeding to Sackett's Harbour to attack Kingston;* and such is the state of the roads in this flat country, in consequence of continual rain, as to render any operations against the enemy extremely difficult, without the aid of a fleet for the transportation of provisions, ammunition and other necessary supplies. The enemy would probably retreat on our approach, and keep out of our reach, being covered by one or more armed vessels. The whole of these embarrassments have resulted from a temporary loss of the command of the lake." The poor old general was plainly very willing to find some cause on which to saddle the effect produced by his infirmities, and after reading the account of the two fresh disasters which now befell him, the reader will not be surprised to find that an order was issued on the 6th July, recalling him from the command of the district; and enjoining on his successor " not to prosecute any offensive operation, until our ascendancy on the lake was re-established."[*] Before closing this subject it may be as well to remind the reader that, at the very time General Dearborn was enumerating the addition of five hundred men to General Vincent's force as a reason for abandoning his plans, he had under his command, at Fort George alone, double the number of regular troops in all Western Canada. Had we not, in our enumeration of his force already shown this, we have a proof of it in Ingersoll's admission. Alluding to Dearborn's recall, he says, " *before* Wilkinson took the command, our forces in Canada, about *four thousand* strong, were shut up in Fort George." At this very time Proctor and Vincent's forces united would not have made up an effective body of two thousand men. And, if we turn to the other end of the lake, we will find the garrisons and other posts equally deficient in point of numbers. What says Armstrong on this head? "1st. Prevost, on his arrival at Prescott, borrowed from that part an escort of soldiers to prevent his being captured on his way to Kingston—a fact utterly inconsistent with the report of his having brought with him large detachments from Quebec and Montreal. 2nd. That Proctor, Barclay, Vin-

---

[*] This Act of executive authority originated with that portion of the House of Representatives most active and influential in supporting the war.

cent and Sheaffe, so far from being in a condition to yield any aid to the attack on Sackett's Harbour, were themselves in great want of reinforcements—Proctor postponing on that account, an attack which he had been ordered to make on Perry's fleet, then fitting out. 3rd. That, when late in the month of May, the British commander-in-chief (induced by the continued absence of the American fleet and army at the head of the lake) made an attack on Sackett's Harbour, he was unable to bring against that post more than seven hundred combatants, conduct utterly unaccountable in an old soldier, having at his disposition a force of either* six or eight thousand men. 4th. That the maximum of the British force at Kingston, in 1813, was one thousand men.† And lastly, that Sheaffe's papers, taken at York, and examined by Col. Connor, aide-de-camp to General Dearborn, 'showed satisfactorily that the garrison at Kingston, during the winter and spring of 1813, was *weak*, and much below the force necessary for its defence.'"

These remarks of Armstrong will serve as a proof of our assertion, that had the Americans been well officered, or had the war been so popular as to have admitted of the choice of generals, from other parties besides the one with whom "war measures" had been the ruling policy, their numbers were on all occasions so overwhelmingly superior as to have precluded the hope of any successful opposition, however gallant might have been the behaviour of the regulars, however determined might have been the militia to die in defence of their hearths and homes, or had even every soldier, regular or militia, possessed individually the energy or spirit of the lamented Brock.

As soon as General Vincent had, by his reinforcements, and the successful issue of the night attack at Stony Creek, been relieved from the embarrassing situation in which he had been placed, he actively recommenced offensive measures, placing the right division of his little force under the command of Lieutenant Colonel Bisshopp, who pushed forward detachments, and took up two positions,

Affair at the Beaver Dam.

commanding the cross roads at the Ten-mile Creek and the Beaver Dam. It was so arranged by preconcerted signals, that their stations could readily support each other. Dearborn finding that these manœuvres had very materially circumscribed the range of his troops, who were now compelled to live on their own resources, determined to check farther encroachments on his ease, and despatched Lieutenant Colonel Bœrstler, with a detachment of nearly seven hundred men, from Fort George, to attack and disperse that portion of Col. Bisshopp's command which had taken up their position in a stone house near the Beaver Dam. This detachment consisted of thirty men of the one-hundred-and-fourth, and were in communication with a party of Indians, who, under the command of Captain Kerr, and about two hundred strong, occupied the woods. Col. Bœrstler in his march came unexpectedly on this body of Indians, who, lining the woods, their numbers partially concealed by the cover, immediately attacked him. The thirty men of the 104th soon came to the assistance of Captain Kerr, and a warm skirmish ensued, which had lasted for about two hours, when Col. Bœrstler dreading an ambuscade, commenced a retreat towards Lundy's Lane, but was immediately attacked from the wood by a small body of about twenty militia, under Col. Thomas Clark, who, accidentally passing, had been attracted by the firing. Col. Bœrstler now began to think that matters looked serious, but instead of retreating as fast as he could, he sent for reinforcements to Fort George, sixteen miles distant.

While waiting for the arrival of these, and making good his position, Lieutenant Fitzgibbon, of the 49th, arrived on the field (if we may apply that expression to a beechwood), and after reconnoitring, and hearing that reinforcements had been sent for, this officer determined on the bold step of summoning the Americans to surrender.* This proposal, doubtless very

---

* As stated by Dearborn.

† A fact ascertained by General Brown during the war, and, subsequently, on a visit to that place

* The circumstances connected with the affair at the Beaver Dam, where Col. Fitzgibbon (then Lieut. Fitzgibbon) gained so much praise for the victory achieved by him over the Americans, was owing to information which Mrs. Secord, the widow of James Secord, Esq., deceased, formerly of Queenston, who was wounded at the battle of that place (13th October, 1812), obtained from private sources of the inten-

much to Lieut. Fitzgibbon's surprise, Col. Bœrstler, seeing no prospect of escaping or saving his wounded, who were by this time pretty numerous, consented to, and terms of capitulation were forthwith agreed on.

Just as these were being drawn up, Major de Haren, who had been sent for by Lieutenant Fitzgibbon, arrived, bringing with him about two hundred and twenty men. This body came up in time to secure the prisoners, but not sufficiently so to save Col. Bœrstler the disgrace of having surrendered to a body, which, with the two hundred Indians, did not half equal that under his command.

Particulars of the capitulation made between

Capitulation of Colonel Bœrstler and five hundred and forty-one American troops. Captain M'Dowell, on the part of Lieut.-Col Bœrstler, of the United States' army, and Major De Haren, of His Britannic Majesty's Canadian regiment, on the part of Lieutenant Colonel Bisshopp, commanding the advance of the British, respecting the force under the command of Lieutenant-Colonel Bœrstler.

Article I. That Lieut.-Col. Bœrstler, and the force under his command, shall surrender prisoners of war.

tion of the American troops to surround and take Fitzgibbon and party, which consisted at that time of a detachment of the 49th regiment, some few militia, and a small body of Indians, to oppose some 500 of the American infantry and a detachment of some 50 of mounted American dragoons. The difficulty of reaching Lieut Fitzgibbon's post is thus related in Mrs. Secord's own words:—" I shall commence at the battle of Queenston, where I was at the time the cannon balls were flying around me in every direction. I left the place during the engagement. After the battle I returned to Queenston, and then found that my husband had been wounded; my house plundered and property destroyed. It was while the Americans had possession of the frontier, that I learned the plans of the American commander, and determined to put the British troops under Fitzgibbon in possession of them, and, if possible, to save the British troops from capture, or, perhaps, total destruction. In doing so, I found I should have great difficulty in getting through the American guards, which were out ten miles in the country. Determined to persevere, however, I left early in the morning, walked nineteen miles in the month of June, over a rough and difficult part of the country, when I came to a field belonging to a Mr. Decamp, in the neighborhood of the Beaver Dam. By this time daylight had left me. Here I found all the Indians encamped; by moonlight the scene was terrifying, and to those accustomed to such scenes, might be considered grand. Upon advancing to the Indians they all rose. and, with some yells, said "Woman," which made me

Article II. That the officers shall retain their arms, horses, and baggage.

Article III. That the non-commissioned officers and soldiers shall lay down their arms at the head of the British column, and shall become prisoners of war.

Artile IV. That the militia and volunteers, with Lieutenant Colonel Bœrstler, shall be permitted to return to the United States on parole.

ANDREW M'DOWELL,
Capt. of the U. S. Light Artillery.
Acceded to and signed,   P. G. BŒRSTLER,
Lieut.-Col. commanding detachment
United States' Army.
P. V. DEHAREN,
Major, Canadian regiment.

tremble. I cannot express the awful feeling it gave me; but I did not lose my presence of mind. I was determined to persevere. I went up to one of the chiefs, made him understand that I had great news for Capt. Fitzgibbon, and that he must let me pass to his camp, or that he and his party would be all taken. The chief at first objected to let me pass, but finally consented, after some hesitation, to go with me and accompany me to Fitzgibbon's station, which was at the Beaver Dam, where I had an interview with him. I then told him what I had come for, and what I had heard—that the Americans intended to make an attack upon the troops under his command, and would, from their superior numbers, capture them all. Benefitting by this information, Capt. Fitzgibbon formed his plans accordingly, and captured about five hundred American infantry, about fifty mounted dragoons, and a field-piece or two was taken from the enemy. I returned home next day, exhausted and fatigued. I am now advanced in years, and when I look back I wonder how I could have gone through so much fatigue, with the fortitude to accomplish it.

(*Certificate.*)

I do hereby certify that Mrs. Secord, the wife of James Secord, of Chippewa, Esq., did, in the month of June, 1813, walk from her house in the village of St. Davids to Decamp's house in Thorold, by a circuitous route of about twenty miles, partly through the woods, to acquaint me that the enemy intended to attempt by surprise to capture a detachment of the 49th regiment, then under my command, she having obtained such knowledge from good anthority, as the event proved. Mrs. Secord was a person of slight and delicate frame, and made the effort in weather excessively warm, and I dreaded at the time that she must suffer in health in consequence of fatigue and anxiety, she having been exposed to danger from the enemy, through whose line of communication she had to pass. The attempt was made on my detachment, by the enemy and his detachment, consisting of upwards of 500 men, with a field-piece, and fifty dragoons were captured in consequence. I write this certificate in a moment of much hurry and from memory, and it is therefore thus brief.

(Signed)   JAMES FITZGIBBON,
Formerly Lieutenant in the 49th Regt.

As soon as General Dearborn heard of Bœrstler's critical situation, he dispatched Col. Christie with a reinforcement of three hundred men. The detachment marched as far as Queenston, where, hearing of Bœrstler's surrender, Col. Christie returned to the camp.

Reinforcements arrive at Queenston, but return to Fort George.

Congress had been in session about a month when the intelligence of this affair reached Washingon, and it served as a sort of climax to the continual tidings of mismanagement and misfortune. Ingersol says, "after a short communion of regret and impatience in the House of Representatives with the Speaker and General Ringold, I was deputed to wait on the President, and request General Dearborn's removal from a command which so far had been thus unfortunate." This remonstrance had the desired effect, and, as we have already seen, Dearborn was recalled, and, according to Ingersol, "the northern army was relieved of a veteran leader, whose age and ill-health, (whatever previous military reputation he might have acquired by distinguished service, bravery, and activity in the war of the Revolution) disqualified him for active and enterprising services, but in his successor, Gen. Wilkinson, did not get a younger, healthier, or more competent commander.

Proceedings in Congress on receipt of news of Bœrstler's surrender.

From the date of Bœrstler's surrender to the end of June, no movements of any importance took place in the Niagara district, the British forces gradually closing round Fort George, and watching carefully the American army, who still occupied that position. A negative good was, however, thus effected, as the services of fully four thousand men were lost to the country, while the expense and labour of supplying so large a body were daily becoming more felt, and increased the feelings of dissatisfaction entertained by the more sensible and reflecting portion of the Union. Two expeditions were undertaken early in July, the result of which proved the benefit derived from keeping the American army cooped up at Fort George.

The first expedition was undertaken by Lieut. Col. Thos. Clark, of the Canadian Militia, on the night of the 4th July —Col. Clark's party crossed over, from Chippewa to Fort Schlosser, and succeeded in capturing the guard stationed there, bringing with them, as the fruits of their enterprise, a large quantity of provisions, one brass gun (a six-pounder), besides several stand of arms, with much ammunition! This affair was but trifling, still it serves to show the zeal of the militia, while the loss of the provisions was a serious blow to the enemy. The success which attended Col. Clark's exploit determined Col. Bisshopp to put in execution the plans he had formed against the important post at Black Rock. On the 11th July, therefore, he crossed over at daybreak with a party of two hundred and forty men, consisting of militia, and drafts from the 8th, 41st and 49th regiments. The surprise of the enemy was complete, and the blockhouses, stores, barracks, dock-yard and one vessel were destroyed, or secured within the Canadian lines. Ingersol, in noticing this, is not very complimentary to his countrymen, "There was a militia force more than sufficient to repel this daring invasion ; but they ran away without resisting it !* Unfortunately in his anxiety to secure as much as possible of the captured stores, Col. Bisshopp delayed his return longer than prudence warranted, and afforded time for the Americans to recover from their surprise and consternation. When retiring to their boats the British were attacked by a strong body of American regulars, militia, and *some Indians*, whom General Porter had collected, and the consequence was, that a heavy loss was experienced before the retreat could be effected— amongst the number of those who died from their wounds, was the gallant commander himself, a most promising young officer, of but twenty-seven years old.

Col. Clark's expedition against Fort Schlosser.

Col. Bisshopp's expedition against Black Rock.

---

* An effect of the Eastern doctrine (on the causes and character of the war), industriously circulated in the Northern and Western frontiers of New York.— *Armstrong's Notes.*

Col. Clark's letter, taken in connection with our previous remarks,

Col. Clark's letter. will show the loss of so many stores actually necessary to the vitality of the American army,* as must have considerably added to the perplexities of the war party at Washington, increasing, as it did, the drainage on the resources of a young country, with a public chest by no means overflowing, and a commerce as effectually suspended as if their whole mercantile marine had been swept away. Nearly one thousand American merchant vessels had been (we thank Ingersol for this information) taken and condemned by the British. Of one hundred thousand and more American seamen, registered at the Custom-house in 1812, a large portion of them were thrown out of employment by the war, to remain idle, discontented, and mischievous, unless they could obtain employment in privateers. Ingersol makes a curious commentary on the avidity with which the Americans seized on and followed up this trade. We call it *trade*, and an inquiry into the character of the parties by whom the privateers were, for the most part, fitted out, will abundantly prove that it was a speculation for individual gain, and not as an injury inflicted on a national enemy, that the fleet which, according to Nile's Register, inflicted such fatal injuries on British commerce, was equipped. Speaking of his countrymen, Ingersol remarks—" This has always been, and will be, not only a maritime but a privateering people. Their *freedom* and their *enterprise*, which is the offspring of their freedom, and their habit of doing many things individually, which in other countries are done exclusively by Government, must always render (mark the delicacy with which he names the trade) *sea volunteers* a numerous and powerful force." We presume that then, as now, the same marauding and republican carelessness of law and public opinion prevailed. We say "as now," for have we not seen within the last two years a most flagrant instance of this buccaneering propensity in the expedition against Cuba? To return, however, to our subject (the descent on Black Rock)

Chippewa,
July 12th, 1813.

*Sir,—I have the honor to report to you, for the information of Major-general de Rottenburg, that the detachment under the command of Lieutenant-colonel Bisshopp, consisting of a detachment of royal artillery, under Lieutenant Armstrong, forty of the King's regiment, under Lieutenant Barstow, one hundred of the 41st, under Captain Saunders, forty of the 49th, under Lieutenant Fitz-Gibbon, and about forty of the 2nd and 3rd Lincoln Militia, embarked at two o'clock on the morning of the 11th instant, to attack the enemy's batteries at Black Rock.

The detachment landed half an hour before day-light, without being perceived, and immediately proceeded to attack the batteries, which they carried with little opposition; the enemy heard the firing at their advanced posts, and immediately retreated with great precipitation to Buffalo.

The block-houses, barracks, and navy-yard, with one large schooner, were burnt; and such of the public stores as could be got off were taken possession of, and carried across the river by the troops. Before the whole of the stores were taken away, the enemy advanced, having been reinforced by a considerable body of Indians, whom they posted in the woods on their flanks and in their advance; they were gallantly opposed by the whole of the troops; but finding the Indians could not be driven from the adjoining woods without our sustaining a very great loss, it was deemed prudent to retreat to the boats, and the troops re-crossed the river under a heavy fire.

I am extremely sorry to add, Lieutenant-colonel Bisshopp fell, severely wounded, on our retreat to the boats; fortunately the detachment did not suffer from it, everything having been arranged and completed previous to his receiving his wounds.

Enclosed are the returns of killed, wounded, and missing, with the exception of those of the 49th regiment and militia, which have not yet been received.

I have also enclosed the returns of the ordnance, and other stores captured.

I have the honor to be, &c.

THOMAS CLARK,
Lieut.-col. 2d Lincoln militia.

To Lieut.-col. Harvey,
Deputy Ad.-gen.

Return of killed, wounded, and missing, on the morning of the 11th instant.

July 13th, 1813.

Total—13 privates killed; 1 inspecting field-officer, 1 Lieutenant-colonel, 1 Captain, 1 Sergeant, 1 Corporal, 19 Privates, wounded; 6 Privates missing.

JOHN HARVEY,
Lieut.-col. D. A. gen.

Return of ordnance destroyed and captured from the enemy at Black Rock, July 12th, 1813.

Total—4 guns, 177 English and French muskets, 1 3-pounder travelling carriage, 6 ammuni-

great as was its success,† still it may be considered to have been dearly purchased by Bisshopp's death. Young and indefatigable in his duties, to his active co-operation much

of General Vincent's successful attempts‡ to enclose General Dearborn and his army within the limits of Fort George, may be ascribed.

---

tion kegs, a small quantity of round and case shot, (quantity not yet known.)

Taken and destroyed.

Two iron 12-pounders, 2 iron 9-pounders.

R. S. ARMSTRONG,
Lieut.-col. R. A.

Return of stores, &c., &c., captured at, and brought from, Black Rock, on the 14th July, 1813.

One hundred and twenty-three barrels of salt, 46 barrels of whiskey, 11 barrels of flour, 1 barrel of tar, 2 large bales of bla.kets, (about 200,) 70 large blankets, loose, 5 casks of clothing; 3 cases, containing 396 soldiers' caps, 16 bars of iron, 1 bar of steel, 1 side sole leather, 7 sides of upper leather, (some of them marked serjeant Fitzgerald, 41st regiment, and taken from Fort Erie, to be returned to the 41st regiment,) 7 large batteaux, 1 large scow.

THOS. CLARK,
Lieut.-col. 2d Lincoln Militia.

†Sir,—I presume that you are willing to award honor to whom honor is due, and I therefore address you to make a small addition to your account of the attack made under Col. Bisshopp on Black Rock. Col. Fitzgibbon has long been known in Canada in both a civil and military capacity, and if he were now present he would be able to give you much interesting and valuable information. At the time of this attack he was a Lieutenant in the 49th, and his daring spirit and energy of character was well known to the whole army. General Vincent had placed him in command of a sort of independent company of Rangers. Volunteers from the different regiments were asked for, and strange to say, so many men of *other regiments* offered that it was difficult to decide who should be permitted to go from the numerous young subs desirous of joining him ; he selected his friend Lieut. Winder of the 49th, now Dr. Winder, Librarian to the House of Assembly at Quebec. Volunteer D. A. McDonell of the 8th. Volunteer Augustus Thompson of the 49th, and another youngster of the 49th, were permitted as a great favor to join his corps. We were all dressed in green uniform made from clothing which had been captured from the enemy ; we called ourselves " Fitzgibbon's green 'uns." We were the first to cross the river on the expedition in question, and Fitzgibbon pushed on so expeditiously, that the block-house was in our possession long before Col. Bisshopp was ready to move forward. For this piece of impertinence we were repaid by being sent on in advance without any breakfast to watch the enemy near Buffalo, while the army was employed in carrying off the stores. As soon as this had been accomplished we were ordered to return and cover the re-embarkation. Col. Bisshopp, who appeared nettled at not having been in front during the advance, seemed now determined to be the last in retiring.

We had all embarked unmolested, but scarcely had we pushed off from the shore, e'er the enemy's Indians commenced firing on us from the bank, to which, unperceived by us, they had crawled. For the Green 'uns to disembark and drive the enemy to the woods required but a few minutes, but we were not fairly seated in the boats again, before the attack was renewed by the Indians, reinforced by the American advance guard. Out we all leaped a second time, and Nichie and his backers were glad to take shelter in the bush again. We now found that we had " Cotched a Tartar "—Porter with his whole force was upon us. " Sauve qui peut," was now the cry, and as a matter of course the rush to the boats was a very devil take the hindmost affair. In the confusion, some oars in the boat in which Col. Bisshopp embarked, were lost overboard, and she drifted down the stream, while the enemy followed on the bank firing into her. The gallant Bisshopp, the darling of the army, received his death wound ; never was any officer, save always the lamented Brock, regretted more than he was.

All the fighting on this occasion was done by the Green 'uns, and if any merit be due, Fitzgibbon is entitled to it. In conclusion, I may as well add, that a part of the " Greens" were over at Fort Schlosser, commanded by Lt. Wir der, in Col. Clark's expedition ; in truth Winder commanded. On the day following the attack on Schlosser, a large detachment crossed from Buffalo, and the remainder of Fitzgibbon's corps, about twenty-five in number, under Thompson, attacked them. They made a running fight out of it of three miles before they reached their boats and got off.

I am, yours,
A GREEN 'UN.

‡Sir,—To your account of the battle of Stony Creek I would like to add a few particulars which may not prove uninteresting to your readers, and you will find that they differ a little from your account of the surprise.

At eleven o'clock at night the Light Company and Grenadiers of the 49th were under arms ; every flint was taken out and every charge was drawn. Shortly after we moved on in sections, left in front, the Light Company leading the way towards the enemy's camp. I had been driven in that afternoon from Stony Creek, and was well acquainted with the ground. The cautious silence observed was most painful ; not a whisper was permitted ; even our footsteps were not allowed to be heard ; I shall never forget the agony caused to the senses by the stealthiness with which we proceeded to the midnight slaughter. I was not aware that any other force accompanied us than the grenadiers, and when we approached near the Creek, I ventured to whisper to Col Harvey, " We are close to the enemy's camp, Sir ;". " Hush ! I know it," was his

This affair, too, led to the Americans throwing off the mask, and, after all the vituperations so freely lavished on the British, making use of the same "savage arm of the service" which they had so bitterly and unceasingly condemned.

In describing the British retreat to their boats, we purposely italicised, in our enumeration of the attacking bodies, the words *some Indians*, in order to direct the reader's attention to the fact that the American Government had called in to their assistance, along the shores of the Niagara, "the ruthless ferocity of the merciless savages," (for this expression see History of the United States, vol. 3, page 228.) The plea for this was the invasion of the United States territory, (" *the pollution of a free soil by tyrant governed slaves*,") but it did not perhaps strike Mr. O'Connor that this admission must sanction on the part of the British an alliance with Indians, also —inasmuch as General Hull had set the example of invasion. The Americans appeared certainly as liberators, but, then, the Canadians were so blind to their interests as not to perceive the blessings of freedom which Hull's proclamation held out ; hence the Indian alliance.

Indian alliance. Reasons assigned for forming it.

When the public journalists of one nation have been collectively descanting on a particular enormity observable in the course of action pursued by another, should that particular course be adopted by the party previously condemning it? It then becomes the duty of the historian to seek into the reasons for the change, and to ascertain either the *cause* or the *apology*.

We have already shown that, from the ruthless character of the border warfare which had so long been waged between the Americans and Indians, it was hopeless to expect that they would at once bury the hatchet, and, along with it, the recollection of all the wrongs and cruelties inflicted on them. It became, therefore, the policy of the Government, seeing that their own past, "ruthless ferocity" precluded any hope of alliance, to prevent the British from seeking that co-operation and friendship denied to themselves. Hence Hull's first proclamation, and the subsequent tirades against "savage warfare," &c.

We have, also, already shown that, inasmuch as Hull's invasion of Western Canada preceded the occupation of, or incursions into, the American territory, Mr. O'Connor's plea,

reply. Shortly after a sentry challenged sharply ; Lieut. Danford and the leading section rushed forward and killed him with their bayonets ; his bleeding corpse was cast aside and we moved on with breathless caution. A second challenge— who comes there?—another rush and the poor sentinel is transfixed, but his agonized dying groans alarmed a third who stood near the watchfire ; he challenged, and immediately fired and fled. We all rushed forward upon the sleeping guard ; few escaped ; many awoke in another world. The excitement now became intense ; the few who had escaped fired as they ran and aroused the sleeping army. All fled precipitately beyond the Creek, leaving their blankets and knapsacks behind.

Our troops deployed into line, and halted in the midst of the camp fires, and immediately began to replace their flints. This, though not a *very* lengthy operation, was one of intense anxiety, for the enemy now opened a most terrific fire, and many a brave fellow was laid low. We could only see the flash of the enemy's firelocks, while we were perfectly visible to them, standing, as we did, in the midst of their camp fires. It was a grand and beautiful sight. No one who has not witnessed a night engagement can form any idea of the awful sublimity of the scene. The first volley from the enemy coming from a spot as "dark as Erebus" seemed like the bursting forth of a volcano. Then again all was

dark and still, save the moans of the wounded, the confused click! click! noise made by our men in adjusting their flints. and the ring of the enemy's ramrods in re-loading. Again the flash and roar of the musketry, the whistling of the bullets and the crash of the cannon—"Chaos has come again." The anxious moments (hours in imagination) have passed ; the tremblingly excited hands of our men have at last fastened their flints ; the comparatively merry sound of the ramrod tells that the charge is driven home ; soon the fire is returned with animation ; the sky is illumined with continued flashes ; after a sharp contest and some changes of position, our men advance in a body and the enemy's troops retire. There were many mistakes made in this action, the two greatest were removing the men's flints and halting in the midst of the camp fires, this is the reason why the loss of the enemy was less than ours, their wounds were mostly made by our bayonets. The changes of position by different portions of each army, in the dark, accounts for the fact of prisoners having been made by both parties. I must give the enemy's troops great credit for having recovered from their confusion, and for having shewn a bold front so very soon after their having been so suddenly and completely surprised.

Yours,
A 49TH MAN.

"The invasion of New York State," cannot be considered tenable ; we must, therefore, look further for the cause of this "unnatural alliance with savages."* Mr. Thomson† declares that it was done " by way of intimidating the British and the Indians, as by the Americans incorporating into their armies, the same kind of force, the habitual stratagems of the savages would be counteracted, and their insidious hostilities defeated," and yet, oddly enough, adds, "in the hope, too, of preventing a recurrence of previous barbarities." Smith,‡ by way of proving this, we suppose, cites the following remarkable instance :—

" Of the influence of a cultivated people," writes Dr. Smith, "whose manners and religion the savages respect, to induce them to resign their inhuman treatment of their prisoners, Major Chappin gave an instructive example immediately after uniting his force with the warriors of the Six Nations. A corps, composed of volunteer militia and of these Indians, had completely put to rout a party of the enemy in the vicinity of Fort George. In a council held before the conflict (for all things must be done among them by common consent), the Indians, by his advice, agreed amongst themselves, besides the obligation of their general treaty, which they recognized, that no one should scalp or tomahawk prisoners, or employ towards them any species of savage inhumanity. Accordingly, after the battle, sixteen wounded captives were committed solely to their management, when, governed by a sacred regard to their covenant, and the benevolent advice of their commander, they exhibited as great magnanimity towards their fallen enemy, as they had shown bravery against their foes in battle."

We can easily understand James's astonishment that any American writer should have been found to promulgate the fact that sixteen British captives, writhing under the anguish of their yet bleeding wounds, were, by the orders of an American officer, "committed solely to the management" of a party of hostile Indians, to determine, by way of experiment, whether those ruthless savages,‖

that faithless and perfidious race would listen to the advice of their white and civilised brethren ; and to ascertain whether the influence of a cultivated people would impose any restraints upon the known habits of Indian warfare. The artful advice to an infuriated mob who had just secured their victim, " Do not nail his ears to the pump," fades in comparison with this example of American feeling for their prisoners. After the battle of the Miami, when the British guard (see chapter nine) in charge of the American prisoners, were overpowered, and some of them killed and wounded in defence of the helpless captives committed to their charge, when forty Americans fell victims to the fury of the Indians, the whole Union resounded with the most exaggerated accounts of British perfidy and cruelty.* This outcry, too, was raised only on the unconfirmed statements of the American press, yet here have we found one of these same historians gravely chronicling an experiment, as to whether the Indians would act the part of good Samaritans, or scalp and otherwise torture their victims. Torture to the feelings of the captives, it must, under all circumstances, have been ; a wanton sporting with the fears of his prisoners on the part of the American officer. James expresses himself very strongly on this subject. "Happily, amidst all that has been invented by the hirelings of the American Government, to rouse the passions of the people and gain over to their side the good wishes of other nations, no British officer stands charged with a crime half so heinous as that recorded to have been committed by the American Major Chappin." It is clear from this passage that James, at any rate, does not attribute the American alliance with the Indians to the desire to render less horrible or cruel the warfare of the red men.

Another reason has been assigned, and we will investigate its probability. We will begin

Lieutenant Eldridge's massacre.

---

* History of the War.
† Sketches of the War.
‡ History of the United States.
‖ We carefully employ none but the terms taught us
§ American writers.

* In our account of the slaughter of Col. Dudley and his party, we adopted Major Richardson's version of the matter (although bearing more hardly on the British), in preference to James's, in which the affair is thus described—"Colonel Dudley and his detachment were drawn into an ambuscade by a body of Indians, stationed in the woods. Here fell the Colonel and the greater part of his men."

with Mr. Thomson's statement.* On the 8th of July Lieutenant Eldridge, of the 13th regiment, was ordered to the support of some American pickets with a detachment of some forty men. In the execution of this service he fell into an ambuscade, and, after a hard contest, his party, with the exception of five, were cut to pieces, by the superior force of *British* and Indians. These five prisoners along with the wounded were then, (according to Mr. Thomson,) "inhumanly murdered," and their persons so savagely mutilated that, "the most temperate recital of the enemy's conduct would, perhaps, scarcely obtain belief." Mr. Thomson here dwells at some length on the atrocities perpetrated—"split skulls," and "torn out hearts" forming part of his catalogue of horrors—he then adds, "Lieutenant Eldridge was supposed to have experienced the same fate."

What were the real facts of this case? Some stores of which the British were in particular want, had been left concealed, at the time of the retreat from Fort George, at a spot not far from an American outpost. The Indian chief Black Bird having been informed of the exigencies of the case, volunteered to bring them into the camp, and he accordingly departed on his expedition with some one hundred and fifty of his warriors. In the performance of his undertaking Lieutenant Eldridge and his party were encountered and captured. After the American officer had surrendered, he drew forth a concealed pistol and shot one of the chiefs, in whose charge he was, through the head, endeavouring to make his escape, for this act of treachery Lieut. Eldridge very deservedly lost his life, and to those who are cognizant of the Indian character it will not appear strange that some of his party should have also paid the penalty of their officer's perfidy. Not one British or Canadian was present on this occasion, (this is proved by Mr. O'Connor himself, in his account,† in which he no where alludes to the British,) yet, Mr. Thomson's rabid feelings have induced him to cite this act of cruelty on the part of the British as a cause for the Indian alliance.

A reference to dates will further disprove Mr. Thomson's statements. "This "act of cruelty" was perpetrated on the 8th of July, now the declaration of war by the six nations of Indians was made three days antecedent, and could not therefore have been occasioned by this "case of barbarity."

"We, the chiefs and counsellors of the Six Nations of Indians, residing in the State of New York, do hereby proclaim to all the war-chiefs and warriors of the Six Nations, that war is declared on our part against the Provinces of Upper and Lower Canada. Therefore, we do hereby command and advise all the war-chiefs to call forth the warriors under them, and put them in motion, to protect their rights and liberties, which our brethren the Americans, are now defending.—*By the Grand Counsellors.*"

Declaration of War, by the Six Nations of Indians.

It would have been far more honest had American writers come boldly forward and justified, on their real grounds, the alliance which they had all along desired to form. They would have been then spared the trouble of inventing, and the disgrace of circulating, all those marvellous tales which disgrace their pages. The credit of being foremost amongst the ranks of these modern Baron Munchausens is certainly due to the government organ, in which the "*Head of the English Church*" is first vehemently denounced as an "ally of hell-hound murderers," and then contrasted with the United States Government. "From the organization of the governmant of the United States, the constant care of every administration has been to better the condition of the Indian tribes, and preserve profound peace with them. Such is the spirit of our republican institutions. We never began a war with them, or placed the tomahawk in their hands. When the British, in alliance with them, ravaged our frontier and committed murders, until then, unheard of, *we advised* this restless *people to peace*, and resisted their importunity to retaliate on the enemy the wrongs they had inflicted. They have been *sometimes employed as spies or guides but in no other capacity*. At this moment (April 1813) the United States could let loose on the British in Canada, upwards of one thousand Indian warriors, impatient for the field of battle, thirsting for blood. But

Real causes of alliance.

the same policy prevails; they are retained by force, or persuaded, or pensioned to remain quiet." What a glorious contrast.

It would appear, however, that the Americans discovered that there is a limit beyond which human patience can no further go— hence the expediency of employing them as a means of counteracting the wiles and stratagems of the hostile tribes, and of gradually instilling into their savage minds the lessons of moderation and christian forbearance. Would it not have been far more honest, we repeat, to have frankly admitted, that by representations, and presents, the object of the Americans had been gained, and that some of the Indian tribes had, forgetting past wrongs, rallied under the American standard. This, however, would not have suited the purposes of the American government, which was, even at the time of completing the treaty with the Indians, meditating farther treachery and violence against the hapless and persecuted red man. At the very time of the completion of the treaty, the government organ writes: "*It appears as though the extermination of the faithless race was indispensable to our safety. We have evidences of their ferocity that it would be criminal to forget.*" What follows is even more at variance with the lessons of moderation and forbearance which the humane and considerate commanders of the American army had it so at heart to inculcate. "In the nature of things it will be impossible for them to defend themselves, nor can Great Britain give any security by treaty. She may abandon or support as policy dictates. Thus the time is at hand when they will be swept away from the face of the country as with the besom of destruction." We can scarcely believe that any one who reads the above, can be at a loss to account for the inveterate and determined hostility evinced by the Indians towards the Americans. Most unfortunately for the case of moderation, and so forth, which American writers are so desirous of establishing, Niles *Register* institutes a comparison between the use of the Indians by the British as analogous to the use of blood hounds in Cuba by the Spaniards,* a most unfortunate comparison.

as in Mrs. Stowe's late work (the world wide known Uncle Tom's Cabin.) '*Proh! pudor!*' the enlightened Americans of the present day are represented as following the same atrocious customs with reference too, not to their enemies, but to those in whom nature has implanted the same burning desire for freedom which we presume inflamed the breasts of a Washington, a Jackson, or a Lawrence.

This digression is, perhaps, scarcely relevant to our subject, but when we find such atrocious paragraphs in American books, professing to be "Historical Registers," we feel bound to retort the calumnies and fix the stigma of cruelty on the nation to which it more properly belongs, "The United States."

American writers may place what colouring they please on this alliance, and may assign any reason they think proper—but the real fact of the case stands thus—the capture of York, the occupation of Fort Erie and Fort George, and Proctor's withdrawal of his forces from the territory of Michigan, gave an appearance of reality to the vapouring and gasconade or the Americans, and enabled them to hold out such reasonable hopes of conquest or plunder as were sufficient to overbalance that deadly animosity which was the most natural feeling for every Indian to cherish, to whom memory had not been denied.

We omitted, in our account of General
General Clay's Mani-   Clay's defeat at the Mi-
festo.   ami, to introduce the
manifesto issued by him previous to that action. It will, however, serve here as an illustration of the lesson of moderation inculcated by the American Commanders. It will be remembered that General Clay's army met with precisely the same fate as their butchered brethren whom they were burning with haste to avenge.

General Orders.

SOLDIERS, You are now about to leave the shores of Kentucky—Many of you can boast that she gave you birth—She is indeed dear to us all.

---

* Below will be found an account of the education of the blood-hounds introduced by the Spaniards into St. Domingo, first to destroy the

Indians and afterwards the fugitive negroes All who have written upon the settlement of America, have endeavored to give immortality to the cruel-

KENTUCKIANS *stand high in the estimation of our common country.* Our brothers in arms, who have gone before us to the scene of action, have acquired a fame, which should never be forgotten by you—a fame worthy your emulation.

I feel conscious you would rather see your country no more, than return to it, under the impression, that by an act of yours, the high character of Kentucky had fallen.

To support this reputation, purchased by valor and by blood, you must with fortitude meet the hardships, and discharge the duties of soldiers. Discipline and subordination mark the real soldier—and are indeed the soul of an army.

In every situation, therefore, the most perfect subordination—the most rigid discharge of duty will be expected from all. Partiality or injustice shall be shown to none.

I have the most perfect confidence in your attachment and support through every difficulty we may encounter.

It is upon you—it is upon your subordination and discipline I rely, for a successful issue of the present campaign. Without this

---

ties of the Spaniards in this particular ; and many British historians are singularly eloquent on this great theme for censure. But who had the astonishing audacity to justify the Spaniards on the plea that these blood-hounds could not be restrained from thrusting their heads into the bowels and tearing out the living hearts of their victims? No one has had the impudence to do this ; but the blame is universally laid where it justly applies, *and the Spaniards, who used the dogs, are considered as responsible for the enormities they committed.*

From the famous speech of Lord Dorchester to the Indians in 1794, to the present day, the British in Canada have constantly trained savages for the very work they are now engaged in. This is not mere assertion. It can be sustained by hosts of testimony ; and will be received as an established fact by an impartial posterity. A war with the United States has always been regarded by the British as a probable event, sooner or later ; and his " gracious majesty's " officers in Canada have been unremittingly employed to attach the biped blood-hounds to themselves, while they excited their hatred to the Americans, by every means in their power.

NOTE.—BLOOD-HOUNDS.

The following is the mode of rearing blood-hounds and the manner of exercising them by chasseurs:—

The moment the blood-hounds are taken from the dam they are confined in kennels, with iron bars in front, like the dens used by showmen for confining wild beasts, where they are sparingly fed on the blood and entrails of animals. As they grow up, their keepers frequently expose in front of their cage a figure resembling a negro, male and female. and of the same color and dress, the body of which contains the blood and entrails of beasts, which being occasionally suffered to gush out, the figure attracts the attention of the dogs as the source of their food. They are then gradually reduced in their meals till, they are almost famished, while the image is frequently exposed to their view; and when they struggle with redoubled ferocity against their prey the image is brought nearer at intervals, till at last it is abandoned to their hunger, and being of wicker work, is in an instant torn to pieces, and thus they arrive at a copious meal. While they gorge themselves with this, the keeper and his colleagues caress and encourage them. By this execrable artifice the white people ingratiate themselves with the dogs, and teach them to regard a negro as their proper prey.—As soon as the young dogs are thus initiated, they are taken out to be exercised on living objects, and are trained with great care, till they arrive at the necessary nicety and exactness in the pursuit of the poor wretches whom they are doomed to destroy. The common use of these dogs in the Spanish islands was in the chase for run-away negroes in the mountains. —When once they got scent of the object, they speedily ran him down and devoured him, unless he could evade the pursuit by climbing a tree, in which case the dogs remained at the foot of the tree yelping in a most horrid manner till their keepers arrived. If the victim was to be preserved for a public exhibition or a cruel punishment, the dogs were then muzzled and the prisoner loaded with chains.—On his neck was placed a collar with spikes inward and hooks outward ; the latter for the purpose of entangling him in the bushes if he should attempt to escape. If the unhappy wretch proceeded faster than his guard, it was construed into an attempt to run from them and he was given up to the dogs who instantly devoured him. Not seldom on a journey of considerable length, these causes were feigned by their keepers to relieve them from their prisoners ; and the inhuman monster, who perpetrated the act, received a reward of ten dollars from the colony on making oath of his having destroyed his fellow-creature ! The keepers, in general, acquire an absolute command over these dogs : but while the French army used them in their late war against St. Domingo, while they had possession of the Cape, the dogs frequently broke loose in that neighborhood, and children were devoured in the public way; and sometimes they surprised a harmless family of laborers (who had submitted and furnished the French themselves with necessaries) at their simple meal, tore the babe from the breast of its mother. and involved the whole party in one common and cruel death, and returned when gorged, with their horrid jaws drenched in human blood. Even the defenceless huts of the negroes have been broken into by these dreadful animals and the sleeping inhabitants have shared a like miserable fate.

confidence and support, we shall achieve nothing honorable or useful.

The same destiny awaits us both. That which exalts or sinks you in the estimation of your country, will produce to me her approbation or condemnation.

Feeling this same common interest, the first wishes of my heart are, that the present campaign should prove honorable to all, and useful to the country.

Should we encounter the enemy—REMEMBER THE DREADFUL FATE OF OUR BUTCHERED BROTHERS AT THE RIVER RAISIN—*that British treachery produced their slaughter.*

The justice of our cause—with the aid of an approving Providence, will be sure guarantees to our success.

GREEN CLAY,

BRIGADIER GENERAL.

The tone of this manifesto, and the spirit breathed in the concluding paragraphs, require no comment on our part. The words in capital letters are exactly as they appeared in General Green Clay's own document. In the teeth of such a manifesto the Americans have dared to impute cruelty to the British, while carefully suppressing the well known fact—that just at this very time General Vincent had sat at the head of a committee by whom, as the best means of putting an end to any cruelties, it had been resolved, that ten dollars should be paid, to every Indian, for every American prisoner brought in alive. This resolution, James declares, appeared in a Boston paper, but we regret to state that not one of the numerous officers and men saved by its instrumentality, ever had the good feeling to acknowledge to what cause their safety was due.

General Proctor and the right division of the army now demand our attention. We cannot, however, concur with Major Richardson, who claims for this corps, the proud title of "the fighting division of Canada." We do not mean by our denial to detract one whit from the laurels won by the right division, but only to assert the claim of the other divisions of the army, whether composed of regulars or militia, and this claim we are borne out in making, if we refer to the various

Proctor's movements in the West.

general orders issued on different occasions from head quarters. The movements of the right division were undoubtedly attended with the most important and beneficial results, and when we consider that their force very rarely exceeded in numbers a single regiment their exertions and energy become more remarkable.

Expedition against Fort Meigs. General Proctor was induced, towards the end of July, to prepare, at the instance of Tecumseth, to repeat his attempt on Fort Meigs. Tecumseth's plan, according to Richardson, was as follows:—"Immediately in rear of Fort Meigs, and at right angles with the river, ran the road to Sandusky, distant about thirty miles, upon, or near, which the chief had been apprized by his scouts that General Harrison, (who with a large portion of his force had left the fort soon after its relief from General Proctor's presence,) was at that moment encamped. Having landed some miles lower down the river, the whole of the Indian force was to march through the woods, and gain, unperceived by the troops in the fort, the Sandusky road, where a sham engagement was to take place, leading the garrison to believe a corps, hastening to their relief, had been encountered, and attacked by the Indians, and inducing them to make a sortie for their rescue. The moment they had crossed the open ground, intervening between their position and the skirt of the wood, we were to rise from our ambuscade, and take them in the rear, making at the same time a rush for the fort, before the enemy could have time effectually to close his gates."

This plan was certainly, to all appearance, a good one, and the attempt was made accordingly, but, whether the Americans suspected the ruse or not, they did not stir from the protection of their fort, although, according to Richardson, the fire had become so animated and heavy, as to leave the British half in doubt whether the battle was a sham or real one.

The surprise of Fort Meigs by stratagem having failed, and as any attempt to reduce it by siege was out of the question, what guns there were, being only light six pounders —it was resolved, (Major Richardson says at Tecumseths' earnest request,) to attempt the reduction of a fort which had been contructed on the west side of the Sandusky river. This fort, about forty miles from the mouth of the river, stood on a rising ground, commanding the river to the east; having a plain to the north and a wood to the west. "The body of the fort was about one hundred yards in length, and fifty in breadth, surrounded. outside of all the other defences, by a row of strong pickets twelve feet high from the ground; each picket armed at the top with a *bayonet*."* Just outside of this fence, with the embankment reaching to the foot of the pickets, was a ditch twelve feet wide, and seven deep, thus forming a glacis of nineteen feet high. The ditch was protected by a bastion and two strong block-houses which completely enfiladed it, thus forming a very sufficient and formidable line of defence. We have no means of ascertaining correctly the number of troops that formed the garrison, but as an American account places them at "an *effective* force of one hundred and sixty rank and file," we may safely and without fear of exaggeration, put the numbers down at two hundred and fifty. Of the British there were three hundred and ninety-one officers and privates. Of the Indians there were but two hundred, and they withdrew to a ravine out of gunshot, almost immediately on the action commencing.

On the first day of August a landing was effected, under an ineffectual discharge from the enemy's guns, and a position taken up in the wood, on the skirt of which the British sixpounders were placed. On the morning of the second a fire was opened on the fort and continued till three, p. m., by which time it having been ascertained that the fire from the light sixes would affect no breach on the stockade, General Proctor resolved to carry the fort by storm. Forming his men accordingly into three columns, about 4 p.m. he began his attack, and although exposed to a most destructive fire, the gallant body reached the ditch. "Not a fascine" says Richardson, "had been provided, and although axes had been distributed among a body of men selected for the purpose, they were so blunt, that it would have been the work of hours to cut through the double line of pickets, even

if an enemy had not been there to interrupt our progress."

In defiance of this difficulty, the axe-men leaped without hesitation into the ditch, and attempted to acquit themselves of their duty; but they were speedily swept away by the guns from the batteries, charged with musket balls and slugs and directed with fatal precision. The troops had established themselves on the edge of the ditch, but it was impossible to scale without the aid of ladders or fascines; and within a few paces of the enemy only, they saw their comrades fall on every hand with no hope of avenging their deaths. The second division had only two officers attached to it. Brevet Lieutenant-colonel Short, of the 41st, was killed while descending the ravine at the head of his column, when, the command devolving on Lieutenant Gordon of the same regiment, that officer encouraging his men, and calling upon them to follow his example, was one of the first in the ditch, and was in the act of cutting the picketing with his sabre, when a ball, fired from a wall-piece, struck him in the breast. Although dangerously wounded, he refused to abandon his post, and continued to animate his men by his example, until a second ball, fired from the same piece, and lodging in his brain, left the division without an officer. The action had continued nearly two hours without producing the slightest impression on the enemy, when the bugles sounded the "cease firing," and the men were ordered to lie flat on the ground on the edge of the ravine. The first division were so near the enemy, that they could distinctly hear the various orders given in the fort, and the faint voices of the wounded and dying in the ditch, calling out for water, which the enemy had the humanity to lower to them on the instant. After continuing in this position until nine o'clock, the columns received an order to effect their retreat in silence, which was done accordingly, the enemy merely firing a few vollies of musketry, producing however no material effect. The troops having been re-embarked the same night, the expedition descended the river, and returned to Amherstburg. Our loss in this affair was severe—three officers, one sergeant, twenty-two rank and file killed; three officers, two sergeants, thirty-six rank and file wounded; and one sergeant, twenty-eight rank and file missing. Of this number, the proportion of the first division alone, consisting principally of the light company of the 41st, which had attacked the strongest point of the position, was five and thirty men.

During the assault, no assistance whatever was afforded by the Indians, who, unaccustomed to this mode of warfare, contented themselves with remaining quiet spectators of the scene.

It is a curious circumstance that we do not find in James, General Proctor's official despatch on this subject. Richardson writes, "The only British document referring to the matter at all, is the following brief notice by Sir George Prevost, evidently founded on a more detailed communication from General Proctor. We give Sir George's general order, and the American official version.* The only one we have been able to get at will be found below in our notes:—

General Order.
Head Quarters, Kingston,
Adjutant General's Office, 3d Sept. 1813.

His Excellency the Commander of the Forces has received a despatch from Major General Proctor, reporting the circumstances of an attack, made by a small portion of regular troops and a body of Indian warriors, on the 2d of August, on the American fort of Lower Sandusky, which, owing to the strength of the enemy's works, which resisted the fire of the light field guns brought against it—so that a practicable breach could not be effected —as also from the want of sufficient co-operation on the part of the Indian warriors, unused to that mode of warfare, the assault was not attended with that brilliant success which has so uniformly signalized the gallant exertions of the right division. The Major General extols the intrepid bravery displayed by the detachment under Brevet Lieutenant Colonel

---

*Copy of a letter from Major Croghan to Gen. Harrison, dated

Lower Sandusky, August 5, 1813.

DEAR SIR,—I have the honor to inform you, that the combined force of the enemy, amounting to at least 500 regulars, and as many Indians, under the immediate command of Gen. Proctor, made its appearance before this place, early on Sunday evening last: and as soon as the General had made such disposition of his troops, as would cut off my retreat (should I be disposed to make one), he sent Col. Elliott, accompanied by Major Chambers, with a flag, to demand the surrender of the fort, as he was anxious to spare the effusion of blood; which he should probably not have in his power to do, should he be reduced to the necessity of taking the place by storm. My answer to the summons was, that I was determined to defend the place to the last extremity, and that no force, however large, should induce me to surrender it. So soon as the flag had returned, a brisk fire was opened upon us, from the gunboats in the river, and from a five and-a-half-inch howitzer, on shore, which was kept up with little intermission throughout the night. At an early hour the next morning, three sixes (which had been placed during the night within 250 yards of the pickets), began to play upon us—but with little effect. About four o'clock P.M., discovering that the fire, from all his guns, was concentrated against the N.W. angle of the fort, I became confident that his object was to make a breach, and attempt to storm the works at that point. I therefore ordered out as many men as could be employed, for the purpose of strengthening that part—which was so effectually secured, by means of bags of flour, sand, &c., that the picketing suffered little or no injury; notwithstanding which, the enemy, about 500, having formed in close column, advanced to assault our works, at the expected point; at the same time making two feints on the front of Captain Hunter's lines. The column which advanced against the north-western angle, consisting of about 350 men, was so completely enveloped in smoke as not to be discovered, until it had approached within 18 or 20 paces of the lines; but the men being all at their posts, and ready to receive it, commenced so heavy and galling a fire as to throw the column a little into confusion; being quickly rallied, it advanced to the outworks, and began to leap into the ditch; just at that moment a fire of grape was opened from our six-pounder (which had been previously arranged, so as to rake in that direction), which, together with the musketry, threw them into such confusion, that they were compelled to retire precipitately to the woods. During the assault, which lasted about half an hour, an incessant fire was kept up by the enemy's artillery (which consisted of five sixes and a howitzer), but without effect. My whole loss, during the siege, was one killed and seven slightly wounded. The loss of the enemy, in killed, wounded, and prisoners, must exceed 150. One Lieutenant Colonel, a Lieutenant, and 50 rank and file, were found in and about the ditch, dead or wounded; those of the remainder, who were not able to escape, were taken off, during the night, by the Indians. Seventy stand of arms and several brace of pistols have been collected near the works. About three in the morning the enemy sailed down the river, leaving behind them a boat, containing clothing and considerable military stores.

Too much praise cannot be bestowed on the officers, non commissioned officers, and privates under my command, for their gallantry and good conduct during the siege.

Yours, with respect,
G. CROGHAN.
Major 17th U.S. Inf. commanding

Short, in endeavoring to force a passage into the enemy's fort, and laments the loss of the brave soldiers who have fallen in this gallant although unsuccessful assault.

Return of killed and wounded.

One captain, one lieutenant, one sergeant, one drummer, twenty-one rank and file killed. One sergeant and twenty-eight rank and file missing. Two captains, one lieutenant, two sergeants, one drummer, thirty-five rank and file wounded.

Killed—Brevet Lieut.-Col. Short, Lieut Gordon, 41st regiment, Lieut. Laussaussiege, Indian department.

Wounded—Capt. Dixon, Royal Engineers, Capt. Muir and Lieut. Macintyre, 41st regiment, all slightly.

By his Excellency's command.

EDWARD BAYNE, Adjutant General.

Although we have such positive evidence as to the share that the Indians had in the attack on the fort at Sandusky, the American writers are determined to drag the Indians within the limits of the ditch which had proved so fatal to the British troops. "The Indians," says Mr. Thomson, "were enraged

American remarks on the Sandusky affair.

and mortified at this unparallelled defeat, and carrying their wounded from the field, they indignantly followed the British regulars to the shipping." In all the account given by this writer in his HISTORY, not the slightest notice is taken of the heroic bravery exhibited by Col. Short and his men, although the most lavish encomias are bestowed on Major Croghan and his "band of *heroes*," who snugly ensconced behind their pickets compelled an army *ten times superior to retreat ingloriously*. Mr. O'Connor, more artful although not more liberal, leaves it to be understood that the Indians joined in the attack. "It is a fact worthy of notice," says this gentleman, "that not one Indian was found amongst the dead, although from three to four hundred were present."

Before following General Proctor's motions, after his retreat, we must return to the Niagara frontier, taking a glance, as we pass, at York and Commodore Chauncey's second descent upon it. The movements also in the lower province demand our attention. So many important events require, however, a fresh chapter.

General Proctor's movements.

CHAPTER XII.

COMMODORE Chauncey having completed the equipment of the *General Pike*, a new vessel of about the same tonnage as the *Wasp*, and manned with a very large crew, about one hundred and twenty of whom had been drafted from the *Constitution*, while the rest of her complement had been made up from other vessels in the Atlantic ports, again appeared on the lake to resume offensive operations. We have been particular in noticing the mode in which the *General Pike* was manned, as a body so large as one hundred and twenty from one vessel, all trained to work together, must have inspired her commander with the greatest confidence, especially when aware that, with the exception of the few thorough bred seamen who had been brought from Great Britain by Sir James Yeo, the remainder of the crews of the British Canadian navy were fresh water seamen, picked up hastily, and possessing few recommendations, save dauntless bravery, and an ardent attachment to the cause in which they had been enlisted. Commodore Chauncey's fleet now consisted of fourteen vessels, making up a force of over twenty-seven hundred tons, and manned by about twelve hundred picked men. Sir James Yeo's fleet was just one third inferior to his adversary in tonnage, guns and men; what his men lacked, however, in numbers and discipline, was in some degree made up by the spirit and zeal which animated them.

Commodore Chauncey's first object was the capture, or destruction, of a considerable quantity of stores that had been collected at Burlington Heights, and which he had ascertained to be but slenderly

Commodore Chauncey's second descent upon York.

Demonstration against the stores at Burlington Heights.

guarded. Col. Harvey, anxious for the protection of these stores, and suspecting, from Chauncey's manœuvres, his designs,. despatched Lieut. Col. Battersby, with part of the Glengarry regiment to strengthen Major Maule, who commanded at Burlington Heights. Col. Battersby by a forced march of extraordinary celerity, arrived with his reinforcement, and the American commodore, finding that his reception was likely to be warmer than he either anticipated or desired, prudently kept his men out of reach of harm, contenting himself with the capture of a few of the neighboring inhabitants. Having ascertained, however, that Col. Battersby's departure had left York undefended, he determined to swell the number of "American victories" by "a second siege and storming. &c." of that place. He accordingly seized his opportunity, and bore away for that port, which he entered on the 31st July.

Amongst the officers whom Commodore Chauncey had embarked for the expedition against Burlington Heights, we find the name of Lieut. Col. Scott. Now, according to Sir George Prevost, Lieut. Col. Scott was at that time an unexchanged prisoner of war, on his parole. Breaking parole is a severe charge to make against an officer, especially one who, as General Scott, has occupied, since, so prominent a place in the world's history, nevertheless, on Mr. James' authority, and with but faint denial of the charge from American historians, we feel compelled to avow our belief that Lieut. Col. Scott did actually forfeit his pledged word of honor as a soldier, on the occasion of the second descent upon York.

Col. Scott breaking parole.

We will now enter on our proof of this charge. All lists of prisoners paroled or exchanged, were necessarily transmitted to the commander-in-chief. In this case it will be found in Sir George Prevost's despatch of the 8th August,* to Lord Bathurst, that *colonel Scott is expressly mentioned as an unparoled prisoner* who had forfeited his pledged word. A faint attempt has been made to clear colonel Scott, from the imputation on the

* This despatch will be found under the next head.

plea that " he believed himself to be an exchanged prisoner," but as no shadow of proof has been brought forward, the defence can not be entertained—The following was the form of parole signed by lieutenant-colonel Scott and others when taken prisoners, " we promise, on honor, not to bear arms, directly or indirectly, against his Britannic Majesty, or his allies, during the present war, until we are regularly exchanged. We likewise engage that the undermentioned non-commissioned officers and privates, soldiers in the service of the United States, who are permitted to accompany us, shall conform to the same conditions." This is no accusation trumped up at this late period to impugn Gen. Scott's character as a man of honor—on the contrary, it was made at the time, and while lieutenant-colonel Scott was yet unknown to fame, and of no more importance in public estimation than any other American officer. It is therefore of consequence, that his friends should, if they can, at least make the attempt to wipe away the imputation.

An extract from James will throw some additional light on the subject, and prove that there were other officers besides colonel Scott, who did not scruple to break their parole, when a convenient opportunity presented itself. " To the doughty quarrel between Mr. President Madison, and general James Wilkinson, * of the American army, we are indebted for some important disclosures relative to the paroled prisoners. The general very candidly tells us, that lieutenant George Read, a witness examined on the part of the prosecution, at the general court martial, held at Troy, in the State of New York, in February, 1814, deposed on oath, " that on the 24th December, 1813, while a prisoner on parole, he received from colonel Larned, an order to repair to Greenbush, in the following words:—

' I am directed by the secretary of war, to call in all the American prisoners of war, at or near this vicinity, to their post, and that the officers join them for drilling, &c.—You will therefore repair to the cantonments at Greenbush, without loss of time.' ' Lieutenant Read further deposeth, that he repaired to Greenbush, in pursuance of the order, and made no objections to doing duty: that on general Wilkinson's arrival at Waterford, in the ensuing January, lieutenant Read called upon him, and exhibited the order received from lieutenant-colonel Larned; that general Wilkinson thought the order very improper, and afterwards issued the following order, dated, Waterford, January, 18th 1814.

' A military officer is bound to obey, promptly, and without hesitation, every order he may receive, which does not affect his honor; but this precious inheritance must never be voluntarily forfeited, nor should any earthly power wrest it from him. It follows that, where an officer is made prisoner, and released on his parole of honor, not to bear arms against the enemy, no professional duties can be imposed on him, while he continues in that condition; and under such circumstances, every military man will justify him for disobedience."

" Such," adds James, "are the principles upon which Mr. Madison conducted the late war. Lieutenant-colonel Scott, although perhaps not one of those American officers, who, like lieutenant Read, ' made no objection to doing duty' in compliance with the shameful order of his Government, certainly gave his parole at Queenston, and yet subsequently appeared in arms, both at Fort George, and at York."

We take pleasure in mentioning, that lieutenant Carr, of the United States army, also a prisoner at Queenston, declined obeying the order to perform duty, on the ground, that it was always contrary to the parole. This meritorious case being an exception, as it would appear, enhances its value; and it ought to operate as a lesson to that government, which could thus stab the reputation of its officers, to facilitate the means of conquest.

It is perfectly clear that Lieutenant-Colonel Scott broke his parole in every sense, as he not only joined what might be called the non-combatants in their usual garrison routine of drills, &c.; but he took, according to Sir George, an active part in the more stirring scenes of the campaign, thus rendering his dereliction from the path of honor doubly flagrant We have found that American writers have been always ready to lay hold of the slightest charge (witness the case of Capt. Manners at Stony Creek) against British

* Wilkinson's Memoirs, vol. 3, page 197.

officers, it will be well for them then in the present case to direct their attention towards clearing the character of one of their most distinguished men from the stain of dishonor resting on it.

To return, however, from our digression, to
Second descent upon York by Chauncey.
Commodore Chauncey whom we left just after his appearance, a second time, before York. This place being left by Colonel Battersby's departure with the Glengarry fencibles, undefended, the Americans landed without opposition and took quiet possession. The first thing done was to lay hold of everything, in the shape of stores, that could possibly be construed into public property, and the decision resting not with a court of judicial enquirers, but rather with men not overburthened with scruples, it may be easily inferred that some private property did by *mistake* find its way to American owners. Their other acts seem to have been attended with the same evidences of republican license, as they opened the gaol and liberated the prisoners, some of whom were in confinement awaiting their trial for capital offences. The few men in the hospital who were so ill as not to bear moving, even in the opinion of American prisoner-hunters, were paroled—the others were removed as trophies won at the " second battle of York." The public store-houses were then all destroyed, and by *mistake* some of the store-houses of the inoffensive inhabitants with large quantities of provisions, were first sacked, and afterwards burnt. This was a fair day's work, and accomplished without so much fighting or loss of life as the capture of the depôt at Burlington would have occasioned. A commander of energy or daring would, perhaps, have been scarcely satisfied to leave himself open to the charge of having been frightened by a handful of men, and prevented, in consequence, from accomplishing an enterprise of some importance. Commodore Chauncey, however, knew better, and as we suppose he must have been the best judge of the value of his character, we leave our readers to form their own estimate of the affair. A second landing was made on the next day, and an *expedition* fitted out which proceeded a *mile or so* up the Don, under the pretext of searching for public stores. The real object was to procure fresh

provisions *cheaply* for the shipping. Having succeeded in all their objects, towards evening they embarked, and the fleet sailed for Niagara, taking with them, or having destroyed, five guns, eleven boats, with a quantity of shot, shells and other military stores. Sir George's dispatch* will bear out all we have asserted relative to the injuries inflicted by the enemy on private individuals, by whom, indeed, this visitation was almost entirely felt. This is a circumstance which must not be lost sight of by the reader, as we shall soon have to show how loud was the outcry raised by both the American people and government when retaliatory measures were adopted by the British. Christie mentions a curious coincidence, viz :—that on the very day the American commander and his troops were burning the barracks and stores at York, Lieut.-Col. Murray was no less actively employed on the same business at Plattsburg—we shall, however, have to treat of this in its proper place.

The American fleet remained quietly at Niagara until the appearance of the British fleet on the 8th of August. Sir James had sailed from Kingston, on the 31st of July with supplies for the army, and having duly landed them, he looked into Niagara in hopes of tempting Commodore Chauncey to leave his anchorage. The challenge was accepted and the Americans bore down on the British line with whom they manœuvred for nearly two

---

* *From Sir G. Prevost to Earl Bathurst.*
Head quarters, Kingston,
Upper Canada, August 8th, 1813.

My Lord,—I have the honour to acquaint your lordship, that the enemy's fleet, of 12 sail, made its appearance off York on the 31st ultimo. The three square rigged vessels, the Pike, Madison, and Oneida, came to anchor in the offing ; but the schooners passed up the harbor, and landed several boats full of troops at the former garrison, and proceeded from thence to the town, of which they took possession. They opened the goal, liberated the prisoners, and took away three soldiers confined for felony : they then went to the hospitals, and paroled the few men that could not be removed. They next entered the store-houses of some of the inhabitants, seized their contents, chiefly flour, and the same being private property. Between 11 and 12 o'clock that night they returned on board their vessels. The next morning, Sunday, the 1st instant, the enemy again landed, and sent three armed boats up the river Don, in search of public stores, of which being disappointed, by sun-set both soldiers and sailors had evacuated the town, the small barrack wood-yard, and store-house, on Gibraltar Point,

days, losing four small vessels during that time, two of them, (the *Julia* and *Growler*) by capture, and the other two, (the *Scourge* of eight guns and the *Hamilton* of nine,) by their being upset in a squall* The entire crews of these vessels, with the exception of sixteen who were saved by the British boa s, were lost. Commodore Chauncey, somewhat disheartened at the loss of four of his vessels, and so many men, bore up for Niagara, from whence he sailed soon after to Sackett's Harbor, where he arrived on the 13th of August. As the reader may be scarcely yet aware of the actual superiority in point of force of the Americans over the British fleet, we will give a few extracts from the Naval Register with the detailed account of the occurrences of the 9th and 10th of August.

We will follow Sir James Yeo through all his operations from the date of the return of the fleet, after the Sackett's Harbor attempt, to the affair now under consideration.

Sir James Yeo on Lake Ontario.

We have already shown the valuable service rendered by Sir James, in the attack on the Americans, at the Forty Mile Creek, where it may be remembered much valuable camp equipage, stores, provisions, &c.—were, thro' his instrumentality, captured. On the 13th (June) he made prizes of two schooners and some boats containing supplies, and learning from some of the prisoners, that there was a depôt of provisions at the Genesee River he directed his course thither, and succeeded in securing the whole. On the 19th he captured another supply of stores and provisions from Great Sodus, and returned on the 29th to Kingston.

On his next cruise, after landing the stores at Burlington we found him, as already described, inviting the American fleet to leave the protection of their batteries We will now quote from the *Naval Chronicle*:

"The Americans, by their own admission, had fourteen vessels, armed, also by their admission, with one hundred and fourteen guns. Nearly one-fourth of the long guns and carronades were on pivot carriages, and were consequently as effective in broadside as twice the number. The fourteen American vessels were manned with eleven hundred and ninety three men."

When Sir James Yeo made his appearance off Niagara, the Americans could scarcely interpret his manœuvres to aught but what they were intended to convey—a challenge—we therefore find that "Commodore Chauncey immediately got under way, and stood out with his fourteen vessels, formed in line of battle; but, as the six British vessels approached, the American vessels, after discharging their broadsides, wore and stood under their batteries. Light airs and calms prevented Sir James Yeo from closing; and, during the

having been first set on fire by them; and at day-light the following morning the enemy's fleet sailed.

The plunder obtained by the enemy upon this predatory expedition has been indeed trifling, and the loss has altogether fallen upon individuals; the public stores of every description having been removed; and the only prisoners taken by them, there, being confined to felons and invalids in the hospital.

The troops which were landed were acting as marines, and appeared to be about 250 men; they were under the command of commodore Chauncey and lieutenant-colonel Scott, an unexchanged prisoner of war on his parole, both of whom landed with the troops. The town, upon the arrival of the enemy, was totally defenceless; the militia were still on their parole; and the principal gentlemen had retired, from an apprehension of being treated with the same severity used towards several of the inhabitants near Fort-George, who had been made prisoners, and sent to the United States. Lieutenant-colonel Battersby, of the Glengarry fencibles, with the detachment of light troops under his command, who had been stationed at York, was, upon the appearance of the enemy's fleet off that place, on the 29th ult. ordered with his detachment and light artillery to proceed for the protection of the depots formed on Burlington Heights, where he had joined major Maule's detachment of the 104th regiment, and concentrated his force on the following evening. The enemy had, during the course of that day, landed from the fleet 500 men, near Brandt's house, with an intention of storming the heights; but finding major Maule well prepared to receive them, and being informed of lieutenant-colonel Battersby's march, they re-embarked, and stood away for York.

My last accounts from major-general De Rottenburg are to the 3d instant, when the enemy's fleet had anchored off Niagara. I have received no tidings of our squadron under sir James Yeo, since its sailing from hence on the 31st ultimo.

I have the honor to be, &c.

GEORGE PREVOST.

Earl Bathurst, &c. &c. &c.

*Christie says, "upset through press of sail in endeavoring to escape."

night, in a heavy squall, two of the American schooners, the *Hamilton* and *Scourge*, upset, and their crews unfortunately perished. On the 9th the two parties were again in sight of each other, and continued manœuvring during that and the succeeding day. On the 10th, at night, a fine breeze sprang up, and Sir James Yeo immediately took advantage of it, by bearing up to attack his powerful opponent; but, just as the *Wolfe* got within gunshot of the *Pike* and *Madison*, these two powerful American ships bore up, fired their stern chase guns, and made sail for Niagara; leaving two fine schooners, the *Julia* and *Growler*, each armed with one long thirty-two and one long twelve pounder on pivots, and manned with a crew of forty men, to be captured without an effort to save them. With his two prizes, and without the loss of a man, and with no greater injury to his ships than a few cut ropes and torn sails, Sir James Yeo returned to Kingston."

We have examined with some care the ministerial organ, (*Niles Register*) for some notice of this affair, with the intention of giving the American account at length, and we were the more desirous of doing this from our having lighted, during our search, on the following choice paragraph—" A Montreal paper speaks of Commodore Chauncey as 'not having learned even the rudiments of war. We have sent him (says the same paper,) a most able teacher (Sir James Yeo) who will carry him through all the inflections peculiar to it in much less time than a school-boy can be taught to conjugate a verb, or understand its principal.'"

"One would think that this paragraph was written by Sir James himself, for it is quite his character. We shall see when Chauncey gets along side of him—*"that's all."*

After reading this elegant extract which will be found on the two hundred and twenty-seventh page of the fourth volume of *Niles Register*, we were quite prepared for finding a full, true, and particular account of Commodore Chauncey's " brilliant victories over an enemy double his force," and perhaps the surest evidence of Sir James Yeo's success may be found in the fact of Commodore Chauncey's *not* having captured the whole British fleet *on paper*. We give an extract of

the Commodore's modest official letter* that the reader may compare it first, with our version, and, secondly, with the only notices in *Niles Register* which bear distinctly on the subject, and which are found in volume five, page twelve. " Commodore Chauncey fell in with the enemy's squadron; of whom, after a good deal of manœuvring, he got the weather gage. *" The British bore away, and he then chased them to Kingston.* " It was thought that the enemy would not give a chance for the combat so earnestly desired by the officers and crews." "It is positively stated that two schooners were captured for want of obedience to orders; perhaps by having too much eagerness to meet the foe. It is agreed upon that our gallant Commodore never yet had the power to bring the enemy to action—his vessels in general sailing much better than ours. The *Sylph*, however, is a valuable auxiliary in catching the foe."

---

*Extract of a letter from Commodore Chauncey to the Secretary of the Navy, dated on board the ship General Pike, at Sackett's Harbor, 13th August, 1813.

SIR,—I arrived here this day with this ship, the Madison, Oneida, Governor Tompkins, Conquest, Ontario, Pert, and Lady of the Lake. The Fair American and Asp I left at Niagara. Since I had the honor of addressing you last, I have been much distressed and mortified; distressed at the loss of a part of the force entrusted to my command, and mortified at not being able to bring the enemy to action. The following movements and transactions of the squadron, since the 6th inst., will give you the best idea of the difficulties and mortifications that I have had to encounter.

On the 7th, at daylight, the enemy's fleet, consisting of two ships, two brigs, and two large schooners, were discovered bearing W.N.W., distant about five or six miles, wind at west. At five, weighed with the fleet, and manœuvred to gain the wind. At nine, having passed to leeward of the enemy's line and abreast of his van ship (the Wolfe), hoisted our colors and fired a few guns, to ascertain whether we could reach him with our shot; finding they fell short I wore and hauled upon a wind upon the starboard tack; the rear of our schooners then about six miles apart. The enemy wore in succession and hauled up on a wind on the same tack, but soon finding that we should be able to weather him upon the next tack, he tacked and made all sail to the northward. As soon as our rear vessels could fetch his wake, tacked and made all sail in chase. In the afternoon the wind became very light, and towards night quite calm. The schooners used their sweeps all the afternoon, in order to close with the enemy, but without success.

One can scarcely wonder at the mistakes into which the too credulous citizens of the Union were led, when the systematic lying of the Government is taken into consideration. The following morceaux will show whether we have affixed too harsh a term to the tissue of misrepresentation that was so sedulously woven round the inhabitants of the Union. They are taken from the principal source of the fictions—The Government Organ.

" The Lady of the Lake, (a flag sent to Kingston) has just returned. The whaling we gave them we find to have been much more serious than we then expected. Sir James Yeo acknowledges to have been beaten by us in each rencounter, and thinks himself lucky that we could not follow the victory up. He says the fighting was done; and that he had given orders to his men to escape from their vessels as soon as they grounded, and that their trains were already laid, for blowing them up. His ships were literally torn to pieces, and a number of officers and men killed and wounded.

" Another account of the battle, says, the fighting was over, and it was only necessary for Commodore Chauncey to take possession, to have completed his victory; but in this he was disappointed by a sudden gale of wind, which drove the enemy's fleet to the head of the lake, under the protection of their batteries. Commodore Chauncey might still have destroyed their fleet; but our, fleet

must, in turn, have inevitably been lost also, and the grand object of the government, the command of the lake, frustrated.

Chauncey might have covered himself with the same imperishable glory, that did Parry; but then he would have unfortunately abandoned the all-important object for which he was contending, and which, by his masterly conduct on that day, was completely and effectually secured to us."

The seemingly careless manner in which the Capture of schooners. capture of the two schooners is disposed of is worthy of remark, it being incidentally brought in as if an affair quite unconnected with the action, (if so petty a skirmish deserved the name) and only arising from an error, the effect of excess of bravery. The last item respecting the *Sylph*, has been most judiciously introduced to cover the admission of "the effects of too much bravery," but still it was not quite enough without the usual contrast of the merits of the respective commanders, so we are gravely told first that Commodore Chauncey partook of a splendid dinner prepared for him, in Washington Hall, New York, in honor of the affair, and in the next paragraph informed that Sir J. Yeo was a blustering bully with whom discretion was the better part of valour, and from whom, as a British official, truth could not be expected.

We are most fortunately enabled to test the value of Commodore Chauncey's official letter, and the remarks of *Niles' Register*, by

---

Late in the afternoon I made the signal of recall, and formed in close order. Wind during the night from the westward, and after midnight squally; kept all hands at quarters and beat to windward in hopes to gain the wind of the enemy. At two A.M. missed two of our schooners; at daylight discovered the missing schooners to be the Hamilton and Scourge. Soon after, spoke the Governor Tompkins, who informed me that the Hamilton and Scourge both overset and sank in a heavy squall, about two o'clock; and, distressing to relate, every soul perished, except sixteen. This fatal accident deprived me at once of the services of two valuable officers, Lieut. Winter and Sailing Master Osgood, and two of my best schooners, mounting together 14 guns. This accident giving to the enemy decidedly the superiority, I thought he would take advantage of it, particularly as by a change of wind he was again brought dead to windward of me. Formed the line upon the larboard tack and hove to. Soon after six A.M. the enemy bore up and set studding-sails, apparently with an intention to bring us to action. When he had approached us within four miles he brought to, on starboard

tack. Finding that the enemy had no intention of bringing us to action, I edged away to gain the land, in order to have the advantage of the land breeze in the afternoon. It soon after fell calm, and I directed the schooners to sweep up and engage the enemy. About noon we got a light breeze from the eastward. I took the Oneida in tow, as she sailed badly, and stood for the enemy. When the van of our schooners was within about one and a half or two miles of his rear, the wind shifted to the westward, which again brought him to windward; as soon as the breeze struck him, he bore up for the schooners in order to cut them off before they could rejoin me; but with their sweeps, and the breeze soon reaching them also, they were soon in their station. The enemy finding himself foiled in this attempt upon the schooners, hauled his wind and hove to. It soon became very squally, and the appearance of its continuing so during the night; and as we had been at quarters for nearly forty hours, and being apprehensive of separating from some of the heavy sailing schooners in the squall, I was induced to run in towards Niagara, and anchor outside the bar. General Boyd very handsomely offered any

the following letter, from one of *General Pike's* officers, which found its way by mistake into the United States *Gazette* of Sept. 6th. The writer, having previously stated the American force at two ships, one brig and eleven schooners, says—" On the 10th, at midnight, we came within gun shot, every man in high spirits. The schooners commenced the action with their long guns which did great execution. At half-past twelve, the commodore fired his broadside, and gave three cheers, which were returned from the other ships, the enemy closing fast. We lay by for our opponent, the orders having been given not to fire till she came within pistol shot,— the enemy kept up a constant fire. Every gun was pointed, every match ready in hand, and the red British ensign plainly to be descried by the light of the moon ; when to our utter astonishment, the commodore wore and stood S. E. leaving Sir James Yeo to exult in the capture of two schooners, and in our retreat which was certainly a very fortunate one for him." Farther comment on the affair is quite unnecessary after this letter, which is the most satisfactory proof we could have adduced, first of the correctness of the account we took from the *Naval Register*—secondly, of the meanness of Commodore Chauncey in

penning the dispatch we have given in our notes, and thirdly, of the utter want of principle of both the American government and their official organ, *Niles' Weekly Register.*—It is almost unnecessary to add that an order was, soon after the appearance of this letter, issued at Washington, forbidding any officer to write, with the intention of publication, any accounts of the operations of the fleet and army.

The officer, who has so opportunely enabled us to add, to the evidence already brought forward, one more proof of the unworthy means adopted by American commanders and their rulers, at Washington, to delude a vain glorious people with ficticious statements of their prowess, has unwittingly raised the veil which the cabinet at Washington would have willingly suffered to remain over Chauncey and his doings. He says, " we proceeded directly," (which, we presume means, after they had done chasing Sir James Yeo to Kingston,) " for Sackett's Harbour, where we victualled and put to sea, the next day, after our arrival, August 14th. On the 16th we discovered the enemy again and hurried to quarters, *again got clear* of the enemy by dint of carrying sail, and returned to Sackett's Harbor. On the 18th we again fell in with the enemy steering for Kingston, and we

assistance in men that I might require. I received 150 soldiers, and distributed them in the different vessels, to assist in boarding or repelling boarders, as circumstances might require. It blew very heavy in squalls during the night. Soon after day discovered the enemy's fleet bearing north ; weighed and stood after him. The wind soon became light and variable, and before 12 o'clock quite calm. At five, fresh breezes from the north, the enemy's fleet bearing north, distant about four or five leagues. Wore the fleet in succession, and hauled upon a wind on the larboard tack. At sundown the enemy bore N.W. by N. on the starboard tack. The wind hauling to the westward I stood to the northward all night in order to gain the north shore. At daylight tacked to the westward, the wind having changed to NN.W. Soon after, discovered the enemy's fleet, bearing S.W. I took the Asp, the Madison, and the Fair American in tow, and made all sail in chase. It was at this time we thought of realizing what we had been so long toiling for ; but before twelve o'clock the wind changed to W.S.W., which brought the enemy to windward ; tacked to the northward ; at three, the wind inclining to the northward, wore to the southward and westward, and made the signal for the fleet to make all sail. At four the enemy bore S.S.W.; bore up and steered for him. At five observed the enemy becalmed under the

land, nearing him very fast with a fine breeze from NN.W. At six formed the order of battle within about four miles of the enemy. The wind at this time very light. At 7 the wind changed to S.W.. and a fresh breeze, which again placed the enemy to windward of me. Tacked and hauled upon a wind on the larboard tack, under easy sail, the enemy standing after us. At nine, when within about two gunshot of our rear, he wore to the southward ; I stood on to the northward under easy sail ; the fleet formed in two lines, a part of the schooners formed the weather line, with orders to commence the fire upon the enemy as soon as their shot would take effect, and as the enemy reached them to edge down upon the line to leeward and pass through the intervals and form to leeward. At about half past ten the enemy tacked and stood after us. At eleven the rear of our line opened his fire upon the enemy ; in about fifteen minutes the fire became general from the weather line, which was returned from the enemy. At half past 11 the weather line bore up and passed to leeward, except the Growler and Julia, which soon after tacked to the southward, which brought the enemy between them and me. Filled the maintopsail and edged two points to lead the enemy down, not only to engage him to more advantage, but to lead him from the Growler and Julia. He, however, kept his wind until he completely separated those

reached the harbor on the 19th. *This is the result of two cruises, the first of which by proper guidance might have decided in our favour the superiority on the lake and consequently in Canada.*"

We take leave of Commodore Chauncey for the present with these two striking instances of his having (according to American writers and official bulletins) chased the British commander all around the lake.

The demonstration against Fort George is

Demonstration against Fort George by Sir George Prevost. very pithily described. by Veritas—"Nothing of moment happened in the centre division,† until joined by Sir George, for a few days, when a grand demonstration was displayed, by marching the enemy up the hill, and down again, which resulted in satisfying him that nothing could be done to dislodge the enemy." We might safely adopt this description, for an examination into the facts will afford very little else to record. Christie handles this subject very fairly, but he is obliged to admit, after attempting a sort

of an excuse for Sir George, that, "the prestige which surrounded his military character improved by the popularity he was acquiring as a chief governor, had been sensibly influenced by his failure at Sackett's Harbour, and the present fruitless "demonstration" as (to cover his second failure) he termed it, dispelled what little confidence in him, as commander of the forces, the army, and those in the country the best able to judge of his abilities as such, previously entertained." The only excuse that even Christie's good nature could find was, that "the whole force in the neighbourhood of Fort George, at that period, did not exceed two thousand men, on an extended line while that of the enemy in Fort George exceeded four thousand." The sum of the whole affair is that, Sir George (for reasons best known to himself, as he has not chosen to make them public) determined to make an attack on Fort George on the 24th August, and a movement was made for an assault upon it. The British drove in the pickets, several of which were taken, advancing to within a short distance of the enemy.

---

two vessels from the rest of the squadron, exchanged a few shot with this ship as he passed, without injury to us, and made sail after our two schooners. Tacked and stood after him. At 12 (midnight) finding that I must either separate from the rest of the squadron, or relinquish the hope of saving the two which had separated, I reluctantly gave up the pursuit, rejoined the squadron then to leeward, and formed the line on the starboard tack. The firing was continued between our two schooners and the enemy's fleet until about one A.M., when, I presume, they were obliged to surrender to a force so much their superior. Saw nothing more of the enemy that night; soon after daylight discovered them close in with the north shore, with one of our schooners in tow, the other not to be seen. I presume she may have been sunk. The enemy showed no disposition to come down upon us, although to windward, and blowing heavy from W. The schooners labouring very much, I ordered two of the dullest to run into Niagara and anchor. The gale increasing very much, and as I could not go into Niagara with this ship, I determined to run to Genesee Bay, as a shelter for the small vessels, and with the expectation of being able to obtain provisions for the squadron, as we were all nearly out, the Medusa and Oneida not having a single day's on board when we arrived opposite Genesee Bay. I found there was every prospect of the gale's continuing, and if it did, I could run to this place and provision the whole squadron with more certainty, and nearly in the

same time that I could at Genesee, admitting that I could obtain provisions at that place. After bringing the breeze as far as Oswego, the wind became light, inclining to a calm, which has prolonged our passage to this day. I shall provision the squadron for five weeks, and proceed up the lake this evening, and when I return again I hope to be able to communicate more agreeable news than this communication contains.

The loss of the Growler and Julia, in the manner in which they have been lost, is mortifying in the extreme; and although their commanders disobeyed my positive orders, I am willing to believe that it arose from an error of judgment and excess of zeal to do more than was required of them; thinking, probably, that the enemy intended to bring us to a general action, they thought, by gaining the wind of him they would have it more in their power to injure and annoy him than they could by forming to leeward of our line. From what I have been able to discover of the movements of the enemy, he has no intention of engaging us, except he can get decidedly the advantage of wind and weather, and as his vessels in squadron sail better than our squadror, he can always avoid an action; unlesss I can gain the wind and have sufficient daylight to bring him to action before dark. His object is, evidently, to harass us by night attacks, by which means he thinks to cut off our small dull sailing schooners in detail. Fortune has evidently favored him thus far. I hope that it will be my turn next, and, although inferior in point of force, I feel very confident of success.

I have the honor to be, Sir, very respectfully, your most obedient servant, ISAAC CHAUNCEY.

---

† Veritas alludes here to the events which occurred after Colonel Bishopp's death.

The Americans, however, not having any particular fancy for fighting where the odds were only two to one, declined leaving their entrenchments, and preferred keeping up a safe and quiet cannonade from the opposite bank of the river. Sir George, then, (not being General Brock) weighed the *pros* and *cons* for an assault, and, unfortunately, for his own credit, decided that to risk an attempt on this port, which was not of sufficient moment, from its dilapidated condition, to compensate the loss that an attack must entail, would be neither prudent nor profitable. He accordingly, as Veritas has it, marched down the hill again and returned to Kingston.

As a military commander, Sir George seems to have lacked most sadly that very essential quality, energy—his personal bravery, no one (not even Veritas) has ever dared to impeach, but still it seems to have been of a negative character, and it is very evident that phrenologists would not have discovered the organ of combativeness to be very largely developed. Christie bears very high testimony as to his worth in his civil capacity. "To the moment of his departure from the province, his popularity with the people, as civil governor, remained unabated. We are well satisfied at being able to quote at least one favorable opinion of Sir George, as Veritas is always unjust, and we think that even James has adopted the fashion of condemning Sir George too readily.

It is now necessary, in order to bring down

Cruise of Commodore Rogers with Congress and President frigates

naval events on the ocean, to the same date as we have already reached with reference to the flotillas on the lake, to visit Boston, from which Commodore Rogers, in the President, sailed in company with the Congress frigate, on the 1st May, 1813. The day after leaving port, the first opportunity of displaying American prowess presented itself in the shape of the British brig sloop Curlew. This was, however, but a transient gleam of good fortune, as the British vessel, according to custom, ran away, and, "by knocking away the wedges of her masts, and using other means to improve her sailing,"* escaped. Captain Head considering, as we suppose, that a British sloop of war was not quite a match,

single-handed, for two large American frigates. Had Commodore Rogers commanded the British sloop, he would doubtless have brought to action and captured both. On the 8th, according to our authorities, "the Congress, whether by intention or accident, parted company."

A glorious opportunity was now presented to Commodore Rogers, and eagerly seized by him, of rivalling his brother commanders in "the chasing" (see Niles Register*) "and capturing of British frigates." The American commodore having the natural sagacity of his countrymen for turning an honest penny, and considering that honor and glory are but names after all, and, to be enjoyed, require prize money, directed his attention to the homeward bound West India fleet. The commodore was, however, too late, and (misfortunes never coming singly), he missed not only the goodly freighted West India-men, but also the opportunity (for which he of course thirsted) of taking at the same time, the Cumberland seventy-four, Captain Thomas Baker. It is much to be regretted, on Commodore Rogers' account, that this happened, as the Cumberland was a very fine vessel, and a fast sailer, and would have been a very desirable acquisition to the American fleet. About the 13th June, the disappointed commodore resolved to seize the "Dragon in its lair," and steered towards the North Sea, looking out keenly for any vessels bound outwards from the St. George's Channel; no prize, however, fell in his way. As the weather was now becoming warm, a cruise in the northern latitudes could not fail to be pleasant, especially as there was a convoy of some five-and-twenty or thirty sail from Archangel to be intercepted, which would unite profit with pleasure. It is a curious circumstance that, in high latitudes, from the state of the atmosphere, objects appear double their real size. It was, no doubt, from this circumstance that the American commodore suffered himself to be chased from his station by, as he thought, "a line of battle ship and a frigate," but in reality by the thirty-two gun frigate Alexandria, Captain Robert Cathcart, and sixteen-gun sloop Spitfire, Captain John

---

* Naval Chronicle, page 112.

* "The brave Rogers is now employed in hunting down British frigates on the ocean."

Ellis. We will take our account of this affair from the same source as the Naval Chronicle, viz., the logs of the two British ships, premising that the commodore had been in the meantime joined by the Scourge. This is proved by Commodore Rogers' letter to the Naval board " at the time of meeting the enemy's two ships, the privateer schooner Scourge, of New York, had joined company." We now give the extracts from the logs :—

"On the 19th July, at 2h. 30m. P. M., latitude at noon 71 ° 52' north, longitude 20 ° 18' east, the Alexandria and Spitfire, standing south-east by south, with a light wind from the northward, discovered a frigate and a large schooner in the north-north east. The two British ships immediately hauled up in chase, and at 5h. 30m. P. M., tacked to the west north west, making the Russian as well as English private signals. At 6h. 15m., the President and her consort, who had hitherto been standing towards the two British ships, tacked from them to the north-west, under all sail, followed by the Alexandria and Spitfire. At 7h. 30m. P. M., the Spitfire was within five miles of the President, who then bore from her north-north-west." If the log of the Spitfire be correct, and that vessel was actually within four miles of the enemy, it would appear extraordinary, but for the phenomenon we have already adverted to, how the commodore could have been deceived, especially as we find it stated in the British logs that the lightness of the night and the clearness of the atmosphere enabled them to keep sight of their adversary. We will now take up the account from the Naval Chronicle.

"On the 20th, at 4h. 30m. P. M., finding that the Spitfire, as well as the President, was gaining upon her, the Alexandria cut away her bower anchor. At 4h. 40m., the Scourge parted company with the President, which was now nearly hull down from the leading British ship. A schooner being unworthy game when a frigate was in sight, the Alexandria and Spitfire continued in pursuit of the President."

"Their attention," says the commodore, "was so much engrossed by the President, that they permitted her (the Scourge) to escape without taking any notice of her.

At 6 P. M., when the Alexandria bore from the Spitfire full two miles south-south-east,

the President bore north, distant only six miles. From this time the American frigate continued gaining upon the Spitfire until 1h. 10 m. P. M., on the 21st; when, thick weather coming on, the latter lost sight both of her consort and her chase. The discharge of four guns however, by the Alexandria, enabled the Spitfire to close. The two British ships again making sail, the sloop, at 2 h. 15 m. P. M., again got sight of the President, in the west-south west, and at 4 P. M. were once more within six miles of her; which, says the commodore, "was quite as near as was desirable." The chase continued during the remainder of the 21st, to the advantage of the American frigate, until 8 A. M., on the 22d, when the Spitfire, a fourth time, got within six miles of the President; who again, by the most strenuous efforts, began increasing her distance.

At 6 P. M., when nearly hull-down from the little persevering sloop, and quite out of sight from the Alexandria, the President fired a gun, hoisted an American ensign at her peak, and a commodore's broad pendant at her main, and hauled upon a wind to the westward. Captain Ellis continued gallantly to stand on, until, at 6 h. 40 m. P. M., Captain Cathcart, who was then eight miles in the east-north-east of his consort, considerately signalled the Spitfire to close. As soon as the latter had done so, sail was again made; and the chase continued throughout that night, and until 10 A.M. on the 23d; when the President had run completely out of sight of both " the line-of-battle ship and the frigate," or, as an American historian says, of the " two line-of-battle-ships,"* which had so long been pursuing her.

Among the prisoners on board the President at the time of the chase, were the master and mate of the British snow Daphne, of Whitby. According to the journal of these men, published in the newspapers, they, as well as many of the President's officers and men, were convinced that the chasing ships were a small frigate and a sloop of war. They describe, in a ludicrous manner, the preparations on board the President, to resist the attack of this formidable squadron. During each of the three days a treble allowance of grog was served out to the crew, and an im-

* Naval Monument, p. 230.

mense quantity of star, chain, and other kinds of dismantling shot got upon deck, in readiness for action. It appears also that when the Eliza Swan whaler hove in sight a few days afterwards, she was supposed to be a large ship of war, and the ceremony with the grog and dismantling shot was repeated. After a very cautious approach on the part of the President, the chase was discovered to be a clump of a merchantman, and made prize of accordingly.

American writers have blustered a good deal about the invincibility and gallant deeds of their navy, and have enlarged most particularly on the events of this very cruise ; and yet, when all the circumstances of the affair are placed before the reader, what a contrast is presented in the conduct of the pursuers and pursued. Commodore Rogers admitted that he was within five miles of his enemy, and yet he dared to pretend that he mistook a vessel of four hundred and twenty-two tons for a large frigate, and (still more barefaced) a small frigate of six hundred and sixty tons for, what? A LINE-OF-BATTLE SHIP !! Brave as Commodore Rogers *might have* been, it is well for him that he did not belong to the British service. Discretion is the better part of valour, and is a most necessary quality for a commander to possess, but, in the present instance, prudence in the commodore appears to have been somewhat akin to puisillanimity, and with our severely dealing public, similar conduct would have been rewarded, not with a public dinner, but a court-martial, the sentence of which would have been disgrace, if not death. It may be considered a most fortunate event for the two British commanders (Cathcart and Ellis) that the Alexandria, from her bad sailing, prevented an encounter, as the two vessels were no match for the American frigate, even after making every allowance for the difference of the commanders, and the engagement must have ended in the capture or destruction of the British vessels. Had this taken place, what an opportunity would have been afforded for magniloquent effusions.—AN AMERICAN FRIGATE CAPTURING A LINE-OF BATTLE SHIP AND A FRIGATE. Such would assuredly have been the most modest version of the affair, if we may judge by the capital that was made out of Commodore Rogers' running away. Not a little dis-

mayed at his narrow escape, Commodore Rogers "determined," says James, "to quit a region where constant daylight afforded an enemy so many advantages over him," we therefore next find him more to the southward, in a position where there was a favourable opportunity for intercepting the trade bound for the Irish channel. Here he cruised until again frightened from his station by a report of a superior force seen in that region. Running up the Channel then, and rounding Ireland, he stood back to his own shores, and, having succeeded in learning the stations of the various British vessels, then cruising off the American coast, from a small schooner which he had captured, was enabled to run safely into Newport, Rhode Island.

We have endeavored to give a fair and unprejudiced account of Commodore Rogers' cruise, and we now propose to give a few extracts from our old friend, the Washington organ. The first statement runs thus :—" The former," (the *President*,) "was reported to have taken the British vessel *Theseus*, with specie." (*The Theseus is rated a seventy-four in Steele's list.*) The *Thetis* frigate mounts thirty-eight guns and must be the vessel alluded to. Two things are note worthy in this paragraph, first, the insinuation respecting the *Theseus*, secondly, the assertion, never contradicted in regard to the *Thetis*. There is very little doubt but that the impression conveyed to the citizens of the United States was that their pet hero Rogers had in all probability captured a seventy-four—certainly a frigate. Could impudence go further than this? The next paragraph is still more amusing—"It is announced officially that Commodore Rogers captured his B. M. brig *Cruizer* of eighteen guns off the Shetland Islands, the *Oberon* was in company but escaped. It was calculated that Rogers had done infinite damage to the Greenland trade. For a considerable time he has given full employment to twenty or thirty of the enemy's vessels of war, and if they do catch him, he will cost them more than he will come to." A postscript to this " bit of truth " goes on to inform us that " he had arrived at Newport, after cruizing *all round and round* the British islands, though they have a thousand vessels of war. It is said that he brought into port a sloop of war, and one of H. M. schooners with twenty-nine merchantmen." Comment on these statements is unnecessary, and so truly absurd are they that, lest we should be suspected of following the example set to us of misrepresenting, we must inform our readers, that our extracts are to be found in the fifth volume of Nile's Register.

The *Congress* after parting company cruised about for a considerable time and then returned to Portsmouth, New Hampshire, where she was blockaded by the *Tenedos*, Captain Parker, who used every means in his power to provoke a meeting. The fate of the *Chesapeake* was not yet, however, forgotten, and the government, mindful of the short career of one thirty-six gun frigate, prudently disarmed and laid up the *Congress* shortly afterwards.

The next event of importance was the capture, August 5th, of the *Dominica* schooner by the Franco-American privateer schooner *Decatur*, commanded by the celebrated Captain Dominique Dixon.* The most discreditable part of this affair appears, at first sight, to be the capture by a privateer, but when it comes to be investigated, it will be found that Lieutenant Barreté (the commander) by his gallant conduct reflected honor rather than disgrace upon the British arms. The *Dominica* mounted twelve guns and had on board fifty-seven men and nine boys. The *Decatur* had the same number of guns, with one hundred and twenty men, and Captain Dixon, knowing the force opposed to him, relied for success upon the arm in which he was almost doubly superior, and carried his opponent by boarding. The obstinate resistance offered by the *Dominica* will be best shown by the list of casualties. Out of her total complement of sixty-six men and boys, the captain, purser, two midshipmen, and thirteen men were killed or mortally wounded, and over forty severely or slightly wounded. The loss of the *Decatur* was nineteen men.

The Dominica and Decatur.

On the 12th of the same month, the *Pelican*, eighteen gun brig-sloop arrived in the Cove of Cork from a cruise, but before the sails were furled, Captain Maples received instructions to put to sea again in quest of an American

The Pelican and Argus.

sloop of war, which had been committing some depredations in the St. George's Channel. About day-break of the 14th, the *Argus* was discovered separating from a ship which she had just set on fire, and standing towards several other merchantmen. The *Pelican* was to windward and bore down under a press of sail, the captain of the *Argus* appearing, by his manœuvres, to invite an engagement. Captain Allen, the commander of the *Argus*, had been first lieutenant of the United States when she captured the *Macedonian*, and had repeatedly expressed his ability to whip any British sloop with an American of equal force, in ten minutes. Let us now examine James' statement of the comparative force of these "anxious candidates for the laurel crown." According to James, " the *Pelican* mounted the usual establishment of her class, sixteen thirty-two pounder carronades, two long sixes, and a twelve pounder boat carronade. But unfortunately, Captain Maples, when recently at Jamaica, had received on board two brass sixes." Having no broadside ports for them, and unwilling to lower them into the hold as ballast, he knocked out two stern ports and mounted them there, "much to the annoyance," says James, " of the man at the helm, and without contributing in the slightest degree to the brig's actual force. The established complement of vessels of the *Pelican's* class was one hundred and twenty men and boys, of this number she lacked the second lieutenant and six men. The *Argus* mounted eighteen twenty-four pound carronades with two long twelves, her crew mustering one hundred and twenty-five strong. The original force had amounted to one hundred and fifty-seven, but thirty-two had been dispatched in prizes.

At 6, A.M., the *Argus* opened her fire, and, after a sharp action of some forty-five minutes duration, was boarded and carried by the British sloop. The *Pelican* had one man killed and five wounded; the *Argus* six killed and eighteen wounded. Amongst the list of the mortally wounded were Captain Allen and two midshipmen. James gives the comparative force thus:—

	Pelican.	Argus.
Broadside guns	9	10
No. of lbs	262	228
Crew. (Men only.)	101	122
Size	tons 385	316

* See vol iv, page 268 of James' Naval History.

The respective forces engaged were so nearly equal that it⁷ is unnecessary to offer any further remark than the admission that whatever superiority there might have been it was on the side of the British, and that Captain Allen fought his vessel bravely under the slight disadvantage, and on his death, which occurred a short time afterwards, his remains were attended to the grave by all the officers, military or naval, in the port.

"Some people excel in powers of endurance, such as the English* evinced at the battle of Waterloo. Others excel in powers of assault such as the French displayed there. But there is no record of a British vessel enduring the terrible blows inflicted on some of the American vessels before yielding." Thus writes Ingersoll, forgetful of the defence made by the *Java*, and still more recently, the *Dominica*, in which last engagement, as we have just seen, the British vessel was not surrendered until her captain and sixty men, out of a crew of sixty-six, lay dead or wounded upon her deck. Mr. Ingersoll, besides these two instances, which we have just cited, might have found a third in the case of the vessel whose capture we are about to relate.

At daylight, on the 5th September, the British brig-sloop *Boxer*, of fourteen guns (twelve eighteen pounder carronades and two sixes) while lying at anchor, near Portland, United States, discovered in the offing a sail, and immediately weighed and stood to sea in pursuit. The strange vessel was soon made out to be an enemy and proved to be the American gunbrig, *Enterprise*, of sixteen guns (fourteen eighteen pounder carronades and two nines) commanded by Lieutenant Burrows. The American vessel, after her superior powers of sailing had been tested, and it had been sufficiently established that should she get beaten it was easy to escape, bore up to engage. At a quarter past three the action commenced, terminating after a severe and protracted contest in the surrender of the *Boxer*. The British vessel measured one hundred and eighty-one tons, (her force we have already shewn) and was manned by sixty men, of whom twelve were absent, and six boys. The *Enterprise* measured two hundred

*By English we presume, Ingersoll means British.

and forty-five tons, and had on board one hundred and twenty men and three boys. The officers of the *Boxer* had the mortification to see four men, during the action, desert their guns, thereby reducing the number of the combatants to forty-four, yet, in spite of all these casualties and the fall of Captain Burrows, early in the action, the vessel was only yielded after a loss of twenty-one men, nearly half the crew. The loss of the *Enterprise* was fourteen killed and wounded, her commander being included amongst the killed. Besides the more than two-fold disparity in crews, the *Enterprise* was altogether a stouter vessel than her antagonist. This will be proved by Commodore Hull's letter* which

* *Extract of a letter from Commodore Hull to Commodore Bainbridge, dated the 10th inst.*

"I yesterday visited the two brigs and was astonished to see the difference of injury sustained in the action. The Enterprize has but one 18 pound shot in her hull, one in her mainmast, and one in her foremast; her sails are much cut with grape shot and there are a great number of grape lodged in her sides, but no injury done by them. The Boxer has eighteen or twenty 18 pound shot in her hull, most of them at the water's edge—several stands of 18 pound grape stick in her side, and such a quantity of small grape that I did not undertake to count them. Her masts, sails and spars are literally cut to pieces, several of her guns dismounted and unfit for service; her top gallant forecastle nearly taken off by the shot, her boats cut to pieces, and her quarters injured in proportion. To give you an idea of the quantity of shot about her, I inform you that I counted in her mainmast alone three 18 pound shot holes, 18 large grape shot holes, 16 musket ball holes, and a large number of smaller shot holes, without counting above the cat harpins.

"We find it impossible to get at the number killed; no papers are found by which we can ascertain it—I, however, counted upwards of 90 hammocks which were in her netting with beds in them, besides several beds without hammocks; and she has excellent accomodations for all her officers below in staterooms, so that I have no doubt that she had one hundred men on board. *We know that she has several of the Rattler's men on board,* and a quantity of wads was taken out of the Rattler, loaded with four large grape shot with a small hole in the centre to put in a cartridge that the inside of the wad may take fire when it leaves the gun. In short, she is in every respect completely fitted and her accommodations exceed any thing I have seen in a vessel of her class."

Remarks.—There have been various opinions respecting the relative force of the vessels, and some ungenerous attempts have been made to diminish the splendour of the victory. The foregoing extracts, we conceive irrefragably settle the question of force and of skill. It appears that in number of men the enemy were equal; in number

we give for two reasons. Firstly, to show the difference of execution done in a close action, where the weight of metal being the same on both sides, the respective stoutness of the timbers would be tested, and secondly to prove 'how ready Commodore Hull was to make statements which he must have seen were untrue. The British brig had upwards of "one hundred men on board, for, "says Captain Hull, I counted upwards of ninety hammocks." Now if the American public did not know, Commodore Hull knew full well that, in the British service, every seaman and marine has two hammocks allowed him[†] yet he was disingenuous enough to pen a statement which he knew, coming from a sort of pet hero, would produce an effect all over the Union. Brave, Captain Hull may have been—most unprincipled, this circumstance clearly proves him to have been. We close this chapter by giving in our notes Lieutenant McCall's really modest, if not quite correct letter,[‡] and with a few observations from James on the difference of the carronades used in the services.

"The established armament of the Boxer was ten carronades; and that number, with her two six-pounders, was as many as the brig could mount with effect or carry with ease. But, when the Boxer was refitting at Halifax, Captain Blyth obtained two additional carronades: had he taken on board, instead of them, twenty extra seamen, the Boxer would have been a much more effective vessel. Against the English ordinary carronade, complaints

have always been made, for its lightness and unsteadiness in action ; but the American carronade of that calibre is much shorter in the breech, and longer in the muzzle : therefore it heats more slowly, recoils less, and carries farther. The same is the case, indeed with all the varieties of the carronade used by the Americans ; and they, in consequence derive advantages in the employment of that ordnance, not possessed by the English ; whose carronades are notoriously the lightest and most inefficient of any in use. If the English carronade, especially of the smaller calibres, had

---

of guns it was well known the enemy were superior ; and the vast difference of execution confirms (if confirmation were wanted) the fact of the high degree of superiority of our seamen in the art of gunnery. And, above all other considerations, it proves that American tars are determined to support their government, in a just war waged in defence of their rights.—*Niles Register.*

†James Naval History.

‡United States Brig " Enterprise,"
Portland, 7th September, 1813.

Sir,—In consequence of the unfortunate death of Lieutenant-Commandant William Burrows, late commander of this vessel, it devolves on me to acquaint you with the result of the cruize. After sailing from Portsmouth on the 1st instant, we steered to the eastward ; and on the morning of the 3rd, off Wood Island, discovered a schooner, which we chased into this harbor, where we anchored. On the morning of the 4th, weighed

anchor and swept out, and continued our course to the eastward. Having received information of several privateers being off Manhagan, we stood for that place ; and on the following morning, in the bay near Penguin Point, discovered a brig getting under way, which appeared to be a vessel of war, and to which we immediately gave chase. She fired several guns and stood for us, having four ensigns hoisted. After reconnoitering and discovering her force, and the nation to which she belonged, we hauled upon a wind to stand out of the bay, and at three o'clock shortened sail, tacked to run down with an intention to bring her to close action. At twenty minutes after 3 P. M., when within half pistol shot, the firing commenced from both, and after being warmly kept up, and with some manœuvering, the enemy hailed and said they had surrendered, about 4 P.M.—*their colors being nailed to the masts, could not be hauled down.* She proved to be his B. M. brig Boxer, of 14 guns. Samuel Blythe, Esq., commander, who fell in the early part of the engagement, having received a cannon shot through the body. And I am sorry to add that Lieutenant Burrows, who had gallantly led us into action, fell also about the same time by a musket ball, which terminated his existence in eight hours.

The Enterprise suffered much in spars and rigging, and the Boxer in spars, rigging, and hull, having many shots between wind and water.

It would be doing injustice to the merit of Mr, Tillinghast, second lieutenant, were I not to mention the able assistance I received from him during the remainder of the engagement, by his strict attention to his own division and other departments. And of the officers and crew generally, I am happy to add, their cool and determined conduct have my warmest approbation and applause.

As no muster roll that can be fully relied on has come into my possession, I cannot exactly state the number killed and wounded on board the Boxer, but from information received from the officers of that vessel, it appears there were between twenty and twenty five killed, and fourteen wounded. Enclosed is a list of the killed and wounded on board the Enterprise. I have the honor to be, &c.

EDWARD R. M'CALL,
Senior Officer.

displayed its imperfections, as these pages have frequently shown that the thirteen-inch mortar was in the habit of doing, by bursting after an hour or two's firing, the gun must either have been improved in form, or thrown out of the service. While on the subject of carronades, we may remark, that even the few disadvantages in the carronade, which the Americans have not been able entirely to obviate, they have managed to lessen, by using,

not only stouter, but double, breechings; one of which, in case the ring-bolt should draw, is made to pass through the timber-head."

We may remark, in conclusion, that none of the praises lavished upon the fine brig *Boxer*, could gain her a place among the national vessels of the United States. She was put up to auction, and sold as a merchant brig; for which service only, and that only in time of peace, she was ever calculated.

CHAPTER XIII.

CONTENTS.

LAKE CHAMPLAIN, the scene which our history now requires us to visit, lies between the northern part of New York State and Vermont. Generally narrow, and only in one place widening out to a breadth of some seventeen or eighteen miles, its mean breadth may be estimated at about six or seven miles, while its length is nearly seventy.

Capture of the *Growler* and *Eagle,* American sloops.

The river Richelieu, by which the waters of the lake find an outlet to the St. Lawrence, runs in a northerly direction, and is nearly useless for the general purposes of navigation, as the bed is full of shoals and rapids, which extend nearly to the *embouchure*, where it mingles its waters with those of the St. Lawrence. This lake belongs to the United States, as (according to James) "the line of demarcation, owing to the ignorance or pusillanimity of the British commissioners employed in 1783, intersected the Richelieu, at the distance of several miles down its course from the lake. The Canadians are, therefore, not only shut out from the lake, but from all water communication with their own territory bordering on Missisquoi bay, formed

by a tongue of land to the eastward. This inconvenience," continues James, "Canadians fully experienced, during the continuance of the several embargoes that preceded the war, when the American gun-boats, stationed at the foot of the lake, prevented the rafts of timber from being floated out of the bay, for passage down the river."

This command of the lake, and particularly the point of junction of the lake and river, was of material service to the Americans, and a battery at Rouse's point would have effectually prevented the passage of any flotilla that the British might have desired to construct for service on Champlain. The sole military post held by the British in that neighbourhood was Isle aux Noix, "a small island, containing only eighty-five acres, situate on the Richelieu, and distant about ten miles from the boundary line." On this island were some small forts and a few block-houses at various points. These defences were garrisoned by detachments from the 13th and 101st regiments, under the command of Major Taylor; a small detachment of artillery was also stationed there. Three gun-boats, built at Quebec, and transported over land, represented the British naval force in that quarter. The Americans with more foresight, and, perhaps, from greater facilities, had, soon after the commencement of the war, armed and equipped several vessels in order to ensure the command of Lake Champlain. Desirous, we suppose of reconnoitring, perhaps with a view of demolishing the fortifications at Isle aux Noix, Lieutenant Sidney Smith with two sloops, manned by seamen from the Atlantic board, presented themselves on the 1st June off Isle aux Noix. Col. Taylor immediately took such measures as resulted in the capture of both. Major Taylor's official letter to General Stovin is short enough to incorporate with our text, and, giving a simple unadorned statement, may be relied on.

Isle Aux Noix.

SIR,—In the absence of Lieutenant-Colonel Hamilton, I have the honor to acquaint you that one of the enemy's armed vessels was discerned from the garrison, at half-past four o'clock this morning, when I judged it expedient to order the three gun-boats under weigh; and before they reached the point above the garrison, another vessel appeared in sight, when the gun-boats commenced firing. Observing the vessels to be near enough the shore for musketry, I ordered the crews of the batteaux and row-boats (which I took with me from the garrison to act according to circumstances) to land on each side of the river, and take a position to rake the vessels; the firing was briskly kept up on both sides; the enemy, with small arms and grape-shot occasionally. Near the close of the action, an express came off to me in a canoe, with intelligence that more armed vessels were approaching, and about three thousand men from the enemy's line, by land. On this information, I returned to put the garrison in the best order for their reception, leaving directions with the gun boats and parties, not to suffer their retreat to be cut off from it; and before I reached the garrison, the enemy's vessels struck their colours, after a well-contested action of three hours and a half. They proved to be the United States' armed vessels Growler and Eagle, burthen from ninety to one hundred tons, and carrying eleven guns each; between them, twelve, eighteen, and sixteen pounder carronades; completely equipped under the orders of the superior officer of the Growler, Captain Sidney Smith, with a complement of fifty men each. They had one man killed and eight wounded; we had only three men wounded, one of them severely, from the enemy's grape-shot on the parties

on shore. The alacrity of the garrison on this occasion calls forth my warmest approbation. Ensigns Dawson, Gibbons, and Humphreys, and acting Quarter-master Pilkington, and men, of the 100th (Prince Regent's) regiment, and Lieutenant Lowe of the marine department, with three gunners of the artillery to each boat, behaved with the greatest gallantry; I am particularly indebted to Captain Gordon of the royal artillery, and Lieutenant Williams, with the parties of the 100th regiment on shore, who materially contributed to the surrender of the enemy. The Growler has arrived at the garrison in good order, and is apparently a fine vessel, and the boats are employed in getting off the Eagle, which was run aground to prevent her sinking. I have hopes she will be saved, but in the meantime have had her dismantled and her guns and stores brought to the garrison. Ensign Dawson, of the 100th regiment, a most intelligent officer, will have the honor of delivering you this.

I have the honor to be, &c.,

GEORGE TAYLOR, Major, 100th regt.

Major-general Stovin,

Commanding at Chambly.

A great blow was inflicted by this capture on the enemy, and it did much to check the intention of invasion from that quarter. It has been shown that the two American vessels were of considerable tonnage and strength, and it was deemed advisable, as their capture now afforded an opportunity for immediate effectual operations on Champlain, not to let the chance pass unprofited by. Whether venturing so far down a river, where it was so narrow as scarcely to afford room for manœuvring (even with the intention we have already alluded to) was strictly prudent, we leave to abler tacticians to decide. We cannot, however, but agree with Christie, that had not the commanders been young and inexperienced men, they would scarcely have undertaken a step which ended so disastrously, and has been generally regarded in the light of a piece of idle bravado.

Whatever might have been the intentions of the American commanders, the effect of their capture was to leave the hospitals, stores, and barracks, which they had been at considerable pains in erecting at different points at Burlington, Plattsburg, Champlain, and Swanton, comparatively assailable, and the commander of the forces determined to add to the blow already inflicted, by such a descent as would at once damage the enemy and divert their attention from the Upper Province.

Descent on posts on Lake Champlain.
The two captured vessels were named the Broke and Shannon, changed afterwards by Admiralty order to Chubb and Finch, and it was determined to man them—This, however, appeared at first an impossibility, as there were no seamen to be procured at or near Isle aux Noix, and none could be spared from the small Ontario fleet. In this emergency, the commander of Her Majesty's brig, Wasp, then lying at Quebec, volunteered for the expedition, which was to deprive commodore McDonough the American Naval Commander of his supremacy.

All preparations having been completed, on the 29th July the expedition left Isle aux Noix for Lake Champlain. The force put in motion was about one thousand strong, consisting of detachments from the 13th, 100th, and 103 regiments, commanded respectively by lieutenant colonels Williams, Taylor and Smith. A small artillery force, under Captain Gordon, and a few of the embodied militia were likewise added, and the whole placed under Lieut.-Colonel John Murray. The success of the expedition was complete, and a landing was effected successively at Plattsburgh, Burlington, Swanton, and Champlain, several store houses and arsenals, and some vessels being destroyed, while large quantities of naval and military stores were captured and removed. "All this, too, was effected in presence of a very superior force, and with scarcely a show of resistance, although the enemy numbered fifteen hundred at Plattsburgh, under General Moore, while Gen. Hamptton was encamped near Burlington, with, as it has been estimated, nearly four thousand men. Colonel Murray's letter, which follows, will show what was accomplished, and the two letters from Captain Everard, (commander of the Wasp,) and Commodore McDonough, will speak for themselves. Had Commodore McDonough been really as anxious as he professed to be, his superior force could easily have prevented the small

British force from effecting the injury they did, and had it not even been possible to prevent all injury, at least the spoiler's return might have been prevented; we give these letters in their regular order, as enumerated above.

From Lieutenant-colonel Murray to Major-general Sheaffe.

Isle aux Noix, August 3d, 1813.

SIR,

The land forces of the expedition that left the province on the 29th July, on an enterprise on Lake Champlain, returned this day, after having fully accomplished the objects proposed, and having carried every order into execution.

The enemy's arsenal and block-house, commissary buildings, and stores at the position of Plattsburgh, together with the extensive barracks at Saranac, capable of containing 4000 troops, were destroyed; some stores were brought off, particularly a quantity of naval stores, shot, and equipments for a large number of batteaux. The barracks and stores at the position of Swanton, on Missisquoi Bay, together with several batteaux at the landing place were destroyed.

A detachment has been sent to destroy the public buildings, barracks, block-houses, &c., at Champlaintown. Every assistance was rendered by the co-operation of captains Everard and Pring, Royal Navy, commanding His Majesty's sloops of war, Broke and Shannon.

I experienced very great benefit from the military knowledge of lieutenant-colonel Williams, (13th regiment, second in command.) I have to report, in the highest terms of approbation, the discipline, regularity, and cheerful conduct of the whole of the troops, and feel fully confident that, had an opportunity offered, their courage would have been equally conspicuous.

General Hampton has concentrated the whole of the regular forces in the vicinity of Lake Champlain, at Burlington, from the best information, said to be about 4500 regular troops, and a large body of militia. The militia force assembled for the defence of Plattsburgh, disbanded on the appearance of the armament. The naval part of the expedition is still cruising on the lake. For any further information, I beg leave to refer you to your aide-de-camp, Captain Loring, and the bearer of this dispatch.

I have, &c.

J. MURRAY, Lieut.-col

To Major-gen. Sir R. H. Sheaffe,
&c., &c., &c.

From captain Everard to Sir George Prevost.

His Majesty's sloop Broke, Lake Champlain, August 3d, 1813.

SIR,

Major-general Glasgow has apprised your excellency of my repairing, with a party of officers and seamen, to man the sloops and gun-boats at Isle aux Noix, in consequence of your letter of the 4th ultimo, addressed to the senior officer of His Majesty's ship at Quebec, stating it to be of great importance to the public service, that an attempt should be made to alarm the enemy on the Montreal frontier, &c.; and agreeably to your wish that I should communicate any thing interesting that might occur, I have the honor to acquaint you, that the object for which the corps under the command of lieutenant colonel Murray had been detached, having been fully accomplished, by the destruction of the enemy's block-house, arsenal, barracks, and public store-houses remaining on the west side of the lake beyond Plattsburg, I stood over to Burlington with the Shannon and the gun-boat, to observe the state of the enemy's force there, and to afford him an opportunity of deciding the naval superiority of the lake. We were close in, on the forenoon of the 2nd, and found two sloops of about 100 tons burthen, one armed with 11 guns, the other 13, ready for sea, a third sloop, (somewhat larger,) lying under the protection of 10 guns, mounted on a bank of 100 feet high, without a breast-work, two scows, mounting one gun each as floating batteries, and several field pieces on the shore. Having captured and destroyed four vessels, without any attempt on the part of the enemy's armed vessels to prevent it, and seeing no prospect of inducing him to quit his position, where it was impossible for us to attack him, I am now returning to execute my original orders.

I have the honor to be, &c.,

THOMAS EVERARD

Commander of His Majesty's sloop, Wasp.

Lieut.-gen. Sir G. Prevost, Bart.,
&c., &c., &c.

From Commodore Macdonough to the American Secretary of the Navy.

United States' sloop President, near Plattsburg, Sept. 9, 1813.

SIR,

I have the honor to inform you, that I arrived here yesterday from near the lines, having sailed from Burlington on the 6th instant, with an intention to fall in with the enemy, who were then near this place. Having proceeded to within a short distance of the lines, I received information that the enemy were at anchor; soon after, they weighed and stood to the northward out of the lake—thus, if not acknowledging our ascendancy on the lake, evincing an unwillingness (although they had the advantage of situation, owing to the narrowness of the channel in which their galleys could work, when we should want room) to determine it.

I have the honor to be, &c.

THOS. MACDONOUGH.

Hon. W. Jones, sec. of the navy.

Lest we should be suspected of exaggeration, and, in truth, it is difficult to comprehend how a superior force should tamely submit to have their arsenals and public store-houses destroyed before their eyes, without even an attempt at resistance—we give an extract from the Washington official organ, which fully corroborates our statements as to the American force:—" *From Lake Champlain.* Our naval force sailed down the lake towards the enemy's line, and returned to Burlington, at which place there were *then collected five thousand regular troops* under General Hampton. Two thousand more were on their march, immediately expected from the Western States. The Plattsburg paper confirms all the accounts of the wanton barbarities of the enemy in that place, and *adds considerably to the amount* of depredations."

It is neither the custom of the Americans to overstate their force, nor to allow the damage to them to be overrated; we contend, therefore that the above extract fully confirms all our statements relative to the affairs on Lake Champlain. With respect to depredations, we have only to remind the reader of the occurrences that took place at York; and, as we proceed in our narration, it will be shown that, whatever apparent acts of severity were committed by the British, they were strictly retaliatory; and we will further prove by Ingersoll's admission that they *were not undeserved.*

There is a very great discrepancy between Christie and Veritas, on the point of supplies for the troops. Veritas writes, "In my last number, I stated, that at one time, in autumn, 1813, our troops at Kingston had not seven days' subsistence. Those at Prescott and Fort Wellington were nearly in a similar situation.

Discrepancy between Christie and the letters of Veritas.

"This was in a great measure owing to a combination of persons, either in the pay of Madison or gratuitously promoting his service. They effected their own purpose, partly by their own example, or by operating on the avarice of the well-affected, by persuading them to withhold supplies so as to get excessive prices. This was the ostensible pretext; but the real motive was to disconcert our military operations, by starving the troops, at the time of the expected invasion, by the forces collecting at Sackett's Harbour."

What says Christie on the same subject, and in reference to the same date. "The army acting upon the extensive line of operations along the frontiers of Upper and Lower Canada, (at the lowest computation one thousand miles from Lake Champlain to Michilimacinac), was, by the able arrangements of Commissary General Sir W. H. Robinson, and the unwearied exertions of the department under his directions, copiously supplied at every point with provisions and commissariat stores of all descriptions."

Now, which of these statements is the correct one? We are inclined to adopt neither. With regard to the statement of Veritas, that interested parties were disposed to hold their stores, in hopes of commanding higher prices, we think it extremely probable; but we are disposed to reject his assumption that it was done to embarrass the movements of our troops and to assist the enemy.

The spirit that prevailed throughout the country, and which enabled our militia to sustain hardships of every description, was too patent, too rife, to permit such a course of action. Had Canadians exhibited a discontented spirit, had the slightest evidences of disaffection been apparent, then there might have been grounds for Veritas's supposition, for supposition we must call it, as his statement is unsupported by any proof that is satisfactory to us. We cannot help ascribing this charge of Veritas to a desire to make an attack even by a side wind, on Sir Geo. Prevost; and we think that the extract we now give will bear us out in the assertion.

To counteract this nefarious plot, it became indispensably necessary to proclaim a modified Martial Law; and in consequence, provisions and forage were taken from the farmers, without their consent; but at very liberal and indeed very high prices, fixed by the Magistrates; the one half of which they would now be happy to get. Many who were duped by the arts of the disaffected, now feel compunction and sorrow at their folly.

This measure created complaints, which were artfully laid hold of by a Junto of disaffected persons, but self styled patriots, who seeing their object likely to be defeated by this prompt and decided measure, became furious in their denunciations against the military in general, but especially General De Rottenburgh and Lieutenant Colonel Pearson, who then commanded at Prescot.

The Chief of this Junto, was a man who had quitted Prescot the moment he heard of war being declared, and resided at Montreal, either from cowardice, or as considering it to afford a wider field for exertions favorable to the views of the enemy. He began his career by libelling every class in this community, and afterwards attacked the officers aforesaid, for doing their duty, in a periodical essay, under the signature of the "Anti-Jacobin," which was at first published in the Courant, but the Editor getting alarmed, at the abusive matter it contained; the work was taken up by a wretched paper called the Spectateur, that had commenced operations upon a congenial plan.

This paper yet continues, but is dwindling into deserved insignificance. The Anti Jacobin has for some time dropped his signature, but occasionally deigns to enlighten his fellow subjects with the fruits of his brain, under anonymous signatures, or under the mask of editorial remarks.

It would occupy too large a space, too enter into a formal discussion of the question about the right of declaring Martial Law, and therefore I shall content myself with observing, that to argue that such a power can in *no case be exercised without a previous Legislative Act*, is as absurd as to say, that an individual has not the right of self-preservation if attacked, but must, instead of defending himself, apply to the civil magistrate for protection, and consequently risk being destroyed before he can obtain that protection.

" General laws apply to ordinary cases, but there are cases that require extraordinary and prompt remedies. Rebellion or invasion assuredly come within the latter class, and during the existence of either of them, or absolute danger thereof, martial-law may be constitutionally proclaimed by the Sovereign or his Representative; and to do so, may be as indispensable to the safety of the state, as the instant application of personal force to the preservation of an individual when attacked.

" That the application of the power aforesaid was not made upon trivial occasion, is manifest ; for the question was reduced to this.—Shall the army be starved at the time the enemy is known to be prepared for, and determined upon immediate invasion ? or shall an authority be exercised to defeat the plots of the disaffected, and thereby save the province against that invasion ? So certainly will every honest and loyal man say yes to the second part of the question, that I venture to assert, that in such a predicament had the officer at the head of the Government, been so neglectful of his duty, as to be dismayed into inaction, by democratic clamour or threats, he would have deserved condign punishment.

" General De Rottenburg, I conceive, was perfectly justified in what he did, from the necessity of the case, and Lieutenant Colonel Pearson in obeying his orders, was also so ; and I have been astonished to learn, that Sir George Prevost, upon finding that the Lieut. Colonel was daily abused and threatened with prosecutions and persecutions by the disaffected Junto, for his zeal in executing his orders about subsisting the troops, cooly observed, that if he had got into a scrape, let him get out of it the best way he can. Sir George's duty was to have enquired whether the Lieut. Colonel had acted from corrupt motives or from zeal in a necessary measure, and if the latter, it was incumbent upon the commander of the Forces to have supported him.

"I have a right to ascribe the conduct of the Junto to disaffection ; for what good subject, when the enemy was at the door, would have taken measures to palsy our means of defence. To give aid to the enemy, is treason, and what more efficient aid could be given, than, what I have mentioned. It only wanted proof, of a correspondence with the enemy, respecting those proceedings, to have made those concerned therein, punishable for High Treason."

We think the reader will fail to discover in this extract any proof of Veritas' assumption, and we repeat that we can see little more in it than a desire to attach some odium to Sir George Prevost.

We will admit that cases did exist of short-commons for the troops. General Proctor's force, for instance, was at this very time suffering for want of provisions; but this, when we come to inquire into the cause, was owing to the great numbers of Indians who, having forsaken their hunting grounds and usual occupations, looked for subsistence for themselves and families to the English commissariat. Had there been no Indians to feed, Proctor would not have required more provisions than could have been easily supplied to him. But, allowing that this and other cases did exist, we still ask for the proof of the animus which caused the deficiency.

Man is naturally selfish, and it would be difficult to find any family, not to speak of nations, where some member or members of it were not actuated by selfish or interested views. Is it to be wondered at, then, that instances occurred, during the war, of parties desiring to drive a bargain with government for their individual benefit? And if there were such, does it necessarily follow that their proceedings were influenced by treasonable motives?

Instances are daily occurring at the present day, and complaints are constantly made, especially on foreign service, of the bad quality of beef supplied to the troops; but does it follow that because the contractors wish to make as much as they can out of their contract, that they are in league with Louis Napoleon or the Czar, to reduce the stamina of the British soldier, so as to render him discontented, or, from sheer weakness, unfitted to resist any future invasion that may be meditated, by either of these Potentates, at some future period?

Without adopting all Christie's statement, we are yet inclined to attach much more value to it, than to that of Veritas, especially as far as relates to the victualling department. Hardships the men had to suffer from want of tents, blankets, clothing, &c. ; but the privations were borne with a cheerful spirit, which did honor to the Canadian soldier, and enabled him to repulse an enemy overwhelmingly superior in point of numbers.

Before leaving, for busier scenes in the west, these waters, we must not omit to mention a trivial event,

Capture of British stores, and affair of boats at Gananoque.

which, like many others of like importance, has been not a little magnified by American historians. Two boats belonging to Commodore Chauncey's squadron, mounting one gun each, and manned by about seventy men, captured a British one gun boat, along with her convoy, consisting of fifteen batteaux, laden with two hundred and thirty barrels of pork, and three hundred bags of bread, bound from Montreal to Kingston, for the relief, we presume, of the troops whom Veritas has described as suffering so much from the machinations of unpatriotic and designing men. The number of prisoners, nine of them sailors, amounted to sixty-seven.

No sooner was intelligence conveyed to Kingston than three gun-boats, under the command of Lieutenant Scott, R.N., with a detachment of the 100th regiment under Capt. Martin, were despatched to intercept the Americans, as well as to recapture the convoy. This turned out an unfortunate affair; it was too late, when the British discovered the enemy, to attack them that day (17th or 18th of July); the attack was accordingly postponed, and early on the next morning the British, who had been, in the meantime, reinforced by another gun-boat, and a detachment of the 41st under Major Frend, ascended Goose Creek in pursuit. The passage up the Creek was, however, obstructed by trees that had been felled and laid across, and the swampy nature of the ground rendered the landing of the troops very difficult; the consequence was, that the expedition returned without success, having lost, principally in their endeavours to land, five men, besides having seventeen wounded. Amongst the killed was Captain Milne, one of Sir George Prevost's aides-de-camp, who had just arrived from head quarters to gain intelligence of the expedition. The American loss is nowhere to be found; but, as might be expected, the British loss is set forth by the veracious American historians, as amounting to sixty or seventy killed, with a commensurate number of wounded.

CHAPTER XIV.

———

For some time before the expedition against Fort Meigs and Fort Stephenson, of which the result was so disastrous, General Proctor had found himself seriously embarrassed by the difficulty of finding food for the large number of Indians who had flocked to his standard. The stores of provisions along the Detroit, which would have amply sufficed for the demand of his own troops, and even of the Indian warriors, were soon exhausted by the necessity of providing food, as well for these claimants, as for the families of the Indians. Other circumstances, too, conspired to increase the difficulty : the absence of the militia from their homes had materially diminished the supply to be expected from the spring crops, as these had, in a great measure been neglected. The American command of the lake precluded all hope of supplies by water, and transportation of stores by land, adequate to meet the demand, was altogether out of the question. The only hope, then, lay in the arrival of such reinforcements from the Lake Ontario fleet as would enable Captain Barclay to open the navigation of the lake to the British. The expectation of all was directed to this point, but neither guns nor men appeared, meanwhile the exigence became hourly more pressing. The

Situation of General Proctor in the west.

Detroit was, however, launched, the forts were dismantled to meet the emergency, and these lumbering guns were fitted in the best manner possible to suit the ports of the *Detroit*, or as we should rather have said the ports were fitted to receive the guns. To complete still farther this botching business. the other four vessels were stripped of part of their armament to complete the equipment of the *Detroit*. Fifty seamen had arrived from Ontario to man the five vessels, with an intimation that no further assistance could be afforded, consequently, General Proctor was compelled to complete the manning of the fleet by a detachment of the 41st regiment.

With a fleet manned and armed in this manner, Captain Barclay found himself compelled by the pressure of circumstances to sally forth upon the lake on the 9th September, to meet a well-provided and almost doubly superior force. The result may be easily anticipated, on the morning of the 10th, the fleets met, and after a bloody and hard struggle, during which, in spite of of all advantages, victory seemed to declare herself on the side of the British, the whole British squadron was captured—Captain Barclay's letter gives a truthful account of the affair.

His Majesty's late Ship Detroit,
Put-in Bay, Lake Erie, Sept. 22d.

SIR,—The last letter I had the honor of writing to you, dated the 6th instant, I informed you, that unless certain intimation

14

was received of more seamen on their way to Amherstburg, I should be obliged to sail with the squadron, deplorably manned as it was, to fight the enemy (who blockaded the port,) to enable us to get supplies of provisions and stores of every description; so perfectly destitute of provisions was the port, that there was not a day's flour in the store, and the squadron under my command were on half allowance of many things, and when that was done there was no more. Such were the motives which induced Major-general Proctor (whom by your instructions I was directed to consult, and whose wishes I was enjoined to execute, as far as related to the good of the country,) to concur in the necessity of a battle being risked under the many disadvantages which I laboured, and it now remains for me, a most melancholy task, to relate to you the unfortunate issue of that battle, as well as the many untoward circumstances that led to the event. No intelligence of seamen having arrived, I sailed on the 9th instant, fully expecting to meet the enemy next morning, as they had been seen among the islands; nor was I mistaken; soon after daylight they were seen in motion in Put-in-bay, the wind was then at S. W. and light, giving us the weather-gage. I bore up for them, in hopes of bringing them to action among the islands, but that intention was soon frustrated, by the wind suddenly shifting to the south-east, which brought the enemy directly to windward. The line was formed according to a given plan, so that each ship might be supported against the superior force of the two brigs opposed to them. About ten the enemy had cleared the islands, and immediately bore up, under easy sail, in a line abreast, each brig being also supported by the small vessels. At a quarter before twelve I commenced the action, by giving a few long guns; about a quarter past, the American Commodore, also supported by two schooners, one carrying four long twelve-pounders, the other a long 32 and 24 pounder, came to close action with the Detroit; the other a brig of the enemy, apparently destined to engage the Queen Charlotte, supported in like manner by two schooners, kept so far to windward as to render the Queen Charlotte's 20-pounder carronades useless, while she was with the Lady

Prevost, exposed to the heavy and destructive fire of the Caledonia and four other schooners, armed with long and heavy guns, like those I have already described. Too soon, alas! was I deprived of the services of the noble and intrepid Captain Finnis, who soon after the commencement of the action fell, and with him fell my greatest support: soon after, Lieutenant Stokoe of the Queen Charlotte, was struck senseless by a splinter, which deprived the whole country of his service at this very critical period. Provincial Lieutenant Irvine, who then had charge of the Queen Charlotte, behaved with great courage, but his experience was much too limited to supply the place of such an officer as Captain Finnis, hence she proved of far less assistance than I expected.

The action continued with great fury until half-past two, when I perceived my opponent drop astern, and a boat passing from him to the Niagara (which vessel was at this time perfectly fresh,) the American commodore, seeing that as yet the day was against him, (his vessel having struck soon after he left her,) and also the very defenceless state of the Detroit, which ship was now a perfect wreck, principally from the raking fire of the gun boats, and also that the Queen Charlotte was in such a situation that I could receive very little assistance from her, and the Lady Prevost being at this time too far to leeward from her rudder being injured, made a noble and alas! too successful an effort to regain it, for he bore up, and, supported by his small vessels, passed within pistol shot, and took a raking position on our bow; nor could I prevent it, as the unfortunate situation of the Queen Charlotte prevented us from wearing; in attempting it we fell on board her. My gallant Lieutenant Garland was now mortally wounded, and myself so severely, that I was obliged to leave deck. Manned as the squadron was, with not more than fifty British seamen, the rest a mixed crew of Canadians and soldiers, who were totally unacquainted with such service, rendered the loss of officers more sensibly felt, and never in any action was the loss more severe; every officer commanding vessels, and their seconds, were either killed or wounded so severely, as to be unable to keep the deck. Lieut. Buchan, of the Lady Prevost, behaved most nobly, and did everything which a brave and experienced officer could do in a vessel armed with twelve-pound carronades, against vessels carrying long guns. I regret to state that he was severely wounded. Lieut. Bignall, of the Dover, commanding the Hunter, displayed the greatest intrepidity ; but his guns being small (two, four, and six pounders) he could be of much less service than he wished. Every officer in the Detroit, behaved in the most exemplary manner. Lieut. Inglis showed such calm intrepidity, that I was fully convinced that, on leaving the deck, I left the ship in excellent hands ; and for an account of the battle, after that, I refer you to his letter which he wrote me, for your information.

Mr Hoffmeister, purser of the Detroit, nobly volunteered his services on deck, and behaved in a manner that reflects the highest credit on him. I regret to add, that he is very severely wounded in the knee. Provincial Lient. Purvis, and the military officers, Lieutenants Garden, of the Royal Newfoundland Rangers, and O'Keefe, of the 41st regiment, behaved in a manner which excited my warmest approbation ; the few British seamen I had behaved with their usual intrepidity, and as long as I was on deck, the troops behaved with a calmness and courage worthy of a more fortunate issue to their exertions.

The weather-gage gave the enemy a prodigious advantage, as it enabled them not only to choose their position, but their distance also, which they did in such a manner as to prevent the carronades of the Queen Charlotte and Lady Prevost from having much effect ; while their long guns did great execution, particularly against the Queen Charlotte. Capt. Perry has behaved in a most humane and attentive manner, not only to myself and officers, but to all the wounded. I trust that although unsuccessful, you will approve of the motives that induced me to sail under so many disadvantages, and that it may be hereafter proved that under such circumstances, the honor of his Majesty's flag has not been tarnished. I enclose the list of killed and wounded.

　　　I have the honor to be &c.
　　　　　(Signed)
　　　　　　R. H. Barclay, Commander,
　　　　　　　and late Senior officer.

In our notes,* Commodore Perry's official letter will be found. This letter we have very little fault to find with, except that it contains no allusion whatever to the bravery evinced by Capt. Barclay and his very inferior force. This inferiority will at once be seen when we give the weight of metal thrown by the American guns, and their number of men, in opposition to the Britsh force.

	Americans.	British.
Weight of metal....lbs	928	459
No. of men..........	580	345

Commodore Perry's acknowledgment of this circumstance, although it might have lessened somewhat his claim to a Nelsonic

---

* U. S: Schr. Ariel, Put-in-Bay,13th Sept. 1813.
SIR,—In my last, I informed you that we had captured the enemy's fleet, on this lake. I have now the honor to give you the most important particulars of the action :—On the morning of the 10th instant, at sun-rise, they were discovered from Put-in-Bay, where I lay at anchor, with the squadron under my command. We got under weigh, the wind light at S. E. which brought us to windward ; formed the line, and bore up. At fifteen minutes before twelve, the enemy commenced firing ; at five minutes before twelve, the action commenced on our part. Finding their fire very destructive, owing to their long guns, and its being mostly directed at the St. Lawrence, I made sail, and directed the other vessels to follow, for the purpose of closing with the enemy —every brace and bow line being soon shot away, she became unmanageable, notwithstanding the great exertions of the sailing-master. In this situation, she sustained the action upwards of two hours, within canister distance, until every gun was rendered useless, and the greater part of the crew either killed or wounded. Finding she could no longer annoy the enemy, I left her in charge of Lieut. Yarnell, who, I was convinced, from the bravery already displayed by him, would do what would comport with the honor of the flag. At half past two, the wind springing up, Captain Elliot was enabled to bring his vessel, the Niagara, gallantly into close action ; I immediately went on board of her, when he anticipated my wish, by volunteering to bring the schooners, which had been kept astern by the lightness of the wind, into close action.

It was with unspeakable pain that I saw, soon after I got on board of the Niagara, the flag of the St. Lawrence come down ; although I was perfectly sensible that she had been defended to the last, and that to have continued to make a show of resistance, would have been a wanton sacrifice of the remains of her brave crew. But the enemy was not able to take possession of her, and circumstances soon permitted her flag again to be hoisted. At forty-five minutes past two, the signal was made for " close action ;" the Niagara being very little injured, I determined to pass through the enemy's line—bore up, and passed

victory, would certainly have raised him in the opinion of every candid reader.

A careful examination of the circumstances connected with this affair, proves that Capt. Barclay lost the day from two causes; the first, that of not being in a position to take possession of the St. Lawrence when she struck; the second, the unfortunate loss of the few naval officers on board the 'fleet. This fact was particularly dwelt upon in the sentence of the court martial which was held on Capt. Barclay and the surviving officers and seamen. We transcribe the sentence pronounced by the court, of which Admiral E. J. Foote was president:

" That the capture of his Majesty's late squadron was caused by the very defective means Capt. Barclay possessed to equip them on Lake Erie; the want of a sufficient number of able seamen, whom he had repeatedly and earnestly requested of Sir James Yeo to be sent to him; the very great superiority of the enemy to the British squadron; and the unfortunately early fall of the superior officers in

---

ahead of their two ships, and a brig, giving a raking fire to them, from the starboard guns and to a large schooner, and sloop, from the larboard side, at half pistol-shot distance. The smaller vessels, at this time, having got within grape and canister distance, under the direction of Capt. Elliot, and keeping up a well directed fire, the two ships, a brig, and a schooner and sloop making a vain attempt to escape.

Those officers and men, who were immediately under my observation, evinced the greatest gallantry; and, I have no doubt but all others conducted themselves as became American officers and seamen. Lieut. Yarnell, 1st of the St. Lawrence, although several times wounded, refused to quit the deck. Midshipman Forest, (doing duty as Lieutenant,) and sailing master Taylor, were of great assistance to me. I have great pain, in stating to you the death of Lieut. Brook, of the marines, and Midshipman Lamb, both of the St. Lawrence, and Midshipman John Clark, of the Scorpion; they were valuable and promising officers. Mr. Hamilton, Purser, who volunteered his services on deck, was severely wounded, late in the action. Midshipman Claxton, and Swartwout, of the St. Lawrence, were severely wounded. On board of the Niagara, Lieutenants Smith and Edwards, and Midshipman Webster, (doing duty as sailing master,) behaved in a very handsome manner. Captain Brevoort, of the army, who acted as a volunteer, in the capacity of a marine officer, on board that vessel, is an excellent and brave officer; and, with his musketry, did great execution. Lieut. Turner, commanding the Caledonia, brought that vessel into action in the most able manner, and is an officer, in all situations, that may be relied on. The Ariel, Lieut. Packet, and Scorpion, sailing master Champlin were enabled to get early into action, and were of great service. Captain Elliot speaks in the highest terms of Mr. Magrath, purser, who had been dispatched in a boat, on service, previous to my getting on board the Niagara; and, being a seaman, since the action has rendered essential service in taking charge of one of the prizes-

Of Captain Elliot, already so well known to the government, it would be almost superfluous to speak:—in this action, he evinced his characteristic bravery and judgment; and, since the close of the action, has given me the most able and essential assistance.

I have the honor to enclose you a return of the killed and wounded; together with a statement of the relative force of the squadrons. The Captain and 1st Lieutenant of the Queen Charlotte, and 1st Lieut. of the Detroit, were killed. Captain Barclay, senior officer, and the commander of the Lady Prevost, severely wounded. The commander of the Hunter and Chippewa, slightly wounded. Their loss, in killed and wounded, I have not been able to ascertain; it must, however have been very great.

I have caused the prisoners, taken on the 10th inst. to be landed at Sandusky; and have requested Gen. Harrison to have them marched to Chillicothe, and there wait, until your pleasure shall be known respecting them.

The St. Lawrence has been so entirely cut up, it is absolutely necessary she should go into a safe harbor; I have, therefore, directed Lieut. Yarnell to proceed to Erie, in her, with the wounded of the fleet; and dismantle, and get her over the bar, as soon as possible.

The two ships, in a heavy sea, this day at anchor, lost their masts, being much injured in the action. I shall haul them into the inner bay, at this place, and moor them for the present. The Detroit is a remarkably fine ship; and is very strongly built; the Queen Charlotte is a much superior vessel to what has been represented;—the Lady Prevost is a large, fine schooner.

I also beg your instructions, respecting the wounded; I am satisfied, sir, that whatever steps I might take, governed by humanity, would meet your approbation;—under this impression, I have taken upon myself to promise Captain Barclay, who is very dangerously wounded, that he shall be landed as near Lake Ontario as possible; and, I had no doubt, you would allow me to parole him; he is under the impression, that nothing but leaving this part of the country will save his life. There is also a number of Canadians among the prisoners—many who have families.

I have the honor, &c.,

O. H. PERRY.

Hon. W. Jones, Sec. Navy.

The Return above alluded to by Commodore Perry, admits the American loss to have been twenty-seven killed, and ninety-six wounded—total one hundred and twenty-three.

the action. That it appeared that the greatest exertions had been made by Captain Barclay, in equipping and getting into order the vessels under his command; that he was fully justified, under the existing circumstances, in bringing the enemy to action; that the judgment and gallantry of Capt. Barclay in taking his squadron into action, and during the contest, were highly conspicuous, and entitled him to the highest praise; and that the whole of the officers and men of his Majesty's late squadron conducted themselves in the most gallant manner; and the court did adjudge the said Captain Robert Henry Barclay, his surviving officers and men, to be most fully and honorably acquitted."

A great deal of bombastive nonsense was circulated by the American press on the subject of Commodore Perry's " victory," and loud was the crowing, but even this was not recompense enough for a grateful country, a resolution was therefore passed in the Senate and House of Representatives to the following effect:

" That the thanks of Congress be, and the same are hereby presented to Captain Oliver Hazard Perry, and through him to the officers, petty officers, seamen, marines, and infantry serving as such, attached to the squadron under his command, for the decisive and GLORIOUS victory gained on Lake Erie on the 10th Sept., in the year 1813, OVER A BRITISH SQUADRON OF SUPERIOR FORCE."

In reference to the " superior force " it is plain that Congress had no grounds whatever for this part of their resolution. No where in Commodore Perry's letter will there be found the slightest allusion to a " superior force," and Yankee commanders were not generally backward in asserting their full claim, and generally much more than their just claims, to the admiration and gratitude of their countrymen. Not even in the ready tool of government, the official organ at Baltimore, is there to be found such assertions as could warrant the addition of this sentence. The thanks of Congress were not, however, deemed sufficient, so the following farther resolutions were unanimously passed:

" Resolved, That the president of the United States be requested to cause gold medals to be struck, emblematical of the action between the two squadrons, and to present them to Captain Perry and Captain Jesse D. Elliot, in such manner as will be most honorable to them, and that the president be farther requested to present a silver medal with suitable emblems and devices to each of the commissioned officers either of the navy or army serving on board, and a sword to each of the midshipmen and sailing masters who so nobly distinguished themselves on that memorable day.

" Resolved, That the president of the United States be requested to present a silver medal with like emblems and devices to the nearest male relative of Lieutenant Jno Brooks of the marines, and a sword to the nearest male relative of midshipmen Henry Lamb, and Thomas Claxton, Junior, and to communicate to them the deep regret which Congress feels for the loss of those gallant men, whose names ought to live in the recollection and affection of a grateful country, and whose conduct ought to be regarded as an example to future generations."

From the last resolution it would appear that Congress thought that honor and medals were sufficient rewards for officers, but that petty officers and seamen not being actuated by the same high spirit, required something more substantial. It was, therefore, resolved, " That three months' pay be allowed, exclusively of the common allowance, to all the petty officers, seamen, marines and infantry, serving as such, who so gloriously supported the honor of the American flag under the orders of their gallant commanders on that signal occasion."

This was a curious distinction to make in a country like the United States, when by the constitution all men are declared to be born free and equal.

We have seen how the American Government rewarded their countrymen, let us now enquire into the reward obtained by Captain Barclay from his country, what recompense was made to him for the noble and chivalrous spirit which urged him to seek an enemy two-fifths his superior. Captain Barclay's appearance at the Court Martial is represented to have drawn tears from the spectators, so mutilated was he. One arm he had lost previously, the second was so badly wounded by a grape shot, that it required artificial support, besides this he had received several flesh body wounds. It will scarcely be believed that, notwithstanding the flattering sentence of the court, and the severity of his wounds, Captain Barclay was only promoted to post rank in 1824, or nearly eleven years after the action.

With the loss of the British fleet vanished all prospect of supplies either of men or provisions, and consequently no hope remained that effectual resistance could be offered to the advance of the enemy, or to his occupation not only of the Michigan territory, but also the western portion of the peninsula. In fact Proctor was at once reduced to the necessity of abandoning all his positions beyond Lake Erie, and by this abandonment he ran the farther risk of being deserted by his Indian allies. Already had a vast number of boats been collected by the Americans, for the purpose of conveying the troops, who had assembled, in the neighbourhood of Forts Sandusky and Meigs, to the number of ten thousand men, across the lake, now that their success had left them undisputed masters in that quarter, when General Proctor found it essential to the safety of his troops to take immediate measures for a retreat. A council of war was held, and the Indian chiefs invited. At this council, General Proctor, after an exposition of the numerical strength of his force, of their position without provisions or other supplies, and the impracticability of procuring the actual necessaries for supporting life, proposed that, as it was utterly impossible to prevent the landing of the enemy in overwhelming force, the forts of Detroit and Amherstburg, together with the various public buildings, should be destroyed, and that the troops and Indians should retire on the centre division at Niagara. It is much to be deplored that this proposition was not acted upon, and that General Proctor suffered himself to be induced by Tecumseth's mingled reproaches and entreaties to change his purpose. Tecumseth's speech, which follows, is said to have been delivered with great energy, and to have produced the most startling effect on his brother Indians, who are described to have started up to a man, brandishing their tomahawks in a most menacing manner:—

"Father,—(he thundered,) listen to your children, you see them now all before you. The war before this, our British father, gave the hatchet to his red children when our old chiefs were alive. They are now all dead. In that war our father was thrown on his back by the Americans, and our father took them by the hand without our knowledge, and we are afraid our father will do so again at this time.

"Summer before last, when I came forward with my red brethren and was ready to take up the hatchet in favour of our British father, we were told not to be in a hurry—that he had not yet determined to fight the Americans.

"Listen! When war was declared, our father stood up and gave us the tomahawk, and told us he was now ready to strike the Americans—that he wanted our assistance; and he certainly would get us our lands back, which the Americans had taken from us.

"Listen! You told us at the same time to bring forward our families to this place—we did so, and you promised to take care of them, and that they should want for nothing, while the men would go to fight the enemy—that we were not to trouble ourselves with the enemy's garrisons—that we knew nothing about them, and that our father would attend to that part of the business. You also told your red children that you would take good care of your garrison here, which made our hearts feel glad.

"Listen! When we last went to the Rapids, it is true we gave you little assistance. It is hard to fight people who live like ground-hogs.

"Father—Listen! Our fleet has gone out; we know they have fought; we have heard the great guns; but we know nothing of what has happened to our father with one arm. Our ships have gone one way and we are much astonished to see our father tying up everything and preparing to run away the other, without letting his red children know what his intentions are. You always told us to remain here and take care of our lands; it made our hearts glad to hear that was your wish. Our great father, the king, is the head, and you represent him. You always told us you would never draw your foot off British ground; but now, father, we see you are drawing back, and we are sorry to see our father doing so without seeing the enemy. We must compare our father's conduct to a fat animal, that carries its tail upon its back, but when afrighted, it drops it between its legs and runs off.

"Listen Father!—The Americans have not yet defeated us by land; neither are we sure that they have done so by water; we therefore wish to remain here, and fight our enemy, should they make their appearance. If they defeat us we will then retreat with our father.

"At the battle of the Rapids, last war, the Americans certainly defeated us; and when we retreated to our father's fort at that place, the gates were shut against us. We were afraid that it would now be the case; but instead of that we now see our British father preparing to march out of his garrison.

"Father! You have got the arms and ammunition which our great father sent for his red children. If you have any idea of going away, give them to us, and you may go in welcome, for us. Our lives are in the hands of the Great Spirit. We are determined to defend our lands, and if it is his will, we wish to leave our bones upon them."

The scene that ensued is described to have been of the most imposing character. Richardson's account says—"The Council room was a large lofty building, the vaulted roof of which echoed back the wild yell of the Indians, while the threatening attitude and diversified costume of these latter formed a striking contrast with the calm demeanor and military garb of the officers grouped around the walls. The most prominent feature in the picture, however, was Tecumseth. Habited in a close leather dress, his athletic proportions were admirably delineated, while a large plume of white ostrich feathers, by which he was generally distinguished, overshadowing his brow, and contrasting with the darkness of his complexion, and the brilliancy of his black and piercing eye, gave a singularly wild and terrific expression to his features. It was evident that he could be terrible."

After some opposition General Proctor prevailed on Tecumseth and his brother chiefs to assent to a second proposal, viz., to retire on the Moravian village, distant nearly half-way between Amherstburg and the outposts of the centre division, and there await the approach of the enemy.

This course of action having been decided on, the troops were immediately set about destroying the fortifications, and various public buildings in Detroit and Amherstburg, and these places presented for some time a scene of cruel desolation. All stores that it was deemed impossible to move were committed to the flames. The work of demolition having been completed, and the baggage waggons and boats sent on in advance, the troops commenced their march; and never was a march set out on, under more dispiriting circumstances.

The situation of the men was deplorable in the extreme; they had been for some time on short allowance; and even their pay had not been regularly received. Arrears were due, to some for six, and to others for nine months. A Canadian winter was fast approaching, and few of the troops had blankets; to all greatcoats were a luxury quite unknown. The same privations which they had experienced during the winter of 1812 were, therefore, likely to be doubly felt during the coming season. To all these real hardships was joined the painful certainty that the families of many of the militia were exposed to similar privations at home.

Under these circumstances, the troops commenced their retreat towards the end of September, and proceeded up the Thames, a river navigable for small craft, up which the boats had already preceded them. On the 27th the American fleet, "composed of sixteen vessels of war and upwards of one hundred boats," received on board General Harrison's division, and landed it, on the afternoon of the same day, at a point three miles below Amherstburg, which post was reached just three days after it had been evacuated by the British.

The two armies, numerically considered, stood thus—The British retreating force consisted of about eight hundred and thirty men, exclusive of five hundred Indians; the Americans mustered fully five thousand men. We have adopted James's statement of the American force, as he seems to have been at much trouble in arriving at something like the truth. "The number of American troops," says James, "with which General Harrison so sanguinely expected to overthrow General Proctor's army does not appear, either in General Harrison's letter or in any of the American accounts, minute as they are in other less important particulars. Perhaps, by putting together such items of numbers as, in the general plan of concealment, may have escaped the notice of the different editors, we shall get within ONE or TWO thousands that landed below Amherstburg 'without opposition.' "

By following out this plan, James has arrived at the number which we have adopted above.

The British movements were extremely slow, as they appear to have been encumbered with a very unnecessary amount of baggage, and, when they arrived at the Moravian village, the pursuing party was but a few leagues behind.

This village, situated on a small plain, offered every facility for defence, being skirted on one side by a thick wood highly favorable to the operations of the Indians, and on the other by the Thames, while immediately in front, a deep ravine, covered with brushwood, and capable of being commanded by artillery, presented an obstacle peculiarly unfavorable to the passage of cavalry, of which a large portion of the advancing columns consisted.

It is impossible to understand the motives which could have induced General Proctor to abandon his original plan of making a stand at this point, and withdrawing his troops into the heart of a wood. It could scarcely have been that he expected by this means to render the cavalry, of which reports averred the major portion of the pursuing force to consist, comparatively useless, as, had even General Proctor been ignorant of the material out of which the American cavalry was formed, the Indians were not in the same state of ignorance, and there can be very little doubt but that this very point was discussed at the meeting, when Tecumseth urged the impolicy of a retreat.

In General Harrison's despatch* he says,

the American backwoodsman rides better than any other people ; a musket or rifle is no impediment, he being accustomed to carry them on horseback from his earliest youth. The Indians knew this as well as General Harrison, and it is not probable but that they put General Proctor in possession of the fact—so acute an observer as Tecumseth was not likely to leave his commander in the dark on so important a point. The British regulars on the other hand were just as ill suited for this irregular kind of bush fighting, where their tactics and previous training would be useless, as their opponents were the reverse. Taking, then, all these points into consideration general Proctor's manœuvres are more and more difficult to be accounted for, especially when we remember that all his former operations had been marked by decision and clear-sightedness. Richardson who was present at the battle, says "on the 5th, at one o'clock in the afternoon, we were within two miles of the Moravian village, but in defiance of that repeated experince which should have taught us the hopelessness of combating a concealed enemy, the troops were ordered to defile into the heart of a wood, not very close it is true, yet through the interstices of which it was impossible for the view to extend itself to a distance of more than twenty paces, much less to discover objects bearing so close a resemblance to the bark and foliage of the trees and bushes, as the costume of the Americans ; whereas on the contrary, the glaring red of the British troops formed a point, in relief, on which the eye could not fail to dwell."

James does not seem to consider the position to have been unfavourable. He says " this position was considered an excellent one ; as the enemy, however numerous his force could not turn the flank of the British, or present a more extended front than theirs," we are rather pleased to be able to bring forward even so slight a palliation as James' opinion, of that unlucky affair, we have not been able to find in any other in-

---

* From major-gen. Harrison to the American secretary at war.

Head-quarters, Detroit, Oct. 9th, 1813.
SIR,--In my letter from Sandwich of the 30th ultimo, I ᵈd myself the honor to inform you that I was preparing to pursue the enemy the follow-

ing day. From various causes, however, I was unable to put the troops in motion until the morning of the 22nd inst., and then to take with me only about 140 of the regular troops—Johnson's mounted regiment, and such of governor Selby's volunteers as were fit for a rapid march,

stance, even the shadow of an excuse offered. Christie says "this disaster to the British arms, seems not to have been palliated by these precautions, and the presence of mind, which, even in defeat reflect lustre on a commander. The bridge and roads in the rear of the retreating army were left entire, while its progress was retarded by a useless and cumbrous load of baggage. Whether the omission sprang from an erroneous contempt of the enemy, or from disobedience of the orders of the commanding officer is not well understood." We are however anticipating, as we have not yet given an account of the battle, if we may so call it.

The disposition of the troops is a point disputed One author asserts that the line formed an obtuse angle; Thompson, that the line was straight. Christie strange to say gives as Proctor's position, the identical one which we have been lamenting that he *did* not occupy. Richardson was present on the occasion, as he was taken prisoner on the field of battle; following him, therefore, we

---

the whole amounting to about 3500 men. To general M'Arthur, (with about 700 effectives) the protecting of this place and the sick was committed; general Cass's brigade, and the corps of lieutenant-col. Ball were left at Sandwich, with orders to follow me as soon as the men received their knapsacks and blankets, which had been left on an island in Lake Erie.

The unavoidable delay at Sandwich was attended with no disadvantage to us. General Proctor had posted himself at Dalson's, on the right side of the Thames, (or Trench) 56 miles from this place, which I was informed he intended to fortify, and wait to receive me. He must have believed, however, that I had no disposition to follow him, or that he had secured my continuance here, by the reports that were circulated that the Indians would attack and destroy this place upon the advance of the army, as he neglected the breaking up the bridges until the night of the 3nd instant. On that night our army reached the river, which is 25 miles from Sandwich, and is one of four streams crossing our route, over all of which are bridges; and they being deep and muddy, are rendered unfordable for a considerable distance into the country. The bridge here was found entire; and in the morning I proceeded with Johnson's regiment to save, if possible, the others. At the second bridge, over a branch of the river Thames, we were fortunate enough to capture a lieutenant of dragoons and 11 privates, who had been sent by general Proctor to destroy them. From the prisoners, I learned that the third bridge was broken up, and that the enemy had no certain information of our advance. The bridge having been imperfectly destroyed, was soon repaired, and the army encamped at Drake's Farm, four miles below Dalson's.

The river Thames, along the banks of which our route lay, is a fine deep stream, navigable for vessels of a considerable burthen, after the passage of the bar at its mouth, over which there is six and a half feet of water.

The baggage of the army was brought from Detroit in boats, protected by three gun-boats, which commodore Perry had furnished for the purpose, as well as to cover the passage of the army over the Thames, or the mouths of its tributary streams; the bank being low and the country generally (prairies) as far as Dalson's, these vessels were well calculated for that purpose Above Dalson's, however, the character of the river and adjacent country is considerably changed. The former, though still deep, is very narrow, and its banks high and woody. The commodore and myself, therefore, agreed upon the propriety of leaving the boats under the guard of 150 infantry; and I determined to trust to fortune and the bravery of my troops to effect the passage of the river. Below a place called Chatham, and four miles above Dalson's, is the third unfordable branch of the Thames; the bridge over its mouth had been taken up by the Indians, as well as that at M'Gregor's Mills, one mile above. Several hundred of the Indians remained to dispute our passage; and upon the arrival of the advanced guard, commenced a heavy fire from the opposite bank of the creek, as well as that of the river. Believing that the whole force of the enemy was there, I halted the army, formed in order of battle, and brought up our two 6-pounders to cover the party that were ordered to cover the bridge. A few shot from those pieces soon drove off the Indians, and enabled us in two hours to repair the bridge and cross the troops. Colonel Johnson's mounted regiment, being upon the right of the army, had seized the remains of the bridge at the mills under a heavy fire from the Indians. Our loss upon this occasion was two killed, and three or four wounded; that of the enemy was ascertained to be considerably greater. A house near the bridge, containing a very considerable number of muskets had been set on fire; but it was extinguished by our troops, and the arms saved. At the first farm above the bridge, we found one of the enemy's vessels on fire, loaded with arms, ordnance, and other valuable stores; and learned they were a few miles a-head of us, still on the right bank of the river. with a great body of Indians. At Bowles' Farm, four miles from the bridge, we halted for the night, found two other vessels and a large distillery filled with ordnance, and other valuable stores, to an immense amount, in flames; it was impossible to put out the fire; two 24-pounders, with their carriages, were taken, and a large quantity of ball and shells of various sizes. The army was put in motion early on the morning of the 5th. I pushed on in advance with the mounted regiment, and requested governor Shelby to follow as expeditiously as possible with the infantry. The governor's zeal, and that of his men, enabled them to keep up with the cavalry, and by nine o'clock we were at Arnold's mills, having taken in the course of the

may safely record that the British were drawn up in line, in a wood, not a very great distance from the Moravian settlement, with the Indians on the right, and a six pounder on the left.

The whole British force thus drawn up amounted to four hundred and seventy six. Originally it numbered about eight hundred and forty—but of these one hundred and seventy four had been just captured in the batteaux, and nearly one hundred and

seventy were either in the hospital or were on duty guarding the baggage.

The American force, even by their own admission, mustered twelve hundred cavalry, nineteen hundred and fifty infantry, and some one hundred and fifty Indians, thus, exclusive of officers, out-numbering Proctor's force seven-fold. General Harrison drew up his orces in two lines, and commenced the attack by a simultaneous charge on both British and Indians, in both cases the first charge

---

morning, two gun-boats and several batteaux, loaded with provisions and ammunition.

A rapid bend of the river at Arnold's mills, affords the only fording to be met with for a considerable distance; but upon examination, it was found too deep for the infantry. Having, however, fortunately taken two or three boats, and some Indian canoes, on the spot, and obliging the horsemen to take a footman behind each, the whole were safely crossed by 12 o'clock. Eight miles from the crossing we passed a farm, where a part of the British troops had encamped the night before, under the command of colonel Warburton. The detachment with general Proctor was stationed near to, and fronting the Moravian town, four miles higher up. Being now certainly near the enemy, I directed the advance of Johnson's regiment to accelerate their march for the purpose of procuring intelligence. The officer commanding it, in a short time, sent to inform me, that his progress was stopped by the enemy, who were formed across our line of march. One of the enemy's waggoners being also taken prisoner, from the information received from him, and my own observation, assisted by some of my officers, I soon ascertained enough of their position and order of battle, to determine that which it was proper for me to adopt.

I have the honour herewith to enclose you my general order of the 27th ult. prescribing the order of march and of battle, when the whole of the army should act together. But as the number and description of the troops had been essentially changed, since the issuing of the order, it became necessary to make a corresponding alteration in their disposition. From the place where our army was last halved, to the Moravian town, a distance of about three miles and a half, the road passes through a beech forest without any clearing, and for the first two miles near to the river. At from 2 to 300 yards from the river, a swamp extends parallel to it, throughout the whole distance. The intermediate ground is dry, and although the trees are tolerably thick, it is in many places clear of underbrush. Across this strip of land, their left *appuyed* upon the river, supported by artillery placed in the wood, their right in the swamp, covered by the whole of their Indian force, the British troops were drawn up.

The troops at my disposal consisted of about 120 regulars, of the 27th regiment, five brigades of Kentucky volunteer militia-infantry, under his excellency governor Shelby, averaging less than

500 men, and colonel Johnson's regiment of mounted infantry, making, in the whole an aggregate something above 3000. No disposition of an army opposed to an Indian force can be safe, unless it is secured on the flanks and in the rear. I had therefore no difficulty in arranging the infantry conformably to my general order of battle. General Trotter's brigade of 500 men formed the front line, his right upon the road, and his left upon the swamp. General King's brigade as a second line, 150 yards in the rear of Trotter's; and Child's brigade, as a corps of reserve, in the rear of it. These three brigades formed the command of major-general Henry; the whole of general Desha's division, consisting of two brigades, were formed *en potence* upon the left of Trotter.

Whilst I was engaged in forming the infantry, I had directed colonel Johnson's regiment, which was still in front, to form in two lines opposite to that of the enemy; and upon the advance of the infantry, to take ground to the left; and, forming upon that flank, to endeavour to turn the right of the Indians. A moments reflection, however, convinced me, that from the thickness of the wood, and swampiness of the ground, they would be unable to do any thing on horseback, and that there was no time to dismount them, and place their horses in security; I therefore determined to oppose my left to the Indians, and to break the British line, at once, by a charge of the mounted infantry; the measure was not sanctioned by any thing that I had seen or heard of, but I was fully convinced that it would succeed. The American back-woodsmen ride better in the woods than any other people. A musket or rifle is no impediment, they being accustomed to carry them on horseback from their earliest youth. I was persuaded, too, that the enemy would be quite unprepared for the shock, and that they could not resist it. Conformably to this idea, I directed the regiment to be drawn up in close column, with its right at the distance of 50 yards from the road, (that it might be in some measure protected by the trees from the artillery,) its left upon the swamp, and to charge at full speed as soon as the enemy delivered their fire. The few regular troops, under their colonel, (Paul,) occupied, in column of sections of four, the small space between the road and the river, for the purpose of seizing the enemy's artillery: and some 10 or 12 friendly Indians were directed to move under the bank. The crotchet formed by the front line and

was repulsed, but a second decided the fate of the day, the British troops giving way first, and the Indians retreating on seeing the fate of their allies, we now take up Richardson.— The result of an affair, against a body of such numerical superiority, and under such circumstances, may easily be anticipated.— Closely pressed on every hand, and principally by a strong corps of mounted riflemen, the troops were finally compelled to give way and, completely hemmed in by their assailants, had no other alternative than to lay down their arms—about fifty men only, with a single officer of the regiment, (Lieut. Bullock) contriving, when all was lost, to effect their escape through the wood. General Proctor, mounted on an excellent charger, and accompanied by his personal staff, sought safety in flight at the very commencement of the action and being pursued for some hours by a detachment of mounted Kentucky riflemen, was in imminent danger of falling into their hands.

The main body of the enemy, who had by this time succeeded in breaking through our centre, and had wheeled up, in order to take the Indians in flank, now moved rapidly upon us in every direction ; so that the resistance the light company had hitherto opposed,

was now utterly hopeless of any successful result. Persuaded, moreover, from the sudden cessation of the firing in that direction, that our centre and left, (for the wood intercepted them from our view) had been overcome, we, at the suggestion and command of Lieutenant Hailes, the only officer with us, prepared to make good our retreat, but, instead of going deeper into the wood as we purposed, we mistook our way, and found ourselves unexpectedly in the road ; when on glancing to the right, we beheld, at a distance of about five hundred yards, the main body of our men disarmed—grouped together, and surrounded by American troops. On turning to the left, as we instinctively did, we saw a strong body of cavalry coming towards us, evidently returning from some short pursuit, and slowly walking their horses. At the head of these, and dressed like his men in Kentucky hunting frocks, was a stout elderly officer whom we subsequently knew to be Governor Shelby, and who, the moment he beheld us emerging from the wood, galloped forward and brandishing his sword over his head, cried out with stentorian lungs, " surrender, surrender, it's no use resisting, all your people are taken, and you had better surrender." There was no alternative. The channel to escape had

---

general Desha's division, was an important point At that place the venerable governor of Kentucky was posted, who, at the age of 66, preserves all the vigour of youth, the ardent zeal which distinguished him in the revolutionary war, and the undaunted bravery which he maintained at King's Mountain. With my aide de camp the acting-assistant adjutant-general, captain Butler, my gallant friend commodore Perry who did me the honour to serve as my volunteer aide de camp, and brigadier general Cass, who having no command, tendered me his assistance, I placed myself at the head of the front line of infantry, to direct the movements of the cavalry, and to give them the necessary support. The army had moved on in this order but a short distance, when the mounted men received the fire of the British line, and were ordered to charge ; the horses in the front of the column recoiled from the fire ; another was given by the enemy, and our column at length getting into motion, broke through the enemy with an irresistible force. In one minute the contest in front was over, the British officers seeing no hopes of reducing their disordered ranks to order and our mounted men wheeling upon them, and pouring in a destructive fire, immediately surrendered. It is certain that only three of our troops were wounded in the charge. Upon the left, however, the contest was more severe with the

Indians. Colonel Johnson, who commanded on the flank of his regiment, received a most galling fire from them, which was returned with great effect. The Indians still further to the right advanced, and fell in with our front line of infantry, near its junction with Desha's division, and for a moment made some impression on it. His excellency governor Shelby, however, brought up a regiment to its support, and the enemy received a severe fire in front, and a part of Johnsons regiment having gained their rear, they retreated with precipitation. Their loss was very considerable in the action, and many were killed in their retreat.

I can give no satisfactory information of the number of Indians that were in action ; but there must have been considerably upwards of 1000.— From the documents in my possession, general Proctor's official letters, (all of which were taken) and from the information of respectable inhabitants of this territory, the Indians kept in pay by the British were much more numerous than has been generally supposed. In a letter to general De Rottenburg, of the 27th ult., general Proctor speaks of having prevailed upon most of the Indians to accompany him. Of these it is certain that 50 or 60 Wyandott warriors abandoned him.

The number of our troops was certainly greater than that of the enemy ; but when it is recol-

been closed by the horsemen in the wood, as well as those in the road, and a surrender was unavoidable. We accordingly moved down to join our captured comrades, as directed by Governor Shelby.

The most serious loss we sustained on this occasion was that of the noble and unfortunate Tecumseth. Only a few minutes before the clang of the American bugles was heard ringing through the forest, and inspiriting to action, the haughty Chieftain had passed along our line, pleased with the manner in which his left was supported, and seemingly sanguine of success. He was dressed in his usual deer skin dress, which admirably displayed his light yet sinewy figure, and in his handkerchief, rolled as a turban over his brow, was placed a handsome white ostrich feather, with which he was fond of decorating himself, either for the Hall of Council or the battle-field. He pressed the hand of each officer as he passed, made some remark in Shawanee, appropriate to the occasion, which was sufficiently understood by the expressive signs accompanying them, and then passed away for ever from our view. Towards the close of the engagement, he had been personally opposed to Colonel Johnson, commanding the American mounted riflemen, and having

severely wounded that officer with a ball from his rifle, was in the act of springing upon him with his tomahawk, when his adversary drew a pistol from his belt and shot him dead on the spot. It has since been denied by the Americans that the hero met his death from the hands of Colonel Johnson. Such was the statement on the day of the action, nor was it ever contradicted at that period. There is every reason to infer then that the merit, (if any merit could attach to the destruction of all that was noble and generous in savage life) of having killed Tecumseth, rests with Colonel Johnson. The merit of having flayed the body of the fallen brave, and made razor strops of his skin, rests with his immediate followers. This too has been denied, but denial is vain.

Discussion relative to the affair at the Moravian town. No affair during the whole war led to such bitter recrimination as that at the Moravian town. The first and principal cause of this was the general order issued by Sir George Prevost, which reflected very severely on the 41st regiment. It is difficult to apportion the censure which the document deserves, or to ascertain whether Sir G. Prevost or Gen. Proctor is the more blameworthy.

lected that they had chosen a position, that effectually secured their flank, which it was impossible for us to turn, and that we could not present to them a line more extended than their own, it will not be considered arrogant to claim for my troops the palm of superior bravery.

(Here follows an enconium upon the officers generally.)

Major Wood, of the engineers, already dististinguished at Fort-Meigs, attended the army with two 6-pounders. Having no use for them in action, he joined in the pursuit of the enemy, and with major Payne of the mounted regiment two of my aides de camp, Todd and Chambers, and three privates, continued it for several miles after the rest of the troops had halted, and made many prisoners.

I left the army before an official return of the prisoners, or that of the killed and wounded was made out. It was, however, ascertained that the former amounted to 601 regulars, including 25 officers. Our loss is seven killed, and 22 wounded, 5 of whom have since died. Of the British troops, 12 were killed, and 22 wounded. The Indians suffered most, 33 of them having been found upon the ground, besides those killed on the retreat.

On the day of the action, six pieces of brass artillery were taken, and two iron 24-pounders

the day before. Several others were discovered in the river, and can be easily procured. Of the brass pieces, three are the trophies of our revolutionary war; they were taken at Saratoga and York, and surrendered by general Hull. The number of small arms taken by us and destroyed by the enemy, must amount to upwards of 5000; most of them had been ours, and had been taken by the enemy at the surrender of Detroit, at the river Raisin, and colonel Dudley's defeat. I believe the enemy retain no other military trophy of their victories than the standard of the 4th regiment. They were not magnanimous enough to bring that of the 41st regiment into the field, or it would have been taken.

You have been informed, sir, of the conduct of the troops under my command in action. It gives me great pleasure to inform you, that they merit also the approbation of their country for their conduct, in submitting to the greatest privation with the utmost cheerfulness.

The infantry were entirely without tents, and for several days the whole army subsisted upon fresh beef, without either bread or salt.

I have the honour to be &c.

W. H. HARRISON.

General John Armstrong,
    secretary of War.

P. S. General Proctor escaped by the fleetness of his horses, escorted by 40 dragoons, and a number of mounted Indians.

General Order, Head Quarters, Montreal—
Nov. 24th 1813.

His Excellency the Commander of the Forces has received an official report from Major General Proctor of the affair which took place on the 5th October, near the Moravian village, and he has in vain sought in it for grounds to palliate the report made to His Excellency by Staff Adjutant Reiffenstein, upon which the General Order of the 18th October was founded—on the contrary, that statement remains confirmed in all the principal events which marked that disgraceful day; the precipitancy with which the Staff Adjutant retreated from the field of action, prevented his ascertaining the loss sustained by the division on that occasion ; it also led him most grossly to exaggerate the enemy's force, and to misrepresent the conduct of the Indian Warriors who, instead of retreating towards Machedash, as he had stated, gallantly maintained the conflict, under their brave Chief Tecumseth, and in turn harassed the American Army on its retreat to Detroit.

The subjoined return states the loss the right division has sustained in the action of the fleet on Lake Erie, on the 10th September and in the affair of the 5th of October, near the Moravian village, in the latter but very few appear to have been rescued by an honorable death, from the ignominy of passing under the American yoke, nor are there many whose wounds plead in mitigation of this reproach. The right division appears to have been encumbered with an unmanageable load of unnecessary, and forbidden private baggage—while the requisite arrangements for the expedition, and certain conveyance of the ammunition and provisions, sole objects worthy of consideration, appear to have been totally neglected, as well as all those ordinary measures resorted to, by officers of intelligence, to retard and impede the advance of a pursuing enemy. The result affords but too fatal a proof of this unjustifiable neglect. The right division had quitted Sandwich on its retreat, on the 26th September, having had ample time, for every previous arrangement, to facilitate and secure that movement. On the 2nd October following, the enemy pursued by the same route, and on the 4th succeeded in capturing all the stores of the division, and on the following day, attacked and defeated it almost without a struggle.

With heart-felt pride and satisfaction the Commander of the Forces had lavished on the Right Division of this Army, that tribute of praise which was so justly due to its former gallantry and steady discipline. It is with poignant grief and mortification that he now beholds its well-earned laurels tarnished, and its conduct calling loudly for reproach and censure.

The Commander of the Forces appeals to the genuine feelings of the British soldier from whom he neither conceals the extent of the loss the Army has suffered, nor the far more to be lamented injury it has sustained, in its wounded honor, confident that but one sentiment will animate every breast, and that zealous to wash out the stain which, by a most extraordinary infatuation, has fallen on a formerly deserving portion of the Army, all will vie to emulate the glorious achievements recently performed, by a small but high spirited and well disciplined division, led by officers possessed of enterprise, intelligence, and gallantry, nobly evincing what British soldiers can perform, when susceptible of no fear, but that of failing in the discharge of their duty.

His Excellency considers it an act of justice, to exonerate most honorably from this censure the brave soldiers of the right division who were serving as marines on board the squadron on Lake Erie. The commander of the forces having received the official report of Capt. Barclay of the action which took place on Lake Erie on the 10th September, when that gallant officer, from circumstances of imperious necessity, was compelled to seek the superior force of the enemy, and to maintain an arduous and long contested action under circumstances of accumulating ill fortune.

Captain Barclay represents that the wind, which was favorable early in the day, suddenly changed, giving the enemy the weather-gage, and that this important advantage was, shortly after the commencement of the engagement, heightened by the fall of Captain Finnis, the commander of the Queen Charlotte. In the death of that intrepid and intelligent officer, Captain Barclay laments the loss of his main support. The fall of Captain Finnis was soon followed by that of Lieut. Stokoe, whose country was deprived of his services at this very critical period of the action, leaving the command of the Queen Charlotte to Provincial Lieutenant Irvine, who conducted himself with great courage, but was too limited in experience to supply the place of such an officer as Capt. Finnis, and in consequence this vessel proved of far less assistance than might be expected.

The action commenced about a quarter before twelve o'clock, and continued with great fury until half past two, when the American commodore quitted his ship, which struck shortly after, to that commanded by Capt. Barclay (the Detroit.) Hitherto the determined valor displayed by the British squadron had surmounted every disadvantage, and the day was in our favor; but the contest had arrived at that period when valor alone was unavailing—the Detroit and Queen Charlotte were perfect wrecks, and required the utmost skill of seamanship, while the commanders and second officers of every vessel were either killed or wounded: not more than fifty British seamen were dispersed in the crews of the squadron, and of these a great proportion had fallen in the conflict.

The American Commodore made a gallant, and but too successful an effort to regain the day. His second largest vessel, the Niagara, had suffered little, and his numerous gun-boats which had proved the greatest source of annoyance during the action, were all uninjured.

Lieutenant Garland, First Lieutenant of the Detroit, being mortally wounded, previous to the wounds of Captain Barclay, obliging him to quit the deck, it fell to the lot of Lieutenant Inglis, to whose intrepidity and conduct the highest praise is given, to surrender His Majesty's ship, when all further resistance had become unavailing.

The enemy, by having the weather gage, were enabled to choose their distance, and thereby avail themselves of the great advantage they derived in a superiority of heavy long guns, but Captain Barclay attributes the resut of the day, to the unprecedented fall of every commander, and second in command, and the very small number of able seamen left in the squadron, at a moment when the judgment of the officer, and skilful exertions of the sailors, were most imminently called for.

To the British seamen Captain Barclay be-
stows the highest praise—*that they behaved like British seamen.* From the officers and soldiers of the regular forces serving as marines, Captain Barclay experienced every support within their power, and states that their conduct has excited his warmest thanks and admiration.

Deprived of the palm of victory when almost within his grasp, by an overwhelming force which the enemy possessed in reserve, aided by an accumulation of unfortunate circumstances, Captain Barclay and his brave crew have, by their gallant daring and self devotion to their country's cause, rescued it's honor and their own, even in defeat."

The 41st Regiment had uniformly behaved so gallantly that this severe censure appears almost uncalled for, and this feeling seems to have pervaded all ranks. No official document, relative to the affair, from general Proctor to Sir George Prevost is to be found, consequently these are no direct proofs that Sir George issued his order in consequence of General Proctor's representations, still, in the line of defence adopted by General Proctor on the court-martial, subsequently held on him, there were precisely such statements brought forward as would have been likely, had they been previously made, to have brought down upon the troops the reprimand conveyed in the General order—we should hesitate co ascribe to General Proctor this underhand proceeding had he not so ungenerously endeavoured on his court-martial to shift the blame from his own shoulders to those of the troops under his command. Whether, however, Sir George Prevost issued his general order, on General Proctor's representations, or not, we cannot help feeling that this order was an ill-advised one. From the facts elucidated afterwards in the court martial, it became apparent that the publishing of it was premature, and this fact seems only to render the hasty conduct of the commander-in-chief more reprehensible. It was clearly his duty, before publishing a document, the tendency of which was to cast odium upon a corps, which he himself admits to have previously won his warmest admiration—to have carefully considered all the information furnished him, and to have distinctly stated whether it was in the representation of their general that the right Division was thus reprimanded.

A cotemporary writes thus relative to the affair, handling Sir George Prevost very severely.

"Well timed indeed, and with a befitting grace does the insulting censure, contained in the opening of the order, emanate from the man who had previously made a descent upon Sackett's Harbour, with a view of destroying the enemy's naval and military works and who at the very moment of accomplishment of the object of the expedition, and when the Americans were retreating, turned and fled with precipitation to his boats, presenting to the troops who were unwilling sharers in his disgrace, the monstrous yet ludicrous anomaly of two hostile armies fleeing from each other at the same time.— Well does it become the leader, who, at Plattsburg, covered the British army with shame, and himself with enduring infamy, by retiring at the head of 15,000 men—chiefly the flower of the Duke of Wellington's army—before a force of Americans not exceeding as many hundreds; and this even at the moment when the commander of these latter was preparing to surrender his trust without a struggle.— Well does it proceed from him, who through timidity and vacillation alone, at an earlier period of the war, entered into a disgraceful armistice with the enemy at the very moment when General Brock was preparing to follow up his successes on the Western frontier, by sweeping the whole southern border of the St. Lawrence. Happily was it devised by the authority to whose culpable inattention and neglect alone was owing the loss of our gallant Barclay's fleet, and the consequent helplessness of that very Right Division he has hesitated not to condemn for a disaster attributable to himself alone. Nay, well and most consistently does the sting issue from the Commander of the Forces, who, on the occasion of the capture of Detroit, and the victory obtained at the river Raisin, ordered Royal salutes to be fired in honor of conquests which had been achieved principally by the 41st Regiment, and whose remarks, even on the occasion of their unavoidable repulse at Sandusky, convey rather a compliment than dispraise."

What added materially to the severity of the reprimand, was the high eulogy pronounced and most deservidly so, on the officers and seaman of Captain Barclay's fleet.

Christie's observations on this unfortunate affair, to be found in our notes,* are pertinent and just, and throw much valuable light on the affair.

---

* General Proctor had, to this time, served with honour and distinction in Upper Canada, and was universally considered a brave and able officer; but his retreat, and the events of this untoward day, blasted his fame and at once ruined him in the public estimation.—Some, however, were of opinion that the severity of the general order, by Sir George Prevost, on the occasion, was premature, and a prejudition of the case of his unfortunate brother in arms, who it was thought before so complete a condemnation from his superior officer, ought to have had the benefit of a trial. This he ultimately did get, but not until upwards of a year after the occurrence alluded to, before the expiration of which, Sir George Prevost himself, had fallen still lower than he, in the public estimation, by his own inglorious retreat from Plattsburgh, more humiliating to the national pride than even Proctor's affair. His retreat and discomfiture were of but a small and isolated division of the army, hitherto distinguished for its gallantry, but which, by the loss of the fleet, becoming destitute of its resources, had no other alternative than a speedy retreat, or an immediate surrender. He took his chance of the former. The retreat, it seems, was ill-conducted; but was, in fact, that of Sir George Prevost, taking all in all, any thing better? He advanced to Plattsburgh, at the head of an effective force of at least twelve thousand troops, the *elite* of the army under his command, recently from France and Spain —men accustomed to victory, and again marching to it, as they believed—well provided with an abundant commissariat, and stores of all kinds, and led on by experienced and able officers.— These, however, on the naval defeat, (the loss of the fleets being, in both cases, the immediate cause of retreat) he countermarched, to their inexpressible humiliation and disgust, without their being allowed once to see, much less co ne in contact with the enemy. A further advance, after the loss of the fleet, was, indeed, out of the question; but nothing could justify the precipitancy of retreat, sacrifice of public stores, and demoralisation in the army that took place in consequence of it. The district of Montreal, was immediately in his rear, and at the short distance of three, or at most four marches from Plattsburgh, upon which he might, it is said, have fallen back at his leisure. It is, however, but justice to remark, time has materially worn down the asperities with which Sir George Prevost was also in his turn prejudged, with respect to this, to say the least of it, most unlucky expedition.

Major general Proctor being tried at Montreal, in December, 1814, on five charges preferred against him for misconduct on this occasion, was found guilty of part of them, and sentenced " to be publicly reprimanded; and to be suspended from rank and pay for six months." It was found " that he did not take the proper measures for conducting the retreat,"—that he had, " in many instances, during the retreat, and in the disposi-

The two defeats, Captain Barclay's and General Proctor's, were productive of the greatest benefit to the Americans, as not only was the whole territory of Michigan, except the port of Michilimacinac, reconquered, but the whole of the western district lost also.

Pour comble de malheur, too, the services of the Indians were lost ; and American editors boast that General Harrison, after the battle of the Thames, made peace with three thousand warriors.

tion of the force under his command, been erroneous in judgment, and in some, deficient in those energetic and active exertions, which the extraordinary difficulties of his situation so particularly required."—" But as to any defect or reproach with regard to the personal conduct of major general Proctor, during the action of the 5th October, the court most fully acquitted him."

His royal highness, the Prince Regent, confirmed the finding of the court, but animadverted upon it rather severely, by the general order issued on the occasion, dated, " Horse Guards, 9th September, 1815," for its " mistaken lenity" towards the accused, as the following extracts will explain :—

" Upon the whole, the court is of opinion, that the prisoner, major general Proctor, has, in many instances during the retreat, and in the disposition of the force under his command, been erroneous in judgment, and in some, deficient in those energetic and active exertions, which the extraordinary difficulties of his situation so particularly required.

" The court doth, therefore adjudge him, the said major general Proctor, to be publicly reprimanded, and to be suspended from rank and pay, for the period of six calender months.

" But as to any defect or reproach, with regard to the personal conduct of major general Proctor, during the action of the 5th October, the court most fully and honorably acquits the said major general Proctor.

" His royal highness, the Prince Regent, has been pleased, in the name, and on the behalf of His Majesty, to confirm the finding of the court, on the 1st, 3d, 4th, and 5th charges.

" With respect to the second charge, it appeared to his royal highness to be a matter of surprise that the court should find the prisoner guilty of the offence alleged against him, while

they, at the same time, acquit him of all the facts upon which that charge is founded ; and yet, that in the summing up of their finding, upon the whole of the charges, they should ascribe the offences of which the prisoner has been found guilty, to error of judgment, and pass a sentence totally inapplicable to their own finding of guilt, which can alone be ascribed to the court having been induced, by a reference to the general good character and conduct of major general Proctor, to forget, through a humane but mistaken lenity, what was due by them to the service.

" Under all the circumstances of the case, however, and particularly those which render it impossible to have recourse to the otherwise expedient measure of re-assembling the court for the revisal of their proceeding, the Prince Regent has been pleased to acquiesce in and confirm so much of the sentence as adjudges the prisoner to be publicly reprimanded; and in carrying the same into execution, his royal highness has directed the general officer, commanding in Canada, to convey to major general Proctor, his royal highness's high disapprobation of his conduct ; together with the expression of his royal highness's regret, that any officer of the length of service, and the exalted rank he has attained, should be so extremely wanting in professional knowledge, and deficient in those active energetic qualities, which must be required of every officer, but especially of one in the responsible situation in which the major general was placed.

" His royal highness, the commader in chief directs, that the foregoing charges preferred against major general Proctor, together with the finding and sentence of the court, and the Prince Regent's pleasure thereon, shall be entered in the general order book, and read at the head of every regiment in his Majesty's service.

" By command of his royal highness the commander in chief.

H. GALVERT, Ad.-general."

CHAPTER XV.

The regulars and militia, who had escaped

Retreat of Proctor and place of rendezvous. captivity or destruction on the unfortunate 5th of October, retreated, as may be easily imagined, in the greatest confusion, to Ancaster, a small village some ten miles from the head of Lake Ontario, and, on the 17th of the same month, they rendezvoused at that place, their numbers, inclusive of seventeen officers, amounting to two hundred and fifty-six. During this retreat, which was effected through an almost unbroken wilderness, the troops suffered the greatest privations and misery, and their appearance as they straggled into the village, was by no means calculated to lessen the feeling of apprehension, which the rumour of the defeat at Moravian town had spread amongst the defenceless inhabitants. To these unfortunates, pillaged houses and their little homesteads destroyed, could not but appear inevitable, and the infection of the panic spread far and wide.

General Armstrong in his observations on

Armstrong's observations on Proctor's defeat. Proctor's retreat and subsequent defeat, seems to have been unaware of that officer's situation previous to the commencement of his retreat, and uninformed as to the manifold difficulties by which he was surrounded.

Proctor's situation at Malden, writes Armstrong, made necessary on his part, a prompt retreat to Vincent, unencumbered with baggage; or a vigorous defence of the post committed to his custody. By adopting the former, he would have saved seven hundred veteran soldiers and a train of artillery, for the future service of his sovereign; by adopting the latter, he would have retained the whole of his Indian allies, (*three thousand combatants*) giving time for the militia of the interior to come to his aid; had the full advantage of his fortress and its munitions, and a chance, at least, of eventual success, with a certainty of keeping inviolate his own self-respect, and the confidence of his followers. Taking a middle course between these extremes, he lost the advantage that would have resulted from either. His retreat began too late—was much encumbered with women, children, and baggage, and at no time urged with sufficient vigour, or protected with sufficient care. Bridges and roads, ferries and boats, were left behind him, neither destroyed nor obstructed; and when, at last, he was overtaken and obliged to fight, he gave to his veterans a formation, which enabled a corps of four hundred mounted infantry, armed with rifles, hatchets, and butcher knives, to win the battle "in a single minute." Conduct like this deserved all the opprobrium and punishment it received, and justly led to General Harrison's conclusion, that "his antagonist had lost his senses."

15

It is plain, we again assert, from these remarks that Armstrong could not have been aware of Proctor's real situaton, and we shall proceed to urge in detail our objections to his conclusions. First as to the prompt retreat to General Vincent, unencumbered with baggage. We have no defence to make of Proctor on this count, too many of our cotemporaries have expressed themselves strongly, in reprobation of the ill judged manner in which the retreat was conducted, to permit us to urge aught in vindication. One fact, however, is remarkable, Veritas the earliest writer on the subject, one by no means sparing in condemnation, and who might have been supposed to be thoroughly acquainted with the pros and cons of the affair, is silent on the point, confining his remarks to a stricture on the severity of Sir George Prevost's general order. This is significant and leads us to pause ere we adopt too readily all that has been said in condemnation of Proctor.

Secondly,—As to the vigorous defence of the post committed to his custody. We have already shown the difficulties by which Proctor was surrounded, and that it was impossible for him to find provisions for his troops as well as for the Indians and their families. Gen. Armstrong lost sight, too, of the fact that "the post" had been to a great degree dismantled of its guns, which had been required to arm Barclay's fleet, and had accordingly been appropriated for that purpose, and captured with that fleet.

Proctor was, we think, to blame for the deposition of his forces at the Moravian town, but even this is, as we have shown, a mere matter of opinion, as the observations, quoted in our last chapter, show. We must not allow one passage in Armstrong to pass unnoticed—it is when he speaks of the formation which enabled *four hundred mounted infantry armed with rifles, hatchets, and butcher knives*, to win the battle in a single minute.

Had we not already shown the overwhelming numbers of Harrison's army, the reader would be led to suppose that a corps of four hundred men, armed hastily with any weapons and horses they could collect, had routed in one minute seven hundred British veterans. We need scarcely go into this subject, as we have both shown the constitution and habits of the body of mounted riflemen (not infantry) and the whole number of Harrison's army, we therefore only direct the reader's attention to the passage as another proof how prone Americans are to misrepresent.

It is not often that we have occasion to commend an American commander for modesty; we must not omit, therefore, on the present occasion to point out an instance of it as occurring in Harrison's despatch. He admits that "the number of our troops was certainly greater than that of the enemy." This is something even for an American General, but the pains he takes to do away with the impression, that numbers had aught to do with the fate of the day, is also noteworthy. Accordingly, he adds, in the next paragraph, "but when it is recollected that they had chosen a position, that effectually secured their flank, which it was impossible for us to turn and that we could not present to them a line more extended than their own, *it will not* be considered arrogant for me to claim for my troops the palm of superior bravery." Can anything be more absurd than this last paragraph? Here were over three thousand Americans opposed to something like four hundred and seventy British, and yet the American General, instead of honestly confessing that by dint of superior numbers he overcame his opponents, descends to the meanness of twaddling about the superior position chosen by Proctor, and claims on that account superior bravery for his men. We should scarcely have noticed this passage in Harrison's despatch had we not found that he thereby gained his object, to throw dust in the eyes of his compatriots. That this was effected is to be discovered in the fact that every town throughout the Union was illuminated, and every church rung out a merry peel on the occasion. All this to be sure might have been a political measure, or, as General Wilkinson calls it, " a military deception," but still it is difficult to imagine that any sober-minded American, in possession of the truth, could or would have seen reason to exult in the circumstance of three thousand five hundred of his countrymen overcoming some four hundred and seventy British and some Indians.

Harrison's end was nevertheless gained, and one of the members for South Carolina, a Mr.

Remarks on Harrison's letter as to numbers.

Cheeves, delivered himself, in the middle of a very long speech, on the conduct of the war, of the following remarkable sentence :—" The victory of Harrison was such as would have secured to a Roman General, in the best days of the Republic, the honors of a triumph." If anything could have made General Harrison ashamed of himself, we think that sentence must have produced the effect.

We had intended to have closed this subject without further remark, but an examination into various documents tempt us to quote them, as they throw much light on an affair which the absence of official returns has left very much in the dark. The communication which led to the correspondence was addressed to Lieutenant Bullock by Major Friend, then in command of the second battalion of the regiment.

Barton Heights, 30th Nov., 1813.

Sir,—I request you will, with as little delay as the nature of the report will admit, furnish me with every circumstance within your knowledge, and that you may have heard from undoubted authority, relative to the late unfortunate affair that took place between Gen. Harrison's army and the 1st battalion 41st regiment, at Moravian town on the 5th of October last, for the purpose of transmitting it to Lieut.-Gen. Champagne. As you are the senior and only officer of the regiment who has escaped from the field, that was in the ranks, it is highly incumbent on you to state most minutely the nature of the ground on which the regiment was formed for action, the manner in which it was formed, the number then of the regiment actually in the field, the number of the enemy opposed to you, and of what they consisted, and what resistance was made by the regiment previous to its defeat, if it had received provisions regularly, was complete in ammunition, and could have got supplies when required, and, in short, every circumstance, that happened from the commencement of the retreat from Amherstburg, relative to the regiment. You cannot be too particular in your statement, as I am sorry to say there are reports afloat disgraceful in the extreme to the regiment, and every individual with it that day. I think it but proper to inform you that I saw Major General Proctor's official report, which highly censures the conduct of the regiment, and in which he says

that he never went into action more confident of success.

I have the honor to be, &c.,
RICHARD FRIEND,
Major Commanding 41st regt.

Lieutenant Bullock's letter, dated Barton Heights, 6th December, 1813. Here follows:—

We proceeded to Moravian town, and, when within 1½ miles of it, were ordered to halt. After halting about five minutes, we were ordered to face to the right about, and advanced towards the enemy in files, at which the men were in great spirits. Having advanced about fifty or sixty paces, we were halted a second time, at which the men appeared dissatisfied, and overhearing some of those nearest to me express themselves to the following effect, 'that they were ready and willing to fight for their knapsacks; wished to meet the enemy, but did not like to be knocked about in that manner, doing neither one thing nor the other,' I immediately checked them, and they were silent. About this time several of the regiment came up without arms or accoutrements, who had escaped from boats cut off by the enemy's cavalry. From these men we learnt that the enemy was within a mile of us, and had a large force of cavalry. We had halted about half an hour, when the Indian alarm was given that the enemy was advancing; most of our men were sitting on the logs and fallen trees by the side of the road. On the alarm being given we were suddenly ordered to form across the road. From the suddenness of the order, apparently without any previous arrangement, the manner in which we were situated when it was given, the way in which it was given, which was 'form up across the road,' and from the nature of the ground, the formation was made in the greatest confusion; so much so, that the Grenadier company was nearly in the centre of the line, and the light company on the right. A second order, as sudden as the first, was given for the grenadiers and No. 1 to march to the rear and form a reserve. The grenadiers and part of Captain Muir's company accordingly formed a second line, about 200 yards in rear of the first, under command of Lieut.-Col. Warburton; the left of it about eight or ten yards to the left of the road, and extending to the right into the woods, formed at extended order, the men placing themselves behind trees, and consequently much separated. The first line I could not distinguish, but from what I have been informed by Lieut. Gardiner, 41st regt., commanding a six-pounder, it was formed in the following manner—a six pounder was placed in the road, having a range of fifty yards, the 41st regiment drawn up on its right, extending in the wood; on each side of the limber of the six-pounder were some of the Canadian Light Dragoons. From the men of the regiment, who escaped from that line, I understand they were not formed at regular extended order but in clusters and in confusion. To the left of the road in which the six-pounder was placed, and parallel to it, ran the River Thames. To the right and left of the road was a remarkably thick forest, and on the right, where we were formed, the ground was free from brushwood for several hundred yards, where cavalry could act to advantage. —My position at this time, (being on the right of the 2nd line) and the thickness of the forest precluded me from noticing the manner in which the enemy attacked the 1st line. The attack commenced about two hours after the order was given to form up across the road. I heard a heavy firing of musketry, and shortly after saw our dragoons retreating together with the limber of the six-pounder—placed on the left of the 1st line. About a minute afterwards I observed that line retreating in confusion, followed closely by the enemy's cavalry, who were galloping down the road. That portion of the 1st line which had escaped the enemy's cavalry, retreated behind the 2d line, which stood fast, and fired an irregular volley obliquing to the right and left, which appeared to check the enemy. The line having commenced firing, my attention was directed to that part of the enemy moving down directly in my front. Hearing the fire slacken, I turned towards the line and found myself remaining with three non commissioned officers of the Grenadier company. The enemy's cavalry had advanced so close, before the reserve could commence firing, from the number of trees, that before a third round could be fired they broke through the left, and the rest not being formed in a manner to repel cavalry, were compelled to retreat. The number of the regiment actually in the field were one lieutenant-colonel, six captains, nine lieutenants, three ensigns, three staff, twenty-six sergeants, eighteen corporals, four drummers, two hundred and ninety-seven rank and file. In what manner the rest of the regiment was distributed you will be made acquainted with by the enclosed statement signed by the Adjutant of the regiment. The number of Indians we had in the field was 800. The number of the enemy I cannot positively affirm, but from the information obtained from individuals of the regiment taken prisoners on that day, and who afterwards escaped; the number could not have been less than 6,000, of which 1,200 or 1,500 were cavalry and mounted riflemen. The number of our dragoons did not exceed 20. Our loss on this occasion was three sergeants, and nine rank and file killed, and thirty-six wounded, that of the enemy, fifteen killed, and from forty to fifty wounded. Having been thus far particular in stating everything to which I was an eye witness, and which has come to my knowledge, I beg leave to remark that, from the well known character of the regiment, any observations emanating from those whose interest it is to cast a direct or indirect reflection upon its conduct, cannot be received with too much distrust.

I have the honor to be, &c.,

RICHARD BULLOCK,

Lieut. 1st Grenadiers.

Major Friend, Comm'g. 2d. Batt. 41st Reg't.

Lieutenant Bullock's letter, contains so clear and full a vindica- James' contradictions on this affair. tion of the troops, that we trust no attempt will be made for the future to cast unfair aspersions on their gallantry. James is somewhat contradictory on this head. He says, after extolling the bravery of the Indians, "had the men of the 41st regiment at all emulated the Indians, the fate of the day might have been changed," and that this was not an improbable event, he assumes, from the American General's claim of superior bravery for his troops.

How does the case stand? Thirty five hundred men beat five hundred; the leader of the larger body, knowing it would be useless to deny that he had the superiority in numbers, endeavors to gloss over the fact by claiming superior bravery, on the score of his thirty-five hundred not having been beaten by the five hundred men; and an English writer admits his claim, on the ground that, as the Americans were used to being beaten, it was a disgrace for five British not to beat thirty-five Americans. In the very next page, after this imputation on the conduct of the troops, James writes:—"The censure passed upon the right division of the Canadian army, by the commander-in-chief, was certainly of unparalleled severity." Now, how could any censure be too severe for unsteadiness in the field? The fact is, James was anxious to have a cut at both Proctor and Sir George Prevost, and, in eagerness to do this, he contradicts himself three times in two pages. Some persons have a most unfortunate mode of assisting their friends when in a difficulty, and James is one of those individuals. He first casts an imputation on the conduct of the 41st, and then, anxious to do away with it, and to shift the blame upon Sir George or General Proctor, he finds the following excuse for them :—

"The ardor which, as Sir George himself admits, and every one else knows, had, till the fatal 5th of October, distinguished the 41st regiment, affords a strong belief that it was not cowardice which made that corps SURRENDER SO TAMELY, no matter to what superiority of force. The privations the troops had undergone, and the marked neglect which had been shown at head-quarters to the representations of their commander, had probably possessed them with an idea that any change would be an improvement in their condition."

James here substitutes the charge of treachery for cowardice, and leaves the regiment no alternative but to be impaled on one or other of the horns of the dilemma he has provided. From this careless writing of James, and from Sir George Prevost's haste to condemn, unheard, General Proctor, American writers have derived much benefit. It enables Ingersol to speak of the "craven mood of the soldiers," and the pusillanimous behaviour of the General." Not satisfied, however, with these hard epithets, Ingersol goes still further, and adds—"No history can deny their characteristic courage, but British murderers and thieves become cowards in Canada. To save themselves they laid down heir arms to an INFERIOR FORCE of raw troops,

while their commander fled in the first moment of encounter." Further comment is unnecessary on a writer who, with Harrison's admission of his superiority in numbers before him, ventures, unsupported by a fact, or even a fiction on the part of his brother historians, to give to the world so daring and unblushing a falsehood.

We feel tempted, in imitation of contemporary writers, to make a further digression in our narrative, in order to place before the reader the character of Tecumseth in its proper light, especially as no words can be found which could be considered too strong when applied in praise of this noble Indian.

Character of Tecumseth.

The Indian warrior Tecumseth was in the forty-fourth year of his age when he fell. " He was of the Shawanee tribe; five feet ten inches high, and, with more than the usual stoutness, possessed all the agility and perseverance of the Indian character. His carriage was dignified; his eye penetrating; and his countenance, even in death, betrayed the indications of a lofty spirit, rather than of the sterner cast. Had he not possessed a certain austerity of manners, he could never have controlled the wayward passions of those who followed him to the battle. He was of a silent habit, but when his eloquence became roused into action by the reiterated encroachments of the Americans, his strong intellect could supply him with a flow of oratory, that enabled him, as he governed in the field, so to prescribe in the council."

Those who consider that, in all territorial questions, the ablest diplomatists of the United States are sent to negotiate with the Indians, will readily appreciate the loss sustained by the latter in the death of their champion.

" The Indians, in general, are full as fond as other savages of the gaudy decoration of their persons; but Tecumseth was an exception. Clothes and other valuable articles of spoil had often been his, yet he invariably wore a deer skin coat and pantaloons. He had frequently levied subsidies to comparatively a large amount, yet he preserved little or nothing for himself. It was not wealth, but glory, that was Tecumseth's ruling passion." The remarks which now follow, must be taken as applicable not to the present but to a past generation :—

"Fatal day, when a Christian people first penetrated the forests, to teach the arts of civilization to the poor Indian! Till then, water had been his only beverage, and himself and his race possessed all the vigor of hardy savages. Now, no Indian opens his lips to the stream that ripples by his wigwam, while he has a rag of clothes on his back, wherewith to purchase rum ; and he and his squaw and his children wallow through the day in beastly drunkenness. Instead of the sturdy warrior, with a head to plan, and an arm to execute vengeance upon the oppressors of his country, we behold the puny besotted wretch, squatting in his house, ready to barter his country, his children, or himself, for a few gulps of that deleterious compound, which, far more than the arms of the United States, is hastening to extinguish all traces of his name and character. Tecumseth himself, in early life, had been addicted to intemperance, but no sooner did his judgment decide against, than his resolution enabled him to quit, so vile a habit. Beyond one or two glasses of wine he never afterwards indulged."

By whom are the savages led? was the question, for many years, during the wars between the Americans and Indians. The name "Tecumseh!" was itself a host on the side of the latter, and the warrior chief, while he signalized himself in all, came off victorious in most, of the many actions in which he had ought and bled. American editors, superadded to a national dislike to the Indians, have some special reasons, which we shall develope presently, for blackening the character of Tecumseh. They say that he neither gave nor accepted quarter. His inveterate hatred to the Americans, considering them, as he did, to have robbed his forefathers of their territory, render such a proceeding, in a savage, not improbable. European history, even of modern date, informs us that the civilized soldier can go into battle with a similar determination. Mr. Thomson says of Tecumseh, that, "when he undertook an expedition, accompanied by his tribe, he would relinquish to them the spoil, though he would never yield the privilege of destroying the victim," and yet it was from an American

publication* that we extracted the account of Tecumseh's killing a brother chief, because the latter wanted to massacre an American prisoner. This trait in Tecumseh's character is corroborated by all the British officers who have served with him.

That it did not however proceed from any good will towards the Americans, was made known, in an extraordinary manner, at the taking of Detroit. After the surrender of the American troops, General Brock desired Tecumseh not to allow the Indians under him to ill-treat the prisoners. Tecumseh promptly replied, "I despise them too much to meddle with them." Nor is there a single act of violence charged to the Indians on that occasion. As a proper contrast to this an American writer,† describing a battle between General Jackson and the Creek Indians, in March 1814, says, "of about one thousand Creeks, only ten of the men are supposed to have escaped with life, sixteen of the Creeks, who had hid themselves, were killed the morning after the battle." The American commander said, in his despatches that he was *determined to exterminate* the tribe, " of course," proceeds the editor, "no quarter was given except to a few women and children."

Few officers in the United States service were so able to command in the field, as this famed Indian Chief. He was an excellent judge of position, and not only knew, but could point out, the localities of the whole country through which he had passed. To what extent he had travelled over the western part of the American continent may be conceived from the well known fact, that he visited the Creek Indians, in the hopes of prevailing on them to unite with their northern brethren, in efforts to regain their country as far as the banks of the Ohio. His facility of communicating the information he had acquired, was thus displayed before a concourse of spectators :—Previously to General Brock's crossing over the Detroit, he asked Tecumseh what sort of a country he should have to pass through, in case of his proceeding farther. Tecumseh taking a roll of elm bark, and extending it on the ground by means of four stones, drew forth his scalping knife, and,

---

* Sketches of the War.
† Political and Historical Register, page 186

with the point, presently sketched upon the bark a plan of the country, its hills, woods, rivers, morasses, and roads, a plan which if it was not as neat was for the purpose required fully as intelligible as if Arrowsmith himself had prepared it. Pleased with this unexpected talent in Tecumseh, also with his having, by his characteristic boldness, induced the Indians, not of his immediate party, to cross the Detroit, prior to the embarkation of the regulars and militia, General Brock, as soon as the business was over, publicly took off his sash, and placed it round the body of the chief. Tecumseh received the honor with evident gratification; but, was the next day, seen without his sash. General Brock, fearing something had displeased the Indian, sent his interpreter for an explanation. The latter soon returned with an account, that Tecumseh, not wishing to wear such a mark of distinction, when an older, and, as he said, an abler, warrior was present, had transferred the sash to the Wyandot chief Round head. Such a man was the unlettered "savage" Tecumseh, such a man it was on whose mangled remains the Kentuckians exercised their savage propensities. Ingersol writes, "when his (Tecumsch's) body was discovered after the battle of the Thames, *known as he was to General* Harrison, and recognized from other Indians among the slain, by pock marks, and a leg once broken and set, pieces of his skin were cut off by some of the Kentucky soldiers, to be kept by them." By way of excuse Ingersol adds, " Indignities to the dead are common to every field of battle. Refined military men, who *might* condemn these Kentucky spoils as barbarous mementos, would sack cities, during days of authorized horrors and licentiousness, which would prove that war is a ferocious departure at best from the laws of humanity." One writes, on the subject, after describing the scalping of Tecumseh, and the cutting of his skin into narrow slips for razor straps, is graceless enough, in the next breath, to lavish oncomiums upon the *humanity of " the Volunteers of Kentucky."* These are his words, "History can record to their honor that, not *merely professing* to be *Christian people,* they *gave a high example of Christian virtues.* For evil they returned not evil. For cruelty they returned mercy and protection." James, when noticing this

paragraph, observes, "had we taken up **Dr.** Smith's book, for the first time, we should have pronounced this an excellent piece of irony." We have, however, produced quite evidence enough to show that whatever atrocities the Indians might have committed, the Americans, as *participes criminis,* should not be the first to cast stones.

Before returning to the Niagara frontier, it will be necessary to Treatment of Prisoners. enter on the subject of the treatment of prisoners, especially as about this time a question arose which not only affected the comfort, but was of grave import to the lives, of many persons on both sides. First, however, as to the treatment of prisoners.

Could the statements of American writers be received, the impression would be conveyed, that, in losing their liberty, the captured British took leave, at the same time, of all the privations and sufferings incident to a state of warfare. A few extracts from the narrative of one of the prisoners taken at the battle of the Thames will show how far this was the case, and whether more credit should be allowed to American claims for liberal conduct towards their prisoners, than as we have just shown, in Tecumseh's instance, they are entitled to when claiming, for the Kentucky volunteers, the character of setting forth a high example of christian virtues and magnanimity towards the dead.

" To describe the fatigue and privations which we endured during our tedious journey would require time and space. The rainy season had already set in, and scarcely a single day passed by without our being literally wet to the skin. Our route lay through an inhospitable tract of country, consisting alternately of gloomy forest and extensive savannah, the latter often intersected by streams fed from the distant mountains, and swollen by the increasing rains.

" Many of the officers were without great coats, having been plundered of nearly everything, as well by the followers of the division, as by the enemy themselves, and although we had a change of linen left, during the whole journey no opportunity was afforded us of having anything washed, so that in a short time many became infected with vermin, which gave the finishing stroke to our calamities. After several weeks of most tedious travelling through this dreary region, some few traces of civilization and cultivation became perceptible, and we finally beheld the banks of the Scioto, overcome, as well may be imagined, with the utmost lassitude. On the opposite shore of this small river stands the town of Chilicothe, the termination of our journey."

So far it will be observed that no extraordinary care was paid to the comforts or even necessaries of the prisoners, but a darker scene has still to be displayed.

After the battle of Queenston twenty-three of the prisoners were recognised as *deserters* and British born subjects, and were sent to England, by the commander-in-chief, for their trial as traitors. The American government, having been made acquainted with the fact, instructed General Dearborn to put an equal number of British soldiers into close confinement as hostages for the safety of the former. In consequence of this measure, the commander of the forces by a general order of October 27th, 1813, proclaimed that he had received the commands of the Prince Regent to put forty-six American officers and non-commissioned officers into close confinement, as hostages for the twenty three soldiers confined by the American government.

General Order, Head quarters, Montreal—
October 27th, 1813.

His Excellency the Governor General and Commander of the Forces, having transmitted to His Majesty's Government a letter from Major General Dearborn, stating that the American Commissary of Prisoners in London had made it known to his Government, that twenty-three soldiers of the 1st, 6th and 13th Regiments of United States Infantry, made prisoners, had been sent to England and held in close confinement as British subjects, and that Major General Dearborn had received instructions from his government, to put into close confinement twenty-three British soldiers, to be kept as hostages for the safe keeping and restoration in exchange for the soldiers of the United States, who had been sent as above stated to England;—in obedience to which instructions, he had put twenty-three British soldiers into close confinement to be kept as hostages; and the persons referred to

in Major General Dearborn's letter being soldiers serving in the American army, taken prisoners at Queenston, who had declared themselves to be British born subjects, and were held in custody in England there to undergo a legal trial.

His Excellency the Commander of the Forces has received the commands of His Royal Highness the Prince Regent, through the Right Honorable the Earl Bathurst, Secretary of State, to lose no time in communicating to Major General Dearborn, that he has transmitted a copy of his letter, and that he is in consequence instructed, distinctly to state to Major General Dearborn, that His Excellency has received the command of His Royal Highness the Prince Regent, forthwith to put in close confinement, forty-six American officers and non-commissioned officers, to be held as hostages for the safe keeping of the twenty-three British soldiers stated to have been put in close confinement by order of the American government.

And he is at the same time to apprize him that if any of the said British soldiers shall suffer death, by reason that the soldiers now under confinement in England have been found guilty, and that the known law, not only of Great Britain, but of every independent state under similar circumstances, has been in consequence executed, he has been instructed to select out of the American officers and non-commissioned officers put into confinement as many as double the number of British soldiers who shall have been so unwarrantably put to death, and cause such officers and non-commissioned officers to suffer death immediately.

And His Excellency is further instructed to notify to Major General Dearborn that the commanders of His Majesty's armies, and fleets on the coast of America have received instructions to prosecute the war with unmitigated severity against all Cities, Towns, and Villages belonging to the United States, and against the inhabitants thereof, if after this communication shall have been duly made to Major General Dearborn, and a reasonable time given for its being transmitted to the American government, that government shall unhappily not be deterred from putting to death any of the soldiers who now are, or who may hereafter be, kept as hostages for the purposes stated in the letter from Major General Dearborn.

His Excellency the Commander of the Forces, in announcing to the troops the commands of His Royal Highness, the Prince Regent, is confident that they will feel sensible, of the parental solicitude which His Royal Highness has evinced for the protection of the person and honor of the British soldier, thus grossly outraged in contempt of justice, humanity, and the Law of Nations, in the persons of twenty-three soldiers placed in close confinement, as hostages for an equal number of traitors who had been guilty of the base and unnatural crime of raising their parricidal arms against that country which gave them birth, and who have been delivered over for legal trial to the just laws of their offended country.

The British soldier will feel this unprincipled outrage, added to the galling insults and cruel barbarities that are, daily, wantonly inflicted on many of his unfortunate comrades, who have fallen into the enemy's hands, as additional motives to excite his determined resolution never to resign his liberty but with his life, to a foe so regardless of all sense of honor, justice and the rights of war.

(Signed,)   EDWARD BAYNES,
Adj't. Gen.

Early in December the commander of the forces received a communication from Major Gen. Wilkinson, by Colonel Macomb, of the United States army, bearing a flag of truce, stating that the Government of the United States adhering unalterably to the principle and purpose declared in the communication of General Dearborn had, by way of reprisal, ordered forty six British officers into close confinement. On receipt of this communication the governor ordered all American officers *without distinction of rank* to be immediately placed in close confinement, and in pursuance of this, Generals Chandler, Winchester and Winder were conveyed from their quarters at Beauport, to Quebec for confinement. At the same time the following order was issued:—

General Order, Adjutant General's Office,
12th December, 1813.

His Excellency the Governor-in-Chief and Commander of the Forces has to announce to the troops under his command, that he has received a communication from Major Gen. Wilkinson, commanding a division of the army of the United States of America, by order of his government, of which the following is an extract:—

"The Government of the United States adhering unalterably to the principle and purpose declared in the communication of General Dearborn to you, on the subject of the twenty-three American soldiers, prisoners of war, sent to England to be tried as criminals; and the confinement of a like number of British soldiers, prisoners of war, selected to abide the fate of the former; has in consequence of the step taken by the British Government, as now communicated, ordered forty-six British officers into close confinement, and that they will not be discharged from their confinement until it shall be known that the forty-six American officers and non-commissioned officers in question are no longer confined."

It would be superfluous to use any argument to refute an assumption so extravagant, unjust, and unprecedented, as to deny the right of a free nation to bring to legal trial, in a due course of law, her own natural born subjects taken in the actual commission of the most heinous offence that man can commit against his king, his country, and his God; that of raising his parricidal arm against his allegiance to his countrymen, by leaguing with their enemies; a crime held in such abhorrence by every civilized nation in Europe, that summary death by the law Martial is its avowed reward, and is inflicted with unrelenting severity by France, the ally of the United States. This pretension must appear to every unprejudiced and upright mind as iniquitous and unjust, as is the retaliation which the Government of the United States has adopted, by placing in close confinement three and twenty British soldiers, as hostages for an equal number of infamous wretches, the unworthy offspring of Great Britain, who, when drawn from the ranks of the enemy, solicited to be suffered to expiate their treason by turning their arms against their employers. These rebels have (with the contempt they merit) been consigned to the infamy and punishment that await them from the just laws of their offended country, while the Government of the United States does not blush to claim these outcast traitors as their own, and outrage the custom of civilized war, in the persons of honourable men, by placing them on a par with rebels and deserters.

No alternative remains to the commander of the forces, in the discharge of his duty to his king, his country, and his fellow soldiers, but to order all the American officers, prisoners of war, without exception of rank, to be immediately placed in close confinement as hostages for the forty-six British officers so confined, by the express command of the supreme authority in that country, until the number of forty-six be completed, over and above those now in confinement.

His Excellency directs that this general order together with that issued on the 27th of October, be read to the troops, that the British soldier may be sensible of the terms on which America has determined to wage this war; confident that he will meet them with proper spirit and indignation; for should he become the prisoner of a foe so regardless of those laws, which for ages have governed civilized nations in war, he would be doomed to a rigorous confinement, and that only preparatory to a more savage scene.

(Signed,)   EDWARD BAYNES,
Adjt-Gen. North America.

We have purposely italicised the words, without *distinction of rank,* as Ingersol has not

Ingersol on reprisal.

scrupled, in his observations on this affair, to endeavour to throw a false colouring over it, and to have recourse to misrepresentation. He writes, "when England took her position on the dogma of *perpetual allegiance.* Gens. Chandler, Winder and Winchester, Colonel Lewis and Major Madison were prisoners on parole near Quebec, but not one of the superior officers was seized as a hostage. A dogma originally applied only to vassals, never enforced against lords, in the feudal ages, from whose dark codes it sprang, England, on the ferocious revival of it, restricted to men in humble stations. No American above the grade of captain was confined. In the first place this is simply untrue as the three generals just mentioned were removed from their

parole at Beauport to Quebec for confinement Again, as to the dogma of perpetual allegiance, it was not the vindication of this dogma which Great Britain at this time desired to assert, but the right of punishing deserters, and of establishing the point that a mere forsaking of the British flag and territory was not sufficient to absolve from the general law of allegiance, or from the military and naval codes in particular, which, in common with those of all nations, awarded the punishment of death to deserters from either service.

Ingersol is not more happy when he cites Moreau, Bernadotte, and Pezzo de Borgo, as cases in point to prove that fugitives from a country may honorably join in warfare against that State. France may be said to have been afflicted with a civil war, in the conducting of which both parties called in allies; but even during those unhappy times victims were not wanting, and Ney's fate tells much more forcibly against Ingersol's position, than Moreau, Bernadotte, and Pozzo de Borgo do for him.

For some time the measures of the respective governments were carried out very rigidly, and many hardships were suffered by the unfortunate victims of this attempt, on the part of the United States, to force Great Britain to consent tamely to regard the desertion of her soldiers and sailors. The final settlement of this affair did not take place till July 1814, but we introduce it here in order to close the subject. The whole correspondence will accordingly be found in our notes,*

*General Order,
Head Quarters, Montreal,
16th April, 1814.

His Excellency the Governor-in-Chief and Commander of the Forces, announces to the troops under his command, that he was pleased to sanction and confirm, on the 15th inst., articles of a convention entered into by Colonel Baynes, Adjutant-General of the Forces, and Brigadier-General Winder of the army of the United States of America, for the mutual release of all prisoners of war, hostages or others, with the exception of the forty-six American officers and non-commissioned officers placed in close confinement as hostages, in conformity to the general order of the 27th of October last, in retaliation for twenty-three British soldiers, confined by the Government of the United States, as hostages for twenty-three British born subjects, taken from the ranks of the enemy, and sent to England for legal trial.

By this agreement it is stipulated that all

and will show how both governments gradually relaxed their respective measures of retaliation, and introduced by degrees a less terrible and menacing state of affairs, the threatened gibbet being removed by the tacit retirement of both belligerents from its proposed erection.

James has been very severe on the Americans for the treatmen of their prisoners, and after enumerating a long list of officers who had been thrown into prison, he asks—" Into what prison? The Penitentiary, along with forty convicts, condemned for murder, rape, forgery, coining, burglary, horse-stealing, &c.' James adds—" Lest the reader should doubt this, he will find in the appendix furnished

---

prisoners of war (the above mentioned alone excepted) shall be mutually exchanged, and delivered at such places as shall be agreed on, with all convenient expedition, and shall be declared, respectively and severally, to be released and free to carry arms, and serve on the 15th day of May next, the same as if they had never been prisoners of war: and it has been further provided, that whatever balance shall appear on the returns of prisoners of war, respectively exchanged or given up on parole, by either party since the commencement of hostilities, the number of prisoners for which an equivalent has not been returned, shall be withheld from all military service, until exchanged.

It is with proud satisfaction that the com mander of the forces feels confident, that this provisional clause can never apply to the army in Canada, from the immense disparity in the number and rank of the prisoners, it has restored to the enemy.

All officers, non-commissioned officers, and soldiers, being prisoners of war, who are not prevented in consequence of their wounds, are commanded to join their respective corps and stations on the 15th day of May next, and to resume their military duties.

(Signed,)   EDWARD BAYNES,
                              Adjutant-General.

General Order,
Head Quarters, Camp at Chambly.
July 2nd, 1814.

Several officers of this army having returned from the United States, where they had been held in close confinement as hostages, and having on their release signed a conditional parole containing a pledge on their part, to return to their captivity at the expiration of a limited period, unless previously exchanged: His Excellency the Governor-in-Chief and Commander of the Forces, considering such parole to be inconsistent with the provisions of a convention for the exchange of prisoners which was entered into by persons duly empowered for that purpose by the Government of the United States, and His Excellency respectively, and has already been carried into complete execution on his part, and has also been in part executed by the American Government,—is pleased to declare that all those officers, whether of the line or Militia are absolved from their parole, under and by virtue of the before mentioned convention:—that they are released and free to serve as if they had never been prisoners of war, and are all and

severally included in the general order of the 16th of April, directing all prisoners of war after the 15th of May to repair to their respective corps and stations, and to resume their military duties.

To destroy any doubts which may by possibility be entertained with regard to the complete execution of the convention above mentioned: to satisfy the nice and scrupulous sensibility with which a British soldier must ever view and examine an act, professing to release him from an obligation in which his honour is implicated, and to remove every apprehension from the minds of those who may come within the scope of the present general order, His Excellency is pleased to authorize the communication to the army under his command, of the principal circumstances attending the commencement, progress, and final conclusion of the convention to which allusion has above been made.

At the solicitation of the Government of the United States, conveyed in a letter from their Secretary of State of the 19th of March, and not less induced by his anxious desire to alleviate the unnecessary severity which the system of retaliation had introduced into the conduct of this war, the Commander of the Forces did not hesitate in acceding to a proposal which seemed to promise the attainment of an object so desirable. In that spirit, and with tnat view, His Excellency consented to the exchange of Brigadier-General Winder, (a hostage) in consequence of that officer having been selected by the President of the United States as an agent vested with full powers to negotiate for an exchange of prisoners of war, as well hostages as others. His Excellency was also pleased to nominate Colonel Baynes as an agent vested with similar powers, on the part of the British army.

The negotiation commenced under the most favourable auspices. The basis and conditions of the convention being left to the discretion of the two officers above mentioned, it was agreed that all prisoners of war, hostages or others (with the sole exception of the British subjects taken from the ranks of the enemy and sent to England for legal trial) should be released in conformity to the regulations of the cartel, General Winder pledging himself that his government entertained the most liberal sentiments, and that the great disparity of prisoners, both with respect to rank and numbers, which the United States would receive and for which they had no equivalent to return, should be withheld from service on parole, until duly exchanged.

This agreement was on the point of being ratified, when a despatch from the American

by the keeper of the prison, a list of convicts, their crimes and sentences." Mr. James actually gives an appendix showing the names of the various prisoners, and the punishment awarded to each offence. Here we are tempted to digress for a moment to show some of the advantages of American law —for instance, we find that for killing a wife by shooting her,

four years' imprisonment is deemed ample punishment, but that for stealing a negro, or a horse, ten and four years and a half are not considered too severe a sentence !

James concludes his observations by remarking—"General Sheaffe did not behave thus to the American forces who surrendered at the battle of Queenston, and many will be

---

Secretary of State, dated Washington the 22nd March, was received by Brig.-Gen. Winder, and was verbally represented by him to convey a positive prohibition to his consenting to the release of the twenty-three British soldiers held in confinement as hostages for the British subjects sent to England for trial, unless it was stipulated that they also should be released, and sent to the United States.

This proposition was instantly answered by a note informing Brigadier-General Winder, that as a new basis had been substituted by the Secretary of State, inadmissible in principle, the negotiation was in consequence at an end, and that his partial exchange as a preliminary measure was also void, and of no effect as emanating from an act which had, from the conduct of the proposing party, become a nullity.

The introduction of this new pretension on the part of the Government of the United States had arrested the progress of the negotiation, when a note from Brigadier General Winder came (No.3) which was acceded to by Colonel Baynes as the basis of a convention (No. 4.)

To ascertain the existence of the power of final ratification on the part of Brigadier General Winder the Commander of the Forces was pleased to direct Colonel Baynes to address to that officer the note (No. 5) and although the answer of Brigadier General Winder, as contained in note (No. 6) did not completely accord with the spirit of candor professed by him, and manifested by His Excellency, nevertheless the fair construction of it was such as to carry to his mind the conviction which it must impress on every honourable man who persues it, that Brigadier General Winder possessed the power of finally ratifying any new agreement for the exchange of prisoners, into which he might think proper to enter.

Under this impression the Commander of the Forces was pleased to declare his assent to the immediate release and exchange of Brigadier General Winder; the negotiation for the exchange of prisoners on the contracted basis imposed by Brigadier General Winder, was recommenced, and the conditions being arranged, a convention was concluded on the 15th April last, and ratified by the contracting parties.

It is under this convention, so begun and ratified, and carried into effect according to the tenor of it, with promptitude and good faith on the part of the Commander of the Forces, and to which no objection has been specified by the American Government, in any of their communications to His Excellency, since the conclusion of it, but which, on the contrary, must have been accepted, since it has been in part executed by that Gov-

ernment, that His Excellency, the Commander of the Forces, has been pleased thus publicly to absolve all the officers and others who have recently returned from the United States from a parole which His Excellency conceives to be inconsistent with the terms of that convention, and which he considers to have been exacted by persons ignorant of its existence, or misconceiving its conditions.

By His Excellency's Command,
Edward Baynes Adjt. General,
British North America.
Montreal, 10th April, 1814.

No. 1.

Colonel Baynes has communicated to His Excellency the Commander of the Forces the purport and extent of the alterations explained by Brigadier General Winder to exist, between the instructions of the 19th March addressed to him by the Secretary of State, and those of the 22nd of the same date received yesterday, and that the omission of the same in the first copy was owing to an error in transcribing it.

His Excellency, however, on reference to the letter of the Secretary of State of the 19th March, addressed to him, as it is stated, "with the view, and in the sincere desire to restore to the mildest practice of civilized nations the treatment of prisoners on both sides," and authorizing Brigadier General Winder, on the part of the United States Government, to conclude an arrangement which may embrace the exchange, as well of those held as hostages, as of other prisoners; and His Excellency learning from that officer that his instructions fully comported with the unqualified tenor of the proposal made in the Secretary of States' letter to him, did not hesitate a moment in acceding to the arrangements therein suggested, and was prepared to waive just grounds which he conceived he had of complaint against the Government of the United States, on the subject of the exchange of prisoners of War, in the hopes of promoting an arrangement so desirable for the cause of humanity and the honor of both nations; and he is much disappointed to find his hopes frustrated by the introduction, at this period of the negotiation, of a claim so totally inadmissible, that had the Secretary of State's letter borne the most distant allusion to it, His Excellency would have felt himself, as he now does, prohibited from proceeding any further on the subject.

The British view the confinement of twenty-three soldiers as the first act of aggression: for the undoubted right which every free nation pos-

surprised that this mode of incarcerating British officers should be realized, not at Verdun in France, but at Kentucky in the United States, the land of liberty." We find the names of thirty officers who were crowded into two small rooms, little larger than the common cells which were seven feet by four. Comment on this is unnecessary.

Before entering on the subject of the impression produced on the centre division, by the intelligence of the disaster which had overwhelmed the right, or northern, division, it will be advisable to conclude the operations which were now undertaken, under Generals Wilkinson and Hampton, in the Lower Province. We may, however, notice, that not-

---

sesses of investigating and punishing the crimes committed by her own natural born subjects, in a due course of law, is too self-evident to require a comment, nor can it, by any distortion of sense, or justice, be construed into a just ground for an act of fair retaliation exercised on twenty-three British Soldiers : the latter are characterized by their patriotism and loyalty, the former stigmatized for their treason and rebellion.

It would be wasting time to enter into any further discussion on this subject. Great Britain has successfully maintained her national right, unsullied for twenty years against the whole world combined ; it is not to be supposed that it is reserved for the United States to stop the course of justice, and to dictate to England what procedure she shall observe towards her own natural born subjects, in her own courts of civil judicature arrested in her own territorities in commission of acts of treason and rebellion.

It is to be remarked, that as the exchange of prisoners of War now proposed by the United States no longer has the general character that was at first proposed, but is specifically to restore quota for quota, it becomes on this ground, incumbent on the part of the British Government, to demand as a preleminary step, a detailed statement of about three thousand prisoners of war, of which the third were of the United States' regular service, captured in Canada during the first Campaign, and given up in good faith to the United States, who at that period, had no British prisoners.—and as all subsequent exchanges on the part of the United States have been acquitted by an equivalent number of prisoners simultaneously exchanged, it is insisted that the American Government is bound by honor and good faith to make full and complete satisfaction for the above debt, in conformity to the 14th article of the cartel, before she can in justice retain, or ask an equivalent for a single British prisoner now in her possession : and for this purpose returns will be prepared, not only of the number of prisoners remaining unexchanged in the possession of either power, but of those given up in good faith by the British Government to the United States, and for which no return has yet been made, or satisfaction offered ; and as it appears from the documents now transmited, that the United States are adding to the number of prisoners placed in restraint as Hostages, His Excellency is left no alternative, and is under the imperious necessity of ordering into close confinement, all the American officers remaining in his possession, not heretofore considered as Hostages.

If the instructions of the Secretary of State

leave to the discretion of Brigadier-General Winder no latitude on the subject of the twenty-three British soldiers considered by Great Britain as the sole just origin of the system of retaliation, the further prosecution of this negotiation, for an exchange of prisoners, must be unavailing, as His Excellency, although prepared to waive all minor considerations, as to meet the American Government on a fair and liberal basis, is at the same time unalterably firm in his determination not to compromise in the slightest degree, that principle of justice and equity upon which the measures of his Government have been framed.

On a former occasion, Colonel Baynes communicated to Major Melville that if the prisoners of war in Canada were not exchanged previous to the arrival of the transports expected early in the Spring, it would become a necessary measure to relieve the Canadas of that charge, and that they would be sent to England ; and on the opening of the river navigation, the prisoners now at Montreal will be sent to Quebec for that purpose.

(Signed)   EDWARD BAYNES,
Col., and Adjt. General.

No. 2.

Brigadier General Winder has received Colonel Baynes' note of this morning, and has read it with close and profound attention, not without considerable surprise and the deepest regret—surprise because it seems to have been expected that the discussions depending between Colonel Baynes and himself were in act to have settled and adjusted a principal question which will no doubt occupy the Congress at Gottenburg—regret because he fears that the beneficial consequences which would result from making exchanges, as far as was practicable under the powers held by General Winder, must be defeated by persisting in the views held out by the note of Colonel Baynes—exchanges which would restore to liberty so many brave and honorable men of both nations, who may otherwise linger out a tedious protracted confinement, finally to be terminated by an inglorious death, and which beside, would have left untouched in the fullest extent, the pretensions of Great Britain, on the question from whence the system of retaliation has arisen.

It appears to Brigadier General Winder, from the note of Colonel Baynes, that he considered an exchange made under the restriction in Brigadier General Winder's power, as an abandonment or compromising the principle in question by the British Government.—Surely, if this were the case, as according to Brigadier General Winder's conception it certainly is not, it would have been

withstanding the defeat sustained in the west, the British still retained undisturbed possession of Michilimacinac, and thereby preserved their influence, to a very material degree, over the Indian tribes in the west.

General Harrison contemplated the reduction of this post, but finding the season far advanced, and more important operations being contemplated, he postponed the movement, especially as he argued that the garrison of this post, cut off from all exterior resources, must necessarily fall. General Harrison seems, however, to have lost sight of the possibility of the garrison being supplied by way of York, or, though with more difficulty, by the Ottawa river. All his disposable forces were

---

an abandonment of it on the part of the American Government, if this restriction had not existed in the power, and would have been an extent of power which, it is confidently believed, His Excellency did not expect would be conferred on the occasion—nor indeed could it be supposed that a power to treat relative to the adjustment of this principle would have been conferred upon a person in the situation, and under the circumstances which Brigadier General Winder was when he received the power.

Brigadier General Winder further supposes that His Excellency had and can have, in the ordinary course of things, no power to settle and adjust this question unless by special delegation, and this if known to the Government of the United States, would have drawn from them a correspondent delegation of power with a view to its adjustment.

But the Government of the United States were aware that His Excellency possessed, as incidental to his military command, the power of making exchanges relative to the prisoners made from and by his command, which did not compromit the principle of the British Government on this point, and therefore had in view to delegate a corresponding power to Brigadier General Winder, as it is considered they have entirely done.

The Government of the United States conceived that a relinquishment of the twenty-three original hostages taken by them would be compromiting the principle on their part, and declined to give a power to this extent—they, on the contrary, do not ask a release of the twenty-three men sent to England, because that would be relinquishing it on the part of the British Government. The power to negotiate upon this question, it is presumed, has been delegated to the commissioners about to assemble at Gottenburg.

But General Winder is at a loss to perceive, that because he does not possess this power a negotiation is to stop, which could originally only have contemplated, and been expected to contemplate, the exchange, as far as could be done without broaching that question. And the letter of the Secretary of State to His Excellency, of the 19th March, and his contemporaneous instructions to Brigadier General Winder, while they look to the largest possible exchange, yet reserve, and express to do so, whole and entire, the right on this system of retaliation, and he most sincerely believes his propositions of yesterday's date entirely attain this object to both parties.

Brigadier General Winder, conscious it would be useless to submit any observation on the other parts of Colonel Baynes' note, as he believes them completely embraced in one of the propositions of his note of yesterday, entirely conformable to Colonel Baynes' wishes; and because, possessing no other powers or instructions than those already communicated, he supposes it more important, at the present moment, to obviate the objections to proceed in the negotiation, which he flatters himself the foregoing remarks will have a tendency to effect, and which unless he can effect, would be time uselessly spent, as no result could flow from it.

Brigadier General Winder submits these remarks in a spirit of unreserved candor and cordiality, and without the loss of a moment ;—and flatters himself, that, viewed by Colonel Baynes with the same spirit, they will be found entitled to strong and conclusive weight.

(Signed)   WM. WINDER,
           Brig. Gen. U. S. Army.

No. 3.
Montreal, April 11th, 1814.

Brigadier-general Winder has received Colonel Baynes's note of this morning, and has read it with the attention which the subject of it was calculate l to awaken, and however much he regrets that he is not able to accomplish all that he hoped and wished, yet he is gratified in believing, that much may be accomplished in strict conformity to the principles upon which his Excellency feels himself bound to act as detailed in Col. Baynes's note of to-day, and also entirely within the powers and instructions which Brigadier-general Winder has received and submitted from his Government. Colonel Baynes' note states, "that the confinement of the twenty-three American officers, and an equal number of non-commissioned officers, is considered as the first stage of retaliation, on the part of the British Government, and will be persevered in so long as the twenty-three soldiers, for which they are held as hostages, are kept in confinement, and cannot be affected by any exchange that does not emancipate the twenty-three British soldiers."

What Brig.-gen. Winder proposes, therefore, in entire conformity to this principle is, that the British officers put into confinement in retaliation for the confinement of the above forty-six American officers and non-commissioned officers shall be released and exchanged to such an extent as an equivalent value of American officers confined in retaliation for them, or who may be prisoners of war, other than the above forty-six, shall be released and exchanged.

Brigadier-General Winder, in his note of the 9th, made his proposition as extensive as he was

therefore moved from the head of Lake Erie to Buffalo, whence they were forwarded to the Niagara district, to join the expedition contemplated against the Lower Province, and in part to supply the detachments which had been already drafted from that district, and conveyed to Sackett's Harbor for the same purpose.

It had been the settled plan of the American Government from the commencement of the war, to make a decisive attack on the Lower Province. We gather this from the correspondence between the officers in command, and the bureau of war at Washington, and we shall proceed to show how this

American Policy.

---

allowed, but considered at the same time, that if, in its whole extent, it was not acceptable to his Excellency he would hold himself ready to embrace any modification of them, which might be more acceptable, and within Brigadier-general Winder's power.

This proposition appearing to Brigadier-general Winder to be so entirely within the principles contained in Col. Baynes' note, he feels the most sanguine assurance of its acceptance, and, without encumbering it with anything else, he hastens to submit it without delay.

(Signed)   WM. WINDER,
Brig. Gen. U. S. Army.

No. 4.

Head Quarters, Montreal,
Adjutant General's Office,
April 12th, 1814.

Colonel Baynes has to acknowledge Brigadier-general Winder's note of the 11th instant, and is commanded to acquaint him, that the commander of the forces consents to an exchange of hostages, and all others, prisoners of war in conformity to the scale of the cartel, under the previous stipulated conditions recited in his note, viz.—That the twenty-three British soldiers first confined as hostages, and the forty-six American officers and non-commissioned officers confined as hostages, in retaliation for the same, remain untouched and be not included in the present proposed exchange.

It appearing that the American Government assert to have placed seventy-seven British officers in confinement as hostages, and the right to retaliate in an equal number, being assumed by the commander of the forces, it would be necessary to place thirty-one American officers in similar restraint, in order to hold seventy-seven to restore in exchange; but to avoid the performance of so unpleasant a task, it is proposed that it be taken for granted that this further act of retaliation has been carried into effect, and that the number of hostages on both sides, being equal in number, amounting to seventy-seven, are declared released as hostages, and placed on the footing of ordinary prisoners of war, to be exchanged as such, in conformity to the cartel.

That this measure take place immediately in Quebec, and with the least possible delay in the United States and Halifax.

The exchange contemplated, is to include every individual held as a prisoner of war connected

with the army of British North America, commencing from the first act of hostilities on either side, excepting only twenty-three British soldiers, and the forty-six American officers and non-commissioned officers to be reserved as hostages; it being further stipulated that the last-mentioned forty-six will be placed on the footing of ordinary prisoners of war, and exchanged as such whenever the twenty-three British soldiers are so released or delivered over for exchange.

The details contained in Brigadier-general Winder's note of the 9th instant are accepted of, as forming the outline for a mutual arrangement for carrying the exchange into effect.

(Signed)   EDWARD BAYNES,
Adjutant-general, B.N.A.

No. 5.

Head Quarters, Montreal,
Adjutant General's Office,
April 12th, 1814.

Colonel Baynes has to acknowledge Brigadier-general Winder's note of the 11th instant, and is commanded to acquaint him, that the commander of the forces has no objection to the principle upon which his exchange is proposed by the Secretary of State as a preliminary measure to his entering upon the proposed negotiation, provided that the basis upon which that negotiation is to be conducted, is in its principle admissible, and holds out a fair and a reasonable prospect of producing the desired end.

His Excellency considered the proposal as stated in the Secretary of State's letter of 19th March as coming under that description, and the accompanying letter of instructions of the same date, comporting with the same, he did not hesitate to grant his consent to the proposed exchange of Brigadier-general Winder, as a proper preliminary measure; but a subsequent communication from the Secretary of the United States, being received by Brigadier-general Winder, and represented by him to have been introduced into the first instructions, alterations in themselves inadmissible in principle, and that the same had been omitted by error in transcribing the first copy, and were therefore to be considered as forming the text and spirit of the proposition. The commander of the forces considered himself absolved from his assent to a document which had, from the act of the proposing party, become a nullity; and thereby cancelling whatever might have emanated from it, and that he was at liberty

determination was carried out—the force employed, the fate which attended the attempt, and the causes which led to the entire failure of a scheme, deliberately planned, long cherished as one of the certain means of reducing the Canadas, and undertaken with every accompaniment of force, that it was in the power of the American Government to impart to it.

---

to revert to the alternative suggested in the Secretary of State's first letter, and reject the proposal *in toto*.

Colonel Baynes is directed to inform Brigadier General Winder, that it is not His Excellency's intention to sanction any partial exchange, except for the express purpose stated in the Secretary of State's letter, with which he thinks it highly expedient and proper to comply, but he must require from that officer a most direct and unequivocal assurance, that he is *authorized to treat and ratify, without further reservation, on the part of his government*, a negotiation on the principles stated in Colonel Baynes' note of the 11th and 12th, and in General Winder's note of the 11th instant—in which case his exchange will be declared full and complete.

Brigadier General Winder will excuse this demand which has become necessary from the doubts which he has himself created, as to the nature and extent of the restriction recently placed upon him by his government.

(Signed,)　　EDWARD BAYNES,
　　　　　　Adjt. Gen. B. N. A.

No. 6.

Montreal, April 13th, 1814.

Brigadier General Winder very much regrets that he should have failed in communicating to Colonel Baynes in the last interview, the extent of the powers communicated to him with requisite precision.

It was the intention of Brigadier General Winder to have stated, that his powers extended without restriction, to propose and agree to an exchange of all British Prisoners of War taken from the command of Sir George Prevost, except the twenty-three men put into confinement in retaliation for the twenty-three men sent to England, to which extent he now assures Colonel Baynes his powers extend, embracing all the subjects contained in Colonel Baynes' notes of the 11th and 12th, and Brigadier General Winder's of the 11th.

As it was not the intention of Brigadier General Winder that his Excellency should have the least

It had been decided that the attack should be made from two points, from the east under General Hampton, with perhaps, the most efficient division that had as yet taken the field during the war; and from the west, under the immediate direction of the commander-in-chief, General Wilkinson.

---

question as to the extent of his powers, he cannot but feel mortified, that an idea should have been entertained for a moment that he intended to render them in the least degree doubtful, and he trusts this avowal will remove all such impressions, and enable Colonel Baynes and himself, upon the adjustment of Brigadier General Winder's exchange, to proceed without delay to the arrangement.

(Signed,)　　WM. WINDER,
　　　　Brig. Gen., U. S. Army.

General Order, Adjutant General's Office,
　　　　　　Head Quarters, Montreal,
　　　　　　　　July 18th, 1814.

His Excellency the Commander of the Forces announces to the troops under his command, that having at the invitation of the American government, deputed Colonel Baynes, Adjutant General, and Lieutenant Colonel Brenton, Provincial Aide-de-camp, to meet on Thursday last at Champlain, Colonel Lear, late Consul General of the United States at Algiers—for the purpose of reconsidering the convention for the exchange of prisoners which had been entered into on the 15th of April last, between Colonel Baynes and Brigadier General Winder; and of removing whatever objections might be made to the due execution of it :—and the said meeting having taken place accordingly, all objections to the said convention were then, and there, completely removed ; and the same was, on the 16th instant, fully and definitively ratified by Colonel Lear, on the part of the United States ; (he having full power for that purpose) with a supplementary clause, by which the twenty-three British soldiers, and the forty-six American officers, the hostages mentioned in the first article of the said convention, are declared to be included in that convention, and are to be released and exchanged, in the same manner as other prisoners of War, mentioned in the same articles, notwithstanding the exception to them therein contained ;—and His Excellency is pleased hereby to direct that this General Order be considered in explanation and confirmation of the said General Orders issued on the 16th and 2nd July, 1814.

EDWARD BAYNES,
Adjt. Gen. N. A.

CHAPTER XVI.

We will follow the fortunes of the commander - in - chief, first, assigning due deference to his rank. The point selected for rendezvous was Grenadier Island, some eighteen miles distant from Sackett's Harbour; this point had been chosen for its contiguity to the St. Lawrence, and at this place, after various casualties, the expedition, amounting to some eight thousand eight hundred men, arrived by the 24th of October. Previous to the arrival of the troops the following correspondence had passed between General Wilkinson and Commodore Chauncey :—

The Expedition under Gen. Wilkinson.

"The main body of the division of the army at this point (Niagara) has sailed to join that at Sackett's Harbour, at the head of the St. Lawrence, with the design to reduce Kingston and Prescott, and to proceed thence to Montreal.

"The main body of the enemy's force is, in this vicinity, at the head of the lake and in York, leaving Kingston very weak.

"The enemy's squadron, beaten and forced to the head of the lake, is not in a situation to attempt the regaining of Kingston harbor,

while the American squadron keeps an eye upon it.

"Under these circumstances, will it be for the interest of the service, that the American squadron should accompany the flotilla with the troops, or shall it watch the British squadron, effect its destruction, and prevent the sudden transport of the division of the enemy by a rapid movement by water to reinforce Kingston ?

"It strikes me, that, in the first case, the enemy being apprised of our intention, by our movements, which cannot be concealed, may, with the aid of their squadron, reach Kingston before our troops are embodied and organized for the attack; and thus the reduction of the place may be spun out to the consumption of the season, and, of course, the main design must fail.

"In the second case, while the American squadron blocks up that of the enemy at the head of the lake, the flotilla will enjoy a free sea, and the British, by being cut off from transport by water, will be thrown back in their arrival at Kingston; long before which period the place must be taken, and our army landed on Montreal Island—no act of God intervening to thwart our intentions."
Fort George, Oct. 1st, 1813.

To this communication a prompt reply was made by Chauncey.

U. S. Ship Pike,
Off Niagara,
Oct. 1st, 1813.

"DEAR SIR,—The reasons you assign, in your memorandum, why the American squadron should remain in this vicinity, in preference to accompanying the flotilla down the lake, are so conclusive, and correspond so exactly

16

with my own ideas and wishes on the subject, that I have no other to offer. I will barely observe that my best exertions shall be used to keep the enemy in check in this part of the lake, or effect his destruction. Yet, with my utmost exertions and greatest vigilance, he may (when favoured by a strong westerly wind) slip past me in the night, and get eighteen or twenty hours start of me down the lake, before I can discover his movement. If that should be the case, I shall lose no time in following him, with so much celerity, as to prevent his interrupting you in your operations upon Kingston."

ISAAC CHAUNCEY.

The Secretary at War (General Armstrong's) observations so entirely coincide with our own view of the case that we are tempted to transcribe them, adopting them fully.

"That a project, giving to the fleet a false position; diverting it from the important duty of covering the descent of an entire division of the army from Fort George to Sackett's Harbor, and thereby directly exposing it to capture or destruction, should have met the high approbation and cordial welcome of the naval commanders, is a problem not easily solved."

Subsequent events confirm this opinion, as Sir James Yeo, who was not the man to allow himself to be confined in port, pushed boldly into the lake, and arrived at Kingston on the 7th. The most unfortunate part of the affair for the British was, that Sir James kept the northern side of the lake, and thus left the boats carrying the division (much dispersed and wholly defenceless) without molestation. Had he been compelled, by adverse winds, to beat down the lake, the probability is great that he must have fallen in with the flotilla, and in such a case the fate of the division would have been sealed.

It had been anticipated by the American commander that General De Rottenburg would have taken measures to reinforce Proctor, and provide for the defence of Malden, but instead of doing so, that general despatched nearly all his effective troops, under convoy of Sir James Yeo, to provide for Kingston.

Having thus brought the Americans to their place of rendezvous, and seen the British reinforcements arrive, in safety, at Kingston, we will accompany the American general-in-chief in the demonstrations, which followed, to his abandonment of the movement against Kingston.

Having only eight thousand men, and the British at Kingston now numbering nearly two thousand, it was deemed advisable to substitute Montreal for the point of attack, especially as Commodore Chauncey volunteered to watch both channels, so as to ensure a quiet sail, or pull, down the river to the flotilla. Unfortunately, however, the American commodore was as little competent to execute one undertaking as the other, and no sooner was the expedition consisting of three hundred large boats, exclusive of schooners, sloops, and twelve heavy gun boats, safely under weigh, than two brigs, two schooners and several gun boats were on the "qui vive" to annoy them. The first detention was at French's Creek, directly opposite the point, at which an army, destined for Kingston, might be supposed to land, here a halt of some five or six days occurred, during which time the flotilla and troops were much annoyed by the teazing British vessels from the bay opposite French Creek. On the 5th November, another start was effected, and a place called Hoag's, four miles below Morrisville, and about fifty from French Creek, was reached. At this point the water procession halted preparatory to passing Fort Wellington, distant six miles farther. The general here drew up, agreeably to established custom, a proclamation, addressed to the inhabitants of the country he was about to conquer. "For its brevity, no less than its moderation," says James, "it far surpasses anything of the sort hitherto promulgated by an American General.

"Proclamation of James Wilkinson, Major General and commander-in-chief of an expedition against the Canadas, to the inhabitants thereof:

"The army of the United States, which I have the honor to command, invaded the province to conquer, and not to destroy; to subdue the forces of his Britannic Majesty, not to war against unoffending subjects. Those, therefore, amongst you who remain quiet at home, should victory incline to the American standard, shall be protected in their persons and property; but those who are found in arms must necessarily be treated as avowed enemies.—To menace is unmanly.—

'To seduce, dishonorable—yet it is just and humane to place these alternatives before you."

On the 7th the powder, ammunition and all the troops, except enough to man the boats strongly, were landed, the boats with muffled oars, and keeping close to the Ogdensburg side, dropping down the river while the troops and ammunition proceeded by land to the Red Mill, fourteen miles below Ogdensburg. The expedition proceeded on the next day, slowly, after a skirmish between twelve hundred American troops, who had been ordered to land under Colonel Macomb, and a party of militia, who had assembled about Fort Matilda, for the purpose of annoying the troops in their passage down the river, which is here not more than five hundred yards wide.

On the 9th of November the flotilla arrived, in the afternoon, at Williamsburg, on the Canadian side. Here the troops already on shore, amounting to some twelve hundred men, were reinforced by General Brown's brigade, with a body of dragoons from the American side.

From this point a detachment, numbering some twenty-nine hundred or three thousand men, was despatched to drive the British troops from the shore, along which they were to march to Barnhartz's, a distance of about twenty miles. A double object was to be effected by this movement, as the boats would be thereby lightened, in their long and perilous descent of the violent rapid called the Long Sault, and would, at the same time, be freed from any annoyance from an enemy on shore. This body proceeded along the banks a few miles, when they unexpectedly found themselves brought to a stand at a place called Chrysler's farm. The impediment in their way was a body of troops who were prepared to dispute the undisturbed march of the Americans.

"Hitherto," says James, "the battles between the British and American troops had been chiefly bush fighting skirmishes. Now they met in an open champaign, where there was no shelter for the American riflemen, no rests for their pieces. All was conducted, as General Wilkinson says, in open space and fair combat."

The best account we can give of the en-gagement, will be found in the respective bulletins of the commanding officers.

From Lieutenant Colonel Morrison to Major General De Rottenburg.

Chrysler's, Williamsburg, Upper Canada, November 12th, 1813.

SIR,—I have the heartfelt gratification to report the brilliant and gallant conduct of the detachment from the centre division of the army, as yesterday displayed in repulsing and defeating a division of the enemy's force, consisting of two brigades of infantry and a regiment of cavalry, amounting to between three and four thousand men, who moved forward, about two o'clock in the afternoon, from Chrysler's point, and attacked our advance, which gradually fell back to the position selected for the detachment to occupy; the right resting on the river, and the left on a pine wood, exhibiting a front of about seven hundred yards. The ground being open, the troops were thus disposed: the flank companies of the 49th regiment, the detachment of the Canadian fencibles, with one field piece, under Lieutenant Colonel Pearson, on the right, a little advanced on the road; three companies of the 89th regiment, under Captain Barnes, with a gun, formed in echellon, with the advance on its left supporting it. The 49th and 89th, thrown more to the rear, with a gun, formed the main body and reserve, extending to the woods on the left, which were occupied by the voltigeurs, under Major Herriot, and the Indians under Lieutenant Anderson. At about half past two the action became general, when the enemy endeavored, by moving forward a brigade from his right, to turn our left, but was repulsed by the 89th, forming *en potence* with the 49th, and both corps moving forward, occasionally firing by platoons. His efforts were next directed against our right, and to repulse this movement the 49th took ground in that direction in echellon, followed by the 89th; when within half musket shot the line was formed, under a heavy but irregular fire from the enemy. The 49th was then directed to charge the gun posted opposite to ours; but it became necessary, when within a short distance of it, to check the forward movement, in consequence of a charge from their cavalry on the right, lest they should wheel about, and fall upon their rear; but they were received in so-gallant a manner by the companies of the 89th, under Captain Barnes, and the well-directed fire of the artillery, that they quickly retreated, and by an immediate charge from those companies one gun was gained. The enemy immediately concentrated their force to check our advance, but such was the steady countenance, and well-directed fire of the troops and artillery, that at about half-past four they gave way at all points from an exceeding strong position, endeavoring by their light infantry to cover their retreat, who were soon driven away by a judicious movement made by Lieutenant Colonel Pearson. The detachment for the night occupied the ground from which the enemy had been driven, and are now moving in pursuit.

I regret to find our loss in killed and wounded has been so considerable; but trust a most essential service has been rendered to the country, as the whole of the enemy's infantry, after the action, precipitately retired to their own shores. It is now my grateful duty to point out to your honor the benefit the service has received from the ability, judgment, and active exertions of Lieutenant Colonel Harvey, the deputy-adjutant general, for sparing whom to accompany the detachment, I must again publicly express my acknowledgments. To the cordial co-operation and exertions of Lieutenant Colonel Pearson, commanding the detachment from Prescott, Lieutenant Colonel Plenderleath, of the 49th, Major Clifford, of the 89th, Major Herriott, of the voltigeurs, and Captain Jackson of the royal artillery, combined with the gallantry of the troops, our great success may be attributed. Every man did his duty, and I believe I cannot more strongly speak their merits than in mentioning, that our small force did not exceed eight hundred rank and file. To Captains Davis and Skinner, of the quarter-master-general's department, I am under the greatest obligations for the assistance I have received from them; their zeal and activity has been unremitting. Lieutenant Hagerman, of the militia, has also, for his services, deserved my public acknowledgements, as has also Lieutenant Anderson, of the Indian department. As the prisoners are hourly bringing in, I am unable to furnish your honor with a correct return of them, but upwards of one hundred are in our possession; neither can I

give an account of the ordnance stores taken, as the whole have not yet been collected.

I have the honor to be, &c.

J. W. MORRISON,
Lieut. Col. 89th, commanding
corps of observation.

Total of killed and wounded—one captain, two drummers, nineteen rank and file, killed; one captain, nine subalterns, six serjeants, one hundred and thirty-one rank and file, wounded; twelve rank and file, missing.

Col. Morrison does not mention the number of troops under his command at Chrysler's farm, but James places them at "eight hundred rank and file, besides Lieutenant Anderson and about thirty Indians, who had accompanied the detachment from Kingston."

The numbers engaged at Chrysler's Farm.

This number General Wilkinson has continued to swell in his official letters* from six-

---

From major-general Wilkinson to the American secretary at war.

HEAD-QUARTERS, FRENCH MILLS,
Adjoining the Province of Lower Canada,
16th November, 1813.

SIR,—I beg leave to refer you to the journal which accompanies this letter, for the particulars of the movements of the corps under my command, down to the St. Lawrence, and will endeavour to exert my unfeeble mind to detail to you the more striking and important incidents which have ensued since my departure from Grenadier Island, at the foot of Lake Ontario, on the 3rd instant.

The corps of the enemy which followed me from Kingston, being on my rear, and in concert with a heavy galley and a few gun-boats, seemed determined to retard my progress. I was tempted to halt, turn about, and put an end to his teasing: but alas! I was confined to my bed. Major-general Lewis was too ill for any active exertions; and above all, I did not dare to suffer myself to be diverted a single day from the prosecution of the views of government. I had written major-general Hampton on the 6th inst., by adjutant-general colonel King, and had ordered him to form a junction with me on the St. Lawrence, which I expected would take place on the 9th or 10th. It would have been unpardonable, had I lost sight of this object an instant. I deemed it of vital importance to the issue of the campaign.

The enemy deserves credit for their zeal and intelligence, which the active universal hostility of the male inhabitants of the country enabled them to employ to the greatest advantage. Thus, while menaced by a respectable force in the rear, the coast was lined with musketry in front, and at every critical part of the river, which obliged me to march a detachment, and this impeded my progress.

teen hundred to two thousand, and not
satisfied even with this amplification, in a
note to his memoirs, written long subsequently, the American General actually ventured to state that, "the enemy showed
twenty five hundred men in battalion, on the
11th, and this force was beaten back, by
seventeen hundred of *undisciplined* troops,
upon a reserve of seven hundred men, making
the whole strength of the enemy thirty-two
hundred men."

To disprove this is easy, and if we take Col.
Walbacks evidence, (who was in the action,
and swore, at the general's court martial,
"That he had a fair view of the enemy, and
and that he supposed the whole, regulars,
militia, and indians to have been between
eleven and twelve hundred men") and compare

it with the testimony of Major-generals Lewis,
Boyd, Covington, and Swartwout, who concurred in opinion "that the British force
amounted to about five hundred," James,
statement may be considered as very nearly
correct. By adding as much to the numbers
given by the four generals, as we deduct from
Walback's, we arrive at James' numbers. This
may fairly be done, as at the Court Martial
one party was doing his best to support
general Wilkinson, while the others were,
perhaps, influenced by opposite feelings.

Having settled this point, we will in turn,
attempt to fix the numbers of Americans.

It has been truly said that—

"A tangled web we weave,
When first we practice to deceive."

and this is literally the case with General

On the evening of the 9th, the army halted a
few miles from the head of Longue Sault. On the
morning of the 10th the enclosed order was issued. General Browne marched, agreeably to
order, and at noon we were apprised, by the reports of his artillery, that he was engaged some
distance below us. At the same time the enemy
were observed in our rear, and their galley and
gun-boats approached our flotilla, and opened a
fire upon us, which obliged me to order a battery
of 18-pounders to be planted, and a shot from it
compelled the enemy's vessels to retire, together
with their troops, after some firing between the
advanced parties. By this time, in consequence
of his disembarking and re-embarking the heavy
guns, the day was so far spent, that our pilots
did not dare to enter the Sault (eight miles a continued rapid), and therefore we fell down about
two miles, and came to anchor for the night.

Early the next morning everything was in readiness for motion ; but having received no intelligence from General Brown, I was still delayed,
as sound precaution required I should learn the
result of his affair, before I committed the flotilla
to the Sault.

At half-past ten A.M., an officer of dragoons
arrived with a letter, in which the General informed me he had forced the enemy, and would
reach the foot of the Sault early in the day. Orders were immediately given for the flotilla to
sail, at which instant the enemy's gun-boats appeared, and began to throw shot among us. Information was at the same time brought me from
Brigadier-general Boyd, that the enemy's troops
were advancing in column. I immediately gave
orders to him to attend them. This report was
soon contradicted. Their gun-boats, however,
continued to scratch us, and a variety of reports
of their movements and counter-movements were
brought to me in succession, which convinced me
of their determination to hazard an attack, when
it could be done to the greatest advantage; and
I therefore resolved to anticipate them. Directions were accordingly sent by that distinguished
officer, Colonel Swift of the engineers, to Brigad-

ier-gen. Boyd, to throw down the detachments of
his command, assigned to him in the order of the
preceding day, and composed of men of his own,
Covington's and Swartwout's brigades, into three
columns, to march upon the enemy, outflank
them if possible, and take their artillery.

The action soon after commenced with the
advanced body of the enemy, and became extremely sharp and galling; and lasted, with occasional pauses, not sustained with great vivacity,
in open space, and fair combat, for upwards of
two hours and a half, the adverse lines alternately
yielding and advancing. It is impossible to say
with accuracy what was our number on the field,
because it consisted of indefinite detachments,
taken from the boats, to render safe the passage
of the Sault.

General Covington and Swartwout voluntarily
took part in the action, at the head of the detachments from their respective brigades, and
exhibited the same courage that was displayed by
Brigadier-general Boyd, who happened to be
the senior officer on the ground. Our force engaged might have reached 1600 or 1700 men,
but actually did not exceed 1800. That of the
enemy was estimated from 1200 to 2000, but did
not probably amount to more than 1500 or 1600 ;
consisting as I am informed, of detachments from
the 49th, 84th, and 104th regiments of the line,
with three companies of the voltigeur and Glengary corps, and the militia of the country, who
are not included in the estimate.

It would be presumptuous in me to attempt to
give you a detailed account of this affair, which
certainly reflects high honor on the valor of the
American soldiers, as no example can be produced of undisciplined men, with inexperienced
officers, braving a fire of two hours and a half,
without quitting the field; or yielding to their antagonists. But, sir, the information I now give
you is derived from officers in my confidence,
who took active parts in the conflict; for, although I was enabled to order the attack, it was
my hard fortune not to be able to lead the troops
I commanded.

Wilkinson. In his first letter that officer declares that "General Boyd's force did not exceed eighteen hundred men." In his second letter, the General discovers and corrects an omission of six hundred men under Lieut. Colonel Upham. In a note to the General's book we meet with the new assertion, " *The force under General Boyd, which engaged the enemy at Chrysler's,* WAS SUPERIOR TO HIM ;" in this case Boyd's force must have *exceeded* thirty-two hundred men. We leave it to the reader to judge and reconcile the conflicting assertions.

From Wilkinson's own notes, we may safely place the numbers of the Americans at twenty-nine hundred men, acting under General Boyd and as assistants to the crews of the flotilla, in navigating the rapids; and making the most liberal allowance for this head, we have still left an American force thrice as great as that of the British, at Chrysler's.

On the evening of the day of battle, the Americans retired to their boats and embarked, proceeding to Barnhartz, near Cornwall, not as had been their intention by a land march, but in crowded boats, exposed to the annoying fire of their pursuers both by land and water.

Leaving, for a short space Gen. Wilkinson, we will follow the fortunes of Gen. Hampton, whom we left, organising an attack, from the eastward, with, as we have previously stated, perhaps the most efficient division that had as yet taken the field during the war. As to numbers we have the authority of the Washington organ, which states that at Burlington " were then collected five thousand regulars, under Major-General Hampton. Two thousand more were on their march and immediately expected from the Eastern States, and several smaller bodies were pushing to that post from other quarters."

Allowing that all these troops, either did not arrive in time, or were not required by the American General, we have still in his

General Hampton's movements—his force.

The disease with which I was assailed on the 2nd of September, on my journey to Fort-George, having, with a few short intervals of convalescence, preyed on me ever since ; at the moment of this action I was confined to my bed, unable to sit on a horse, or to move ten paces without assistance. I must, however, be pardoned for trespassing on your time by a few remarks in relation to this affair. The objects of the British and American commanders were precisely opposed, the first being bound by the instructions of his government, and the most solemn obligations of duty, to precipitate his descent of the St. Lawrence by every practicable means, because this being effected, one of the greatest difficulties opposed to the American army would be surmounted ; and the former by duties equally imperious, to retard it, and if possible to prevent such a descent. He is to be accounted victorious who effected this purpose. The British commander having failed to gain either of the objects, can lay no claims to the honors of the day. The battle fluctuated, and the victory seemed at different times inclined to the contending corps. The front of the enemy was at first forced back more than a mile, and though they never regained the ground they lost, their stand was permanent, and their charges resolute. Amidst these charges, and near the close of the contest, we lost a field-piece by the fall of the officer who was serving it with the same coolness as if he had been at parade, or at a review. This was lieutenant Smith, of the light artillery, who in point of merit stood conspicuous. The enemy having halted, and our troops having again formed in battalia, front to front, and the fire having ceased on both sides, we resumed our position on the bank of the river, and the infantry being much fatigued, the whole were re-imbarked, and proceeded down the river without further annoyance from the enemy or their gun boats, while the dragoons with five pieces of light artillery marched down the Canada shore without molestation.

It is due to his rank, merit, and services, that I should make particular mention of brigadier-general Covington, who received a mortal wound directly through his body, while animating his men, and leading them to the charge. He fell where he fought, at the head of his men, and survived but two days.

The next day the flotilla passed through the Sault, and joined that excellent officer, brigadier-gen. Brown, at Barnhartz, near Cornwall, where he had been instructed to take post and wait my arrival, and where I confidently expected to hear of major-general Hampton's arrival on the opposite shore.

But immediately after I had halted, col. Atkinson, inspector-general of the division under major-general Hampton, waited on me with a letter from that officer, in which, to my unspeakable mortification and surprise, he declined the junction ordered—and informed me he was marching to Lake Champlain, by way of co-operation in the proposed attack upon Montreal. This letter, together with a copy of that to which it is in answer, were immediately submitted to a council of war, composed of many general officers, and the colonel commanding the elite, the chief engineer and adjutant-general, who immediately gave it as their opinion, that the attack on Montreal should be abandoned for the present season, and the army near Cornwall be immediately crossed to the American shore, for taking up winter quarters, and that this place afforded an eligible position for such quarters. I acquiesced in this

letter, to the Secretary of War, of the 12th October, very satisfactory proofs not only as to numbers, but also as to efficiency.

" Four 'thousand *effective* infantry, and a well appointed train of artillery, ought to inspire you with some reliance upon our army."

Here is evidence to substantiate our assertion, and be it remarked that there is no proof that the expected reinforcements did not arrive, as General Hampton speaks only of effective infantry, and would not be likely to include the raw levies which were pouring in on him in the category of effectives. Neither is mention made of cavalry, although a force without which American movements were seldom attempted.

On the 22nd October, General Hampton reached the junction of the Outarde and Chateauguay rivers. Here Col. De Salaberry was prepared to check their further advance with literally a handful of Canadians, and most judiciously does he seem to have posted himself. According to Christie, " In his rear there was a small rapid, where the river was fordable ; this he covered with a strong breastwork and a guard, keeping at the same time a strong picquet of the Beauharnois militia,

in advance on the right bank of the river, lest the enemy approaching under cover of the forest, might cross the ford and dislodge him from his ground."

Hampton, perceiving the importance of forcing this position, ordered Colonel Purdy on the night of the 25th, with a strong body to fall on De Salaberry's rear, while he attacked him in front with the main body. Fortunately Purdy got bewildered in the woods, and did not gain the point of attack as desired. In the morning General Hampton, with from three thousand five hundred to four thousand men under General Izard, advanced, expecting every hour to see the effects of Purdy's attack from the rear. This advance was gallantly met by De Salaberry, and checked the American skirmishers retreating on the main body. This retreat was mistaken for a flight and the advancing body wavered, De Salaberry remarking that, from numbers he must be speedily outflanked, resorted to a ruse which proved completely successful. He ordered the buglers placed at intervals to sound an advance, which

---

opinion, not from the shortness of the stock of provisions, (which had been reduced by the acts of God,) because our meat had been increased five days, and our bread had been reduced only two days ; and because we could, in case of extremity, have lived on the enemy, but because the loss of the division under major-general Hampton weakened my force too sensibly to justify the attempt.

In all my measures and movements of consequence, I have taken the opinion of my general officers, which have been accordant with my own.

I remained on the Canadian shore till the next day, without seeing or hearing from the powerful force of the enemy in our neighbourhood, and the same day reached this position with the artillery and infantry.

The dragoons have been ordered to Utica and its vicinity, and I expect are 50 or 60 miles on the march. You have, under cover, a summary abstract of the killed and wounded in the affair of the 11th instant, which will soon be followed by a particular return ; in which, a first regard will be paid to individual merit. The dead rest in honor, and the wounded bleed for their country, and deserve its gratitude, With respect,

I have the honor to be, sir,
Your obedient servant,
JAS. WILKINSON.

Here follows a statement of the killed and wounded;—*Killed.* 102.— *Wounded*, 236.

Hon. J. Armstrong, &c. &c. &c.

From general Wilkinson to the American secretary at war.

Head-quarters, French Mills, Nov. 18, 1813.

SIR,—I beg this may be considered as an appendage to my official communication respecting the action of the 11th instant.

I last evening received the enclosed information, the result of the examination of sundry prisoners taken on the field of battle, which justifies the opinion of the general officers who were in the engagement. This goes to prove that, although the imperious obligations of duty did not allow me sufficient time to rout the enemy, they were beaten ; the accidental loss of one field-piece notwithstanding, after it had been discharged 15 or 20 times. I have also learned, from what has been considered good authority, but I will not vouch for the correctness of it, that the enemy's loss exceeded 500 killed and wounded.

The enclosed report will correct an error in my former communication, as it appears it was the 89th, and not the 84th, British regiment, which was engaged on the 11th I beg leave to mention, in the action of the 11th, what, from my severe indisposition, I have omitted.

Having received information, late in the day, that the contest had become somewhat dubious, I ordered up a reserve of 500 men, whom I had ordered to stand by their arms, under lieutenant-col. Upham, who gallantly led them into action, which terminated a few minutes after their arrival on the ground. With great consideration and respect, I have the honor to be, &c.

JAMES WILKINSON.

Hon. John Armstrong, secretary at war.

had the effect of checking the ardor of the enemy, and, just at this moment, a company of the Provincial militia, hitherto concealed, opened an unexpected fire on the main body. This almost flank fire, and the extended line along which the bugles appeared to sound, possessed General Hampton and his army with the idea that a powerful body was in front and on the flanks, and the Americans were thrown into the utmost disorder, and a tumultuous and precipitate retreat ensued—leaving Col. DeSalaberry, with scarcely three hundred Canadians, master of the field. About the close of the affair Sir George Prevost and General DeWatteville arrived on the ground.

Even Ingersol is compelled to remark respecting this affair, "Encomium on the prowess of Col. De Salaberry and his Canadian countrymen is probably well founded. It is true that a few hundred of them worsted an army of between four and five thousand American regulars, when General Hampton had been for some time assiduously preparing for active service, and the bubble of Canadian conquest burst and evaporated, if not forever, at any rate for that war."

A more detailed account will be found in the following general order of October 27th:

HEAD-QUARTERS,
A Fourche, on Chateauguay river.
Oct. 27th, 1813.

GENERAL ORDERS.—His excellency the governor-in-chief and commander of the forces has received from major-general De Watteville, the report of the affair which took place at the advanced position of his post, at 11 o'clock on Tuesday morning, between the American army under the command of major-general Hampton, and the advanced pickets of the British thrown out for the purpose of covering working parties, under the direction of lieut. col. De Salaberry; the judicious position chosen by that officer, and the excellent disposition of his little band, composed of the light infantry of Canadian fencibles, and two companies of Canadian voltigeurs, repulsed with loss the advance of the enemy's principal column commanded by gen. Hampton in person; and the American light brigade under col. M'Carty, was in a like manner checked in its progress on the south side of the river, by the gallant and spirited advance of the flank company 3d battalion embodied militia,

under captain Daly, supported by captain Bruyers' company of Sedentary militia. Captains Daly and Bruyers being both wounded, and their companies having sustained some loss, their position was immediately taken up by a flank company of the first battalion embodied militia. The enemy rallied and repeatedly returned to the attack, which terminated only with the day in his complete disgrace and defeat, being foiled by a handful of men not amounting to a *twentieth* part of the force opposed to them; but which, nevertheless, by their determined bravery maintained their position, and effectually protected the working parties, who continued their labors unmolested. Liet. col. De Salaberry reports having experienced the most able support from captain Ferguson, in command of the light company Canadian Fencibles, and also from captain Jean Bapt. Duchesnay, of the two companies of Voltigeurs; from captain Lamoote and adjutants Hebden and O'Sullivan, and from every officer and soldier engaged, whose gallantry and steadiness were conspicuous and praiseworthy in the highest degree.

His excellency, the governor-in-chief and commander of the forces, having had the satisfaction of himself witnessing the conduct of the troops on this brilliant occasion, feels it a gratifying duty to render them that praise which is so justly their due; to major-general De Watteville for the admirable arrangement established by him for the defence of his post; to lieut. col. De Salaberry, for his judicious and officerlike conduct displayed in the choice of position and arrangement of his force; to the officers and men engaged with the enemy the warmest acknowledgments of his Excellency are due, for their gallantry and steadiness, and to all the troops at the station the highest praise belongs, for their zeal, steadiness, and discipline, and for the patient endurance of hardship and privation which they have evinced. A determined perseverance in this honorable conduct cannot fail of crowning the brave and loyal Canadians with victory, and hurling disgrace and confusion on the head of the enemy that would pollute their happy soil.

By the report of prisoners, the enemy's force is stated at 7,500 infantry, 400 cavalry, and ten field pieces. The British advanced force actually engaged, did not exceed *three hundred*. The enemy suffered severely from our fire, as well as from their own; some detached corps having fired upon each other by mistake in the woods.

Canadian light company had 3 rank and file killed--1 sergeant, 3 rank and file wounded.

Voltigeurs, 4 rank and file wounded.

Third battalion, flank company, 1 captain wounded—2 rank and file killed, 6 wounded, and four missing.

Chateauguay Chasseurs, 1 captain wounded.

Total—5 rank and file killed—2 captains, 1 sergeant, 13 rank and file wounded, and 4 missing.

Officers wounded—captain Daly, 3d embodied militia, twice wounded severely, but not dangerously. Captain Bruyers, Chateauguay chasseurs, slightly.

(Signed)   EDWARD BAYNES, adj. gen.

After his repulse at Chateauguay, General Hampton retreats. Hampton retreated to his late position; and, on assembling a council of war, it was determined to fall back on their former position at Four Corners, so as to keep open the communication with the United States, and, at the same time, be in readiness, if possible, to renew an attack on the enemy. The retreat was much impeded and harrassed by the Canadian militia,* who hung on their rear; and, indeed, so great had been the fatigues and privations experienced by the Eastern division, from constant attacks and the inclemency of the season, that General Hampton, deeming farther co-operation with General Wilkinson impossible, shortly after fell back upon Plattsburg, and retired to winter quarters.

We will now return to General Wilkinson, whom we left, near Cornwall, awaiting the arrival of General Hampton.

Wilkinson retires to winter quarters. General Wilkinson was not kept very long in suspense, as on the 12th November, a letter from Hampton made its appearance, "*blasting*," according to the commander-in-chief," all his

hopes, and destroying every prospect of the campaign." A council of war was called on the receipt of this communication, and it was determined that "the conduct of Major General Hampton, in refusing to join his division to the troops descending the St. Lawrence (to carry an attack on Montreal,) rendered it expedient to move the army to French Mills, on Salmon river."

This determination was carried into effect on the 13th.

General order. The retreat of the two American generals, with their forces, having removed every appearance of danger, the commander of the forces, by a general order of the 17th November, dismissed the Sedentary Militia, with due acknowledgements of the loyalty and zeal which they had manifested.*

The failure of an invasion planned on so great a scale was with difficulty apologised for by the public journals in the pay of government; but the Boston Gazette, not having a share of government patronage, was enabled to speak out boldly; and we transcribe an extract from that journal:—

"Every hour is fraught with doleful tidings—humanity groans from the frontiers. Hampton's army is reduced to about two thousand, Wilkinson's cut up and famishing; crimination and recrimination are the order of the day. Democracy has rolled herself up in weeds, and laid down for its last wallowing in the slough of disgrace. Armstrong the cold-

---

* Sir George Prevost, in his official despatch on this occasion, solicited from the Prince Regent, as a mark of his gracious approbation of the embodied battalions of the Canadian militia, five pairs of colors, for the 1st, 2nd, 3rd, 4th, and 5th battalions, which was accordingly granted.

* "Head Quarters, Lachine,
       November 17th, 1813.

"General Order.—The divisions of sedentary militia called out by the general order of the 8th instant, are to be disbanded and to return to their respective homes, in the following order.

"His excellency the governor in chief and commander of the forces, in dispensing, for the present, with the further services of the militia, feels the greatest satisfaction in acknowledging the cheerful alacrity with which they have repaired to their respective posts, and the loyalty and zeal they have manifested at the prospect of encountering the enemy—although he has been checked in his career by the bravery and discipline of his Majesty's troops in the Upper Province, and thus frustrated in his avowed intention of landing on this island, his excellency feels confident that had he been enabled to reach it, whatever might have been his force, he would have met with that steady and determined resistance from the militia of the province, which would have terminated his third attempt for its invasion, like those which preceded it, in defeat and disgrace.

blooded director of all the military anarchy, is chopfallen."

The Boston Gazette was not the only plain spoken journal in this respect. Similar ridicule assailed government from all parts of the north and east, and announced that "complete ruin from Champlain to Erie,† marked the retrograde of American arms, closing the year 1813 with a destructive invasion."

It will be now interesting to inquire into the causes of the failure, and to ascertain how far it was attributable to the gallantry of the defenders, and in what degree to be ascribed to the disputes or imbecility of the American generals.

It appears as if an overruling Providence had ordained that, by means of inefficient leaders, the expeditions, from which the greatest results were expected, should be precisely those to be frustrated and covered with ignominy and shame. Hull, Dearborn, and Smyth have alike been found the most energetic of leaders in their proclamations, but just the reverse in the hour of action, and so it was in the present instance. The American government committed the fatal mistake of entrusting the command of the most important expedition ever sent forth since the formation of the Republic, to two generals most heartily

Causes of the failure of the expeditions.

jealous of each other, and political enemies; the Secretary at War being at the same time, if we are to judge by his writing, an opponent of the commander-in-chief of the expedition. The result of this we have seen.

The failure is to be ascribed to two causes. General Wilkinson's incompetence, and Hampton's anxiety to secure to himself the honors of the expedition.

Of the first we have the most abundant evidence furnished at the court martial held on General Wilkinson.

The testimony of Mr. Thime on that trial prove these facts.

"1st. That the General began his expedition without knowing whether he carried with his army of eight thousand men, subsistence sufficient for five days or for fifty.

"2ndly. That his attention to this important subject was first awakened at Grenadier Island, in consequence of the supposed effect of a storm on the provision boats.

"3rdly. That, although apprised that the loss was great, he adopted no measures to remedy that disaster."

Nor was this all that was proved. In the General's diary it is stated that, on the 7th of November, having passed all the preceding night in the open air, he was

---

" The Montreal Volunteers, to march from Lachine, at 10 o'clock to-morrow morning, to Montreal.

" The 1st batt. of Montreal militia, at 8 o'clock on Friday morning.

" The 2d batt. at 10 o'clock, and the 3d batt., at 12 o'clock, on the same day.

" The above corps are to remain embodied until the 24th instant, on which day a corps of the line will relieve them.

" On the 20th instant, colonel McGill will allow the whole of the men belonging to the second class of sedentary militia to return to their respective homes—Upon proper certificates being produced to the commissariat of Montreal, each captain or commanding officer of a company of sedentary militia is to receive for every private man, returning home, at the rate of 1s. 3d. currency, and non-commissioned officers in that proportion, for every five leagues that they have to travel—this allowance is, for that period, in lieu of pay and rations.

" Colonel La Croix's division, now at Lower Lachine, is to march from thence on the 20th instant, so as to arrive on the Champ de Mars,

† In allusion to the British descent on the Niagara frontier.

at Montreal, by 10 o'clock in the morning of that day, for the purpose of piling their arms, and returning in store their accoutrements, ammunition, blankets, haversacks, and canteens.

" Lieut. col. M'Kenzie's battalion will march from its present quarters so as to arrive on the Champ de Mars, at 12 o'clock the same day,—and lieut. col. Leprohon's at 2 o'clock.

" Lieut. col. Cuthbert's is to arrive on the Champ de Mars, at 10 o'clock on the 21st inst.—The battalion placed under the command of lieut. col. Boucherville will leave the ground it at present occupies on the 12th, and proceed to Montreal on its route to Three Rivers.—The one confided to the command of lieut. col. Deschambault will commence falling back to Montreal on the 23d instant.—The remaining battalions of the sedentary militia are to commence their march for their respective parishes on the 23d.

" The quarter-master general of the forces will make the necessary arrangements for relieving captain Platt's troop of Volunteer Cavalry from its present duty, on or before the 24th instant when it is to return to Montreal for the purpose of being disarmed until further orders.

" By his excellency's command,
                    EDWARD BAYNES,
                        Adjt.-general."

in consequence thereof much indisposed. The statements which follow will show to what cause the General's indisposition was really to be ascribed.

"On or about the 6th of November, 1813, (the night the American troops passed Ogdensburgh and Prescott,) having received orders to muffle the oars, and leave men enough barely sufficient to man the boats, we marched the remainder by land below Ogdensburgh. When we arrived, as we thought, near the place where we were to meet the boats, (say a mile below Ogdensburgh,) we halted at a small house near the river (D. Thorp's); and while there, discovered a boat approaching the shore. Major Forsyth hailed the crew, and on explanation was informed it was General Wilkinson's boat. The Major, myself, and others, met the General at the water's edge, and asked if he wished to come on shore. Indicating that he did, Forsyth and myself took him by the arms to assist him out of the boat, and up the bank. We found him most abominably intoxicated, and hurried him into the house; during which time, he was muttering the most desperate imprecations against the enemy—saying, that if they did not cease firing, he would blow to dust the whole British garrison, and lay waste their country. After seating him on a chair near the fire, the major and myself retired to consult what was best to be done, under the present situation of the commander-in-chief; when we concluded to detail and post a guard near the door of the house, to keep out both citizens and soldiers. I made the detail and posted the sentinel, and soon afterward perceiving the General to nod, and apprehending that he would fall into the fire, I proposed laying him on something like a bedstead that was in the room, and having done so, he was, in a very short time, in a sound sleep. The time to the best of my recollection, at which we received the General, was about two o'clock in the morning. For some time after this occurrence, he was not very accessible; it was said that he was in bad health."

The above is a statement made by Major Birdsall.

"Owin Chatfield deposeth and saith, that, on the night the American army passed Prescott, this deponent went to the house of Daniel Thorp. This deponent farther saith, that

General James Wilkinson was there, and in a state of intoxication; and that his deportment, and obscene and vulgar conversation, but too plainly manifested his being in that situation. This deponent farther saith, that the General sung several obscene and vulgar songs; and farther saith not.

(Signed)   Owin Chatfield.

Sworn before me at the village of Ogdensburgh, this 17th of July, 1835.

John Scott,
Justice of the Peace, &c.

"Daniel Thorp deposeth and saith, that he lives about a mile below the village of Ogdensburgh, and that, on the night the American army passed Prescott, General James Wilkinson came to the house of deponent in a state of intoxication, as deponent verily believed at the time, and which he still believes; and that soon after his arrival at deponent's house, the General was put to bed. This deponent farther saith, that the General remained at his house several hours, and that, during his stay there, his behaviour was very unlike a gentleman, and his conversation very vulgar and obscene.

(Signed)   Daniel Thorp.

Sworn before me, this 18th of July, 1819.

John Scott,
Justice of the Peace, &c."

Were this proof not sufficient, there is that of General Boyd, who deposed at the trial "that he sought an interview with the general commanding, for the purpose of reporting the occurrences of the day, and receiving such new orders as they might suggest, and found an aide-de-camp at the door instructed to announce that the chief of the army was not in a condition, to receive visits, give orders, or even listen to a reporting officer, just returned from a field of battle."

The opinion the reader must have formed of the General's capability for command after these extracts, will enable him to arrive at a very sufficient conclusion as to the main cause of the failure. We have, however, a farther cause—the gallantry of the men "who," according to Ingersol, "in brigs, schooners, gun boats and gallies, led by the gallant Captain Mulcaster, gave our craft no repose or respite from attack." This, too, although Chauncey had boasted that he was to destroy Sir James Yeo's squadron, and *ensure a safe passage for the flotilla down the river.* So much for Chaunceyan gasconade.

Ingersol, in mentioning Wilkinson's diary, calls it "the Odyssey of a calamitous voyage, by a bed-ridden general and his tempest tossed followers, who were continually assailed by vigilant and skilful enemies on the water, and from batteries along the shores, at every turn."

The highest meed of praise we can award to the Brito-Canadian defenders of their soil and perhaps the most reliable, as it comes from an enemy, is simply to transcribe a passage from Ingersoll.

"The British and Canadian troops deserve great credit for the persevering and invincible spirit in which they met a formidable invasion, fortified every pass on the St. Lawrence, seized every opportunity of harassing, impeding, and assailing our army, until at last they, more than storms, and casualties, *more than Hampton's defection,* forced it to dishonored defeat, when, well led, there was every pledge of victory." We need add nothing to such commendation.

The reasons assigned by General Hampton, General Hampton. in vindication of his disobedience, were want of food for men ; forage, for cattle and horses, and means of transporting more of the former than each soldier could carry on his back. These excuses can be doubly disproved, first by Hampton's own letter to Wilkinson in answer to one from that general, complaining of scarcity of provisions. Hampton, in that letter, so far from setting forth any scarcity on his part, distinctly says, "I hope to be able to prevent your starving ;" and then continues, "besides rawness and sickness, my troops have endured fatigues equal to a winter campaign in the late snows and bad weather, and are sadly depressed and fallen off." When thus complaining, it is not likely that Hampton would have omitted to add to his complaint of "fatigues undergone," that scarcity of provisions, had such really existed. This point established, we may safely adduce as the second means of disproof, the testimony given given at Wilkinson's trial by various officers. First, General Bissel deposed—

"That he reached the Four Corners with his regiment, on the 15th November, from St. Regis—that the marching was generally dry, the roads frozen, and part of them sandy —that, for a few miles through the woods, the frost, in some places, yielded to loaded waggons—that he had a number of horses with his regiment, but found no difficulty in procuring supplies for them, his quartermaster purchasing a considerable quantity of hay and corn, within three miles of the Four Corners."

Colonel Thomas, quartermaster-general of Hampton's army, deposeth—"That there was always on hand full supplies of hard bread, flour, salt pork, and beef, and beef cattle with the army ; and that he was always competent to furnish means of transportation for said army, wherever it might be ordered to move, as well after as before General Wilkinson's order to General Hampton to join the army on the St. Lawrence."

Major Wadsworth, issuing commissary, deposeth—"That he had constantly a full supply for the troops, of hard bread, flour, salt pork, and beef ; and after the first of October, constantly with the army, a considerable number of beef cattle. About the 10th of November, when the division moved from Chateauguay (Four Corners) to Plattsburgh, there was in deposit forty-five days' provision of bread and flour, a considerable quantity of salt meat, and at the Four Corners and its vicinity, seven or eight hundred head of fat cattle."

Captain Conkling, of the 4th U. S. infantry deputy quartermaster, being asked by the court what time it would have taken to remove the division, with its provision and baggage, from the Four Corners to St. Regis, on the St. Lawrence, deposeth—"That he did not exactly know the distance between the two places, but if twenty-five miles, as reported, it would have taken three days."

The real secret of the failure was the jealousy of the two commanders and the secretary at war, Wilkinson's jealousy of Armstrong's authority being as sensitive, as Hampton's of Wilkinson. As early as the 24th of August, Wilkinson, according to Ingersol, wrote to Armstrong requesting that he would not interfere with his arrangements, or give orders within the district of his command, meaning, of course, that he wished Hampton to receive no orders save through him.

Two heads on the same shoulders make a monster. Happily for Canada, this great expedition, nay the whole campaign, was a monster with three heads, biting and barking at each other with a madness which destroyed them all, disgraced the country, and saved Canada. Discord was a leprosy in the very heart of the undertaking, and to this fully as much as to Canadian gallantry, great as it undoubtedly was, is to be ascribed the failure of the long cherished schemes and hopes of the war party.

The sad intelligence of the catastrophe on the Thames reached General Vincent about the 9th October, and that active officer, in order to secure a central position, so as either to co-operate with the remains of Proctor's army, or renew operations on the Niagara frontier, immediately moved his troops from the cross roads to Burlington heights, where Proctor joined him with the small remnant of his division. This movement has been described by American historians thus—

Impression produced on the centre division by the disaster of the right.

"General McClure, with the New York militia, volunteers, and Indians, succeeded in driving the British army from the vicinity of Fort George, and pursued them as far as the Twelve Mile Creek."

The subsequent conduct of General McClure and his army will satisfy the reader as to the probability of this statement.

The effect produced on Sir George Prevost by the tidings of Proctor's discomfiture was an order to Vincent, to commence his retreat without delay, and to evacuate all the British posts beyond Kingston. A council of war, held at Burlington heights, decided, however, upon an opposite course of action, and it was determined to defend the western peninsula at all hazards. James's remarks on this order of Prevost are forcible and just:—

Prevost's instructions.

"Fatal, indeed, would have been the retreat. There was still a considerable number of sick, both at Burlington heights and at York; and, considering the season of the year and the state of the roads, the whole of them must have been left to the protection of the enemy. Nor, for the same reason, could the ordnance, ordnance stores, baggage, and pro-

visions have followed the army; and yet the garrison at Kingston, upon which place the troops were directed to retire, had, at this time, scarcely a week's provision in store. This abandonment, too, of territory so soon following up the affair at the Moravian village, what would the Indians have thought of us? In short, it will not bear reflection."

A very spirited occurrence grew out of one of the effects produced by Proctor's discomfiture. Two companies of the 100th regiment, which had been stationed at Charlotteville, in the London district, had been ordered to join the main body at Burlington heights, and orders had also been issued to disembody the militia. The officer, however, to whom the execution of this duty had been entrusted, knowing that a body of American marauders, with some disaffected Americo-Canadians, had been committing outrages on the inhabitants, left a supply of arms and ammunition with some of the militia officers and privates. Col. Bostwick, of the Oxford militia, determined to put down the marauders, and having, accordingly, mustered forty-five men, he marched, towards the end of October, against, and fortunately fell in with, them, on the shore of Lake Erie, about nine miles from Dover. An engagement ensued, in which several of the gang were killed and wounded, and eighteen taken prisoners. These eighteen were tried and fifteen convicted of high treason—of this number eight were executed, and seven transported. The whole affair was very creditable, planned with considerable judgment, and carried out in a most spirited manner. The President of Upper Canada was so pleased with it that he issued a general order,* in commendation of the spirit and zeal displayed.

---

* "*District general order.*
District head-quarters,
Kingston, 35th November, 1813.
The major-general commanding, and president, having received from major-general Vincent a report of the very gallant and patriotic conduct of lieutenant-colonel Bostwick, and an association of 45 officers and men of the militia of the county of Norfolk, in capturing and destroying a band of traitors, who, in violation of their allegiance, and of every principle of honor and honesty, had leagued themselves with the enemies of their country, to plunder and make prisoners the peaceable and well disposed inhabitants of the province, major-general De Rottenburg requests that colonel Bostwick, and every individual of the association, will accept his best thanks for their

This general order we cannot but regard as a severe commentary on the policy of Sir George Proctor, which would have given up the whole peninsula without striking a single blow in its defence.

The inhabitants in the neighborhood of Fort George having represented to Gen. Vincent how exposed they were to the predatory attacks of General McClure's militia, who were pillaging their farm houses and destroying their barns, he determined to check these depredations and injuries. Colonel Murray was accordingly ordered to make a demonstration with three hundred and seventy-nine rank and file of the 100th regiment, about twenty volunteers, and seventy Indians led by Colonel Elliott, as far as the Forty Mile Creek, beyond which he was forbidden to proceed. This movement had the effect of making General McClure, who was posted at Twenty Mile Creek, decamp with considerable haste. Observing the effects of his demonstration, Col. Murray solicited and obtained permission to extend his march, first to the Twenty, and subsequently to the Twelve Mile Creeks. These approaches on Murray's part so alarmed the American General, by this time driven back to Fort George, as to induce him to adopt the atrocious measures which led to such just and prompt, and merited, though severe retaliation.

General McClure, having heard of the disastrous termination to Wilkinson's expedition, and dreading a similar fate, determined to evacuate Fort George. Even this step, however, was not considered by the American General as affording sufficient security; he feared lest Fort Niagara might be endangered should he leave a shelter for the advancing troops, and acting under this impulse, he wantonly destroyed the flourishing village of Newark, and then ignobly fled into his own territory.

Movements of Colonel Murray.

Destruction of Newark, now Niagara.

The winter of 1813 had set in unusually early, and for several days previous to the 10th December, the cold had been very severe, and deep snow covered the ground. It was in such weather that General McClure resolved to execute his barbarous plans. Half an hour's notice this second Davoust gave to the unfortunate inhabitants for preparation. This brief space was all that was accorded to the villagers to save their furniture, their babes, and their bed-ridden. This interval passed, the merciless incendiaries came round and executed their merciless orders. James's indignation at this affair is very great, when describing the burning of Newark:—

"Out of the one hundred and fifty houses of which Newark had consisted, all, save one, were levelled to the dust. Such articles of furniture and other valuables as the incendiaries could not, and the inhabitants had neglected or been unable, to carry away, shared the general fate. Of Counsellor Dickson's library, which had cost him between five and six hundred pounds sterling, scarcely a book escaped. Mr. Dickson was at this time a prisoner in the enemy's territory, and his wife lay on a sick bed. The villains—how shall we proceed?—took up the poor lady, bed and all, and placed her upon the snow before her own door; where, shivering with cold, she beheld her house and all that was in it consumed to ashes! Upwards of four hundred helpless women and children, without provisions, and in some instances with scarcely clothes upon their backs, were thus compelled, after being the mournful spectators of the destruction of their habitations, to seek shelter at a distance, and that in such a night, too! The reader's imagination must supply the rest."

zeal and loyalty in planning, and gallantry in carrying into execution, this most useful and public spirited enterprise.

"The major-general and president hopes, that so striking an instance of the beneficial effect of unanimity and exertion in the cause of their country, will not fail of producing a due effect on the militia of this province. He calls upon them to observe how quickly the energetic conduct of 45 individuals has succeeded in freeing the inhabitants of an extensive district from a numerous and well armed banditti, who would soon have left them neither liberty nor property. He reminds them that, if so much can be effected by so small a number, what may not be expected from the unanimous exertions of the whole population, guided and assisted by a spirit of subordination, and aided by his majesty's troops, against an enemy who comes for no other purpose than to enslave, plunder, and destroy.

By order,
H. N. MOORSOM,
Lieutenant A. D. A. G."

We will reserve our comments on this proceeding until we have accompanied the respective forces through the movements which quickly succeeded the destruction of Newark.

With such haste did McClure retreat, that the fortifications at Fort George, which had been repaired since their occupation by the Americans in May were left comparatively uninjured. He was in too much haste to destroy the magazines, or even to remove his tents, of which a sufficiency for fifteen hundred men were left standing—even the destruction of the new barracks, recently erected on the Niagara, was not deemed necessary.

Had McClure not retreated with such precipitancy, the indignation of the soldiers, as they beheld the smoking ruins of the beautiful and flourishing village, would have burst like a thunder stroke upon the heads of the American General and his troops.

Colonel Murray gives the following account of his march and occupation of Fort George :

" *From colonel Murray to major-general Vincent.*"

Fort-George, Dec. 12, 1813.

Sir,—Having obtained information that the enemy had determined on driving the country between Fort George and the advance and was carrying off the loyal part of the inhabitants, notwithstanding the inclemency of the season, I deem it my duty to make a rapid and forced march towards him with the light troops under my command, which not only frustrated his designs, but compelled him to evacuate Fort George, by precipitately crossing the river, and abandoning the whole of the Niagara frontier. On learning our approach, he laid the town of Newark in ashes, passed over his cannon and stores, but failed in an attempt to destroy the fortifications, which are evidently so much strengthened whilst in his possession, as might have enabled general M'Clure (the commanding officer) to have maintained a regular siege ; but such was the apparent panic, that he left the whole of his tents standing.

I trust the indefatigable exertions of this handful of men have rendered an essential service to the country, by rescuing from a merciless enemy, the inhabitants of an extensive and highly cultivated tract of land, stored with cattle, grain, and provisions, of every description ; and it must be an exultation to them to find themselves delivered from the oppression of a lawless banditti, composed of the disaffected of the country, organized under the direct influence of the American government, who carried terror and dismay into every family.

I have the honor to be &c.

J. MURRAY,
Colonel.

To major-general Vincent, &c.

Sir George Prevost, relieved, by the unexpected termination of Wilkinson's expedition, from all further apprehension with regard either to Montreal or Kingston, now hastened to take such measures as would counterbalance the success which had attended General Harrison's movements, and secure the maintenance of the commanding positions yet held at Stony Creek and Burlington Heights.

Movements in the West.

Early in November Lieutenant General Drummond and Major General Riall had arrived from England; the former to relieve De Rottenburg in the military command and presidency in the Upper Province. Both these officers arrived at General Vincent's head quarters at St. David's, soon after the re-occupation of Fort George, and at the crisis when Col. Murray's energy and decision had been so ably manifested.

Colonel Murray proposed to General Drummond a retaliatory attack upon the opposite lines ; and the proposal not only met with the cordial approbation of General Drummond, but his hearty sanction. Without waiting, therefore, for the permission of Sir George Prevost, he instructed Colonel Murray to carry his plans into immediate operation. This decision was right, as the delay necessary for waiting the orders of the commander in chief might have enabled the enemy to recover from his panic, and the opportunity for striking a vigorous blow and avenging the conflagration of Newark, might have been thus lost. Orders were therefore given for prompt and vigorous measures, to be carried out by Col. Murray and General Riall. Col. Murray's despatch gives a clear and unexaggerated account of the surprise of Fort Niagara :—

Attack on Fort Niagara.

From the same to lieutenant-general Drummond.

Fort Niagara, Dec. 19, 1813.

SIR,—In obedience to your honor's commands, directing me to attack Fort Niagara, with the advance of the army of the right, I resolved upon attempting a surprise. The embarkation commenced on the 18th, at night, and the whole of the troops were landed three miles from the fort, early on the following morning, in the following order of attack :—Advanced guard one subaltern and 20 rank and file; grenadiers 100th regiment; royal artillery, with grenadiers; five companies 100th regiment, under lieutenant-colonel Hamilton, to assault the main gate, and escalade the works adjacent ; three companies of the 100th regiment, under captain Martin, to storm the eastern demi-bastion; captain Bailey, with the grenadiers royal Scots, was directed to attack the salient angle of the fortification ; and the flank companies of the 41st regiment were ordered to support the principal attack.—Each party was provided with scaling ladders and axes. I have great satisfaction in acquainting your honor, that the fortress was carried by assault in the most resolute and gallant manner, after a short but spirited resistance.

The highly gratifying but difficult duty remains, of endeavoring to do justice to the bravery, intrepidity, and devotion of the 100th regiment to the service of their country, under that gallant officer lieutenant-colonel Hamilton, to whom I feel highly indebted for his cordial assistance. Captain Martin, 100th regiment, who executed the task allotted to him in the most intrepid manner, merits the greatest praise ; I have to express my admiration of the valour of the royals, grenadiers, under captain Bailey, whose zeal and gallantry were very conspicuous. The just tribute of my applause is equally due to the flank companies of the 41st regiment, under lieutenant Bullock, who advanced to the attack with great spirit. The royal artillery under lieutenant Charlton, deserve my particular notice. To captain Elliot, deputy-assistant-quarter-master-general, who conducted one of the columns of attack, and superintended the embarkation, I feel highly obliged. I cannot pass over the brilliant services of lieutenant Dawson and Captain Fawcett 100th, in command of the advance and grenadiers, who gallantly executed the orders entrusted to them, by entirely cutting off two of the enemy's piquets, and surprising the sentries on the glacis and at the gate, by which means the watchword was obtained, and the entrance into the fort greatly facilitated, to which may be attributed in a great degree our trifling loss. I beg leave to recommend these meritorious officers to your honors protection. The scientific knowledge of lieutenant Gengruben, royal engineers, in suggesting arrangements previous to the attack, and for securing the fort afterwards, I cannot too highly appreciate. The unwearied exertions of acting quarter-master Pilkington, 100th regiment, in bringing forward the materials requisite for the attack, demand my acknowledgements. Captain Kirby, lieutenants Ball, Scroos, and Hamilton, of the different provincial corps, deserve my thanks. My staff-adjutant, Mr. Brampton, will have the honor of presenting this despatch, and the standard of the American garrison ; to his intelligence, valor, and friendly assistance, not only on this trying occasion, but on many former, I feel most grateful. Our force consisted of about 500 rank and file. Annexed is a return of our casualities, and the enemy's loss in killed, wounded, and prisoners. The ordnance and commissariat stores are so immense, that it is totally out of my power to forward to you a correct statement for some days, but 27 pieces of cannon, of different calibres, are on the works, and upwards of 3000 stand of arms, and many rifles in the arsenal. The store-houses are full of clothing and camp equipage of every description.

J. MURRAY,

Colonel.

His honor lieutenant-gen, Drummond, &c.

CHAPTER XVII.

General McClure's letter to the American Secretary at War will be found in our notes.*

On the same morning on which the surprise of Fort Niagara was effected, General Ryall crossed over to Lewiston with about five hundred rank and file, and, almost without opposition, entered and fired it. The small villages of Youngstown, Manchester, and Tuscarora, as soon as the inhabitants had deserted them, shared the same fate as had been awarded to Newark.

The conflagration thus lighted up along the shores of the Niagara spread such terror that General McClure, not daring, or caring, to expose himself to the dangers which he had provoked, resigned the command of the regulars and militia, now assembling from all parts, to Major General Hall, and on the morning of the 29th, that General occupied Buffalo with some two thousand troops.

On the morning of the 28th, the indefatigable Drummond was at Chippewa, and on the next day within two miles of Fort Erie, when he set about reconnoitering the enemy's position at Black Rock, with a view, to pursue, still further, his work of retaliation and annoyance. Accordingly, on the night of the 30th, Gen. Ryall, with five hundred and forty regulars, fifty volunteer militia, and one hundred and twenty Indians, crossed the Niagara, and landed without opposition about two miles from Black Rock. The events which then took place will be found in full detail in Gen. Ryall's letter:—

From Major General Ryall to Lieutenant General Drummond.

Niagara frontier, near Fort Erie,
January 1st, 1814.

SIR,—I have the honor to report to you, that agreeably to the instructions contained in your letter of the 29th ult., and your general order of that day, to pass the river

---

* " *From brigadier-general M'Clure to the American secretary of war.*
Head-quarters, Buffalo,
Dec. 22d, 1813.

SIR,—I regret to be under the necessity of announcing to you the mortifying intelligence of the loss of Fort Niagara. On the morning of the 19th instant, about four o'clock, the enemy crossed the river at the Five mile Meadows in great force, consisting of regulars and Indians, who made their way undiscovered to the garrison, which from the most correct information I can

collect, was completely surprised. Our men were nearly all asleep in their tents; the enemy rushed in, and commenced a most horrible slaughter. Such as escaped the fury of the first contest, retired to the old mess-house, where they kept up a destructive fire upon the enemy until a want of ammunition compelled them to surrender. Although our force was very inferior, and comparitively small indeed, I am induced to think that the disaster is not attributable to any want of troops, but to gross neglect in the commanding officer of the fort, captain Leonard, in not preparing, being ready, and looking out for the expected attack.

I have not been able to ascertain correctly the number of killed and wounded. About 20 regu-

17

Niagara, for the purpose of attacking the enemy's force, collected at Black Rock and Buffalo; and carrying into execution the other objects, therein mentioned, I crossed the river in the following night, with four companies of the King's Regiment, and the light company of the 89th, under Lieutenant Colonel Ogilvie; two hundred and fifty men of the 41st regiment, and the grenadiers of the 100th, under Major Friend; together with about fifty militia volunteers and a body of Indian warriors. The troops completed their landing about twelve o'clock, nearly two miles below Black Rock; the light infantry of the 89th being in advance, surprised and captured the greater part of a piquet of the enemy, and secured the bridge over the Conguichity Creek, the boards of which had been loosened, and were ready to be carried off had there been time given for it. I immediately established the 41st and 100th grenadiers in position beyond the bridge, for the purpose of perfectly securing its passage: the enemy made some attempts during the night upon this advanced position, but were repulsed with loss.

At daybreak I moved forward, the King's Regiment and light company of the 89th leading, the 41st and grenadiers of the 100th being in reserve. The enemy had by this time opened a very heavy fire of cannon and musketry on the Royal Scotts, under Lieut. Colonel Gordon, who were destined to land above Black Rock, for the purpose of turning his position, while he should be attacked in front by the troops who landed below; several of the boats having grounded, I am sorry to say this regiment suffered some loss, and was not able to effect its landing in sufficient time to fully accomplish the object intended, though covered by the whole of our field guns, under Captain Bridge, which were placed on the opposite bank of the river.

The King's and 89th, having in the meantime gained the town, commenced a very spirited attack upon the enemy, who were in great force, and very strongly posted. The reserve having arrived on the ground, the whole were shortly engaged. The enemy maintained his position with very considerable obstinacy for some time; but such was the spirited and determined advance of our troops, that he was at length compelled to give way, was driven through his batteries, in which were a twenty-four-pounder, three twelve-pounders, and one nine-pounder, and pursued to the town of Buffalo, about two miles distant; he here shewed a large body of infantry and cavalry, and attempted to oppose our advance by the fire of a field piece, posted on the height, which commanded the road; but

lars have escaped out of the fort, some badly wounded. Lieutenant Beck, 24th regiment is killed, and it is said three others.

You will perceive sir, by the enclosed general orders, that I apprehended an attack, and made the necessary arrangements to meet it; but have reason to believe, from information received by those who have made their escape, that the commandant did not in any respect comply with those orders.

On the same morning a detachment of militia, under major general Bennett, stationed at Lewistown Heights, was attacked by a party of savages; but the major and his little corps, by making a desperate charge, effected their retreat, after being surrounded by several hundreds, with the loss of six or eight, who doubtless were killed; among whom were two sons of captain Jones, Indian interpreter. The villages of Youngstown, Lewistown, Manchester, and the Indian Tuscarora village, were reduced to ashes, and the inoffensive inhabitants who could not escape, were, without regard to age or sex, inhumanly butchered, by savages headed by British officers painted. A British officer who was taken prisoner, avows that many small children were murdered by the Indians.

Major Mallory, who was stationed at Schlosser,

with about 40 Canadian volunteers, advanced to Lewistown Heights, and compelled the advanced guard of the enemy to fall back to the foot of the mountain. The major is a meritorious officer; he fought the enemy two days, and contested every inch of ground to the Tanawanty Creek. In these actions lieutenant Lowe, 23d regiment of the United States army, and eight of the Canadian volunteers, were killed. I had myself, three days previous to the attack on the Niagara, left with a view of providing for the defence of this place, Black Rock, and the other villages on this frontier.

I came here with the troops, and have called out the militia of Genessee, Niagara, and Chatauqua countries, en masse

This place was then thought to be in imminent danger, as well as the shipping, but I have no doubt is perfectly secure. Volunteers are coming in great numbers; they are, however, a species of troops that cannot be expected to continue in the service for a long time. In a few days 1000 detatched militia, lately drafted, will be on.

I have the honour to be, &c.
G. M'CLURE,
Brig.-gen. com.
Hon. J. Armstrong, sec. at war."

finding this ineffectual, he fled in all directions, and betaking himself to the woods, further pursuit was useless. He left behind him one six-pounder brass field piece, and one iron eighteen and one iron six-pounder, which fell into our hands. I then proceeded to execute the ulterior object of the expedition, and detached Captain Robinson, of the King's, with two companies, to destroy two schooners and a sloop, (part of the enemy's late squadron,) that were on shore a little below the town, with the stores they had on board, which he effectually completed. The town itself, (the inhabitants having previously left it,) and the whole of the public stores, containing considerable quantities of cloathing, spirits, and flour, which I had not the means of conveying away, were then set on fire, and totally consumed; as was also the village of Black Rock, on the evening it was evacuated. In obedience to your further instructions, I have directed Lieutenant Colonel Gordon to move down the river to Fort Niagara, with a party of the 19th light dragoons, under Major Lisle, a detachment of the Royal Scots, and the 89th light company, and destroy the remaining cover of the enemy upon his frontier, which he has reported to have been effectually done. From every account I have been able to collect, the enemy's force opposed to us was not less than from two thousand to two thousand five hundred men; their loss in killed and wounded, I should imagine from three to four hundred; but from the nature of the country, being mostly covered with wood, it is difficult to ascertain it precisely; the same reason will account for our not having been able to make a greater number of prisoners than one hundred and thirty.

I have great satisfaction in stating to you the good conduct of the whole of the regular troops and volunteer militia; but I must particularly mention the steadiness and bravery of the King's Regiment, and 89th light infantry. They were most gallantly led to the attack by Lieutenant Colonel Ogilvie, of the King's, who, I am sorry to say, received a severe wound, which will for a time deprive the service of a very brave and intelligent officer. After Lieutenant Colonel Ogilvie was wounded, the command of the regiment devolved on Captain Robinson, who, by a very judicious movement to his right, with the three bat-

talion companies, made a considerable impression on the left of the enemy's position. I have every reason to be satisfied with Lieutenant Colonel Gordon, in the command of the Royal Scotts, and have much to regret, that the accidental grounding of his boats deprived me of the full benefit of his services; and I have also to mention my approbation of the conduct of Major Friend, commanding the 41st, as well as that of Captain Fawcett, of the 100th grenadiers, who was unfortunately wounded. Captain Barden, of the 89th, and Captain Brunter, of the king's light infantry companies, conducted themselves in the most exemplary manner. Lieutenant Colonel Elliott, in this, as well as on other occasions, is entitled to my highest commendations, for his zeal and activity as superintendent of the Indian department; and I am happy to add, that, through his exertions, and that of his officers, no act of cruelty, as far as I could learn, was committed by the Indians towards any of their prisoners. I cannot close this report without mentioning, in terms of the warmest praise, the good conduct of my aide-de-camp, Captain Holland, from whom I received the most able assistance throughout the whole of these operations. Nor can I omit mentioning my obligations to you for acceding to the request of your aide-de-camp, Captain Jervoise, to accompany me. He was extremely active and zealous, and rendered me very essential service. I enclose a return of the killed, wounded, and missing, and of the ordnance captured at Black Rock and Buffalo.

P. RYALL,
Major General.

Lieutenant General Drummond, commanding the forces, Upper Canada.

The return enclosed by General Ryall showed a loss of thirty-one killed, seventy-two wounded, besides nine missing. The American loss it is impossible to arrive at, as all the information afforded by General Hall's letter is "many valuable lives were lost." General Hall's letter is short, but, short as it is, it serves as an additional proof how determined the writers of bulletins were, that American troops should never be supposed to succumb, except to superior forces.

Return of killed and wounded in attack on Fort Niagara.

We will give first General Hall's letter, and, as a commentary on it, Gen. Armstrong's remarks will fully answer our purpose.

"I have only time to acknowledge the receipt of your letter of the 25th inst., and to add, that this frontier is wholly desolate. The British crossed over, supported by a strong party of Indians, a little before day this morning, near Black Rock; *they were met by the militia under my command with spirit; but were overpowered* by the numbers and discipline of the enemy, the militia gave way, and fled on every side; every attempt to rally them proved ineffectual.

The enemy's purpose was obtained, and the flourishing village of Buffalo was laid in ruins. The Niagara frontier now lies open and naked to our enemies. Your judgment will direct you what is most proper in this emergency. I am exhausted with fatigue, and must defer particulars till to-morrow. Many valuable lives are lost."

Such is General Hall's letter, now for Armstrong. After describing the fall of Fort Niagara, but here we must pause for a a moment to examine into the truth of Armstrong's assertions respecting the fall of Fort Niagara

The General observes, "Murray's movement, in a view strictly military, was well conducted and merits applause, but the use subsequently made by that officer of his adversary's crime, or of his own good fortune, cannot fail to degrade him both as a man and a soldier; since, "what has been gained in either character, and has been gained without loss or resistance, should be held without bloodshed." Yet of the sleeping, unarmed, and unresisting garrison of Fort Niagara, sixty-five men were killed and fourteen, wounded. More than two-thirds of whom were hospital patients.

Here is a direct charge which is substantiated by no other American writer, Ingersol excepted. No allusion to such a circumstance will be found in McClure's despatch, except the passage "the enemy rushed in and commenced a most horrible slaughter." Let us examine the circumstances. McClure was anxious to make the best excuse he could for himself, and has shown that he was very ready to place all the blame on Captain Leonard for not being ready and prepared for the attack; still, he says not one word as to the massacre of hospital patients implied by General Armstrong. Is it probable that he would have let slip so favourable an opportunity of arresting enquiry into the fall of the fort, had so outrageous an act been commited. It would have been the best mode possible of exciting national indignation, and, under cover of the clamour, the question as to capability in the defence of the post would have been forgotten.

What do other American writers say on the subject? Dr. Smith, to whom we have, on more than one occasion, referred, and with whose animus the reader must by this time be pretty well acquainted, merely states that, in the month of January Fort Niagara was surprised and captured. Mr. Thomson is more particular, and after the usual introduction of "Indian warriors" states amongst the enumeration of horrors, that "*the women of the garrison were stripped of their clothing, and many of them killed.*" This statement is bad, and false enough to prove most conclusively that the writer was anxious to make a case out against the British. Is it likely then, we ask, that the slaughter of unarmed hospital patients, had such really occurred, would have been passed over in silence by this malevolent and inventive writer.

This assertion of General Armstrong's may fairly be classed, for meanness and falsehoods with that of General McClure, respecting "British officers painted like Indians." Where General McClure obtained this information we are at a loss. It is not to be found in any American writer, with the exception of Mr. O'Connor, and bears so distinctly the stamp of having been fabricated by a man, who was frightened out of his wits, that it is scarcely necessary to enter further into the matter.

We have said enough on the subject to show that General Armstrong has here, without due deliberation or attention, stated what a very short enquiry would have convinced him to be untrue. We will, then, return to Hall's letter. Armstrong says, "the success of this part of the enterprise (the capture of Fort Niagara) being ascertained, Ryall proceeded to execute what remained of the plan; *and it must be admitted with little more of opposition from any quarter than if the justice of the proceeding, both as to character and extent, had been unquestionable.* Beginning with the villages and intermediate houses on the bank of the river, all were sacked and burned from Youngstown to Buffalo, both included ; and so universal was the panic produced by the invasion, that had it not been stayed by *the voluntary retreat of the enemy,* a large portion of the frontier would in a few days more have been left without a single inhabitant ; so true it is, that FEAR BETRAYS, LIKE TREASON.

The italics in the above quotation are ours, the last portion in capitals, is Armstrong's own ; and the whole extract is a pretty convincing proof that in his estimation, fear of the enemy had rather more to do with the retreat of the Americans, than the overwhelming numbers of the British invaders.

With a few extracts from Ingersol, we will close, the sketch of operations on the Niagara frontier.

"Both sides of the Niagara, says Ingersol" had been from April to December distracted by the disgraceful hostilities of border warfare, in which the Americans were the aggressors, and doomed to be the greatest sufferers. Western New York was, before the year ended, desolated by British reaction, transcending American aggression, which we cannot deny provoked, however severe, that retaliation."

This admission, coming from a writer who so readily endorses the unfounded assertion of Armstrong, may be taken as very fair testimony as to which party was the first to violate the recognized rules of warfare.

Ingersol is very severe on the conduct of the American militia, along the Niagara frontier. "Our loss of character was greater than that of life and property. General Cass ascertained that the troops reported to have done the devastation, were but six hundred and fifty men, regulars, militia, and Indians— the latter helpless for taking a fort except by suprise, the militia not much more to be feared ; so that our nearly four hundred regulars in the fort had been easily conquered by an equal, perhaps less number ; to oppose whom, we had between twenty-five hundred and three thousand militia, all, except very few of them, behaving, said General Cass, in the most cowardly manner.

With such a condemnation, from one of their own writers, on their conduct, we find it hard to understand how, at the present day, the productions of such writers as Thomson, Smith and O'Connor, are tolerated by enquiring or impartial readers, who desire to ascertain the real amount of glory due to America.

No one regretted more deeply than Sir George Provost, the savage mode of warfare which the Americans, by their departure from the customary usages of warfare, had compelled him to sanction, and so soon as something like a just punishment had been inflicted on them, he issued the following proclamation, in which will be found, commented on with considerable precision and ability, the progress of the war on the part of the enemy :—

Proclamation of Sir George Provost.

" By his Excellency Lieut. General Sir George Prevost, Baronet, commander of his Majesty's forces in North America, &c., &c., &c.

" To the inhabitants of his Majesty's provinces in North America.

" A PROCLAMATION.

" The complete success which has attended his Majesty's arms on the Niagara Frontier, having placed in our possession the whole of the enemy's posts on that line, it became a matter of imperious duty to retaliate on America, the miseries which the unfortunate inhabitants of Newark had been made to suffer from the evacuation of Fort George.

The villages of Lewiston, Black Rock, and Buffalo have accordingly been burned.

" At the same time the commander of the forces sincerely deprecates this mode of warfare, he trusts that it will be sufficient to call the attention of every candid and impartial person amongst ourselves and the enemy, to the circumstances from which it has arisen, to satisfy them that this departure from the established usages of war, has originated with America herself, and that to her alone, are justly chargeable, all the awful and unhappy consequences which have hitherto flowed, and are likely to result, from it.

" It is not necessary to advert to the conduct of the troops employed on the American coast, in conjunction with his Majesty's squadron, under Admiral Sir John B. Warren, since, as they were neither within the command, nor subject to the control of his excellency, their acts cannot be ascribed to him, even if they wanted that justification which the circumstances that occasioned them so amply afford.

"It will be sufficient for the present purpose, and in order to mark the character of the war, as carried on upon the frontiers of these provinces, to trace the line of conduct observed by his excellency, and the troops under his command, since the commencement of hostilities, and to contrast it with that of the enemy.

"The first invasion of Upper Canada took place in July, 1812, when the American forces under brigadier general Hull, crossed over and took possession of Sandwich, where they began to manifest a disposition so different from that of a magnanimous enemy; and which they have since invariably displayed, in marking out, as objects of their peculiar resentment, the loyal subjects of his Majesty, and in dooming their property to plunder and conflagration.

"Various instances of this kind occurred, both at Sandwich and in its neighborhood, at the very period when his Majesty's standard was waving upon the fort of Michilimackinac, and affording protection to the persons and property of those who had submitted to it:— Within a few weeks afterwards, the British flag was also hoisted on the fortress of Detroit, which, together with the whole of the Michigan territory, had surrendered to his Majesty's arms.

"Had not his excellency been actuated by, sentiments far different from those which had influenced the American government, and the persons employed by it, in the wanton acts of destruction of private property, committed during their short occupation of a part of Upper Canada, his excellency could not but have availed himself of the opportunity which the undisturbed possession of the whole of the Michigan territory, afforded him of amply retaliating for the devastating system which had been pursued at Sandwich and on the Thames.

"But strictly in conformity to the views and disposition of his own government, and to that liberal and magnanimous policy which it had dictated, he chose rather to forbear an imitation of the enemy's example, in the hope, that such forbearance would be duly appreciated by the goverement of the United States,

and would produce a return to more civilised usages of war.

"The persons and property, therefore, of the inhabitants of the Michigan terriory, were respected, and remained unmolested.

"In the winter of the following year, wher the success which attended the gallant enter prise against Ogdensburgh had placed that populous and flourishing village in our possession, the generosity of this British character was again conspicuous, in the scrupulous preservation of every article which could be considered as private property, such public buildings only being destroyed as were used for the accommodation of troops and for public stores.

"The destruction of the defences of Ogdensburgh, and the dispersion of the enemy's force in that neighbourhood, laid open the whole of their frontier on the St. Lawrence, to the incursions of his Majesty's troops, and Hamilton, as well as the numerous settlements on the banks of the river, might, at any hour, had such been the disposition of his Majesty's government, or of those acting under it, been plundered and laid waste.

"During the course of the following summer, by the fortunate result of the enterprise against Plattsburgh, that town was for several hours in the complete possession of our troops, there not being any force in the neighborhood which could attempt a resistance.—Yet even there, under circumstances of strong temptation, and when the recent example of the enemy in the wanton destruction at York, of private property, and buildings not used for military purposes, must have been fresh in the recollection of the forces employed on that occasion, and would have justified a retaliation on their part, their forbearance was strongly manifested, and the directions his excellency had given to the commander of that expedition, so scrupulously obeyed, that scarcely can another instance be shewn in which, during a state of war, and under similar circumstances, an enemy, so completely under the power and at the mercy of their adversaries, had so little cause of complaint.

"During the course of the same summer, forts Schlosser and Black Rock, were surprised and taken by a part of the forces under the command of Major General De Rottenburg, on the Niagara frontier, at both of which places personal property was respected, and the public buildings were alone destroyed.

"It was certainly matter of just and reasonable expectation, that the humane and liberal course of conduct pursued by his Excellency on these different occasions, would have had its due weight with the American government, and would have led it to have abstained, in the further porsecution of the war, from any acts of wantonness or violence, which could only tend unnecessarily to add to its ordinary calamities, and to bring down upon their own unoffending citizens a retaliation, which, though distant, they must have known would await and certainly follow such conduct.

"Undeterred, however, by his Excellency's example of moderation, or by any of the consequences to be apprehended from the adoption of such barbarous measures, the American forces at Fort George, acting, there is every reason to believe, under the orders, or with the approbation of their government, for some time previous to their evacuation of that fortress, under various pretences, burned and destroyed the farm houses and buildings of many of the respectable and peaceable inhabitants of that neighborhood. But the full measure of this species of barbarity remained to be completed at a season when all its horrors might be more fully and keenly felt, by those who were to become the wretched victims of it.

"It will hardly be credited by those who shall hereafter read it in the page of history, that in the enlightened era of the nineteenth century, and in the inclemency of a Canadian winter, the troops of a nation calling itself civilized and christian, had wantonly, and without the shadow of a pretext, forced four hundred helpless women and children to quit their dwellings, and be the mournful spectators of the conflagration and total destruction of all that belonged to them.

"Yet such was the fate of Newark on the 10th of December, a day which the inhabitants of Upper Canada can never forget, and the recollection of which cannot but nerve their arms when again opposed to their vindictive foe. On the night of that day, the American troops under Brigadier General M'Clure, being about to evacuate Fort George, which they could no longer retain, by an act of inhumanity disgraceful to themselves and to the nation to which they belong, set fire to upwards of 150 houses, composing the beautiful village of Newark, and burned them to the ground, leaving without covering or shelter, those 'innocent, unfortunate, distressed inhabitants,' whom that officer, by his proclamation, had previously engaged to protect.

"His Excellency would have ill consulted the honor of his country, and the justice due to His Majesty's injured and insulted subjects, had he permitted an act of such needless cruelty to pass unpunished, or had he failed to visit, whenever the opportunity arrived, upon the inhabitants of the neighboring American frontier, the calamities thus inflicted upon those of our own.

"The opportunity has occurred, and a full measure of retaliation has taken place, such as it is hoped will teach the enemy to respect, in future, the laws of war, and recal him to a sense of what is due to himself as well as to us.

"In the further prosecution of the contest to which so extraordinary a character has been given, his Excellency must be guided by the course of conduct which the enemy shall hereafter pursue. Lamenting as his Excellency does, the necessity imposed upon him of retaliating upon the subjects of America the miseries inflicted on the inhabitants of Newark, it is not his intention to pursue further a system of warfare so revolting to his own feelings, and so little congenial to the British character, unless the future measures of the enemy should compel him again to resort to it.

"To those possessions of the enemy along the whole line of frontier which have hitherto remained undisturbed, and which are now within his Excellency's reach, and at the mercy of the troops under his command, his Excellency has determined to extend the same forbearance and the same freedom from rapine and plunder, which they have hitherto experienced; and from this determination the future conduct of the American government shall alone induce his Excellency to depart.

"The inhabitants of these provinces will, in the mean time, be prepared to resist, with firmness and with courage, whatever attempts the resentment of the enemy, arising from their disgrace and their merited sufferings, may lead them to make, well assured that they will be powerfully assisted at all points by the troops under his Excellency's command, and that prompt and signal vengeance will be taken for every fresh departure by the enemy, from that system of warfare, which ought alone to subsist between enlightened and civilized nations.

"Given under my hand and seal at arms at Quebec, this 12th day of January, 1814.

"GEORGE PREVOST.

" By His Excellency's command,

E. B. BRENTON."

We must now change the scene and transport the reader from the shores of the mighty St. Lawrence and Niagara to the Chesapeake. Along these shores thirty years of uninterrupted peace had effected wonders, and towns had rapidly sprung up, raised into prosperity by the facilities for commerce afforded by this magnificent estuary and its tributary streams. These towns and villages were then, as now* wholly unprepared to offer any resistance to an armed force, the arrival of the British fleet, therefore, under Admiral Warren, towards the latter end of March, 1803, in their comparatively defenceless waters, spread an undefined but half fearful impression.

American writers have not scrupled to characterize the proceedings of Admiral Warren, or rather of his second in command, Sir George Cockburn, as a series of maurauding attacks, comparable only to those of the Bucaneers two centuries before; a little consideration will, however, show that the writers preferring these charges, have lost sight of Hull and Smyth's proclamations, on their invasion of Canada. These manifestoes, or rather denunciations, the reader doubtless remembers the import of, and it is therefore needless to refer again to them, or to quote a second time their vapourings or threats. That these threats were not carried into execution was owing

*Occurrences in Chesapeake Bay, and its tributary rivers.

not to the conciliatory spirit of the invaders, but simply to the fact that, ere the ink was dry on the proclamations, the invaders were either prisoners, or had retreated ingloriously to their own territories; we have besides, abundant proof from the behaviour of the American soldiery, when in occupation of the Niagara district, what would have been their line of conduct to the inhabitants of these sections of country, had they encountered any opposition, and if the inhabitants along the shores of the Chesapeake Bay, suffered from some of the inevitable evils of warfare, the cause must be sought for from two sources.

As we have, on more than one occasion, shown, from Washington and Baltimore issued the most mendacious and inflated accounts of the exploits of both American naval and land expeditions. The Government organs on no occasion suffered the truth to transpire in case of defeat, and when victory had been achieved, the conquest was magnified to such a degree as to inspire a feeling of invincibility. It is scarcely to be wondered at, then, that every farmer or blacksmith imagined, that in case of attack, there was but the necessity to offer a show of resistance, and that the Britishers would run away. To this cause then which led them to tempt, and even provoke, attacks was in the first place attributable some of the severities enforced in this quarter.

A second reason is, perhaps, to be found in the fact that sailors, whatever their discipline on board, are very apt to indulge in a little more license than their red-coated brethren. The expeditions along the shores of the Chesapeake necessarily comprehended many bluejaekets, and many of the complaints made by the inhabitants must, we fear, be ascribed to Jack Tar's thoughtlessness. It must, at the same time, be observed that every trifle has been magnified and distorted by American writers. If a sailor or soldier, straggling from his party, and relieved from the watchful and supervising eye of his commander, robbed a hen roost, or made free with a sucking pig, it was immediately magnified into wholesale wanton destruction of property and the tale, in all probability, received so rich a colouring that the unfortunate offender would be at a loss to know again his own exploit.

In our account of the proceedings in this quarter, we will simply confine ourselves to

---

*NOTE—We say as now, for to any one conversant with the subject, it must be evident that the defences near Point Comfort, called Riprapton or Rip Raps, are wholly inadequate to the purpose, and would prove but an insufficient means for the protection of the Chesapeake.

laying before the reader the official documents bearing upon the several expeditions, making on each any comments necessary, and giving, if possible, at the same time the American version of each. We shall also endeavour to show that the attacks made by the British, and represented as marauding expeditions, were actually attacks on positions which the Americans had hastily fortified with the intention of annoyance.

The first exploit effected was the cutting out of four armed schooners, lying at the mouth of the Rappahanock river, by an expedition of five boats under the command of Captain Polkinghorne, of the St. Domingo. This exploit was very gallantly executed, and James in his Naval occurrences, (page 367,) gives a full account of it,—we will, however, pass on to more important enterprises. The first of these was an expedition, undertaken a few days after, to destroy a depôt of military stores, the foundries, and public works at a place called French Town, a considerable distance up the river Elk.* Admiral Cockburn's letter to Admiral Warren will, however, give this occurrence in detail:—

His Majesty's sloop Fantome in the Elk River, 20th April, 1813.

SIR,—I have the honor to acquaint you, that, having yesterday gained information of the depôt of flour (alluded to in your note to me of the 23rd inst.) being with some military and other stores, situated at a place called French-Town, a considerable distance up the river Elk, I caused his Majesty's brigs, Fantome, and Mohawk, and the Dolphin, Racer, and Highflyer tenders, to be moored, yesterday evening, as far within the entrance of this river as could be prudently effected after dark; and at eleven o'clock last night, the detachment of marines now in the advanced squadron, consisting of about 150 men, under captains Wybourn and Carter, of that corps, with five artillery men, under first-lieutenant Robertson of the artillery, (who eagerly volunteered his valuable assistance on this occasion,) proceeded in the boats of the squadron, the whole being under the immediate direction of lieutenant G. A. Westphall, first of the Marlborough, to take and destroy the afore-

said stores: the Highflyer tender, under the command of lieutenant T. Lewis, being directed to follow, for the support and protection of the boats, as far and as closely as he might find it practicable.

Being ignorant of the way, the boats were unfortunately led up the Bohemia River, instead of keeping in the Elk; and, it being daylight before this error was rectified, they did not reach the destined place till between 8 and 9 o'clock this morning, which occasioned the enemy to have full warning of their approach, and gave him time to collect his force, and make his arrangements for the defence of his stores and town; for the security of which, a 6-gun battery had lately been erected, and from whence a heavy fire was opened upon our boats the moment they approached within its reach; but the launches, with their carronades, under the orders of lieutenant Nicholas Alexander, first of the Dragon, pulling resolutely up to the work, keeping up at the same time a constant and well-directed fire on it; and the marines being in the act of disembarking on the right, the Americans judged it prudent to quit their battery, and to retreat precipitately into the country, abandoning to their fate French-Town and its depôts of stores; the whole of the latter, therefore, consisting of much flour, a large quantity of army-clothing, of saddles, bridles, and other equipments for cavalry, &c. &c., together with various articles of merchandize, were immediately set fire to, and entirely consumed, as were five vessels lying near the place; and the guns of the battery being too heavy to bring away, were disabled as effectually as possible by Lieutenant Robertson and his artillery-men; after which, my orders being completely fulfilled, the boats returned down the river without molestation; and I am happy to add, that one seaman, of the Maidstone, wounded in the arm by a grape-shot, is the only casualty we have sustained.

To lieutenant G. A. Westphall, who has so gallantly conducted, and so ably executed, this service, my highest encomiums and best acknowledgements are due; and I trust, sir, you will deem him to have also thereby merited your favourable consideration and notice. It is likewise my pleasing duty to acquaint you, that he speaks in the highest terms of

---

In our next we promise a Map of this locality, so that the reader may trace the proceedings.

every officer and man employed with him on this occasion; but particularly of the very great assistance he derived from lieutenant Robertson, of the artillery; lieutenant Alexander, of the Dragons; lieutenant Lewis, of the Highflyer; and Captains Wybourn and Carter of the royal marines.

I have now anchored the above mentioned brigs and tenders near a farm, on the right bank of this river, where there appears to be a considerable quantity of cattle, which I intend embarking for the use of the fleet under your command; and if I meet with no resistance or impediment in so doing, I shall give the owner bills on the victualling-office for the fair value of whatsoever is so taken; but should resistance be made, I shall consider them as a prize of war, which I trust will meet your approbation; and I purpose taking on board a further supply for the fleet to-morrow, on similar terms, from Specucie Island, which lies a little below Havre-de-Grace, and which I have been informed is also well stocked.

I have the honor to be, &c.

G. COCKBURN, Rear-admiral.

To the right hon. admiral Sir J. B. Warren, bart. K. B., &c.

Although the strictest orders were issued by the Rear Admiral, to land without molestation to the unopposing inhabitants, and although these orders were enforced with the greatest severity, still we find our old friends, the writers of the *History of the War* and *Sketches of the War*, ready as ever to malign and misstate. The author of the *History of the United States*, however, outdoes them both, and shines conspicuous in his task of distortive misrepresentation. So totally careless of truth is he as to represent public stores as belonging to merchants of Baltimore and Philadelphia, and this in direct opposition to Gen. Wilkinson's statement, who distinctly says:—

"By the defective arrangements of the war department, he [rear Admiral Cockburn] succeeded in destroying the military equipments and munitions found there; of which, I apprehend, the public never received any correct account.*

The same system of false colouring, will be found to pervade these writers works whenever the occurrences on the Chesapeake are

in question. The National vanity received here its sorest wound, and Americans were here first taught the proper value of their militia.

The defeats along the lake shores, and the various repulses, had been all so glossed over, that the idea of militia not being equal to the most disciplined soldiery, was never entertained! when, therefore, the fact was forced on them, a bitterness of feeling was engendered, which, like an unwholesome tumour, found vent, in the discharge of the most violent matter.

A second expedition was soon forced upon the commanding officer, by the absurd temerity of the inhabitants of Havre de Grace.— The rule laid down by the British Admiral was, that all supplies should be paid for, at full market price, but that all such supplies must be forthcoming, that is without serious inconvenience to parties supplying, but that, should resistence be offered, the village or town would then be considered as a fortified place, and the male inhabitants as soldiers, the one to be destroyed, the other with their property to be captured or destroyed.

The inhabitants of French Town had experienced the benefit of this arrangement, and taking no part in the contest, remained unmolested. The inhabitants of Havre de Grace, not so prudent, received a severe lesson.—

Descent on Havre de Grace.   The British Admiral, deeming it necessary, to draw his supplies from a place called Specucie Island, where cattle and provisions were abundant, was obliged to pass in sight of Havre de Grace, a village on the west side of the Susquehanna, a short distance above the confluence of that river with the Chesapeake. The inhabitants of this place, possessed, very probably, to a great extent, an idea of their valor, and qualifications for becoming soldiers, and had consequently erected a six gun battery, and, as if to attract particular attention, had mounted a large American Ensign.— Most probably, however, neither, the Ensign nor the battery would have attracted attention had the erectors thereof, remained quiet, but instead of this a fire was opened upon the British ships, although they were far beyond the range of the guns. This provocation the Admiral determined to resent, he consequently determined to make the town of Havre de

Grace and the battery the objects of his next attack.

Full details of the reasons for, and objects of the attack, will be found in Admiral Cockburn's second letter which follows:

" His Majesty's ship Maidstone,
Tuesday night, 3d May, 1813, at anchor
off Turkey Point.

"SIR,—I have the honor to inform you, that whilst anchoring the brigs and tenders off Specucie Island, agreeably to my intentions notified to you in my official report of the 29th ultimo, No. 10, I observed guns fired, and American colours hoisted, at a battery lately erected at Havre de Grace, at the entrance of Susquehanna River. This, of course, immediately gave to the place an importance which I had not before attached to it, and I therefore determined on attacking it after the completion of our operations at the island; consequently, having sounded in the direction towards it, and found that the shallowness of the water would only admit of its being approached by boats, I directed their assembling under Lieutenant Westphall, (first of the Marlborough,) last night at 12 o'clock, alongside the Fantome: when our detatchments of marines, consisting of about 150 men, (as before,) under Captains Wybourn and Carter, with a small party of artillerymen, under Lieutenant Robinson, of the artillery, embarked in them; and the whole, being under the immediate direction of Captain Lawrence, of the Fantome, (who, with much zeal and readiness, took upon himself, at my request, the conducting of this service,) proceeded toward Havre de Grace, to take up, under cover of the night, the necessary position for commencing the attack at the dawn of day. The Dolphin and Highflyer tenders, commanded by Lieutenants Hutchinson and Lewis, followed for the support of the boats, but the shoalness of the water prevented their getting within six miles of the place. Captain Lawrence, however, having got up with the boats, and having very ably and judiciously placed them during the dark, a warm fire was opened on the place at daylight from our launches and rocket-boats, which was smartly returned from the battery for a short time; but the launches constantly closing with it, and their fire rather increasing than decreasing, that from the battery soon began to slacken; and Captain Lawrence observing

this, very judiciously directed the landing of the marines on the left; which movement, added to the hot fire they were under, induced the Americans to commence withdrawing from the battery, to take shelter in the town.

"Lieut. G. A. Westphall, who had taken his station in the rocket-boat close to the battery, therefore now judging the moment to be favourable, pulled directly up under the work, and landing with his boat's crew, got immediate possession of it, turned their own guns on them, and thereby soon caused them to retreat, with their whole force, to the farthest extremity of the town, whither, (the marines having by this time landed,) they were pursued closely; and no longer feeling themselves equal to an open and manly resistance, they commenced a teasing and irritating fire from behind the houses, walls, trees, &c.: from which, I am sorry to say, my gallant first-lieutenant received a shot through his hand whilst leading the pursuing party; he, however, continued to head the advance, with which he soon succeeded in dislodging the whole of the enemy from their lurking places, and driving them for shelter to the neighboring woods; and whilst performing which service, he had the satisfaction to overtake, and with his remaining hand to make prisoner and bring in a captain of their militia. We also took an ensign and some armed individuals; but the rest of the force, which had been opposed to us, having penetrated into the woods, I did not judge it prudent to allow of their being further followed with our small numbers; therefore, after setting fire to some of the houses, to cause the proprietors, (who had deserted them, and formed part of the militia who had fled to the woods,) to understand, and feel, what they were liable to bring upon themselves, by building batteries, and acting towards us with so much useless rancour, I embarked in the boats the guns from the battery, and having also taken and destroyed about 130 stand of small arms, I detached a small division of boats up the Susquehanna, to take and destroy whatever they might meet with in it, and proceeded myself with the remaining boats under Captain Lawrence, in search of a cannon foundry, which I had gained intelligence of, whilst on shore at Havre de Grace, as being situated about three or four miles to the northward, where we found it accordingly; and getting possession of it without difficulty, commenced instantly its destruction, and that of the guns and other materials we found there, to complete which occupied us during the remainder of the day, as there were several buildings, and much complicated heavy machinery, attached to it; it was known by the name of Cecil, or Principic foundry, and was one of the most valuable works of the kind in America; the destruction of it, therefore, at this moment, will, I trust, prove of much national importance.

In the margin* I have stated the ordnance taken and disabled by our small division this day, during the whole of which we have been on shore in the centre of the enemy's country, and on his highroad between Baltimore and Philadelphia. The boats which I sent up the Susquehanna, returned after destroying five vessels on it, and a large store of flour; when everything being completed to my utmost wishes, the whole division re-embarked and returned to the ships, where we arrived at 10 o'clock, after having been 22 hours in constant exertion, without nourishment of any kind; and I have much pleasure in being able to add, that excepting Lieutenant Westphall's wound, we have not suffered any casualty whatever.

The judicious dispositions made by Captain Lawrence, of the Fantome during the preceding night, and the able manner in which he conducted the attack of Havre in the morning, added to the gallantry, zeal, and attention, shewn by him during this whole day, must justly entitle him to my highest encomiums and acknowledgements, and will, I trust, ensure to him your approbation; and I have the pleasure to add, that he speaks in the most favourable manner of the good conduct of all the officers and men employed in the boats under his immediate orders, particularly of Lieutenants Alexander and Reed, of the Dragon and Fantome, who each commanded a division; of Lieutenant G. A. Westphall,

whose exemplary and gallant conduct it has been necessary for me already to notice in detailing to you the operations of the day. I shall only now add that, from a thorough knowledge of his merits, (he having served many years with me as first lieutenant,) I always, on similar occasions, expected much from him, but this day he even outstripped those expectations; and though in considerable pain from his wound, he insisted on continuing to assist me to the last moment with his able exertions. I therefore, sir, cannot but entertain a confident hope that his services of to-day, and the wound he has received, added to what he so successfully executed at Frenchtown, (as detailed in my letter to you of the 29th ultimo,) will obtain for him your favourable consideration and notice, and that of my Lords Commissioners of the Admiralty. I should be wanting in justice did I not also mention to you, particularly, the able assistance afforded me by Lieutenant Robertson, of the artillery, who is ever a volunteer where service is to be performed, and always foremost in performing such service, being equally conspicuous for his gallantry and abihty; and he also obliged me by superintending the destruction of the ordnance taken at the foundry. To Captains Wybourn and Carter, who commanded the marines, and shewed much skill in the management of them, every praise is likewise due, as are my acknowledgements to Lieutenant Lewis, of the Highflyer, who not being able to bring his vessel near enough to render assistance, came himself with his usual active zeal to offer his personal services. And it is my pleasing duty to have to report to you, in addition, that all the other officers and men seemed to vie with each other in the cheerful and zealous discharge of their duty, and I have, therefore, the satisfaction of recommending their general good conduct, on this occasion, to your notice accordingly.

I have the honor to be, &c.

G. COCKBURN, Rear-Adm.

To the Right Hon. Admiral Sir J. B. Warren, Bart. and K.B., &c.

The descent of the British on Havre de Grace has more than any other event of the war afforded an opportunity for exaggeration and misrepresentation—each particular dealer in these articles has, however, happily for the truth, contrived so to tell his story as to con-

---

* Taken from the battery at Havre de Grace—6 guns, 12 and 6-pounders.

Disabled, in battery for protection of foundry—5 guns, 24-pounders.

Disabled, ready for sending away from foundry—28 guns, 32-pounders.

Disabled, in boring-house and foundry—8 guns and 4 carronades of different calibres.

Total—51 guns, and 130 stand of small arms.

tradict his neighbour, and we are thus enabled to refute, most convincingly, the random and malevolent statements put forth. The North American Review states, that for three weeks the inhabitants of Havre de Grace had been making preparations, and that the militia of the district had been called out. An extract from this review will show that the demonstration of the Havre de Gracians was not the unpremeditated movement of men hastily summoned together for mutual defence, but was a preconcerted arrangement.

"The militia, amounting to about two hundred and fifty, were kept to their arms all night; patroles were stationed in every place where they could possibly be of any service; and the volunteers were at their guns, with a general determination to give the enemy a warm reception." We make this quotation to show, not that these men were wrong in taking up arms for the preservation of their hearths and homes, but to prove that any severities on the part of the British, were not exercised upon unoffending or defenceless inhabitants, but actually formed part and parcel of the miseries always attendant on a state of warfare. Another object gained by the quotation is to convict the writers of the "Sketches of the War," History of the War," and "History of the United States" of wilful distortion of the truth. One of these writers states that they "attacked, plundered, and burnt the neat and flourishing *but unprotected* village of Havre de Grace; for which outrage *no provocation had* been given, nor could excuse be assigned" Admiral Cockburn's letter, and the remarks in the Review, show whether the village or town was either unprepared for, or unexpectant of, an attack. This last extract will therefore suffice as a sample of the other accounts.

But this system of mis-statement was not confined to journalists or historians, Mr. Munroe in his official communication to Sir Alexander Cochrane, in the teeth of the fact that six pieces of cannon and one hundred and thirty stand of arms had been captured, persists in describing the inhabitants as unarmed. One writer a Mr. O'Connor in his zeal to prove at once the bravery of the defenders, and the deliberate atrocity of the assailants—first descants upon the vigorous preparations made, and the resolute defence,

and then winds up by declaring that "it is not easy to assign any cause, other than the caprice of its projector, for this violent attack on an *unoffending and defenceless* village. No reason of a public nature could have induced it. No public property was deposited there, nor were any of its inhabitants engaged in *aiding* the prosecution of the war."

It would be idle and unnecessary after these quotations to add anything more on this subject, and we shall accordingly pass on to the next instance of atrocity perpetrated by the British. We will just call attention to one point more connected with this affair, which is, that but one American writer thought the loss of forty-five pieces of cannon, chiefly thirty-two's and twenty-four pounders, of sufficient consequence to give it a place in his history.

The third expedition undertaken for the purpose of capturing or destroying public property, set out on the night of the 5th May. The destination of this expedition was to the villages of Georgetown and Fredericktown, situated on the opposite banks of the river Sassafras, and nearly facing each other. The official letter will, however, furnish the most correct details.

H. M. S. Maidstone, off the Sassafras river, May 6th, 1813.

Sir,—I have the honour to acquaint you, that understanding Georgetown and Fredericktown, situated up the Sassafras river, were places of some trade and importance, and the Sassafras being the only river or place of shelter for vessels at this upper extremity of the Chesapeake, which I had not examined and cleared, I directed, last night, the assembling the boats alongside the Mohawk, from whence with the marines, as before, under captains Wybourn and Carter, with my friend lieutenant Robertson, of the artillery, and his small party, they proceeded up this river, being placed by me for this operation, under the immediate directions of captain Byng of the Mohawk.

I intended that they should arrive before the above mentioned towns by dawn of day, but in this I was frustrated by the intricacy of the river, our total want of local knowledge in it, the darkness of the night, and the great distance the towns lay up it; it, therefore, unavoidably became late in the morning before we approached them, when, having intercepted a small boat with two inhabitants, I directed captain Byng to halt our boats about two miles below the town, and I sent forward the two Americans in their boat to warn their countrymen against acting in the same rash manner the people of Havre-de-Grace had done; assuring them if they did, that their towns would inevitably meet with a similar fate; but, on the contrary, if they did not attempt resistance, no injury should be done to them or their towns; that vessels and public property only would be seized; that the strictest discipline would be maintained; and that, whatever provisions or other property of individuals I might require for the use of the squadron, should be instantly paid for in its fullest value. After having allowed sufficient time for this message to be digested, and their resolution taken thereon, I directed the boats to advance, and I am sorry to say, I soon found the more unwise alternative was adopted; for on our reaching within about a mile of the town, between two projecting elevated points of the river, a most heavy fire of musketry was opened on us from about 400 men, divided and entrenched on the two opposite banks, aided by one long gun. The launches and rocket-boats smartly returned this fire with good effect, and with the other boats and the marines I pushed ashore immediately above the enemy's position, thereby ensuring the capture of the towns or the bringing him to a decided action. He determined, however, not to risk the latter; for the moment he discerned we had gained the shore, and that the marines had fixed their bayonets, he fled with his whole force to the woods, and was neither seen nor heard of afterwards, though several were sent out to ascertain whether he had taken up any new position, or what had become of him. I gave him, however, the mortification of seeing, from wherever he had hid himself, that I was keeping my word with respect to the towns, which (excepting the houses of those who had continued peaceably in them, and had taken no part in the attack made on us) were forthwith destroyed, as were four vessels laying in the river, and some stores of sugar, of lumber, of leather, and of other merchandize. I then directed the re-embarkation of our small force, and we pro-

ceeded down the river again, to a town I had observed, situated in a branch of it, about half way up, and here I had the satisfaction to find, that what had passed at Havre, George-town, and Fredericktown, had its effect, and led these people to understand, that they had more to hope for from our generosity, than from erecting batteries, and opposing us by means within their power; the inhabitants of this place having met me at landing, to say that they had not permitted either guns or militia to be stationed there, and that whilst there I should not meet with any opposition whatever. I therefore landed with the officers and a small guard only, and having ascertained that there was no public property of any kind, or warlike stores, and having allowed of such articles as we stood in need of being embarked in the boats on payment to the owner of their full value, I again re-embarked, leaving the people of this place well pleased with the wisdom of their determination on their mode of receiving us. I also had a deputation from Charlestown, in the north-east river to assure me that that place is considered by them at your mercy, and that neither guns nor militia-men shall be suffered there; and as I am assured that all the places in the upper part of the Chesapeake have adopted similar resolutions, and that there is now neither public property, vessels, or warlike stores remaining in this neighbourhood, I propose returning to you with the light squadron to-morrow morning.

I am sorry to say the hot fire we were under this morning cost us five men wounded one only, however, severely; and I have much satisfaction in being able to bear testimony to you of the zeal, gallantry, and good conduct of the different officers and men serving in this division. To Captain Byng, of the Mohawk, who conducted the various arrangements on this occasion, with equal skill and bravery, every possible praise is most justly due, as well as to Captains Wybourn, Carter, Lieutenant Robertson, of the Artillery, and Lieutenant Lewis, of the Highflyer; Lieutenant Alexander, of the Dragon, the senior officer under Captain Byng, in command of the boats, deserves also that I should particularly notice him to you for his steadiness, correctness, and the great ability with which he always executes whatever service is entrusted to him; and I must beg permission of seizing this opportunity of stating to you how much I have been indebted to Captain Burdett, of this ship, who was good enough to receive me on board the Maidstone, when I found it impracticable to advance higher in the Marlborough, and has invariably accompanied me on every occasion whilst directing these various operations, and rendered me always the most able, prompt, and efficacious assistance.

I have the honor to be, &c.

G. COCKBURN, Rear-Ad.

'To the Right Hon. Sir J. B. Warren, Baronet, K. B. &c.

Whatever severities were used towards the inhabitants of these villages, the chastisement was merited. The British had evinced the desire to respect private property, and had even sent on two of their own countrymen to apprise the villagers of their disposition. The Americans returned a submissive message, alleging that they were without the means of defence, whilst they were preparing a warm reception for their visitors. In short they laid a trap for the British, in which they were themselves caught, inasmuch as they lost their property, which would otherwise have been respected. This was so clearly established that even American writers have been able to make very little of it, and they have, accordingly, contented themselves with general charges of British cruelty and so forth.

One end was gained by the example made of Havre de Grace and the two villages, as deputations praying for mercy began now to be sent to the British commander from the other places in the neighbourhood of the Chesapeakes. This disposition on the part of the inhabitants has been construed into "treachery" by the author of "the War," and most unjustly so. The British were in force, the militia who should have opposed them were too few in number and generally too undisciplined, if not lacking in courage, to offer any effectual resistance. What then remained for the poor people but to make the best terms possible, so as to avert the fate which had overtaken three places already mentioned. Still more unfair is it to call the British unprincipled marauders, as on no occasion was any severity observed except

when by making resistance the town or village fell under the category of "places taken by storm."

The great object of the attacks made by such journals as the "National Advocate," "Democratic Press," and others of the same stamp, was to lower the character of British troops and of Britain, in the estimation of Europe, and, at the same time, by the recital of these outrages to influence the feelings of western patriots. James, who was in a situation to ascertain the truth declares that "American citizens of the first consequence in Baltimore, Annapolis and Washington, when they have gone on board the British Chesapeake squadron, as they frequently did, with flags, to obtain passports, or ask other favours, and these inflammatory paragraphs were shown to them, never failed to declare with apparent shame, that they had been penned without the slightest regard to truth; but merely to instigate their ferocious countrymen in the Western States to rally round the American standard." Fortunately the task of disproving all these charges is easy, as the North American Review bears the following testimony to the behaviour of the invaders.

"They, (the British,)," says the Review, were always desirous of making a fair purchase, and of paying the full value of what they received; and it is no more than justice to the enemy to state that, in many instances, money was left behind, in a conspicuous place, to the full amount of what had been taken away.*

One very material difference may be observed between the proclamations we have seen issued by General Hull, on the first invasion of Canada, and Sir George Cockburn's addresses to the Americans. The first, invited the Canadians to turn traitors, threatening them, in case of non-compliance, with all the horrors of war, the English Admiral merely asked them for their own sakes not to oppose a superior force.

The next object of importance was the cutting out of the American Schooner Surveyor, by the boats of the Nacissus. This was a very spirited thing on both sides, and so impressed was Lieutenant Crerie with the gal-

Cutting out of the Surveyor Schooner.

*North American Review, vol. 5. V. P. 153.

lantr, of the American Commander, Captain Travis, that he returned him his sword with the following letter:—

From Lieutenant CRERIE to Captain TRAVIS.

His Majesty's ship Narcissus, June 13th, 1813.

SIR,—Your gallant and desperate attempt to defend your vessel against more than double your number, on the night of the 12th instant, excited such admiration on the part of your opponents, as I have seldom witnessed, and induces me to return you the sword you had nobly used, in testimony of mine Our poor fellows have severely suffered, occasioned chiefly, if not solely, by the precaution you had taken to prevent surprise; in short, I am at a loss which to admire most, the previous engagement on board the Surveyor, or the determined manner by which her deck was disputed, inch by inch.

I am, Sir, with much respect, &c.

JOHN CRERIE.

Captain S. Travis, U. S. Cutter, Surveyor.

Towards the middle of June, the Naval Commander at Norfolk, Com. Cassin deemed it advisable to attempt the destruction or capture of the Junon, forty-six gun frigate, then anchored in Hampton Roads, and from which boat expeditions had been dispatched to destroy the shipping in James' River.

Attack on Junon by flotilla.

An attack was made on the 20th by the American flotilla,* armed with some thirty

*From Commodore CASSIN to the American Secretary of the Navy.

Navy Yard, Gosport, June 21, 1813.

SIR,—On Saturday. at 11 P. M., Captain Tarbell moved with the flotilla under his command consisting of 15 gun-boats, in two divisions, Lieutenant John M. Gardner, 1st division, and Lieutenant Robert Henley, the 2nd, manned from the frigate, and 50 musketeers, ordered from Craney Island by General Taylor, and proceeded down the River; but adverse winds and squalls prevented his approaching the enemy until Sunday morning at four, when the flotilla comenced a heavy galling fire on a frigate, at about three quarters of a mile distance, lying well up the roads, two other frigates lying in sight. At half past four, a breeze sprung up from E.N.E. which

guns, and manned with about five hundred men. The Junon was becalmed and as the flotilla did not venture within reach of her carronades, the action was confined to a distant cannonade. It, however, lasted a sufficiently long time to warrant Commodore Cassin's writing the letter which we have given in our notes. One statement of the doughty Commodore is particularly ridiculous, viz., that the Junon was almost reduced to a sinking state, the fact being that she received two shots only in her hull, and had but one man killed.

enabled the two frigates to get under way—one a razee or very heavy ship, and the other a frigate—and to come nearer into action. The boats in consequence of their approach, hauled off, though keeping up a well directed fire on the razee and the other ship. which gave us several broadsides. The frigate first engaged, supposed to be the Junon, was certainly severely handled—had the calm continued one half hour, that frigate must have fallen into our hands, or been destroyed. She must have slipped her mooring so as to drop nearer the razee, who had all sail set, coming up to her with the other frigate. The action continued one hour and a half with three ships. Shortly after the action, the razee got alongside of the ship, and had her upon a deep careen in a little time, with a number of boats and stages round her. I am satisfied considerable damage was done to her, for she was silenced some time, until the razee opened her fire, when she commenced. Our loss is very trifling. Mr. Allison, master's mate, on board 139, was killed early in the action, by an 18 pound ball, which passed through him and lodged in the mast. No. 154 had a shot between wind and water. No. 67 had her franklin shot away, and several of them had some of their sweeps and stancheons shot away—but two men slightly injured from the sweeps. On the flood tide several ships of the line and frigates came into the roads, and we did expect an attack last night. There are now in the roads 13 ships of the line and frigates, one brig and several tenders.

I cannot say too much for the officers and crews on this occasion; for every man appeared to go into action with much cheerfulness, apparently anxious to do his duty and resolved to conquer. I had a better opportunity of discovering their actions than any one else, being in my boat the whole of the action.

I have the honor to be, &c.

JOHN CASSIN.

Hon. W. Jones, &c.

CHAPTER XVIII.

As MAY be supposed, the blockade of the Chesapeake, and the threatening position taken up by the fleet, off Hampton Roads, placed the Americans on the *qui vive*, especially as many tongued rumour had been busied in ascribing plans and intentions of every description to the British Admiral.

The flotilla had failed in their attack on the Junon, thereby demonstrating that gun boats alone could effect nothing : the Constellation could not venture from under the batteries, and as there was, consequently, really no force by which the British could be attacked by water, the Americans were compelled to endure the sight of a hostile squadron daily before their eyes, with the mortifying conviction forced on them, that, inasmuch as they had been fomenters of the war, so were they now the principal sufferers —So strict was the blockade that it was not only impossible for any vessel to escape the cruisers which guarded the passage between Cape Henry and Cape Charles, but it was an enterprise attended with great risk for any vessel to leave the James, Elizabeth, York, or in fact, any of the rivers which disembogue into the Chesapeake bay.

All that was, under these circumstances, left for the Americans was to prepare against attacks, and we accordingly find in "Sketches of the war" that upwards of ten thousand militia were assembled round Norfolk and its vicinity, the points against which an attack

was most likely to be directed. With the whole coast thus on the alert it was not to be expected that the preparations which were openly made towards the end of June by the British Squadron would escape observation. "Accordingly," as James has it "Craney Island being rather weakly manned, the commanding officer at Norfolk sent one hundred and fifty of the Constellation's seamen and marines, to a battery of eighteen pounders in the north west, and about four hundred and eighty Virginia Militia, exclusive of officers, to reinforce a detachment of artillery, stationed with two twenty four and four six pounders on the west side of the island. Captain Tarbell's fifteen gun boats were also moored in the best position for contributing to the defence of the post." It will thus be seen that very formidable preparations for the defence of this port were adopted, and the following despatch from Admiral Warren to Mr Croker announcing the failure of the attack on Craney Island will not wholly be unprepared for.

From Admiral Warren to Mr. Croker.

San Domingo, Hampton-roads,

Chesapeake, June 24, 1813.

SIR,—I request you will inform their lordships, that, from the information received of the enemy's fortifying Craney Island, and it being necessary to obtain possession of that place, to enable the light ships and vessels to proceed up the narrow channel towards

18

Norfolk, to transport the troops over on that side for them to attack the new fort and lines in the rear of which the Constellation frigate was anchored, I directed the troops under Sir Sydney Beckwith to be landed upon the continent within the nearest point to that place, and a reinforcement of seamen and marines from the ships; but upon approaching the island, from the extreme shoalness of the water on the sea side, and the difficulty of getting across from the land, as well as the island itself being fortified with a number of guns and men from the frigate and militia, and flanked by fifteen gun-boats, I considered, in consequence of the representation of the officer commanding the troops, of the difficulty of their passing over from the land, that the persevering in the attempt would cost more men than the number with us would permit, as the other forts must have been stormed before the frigate and dock-yard could have been destroyed; I therefore ordered the troops to be re-embarked.

I am happy to say, the loss in the above affair, (returns of which are enclosed) has not been considerable, and only two boats sunk.

I have to regret, that Captain Hanshett, of His Majesty's ship Diadem, who volunteered his services, and led the division of boats with great gallantry, was severely wounded by a ball in the thigh.

The officers and men behaved with much bravery and if it had been possible to have got at the enemy, I am persuaded would have soon gained the place.

I have the honor to be, &c.
J. B. WARREN.
J. W. Croker, Esq.

A return of officers, seamen, and marines, belonging to His Majesty's ships, killed, wounded, and missing, in the attack on Craney Island, June 22d.

Killed, none—wounded, eight—missing, ten.

Return of land forces killed, wounded, and missing, in same attack.

Killed, six—wounded, sixteen—missing, one hundred and four.

The policy of making this attack has been very much questioned, and some of James' objections appear to have a considerable show of reason. He says, "There can be only one opinion, surely, about the wisdom of

sending boats, in broad-day-light, to feel their way to the shore, over shoals and mud banks, and that in the teeth of a very formidable battery.—* But still had the veil of darkness been allowed to screen the boats from view, and an hour of the night chosen, when the tide had covered the shoals with deep water, the same little party might have carried the batteries, and a defeat as disgraceful to those that caused, as honorable to those that suffered in it, been converted into a victory. As it was the victory at Craney Island, dressed up to advantage in the American Official account, and properly commented on by the Government editors, was hailed throughout the Union as a glorious triumph fit for Americans to achieve."

We fully concede with many of James' objections, especially as to the injudicious selection of open daylight and an ebb tide. And although the particulars of the casualties are not given in Admiral Warren's despatch, yet other sources show that it was precisely to these causes that the failure was to be attributed.

In the first place there was an open parade of boats and an unwonted bustle round the British vessels; This was of course not unobserved by the enemy, who thus had time afforded to them to mature their plans of defence. In the second place the first part of the expedition of some seventeen or eighteen boats with about eight hundred men, under Sir Sydney Beckwith, was landed at a place called Peg's point, an untenable position, and from whence a movement, in support of the main body, could not be made. After remaining in this position for some time, the troops were re-embarked and returned to the fleet. The actual attack was made by a body about equally strong as the first division, and we would observe here, that it was made contrary to the opinion and advice of Captains Hanshett, Maude, and Romilly, however, overruled by the decision of Captain Perchell, the senior officer. It will thus be seen that the commanding officer had just half the force he calculated on for

*Here James indulges in a bit of the patriotic, about British basing their hopes of success on valour, not numbers, which we can afford to leave out. * * * * *

the demonstration, a fact that must not be forgotten when we come to compare American accounts. From the shallowness of the water, the tide being out, some of the boats got aground on a mud bank some hundred and fifty yards from the muzzles of the guns manned by the Constellation's men. In this position it is not very wonderful that two of the boats were sunk and many of the crews killed, especially when we add that the boats were ashore so close to the beach that the American Marines and Militia, by wading in a short distance, could pick off the men while struggling in the water. Admiral Warren's wording of his despatch is about as absurd as some of the American accounts. The Admiral slurs over the real reasons why his men were obliged to abandon the enterprise, but it would have been much more creditable if he had confessed honestly that the attack, injudiciously planned, was a total failure. His account, glossing over the affair, differs so widely from those of American writers that the reader is tempted to enquire farther, and the consequence is, that the Admiral is convicted of the very fault with which we charge—Thompson, O'Connor, Smith and Ingersol.

We have fairly stated the British force, and their loss; we will now examine the American version of the affair. One* makes the British force, that landed in front of the Island battery, consist of four thousand men, but forgetting shortly after his random figures, in the next page he states "that three thousand British soldiers, sailors and marines were opposed to four hundred and eighty Virginia militia, and one hundred and fifty sailors and marines." Mr. O'Connor reduces the force at Craney Island to fifteeeen hundred men, only thus doubling them, but to make his country some amends for this, he quadruples the force that landed on the main, stating them at three thousand strong. Commodore Cassin in a postscript to one of his letters adopts the same number, and even Ingersol, who from having been the latest writer has had more opportunity afforded of learning the truth, falls into the same error and makes the British troops twenty-five hundred strong, *adding besides fifty boats full of men.*

*Sketches of the War—p. 215.

It is also note worthy that in not one of the accounts is there one allusion to the boats having grounded, the sole cause of the failure, as experience had proved that the militia could not be depended on in an attack by regular troops. The Niagara frontier sufficiently proves the correctness of this assertion. Armstrong's account differs considerably from the others, but even he falls into a mistake. He states, "the disposable force of the enemy was divided into two corps, one of which, embarked into boats, and carried directly to its object, attempted to make good a descent on the northern side of the Island; while the other landed on the main, and *availing itself of a shoal, which, at low water, was fordable by infantry,* forced its way to the western side. Though made with a considerable degree of steadiness, both attacks failed.

The mistake, made in this paragraph, is that the troops crossed from the main land to the Island, and took part in the attack. That this was not the case is certain from the fact that the other writers, whose various accounts we have been criticising, make no mention of a fact which would assuredly not have been lost sight of by them, desirous as they were of making as great a parade of national valor as possible.

Looking at the descent on Craney Island in the most favorable light it can be regarded in no other light than as a badly planned demonstration, to be regretted for two reasons, —one, the loss of life and honor to the British—the other, that an opportunity was afforded to American writers of asserting that the attack on Hampton and the outrages committed there were in revenge for the failure at Craney Island.

We have already stated that large bodies of troop had been collected in and around Norfolk, and as it was supposed that a considerable body was stationed at Hampton, it was resolved that an attack should be made on that post; accordingly, on the night of the 25th of June, about two thousand men, under the command of Sir Sidney Beckwith, in a division of boats, covered by the Mohawk Sloop, landed, and, after some resistance, carried by storm the enemy's defences.

The two despatches from admiral Warren and Sir Sidney Beckwith will be found to contain all necessary particulars of the attack, differing but little, in these points from American accounts.

San Domingo, Hampton-roads, Chesapeake,
June 27th, 1813.

SIR,—I request to inform their lordships, that the enemy having a post at Hampton, defended by a considerable corps, commanding the communication between the upper part of the country and Norfolk; I considered it advisable, and with a view to cut off their resources, to direct it to be attacked by the troops composing the flying corps attached to this squadron; and having instructed rear-admiral Cockburn to conduct the naval part of the expedition, and placed captain Pechell with the Mohawk sloop and launches, as a covering force, under his orders, the troops were disembarked with the greatest zeal and alacrity.

Sir Sydney Beckwith commanding the troops, having most ably attacked and defeated the enemy's force, and took their guns, colours, and camp, I refer their lordships to the quarter-master-general's report, (which is enclosed,) and that will explain the gallantry and behaviour of the several officers and men employed upon this occasion, and I trust will entitle them to the favour of his royal highness the prince regent, and the lord's commissioners of the Admiralty.

Sir Sydney Beckwith having reported to me that the defences of the town were entirely destroyed, and the enemy completely dispersed in the neighbourhood, I ordered the troops to be re-embarked, which was performed with the utmost good order by several officers of the squadron under the orders of rear-admiral Cockburn.

I have the honour to be,
JOHN BORLASE WARREN.
John Wilson Croker, Esq.

—

No. 15.

From quarter-master-general Sir Sydney Beckwith to Admiral Warren.

His majesty's ship San Domingo, Hampton-roads, June 28, 1813.

SIR,—I have the honour to report to you, that in compliance with your orders to attack the enemy in town and camp at Hampton, the troops under my command were put into light sailing vessels and boats, during the night of the 25th instant, and by the excellent arrangements of rear-admiral Cockburn, who was pleased in person to superintend the advance under lieutenant-colonel Napier, consisting of the 102d regiment, two companies of Canadian Chasseurs, three companies of marines from the squadron, with two 6-pounders from the marine artillery, were landed half an hour before daylight the next morning, about two miles to the westward of the town, and the royal marine battalions, under lieutenant-colonel Williams, were brought on shore so expeditiously that the column was speedily enabled to move forward.

With a view to turn the enemy's position, our march was directed towards the great road, leading from the country into the rear of the town. Whilst the troops moved off in this direction, rear-admiral Cockburn, to engage the enemy's attention, ordered the armed launches and rocket-boats to commence a fire upon their batteries; this succeeded so completely, that the head of our advanced guard had cleared a wood, and were already on the enemy's flank before our approach was perceived. They then moved from their camp to their position in rear of the town, and here they were vigorously attacked by lieutenant colonel Napier, and the advance; unable to stand which, they continued their march to the rear of the town, when a detachment, under lieutenant-colonel Willams, conducted by captain Powell, assistant-quarter-master-general, pushed through the town, and forced their way across a bridge of planks into the enemy's encampment, of which, and the batteries immediate possession was gained. In the mean time some artillerymen stormed and took the enemy's remaining field-pieces.

Enclosed I have the honour to transmit a return of ordnance taken. Lieutenant-colonel Williams will have the honour of delivering to you a stand of colours of the 68th regiment, James city light infantry, and one of the first battalion 85th regiment. The exact numbers of the enemy it is difficult to ascertain.

From the woody country, and the strength of their positions, our troops have sustained some loss; that of the enemy was very considerable—every exertion was made to collect the wounded Americans, who were attended to by a surgeon of their own, and by the British surgeons, who performed amputations on such as required it, and afforded every assistance in their power. The dead bodies of such as could be collected, were also carefully buried.

I beg leave on this occasion to express the obligations I owe to lieutenant-colonel Napier, and lieutenant-colonel Williams, for their kind and able assistance; to major Malcolm and captain Smith, and all the officers and men, whose zeal and spirited conduct entitle them to my best acknowledgements.

SYDNEY BECKWITH, Q. M. G.

Return of ordnance stores taken.

Four twelve-pounders in camp.

Three six-pounders   do.

Three artillery waggons and horses.

Return of the killed and wounded.—Five killed, twenty-three wounded and ten missing.

James' observations on this affair are worth attention as he does not attempt to conceal the fact, that acts of rapine and violence were committed, unauthorized by the laws of legitimate warfare. James writes, "The Foreign renegadoes (les Chasseurs Britaniques) forming part of the advanced force, commenced perpetrating upon the defenceless inhabitants acts of rapine and violence which unpitying custom has, in some degree, rendered inseparable from places that have been carried by storm, but which are as revolting to human nature, as they are disgraceful to the flag which would sanction them. The instant these circumstances of atrocity reached the ears of the British commanding officer, orders were given to search for, and bring in all the Chasseurs," which was done.

It will be as well to remark in palliation of this, that, immediately after the storming of Hampton, the Commander of the Chasseurs, Captain Smith, waited on the Commander-in-Chief, and informed him that his men, on being remonstrated with respecting their outrageous conduct, declared it to be their intention to give no quarter to Americans, in consequence of their comrades having been so cruelly shot at whilst struggling in the water, and unarmed, before the batteries at Craney Island. The Admiral on learning from Captain Smith his conviction, that his men would act as they had declared they would, was compelled, although short of troops, to embark and send them from the American coast.

We do not pretend to extenuate the ex-cesses committed, and deplore as heartily as any American that such should have occurred, still we must point out that these grave errors were but the fruit of the seed which Americans themselves had sown; besides, we can adduce from their own journals clear proof that, although many excesses occurred, still these actions have been grossly exaggerated by their historians. The Georgetown *Federal Republican*, of July 7th, a journal published under the very eye of the Government at Washington, testifies "that the statement of the women of Hampton being violated by the British, turns out to be false. A correspondence upon that subject and the pillage said to have been committed there, has taken place between General Taylor and Admiral Warren. Some plunder appears to have been committed, but it was confined to the Chasseurs. Admiral Warren complains, on his part, of the Americans having continued to fire upon the struggling crews of the barges, after they were sunk."

It might have been expected that, when penning their violent philippics against British cruelty and atrocity, this testimony would have had some weight with the denouncers of Admiral Cockburn and his men, but we regret to be compelled to state that in no American history from which we quote, nor in any other, that we have seen or heard of, does this exculpation of the British appear.

Admiral Warren, having effectually succeeded in annihilating the trade along the whole coast of the Chesapeake Bay, dispatched Admiral Cockburn, in the Sceptre 74, with the Romulus, Fox and Nemesis all *armèis en flute* to Ocracock, in North Carolina, for the purpose of striking a blow on the commerce carried on in the adjacent ports. On the 12th of July the expedition arrived off Ocracock, and preparations for landing were promptly arranged. On the morning of the 13th the troops were embarked under the command of Lieutenant Westphall, first of the Sceptre, and making for shore, after some opposition succeeded in capturing two privateers, the Atlas of Philadelphia, of ten guns, and the Anaconda of New York, of 18 long nines. These vessels took possession of, the troops landed, and without opposition entered Portsmouth. The destruction of the two letters of marque having been accomplished, Admiral

Cockburn re-embarked his men, finding that but few public stores were contained in the place, and that the inhabitants appeared peaceably disposed and disinclined to draw on themselves the chastisement which had attended the resistance made by some of the villages on the Chesapeake Bay.

The operations of the Southern Squadron were completed by the descent on Portsmouth and the British Admiral was satisfied that he had inflicted a blow on American commerce, which it would require years of prosperity to repair. In point of fact the great outlet by which American commerce found a passage had been hermetically sealed and the commerce of Delaware and Maryland, Virginia and North Carolina, may be said to have been virtually extinguished. We will accordingly once more change the scene and again visit the Canadas.

We now transport the reader from a Southern June to a Canadian December, when we find Lieutenant Metcalf and twenty-eight militia capturing thirty-nine regulars, near Chatham. This exploit was but trifling, yet it is noteworthy as it proved that General Harrison's occupation of the western peninsula had but served to infuse fresh spirit, and to render the opposition more determined. General Drummond was so satisfied with the gallantry displayed by Lieutenant Metcalfe, that he promoted him.

Another circumstance, which, however, was to be expected, must here be noticed No American has thought it necessary to mention this little expedition, although we hear numerous instances of more trifling affairs being duly chronicled. This, however, would have reflected no credit, hence the universal silence. The next affair was an attempt made by Captain Lewis Basden, commanding the light company of the 89th, and a detachment of the Rangers and Kent militia, under the command of Captain Caldwell, to check the invasion of the Americans along the Detroit and Lake Erie Shores. General Armstrong gives rather a lengthy account of this inroad of the Americans, and observes, " having a worthless object, it ought not to have been adopted. For of what importance to the United States would have been the capture or destruction of a blockhouse, in the heart of an enemy's country more than one hundred miles distant

from the frontier, and which, if held, would have been difficult to sustain, and, if destroyed, easily reinstated." The Americans hearing of the approach of the British party retreated, but were compelled to make a stand, which they did intrenching themselves so effectually that their assailants were compelled to retreat with a loss of sixty-five killed and wounded, amongst them Lieut. Basden. As a proof of the sheltered position of the Americans we may mention that their loss only amounted to four killed and four wounded. The demonstration had, however, the effect of compelling the Americans to abandon any further advance and to retreat as fast as they could. Colonel Butler, the originator of the expedition, has written rather an exaggerated account of it to General Harrison, and he has not failed to reduce Americans by twenty in number, adding at the same time about forty to the British. His letter will, however, speak for itself:—

DEAR SIR—

By Lieutenant Shannon of the 27th Regt., United States' infantry, I have the honor of informing you, that a detachment of the troops under my command, led by Captain Holmes, of the 24th United States' infantry, has obtained a signal victory over the enemy.

The affair took place on the 4th instant, about 100 miles from this place, on the river de French. Our force consisted of no more than 160 Rangers and mounted infantry. The enemy, from their own acknowledgement, had about 240. The fine light company of the Royal Scots is totally destroyed; they led the attack most gallantly, and their commander fell within ten paces of our front line. The light company of the 89th has also suffered severely; one officer of that company fell, one is a prisoner, and another is said to be badly wounded.

In killed, wounded, and prisoners, the enemy lost about 80, whilst on our part there were but four killed, and four wounded. This great disparity in the loss on each side is to be attributed to the very judicious position occupied by Captain Holmes, who compelled the enemy to attack him at great disadvantage. This even, more gallantly merits the laurel.

Captain Holmes has just returned, and will

furnish a detailed account of the expedition, which shall immediately be transmitted to you.

Very respectfully,
Your most obedient Servant,
H. BUTLER,
Lieut.-Col. Commandant at Detroit.
Major-General Harrison.

Enemy's forces, as stated by the prisoners.

Royal Scots,	101
89th Regiment,	45
Militia,	50
Indians,	40 to 60
	236

We are rather at a loss to guess whether the information, as to force was gained from the one wounded man who fell into Captain Holmes' hands. The return made by the British, shows a loss of fifty-seven instead of eighty killed and wounded, and the only prisoner was a volunteer, who, poor fellow, had only just joined and could scarcely be expected to have had much time to learn particulars as to force.

Again we must, for a short space, leave the west and follow the movement to farther east. We must not omit, however, to chronicle a mistake into which Major General Browne was led, and which must have tended, materially, to lower American Commanders in the estimation of their men.

Wilkinson's memoirs show clearly, as explained by a letter of General Armstrong, of date the 20th January, that it was contemplated to open the campaign of 1814 by a pretended demonstration in the Upper Canadian peninsula. A twofold object was to be accomplished by this, as to defend the frontier ports along the Niagara would require the union of all the troops in Western Canada, and it would be rendered difficult, if not impossible, to make any demonstrations against Amherstburg, Detroit, or the shipping at Erie and Put-in-bay. Again, this attack would prevent the possibility of any re-inforcements being sent to the lower Province, in case attacks should be contemplated on Kingston, Montreal, or Quebec.

The real orders to General Browne, were, "you will immediately consult with Commodore Chauncey, about the readiness of the fleet, for a descent on Kingston, the moment

the ice leaves the lake. If he deems it practicable, and you think you have troops enough to carry it, you will attempt the expedition. In such an event, you will use the enclosed as a *ruse de guerre.*"

The instructions to be used in this manner were " public sentiments will no longer tolerate the possession of Fort Niagara by the enemy. You will therefore move the division which you brought from French Mills, and invest that post. Governor Jenkins will co-operate with his five thousand militia ; and Colonel Scott, who is to be made a brigadier, will join you. You will receive your instructions at Onondaga hollow." Poor General Browne, knowing that he would have to wait for some months ere the fleet could move, was induced to mistake the real object of attack, and accordingly marched forthwith his troops, two thousand strong from Sackett's Harbour westward, to the point where he was to receive his instructions ; here he was undeceived and had to march back again through the most wretched roads to Sackett's Harbour. This marching and countermarching could not have inspired much confidence in the minds of the soldiery, when the time for action in the western peninsula really did arrive.

During all this time General Wilkinson had been at Plattsburg nursing his wrath against the Canadians and British for the reception which they had accorded to him in his expedition down the St. Lawrence. Finding it impossible, we presume, to restrain his desire for revenge, the General, on the 19th March, advanced with his army from Plattsburg to Swanton, Vermont, near to Missisquoi Bay, on Lake Champlain. On the 22d the General crossed the boundary and took possession of Philipsburg, a village just within the lines. On the 26th, the General re-crossed the lake for the purpose of striking a blow in another and more favorable direction, and we find him on the 29th, at the head of four thousand men holding a council of war to deliberate on an attack to be made on a British force stationed at La Colle Mill, about eight miles from Champlain. We here give the proceedings of the council, and the general order, which was the result of these deliberations.

Minutes of a council of war held at Champlain the 29th of March, 1814.

Present—Brigadier-general Macomb, brigadier-general Bissell, brigadier-general Smith, colonel Atkinson, colonel Miller, colonel Cummings, major Pitts, major Totten.

Major-general Wilkinson states to the council, that, from the best information he can collect, the enemy has assembled at the Isle aux Noix and La Colle Mill 2500 men, composed of about 2000 regular troops and 500 militia, of whom, after leaving a garrison of 200 men at Isle aux Noix, 1800 regulars and 500 militia may be brought into action. The corps of the United States, now at this place, consists of 3999 combatants, including 100 cavalry, and 304 artillerists, with 11 pieces of artillery. The objects of the enemy are unknown, and the two corps are separated nine miles. Under these circumstances the major general submits the following questions for the consideration and opinion of the council·

First—Shall we attack the enemy? and in such case do the council approve the order of march and battle hereunto annexed, with the general order of the day?

Second—When and by what route shall the attack be made, on the plan of the intermediate country hereunto annexed?

Third—Shall a single attack be made with our force combined; or shall two attacks be made; or shall we feint on the right by the shore of the Sorel, or to the left by Odell's mill, to favour the main attack?

The general will be happy to adopt any advantageous change which may be proposed by the council, or be governed by their opinions.

The council is of opinion, that the light troops should cover a reconnoissance towards La Colle Mill; and if it is found practicable, the position should be attacked, and the enemy's works destroyed; that the whole army move to support the light troops; that the order of battle is approved, and the manner and mode of attack must be left entirely with the commanding general.

ALEX. MACOMB,
TH. A. SMITH,
D. BISSELL,
R. PURDY,
JAMES MILLER,
T. H. PITTS,
H. ATKINSON,
JOSEPH G. TOTTEN.

Under existing circumstances my opinion is, that we go as far as La Colle Mill, designated in the map, to meet the enemy there, and destroy their block-house and the mill in which they are quartered.

M. SMITH, col. 29th inf.

No. 18.

American general order of the 29th *of March.*

Head-quarters, Champlain, 29th March, 1814.

The army will enter Canada to-morrow to meet the enemy, who has approached in force to the vicinity of the national line of demarcation; the arms and ammunition are therefore to be critically examined, and the men completed to 60 rounds. The commanding officers of corps and companies will be held responsible for the exact fulfilment of this essential order. The troops to be completed to four days' cooked provisions, exclusive of the present; and it is recommended to the gentlemen in commission to make the same provision. No baggage will be taken forward, excepting the bedding of the officers. Let every officer, and every man, take the resolution to return victorious, or not at all: for, with double the force of the enemy, this army must not give ground.

Brigadier-general Macomb having joined with his command, the formation of the troops must necessarily be modified. They are therefore to be formed into three brigades; the first, under general Macomb, consisting of his present command, with the addition of colonel M. Smith's consolidated regiment; second and third, under the command of brigadier-general Smith and Bissell, consisting of the troops already consigned to them. The order of march and battle will be furnished the brigadier-generals, and commanding officers of regiments, by the adjutant-general.

The transport permit will be immediately returned for, and distributed by, regiments.

On the march, when approaching the enemy, or during an action, the men are to be profoundly silent, and will resolutely execute the commands they may receive from the officers. In every movement which may be made, the ranks are to be unbroken, and there must be no running forward or shouting. An officer will be posted on the right of each platoon, and a tried serjeant will form a supernumerary rank, and will instantly put to death any man who goes back. This formation is to take place by regiments and brigades, in the the course of the day, when the officers are to be posted.

Let every man perfectly understand his place; and let all bear in mind what they owe to their own honor and to a beloved country, contending for its rights, and its very independence as a nation.

The officers must be careful that the men do not throw away their amunition: one deliberate shot being worth half a dozen hurried ones; and they are to give to the troops the example of courage in every exigency which may happen.

In battle there must be no contest for rank or station, but every corps must march promptly and directly to the spot, which it may be directed to occupy. The troops will be under arms at reveillée to-morrow morning, and will be ready to march at a moment's warning.— All orders from the adjutant and inspector-general's department; from captain Rees, assistant–deputy–quarter–master–general; and major Lush and captain Nourse, extra aides de camp to general Wilkinson, will be respected as coming from the commanding general himself.   Signed, by order,

W. CUMMINGS, adj. gen.

We have on several occasions been reminded of the old saying, *montes parturiunt nascitur ridiculus mus,* when chronicling the sayings (*not doings,*) of American commanders, but in no instance have we found more ridiculous results following inflated professions. The proclamation breathed the very spirit of valour, and the orders to conquer or to die were most explicit. A retreat was not to be thought of, and in case any craven spirit should exist amongst the four thousand, (save one,) breasts animated with Wilkinsonian ardour, (perhaps as James has it "*as an additional stimulus to glory*") à picked man was chosen to whom instructions were given to put to death "any man who goes back."— What could promise more fairly for the annihilation of the twenty-three hundred British-ers. One is almost forced to believe that this proclamation had been drawn up under the supervision of the Cabinet at Washington.— Let us examine, however, before following the steps of the heroes who had just set out, through snow and mud, on the fourth invasion of Canada, how the case really stood.—

For this purpose a passage from James will be sufficient:—

" At St. John's, distant about fourteen miles from the Isle aux Noix, and twenty-one from La Colle river were stationed under the command of lieutenant colonel Sir William Williams, of the 13th regiment, six batalion companies of that regiment, and a battalion of Canadian militia; numbering altogether, about seven hundred and fifty rank and file. At Isle aux Noix, where lieutenant colonel Richard Williams, of the Royal marines, commanded, were stationed the chief part of a battalion of that corps, and the two flank companies of the 13th regiment; in all about five hundred and fifty rank and file. The garrison of La Colle Mill, at which major Handcock, of the 13th regiment, commanded, consisted of about seventy of the marine corps, one corporal, and three marine artillerymen, captain Blake's company of the 13th regiment, and a small detachment of frontier light infantry under captain Ritter; the whole not exceeding one hundred and eighty rank and file. At Whitman's, on the left bank of the Richelieu, distanced about two miles from the Mill, and communicating with Isle aux Noix, was the remaining battalion company of the Canadian fencibles, under captain Cartwright, and a battalion company of Voltigeurs were stationed at Burtonville, distant two miles up La Colle river, and where there had been a bridge, by which the direct road into the province passed."

On a review of these numbers it will be found that there were not altogether more than seventeen hundred and fifty regulars and militia within a circle of twenty five miles in diameter, yet general Wilkinson in the estimate presented to the council numbers the troops at Isle aux Noix, and La Colle, alone, at twenty five hundred and fifty, and designates them all as regular troops with the exception of two companies. Before entering on the expedition we will give a description of this famous post against which four thousand valiant Americans were marching.

The Mill at La Colle was built of stone with walls about eighteen inches thick, having a wooden or shingled roof, and consisting of two stories. It was in size about thirty-six feet by fifty, and situate on the south bank of La Colle river; which was then fro zen over nearly to its mouth, or junction with the Richelieu, from which the Mill was about three quarters of a mile distant. The Mill had been placed in a state of defence, by filling up the windows with logs, leaving horizontal interstices to fire through. On the north bank of the river, a little to the right of the Mill, and with which it is communicated by a wooden bridge, was a small house, converted into a block house, by being surrounded with a breast-work of logs. In the rear of this temporary block house was a large barn, to which nothing had been done, and which was not even musket proof. The breadth of the cleared ground, to the southward of the Mill, was about two hundred, and that to the northward, about one hundred yards, but in the flanks the woods were much nearer. The reader has now before him the position and strength of the Mill, the number of troops available for its defence, and the number of the assailants. These points then haing been settled, we will accompany General Wilkinson on that march which was to result in victory or death.

The Americans commenced the expedition by setting out in a wrong direction, and instead of La Colle found themselves at Burtonville, where they attacked and drove in a small piquet. This mistake discovered, the march was resumed but again in a wrong direction. At last, however, they got on the main road near Odelltown, about three miles from La Colle. This road was found almost impassable for the troops, in consequence of the trees on either side having been feiled, and before the march could be pursued, the axe-men were compelled to cut up and remove the obstruction. While this operation was going on, a piquet sent forward by Major Handcock, opened a severe fire and killed and wounded several men. At last, however, the Mill was reached and by half-past one in the afternoon the American commander had invested the fortress with his nearly four thousand men. As the General very naturally expected that the one hundred and eighty men who composed the garrison, would attempt to escape, six hundred, under Colonel Mills, were sent across in rear of the Mille, to cut off all chance of a retreat. A heavy fire was then opened from an 18-12 and 6 pounder battery, also from a 5½ inch howit-

zer. By this time the two flank companies of the 13th had arrived at the scene of action, and a gallant charge was made by them on the battery, but the overpowering fire kept up compelled them to retreat and recross the river. A second charge was now made by the Fencibles and the Voltigeurs, with the remnant of the two companies of the 13th. This charge was so vigorous that the artillerymen were driven from their guns which were only saved from capture by the heavy fire of the infantry. The evidence as to the gallantry of the British and Canadians is fortunately to be found in the proceedings at General Wilkinson's court martial. Lieutenant-Colonel McPherson who commanded the artillery, deposed on that occasion that, "the ground was disputed inch by inch, in our advance to the mill; and the conduct of the enemy, that day, was distinguished by desperate bravery. As an instance one company made a charge on our artillery, and at the same instant, received its fire, and that of two brigades of infantry." Lieutenant-Col. Totten, of the Engineers, and Brigadier General Bissell might both be also cited as bearing the same testimony. Despite, however, this gallantry, it became apparent to Major Handcock that farther attempts on the guns, in the teeth of such overwhelming superiority in numbers, would be but to sacrifice valuable lives, the men were accordingly withdrawn to act on the defensive. Here we must correct a statement made by General Wilkinson, in his trial, viz., that he had to contend against not only Captain Pring's two sloops, but also two gun-boats at the back of the mill. We assert on the authority of James, and Wilkinson's own memoirs, (vol. 3, p 235,) that not one American officer stated anything of the kind, and that Colonel Totten swore positively "that the fire from the gunboats was perfectly useless, fifty or a hundred feet above their heads."

It was by this time about dusk, but although the fire of the besieged had slackened for want of powder, the enemy made no attempt to carry the Mill by storm, but retired from the field. Thus ended the fourth great invasion of Canada.

It would almost seem impossible for any historian, however unprincipled to represent this affair in any other light than as a check of a large by a small body, but nothing, it appears, was too difficult for true patriots, who desired to place their country in the most favorable light. Accordingly we find Messrs. Thompson, O'Connor and Smith explaining away and smoothing the failure of the attack until in their skilful hands, the affair almost assumes the character of a victory. Mr. O'Connor contends that the enemy must not be permitted to claim a victory because circumstances "*concurred to render it nearly impossible to drive him from his cowardly stronghold.*" Instead of one hundred and eighty, Dr. Smith places two thousand five hundred men within the Mill, although it is difficult to imagine how so many men could be packed in a building fifty by thirty-six feet —[considering that there were two stories to the Mill, this would be somewhere about an allowance of one and a half feet to each individual.] As the account which has been just given is necessarily imperfect, a despatch from Colonel Williams to Sir George Provost, is added, which will be found to be detailed and perhaps more satisfactory.

From Lieutenant-Colonel Williams to Sir G Prevost.

La Colle, March 13, 1814.

SIR,—I beg leave to acquaint you, that I have just received from Major Handcock, of the 13th Regiment, commanding at the block-house on La Colle river, a report, stating that the out-posts on the road from Burtonville and La Colle mill, leading from Odell-town, were attacked at an early hour yesterday morning by the enemy in great force, collected from Plattsburgh and Burlington, under the command of Major-General Wilkinson. The attack on the Burtonville road was soon over, when the enemy shewed themselves on the road from the mill that leads direct to Odell-town, where they drove in a piquet stationed in advance of La Colle, about a mile and a half distant; and soon after the enemy established a battery of three guns (12-pounders) in the wood. With this artillery they began to fire on the mill, when Major Handcock, hearing of the arrival of the flank companies of the 13th Regiment at the block-house, ordered an attack on the guns; which, however, was not successful, from the wood being so thick and so filled with men. Soon after, another op-

portunity presented itself, when the Canadian Grenadier Company, and a company of the Voltigeurs, attempted the guns; but the very great superiority of the enemy's numbers, hid in the woods, prevented their taking them.

I have to regret the loss of many brave and good soldiers in these two attacks, and am particularly sorry to loose the service, for a short time, of Captain Ellard, of the 13th Regiment, from being wounded while gallantly leading his company. The enemy withdrew their artillery towards night-fall, and retired, towards morning, from the mill, taking the road to Odell-town.

Major Handcock speaks in high terms of obligation to Captain Ritter, of the Frontier Light Infantry, who, from his knowledge of the country, was of great benefit. The marine detachment, under Lieutenants Caldwell and Barton, the Canadian Grenadier Company, and the company of Voltigeurs, as well as all the troops employed: the Major expresses himself in high terms of praise for their conduct, so honourable to the service.

Major Handcock feels exceedingly indebted to Captain Pring, R.N., for his ready and prompt assistance, in mooring up the sloops and gun-boats from Isle au Noix, to the entrance of the La Colle river, the fire from which was so destructive. Lieutenants Caswick and Hicks, of the royal navy, were most actively zealous in forwarding two guns from the boats, and getting them up to the mill.

To Major Handcock the greatest praise is due, for his most gallant defence of the mill against such superior numbers; and I earnestly trust it will meet the approbation of his excellency the Commander-in-chief of the Forces. I have the honour to transmit a list of the killed and wounded of the British: that of the enemy, from all accounts I can collect from the inhabitants, must have been far greater.

I have the honor to be, &c.,

WILLIAM WILLIAMS,

Lieut.-Col. 13th Reg.,

commanding at St. John's.

List of killed, wounded, and missing, in action at La Colle mill, on the 30th March, 1814.

11 rank and file, killed; 1 captain, 1 subaltern, 1 sergeant, 43 rank and file, wounded; 4 rank and file missing.

Note—1 Indian warrior killed, 1 wounded.

R. B. HANDCOCK, Major.

A comparison between Col. Williams modest letter, and Mr. O'Connor's version of the same affair will not be uninteresting to the reader:

"The issue of this expedition," says Mr. O'Connor, "was unfortunate, although in its progress it did honor to the Americans engaged. The enemy claimed a victory, and pretended to gather laurels, only because he was not vanquished. General Wilkinson, at the head of his division, marched from Champlain with the intention of reducing the enemy's FORTRESS at the river La Colle.

"About eleven o'clock, he fell in with the enemy at Odell-town, three miles from La Colle, and six* from St. John's. An attack was commenced by the enemy on the advance of the army under Colonel Clarke and Major Forsyth. Col. Bissell came up with spirit, and the enemy was forced to retire with loss. General Wilkinson took part in this action, and bravely advanced into the most dangerous position, declining frequently the advice of his officers to retire from imminent danger. The enemy having used his congreve rockets without producing any effect, retired to La Colle, where he was pursued. At this place an action was expected; but the enemy whose force, when increased by a reinforcement from the Isle aux Noix, amounted to at least twenty-five hundred men, mostly regulars, *declined meeting the American force, although much inferior in numbers and means of warfare.*

"Several sorties were made by the enemy, but they were resisted with bravery and success. The conduct of every individual attached to the American command, was marked by that patriotism and prowess, which has so often conquered the boasted discipline, long experience, and military tactics of an enemy who dared not expose his "*invincibles*"† to the disgrace of being defeated by a less numerous force of Yankee woodsmen."‡

This extract we would not venture to give without naming also the very page from which it was taken. Would any one, we ask, believe it possible that this writer was describing the repulse of four thousand Americans in an attack on *a mill*, garrisoned by one hundred and

eighty British—with somewhere about twelve hundred regulars and militia stationed in the vicinity. Even General Wilkinson was compelled to allow, on his trial, that the building was defended by a garrison of, not eighteen hundred regulars and five hundred militia, but of six hundred veteran troops.

Col. McPherson's testimony on the same occasion showed that in his estimation, at all events, the gallantry so much vaunted by Mr. O'Connor was not displayed, and he declared "that the army should have attempted to force a passage into the mill, and employed the bayonet at every sacrifice, or have renewed the attack, with heavier ordnance, at daylight the next morning."

How Messrs. O'Connor, Smith, and Thompson could, with the proceedings of General Wilkinson's trial open to the world, venture to put forth their statements would puzzle any one unaccustomed to their through thick and through thin style of laudation and apology.

James is very severe upon the poor General for the note which he put forward in answer to Col. McPherson's assertion that "the bayonet ought to have been employed." To take such a post, wrote Wilkinson, with small arms, has often been attempted, but never succeeded, from the time of Xenophon who failed in the attempt down to the present day. Xenophon himself was baffled in an attempt against a Castle in the plain of Caicus, and also in his attack on the metropolis of the Drylanes, and in times modern as well as ancient, we have abundant examples of the failure of military enterprises, by the most distinguished chiefs."

Before giving James's comments on this note we would suggest to General Wilkinson and his three apologists that an attack on a Stone Castle with narrow slits for the double purpose of admitting light and discharging arrows, cross-bolts, or javelins, and an attack on a Mill, (where is not usually a lack of good sized windows,) with musketry and a well served battery of three heavy guns, are not quite one and the same thing. As the General has gone so far out of his way to find an excuse, we also may be excused for travelling back a few years, in order to confute his assertions. In that veracious historical

* We presume Mr. O'Connor means twenty-six miles.
† These italics are Mr. O'Connor's.
‡ History of the War, page 219.

work generally known as Ivanhoe,* we have an instance of a stone castle being carried by a rabble armed with bows, bill hooks, and spears, assisted only by one Knight. Now if such deeds of *derring do* could be effected by the brave foresters of olden times, we opine that American woodsmen, especially when aided by a General *whom it was difficult to keep out of danger*, should have at least attempted one onslaught. The whole passage, however, is too ridiculous to laugh at, we will therefore return to James, who, commenting on the General's note in justification, observes "General James Wilkinson, of the United States Army, then has the effrontery to compare his disgraceful discomfiture before a Canadian grist mill, with what occurred to—Lord Wellington at Burgos—Bonaparte at St. Jean D'Acre—and General Graham at Burgos. James here declares himself to be as sick of the Bobadil General, as he presumes his readers to be.

We have dwelt sufficiently long on this subject, and will therefore but remark that Wilkinson returned after his repulse to his old quarters, relieving the Canadians from fear, not of his men as soldiers, but as marauders and pillagers, quite as expert as the much abused sailors and soldiers of the Chesapeake squadron.

The next event which occurred was one for which Sir George Prevost has been severely blamed. Commodore McDonough had just launched a ship and a brig, both destined for service in Lake Champlain—and had also collected a great store of provisions and munitions of war at Vergennes, Vermont. On the 9th May Captain Pring judging that the ice was sufficiently broken to allow his using the flotilla under his command, determined to attack the place and destroy at once the ships and stores. He, however, found the enemy in too great force for him to effect any movement, as he was without troops to attack the enemy on shore, he was therefore compelled to return to Isle Aux Noix.

James remarks on this affair: "had a corps of eight or nine hundred men been spared, the lives of Downie and his brave comrades

*We contend that Ivanhoe is quite as reliable authority as either Smith, O'Connor, or Thompson.

would have been saved in the September following, and all the attendant circumstances, still so painful to reflect upon, would have been averted. Veritas in his letters speaks still more plainly, "Captain Pring applied to Sir George for troops—as usual the application was refused—but when Captain Pring returned, and reported to Sir George *what might have been done by a joint attack then*, he was offered assistance, to which offer the Captain replied, that it was *then too late*, as the enemy had taken alarm and prepared accordingly." Sir George's mistake in not despatching troops, whether asked for or not, on this expedition, will be more clearly understood when we reach that part of our narrative, relating to the attack in which Captain Downie lost his life.

From the River Richelieu we must transport the reader to Ontario, and follow the fortunes of the expedition against Oswego, a place, next to Sackett's Harbour, of the most importance to the enemy, and at which it was supposed that large quantities of naval stores had been deposited. On the 3rd of May the fleet under the command of Sir James Yeo, embarked at Kingston, a body of one thousand and eighty men, all included, and on the 4th, General Drummond himself embarked. At three o'clock in the afternoon of the 4th the fleet had arrived sufficiently near Oswego to open their fire, and preparations were at the same time made for disembarking the troops; this movement, however, was frustrated by a gale springing up which compelled them to claw off a lee shore, and gain an offing. The three despatches which follow, will convey a very clear idea of the proceedings which took place as soon the weather moderated. The first is from General Drummond.

H. M. S. Prince Regent
Oswego, May 7.

SIR—I am happy to have to announce to your Excellency the complete success of the expedition against Oswego. The troops mentioned in my despatch of the 3rd instant; viz, six companies of De Wattevilles regiment, under Lieutenant Colonel Fischer, the light company of the Glengarry light infantry, under Captain Mc Millan, and the whole of the second battallion royal marines, under Lieutenant Colonel Malcolm, having been embarked with a detachment of the royal artillery under captain Cruttenden, with two field-pieces, a detachment of the rocket company under Lieutenant Stevens, and a detachment of sappers and miners under Lieutenant Gosset, of the royal engineers, on the evening of the 3rd instant, I proceeded on board the Prince Regent at day-light on the 4th, and the squadron immediately sailed; the wind being variable, we did not arrive off Oswego until noon the following day. The ships lay to, within long gun-shot of the battery, and the gun-boats under captain Collier were sent close in, for the purpose of inducing the enemy to shew his fire, and particularly the number and position of his guns. This service was performed in the most gallant manner, the boats taking a position within point-blank shot of the fort, which returned the fire from four guns, one of them heavy. The enemy did not appear to have any guns mounted on the town-side of the river.

Having sufficiently reconnoitred the place, arrangements were made for its attack, which it was designed should take place at eight o'clock that evening; but at sun-set a very heavy squall blowing directly on the shore, obliged the squadron to get under weigh, and prevented our return until next morning; when the following disposition was made of the troops and squadron by commodore sir J. Yeo and myself. The Princess Charlotte, Wolfe,* and Royal George,† to engage the batteries, as the depth of water would admit of their approaching the shore; the Sir Sidney Smith‡ schooner, to scour the town, and keep in check a large body of militia, who might attempt to pass over into the fort; the Moira§ and Melville¶ brigs, to tow the boats with the troops, and then cover their landing, by scouring the woods on the low point towards the foot of the hill, by which it was intended to advance to the assault of the fort.

Captain O'Connor had the direction of the boats and gun-boats destined to land the troops, which consisted of the flank companies of De Watteville's regiment, the company of the Glengarry light infantry, and the second battalion of the royal marines, being all that could be landed at one embarkation. The

four battalion companies of the Regiment De Watteville, and the detachment of artillery remaining in reserve on board the Princess Charlotte and Sir Sidney Smith Schooner.

As soon as every thing was ready, the ships opened their fire, and the boats pushed for the point of disembarkation, in the most regular order. The landing was effected under a heavy fire from the fort, as well as from a considerable body of the enemy, drawn up on the brow of the hill and in the woods. The immediate command of the troops was entrusted to Lieutenant-Colonel Fischer, of the regiment of De Watteville, of whose gallant, cool, and judicious conduct, as well as of the distinguished bravery, steadiness, and discipline of every officer and soldier composing this small force, I was a witness, having, with commodore sir James Yeo, the deputy-adjutant-general, and the officers of my staff, landed with the troops.

I refer your excellency to Lieut.-Col. Fischer's letter enclosed, for an account of the operations. The place was gained in ten minutes from the moment the troops advanced. The fort being every where almost open, the whole of the garrison, consisting of the third battalion of artillery, about 400 strong, and some hundred militia, effected their escape, with the exception of about 60 men, half of them severely wounded.

I enclose a return of our loss, amongst which I have to regret that of Captain Haltaway, of the royal marines. Your excellency will lament to observe in the list the name of that gallant, judicious, and excellent officer, captain Mulcaster, of the royal navy, who landed at the head of 200 volunteer seamen from the fleet, and received a severe and dangerous wound, when within a few yards of the guns, which he was advancing to storm, which I fear will deprive the squadron of his valuable assistance for some time at least.

In noticing the co-operation of the naval branch of the service, I have the highest satisfaction in assuring your excellency, that I have throughout this, as well as on every other occasion, experienced the most zealous, cordial, and able support from sir James Yeo. It will be for him to do justice to the merits of those under his command; but I may nevertheless be permitted to observe, that nothing could exceed the coolness and gallant-try in action, or the unwearied exertions on shore, of the captains, officers, and crews of the whole squadron.

I enclose a memorandum of the captured articles that have been brought away, in which your excellency will perceive with satisfaction seven heavy guns, that were intended for the enemy's new ship. Three 32 pounders were sunk by the enemy in the river, as well as a large quantity of cordage, and other naval stores. The loss to them, therefore, has been very great; and I am sanguine in believing that by this blow, they have been deprived of the means of completing the armament, and particularly the equipment, of the large man of war, an object of the greatest importance.

Every object of the expedition having been effected, and the captured stores embarked, the troops returned in the most perfect order on board their respective ships, at four o'clock this morning, when the squadron immediately sailed; the barracks in the town, as well as those in the fort, having been previously burnt, together with the platforms, bridge, &c and the works in every other respect dismantled and destroyed, as far as practicable.

I cannot close this dispatch without offering to your excellency's notice the admirable and judicious manner in which lieutenant-colonel Fischer formed the troops, and led them to the attack; the cool and gallant conduct of lieutenant-colonel Malcolm, at the head of the second battalion royal marines; the intrepidity of captain de Berzey, of the regiment de Watteville, who commanded the advance; the zeal and energy of lieutenant colonel Parson, inspecting field-officer, who with major Smelt, of the 103rd regiment, had obtained a passage on board the squadron to Niagara, and volunteered their services on the occasion; the gallantry of captain M'Millan, of the Glangarry light infantry who covered the left flank of the troops in advance; and the activity and judgment of captain Cruttenden, royal artillery; brevet-major De Courten, of the regiment de Watteville; lieutenant Stevens, of the rocket company; lieut. Gosset, royal engineers, each in their respective situations.

Lieutenant-colonel Malcolm has reported in high terms the conduct of lieutenant Lawrie, of the royal marines, who was at the head of the first men who entered the fort; and I had an opportunity of witnessing the bravery of lieutenant Hewett, of that corps, who climbed the flag-staff and pulled down the American ensign which was nailed to it. To lieutenant-colonel Harvey, deputy-adjutant-general, my warmest approbation is most justly due, for his unremitting zeal and useful assistance. The services of this intelligent and experienced officer have been so frequently brought under your excellency's observation before that it would be superfluous my making any comment on the high estimation in which I hold his valuable exertions.

Captain Jervois, my aide-camp, and lieutenant-colonel Hagerman, my provincial aide de camp, the only officers of my personal staff who accompanied me, rendered me every assistance.

Captain Jervois, who will deliver to your excellency, with this despatch, the American flag taken at Oswego, is fully able to afford every further information you may require; and I avail myself of the present opportunity strongly to recommend this officer to the favorable consideration of his royal highness the commander in chief.

I have the honor to be, &c.,

GORDON DRUMMOND.

Col Fischar's letter to Colonel Harvey, and that from Sir James Yeo to McCroker, being more explanatory, will furnish still more conclusive evidence, as to the importance of this affair.

From lieutenant-colonel Fischer to lieutenant-colonel Harvey.

H. M. S. Prince Regent, off Oswego,
SIR, Lake Ontario, May 7.

It is with heartfelt satisfaction that I have the honor to report to you, for the information of lieutenant-general Drummond, commanding, that the troops placed under my orders for the purpose of storming the fort at Oswego, have completely succeeded in this service.

It will be superfluous for me to enter into any details of the operations, as the lieutenant-general has personally witnessed the conduct of the whole party; and the grateful task only remains to point out for his approbation, the distinguished bravery and discipline of the troops.

The second battalion of royal marines

formed their column in the most regular manner, and, by their steady and rapid advance, carried the fort in a very short time. In fact, nothing could surpass the gallantry of that battalion, commanded by lieutenant-colonel Malcolm; to whose cool and deliberate conduct our success is greatly to be attributed.

The lieutenant-colonel reported to me, in high terms, the conduct of lieutenant James Laurie, who was at the head of the first men who entered the fort. The two flank companies of De Watteville's, under captain De Berzey, behaved with spirit, though labouring with more difficulties during their formation, on account of the badness of the landing place, and the more direct opposition of the enemy. The company of Glengarry light infantry, under captain M'Millan, behaved in an equally distinguished manner, by clearing the wood, and driving the enemy into the fort. I beg leave to make my personal acknowledgements to staff-adjutant Greig, and lieutenant and adjutant Mermet, of De Watteville's, for the zeal and attention to me during the day's service. Nor can I forbear to mention the regular behavior of the whole of the troops during their stay on shore, and the most perfect order in which the re-embarkation of the troops has been executed, and every service performed.

I enclose herewith the return of killed and wounded, as sent to me by the different corps.

I have the honor to be, &c.,

V. FISCHER,
Lieut.-col. De Watteville's regiment.
Lieut.-col. Harvey,
Deputy-adjutant-general.

Return of killed and wounded of the troops in action with the enemy at Oswego, on the 10th of May, 1814.

Total—1 captain, 2 sergeants, 1 drummer, 15 rank and file, killed; 1 captain, 1 subaltern, 2 sergeants, 58 rank and file, wounded.

J. HARVEY,
Lieut.-col. dep.-adj.-gen.

Return of the killed and wounded of the royal navy at Oswego, May 6.

3 seamen, killed; 2 captains, 1 lieutenant, 1 master, 7 seamen, wounded.

Total—3 killed; 11 wounded.

J. LAWRIE, sec.

His majesty's brig Magnet, (late Sir Sidney Smith, Off Oswego, U. S. May 7.

Return of ordnance and ordnance-stores, taken and destroyed at Oswego, Lake-Ontario, the 6th May, 1814, by his majesty's troops under the command of lieut. genl. Drummond.

Taken;—3 32-pounder iron guns, 4 24-pounder iron guns, 1 12-pounder iron gun, 1 6-pounder iron gun.—Total 9.

Destroyed;—1 heavy 12 pounder, 1 heavy 6-pounder.—Total 2.

Shot;—81 42-pounder, round; 32 32-pounder, round; 36 42-pounder, canister; 42 32-pounder, canister; 30 24-pounder, canister; 12 42-pounder, grape; 48 32-pounder, grape; 18 24-pounder, grape.

Eight barrels of gunpowder, and all the shot of small calibre in the fort, and stores, thrown into the river.

EDWARD CRUTTENDEN, captain,
commanding royal artillery.
E. BAYNES, adj.-general.

Memorandum of provisions stores, captured.

One thousand and forty-five barrels of flour, pork, potatoes, salt, tallow, &c. &c. 70 coils of rope and cordage; tar, blocks, (large and small,) 2 small schooners, with several boats, and other smaller craft.

NOAH FREER, mil. Sec.

CHAPTER XVIII.—*Continued.*

It will be as well, before giving Sir James Yeo's official account, to make a few observations on the American version of the descent on Oswego. It is worthy of remark, that Gen. Drummond distinctly states, that the vessels anchored at long gun shot of the batteries, and that the reconnoisance of the morning was only intended as a feint to enable him to discover where the enemies' batteries were, and what was their force ; this effected, Sir James Yeo would then be enabled, on the withdrawal of his gun-boats, to place his vessels in the most commanding situations. This retirement of the gun-boats, however, appears to have afforded General Armstrong and others an opportunity of palliating the defeat, by claiming a sort of victory on the first day. The General says, " The larger vessels took a position for battering the fort, and soon after, opened upon it a heavy fire ; while fifteen boats, *crowded with infantry,* moved slowly to the shore. When arrived within the range of Mitchell's* shot, a fire upon them was commenced, which in a few minutes compelled them to withdraw. A second attempt, made in the same way, was not more successful ; when ships, boats, and troops retired *en masse,* and stood out of the harbour."

It will be seen by this extract, that the ships were not within reach of the American guns, why then did General Armstrong omit to mention the cause which compelled the British vessels to withdraw ? and why does he contradict himself by leaving it to be inferred, that the withdrawal was occasioned by the fire, and should therefore be considered in the light of a repulse.

Again, too, the General states that, on the occasion of the second landing, " every foot of ground was well contested with the head of the British column, for half an hour, after which no farther annoyance was given to the retreat, which was effected with coolness and courage."

We do not exactly understand how the General could have been so rash as to claim for the defendants at Oswego either coolness or courage, when one of the American officers, who was in the action, in a letter dated "Oswego Falls," writes thus:—"The militia thought best to leave us, *I do not think they fired a gun.*" James mentions this same letter, which he speaks of as having been published in the newspapers of the day.

Another circumstance, which occurred that same afternoon, afforded also great cause

---

* The Commander at Oswego.

for self laudation on the part of the Americans. The British fleet found it necessary, in consequence of a heavy gale from the north-west, to claw off a lee shore, without delaying to hoist up all their boats, some of which were cut loose, and drifted on shore. This was done to prevent getting embayed; and to every one, who may remember the situation of Oswego, the necessity of this will be apparent, especially when it is farther borne in mind, that a lee shore, on these lakes, even in a moderate gale, is so much dreaded, that, even at the present day, despite the superior build of vessels, and increased skill in seamanship, vessels are sometimes compelled to leave their anchorage twice or three times, and that it often takes a fortnight, or perhaps longer, to take in a load which a couple of days in fair weather would be sufficient for. The American Retreat of the fleet. writers represent these boats as prizes. Smith, O'Connor, and Thompson, all mention the retreat of the British fleet, but not one of them had the honesty to state the cause.

Another point to be commented on is the discrepancy as to numbers. General Brown declares, that over three thousand were landed; Mr. O'Connor reduces this number to two thousand; Smith states the numbers at between two and three thousand. Mr. Thompson only mentions seventeen hundred; and the American officer, whom we have already mentioned, estimates the number at twelve hundred. Armstrong eschews numbers, and merely mentions fifteen boats crowded with men.

These same writers have been quite as determined to reduce their own, as to swell the numbers of their opponents; and appear accordingly, one and all, to have carefully omitted in their list of combatants the militia, and to have confined their statement as to numbers to that of the regulars alone. We accordingly find that three hundred men, and no more, formed the heroic band who, for half an hour, resisted, according to General Brown, the onslaught of more than three thousand men. The same policy was observed with regard to the captured articles, and the government organs were most assiduous in their attempts to represent the amount of loss "as most trifling." This proceeding afforded an opportunity to the opposition or federal papers of the day to tax government with wilfully deceiving the people. We have already shown what really was captured, and will now give in contrast the American accounts.

Mr. Thompson says:—"The enemy took possession of the fort and barracks, but for the little booty which he obtained, consisting of a few barrels of provisions and whiskey, he paid much more than an equivalent." Smith declares that we captured "nothing but a naked fort." O'Connor admits eight pieces of cannon, and stores worth *one hundred dollars*.

The returns made by the British are borne out by an American writer from Onondago, who estimates the amount at over forty thousand dollars.

The last point worthy of note is that, although the British troops remained for nearly 24 hours in the place, we do not find any complaint against them on the part of a single American writer. This was highly creditable to the troops, marines and seamen, and affords a very marked contrast to the behaviour of some Americans in an affair at Long Point, which we shall shortly have to relate. We will now give Sir James Yeo's version of the affair, and in our notes will be found* the general order issued by the American commander, General Brown.

From Sir James L. Yoe to Mr. Croker.

Sir,—My letter of the 15th of April last will have informed their lordships, that his Majesty's ships, Prince Regent and Princess Charlotte, were launched on the preceeding day! I now have the satisfaction to acquaint you, for their Lordship's information, that the squadron, by the unremitting exertions of the officers and men under my command, were ready on the 3rd instant, when it was determined by lieutenant-general Drummond and myself, that an immediate attack should be made on the forts and town of Oswego: which, in point of position, is the most formidable I have seen in Upper Canada; and where the enemy had, by river navigation, collected from the interior several heavy guns, and naval stores for the ships, and large depots of provisions for their army.

At noon, on the 5th, we got off the port, and were on the point of landing, when a heavy gale from the N. W. obliged me to gain an offing. On the morning of the 6th, everything being ready, 140 troops, 200 seamen armed with pikes, under Captain Mulcaster, and 400 marines were put into the boats. The Montreal and Niagara took their stations abreast, and within a quarter of a mile, of the fort; the Magnet opposite the town, and the Star and Charwell to cover the landing, which was effected under a most heavy fire of round, grape, and musketry, kept up with great spirit. Our men having to ascend a very steep and long hill, were consequently exposed to a destructive fire. Their gallantry overcoming every difficulty, they soon gained the summit of the hill; and, throwing themselves into the fosse, mounted the ramparts on all sides, vieing with each other who should be foremost. Lieutenant Laurie, my secretary, was the first who gained the ramparts; and lieutenant Hewitt climbed the flag-staff under a heavy fire, and in the most gallant style struck the American colours, which had

been nailed to the mast. My gallant and much esteemed friend, captain Mulcaster, led the seamen to the assault with his accustomed bravery; but I lament to say, he received a dangerous wound in the act of entering the fort, which I apprehend will, for a considerable time, deprive me of his valuable services. Mr. Scott, my first lieutenant, who was next in command, nobly led them on; and soon gained the ramparts. Captain O'Connor, of the Prince Regent, to whom I entrusted the landing of the troops, displayed great ability and cool judgment; the boats being under a heavy fire from all points.

Captain Popham, of the Montreal, anchored his ship in a most gallant style, sustaining the whole fire until we gained the shore. She was set on fire three times by red-hot shot, and much cut up in her hull, masts, and rigging; Captain Popham received a severe wound in his right hand, and speaks in high terms of Mr. Richardson, the master, who, from a severe wound in the left arm, was obliged to undergo amputation at the shoulder joint.

Captain Spilsbury, of the Niagara; Captain Dobbs, of the Charwell; Captain Anthony of the Star: and Captain Collier of the Magnet, behaved much to my satisfaction. The second battalion of royal marines excited the admiration of all; they were led by the gallant Col. Malcolm, and suffered severely. Captain Holloway, doing duty in the Princess Charlotte, gallantly fell at the head of his company. Having landed with the seamen and marines, I had great pleasure in witnessing not only the zeal and prompt attention of the officers to my orders, but also the intrepid bravery of the men, whose good and temperate conduct, under circumstances of great temptation, (being a whole night in the town, employed loading the captured vessels with ordnance, naval stores, and provisions) most justly claim my high approbation and acknowledgment. And I here beg leave to recommend to their lordships' notice the service of my first lieutenant, Mr. Scott; and of my aid-de-camp, acting lieutenant Yoe, to whom I beg leave to refer their lordships for information; nor should

Lieutenant-Colonel Mitchell had, in all, less than 300 men; and the fosse of the enemy, by land and water, exceeded 3000.

R. JONES, assistant-adjt.-gen.

the meritorious exertions of acting lieutenant Griffin, severely wounded in the arm, or Mr. Brown, both of whom were attached to the storming party, be omitted. It is a great source of satisfaction to me to acquaint their lordships, that I have on this and all other occasions, received from Lieut-Gen. Drummond that support and attention, which never fail in securing perfect cordiality between the two services.

I herewith transmit a list of the killed and wounded, and of the ordnance, naval stores, and provisions, captured and destroyed by the combined attack on the 6th instant.

I have the honour to be, &c.,

JAMES LUCAS YEO,
Commodore and Commander in Chief.

J. W. Croker, Esq., &c.

A list of officers and seamen, of his Majesty's fleet on Lake Ontario, killed and wounded at Oswego, on the 6th of May, 1814.

Three seamen, killed; 2 captains, 1 lieutenant, 1 master, 7 seamen, wounded.
Total—3 killed, 11 wounded.

A statement of ordnance, naval stores, and provisions, brought off and destroyed in a combined attack of the sea and land forces on the town and fort of Oswego, on the 6th May, 1814.
Ordnance Stores brought off:—Three long 32-pounder guns; four long 24 pounders.
A quantity of various kinds of Ordnance Stores.
Naval Stores and Provisions:—3 schooners; 300 barrels of flour, 500 barrels of pork, 600 barrels of salt, 500 barrels of bread.
A quantity of large rope.
Destroyed:—Three long 24-pounder guns, one long 12-pounder gun, two long 6-pounder guns.
One schooner, and barracks and other public buildings.

J. L. YEO,
Commodore and Commander-in Chief.

The statement of stores captured, given by Sir James Yeo, corresponds pretty closely with the returns made by the other officers; and, as all the articles enumerated in the lists would have to be accounted for, it is not very likely that any addition to them would have been made, which could only result in heavy expenses to the parties thus increasing the honour of their exploits by a direct taxation on their pockets.

The British loss at Oswego was severe—eighty-two killed and wounded. That the Americans, however, were not suffered to retreat quite so coolly as is represented, may be inferred from the fact that their own accounts return sixty-nine killed and wounded, while sixty prisoners were captured.

The style in which Armstrong winds up his account of this affair is very amusing, especially when taken in contrast with his version of another occurrence which happened shortly after. "On the morning of the 7th, having collected the small booty afforded by the post, and burned the barracks, the fleet and army of the enemy *abandoned* the enterprise, and returned to Kingston." One would scarcely imagine that the enterprise thus carelessly spoken of had cost the Americans forty thousand dollars, besides a heavy loss both of life and in prisoners.

The other occurrence alluded to above took place on the 30th May, and strikingly illustrates General Armstrong's unfair mode of writing history.

By the capture of a boat, Sir James Yeo learned that eighteen other boats, each armed with two guns, twenty-four pounders, were waiting at Sandy Creek for an opportunity of reaching Sackett's Harbour. Sir James accordingly despatched Captains Popham and Spilsbury with one hundred and eighty seamen and marines to intercept them or cut them out. The party having reached the creek where they had ascertained that the enemy were, commenced the passage up, but were attacked from the shore by a large party of riflemen, one hundred and fifty in number, besides militia, infantry, and cavalry, mustering some two hundred strong. The British were here fairly caught in a trap, and all that remained for them was to fight their way back; and to do this, parties were landed on both banks, in order to drive back the enemy from a situation commanding the passage of the boats. This attempt was gallantly made, but numbers prevailed, and the result of the affair was the destruction or capture of the whole party. As a proof, however, of the resistance, it will suffice to state that the killed and wounded amounted to more than one-third of the party. That the Americans must have had Indians as their allies, is evident from the conclusion of Captain Popham's official despatch:—"The exertions of the American officers of the rifle corps, commanded by Major Appling, in saving the lives of many of the officers and men, whom *their own men and the Indians were devoting to death*, were conspicuous, and claim our warmest gratitude."

Armstrong begins his statement of the affair by styling it an "achievement" accomplished by Major Appling and one hundred and thirty-two men, omitting all mention of either militia or Indians, and he declares that the whole British party fell into the hands of the Americans without the loss of a single man of their party. The probability of this the reader can judge of, when it is borne in mind that a hand-to-hand conflict occurred on both banks of the river, and that the British were only overpowered by numbers. The same disregard of truth, however, which caused Armstrong to suppress all mention of the militia and infantry, would doubtless prompt him to conceal the American loss, whatever it might have been.

An occurrence on the shores of Lake Erie, to which we have already alluded, does not reflect quite so much credit on the national character as did Major Appling's and his officers' conduct. Early in March, General Drummond had quartered at the inconsiderable village of Dover a small body of dragoons. This was done by way of establishing an outpost, so that the Americans might not be enabled, having the command of the Lake, to land, without opposition or notice, troops, at a post so close to Burlington heights, the grand centre of the British position, and the depot for the troops on the Niagara line.

Fear of another attack on the part of the

British had induced the American commander to concentrate about Buffalo and Erie (where the fleet lay) a large body of troops. One of the American officers, a Colonel Campbell, judging, doubtless, that it was a pity so many men should remain inactive, saw, in the occupation of Dover, an opportunity of distinguishing himself and benefiting his country. Taking, then, full five hundred United States infantry, he crossed over from Erie on the 13th May, and, the British troops retiring before him, destroyed the mills, distilleries, and houses in the village. Mr. Thornton says: "A *squadron* of British dragoons stationed at the place fled at the approach of Colonel Campbell's *detachment*, and abandoned the women and children, who experienced humane treatment from the Americans."

If the burning of stores, barns, and dwelling houses of peaceable and unresisting inhabitants be included in Mr. Thornton's category of humane treatment, we should like to be enlightened as to what would be considered harsh treatment. As a proof, however, that even the Americans were ashamed of the transaction, we have only to mention that a court of inquiry, of which General Scott was president, was instituted to take the facts into consideration, and that their decision was, "that in burning the houses of the inhabitants, Colonel Campbell had greatly erred; but this error they imputed to the recollection of the scenes of the Raisin and the Miami, in the Western territories, to the army of which Colonel Campbell was at that time attached, and to the recent devastation of the Niagara frontier."

The court appears to have had most convenient memories, or they could scarcely have forgotten that an act very similar to the present had alone caused the destruction along the banks of the Niagara. We learn from the transaction, that the American military tribunals of that day looked upon pillage and destruction of private property, only a "trifling error." We will have occasion to notice in what light the destruction of the public buildings at Washington was regarded, and whether the course of the British Generals is so lightly considered.

Early in April an expedition was organized, having for its object an attack on a new post established at Matchadash, and the recapture of Michilimackinac. The expedition, however, in consequence, says Armstrong,* of a discrepancy in the Cabinet at Washington, was not despatched until the 3rd of July, at which time a detachment of regular troops and militia, under the command of Colonel Crogan, was embarked on board of the fleet, which sailed soon after from Detroit for Matchadash.

Expeditions against Machilimackinac and Matchadash.

The idea of attacking Matchadash was very soon abandoned, in consequence of sundry impediments, writes Armstrong, " arising from shoals, rocks, dangerous islands, perpetual fogs, and bad pilotage," and the safer and easier plan of an attack on the North-West Company's settlement at St. Mary's substituted. This part of the expedition was entrusted to Captain Holmes of the United States Army, and Lieutenant Turner of the United States Navy, and very effectually the work entrusted to them was executed, as every house at the post was destroyed, no public buildings of any description being there to warrant this atrocious outrage. The horses and cattle were killed, and even the provisions and garden stuff, which could not be removed, were destroyed, with a view of thoroughly ruining the post.

Messrs Thomson and Smith are particularly reserved as to the conduct of their countrymen at St. Mary's, but Mr. O'Connor boldly declares that " the property destroyed was, according to the maritime law of nations, as recognized in the English courts, good prize, as well as because the Company's agent, Johnson, *acted the infamous part of a traitor,* having been a citizen and magistrate of the Michigan territory, before the war, and at its commencement, and now discharging the functions of magistrate under the British Government."

This position of Mr. O'Connor's, that *merchandise on shore as well as afloat is good prize,* must not be lost sight of, as the same writer will be found laying down a very different interpretation of what constitutes " good prize," when the proceedings of the British in the Chesapeake are under his consideration.

---

* *Letter from the Secretary of War to the President.—April 31st, 1814.*

SIR : So long as we had reason to believe that the enemy intended and was in condition to re-establish himself on the Thames, and open anew his intercourse with the Indian tribes of the west, it was, no doubt, proper to give to our naval means a direction which would best obstruct or defeat such movement or designs. An order has been accordingly given by the navy department, to employ the flotilla, in scouring the shores of the more western lakes, in destroying the enemy's trading establishment at St. Joseph's, and in recapturing Fort Michilimackinac. As, however, our last advices show, that the enemy has no efficient force westward of Burlington bay, and that he has suffered the season of easy and rapid transportation to escape him, it is evident that he means to strengthen himself on the peninsula, and make Fort Erie, which he is now repairing, the western extremity of his line of operation. Under this new state of things, it is respectfully submitted, whether another and better use cannot be made of our flotilla ?

In explaining myself, it is necessary to premise that, the garrisons of Detroit and Malden included, it will be practicable to assemble on the shores and navigable waters of Lake Erie, five thousand regular troops, and three thousand volunteers and militia, and that measures have been taken to produce this effect on or before the 10th day of June next. Without, however, the aid of naval means, this force will be comparatively inoperative, and necessarily dispersed, but with such aid, competent to great objects.

Lake Erie on which our dominion is undisputed, furnishes a way scarcely less convenient for approaching the heart of Upper Canada than Lake Ontario. Eight, or even six thousand men landed in the bay between Point Abino and Fort Erie. and operating either on the line of the Niagara, or more directly [if a more direct route is found], against the British post at the head of Burlington bay, cannot be resisted with effect, without compelling the enemy so to weaken his more eastern posts, as to bring them within reach of our means at Sackett's Harbour and Plattsburgh.

In choosing between this object and that to which the flotilla is now destined, there cannot, I think, be much, if any, hesitation. Our attack, carried to Burlington and York, interposes a barrier, which completely protects Malden and Detroit— makes doubtful and hazardous the enemy's intercourse with the western Indians, reduces Mackinac to a possession perfectly useless, renders probable the abandonment of Fort Niagara, and takes from the enemy half his motive for continuing the naval conflict on Lake Ontario. On the other hand, take Mackinac, and what is gained, but Mackinac itself.

I have the honour to be, &c.,

(Signed,)   JOHN ARMSTRONG.

What, too, could the American Government have thought of the monstrous position laid down, that a man, who deserted, "played the infamous part of a traitor." What a bitter satire is this of Mr. O'Connor's on the whole American Government? and even more particularly direct does his shaft fly against the commanders of the vessels who had captured, either in merchantmen or vessels of war, British subjects, and who had employed every means short of death to force them to abandon their national flag.

It must not be forgotten that there was not a military or naval man of any description at St. Mary's, to warrant this conduct on the part of the Americans; and there is very little room for doubt but that the course adopted was in revenge for the failure of the principal object of the expedition, which was to get hold of the North-West furs, which scheme was, however, happily frustrated.

"This service," says Armstrong, "being soon and successfully performed, the fleet sailed for Michilimacinac, and, on the 26th, anchored off that island."

The laboured attempt of Armstrong to invest this post with all the defences that citadels like Quebec possess, is so ludicrous, that we are tempted to transcribe the whole passage :—

"After a short reconnoissance, and a few experiments, three discoveries, altogether unlooked for, were made—

1st, That, from the great elevation of the fort, its walls could not be battered by the guns of the shipping.

2d, That, from the steepness of the ascent, any attempt to carry the fort by storm would probably fail.

3d. That should this mode of attack succeed, it would be useless, inasmuch as every foot of its interior was commanded by guns placed on higher ground.

These facts, leaving no hope of success but from an attack of the upper battery, the troops were landed on the 4th August, and conducted to the verge of an old field; indicated by the inhabitants as the position which would best fulfil the intention of the movement, when, to Croghan's surprise, he found himself anticipated by the enemy; and in a few minutes, assailed in front from a redoubt mounting four pieces of artillery, and in flank, by one or more Indian attacks made from the surrounding woods. Succeeding, at last, in repulsing these, and in driving the enemy from the cleared ground, it was soon discovered that the position was not such as was at all proper for a camp of either siege or investment, being of narrow surface, skirted in the whole circumference by woods, intersected by deep ravines, and furnishing only a difficult and perilous communication with the fleet. Croghan, at once and wisely, withdrew to the Lake shore and re-embarked the troops. Our loss on the occasion was not great, numerically considered; but became deeply interesting by the fate of Capt. Holmes, a young man of high promise, universally respected and regretted."

All this reads well, and doubtless produced the desired effect; but what were the real facts? That the Americans made a feint of landing in one quarter, in which direction the British troops hastened, the real landing having been effected elsewhere almost without opposition. A short time, however, after the landing, the Americans were attacked by a body of Indians, and compelled to retreat, the British troops having no share in the action, the whole credit of which belongs to the Indians. Had the garrison been present to co-operate, there is no doubt but that the whole party would have been captured or killed. The savage and ruthless Holmes, the author of all the ravages at St. Mary's, met a well-deserved fate, being shot during the skirmish.

Armstrong and others have done their utmost to gloss over this repulse, by representing Michilimacinac as an isolated post, having no influence, direct or indirect, on the war. This sort of argument is very convenient *after* defeat, but the question naturally arises, why did the American Government despatch one thousand troops (for such was the number, and not five hundred, as represented by Armstrong and others,) against so unimportant a post?

In Lieutenant-Col. Macdonald's despatch to Sir George Prevost, it will be found that the Indians did not receive the credit to which they were entitled, but both Veritas' Letters, and Sketches of the War admit that the repulse was effected by the Indians.

Colonel Macdouall's despatch states:—

From Lieutenant-Colonel M'Douall to Sir George Prevost.

SIR,
                        Michilimacinac, August 14, 1814.

I have reported to lieutenant-general Drummond the particulars of the attack made by the enemy on this post on the 4th instant. My situation was embarrassing. I knew that they could land upwards of 1,000 men ; and after manning the guns at the fort, I had only a disposable force of 140 to meet them, which I determined to do, in order as much as possible to encourage the Indians, and having the fullest confidence in the little detachment of the Newfoundland regiment. The position I took up was excellent, but at an unavoidable and too great a distance from the forts, in each of which I was only able to leave 25 militiamen. There were likewise roads upon my flanks, every inch of which were known to the enemy, by means of the people formerly residents of this island, who were with them. I could not afford to detach a man to guard them.

My position was rather too extensive for such a handful of men. The ground was commanding, and, in front, clear as I could wish it. On both our flanks and rear, a thick wood. My utmost wish was, that the Indians would only prevent the enemy from gaining the woods upon our flanks, which would have forced them upon the open ground in our front. A natural breastwork protected my men from every shot ; and I had told them that, on a close approach of the enemy, they were to pour in a volley, and immediately charge ; numerous as the enemy were, all were fully confident of the result.

On the advance of the enemy, my 6-pounder and 3-pounder opened a heavy fire upon them, but not with the effect they should have had : being not well manned, and for want of an artillery-officer, who would have been invaluable to us. They moved slowly and cautiously, declining to meet me in the open ground, but gradually gaining my left flank, which the Indians permitted, without firing a shot. I was even obliged to weaken my small front, by detaching the Michigan fencibles to oppose a party of the enemy, which were advancing to the woods on my right. I now received accounts from Major Crawford, of the militia, that the enemy's two large ships had anchored in the rear of my left, and that troops were moving by a road in that direction towards the forts. I, therefore, immediately moved, to place myself between them and the enemy, and took up a position effectually covering them ; from whence, collecting the greater part of the Indians who had retired, and taking with me Major Crawford and about 50 militia, I again advanced to support a party of the Fallsovine Indians ; who, with their gallant chief, Thomas, had commenced a spirited attack upon the enemy ; who, in a short time, lost their second in command and several other officers ; seventeen of whom we counted dead upon the field, besides what they carried off, and a considerable number wounded. The enemy retired in the utmost haste and confusion, followed by the troops, till they found shelter under the very powerful broadside of their ships, anchored within a few yards of the shore. They re-embarked that evening, and the vessels immediately hauled off.

I have the honor, &c.
            R. M'DOUALL, lieutenant-colonel.
His Excellency Sir George Prevost, &c.

Mr. Thomson, in Sketches of the War, does not use his own language, but quotes from Captain Sinclair's letters the following passage—" Michilimacinac is, by nature, a perfect Gibraltar, being a high inaccessible rock on every side, except the west ; from which, to the heights, you have nearly two miles to pass through a wood, so thick, that our men were shot down in every direction, and within a few yards of them, *without being able to see the Indians*, who did it. * * * Several of the commanding officers were picked out, and killed or wounded by the savages, without seeing any of them. The men were getting lost and falling into confusion, natural under such circumstances ; which demanded an immediate retreat, or a total defeat, and a general massacre must have ensued," This was conducted in a masterly manner by Col. Croghan, who had lost that *valuable and ever to be lamented officer*, Major Holmes, who, with Capt. Van Horn, was killed by the Indians."

It is worthy of remark that to the Indians is here given the credit of this repulse, and had this really not been the case, there is no doubt but that Mr. Thomson would gladly have swelled the roll of difficulties which the Americans had to contend against. As it is, Mr. Thomson declares "that the Indians alone exceeded the strength of Col. Croghan's detachment, and that this intrepid young officer was compelled to withdraw his forces after having sustained a loss of sixty-six killed and wounded."

There were but fifty Indians on the island at the time of the attack, so that Mr. Thomson's "*intrepid young officer*," the hero of Sandusky, did not cover himself with laurels on the occasion.

Shortly after the arrival of Col. McDouall at Michilimacinac, he was joined by so many of the Western Indians, that he felt warranted in despatching a party to attack the late Indian post of Prairie du Chien, some four hundred and fifty miles from Michilimacinac, on the Mississippi, which had been lately taken possession of by Gen. Clark. A St. Louis paper states that "every attention was directed to the erection of a temporary place calculated for defence, that a new fort was progressing, and that the defence was entrusted to one hundred and thirty-four dauntless young fellows from the country." Besides these dauntless young fellows, we know that sixty rank and file of the 7th regiment were present. All this preparation shows the importance attached to the post, and makes it the more strange that no American author should have alluded to the expedition despatched against it.

Attack on the post of Prairie du Chien.

The object in making this attack was to remove the possibility of an unexpected attack on Michilimacinac from the rear. Col. McKay's dispatch to Col. McDouall will be found sufficiently explanatory without further comment from us.

From Lieutenant-Colonel M'Kay to Lieutenant-Colonel M'Douall

Prairie du Chien, Fort M'Kay.
SIR,   July 27, 1814.

I have the honour to communicate to you, that I arrived here on the 17th instant at 12 o'clock; my force amounting to 650 men: of which, 150 were Michigan fencibles, Canadian volunteers, and officers of the Indian department, the remainder Indians.

I found that the enemy had a small fort, situated on a height, immediately behind the village, with two blockhouses, perfectly safe from Indians, and that they had 6 pieces of cannon, and 60 or 70 effective men, officers included. That, lying at anchor in the middle of the Mississippi, directly in front of the fort, there was a very large gun-boat, called Governor Clark, gun-boat No. 1, mounting 14 pieces of cannon, some 6 and 3 pounders, and a number of cohorns, manned with 70 or 80 men with muskets, and measuring 70 feet keel. This floating blockhouse is so constructed, that she can be rowed in any direction, the men on board being perfectly safe from small arms, while they can use their own to the greatest advantage.

At half-past 12 o'clock, I sent captain Anderson with a flag of truce, to invite them to surrender, which they refused. My intention was not to have made an attack till next morning at day-light; but, it being impossible to control the Indians, I ordered our gun to play upon the gun-boat, which she did with a surprizing good effect; for, in course of three hours, the time the action lasted, she fired 86 rounds, two-thirds of which went into the Governor Clark. They kept up a constant fire upon us, both from the boat and fort. We were an hour between two fires, having run our gun up within musket-shot of the fort, from whence we beat the boat out of her station. She cut her cable and ran down the current, and was sheltered under the island. We were obliged to desist, it being impossible, with our little barges, to attempt to board her, and our only gun in pursuit of her would have exposed our whole camp to the enemy; she therefore made her escape.

On the 19th, finding there were only six rounds of round shot remaining, including three of the enemy's we had picked up, the day was employed in making lead bullets for the gun, and throwing up two breast-works : one within 700 yards, and the other within 450 yards of the fort. At six in the evening, every thing being prepared, I marched to the first breast-work, from whence I intended throwing in the remaining six rounds. At the moment, the first ball was about being put into the cannon, a white flag was put out at the fort, and immediately an officer came down with a note and surrendered. It being too late I deferred making them deliver up their arms in form till morning, but immediately placed a strong guard in the fort, and took possession of the artillery; From the time of our landing till they surrendered, the Indians kept up a constant but perfectly useless fire, upon the fort : the distance from whence they fired was too great to do execution, even had the enemy been exposed to view.

I am happy to inform you, that every man in the Michigan fencibles, Canadian volunteers, and officers in the Indian department, behaved as well as I could possibly wish ; and, though in the midst of a hot fire, not a man was even wounded except three Indians; that is, one Puant, one Fallsovine, and one Sioux, all severely, but not dangerously.

One lieutenant, 24th U. S. regiment; one militia captain, one militia lieutenant, three serjeants, three corporals, two musicians, 53 privates, one commissary, and one interpreter, have been made prisoners, One iron 6-pounder, mounted on a garrison, carriage ; one iron 3-pounder, on a field carriage; three swivels, 61 stand of arms, four swords, one field-carriage for 6-pounder, and a good deal of ammunition ; 28 barrels of pork, and 46 barrels of flour: these are the principal articles found in the fort when surrendered.

I will now take the liberty to request your particular attention to captains Rollette and Anderson ; the former for his activity in many instances, but particularly during the action. The action having commenced unexpectedly, he ran down from the upper end of the village, with his company, through the heat of the fire to receive orders; and before and since, in being instrumental in preserving the citizens from being quite ruined by pillaging Indians ; and the latter, for his unwearied attention in keeping everything in order during the route, and his activity in following up the cannon during the action, and assisting in transporting the ammunition. Lieutenant Portier, of captain Anderson's company ; lieutenants Graham and Brisbois, of the Indian department ; captain Dean of the Prairie · du Chien militia ; and lieutenant Powell, of the Green Bay, all acted with courage and activity, so becoming Canadian militia or volunteers. The interpreters also behaved well, but particularly M. St. Germain, from the Sault St. Marie, and M. Rouville, Sioux interpreter : they absolutely prevented their Indians committing any outrage in the plundering way. Commissary Honoré, who acted as lieutenant in captain Rollette's company whose singular activity in saving and keeping an exact account of provisions surprised me, and without which we must unavoidably have lost much of that essential article. The Michigan fencibles, who manned the gun, behaved with great courage, coolness, and regularity. As to the serjeant of artillery, too much cannot be said of him ; for the fate of the day, and our success are to be attributed, in a great measure, to his courage, and well-managed firing.

Since writing the foregoing, a few Sanks have arrived at the rapids, at the Rock river, with two Canadians, and bring the following information : On the 21st instant, six American barges, three of which were armed, were coming up and encamped in the rapids ; that, in the course of the night, the party of Indians having the four bags of gunpowder I sent from this on the 17th, reached them. The barges being encamped at short distances from each other, they, on the 22d, early in the morning, attacked the lowest, and killed, about 100 persons, took five pieces of cannon, and burnt the barge : the other barges seeing this disaster, and knowing there were British troops here, ran off. This is, perhaps, one of the most brilliant actions, fought by Indians only, since the commencement of the war.

I have, &c.

W. M'KAY, Lieutenant-colonel.

Lieutenant-colonel M'Douall,
    commanding at Michilimacinac.

This notice of the Indians would have come with a better grace from Col. McKay, had he not previously stated that the fire incessantly kept up by them was perfectly useless, from their being *so far off*, while, in the very next paragraph, he admits that not a man, except *three Indians*, was wounded. How is this reconcilable with the respectful distance which they observed? and did it not occur to Col. McKay, when stating that his red allies got wounded, that he was thereby admitting the fact of their being under fire?

Attack on and destruction of the Nancy at Nottawasaga.

Captain Sinclair after the repulse at Michilimacinac, thinking, we presume, that it would not answer to return empty-handed, and having missed the furs at St. Mary's and St. Joseph's, determined to make a third attempt to acquire laurels and booty by a descent on a block house, two miles up the Nottawasaga, situate on the south-east side of the river, which here runs parallel to, and forms a narrow peninsula with, the shore of Gloucester Bay. The success of the expedition was complete, so far as the destruction of the block house, but neither the Nancy, her men, nor the furs rewarded the prowess of captain Sinclair and his party, as lieutenant Worsely, who commanded, burned the Nancy, a small trading schooner belonging to the North West Company, to prevent the enemy taking possession of her, and, as the block house had been set fire to by a shell, he himself retired with his party up the river. The whole of the North West Company's valuable furs had been previously despatched up the French river, so that the sole reward reaped on the occasion was the destruction of a log block house, and the destruction of a schooner some eighty or a hundred tons burthen. Although no benefit was reaped by the Americans in this affair, it was productive of ultimate good to the British, as,

when captain Sinclair departed for Lake Erie, he left the two American Schooners, Tigress and Scorpion, to blockade the Nottawasaga, hoping thereby, as it was the only route by which provisions or supplies of any description could be forwarded to Michilimacinac, that he should be thus enabled to starve out a place which had successfully resisted an attack by arms. In obedience, probably, to orders, the schooners took a trip to the neighbourhood of St. Joseph's, and were discovered by some Indians, who disclosed the fact of their presence to lieutenant Worsley, with the additional information that they were fifteen miles apart. Acting on this information, lieutenant Worsley proceeded to take the measures which will be found detailed in the following despatch :—

From Lieutenant Bulger to Lieutenant-Colonel M'Douall.

Michilimacinac, September 7, 1814.

SIR,

I have the honor to report to you the particulars of the capture of the United States' schooners, Scorpion and Tigress, by a detachment from this garrison, under the command of Lieutenant Worsley, of the royal navy, and myself.

In obedience to your orders, we left Michilimacinac on the evening of the 1st instant, in four boats, one of which was manned by seamen under Lieutenant Worsley, the others by a detachment of the royal Newfoundland regiment, under myself, Lieutenants Armstrong, and Radenhurst. We arrived near the Détour about sun-set on the following day; but nothing was attempted that night, as the enemy's position had not been correctly ascertained. The troops remained the whole of the 3rd instant concealed amongst the woods, and, about 6 o'clock that evening, began to move towards the enemy. We had to row about six miles, during which the most perfect order and silence reigned. The Indians who accompanied us from Macinac, were left about three miles in the rear. About 9 o'clock at night we discovered the enemy, and had approached to within 100 yards before they hailed us. On receiving no answer, they opened a smart fire upon us, both of musketry and of the

24-pounder. All opposition, however, was in vain; and in the course of five minutes, the enemy's vessel was boarded and carried, by Lieutenant Worseley and lieutenant Armstrong on the starboard-side, and my boat and Lieutenant Radenhurst's on the larboard. She proved to be the Tigress, commanded by sailing-master Champlin, mounting one long 24-pounder, and with a complement of 30 men. The defence of this vessel did credit to her officers, who were all severely wounded. She had three men wounded and three missing, supposed to have been killed and thrown immediately overboard. Our loss is two seamen killed, and several soldiers and seamen slightly wounded.

On the morning of the 4th instant the prisoners were sent in a boat to Macinac, under a guard, and we prepared to attack the other schooner, which we understood was anchored 15 miles further down. The position of the Tigress was not altered; and, the better to carry on the deception, the American pendant was kept flying. On the 5th instant, we discerned the enemy's schooner beating up to us; the soldiers I directed to keep below, or to lie down on the deck, to avoid being seen. Every thing succeeded to our wish; the enemy came to anchor about two miles from us in the night; and, as day dawned on the 6th instant, we slipt our cable, and ran down under our jib and foresail. Every thing was so well managed by Lieutenant Worseley, that we were within ten yards of the enemy before they discovered us. It was then too late; for, in the course of five minutes, her deck was covered with our men, and the British flag hoisted over the American. She proved to be the Scorpion, commanded by Lieutenant Turner, of the United States' navy; carrying one long 24-pounder in her hold, with a complement of 32 men. She had two men killed, and two wounded. I enclose a return of our killed and wounded, and am happy to say that the latter are but slight.

To the admirable good conduct and management of Lieutenant Worseley, of the royal navy, the success is to be in a great measure attributed; but I must assure you, that every officer and man did his duty.

I have the honor to be, &c.

A. H. BULGER,
Lieutenant Royal Newfoundland Regiment.
To Lieutenant-Colonel Mc'Douall, &c. &c.

Return of killed and wounded of the troops, employed in the capture of the United States' schooners, Scorpion and Tigress, on the 3rd and 6th of September, 1814.

Royal Artillery;—1 rank and file, wounded.
Royal Newfoundland Regiment;—1 Lieutenant, 6 rank and file, wounded

Officer wounded.
Lieutenant Bulger, slightly,
N.B. Three seamen killed.

Lieutenant Bulger does not mention in his despatch anything relative to the value of these schooners, which were appraised shortly after, by the proper officers, and valued at sixteen thousand pounds sterling. As all mention of force is also omitted, it will be as well to state that the party consisted of lieutenant Worseley, one midshipman, one mate, and seventeen seamen, with lieutenant Bulger and fifty rank and file. Besides this number, there were forty-one others taken from the Indian department, the commissariat, &c., besides three Indian chiefs. The American versions of this affair, which was made the subject of a court of investigation by their government, fully sustain their character for fertility of invention. Before the court, the British force was made to consist of three hundred soldiers, sailors and Indians. Mr. Thomson supplies lieutenant Worseley with two hundred and fifty Indians, a hundred and fifty sailors, and a detachment of the Newfoundland regiment. Mr. O'Connor mentions no numbers, but introduces instead the following statement.

" Captain Arthur Sinclair, commanding the United States' naval force on the upper lakes, states in a letter to the Secretary of the Navy, on the authority of sailing master Champlin, that ' the conduct of the enemy to their prisoners (the crew of the Tigress), and the inhuman butchery of those who fell into their hands, at the attack on Michilimacinac, has been barbarous beyond a parallel. ` The former have been plundered of almost every article of clothing they possessed ; the latter had their hearts and livers taken out, which were *actually cooked and feasted* on by the savages ; and *that too in the quarters of the British officers, sanctioned* by Col. McDouall.' "

It is only necessary to remark on this extraordinary fabrication of Mr. O'Connor's, that there were no prisoners taken at Michilimacinac, and that in the proceedings, as reported by American journals, of the court of enquiry that tried the officers and crew of the Tigress, no such proceedings were even hinted at. Is it probable that such conduct, had it occurred, would have been passed over in silence, affording, as it would have done, such an opportunity of stigmatizing the British ? The answer is obvious, yet we find that Mr. O'Connor's book, with the atrocious statement uncontradicted, has passed through many editions, and is even now a class book of history in the United States.

In regard to the numbers, the statements furnished by authorities who wrote on the subject at the time, have enabled us to disprove the American exaggerations, by giving the correct numbers.

Naval proceedings. We must now pass, for the present, from the operations by land, and take a glance at the occurrences that had taken place during the last few months. We must not omit, however, to notice one statement of Ingersol's relative to the capture of the Argus by H. M. Brig the Pelican, which we have already touched upon.

In extenuation of the loss of the Argus, Ingersol states "that on the 13th August, the Argus captured a vessel loaded with wine, of which too free use was made by the American crew, soon after which her flag was, not ingloriously, struck, after an engagement with the English brig of war Pelican, Capt. Maples."

Now what inference is to be drawn from this passage? Is it to be construed into a confession that the American captain resorted to an attempt to give his crew what is commonly styled Dutch courage, or should it be taken as a very severe reproof upon the discipline of the crew of the Argus ? Ingersol knew full well, when he attempted this ridiculous excuse, that when a merchant vessel is taken by a man of war, that, should she not be destroyed, a prize crew is put on board of her, and she is despatched to the nearest port; had he, therefore mentioned as a reason why the prize was recaptured, that the prize crew got drunk, it would have been of no unusual occurrence. Again, how were the crew of the Argus to have got at the wine ; the prize was not taken by boarding, but by a gun fired across her bows, and so soon as a boat's crew was put on board of her, the Pelican being discovered, the boat's crew were recalled, and the brig set on fire. Is it probable that the captain and officers of the Argus would be so remiss in their duties as not to notice the boat's crew bringing back from the prize so much wine as to intoxicate a whole crew, and keep them in that state for twenty-four hours, the time that elapsed between the capture of the brig and the going into action. The whole idea is absurd, and only furnishes another instance of what American writers will resort to in order to bolster up any national dishonour or defeat.

On the 24th of May Commodore Decatur, Decatur's cruise in the United States, with Macedonian and sloop Hornet. commanding the United States forty-four-gun frigate, with the Macedonian, thirty-eight, and the Hornet, eighteen gun sloop, started for the East Indies from New York. By the 1st June, the American squadron had got through the intricacies of Long Island sound, by which passage they were forced to endeavour to get out, Sandy Hook being blockaded, and they stood out to sea. At nine a. m., however, they were discovered by H. M. ship Valiant, seventy-four guns, in company with the eighteen-pounder, forty-gun frigate Acasta, and immediately chased. Here was a glorious opportunity for Commodore Decatur ; he had been thirsting for an opportunity to tackle single-handed to a British seventy-four; and as according to American accounts the Macedonian was as fine a frigate as the British had ever built, the Acasta was just her match, and if any slight make-weight might have been required, it was amply supplied by the Hornet. What then did Commodore Decatur do? He ran back to New London, being compelled to start a great part of his water, and throw his provisions overboard, to escape capture. The Commodore did not attempt to increase the force in pursuit, but the American papers did; and it was, accordingly, circulated through the Union, that three vessels had chased, a razee being added to the real number.

An attempt was made a short time after the chase of Decatur and his squadron, to blow up the Ramilies, seventy-four, then at Anchor at Fisher's Island. James gives the following account of this occurrence.

Attempt to blow up the Ramilies, at Fisher Island.

Two merchants of New York, encouraged by a promise of reward from the American Government, formed a plan for destroying the Ramilies, Captain Sir Thomas Masterman Hardy. A schooner named the Eagle was laden with several casks of gunpowder, having trains leading from a species of gun lock, which, upon the principle of clockwork, went off at a given period after it had been set. Above the casks of powder, and in full view at the hatchway, were some casks of flour, it being known at New York that the Ramilies was short of provisions, and naturally supposed that Captain Hardy would immediately order the vessel alongside, in order to get the ship's wants supplied."

" Thus murderously laden, the schooner sailed from New York and stood up the sound. On the 25th, in the morning, the Eagle approached New London, as if intending to enter that river. The Ramilies dispatched a boat, with thirteen men, under lieutenant John Geddes, to cut her off. At eleven, a. m., lieutenant Geddes boarded the schooner, and found that the crew, after having let go her only anchor, had abandoned their vessel and fled to the shore.

The lieutenant brought the fatal prize near the Ramilies, and Sir Thomas ordered him to place the vessel alongside of a trading sloop, which had been recently captured, and lay a short distance off.

The lieutenant did as he was ordered, and at 2 h. 30 m., p. m., while he and his men were in the act of securing her, the schooner blew up with a tremendous explosion. The poor lieutenant and ten of the fine fellows, who were with him, perished; and the remaining three men escaped only with being shockingly scorched.

Both James and Brenton are very severe in their animadversions on this head, and James declares that he fully concurs with Brenton in the following remark:—

"A quantity of arsenic placed amongst the food, would have been so perfectly compatible with the rest of the contrivance, that we wonder it was not resorted to. Should actions like these receive the sanction of Government, the science of war, and the law of nations, will degenerate into the barbarity of the Algerines ; and murder and pillage will take the place of kindness and humanity to our enemies."

We confess we are not of this opinion. We see in this transaction nothing more than the modified use of fire ships, and cannot see the difference between this scheme and the Emperor of Russia sinking submarine charges to blow up vessels attempting the passage to Cronstadt. Some eminent writers on the subject, such as Wolf, &c., have asserted that war legalizes any violence, and that fraud and poison may be employed against enemies ; Grotius, Vatel, and other authorities have defined the legitimate mode of war to be the employment only of such force as is necessary to accomplish the end of war—rather an ambiguous definition. Leaving, however, this nice point to be settled by the peace congress, we would direct attention to Ingersol's inconsistency on this subject. He is very eloquent on the employment of the Indians by the British, and declares that "God and nature put no such means in men's hands; shocking to every lover of honorable war. In vain has religion been established if these acts of cruelty are permitted."

Now surely the employment of Indians was no more shocking to every lover of honorable war, than the attempt to blow up the Ramilies. Yet we find Ingersol reprobating the one and passing over the other.

We are more honest than Ingersol, and can find no difference between a shell thrown into Odessa, and a fire-ship sent into Cronstadt or Sebastopol. Every Christian must deplore war as a calamity, but so long as the necessity of a thing, so opposed to every Divine law as a state of warfare, is recognized by nations, we cannot see how it is to be regulated by Christian rules.

Perhaps one of the most signal instances American boasting in reference to the course of the President. of unblushing effrontery occurred in the case of the President, Commodore Rodgers. The President was on her return from her third cruise, and having passed the Delaware was standing for New York, "when," says the Commodore, "I saw nothing until I made Sandy Hook, when I again fell in with *another of the enemy's squadrons;* and by some unaccountable cause, was permitted to enter the bay, although in the presence of a decidedly superior force, after having been obliged to remain outside, seven hours and a half, waiting for the tide."

This assertion of the Commodore's was not sufficient for the officers of the President, who improved on the story, and asserted that seeing a large ship to windward they "backed the maintopsail and cleared for action. The strange sail came down within gun-shot, and hauled her wind on the starboard tack. We continued, with our maintopsail to the mast, three hours, and, seeing no probability of the seventy-four gun ship's bearing down to engage, the President gave her a shot to windward, and hoisted our colours; when she bore up for us reluctantly. When within half gun-shot, backed her maintopsail. At this moment, all hands were called to muster aft, and the Commodore said a few but expressive words, though it was unnecessary; for what other stimulant could true Americans want, than fighting gloriously in the sight of their native shore, where hundreds were assembled to witness the engagement."

"The commander of the seventy-four," adds the writer of this veracious document, "had it in his power, for five hours, to bring us at any time to an engagement, our maintopsail to the mast during that time. It was afterwards ascertained that the ship which declined the battle with the President, was the Plantagenet, seventy-four, Captain Lloyd. The reason given by Captain Lloyd for avoiding an engagagement was that his crew were in a state of mutiny."

One would almost think that this was invention enough to put forth on an imaginary subject; not so, however, as another American writer declares that "Captain Lloyd after returning to England had several of his sailors tried and executed on this charge."

Unfortunately for the truth of these statements, the Plantagenet, on the day that Commodore Rodgers was off the Hook, was off Barbadoes, at least sixteen hundred miles distant. Again, the crew of the Plantagenet was one of the finest in the service, and no such trials took place on her return home. The vessel that was magnified into a seventy-four by the diseased imagination of Rodgers and his officers, was the thirty-eight gun frigate Loire, Captain Thomas Brown, and his reasons for not bringing the President to action were, that he had seventy-four men away in prizes, and forty in sick bay, thus leaving out of three hundred and thirty two men, only two hundred and seventeen to go into action with a vessel carrying four hundred and seventy.

We have lost sight of the Essex, thirty-two Cruise of the Essex. gun frigate, Capt. Porter, who sailed towards the end of 1812, on a cruise to the Pacific. The Essex was to have made this cruise in company with the Constitution and Hornet, but not meeting with these vessels at the rendezvous, Captain Porter proceeded alone, and on the 14th of March, having captured the British packet Norton, with eleven thousand pounds sterling on board, arrived at Valparaiso, on the coast of Chili.

Having revictualled his ship, Capt. Porter stood over to the Gallipagos, where he captured twelve whalers. Two of these the American commander armed and manned as cruisers, the manning part of the operation being completed by inducing several of the crews of the whale ships to desert, and by taking several Americans out of a Peruvian vessel. The larger of these vessels, newly christened the Essex Junior, was armed with twenty guns (ten long sixes, and ten eighteen pound carronades) and a complement of ninety-five men.

It does not appear that Capt. Porter was very successful between this time and the beginning of 1814, when we find him still in company with the Essex Junior in Valparaiso.

On the 8th of February the British thirty-six gun frigate Phœbe, Captain Hillyar, and the eighteen gun sloop, Cherub, Captain Tucker, long in pursuit of Captain Porter, discovered his vessels at anchor with two of the prizes, stood into and anchored in the port. With the usual policy of his country, Captain Porter began to tamper with the British seamen, by hoisting at his fore-top-gallant mast head a white flag, with the motto, "Free Trade and Sailors' Rights." This was answered by Captain Hillyar, who ran up a St. George's ensign, with the motto "God and Country; British Sailors' Best Rights; Traitors offend both." Three or four days after, Captain Porter returned to the attack by hoisting a flag, on which was inscribed "God, our Country, and Liberty; Tyrants offend both."

After remaining sometime in harbour, and making several ineffectual attempts to escape from his watchful antagonist, Capt. Porter, on the 27th of March, was blown out of the Harbour, followed immediately by both British vessels, and, after an attempt to run his vessel on shore, easily captured; the Essex junior having been secured also. Captain Porter and part of his crew succeeded in es-

caping to shore, taking with them part of the specie. This, however, was only partially effected, from their boats having been much cut up by the fire of the Phœbe. The loss of the two British vessels was five killed and ten wounded. Captain Porter asserted that he had fifty-eight killed and sixty-six wounded, and there is no means of disproving the assertion. "The battered state of the Essex," declared Captain Porter, "must prevent her ever reaching England." In spite, however, of the assertion, she was safely anchored in Plymouth Sound. The superiority was decidedly in favour of the British.(not more so, however, than in the three first actions of the war, the advantage was the other way), so there is no room for further observation on the matter, than to examine what became of the prizes taken by the Essex. The Essex junior, we have just seen recaptured; another, the Georgiana, armed with sixteen guns, and a prize crew of over forty men, was fitted up with spermacetti oil taken from the others, and despatched to the United States; her passage was cut short in the West Indies by the Barossa frigate. The cargo was valued at one hundred thousand dollars. The Policy and New Zealander were filled with all the oil from the other ships, and sent home. They were, however, both recaptured, with their prize crews—the first by the Loire, the second by the Belvidera. The Rose and Charlton were given up to the prisoners; the Sir Andrew Hammond was taken by the Cherub; the Hector, Greenwich, and Catherine got burned, and the Seringapatam was run away with by her crew, who delivered her to her owners in payment of salvage. It will thus be seen that, a balance being struck, the result would not be very favourable to the American Government, the loss of the Essex being taken into consideration; not to speak of the valuable services of Captain David Porter, of whose talents as a despatch-writer we will furnish the reader with an example in our next chapter.

CHAPTER XIX.

WE give below, as promised in our last Captain David Porter as a writer of despatches. chapter, Capt. Porter's lengthy vindication of himself for the loss of the Essex, and we to have been particularly struck with the display of motto flags, and the number of jacks at the mast heads, apparently quite forgetful that he acknowledges to have sported an equal number himself. An ensign and motto flag at the gaff, another motto flag, "free trade and equal rights," at the fore, an ensign in the mizen rigging, and think that a more extraordinary production for mingled cunning and blundering it would be difficult to find. Captain Porter appears

---

* *Letter from Captain Porter to the Secretary of the Navy.*

ESSEX JUNIOR, July 3rd, 1814
at Sea.

SIR,—I have done myself the honour to address you repeatedly since I left the Delaware ; but have scarcely a hope that one of my letters has reached you; therefore consider it necessary to give you a brief history of my proceedings since that period.

I sailed from the Delaware on the 27th of October, 1812, and repaired with all diligence (agreeably to instructions from Commodore Bainbridge) to Port Praya, Fernando de Noronho, and Cape Frio ; and arrived at each place on the day appointed to meet him. On my passage from Port Praya to Fernando de Noronho, I captured his Britannic Majesty's packet Nocton ; and after taking out about 71,000 pounds sterling in specie, sent her under command of Lieutenant Finch for America. I cruized off Rio de Janeiro, and about Cape Frio, until the 12th of January, 1818, hearing frequently of the Commodore, by vessels from Bahia. I here captured but one schooner, with hides and tallow—I sent her into Porto Rico. The Montague, the Admiral's ship, being in pursuit of me, my provisions now getting short, and finding it necessary to look out for a supply,

to enable me to meet the Commodore by the 1st of April, off St. Helena, I proceeded to the island of St. Catharines (the last place of rendezvous on the coast of Brazil) as the most likely to supply my wants, and at the same time afford me that secrecy necessary to enable me to elude the British ships of war on the coast, and expected there. I here could procure only wood, water and rum, and a few bags of flour ; and hearing of the Commodore's action with the Java,the capture of the Hornet by the Montague, and a considerable augmentation of the British force on the coast, and of several being in pursuit of me, I found it necessary to get to sea as soon a possible. I now, agreeably to the Commodore's plan, stretched to the southward, securing the coast so far as Rio de la Plata. I heard that Buenos Ayres was in a state of starvation, and could not supply our wants ; and that the government of Montevideo was very inimical to us. The Commodore's instructions now left it completely discretionary with me what course to pursue, and I determined on following that which had not only met his approbation, but the approbation of the then secretary of the navy. I accordingly shaped my course for the Pacific ; and after suffering greatly from short allowance of provisions, and heavy gales off Cape Horn (for which my ship and men were badly provided) I arrived at Valparaiso on the 14th of March, 1813. I here took in as much jerked beef and other provisions, as my ship would conve-

and several jacks hoisted in different parts of the ship—all these are mentioned by Capt. Porter, and had he not acknowledged it,

James' Naval History would have furnished the information.

We should scarcely note such a trifle, were

niently stow, and ran down the coast of Chili and Peru; in this track I fell in with a Peruvian corsair, which had on board twenty-four Americans as prisoners, the crews of two whale ships, which she had taken on the coast of Chili. The captain informed me, that, as the allies of Great Britain, they would capture all they should meet with, in expectation of a war between Spain and the United States, I consequently threw all his guns and ammunition into the sea, liberated the Americans, wrote a respectful letter to the viceroy, explaining the cause of my proceedings, which I delivered to her captain. I then proceeded for Lima and re-captured one of the vessels as she was entering the port. From thence I proceeded for the Gallipagos Islands, where I cruized from the 17th of April, until the 3rd of October, 1813; during which time I touched only once on the coast of America, which was for the purpose of procuring a supply of fresh water, as none is to be found among those islands, which are, perhaps, the most barren and desolate of any known.

While among this group, I captured the following British ships, employed chiefly in the spermaceti whale fishery:—

LETTERS OF MARQUE.

	Tons.	Men.	Guns.	Pierced for.
Montezuma	270	21	2	
Policy	175	26	10	18
Georgiana	280	25	6	18
Greenwich	388	25	10	20
Atlantic	355	24	8	20
Rose	220	21	8	20
Hector	270	25	11	20
Catharine	270	29	8	18
Seringapatam	357	31	14	26
Charlton	274	21	10	18
New Zealander	259	23	8	18
Sir A. Hammond	301	31	12	18
	3,456	302	107	

As some of those ships were captured by boats, and others by prizes, my officers and men had several opportunities of showing their gallantry,

The Rose and Charlton were given to the prisoners, the Hector, Catharine and Montezuma, I sent to Valparaiso, where they were laid up; the Policy, Georgiana and New Zealander, I sent for America; the Greenwich I kept as a store ship, to contain the stores of any other prizes, necessary for us; and the Atlantic, now called Essex Junior, I equipped with twenty guns, and gave comand of her to lieutenant Downes,

Lieutenant Downes had conveyed the prizes to Valparaiso, and on his return brought me letters informing me, that a squadron under the command of commodore James Hillyar, consisting of the frigate Phœbe, of thirty-six guns,

the Racoon and Cherub sloops of war, and a store-ship of twenty guns, had sailed on the 6th of July for this sea. The Racoon and Cherub had been seeking me for some time on the coast of Brazil, and on their return from their cruize, joined the squadron sent in search of me to the Pacific. My ship, as it may be supposed, after being near a year at sea, required some repairs to put her into a state to meet them; which I determined to do, and bring them to action if I could meet them on nearly equal terms. I proceeded now in company with the remainder of my prizes, to the island of Nooaheevah or *Madison's* island, lying in the *Washington* group, discovered by a captain Ingraham, of Boston; here I caulked and completely overhauled my ship, made for her a new set of water casks, her old ones being entirely decayed, and took on board from my prizes provisions and stores for upwards of four months, and sailed for the coast of Chili on the 12th of December, 1813. Previous to sailing, I secured the Seringapatam, Greenwich and Sir Andrew Hammond under the guns of a battery, which I erected for their protection, (after taking possession of this fine island for the United States, and establishing the most friendly inercourse with the natives,) I left them under the charge of lieutenant Gamble of the marines, with twenty-one men, with orders to repair to Valparaiso, after a certain period.

I arrived on the coast of Chili on the 12th of January, 1814; looked into Conception and Valparaiso, found at both places only three English vessels, and learned that the squadron which sailed from Rio de Janeiro for that sea had not been heard of since their departure, and were supposed to be lost in endeavouring to double Cape Horn.

I had completely broken up the British navigation in the Pacific; the vessels which had not been captured by me, were laid up and dare not venture out. I had afforded the most ample protection to our own vessels, which were on my arrival, very numerous and unprotected. The valuable whale fishery there is entirely destroyed, and the actual injury we have done them may be estimated at two and half millions of dollars, independent of expenses of the vessels in search of me. They have furnished me amply with sails, cordage, cables, anchors, provisions medicines and stores of every description; and the slops on board them have furnished clothing for the seamen. We had, in fact, lived on the enemy since I had been in that sea, every prize having proved a well found store-ship for me. I had not yet been under the necessity of drawing bills on the department for any object, and had been enabled to make considerable advances to my officers and crew on account of pay.

For the unexampled time we had kept the sea, my crew had continued remarkably healthy.

it not a part of the ridiculous pretension and sneering which prevailed, and which laid American officers open to the charge that misrepresentation and false writing formed part of an American officer's duty to his country. Captain Porter declares that, in

I had but one case of the scurvy, and had lost only the following men by death ; viz. :

John S. Cowan, lieut. Robert Miller, surgeon. Levi Holmes, o. seaman: Edward Sweeny do. Samuel Groce, seaman. James Spafford, gunner's mate. Benjamin Geers, } quarter gunners. John Rodgers, Andrew Mahan, corporal of marines. Lewis Price, private marine.

I had done all the injury that could be done the British commerce in the Pacific, and still hoped to signalize my cruize by something more splendid before leaving that sea, I thought it not improbable that commodore Hillyar might have kept his arrival secret, and believing that he would seek me at Valpariso as the most likely place to find me, I therefore determined to cruize about that place, and should I fail of meeting him, hoped to 1 e compensated by the capture of some merchant ships, said to be expected from England.

The Phœbe, agreeably to my expectations, came to seek me at Valpariso, where I was anchored with the Essex, my armed prize the Essex Junior, under the command of lieutenant Downes, on the look out off the harbour ; but, contrary to the course I thought he would pursue, commodore Hillyar brought with him the Cherub sloop of war, mounting 28 guns, 18 32 pound carronades, 8 24's and 2 long 9's on the quarter-deck and fore-castle, and a complement of 180 men. The force of the Phœbe is as follows : 30 long 18 pounders, sixteen 32 pound carronades, one howitzer, and six 3 pounders in the tops, in all 53 guns, and a complement of 320 men, making a force of 81 guns and 500 men ; in addition to which they took on board the crew of an English letter of marque laying in port. Both ships had picked crews, and were sent into the Pacific, in company with the Racoon of 22 guns and a store ship of 20 guns, for the express purpose of seeking the Essex, and were prepared with flags bearing the motto, "God and country ; British sailors' best rights—Traitors offend both." This was intended as a reply to my motto "Free Trade and sailors' Rights," under the erroneous impression that my crew were chiefly Englishmen, or to counteract its effect on their own crews. The force of the Essex was 46 guns, forty 32 pound carronades, and six long 12's, and her crew, which had been much reduced by prizes, amounted only to 255 men. The Essex Junior, which was intended only as a store-ship mounted twenty guns, ten 18 pound carronades, and ten short 6's, with only 60 men on board. In reply to their motto, I wrote at my mizen, "God, our Country and Liberty ; Tyrants offend them."

On getting their provisions on board, they went off the port for the purpose of blockading me, where they cruized for near six weeks ; during which time I endeavoured to provoke a challenge, and frequently, but ineffectually, to bring the Phœbe alone to action, first with both my ships, and afterwards with my single ship, with both crews on board. I was several times under way, and ascertained that I had greatly the advantage in point of sailing, and once succeeded in closing within a gun-shot of the Phœbe, and commenced a fire on her, when she ran down for the Cherub, which was two and a half miles to leeward ; this excited some surprize and expressions of indignation, as previous to my getting under way, she hove to off the port, hoisted her motto flag and fired a gun to windward. Commodore Hillyar seemed determined to avoid a contest with me on nearly equal terms, and from his extreme prudence in keeping both his ships ever after constantly within hail of each other, there were no hopes of any advantages to my country from a longer stay in port. I therefore determined to put to sea the first opportunity which should offer ; and I was the more strongly induced to do so, as I had gained certain intelligence that the Tagus rated 38, and two other frigates, had sailed for that sea in pursuit of me ; and I had reason to expect the arrival of the Racoon from N.W. coast of America where she had been sent for the purpose of destroying our fur establishment on the Columbia. A rendezvous was appointed for the Essex Junior, and every arrangement made for sailing, and I intended to let them chase me off, to give the Essex Junior an opportunity of escaping. On the 28th March, the day after this determination was formed the wind came on to blow fresh from the southward, when I parted my larboard cable and dragged my starboard anchor directly out to sea. Not a moment was to be lost in getting sail on the ship. The enemy were close in with the point forming the west side of the bay ; but on opening them, I saw a prospect of passing windward, when I took in my top-gallant-sails, which were set over single reefed top-sails, and braced up for this purpose ; but on rounding the point a heavy squall struck the ship and carried away her main-top-mast, precipitating the men who were aloft into the sea, who were drowned. Both ships now gave chase to me, and I endeavoured in my disabled state to regain the port ; but finding I could not recover the common anchorage, I ran close into a small bay, about three-quarters of a mile to leeward of the battery on the east side of the harbour, and let go my anchor within pistol shot of the shore, where I intended to repair my damages as soon as possible. The enemy continued to approach, and shewed an evident intention of attacking, regardless of the neutrality of the place where I was anchored, and the caution observed in their approach to the attack of the crippled Essex was truly ridiculous, as was their

half an hour, he disabled, with three guns only, both his opponents, so as to compel them to haul off to repair damages ; this as-

sertion may, and doubtless will, be readily adopted by readers who know nothing of what three twelve-pounders can effect in the

display of their motto flags, and the number of jacks at all the mast-heads. I, with as much expedition as circumstances would admit of, got my ship-ready for action, and endeavoured to get a spring on my cable, but had not succeeded, when the enemy, at 54 minutes after 3 P.M. made his attack, the Phœbe placed herself under my stern, and the Cherub on my starboard bow ; but the Cherub soon finding her situation a hot one, bore up and run under my stern also ; where both ships kept up a hot raking fire, I had got three long 12 pounders out of the stern ports, which were worked with so much bravery and skill, *that in half an hour we so disabled both as to compel them to haul off to repair damages.* In the course of this firing, I had, by the great exertions of Mr. Edward Barnewall, the acting sailing-master, assisted by Mr. Linscott, the boatswain, succeeded in getting springs on our cable three different times ; but the fire of the enemy was so excessive, that before we could get our broad-side to bear, they were shot way and thus rendered useless to us. My ship had received many injuries, and several had been killed and wounded—but my brave officers and men, notwithstanding the unfavorable circumstances under which we were brought to action, and the powerful force opposed to us, were no ways discouraged—all appeared determined to defend their ship to the last extremity, and to die in preference to a shameful surrender. *Our gaff, with the ensign and the motto flag at the mizen, had been shot away, but Free trade and Sailors' Rights, continued to fly at the fore. Our ensign was replaced by another—and to guard against a similar event, an ensign was made fast in the mizen-rigging, and several jacks were hoisted in different parts of the ship.* The enemy soon repaired his damages for a fresh attack ; he now placed himself, with both his ships, on my starboard quarter, out of the reach of my carronades, and where my stern guns could not be brought to bear—he there kept up a most galling fire, which it was out of my power to return, when I saw no prospect of injuring him without getting under way and becoming the assailant. My top-sail sheets and haulyards were all shot away, as well as the jib and fore-top-mast-stay-sail-haulyards. The only rope not cut was the flying-jib-haulyards—and that being the only sail I could set, I caused it to be hoisted, my cable to be cut, and ran down on both ships, with an intention of laying the Phœbe on board.

The firing on both sides was now tremendous ; I had let fall my foretopsail and foresail, but the want of tacks and sheets rendered them almost useless to us—yet we were enabled for a short time to close with the enemy ; and although our decks were now strewed with dead and our cockpit filled with wounded —although our ship had been several times on

fire, and was rendered a perfect wreck, we were still encouraged to hope to save her, from the circumstance of the Cherub, from her crippled state, being compelled to haul off. She did not return to close action again, although she had it apparently in her power to do so, but kept up a distant firing with her long guns. The Phœbe, from our disabled state, was enabled however, by edging off, to choose the distance which best suited her long guns, and kept up a tremendous fire on us, which mowed down my brave companions by the dozen. Many of my guns had been rendered useless by the enemy's shot, and many of them had their whole crews destroyed —we manned them again from those which were disabled, and one gun in particular was three times manned—fifteen men were slain at it in the course of the action ! but strange as it may appear, the captain of it escaped with only a slight wound. Finding that the enemy had it in his power to choose his distance, I now gave up all hopes of closing with him, and, as the wind for the moment, seemed to favour the design, I determined to endeavour to run her on shore, land my men and destroy her. Every thing seemed to favour my wishes. We had approached the shore within musket shot, and I had no doubt of succeeding, when in an instant the wind shifted from the land (as it is very common in this port in the latter part of the day) and payed our head down on the Phœbe, where we were again exposed to a dreadful raking fire. My ship was now totally unmanageable : yet as her head was toward the enemy, and he to the leeward of me, I still hoped to be able to board him. At this moment Lieut. Downes came on board to receive my orders, under the impression that I should soon be a prisoner. He could be of no use to me in the then wretched state of the Essex ; and finding (from the enemy's putting his helm up) that my last attempt at boarding would not succeed, I directed him after he had been ten minutes on board, to return to his own ship, to be prepared for defending and destroying her in case of attack. He took with him several of my wounded, leaving three of his boat's crew on board to make room for them.—The Cherub now had an opportunity of distinguishing herself, by keeping up a hot fire on him during his return. The slaughter on board my ship had now become horrible, the enemy continued to rake us, and we unable to bring a gun to bear. I therefore directed a hawser to be bent to the sheet anchor, and the anchor to be cut from the bows to bring her head round : this succeeded. We again got our broadside to bear, and as the enemy was much crippled and unable to hold his own, I have no doubt he would have drifted out of gun shot before he discovered we had anchored, had not the hawser unfortunately parted. My ship had taken fire several times

teeth of a heavy fire of long eighteens, but cannot impose upon any one else. Other accounts were received of this engagement than those furnished by the officers engaged on either side, and, in the private letters from some of the on-lookers, not one syllable is

during the action, but alarmingly so forward and aft at this moment, the flames were bursting up each hatchway, and no hopes were entertained of saving her ; our distance from the shore did not exceed three quarters of a mile, and I hoped many of my brave crew would be able to save themselves, should the ship blow up, as I was informed the fire was near the magazine, and the explosion of a large quantity of powder below served to increase the horror of our situation—our boats were destroyed by the enemy's shot; I therefore directed those who could swim to jump overboard, and endeavour to gain the shore. Some reached it—some were taken by the enemy, and some perished in the attempt ; but most preferred sharing with me the fate of the ship. We, who remained, now turned our attention wholly to extinguishing the flames ; and when we had succeeded went again to our guns, where the firing was kept up for some minutes, but the crew had by this time become so weakened, that they all declared to me the impossibility of making further resistance, and entreated me to surrender my ship to save the wounded, as all further attempt at opposition must prove ineffectual, almost every gun being disabled by the destruction of their crews. I now sent for the officers of divisions to consult them ; but what was my surprize to find only acting Lieut. Stephen Decatur M'Knight remaining, (who confirmed the report respecting the condition of the guns on the gun deck—those on the spar deck were not in a better state). Lieut. Wilmer, after fighting most gallantly through the action, had been knocked overboard by a splinter while getting the sheet anchor from the bows and was drowned. Acting Lieut. John G. Cowell had lost a leg ; Mr. Edw. Barnewall, acting sailing master had been carried below after receiving two severe wounds, one in the breast and one in the face ; and acting Lieut. William H. Odenheimer had been knocked overboard from the quarter an instant before, and did not regain the ship until after the surrender. I was informed that the cockpit, the steerage, the wardroom and the berth deck could contain no more wounded ; that the wounded were killed while the surgeons were dressing them, and that unless something was speedily done to prevent it, the ship would soon sink from the number of shot holes in her bottom. And on sending for the carpenter he informed us that all his crew had been killed or wounded, and that he had once been over the side to stop the leaks when his slings had been shot away, and it was with difficulty he was saved from drowning. The enemy from the smoothness of the water, and the impossibility of our reaching him with our carronades, and the little apprehension that was excited by our fire which had now become much slackened, was enabled to take aim at us as at a target ; his shot never missed our hull,

and my ship was cut up in a manner which was perhaps, never before witnessed—in fine, I saw no hopes of saving her, and at 20 minutes after 6 P.M. gave the painful order to strike the colours. 75 men, including officers, were all that remained of my whole crew, after the action, capable of doing duty, and many of them severely wounded, some of whom have since died. The enemy still continued his fire, and my brave though unfortunate companions, were still falling about me. I directed an opposite gun to be fired, to shew them we intended no further resistance ; but they did not desist ; four men were killed at my side, and others in different parts of the ship. I now believed he intended to shew us no quarter, and that it would be as well to die with my flag flying as struck, and was on the point of again hoisting it, when about ten minutes after hauling the colours down he ceased firing.

I cannot speak in sufficiently high terms of the conduct of those engaged for such an unparalleled length of time, under such circumstances, with me, in the arduous and unequal contest. Let it suffice to say that more bravery, skill, patriotism and zeal were never displayed on any occasion. Every one seemed determined to die in defence of their much loved country's cause, and nothing but views of humanity could ever have reconciled them to the surrender of the ship ; they remembered the wounded and helpless shipmates below. To acting lieutenants M'Knight and Odenheimer I feel much indebted for their great exertions and bravery throughout the action in fighing and encouraging the men at their divisions, for the dexterous management of the long guns, and for their promptness in remanning their guns as their crews were slaughtered. The conduct of that brave and heroic officer, acting lieutenant John G. Cowell, who lost his leg in the latter part of the action, excited the admiration of every man in the ship, and after being wounded would not consent to be taken below until loss of blood rendered him insensible. Mr. Edward Barnewell acting sailing master, whose activity and courage was equally conspicuous, returned on deck after his first wound, and remained after receiving his second until fainting with loss of blood. Mr. Samuel B. Johnson who had joined me the day before, and acted as marine officer, conducted himself with great bravery, and exerted himself in assisting at the long guns ; the musketry after the first half hour being useless, from our long distance.

Mr. M. W. Bostwick, whom I had appointed acting purser of the Essex Junior, and who was on board my ship, did the duties of aid, in a manner which reflects on him the highest honour, and midshipmen Isaacs, Farragut and Ogden, as well as acting midshipmen James Terry, James R. Lyman and Samuel Duzenbury, and master's mate William Pierce exerted themselves

mentioned of the British vessels hauling off to repair damages. Again, Captain Porter endeavours to insinuate that he was attacked in a neutral port, although confessing, a dozen lines above, that he was unable to recover the common anchorage.

in the performance of their respective duties and gave an earnest of their value to the service; the three first are too young to recommend for promotion, the latter I beg leave to recommend for confirmation as well as the acting lieutenants, and Messrs. Barnewall, Johnston and Bostwick.

We have been unfortunate, but not disgraced. The defence of the Essex has not been less honorable to her officers and crew, than the capture of an equal force, and I now consider my situation less unpleasant than that of commodore Hillyar, who, in violation of every principle of honour and generosity, and regardless of the rights of nations, attacked the Essex in her crippled state; within pistol shot of neutral shore; when for six weeks I had daily offered him fair and honorable combat, on terms greatly to his advantage; the blood of the slain must be on his head, and he has yet to reconcile his conduct to heaven, to his conscience and to the world.

My loss has been dreadfully severe, 58 killed or have since died of their wounds; and among them lieutenant Cowell; 39 were severely wounded, 27 slightly, and 31 are missing; making in all 154, killed, wounded, and missing, a list of whose names is annexed.

The professional knowledge of Dr. Richard Hoffman, acting surgeon, and Doctor Alexander Montgomery, acting surgeon's mate, added to their assiduity and the benevolent attentions and assistance of Mr. D. P. Adams, the chaplain, saved the lives of many of the wounded, those gentlemen have been indefatigible in their attentions to them; the two first I beg leave to recommend for confirmation, and the latter to the notice of the department.

I must in justification of myself observe, that with our six twelve pounders alone we fought this action, our carronades being almost useless.

The loss in killed and wounded has been great with the enemy; among the former is the first lieutenant of the Phœbe, and of the latter captain Tucker of the Cherub, whose wounds are severe. Both the Essex and Phœbe were in a sinking state, and it was with difficulty they could be kept afloat until they anchored in Valparaiso next morning. The battered state of the Essex, will, I believe, prevent her ever reaching England, and I also think it will be out of their power to repair the damages of the Phœbe so as to enable her to double Cape Horn. All the masts and yards of the Phœbe and Cherub are badly crippled, and their hulls much cut up; the former had eighteen twelve pound shot through her below her water line, some three feet under water. Nothing but the smoothness of the water saved both the Phœbe and Essex.

I hope Sir, that our conduct may prove satisfactory to our country, and that it will testify it by obtaining our speedy exchange, that we may again have it in our power to prove our zeal.

Commodore Hillyar, I am informed, has thought proper to state to his Government that the action lasted only 45 minutes; should he have done so, the motive may be easily discovered —but the thousands of disinterested witnesses who covered the surrounding hills can testify that we fought his ships for two hours and a half; upwards of fifty broadsides were fired by the enemy agreeable to their own accounts, and upwards of seventy five by ours; excepting the few minutes they were repairing damages the firing was incessant.

Soon after my capture I entered into an agreement with commodore Hillyar to disarm my prize the Essex Junior, and proceed with the survivors of my officers and crew in her to the United States, taking with me all her officers and crew. He consented to grant her a passport to secure her from recapture. The ship was small and we knew we had much to suffer, yet we hoped soon to reach our country in safety, that we might again have it in our power to serve it. This arrangement was attended with no additional expence, as she was abundantly supplied with provisions and stores for the voyage.

In justice to commodore Hillyar, I must observe, that, although I can never be reconciled to the manner of his attack on the Essex, or to his conduct before the action, he has, since our capture shewn the greatest humanity to my wounded, whom he permitted me to land on condition that the United States should bear their expenses, and has endeavoured as much as lay in his power to alleviate the distresses of war by the most generous and delicate deportment towards myself and officers and crew; he gave orders that the property of every person should be respected—his orders, however, were not so strictly attended to as might have been expected; besides being deprived of books, charts, &c. &c., both myself and officers lost many articles of our clothing, some to a considerable amount. I should not have considered this last circumstance of sufficient importance to notice, did it not mark a stirking difference between the navy of Great Britain and that of the United States, highly creditable to the latter.

By the arrival of the Tagus, a few days after my capture, I was informed that besides the ships which had arrived in the Pacific in pursuit of me, and those still expected, others were sent to cruize for me in the China seas, off New Zealand, Timor and New Holland, and that another frigate was sent to the River la Plata.

To possess the Essex it has cost the British government near six millions of dollars, and yet, sir, her capture was owing entirely to accident; and if we consider the expedition with which naval contests are now decided, the action is a

HISTORY OF THE WAR OF 1812.

It may not be, perhaps, known to every one, that in the English merchant service a different style of painting their vessels prevailed at that time to what was adopted in the United States. In British vessels imitation port holes were painted, whilst in American, a plain white or red riband was painted from stem to stern. Captain Porter knew perfectly well when making his statement of his capture of twelve letters of marque, that he would not deceive sailors, especially as he admits that the vessels were employed in the spermaceti whale fishery.

To any one who has ever seen the decks of a vessel while on the fishing grounds and the state of her decks, the absurdity of Capt. Porter's representing vessels of one hundred and seventy-five tons as carrying ten guns, or being pierced for eighteen, is simply ridiculous. We have, however, shown on a previous occasions an attempt by would-be American Nelsons to swell the capture of West India droghers and other coasting vessels, into "gallant and successful carrying of H. M. S. armed vessel, of fifteen tons, twelve guns, and ninety men." Such, in sooth, is very much the spirit in which Capt. Porter dictated his report; the gallant commander forgot, however, in his estimate of the cost to the British Government of the capture of the Essex, to record the fact of the ultimate re-capture of many of the vessels, and of all their cargoes.

Captain Porter must have had a prodigious opinion of his own prowess, if we may judge by the number of vessels which he represents as having been equipped, manned, and despatched to various parts of the world, for no other purpose than that of capturing the redoubtable Captain David Porter—six millions of dollars spent in despatching fresh vessels to the Pacific, besides those already there, to the Chinese Seas, to Timor, to New Zealand, to New Holland, and as if one side of the continent might be insufficient to restrain Captain Porter's ardour, vessels to the Rio de la Plata were also found necessary. A Russian squadron, at the present time supposed to be cruising somewhere in our Indian possessions, has not excited half the alarm, nor do we find that half the preparations have been made, which were deemed necessary to ensure the capture of our American frigate. Enough, however, of Captain David Porter and his ridiculous attempt at self-glorification.

The Americans, not yet satisfied that the chance of conquering Canada was hopeless, determined, early in 1814, to make another attempt. We find, accordingly, that, from the beginning of April to the end of June, General Brown, the American commander, was actively engaged in preparing his army of invasion. Towards the end of June, the Secretary at War, at

Fifth invasion of Canada by a United States army.

---

dishonour to them. Had they brought their ships boldly into action with a force so very superior, and having the choice of position, they should either have captured or destroyed us in a fourth the time they were about it.

During the action, our consul general, Mr. Poinsett, called on the governor of Valparaiso, and requested that the batteries might protect the Essex. This request was refused, but he promised that if she should succeed in fighting her way to the common anchorage he would send an officer to the British commande and request him to cease firing, but declined using force under any circumstances, and there is no doubt of a perfect understanding existing between them; this conduct added to the assistance given to the British, and their friendly reception after the action, and the strong bias of the faction which govern Chili in favour of the English, as well as their hostility to the Americans, induced Mr. Poinsett to leave that country. Under such circumstances, I did not conceive it would be proper for me to claim the restoration of my

ship, confident that the claim would be made by my government to more effect. Finding some difficulty in the sale of my prizes, I had taken the Hector and Catharine out to sea and burnt them with their cargoes.

I exchanged lieutenant M'Knight, Mr. Adams, and Mr. Lyman and eleven seamen for part of the crew of the Sir Andrew Hammond, and sailed from Valparaiso on the 27th April, where the enemy were still patching up their ships to put them in a state for proceeding to Rio de Janeiro previous to going to England.

Annexed is a list of the remains of my crew to be exchanged, as also a copy of the correspondence between commodore Hillyar and myself on that subject. I also send you a list of the prisoners I have taken during my cruize, amounting to 343.

I have the honor to be, &c.   D. PORTER.

The honorable Secretary of the
    navy of the United States,
    Washington.

Washington, judging, it may be supposed, from Brown's despatches, that sufficient preparations had been made, issued his fiat "to carry Fort Erie, and beat up the enemy's quarters at Chippewa;" adding, however, the prudent proviso that "in case his (the British) fleet gets the control of Lake Ontario, you are immediately to re-cross the strait." A few of the heads of General Armstrong's "heads of plan of campaign" are interesting, as they show how very certain the Secretary at War had made himself that all his plans were to succeed. The first was, That such portions of the Erie fleet, and of the garrison at Detroit, as the officer commanding may deem necessary for the purpose, be despatched without delay to the western lakes, with orders to attack or capture a British fort or depot, established at Matchadash Bay, on Lake Huron; recapture Michilimacinac, &c. These orders very explicit, and doubtless, when issued, General Armstrong considered them as already executed. We showed, however, in our last chapter the miserable failure which attended all the operations undertaken in this direction, and that the Americans, instead of crowning themselves with glory and rich furs, reaped only a harvest of defeat and disgrace.

Simultaneous orders were also issued to bring all surplus vessels on Lake Erie to assist in transporting the left division to the Canadian shore, and that such division, after landing, should "be marched as expeditiously as possible on the British position at Burlington Bay, to siege and fortify that post, and, having thus cut the enemy's line of land communication between York and Fort George, await the arrival and co-operation of the Ontario fleet." This was, of course, assuming that Chauncey had disposed of Sir James Yeo and his fleet, and that such would be the case, Armstrong does not appear to have doubted, as he adds, " The commanders of the two armies will have within their choice, a speedy investment of Fort George and Niagara; rapid descent on Sackett's Harbour; a junction with the brigade at that post, and a direct attack on Kingston."

Having completed his arrangements, Gen. Brown, on receipt of Gen. Armstrong's instructions, issued the following general order, dated July 2d, 1814:—

General Brown's proclamation or general order.

"Major-Gen. Brown has the satisfaction to announce to the troops of his division on the frontier, that he is authorized by the orders of his Government, to put them in motion against the enemy. The first and second brigades, with the corps of artillery, will cross the strait before them, this night, or as early to-morrow as possible. The necessary instructions have been given to the brigadiers, and by them to the commanding officers of regiments and corps,

Upon entering Canada the laws of war will govern; men found in arms, or otherwise engaged in the service of the enemy, will be treated as enemies; those behaving peaceably, and following their private occupations, will be treated as friends. Private property, in all cases, will be held sacred; public property, whenever found, will be seized and disposed of by the commanding general. Our utmost protection will be given to all who join, or who evince a desire to join us.

Plundering is prohibited. The Major-General does not apprehend any difficulty on this account, with the regular army and volunteers who press to the standard of their country, to avenge her wrongs, and to gain a name in arms. Profligate men, who follow the army for plunder, must not expect that they will escape the vengeance of the gallant spirits who are struggling to exalt the national character. Any plunderer shall be punished with death who may be found violating this order."

After the specimen of humanity afforded by the party under Colonel Campbell, who landed on the 13th May, at Dover, General Brown's assertion that from the United States regulars, he apprehended nothing on the score of marauding or plundering, appears supremely ridiculous. It must be borne in mind that the detachment in question was not composed of profligate men, who followed the army for plunder, but of United States regular infantry, the absurdity is therefore heightened when it is remembered that, so notorious was the conduct of these men, that it was found necessary, for appearance' sake, to hold a court of enquiry, and that the result of said enquiry was, not a disproof of excesses having been committed, but merely that there were extenuating circumstances. Another point worthy of remark in this general order is the invitation held out to the Canadians to turn traitors. By thus stooping to invite men to commit a most dastardly action, the American General decidedly lowered his own and the character of the troops he commanded. We have found, however, that the same course was adopted on every occasion when temptation could be extended, and from this fact the only inference to be drawn is that the Americans possessed no very keen sense of honor themselves, and, perhaps, from not knowing what honesty meant, were also inclined to give others credit for not being burthened with the commodity.

The force assembled by General Brown, so far as we can gather General Brown's force. from the various American accounts, amounted to at least a body of three thousand regular infantry, besides about a thousand volunteers and Indians, making in all a force of some four thousand one hundred men. This number included four hundred artillery and a squadron of dragoons. Besides this regular force there were, according to James, "between Erie and Lewiston, the 1st regiment of infantry, a regular rifle corps, and from two to three hundred volunteers, under Colonel Swift." These two bodies mustered collectively five thousand strong, and even this is not all, as the militia of the district are not included, nor the regular force which Commodore Chauncey was expected to bring from Sackett's Harbour. It is clear, then, that Gen. Armstrong expected that the attack would be made by a force of at least ten thousand men.

Fortunately for Upper Canada, these overwhelming numbers were prevented, in consequence of Chauncey's not acquiring a superiority in Lake Ontario, from uniting, and the two divisions which crossed the strait did not much exceed four thousand men. Even these numbers, however, were fearful odds when the strength of their opponents is considered ; the British troops mustering, along the whole Niagara frontier, only seven-

teen hundred and eighty rank and file, out of which number, too, the garrisons at Forts Erie, George, Missisagu, and Niagara must be subtracted, leaving an available force of seven hundred and sixty regulars at General Riall's disposal. To this number must, however, be added three hundred sedentary militia and as many Indians, in all thirteen hundred and fifty men to oppose an invading force of four thousand. General Riall was compelled, besides, to almost strip the forts of their garrisons when marching against Brown at Chippewa.

It appears as if Canada owed almost as much to the incapacity or differences of the American commanders, as was due to the gallantry of the troops. We have shown that this was the fact in previous invasions, and it would appear that the present attempt did not furnish an exception. This conclusion may be deduced from the following extract from General Brown's memoranda of occurrences in the campaign of 1814, on the Niagara :—

" Toward the evening of the 2nd, General Ripley (the second in command) appeared to be much discomposed. He objected to the division made of the transports, and complained that he would not be able to cross with sufficient force ; that the principal fighting would be above the fort where he was ordered to land, and that he had seen lights during the night and smoke during the day, for some time past. Gen. Brown endeavoured to satisfy him, but in vain. He (Ripley) tendered his resignation, which was not accepted, as the General was inflexibly determined that the army should cross agreeably to the arrangements he had made."

It is difficult to understand on what grounds the American General could have based his objections. By their spies the Americans were fully informed as to the smallness of the numbers that could be mustered against them, and, in fact, they were in this instance too well served by their spies, by whom they were led to believe that the British did not amount to one thousand men, regulars, militia, and Indians all included. That this was the case was proved by General Brown dividing his force, in order to prevent the possibility of the garrison at Fort Erie escaping.

Whatever were Ripley's reasons for dissatisfaction, it is certain that the movement of his division across the river was made more slowly than that of the other, under General Scott. It is absolutely necessary not to pass over these indications of want of unanimity among the American commanders, as it would otherwise be laying ourselves open to the same charges that are so justly preferred against American historians of distorting the truth. This insinuation must be particularly guarded against by the English chronicler of the war, inasmuch as it generally falls to his lot to recount the defeat of large bodies of Americans by very inferior force ; hence other reasons must be sought than the mere difference in the bravery of the troops, and these are very readily found in the incapacity and quarrels of the commanders.

The two divisions having crossed on the 3rd of July, invested Fort Erie, which, being incapable of actual defence, both from the nature of the fortifications and the smallness of its garrison, was at once surrendered. Here we would direct attention to that part of General Brown's despatch where it is stated that "Fort Erie did not, as I assured you it should not, detain me a single day." This is particularly absurd, when it is remembered that, by American accounts, the garrison only amounted to one hundred and seventy, and that General Wilkinson in his memoirs distinctly states that "Fort Erie was in a defenceless condition."

The American divisions landed, one a mile and a half above, and the other the same distance below Erie, so that no opposition could be brought to bear from the guns of the fort; and, on its surrender, the garrison was promptly despatched across the river, and marched into the interior of New York State, a detachment of artillery and a few infantry being left as a garrison ; three armed schooners, under the command of Lieutenant Kennedy, being stationed as a further security under its walls.

It was not until 8 A.M. that General Riall received the intelligence of the Americans having landed, and he instantly, on receipt of the information, ordered five companies of the Royal Scots to advance as a reinforcement of the post. The advance of this body was, however, checked by the intelligence of the surrender of the fort. General Riall then determined on an immediate attack, but was induced, by its being represented to him that the 8th regiment was hourly expected from York (now Toronto), to postpone the attack until the morning of the 4th. On the morning of the 4th the attack was accordingly made.

In the letters of *Veritas*, some very pertinent remarks are made on this subject, which we transcribe:— "General Riall's attack upon the enemy, under so great a disproportion of force, as probably five to one, has been censured by many; but the probability is, that if he had not done so, and broke in upon their plan of operations, by that daring and unexpected manœuvre, they, probably, without the aid of their fleet, would (by appearing to threaten an attack upon our lines at Chippewa) have marched to the left, and have actually cut off our communication with Burlington, as originally intended.

"In this view of the subject, his attack was fortunate, and the retreat afterwards made by him is deserving of credit, from having been effected in good order, without loss of men, artillery, stores, or baggage ; so that the confidence of his troops remained unabated. Had he retreated in the first instance without fighting, the probability is that his men would have been dispirited, as considering such a retrograde movement then premature."

We fully concur with the opinions expressed by *Veritas*, which we think are fully borne out by a consideration of the plans laid down by the Secretary at War, and the adoption of this movement by General Riall, when ignorant of the force of the enemy, can only be considered as a proof of the judgment and bravery of that officer, who was only anxious to prevent a junction with the force that might be expected in the fleet.

From Major-General Riall to Lieutenant-General Sir G. Drummond.

Chippewa, July 6.

SIR,—I have the honour to inform you that the enemy effected a landing on the morning of the 3d instant at the ferry, opposite Black Rock, having driven in the picquet of the garrison of Fort Erie. I was made acquainted with the circumstance about eight in the morning, and gave orders for the immediate advance to Chippewa of five companies of the royal Scots, under Lieutenant-Colonel Gordon, to reinforce the garrison of that place. Lieutenant-Colonel Pearson had moved forward from thence with the light companies of the 100th, some militia, and a few Indians, to reconnoitre their position and numbers; he found them posted on the ridge parallel with the river, near the ferry, and in strong force. I received instructions from Major Buck, that they had also landed a considerable force above Fort Erie. In consequence of the King's regiment, which I had every reason to expect the day before from York, not having arrived, I was prevented from making an attack that night.

The following morning, the 4th, a body of their troops were reported to be advancing by the river; I moved to reconnoitre, and found them to be in considerable force, with cavalry and artillery, and a large body of riflemen. Lieutenant-Colonel Pearson was in advance during this reconnoisance with the light company of the royal Scots, and the flank company of the 100th, and a few of the 19th light dragoons, four of whom, and eight horses, were wounded in a skirmish with the enemy's riflemen.

Having been joined by the King's regiment on the morning of the 5th, I made my dispositions for attack at four o'clock in the afternoon. The light companies of the royal Scots, and 100th regiment, with the second Lincoln militia, formed the advance under Lieutenant-Colonel Pearson. The Indian warriors were, throughout, on our right flanks in the woods. The troops moved in three columns, the third (the King's regiment) being in advance. The enemy had taken up a position with his right resting on some buildings and orchards, close on the river Niagara, and strongly supported by artillery; his left towards the wood, having a considerable body of riflemen and Indians in front of it.

Our Indians and militia were shortly engaged with the enemy's riflemen and Indians, who at first checked their advance: but the light troops being brought to their support, they succeeded, after a sharp contest, in dislodging them, in a very handsome style. I placed two light twenty-four pounders and a five-and-a-half inch howitzer against the right of the enemy's position, and formed the royal Scots and 100th regiment, with the intention of making a movement upon his left, which deployed with the greatest regularity, and opened a very heavy fire. I immediately moved up the King's regiment to the right, while the royal Scots and 100th regiment were directed to charge the enemy in front, for which they advanced with the greatest gallantry, under a most destructive fire. I am sorry to say, however, in this attempt they suffered so severely, that I was obliged to withdraw them, finding their further efforts against the superior numbers of the enemy would be unavailing. Lieutenant Colonel Gordon and Lieutenant-Colonel the Marquis of Tweeddale, commanding these regiments, being wounded, as were most of the officers belonging to each. I directed a retreat to be made upon Chippewa, which was conducted with good order and regularity, covered by the King's regiment, under Major Evans, and the light troops under Lieutenant Colonel Pearson; and I have pleasure in saying, that not a single prisoner fell into the enemy's hands, except those who were disabled from wounds. From the report of some prisoners, we have made the enemy's force to amount to about six thousand men, with a very numerous train of artillery, having been augmented by a very large body of troops, which moved down from Fort Erie immediately before the commencement of the action. Our own force, in regular troops, amounted to about fifteen hundred, exclusive of the militia and Indians, of which last description there were not above three hundred. Fort Erie, I understand, surrendered upon capitulation, on the 3d inst. Although this affair was not attended with the success which I had hoped for, it will be gratifying to you to learn that the officers and men behaved with the greatest gallantry. I am particularly indebted to Lieutenant-Colonel Pearson for the very great assistance I have received from him, and for the manner in which he led his light troops into action.

Lieutenant-Colonel Gordon, and Lieutenant-Colonel the Marquis of Tweeddale, and Major Evans, commanding the King's regiments, merit my warmest praise for the good example they showed at the head of their respective regiments.

The artillery, under the command of Capt. Macconnochie, was ably served. and directed with good effect; and I am particularly obliged to Major Lisle, of the 19th light dragoons, for the manner in which he covered and protected one of the twenty-four-pounders which had been disabled. I have reason to be highly satisfied with the zeal, activity, and intelligence of Captain Holland, my aide-de-camp, Captain Eliot, deputy-assistant quarter-master-general; staff-adjutant Greig; and Lieutenant Fox, of the royal Scots, who acted as Major of brigade during the absence of Major Glegg at Fort George. The conduct of Lieutenant-Colonel Dixon, of the 2d Lincoln militia, has been most exemplary; and I am very much indebted to him for it, on this as well as on other occasions, in which he has evinced the greatest zeal for his Majesty's service. The conduct of the officers and men of this regiment has also been highly praiseworthy. Lieutenant-Colonel Pearson has reported to me, in the most favourable terms, the excellent manner in which Lieut. Horton, with a part of the 19th light dragoons, observed the motions of the enemy, while he occupied the position he took on his first landing, and during his advance to this place.—I have, &c.,

P. RIALL, Major-Gen.

General Brown's despatch is short,* but

General Brown's despatch.

is remarkable for one feature, viz., that, even with the knowledge of his own strength, he

---

Chippewa Plains, July 6, 1814.

SIR,—Excuse my silence; I have been much engaged; Fort Erie did not, as I assured you it should not, detain me a single day. At eleven o'clock on the night of the 4th, I arrived at this place with the reserve, General Scott having taken the position about noon with the van. My arrangements for turning and taking in the rear the enemy's position east of Chippewa was made, when Major-General Riall, suspecting our intention, and adhering to the rule that it

could not have been very sanguine of ultimate success. The General distinctly states that, with his gallant and accomplished troops, he will break down all opposition between him and Lake Ontario; but he is careful to qualify this admission by adding that "if joined by the fleet, all will be well," but that, if such junction should not take place, he will endeavour to avoid disgrace.

Some of the American accounts of the battle of Chippewa are worthy of notice for their outrageous extravagance. Mr. O'Connor, for instance, states that the British regulars suffered defeat from an inferior force, principally volunteers and militia, inferior in everything but courage to the vanquished enemy. Yet this same writer was in possession of official documents which particularized the presence of four regiments of regular infantry and a corps of artillery, and the fact of these bodies having suffered severely in the engagement. This statement was made, too, in direct opposition to General Wilkinson's account, which states the effective strength of General Scott's brigade alone at eleven hundred regular infantry, and the force that crossed the strait under General Brown at about three thousand five hundred men, including twenty-seven hundred regulars.†

---

is better to give than to receive an attack, came from behind his works about five o'clock in the afternoon of the 5th in order of battle. We did not baulk him. Before six o'clock his line was broken and his forces defeated, leaving on the field 400 killed and wounded. He was closely pressed, and would have been utterly ruined, but for the proximity of his works, whither he fled for shelter.

The wounded of the enemy, and those of our own army, must be attended to. They will be removed to Buffalo. This, with my limited means of transportation, will take a day or two, after which I shall advance, not doubting but that the gallant and accomplished troops I lead, will break down all opposition between me and Lake Ontario, when, if met by the fleet, all is well—if not, under the favor of heaven, we shall behave in a way to avoid disgrace. My detailed report shall be made in a day or two.

I am, with the highest respect, &c.,

JACOB BROWN.

Hon. Secretary of War.

† Wilkinson's Memoirs, Vol. I., pages 646, 652, 654, 658.

One of the strongest proofs that can be Movements of the American adduced of the Ameri-
army. cans *not having gained* *a victory* at Chippewa, is that General Brown romained from the 4th to the 8th before he could summon up resolution to make another attempt against General Riall, who still maintained his position at Chippewa. On the 8th the American General resolved on a forward movement, and after a slight skirmish with some of General Riall's artillery (a small body of men with two guns), the Chippewa creek was crossed, and the Americans advanced as far as Queenston, General Riall retreating to Fort George.

From the 8th of July to the 23rd of the General Brown's inaction month, General Brown, and timidity. with his enormous force, was content to remain without striking a blow, unless an occasional demonstration before Forts George and Mississaga, or the wanton conflagration of the village of St. David's, be considered as such. During this time, the American General wrote the most moving letters to Commodore Chauncey, almost imploring his co-operation.

"All accounts agree," writes Gen. Brown, "that the force of the enemy at Kingston is very light. Meet me on the Lake shore, north of Fort George, with your fleet, and we will be able, I have no doubt, to settle a plan of operations that will break the power of the enemy in Upper Canada, and that in the course of a short time. At all events, let me hear from you. I have looked for your fleet with the greatest anxiety since the 10th. *I do not doubt my ability to meet* the enemy in the field, and to march in any direction over his country, your fleet carrying for me the necessary supplies. We can threaten Forts George and Niagara, and carry Burlington Heights and York; and proceed direct to Kingston, and carry that place. For God's sake, let me see you."[*]

This letter is remarkable for many reasons, Brown's letter to Chauncey. not the least curious of which is the pathetic and almost touching appeal of a general, with four thousand men at his back, to a naval commander to bring him four thousand more,

to enable him to go in pursuit of an enemy, not mustering more than half his number. The mingled promises and intreaties are very amusing; in one paragraph Chauncey is assured of his (General Brown's) "ability to meet the enemy in the field," and in the very next sentence he is entreated "for God's sake" to come to assist in threatening Fort George, a fortification which was abandoned by General MacClure, with a garrison of two thousand men, on account of its untenability, This, too, at a time when the garrison did not number five hundred men, and the force that could be brought against it reached four thousand. Another very ridiculous feature in this letter is the promise to Chauncey that, if he will only come and help, after the upper peninsula is cleared, the army *will proceed to Kingston and carry the place*, this, too, from a man who remained with a force quadruple the strength of that opposing him for thirteen days, without mustering up sufficient courage to attempt more brilliant enterprises than the burning of an unprotected village, and the plundering of a few scattered farm houses. We have, however, occupied too much space already with the proceedings of such a commander as General Brown, and we very willingly accompany him back to Chippewa, to which place he retreated on the 24th, while under a violent fit of apprehension of his four thousand men being surrounded or intercepted. We gladly turn from such an exhibition of American generalship to General Riall, who, after throwing re-inforcements into Forts George and Mississaga retired towards Burlington heights, where he expected to be joined by the 103rd regiment, and the flank companies of the 104th. This meeting taking place, however, at the twenty mile creek, General Riall, instantly retraced his steps, and took up a position about thirteen miles from the American army.

We will leave the two armies thus posted, while we notice the atrocities perpetrated by the Americans during their three weeks campaign in the Niagara district. In doing this we will take no one sided British account, but a letter from an American officer, a major McFarland; we may also refer to

---

[*] Wilkinson's Memoirs, Vol. I., page 666.

the fact, that an American officer, Colonel Stone, was dismissed the service by the sentence of a Court Martial, for the wanton destruction of St. David's. Major McFarland writes :—

" The militia and Indians plundered and burnt everything. The whole population is against us, not a foraging party, but is fired on, and not unfrequently returns with missing numbers. This state was to be anticipated. The militia have burnt several private dwelling houses, and, on the 19th instant, burnt the village of St. David, consisting of about thirty or forty houses. This was done within three miles of camp; and my battalion was sent to cover the retreat, as they (the militia) had been sent to scour the country, and it was presumed they might be pursued. My G–d! what a service. I never witnessed such a scene; and had not the commanding officer of the party, lieutenant colonel Stone, been disgraced, and sent out of the army, I should have resigned my commission."

Lest our readers should imagine that Major McFarland was one of the parties disaffected to the war, and whose report would consequently not be trustworthy, we give a few more extracts from his letter :— " He declares that he desires no better fun than to fight the British troops whom, according to James, this same Major politely calls cut-throats."—he also glories in being a " staunch American." " What then" asks James, " must have been the scenes and sufferings that could excite compassion in such a breast."

To return, however, to the two generals. On learning that General Brown had retreated, General Riall advanced with his augmented force, now nearly one thousand strong, and took up a position near Lundy's Lane (about a mile from the Falls), and about two and a half miles from the American position. The American commander, having been instructed that General Riall had crossed over from Queenston to Lewiston, to effect a diversion, and that a small party occupied Lundy's Lane, determined by a counter diversion to advance on that post. He accordingly despatched General Scott with eleven hundred rank and file

against the enemy, with special orders to "report if the enemy appeared," and to apply for assistance if necessary. General Scott, having learned that the force occupying Lundy's Lane was more than a mere patrolling party, reported it to General Brown, who immediately pressed forward to support him. General Riall, on the advance of this superior force, very prudentially gave orders to retire on Queenston. Assistance was, however, nearer at hand than General Riall could have hoped or anticipated.

No sooner had General Drummond heard of the landing of a large American force, and the result of the battle at Chippewa, than he hastened from Kingston to York, which place he left on the evening of the 24th, arriving at Fort Niagara on the next morning. The greatest energy seems to have characterized General Drummond's motions, and we find him first dispersing Colonel Swift and his party of volunteers, and then rapidly advancing with about eight hundred rank and file to the support of General Riall.

When within a short distance of Lundy's Lane, General Drummond learned that the force under General Riall was in retreat, and his first act was to change the retreat into an advance upon the position so lately abandoned, and the position was again occupied when the American troops were within half a mile of it. For the particulars of this action we will, however, refer our readers to General Drummond's despatch :—

From Lieutenant-general Drummond to Sir G. Provost.

Head Quarters, near Niagara Falls,
Sir,   July 27, 1814.

I embarked on board his majesty's schooner Netley, at York, on Sunday evening the 24th inst., and reached Niagara at day-break the following morning. Finding, from lieutenant-colonel Tucker, that major-general Riall was understood to be moving towards the Falls of Niagara to support the advance of his division, which he had pushed on to that place on the preceding evening, I ordered lieutenant-colonel Morrison, with the 89th regiment and a detachment of the royals and king's, drawn from Fort George and Mississaga to proceed to the same point in order that, with the united force I might act against the enemy (posted at Street's Creek, with his advance at Chippewa) on my arrival if it should be found expedient.— I ordered lieutenant-colonel Tucker, at the same time to proceed up the right bank of the river, with 300 of the 31st, about 200 of the royal Scots, and a body of Indian warriors, supported (on the river) by a party of armed seamen, under captain Dobbs, royal navy. The object of this movement was to disperse or capture, a body of the enemy encamped at Lewiston. Some unavoidable delay having occurred in the march of the troops up the right bank, the enemy had moved off previous to lieutenant-colonel Tucker's arrival. I have to express myself satisfied with the exertions of that officer.

Having refreshed the troops at Queenstown, and having brought across the 41st, royals, and Indians, I sent back the 41st and 100th regiments, to form the garrisons of forts George, Mississaga, and Niagara, under lieutenant-colonel Tucker, and moved with the 89th, and detachments of the royals and king's, and light company of the 41st, in all about 800 men, to join major-general Riall's division at the Falls.

When arrived within a few miles of that position, I met a report from major-general Riall that the enemy was advancing in great force. I immediately pushed on, and joined the head of lieutenant-colonel Morrison's columns just as it reached the road leading to the Beaver Dam, over the summit of the hill at Lundy's Lane. Instead of the whole of major-general Riall's division, which I expected to have found occupying this position, I found it almost in the occupation of the enemy, whose columns were within 600 yards of the top of the hill, and the surrounding woods filled with his light troops. The advance of major-general Riall's division, consisting of the Glengarry light infantry and incorporated militia, having commenced a retreat upon Fort George, I countermanded these corps, and formed the 89th regiment, the royal Scots detachment, and the 41st light company, in the rear of the hill, their left resting on the great road; my two 24 pounder brass field guns a little advanced, in front of the centre, on the summit of the hill; the Glengarry light infantry on the right; the battalion of incorporated militia, and the detachment of the king's regiment on the left of the great road; the squadron of the 19th light dragoons in the rear of the left, on the road. I had scarcely completed this formation when the whole front was warmly and closely engaged. The enemy's principal efforts were directed against our left and centre. After repeated attacks, the troops on the left were partially forced back, and the enemy gained a momentary possesion of the road. This gave him, however, no material advantage, as the troops which had been forced back formed in the rear of the 89th regiment, fronting the road, and securing the flank. It was during this short interval that major-general Riall, having received a severe wound, was intercepted as he was passing to the rear, by a party of the enemy's cavalry, and taken prisoner.— In the centre, the repeated and determined attacks of the enemy were met by the 89th regiment, the detachments of the royals and king's, and the light company of the 41st regiment, with the most perfect steadiness and intrepid gallantry, and the enemy was constantly repulsed with very heavy loss.— In so determined a manner were their attacks directed against our guns, that our artillerymen were bayonetted by the enemy while in the act of loading, and the muzzles of the enemy's guns were advanced within a few yards of ours. The darkness of the night during this extraordinary conflict, occasioned several uncommon incidents: our troops having for a moment been pushed back, some of our guns remained for a few minutes in the enemy's hands; they, however, were not only quickly recovered, but the two pieces (a 6-pounder and a 5½ inch howitzer) which the enemy had brought up, were captured by us, together with several tumbrils, and in limbering up our guns at one period, one of the enemy's 6-pounders was put by mistake on a limber of ours, and one of our 6-pounders limbered on one of his: by which means the pieces were exchanged; and thus, though we captured two of his guns, yet, as he obtained one of ours, we have gained only one gun.

About 9 o'clock, (the action having commenced at 6,) there was a short intermission of firing, during which it appears the enemy was employed in bringing up the whole of his remaining force; and he shortly afterwards renewed his attack with fresh troops, but was everywhere repulsed with equal gallantry and success. About this period the remainder of major-general Riall's division, which had been ordered to retire on the advance of the enemy, consisting of the 103d regiment, under Colonel Scott; the head-quarter division of the royal Scots; the head-quarter division of the 8th, or king's; flank companies of the 104th; and some detachments of militia, under lieutenant Colonel Hamilton, inspecting field officer, joined the troops engaged; and I placed them in a second line, with the exception of the royal Scots and flank companies of the 104th, with which I prolonged my line in front to the right, where I was apprehensive of the enemy outflanking me.

The enemy's efforts to carry the hill were continued till about midnight, when he had suffered so severely from the superior steadiness and discipline of his majesty's troops, that he gave up the contest, and retreated with great precipitation to his camp beyond the Chippewa. On the following day he abandoned his camp, threw the greater part of his baggage, camp equipage, and provisions, into the Rapids, and having set fire to Street's mills, and destroyed the bridge at Chippewa, continued his retreat in great disorder towards Fort Erie. My light troops, cavalry, and Indians are detached in pursuit, and to harass his retreat, which I doubt not he will continue until he reaches his own shore.

The loss sustained by the enemy in this severe action cannot be estimated at less than 1,500 men, including several hundred of prisoners left in our hands; his two commanding generals, Brown and Scott, are said to be wounded, his whole force, which has never been rated at less than 5,000, having been engaged.

Enclosed I have the honour to transmit a return of our loss, which has been very considerable. The number of troops under my command did not, for the first three hours, exceed 1600 men; and the addition of the troops under Colonel Scott, did not increase it to more than two thousand eight hundred of every description.

A very difficult, but at the same time a most gratifying duty remains, that of endeavouring to do justice to the merits of the officers and soldiers by whose valor and discipline this important success has been obtained. I was, very early in the action, deprived of major-general Riall, who, I regret to learn, has suffered the amputation of his arm* and whose bravery, zeal, and activity, have always been conspicuous.

To lieutenant-colonel Harvey, deputy-adjutant-general, I am so deeply indebted for his valuable assistance previous to, as well as his able and energetic exertions during, this severe contest, that I feel myself called upon to point your excellency's attention to the distinguished merits of this highly deserving officer, whose services have been particularly conspicuous in every affair that has taken place since his arrival in this province. The zeal and intelligence displayed by major Glegg, assistant-adjutant-general, deserve my warmest approbation. I much regret the loss of a very intelligent and promising young officer, lieutenant Moorsom, 104th regiment, deputy-assistant-adjutant-general, who was killed towards the close of the action. The active exertions of captain Eliot, deputy-assistant-quarter-master-general, of whose gallantry and conduct I had occasion on two former instances to remark, were conspicuous. Major Maule and lieut. Le Breton of the quarter-master-general's department were extremely useful to me : the latter was severely wounded.

Amongst the officers from whose active exertions I derived the greatest assistance, I cannot omit to mention my aides-de-camp, captains Jervoise and Loring, and captain Holland, aide-de-camp to major-general Riall. Captain Loring was unfortunately taken prisoner by some of the enemy's dragoons, whilst in the execution of an order.

In reviewing the action from its commencement, the first object which presents

* It was afterwards ascertained, that major-general Riall, though severely wounded, did not lose his arm.

itself, as deserving of notice, is the steadiness and good conduct of the squadron of the 19th light dragoons, under major Lisle, and the very creditable and excellent defence made by the incorporated militia-battalion, under lieutenant-colonel Robinson, who was dangerously wounded, and a detachment of the 8th (king's regiment,) under colonel Campbell. Major Kirby succeeded lieutenant-colonel Robinson in the command of the incorporated militia-battalion, and continued very gallantly to direct its efforts.

AMERICAN VERSIONS OF THE BATTLE OF BRIDGE-
WATER.

Copy of a letter from an officer in the army to his friend in Alexandria, dated Fort Erie U. C. July 28.

On the 23d I found myself so far recovered as to join the army at Queenston Heights, although that part of my foot which was fractured will never be of much service. On the 24th we retired to Chippewa, and on the 25th at half-past 4 P. M. our first brigade commanded by General Scott, engaged the enemy's advance, about 2½ miles from Chippewa ; the main body of both armies soon supported the advances, and a tremendous battle was fought lasting 5 hours and 23 minutes, mostly within half musket, and sometimes within pistol shot, which ended in the enemy's total defeat, leaving 2 brass 24 pounders and 1 brass 6 pounder in our possession. We kept the battle ground until midnight, when having removed our wounded and part of our dead, we retired to Chippewa, taking with us his brass 6 pounder. We were unable to bring off his two 24 pounders from a want of horses; almost all ours being killed, and our pieces were generally taken off with bricoles. The enemy's loss in killed, wounded and prisoners must be about 12 or 1300. Of prisoners we have taken major general Riall, Gen. Drummond's aid de camp, 19 officers and 350 or 400 men. His force engaged was by their own account about 4,500 regulars, besides his Indians, &c., commanded by Lieut. Gen. Drummond and Maj. Gen. Riall. We had not an Indian engaged and our force did not exceed twenty-eight hundred men : our loss is severe. Generals Brown and Scott, and an aid of each with several field officers are wounded —several other officers killed, among whom was my captain [Ritchie]—he was wounded in the body, but refused to quit his piece, when a cannon shot took most of his head off All the men at his piece were killed or wounded. He was brother to the editor of the Richmond Enquirer, and formerly lived in Alexandria.

The battle of NIAGARA, says the Albany Argus, commands, like the achievements of our naval heroes, the admiration of all classes of the American people, a few excepted; and the most bitter revilers of the army are impelled by the strong current of applause, to admit that the heroes of Niagara merit the warmest thanks and gratitude of their country. The captured officers of the enemy with an ingenious candor that reflects upon them honour, declare, that there was exhibited on our part not only the most undaunted bravery, but a proficiency in tactics and military skill, seldom surpassed by the most veteran armies.

From major-general Brown to the American secretary of war.

(No date.)

SIR,—Confined as I was, and have been, since the last engagement with the enemy, I fear that the account I am about to give may be less full and satisfactory than under other circumstances it might have been made. I particularly fear that the conduct of the gallant men it was my good fortune to lead will not be noticed in a way due to their fame, and the honour of our country.

You are already apprised, that the army had, on the 25th ult. taken a position at Chippewa. About noon of that day, colonel Swift, who was posted at Lewiston, advised me, by express, that the enemy appeared in considerable force in Queenston, and on its heights ; that four of the enemy's fleet had arrived on the preceding night, and were then lying near Fort Niagara ; and that a number of boats were in view, moving up the strait. Within a few minutes after this intelligence had been received, I was further informed by captain Denmon, of the quarter–master's department, that the enemy were landing at Lewiston, and that our baggage and stores at Schlosser, and on their way thither, were in danger of immediate capture.

It is proper here to mention, that having received advices as late as the 20th, from general Gaines, that our fleet was then in port, and the commodore sick, we ceased to look for co-operation from that quarter, and determined to disencumber ourselves of baggage. and march directly to Burlington Heights. To mask this intention, and to draw from Schlosser a small supply of provisions, I fell back upon Chippewa. As this arrangement, under the increased force of the enemy, left much at hazard on our side of the Niagara, and as it appeared by the before stated information, that the enemy was about to avail himself of it, I conceived that the most effectual method of recalling him from the object was to put myself in motion towards Queenston. General Scott, with the 1st brigade, Towson's artillery, and all the dragoons and mounted men, were accordingly put in march on the road leading thither, with orders to report if the enemy appeared, and to call for assistance, if that was necessary.

The 25th regiment, under major Jessup, was engaged in a most obstinate conflict with all

21

This battalion has only been organized a few months, and, much to the credit of captain Robinson, of the king's regiment, (pro-vincial lieutenant-colonel), has attained a highly respectable degree of discipline.

In the reiterated and determined attacks that remained to dispute with us the field of battle. The major, as has been already stated, had been ordered by general Scott, at the commencement of the action, to take ground to his right. He had succeeded in turning the enemy's left flank,—had captured (by a detachment under captain Ketchum) general Riall, and sundry other officers, and shewed himself again to his own army, in a blaze of fire, which defeated or destroyed a very superior force of the enemy. He was ordered to form on the right of the 2nd regiment. The enemy rallying his forces, and as is believed, having received reinforcements, now attempted to drive us from our position, and regain his artillery. Our line was unshaken, and the enemy repulsed. Two other attempts, having the same object, had the same issue. General Scott was again engaged in repelling the former of these; and the last I saw of him on the field of battle, he was near the head of his column, and giving to its march a direction that would have placed him on the enemy's right. It was with great pleasure I saw the good order and intrepidity of general Porter's volunteers from the moment of their arrival, but during the last charge of the enemy those qualities were conspicuous.

On the general's arrival at the Falls, he learned that the enemy was in force directly in his front, a narrow piece of wood alone intercepting his view of them. Waiting only to give this information, he advanced upon them. By the time assistant-adjutant-general Jones had delivered this message, the action began, and before the remaining part of the division had crossed the Chippewa, it had become close and general between the advanced corps. Though general Ripley with the 2nd brigade, major Hindman with the corps of artillery, and general Porter, at the head of his command, had respectively pressed forward with ardor, it was not less than an hour before they were brought to sustain general Scott, during which time his command most skillfully and gallantly maintained the conflict. Upon my arrival I found that the general had passed the wood, and engaged the enemy on the Queenstown road, and on the ground to the left of it, with the 9th, 11th and 22nd regiments, and Towson's artillery.

The 25th had been thrown to the right to be governed by circumstances. Apprehending that these corps were much exhausted, and knowing that they had suffered severely, I determined to interpose a new line with the advancing troops, and thus disengage general Scott, and hold his brigade in reserve. Orders were accordingly given to General Ripley. The enemy's artillery at this moment occupied a hill which gave him great advantages, and was the key of the whole position. It was supported by a line of infantry. To secure the victory, it was necessary to carry this artillery, and seize the height. This duty was assigned to colonel Miller, while, to favor its execution, the 1st regiment, under the command of colonel Nicholas, was directed to menace and amuse the infantry. To my great mortification, this regiment, after a discharge or two, gave way, and retreated some distance before it could be rallied, though it is believed the officers of the regiment exerted themselves to shorten the distance.

Stimulated by the examples set them by their gallant leader, by Major Wood, of the Pennsylvania corps, by Colonel Dobbin, of New York, and by their officers generally, they precipitated themselves upon the enemy's line, and made all the prisoners which were taken at this point of the action.

Having been for some time wounded, and being a good deal exhausted by loss of blood, it became my wish to devolve the command on General Scott, and retire from the field; but on inquiry, I had the misfortune to learn that he was disabled by wounds; I therefore kept my post, and had the satisfaction to see the enemy's last effort repulsed. I now consigned the command to General Ripley.

While retiring from the field, I saw and felt that the victory was complete on our part, if proper measures were promptly adopted to secure it. The exhaustion of the men was, however, such as made some refreshment necessary. They particularly required water. I was myself extremely sensible of the want of this necessary article. I therefore believed it proper that general Ripley and the troops should return to camp, after bringing off the dead, the wounded, and the artillery; and in this I saw no difficulty, as the enemy had entirely ceased to act. Within an hour after my arrival in camp, I was informed that general Ripley had returned without annoyance and in good order. I now sent for him. and, after giving him my reasons for the measure I was about to adopt, ordered him to put the troops into the best possible condition; to give them the necessary refreshment; to take with him the piquets and camp guard, and every other description of force, to put himself on the field of battle as the day dawned, and there to meet and beat the enemy if he again appeared. To this order he made no objection, and I relied upon its execution. It was not executed. I feel most sensibly how inadequate are my powers in speaking of the troops, to do justice either to their merits or to my own sense of them. Under abler direction, they might have done more and better.

From the preceding detail, you have now evidence of the distinguished gallantry of Generals Scott and Porter, of Colonel Miller, and Major Jessop.

which the enemy made on our centre, for the purpose of gaining, at once, the crest of the position, and our guns, the steadiness and intrepidity displayed by the troops allotted for the defence of that post, were never surpassed; they consisted of the 2d battalion of the 89th regiment, commanded by lieutenant-colonel Morrison, and, after the lieutenant-colonel had been obliged to retire from the field by a severe wound, by major Clifford; a detachment of the royal Scotts, under lieutenant Hemphill, and after he was killed, lieutenant Fraser; a detachment of the 8th, (or King's), under captain Campbell; light company 41st regiment, under captain Glew; with some detachments of militia under lieutenant-colonel Parry, 103rd regiment. These troops repeatedly, when hard pressed, formed round the colour of the 89th regiment, and invariably repulsed the desperate efforts made against them. On the right, the steadiness and good conduct of the 1st battalion of royal Scotts, under lieutenant Gordon, on some very trying occasions excited my admiration. The king's regiment, 1st battalion, under major Evans, behaved with equal gallantry and firmness, as did the light company of the royals, detached under captain Stewart; the grenadiers of the 103d, detached under captain Browne; and the flank companies of the 104th, under captain Leonard; the Glengarry light infantry, under lieutenant-colonel Battersby, displayed most valuable qualities as light troops; colonel Scott, major Smelt, and the officers of the 103d, deserve credit for their exertions in rallying that regiment, after it had been thrown into momentary disorder.

Lieutenant-colonel Pearson, inspecting field-officer, directed the advance with great intelligence; and lieutenant-colonel Drummond, of the 104th, having gone forward with my permission, early in the day, made himself actively useful in different parts of the field, under my direction. These officers are entitled to my best thanks, as is Lieutenant-colonel Hamilton, inspecting field-officer, for his exertions after his arrival with the troops under Colonel Scott. The field artillery, so long as there was light, was well served.

The credit of its efficient state is due to captain Mackonochie, who has had charge of it since its arrival with this division. Captain M'Lauchlan, who has care of the

---

Of the 1st brigade, the chief, with his aide de camp, Worth, his major of brigade, Smith, and every commander of battalion were wounded.

The 2d brigade suffered less; but, as a brigade, their conduct entitled them to the applause of their country. After the enemy's strong position had been carried by the 21st and the detachments of the 17th and 19th, the 1st and 23d assumed a new character. They could not again be shaken or dismayed. Major M'Farland, of the latter, fell nobly at the head of his battalion.

Under the command of General Porter, the militia volunteers of Pennsylvania and New York stood undismayed amidst the hottest fire, and repulsed the veterans opposed to them. The Canadian volunteers, commanded by Colonel Wilcox, are reported by General Porter as having merited and received his approbation.

The corps of artillery, commanded by Major Hindman, behaved with its usual gallantry. Captain Towson's company, attached to the 1st brigade, was the first and last engaged, and during the whole conflict maintained that high character which they had previously won by their skill and valour. Captains Biddle and Ritchie were both wounded early in the action, but refused to quit the field. The latter declared that he never would leave his piece; and, true to his engagement, fell by its side, covered with wounds.

The staff of the army had its peculiar merit and distinction; Colonel Gardiner, adjutant-general, though ill, was on horseback, and did all in his power; his assistant, Major Jones, was very active and useful. My gallant aides de camp, Austin and Spencer, had many and critical duties to perform, in the discharge of which the latter fell. I shall ever think of this young man with pride and regret; regret that his career has been so short—pride that it has been so noble and distinguished.

The engineers, Majors Macrae and Wood, were greatly distinguished on this day, and their military talent was exerted with great effect; they were much under my eye, and near my person, and to their assistance a great deal is fairly to be ascribed; I most earnestly recommend them, as worthy of the highest trust and confidence. The staff of Generals Ripley and Porter discovered great zeal and attention to duty. Lieutenant E. B. Randolph, of the 20th regiment, is entitled to notice; his courage was conspicuous.

I enclose a return of our loss; those noted as missing may generally be numbered with the dead. The enemy had but little opportunity of making prisoners.

I have the honor to be, Sir, &c.,

JACOB BROWN.

Hon. John Armstrong, Secretary at War.

batteries at Fort Mississaga, volunteered his servces in the field on this occasion. He was severely wounded. Lieutenant Tomkins deserves much credit for the way in which two brass 24 pounders, of which he had charge were served ; as does serjeant Austin of the rocket company, who directed the Congreve rockets, which did much execution. The zeal, loyalty, and bravery with which the militia of this part of the province had come forward to co-operate with his majesty's troops in the expulsion of the enemy, and their conspicuous gallantry in this, and in the action of the 5th instant, claim my warmest thanks.

I cannot conclude this despatch without recommending, in the strongest terms, the following officers, whose conduct during the late operations has called for marked approbation ; and I am induced to hope that your excellency will be pleased to submit their names for promotion to the most favourable consideration of his royal highness the prince regent ; viz : Captain Jervoise my aide-de-camp ; captain Robinson, 8th (king's) regiment, (provincial lieutenant-colonel), commanding the incorporated milita ; captain Eliot, deputy assistant-quarter-master-general ; captain Holland, aide-de-camp to major-general Riall ; and captain Glew, 41st regiment.

This despatch will be delivered to you by captain Jervoise, my-aide-de-camp, who is fully competent to give your excellency every further information you may require.

I have the honour to be, &c.

GORDON DRUMMOND,

Lieutenant-general., &c.

His Excellency Sir G. Prevost.

CHAPTER XX.

Of all the battles that were fought during the war, none could be compared with that of Lundy's Lane for the obstinacy both of attack and defence exhibited on both sides. At Chippewa the contest was decided principally by musketry, but at Lundy's-lane the Americans, for the first time, ventured to cross bayonets with Britsh troops, and the issue of the combat then taught them, whatever their moral courage, their physical inferiority to British and Canadian troops.

The battle of Bridgewater, or Lundy's Lane, and its results.

This battle may almost be styled an impromptu engagement, inasmuch as the American General, in ordering the advance in the first instance, was without correct information, as to the force opposed to him. This we learn from Wilkinson, who distinctly states that it was reported to General Scott, "that the enemy could not be in force," and that, consequently, that officer "pressed forward with ardor," to attack the British.

If ever one army was fairly beaten by another, the battle of Lundy's-lane furnishes us with such an instance; that is, if remaining in possession of the field while your adversary retreats precipitately and in disorder, be considered as a proof of victory; General Drummond was attacked by a superior force, and, through the gallantry of his troops, he not only sustained his position, but, on the next morning, when General Ripley* received instructions from General Brown to make another attack, he was found so well prepared to repel it, that the attack was not made; the front, too, shown by the British being so formidable, that a retreat on the part of the Americans was found necessary, this retreat not being, as American writers represent, orderly, but marked with the destruction of military stores of various kinds.

That the American loss was severe can be proved by the fortunate admission of Ingersol, who says, † "Those who had sunk exhausted, those gone to take care of the wounded, the numbers who, in all battles, stray from their places, those left in camp when the rest went out to battle; all those diminutions left, in the judgment of reliable officers, not more *than a thousand fighting men* embodied, when they were marched back to Chippewa." That the loss was so severe, we, cannot, for a moment believe, when we consider the numbers of the Americans engaged; we can only, therefore, look on this statement of Ingersol's as an attempt at an excuse for the retreat of a superior body before an inferior.

If ever a writer earned a pension from his devotion to his "country's cause," Ingersol is that man. Nothing has sufficed to withstand the onslaught of his pen on the character and morale of the British, and a few extracts, taken in connection with Drummond's despatch, will not be found unamusing. We are first informed, page 99, that "General Brown, when the victory of Bridgewater, so far as could be judged from all circumstances, was complete, was with difficulty supported on his horse as he retired to Chippewa." We presume that Mr. Ingersol on reading over this paragraph considered it necessary to account for General Brown and his army's retreat to Chippewa, accordingly on page 100, we find it stated that "The struggle was over. Pride of success was supplanted by bodily exhaustion, anxiety

---

* Wilkinson, Vol 1. Appendix 9.

† Page 99, Historical sketch of the second war.

for repose from excessive toil, and relief from tormenting thirst. The Americans, therefore, BUT AS VICTORS were marched to their encampment, as Brown had directed, though without the cannons captured." When we consider that the Americans had made a leisurely march of it to Lundy's-lane, that they went fresh into action, with the knowledge that strong reinforcements were at hand, and that they expected to encounter a vastly inferior force, Ingersol's twaddle about the want of water and so forth, is very absurd. The major part of the British forces engaged at Lundy's-lane had made a forced march of fourteen miles, and had gone into action literally out of breath and exhausted with fatigue, yet we do not find one word in General Drummond's despatch relative to the "necessity of repose from excessive toil." Again, we are told by Ingersol, that for want of horses, harness, drag ropes, and other contrivances, the inestimable trophies (the captured guns) fell at last into the hands of the British, who returned to the hill, soon after the Americans left it. Mr. Ingersol further accounts for the capture of an American howitzer, by indignantly denying General Drummond's statement. That officer, in his despatch, stated "a howitzer, which the enemy brought up, was captured by us." To this Ingersol responds—"They *captured nothing, but merely found a cannon accidentally left*, when an hour after the enemy's retreat, their conquerors in complete and undisturbed possession of the guns and the field, slowly and in perfect order, left it and them, to return to the indispensable repose of their camp."

It has been our good fortune to converse with several of the officers who distinguished themselves in the battle of Lundy's-lane, and by all we have been assured, that, so far from the American troops leaving the hill, leisurely, and voluntarily abandoning the guns, as Ingersol represents, the real state of the case was, that the Americans did abandon both the top of the hill and the guns, but that it was because a vigorous bayonet charge compelled them, and that the guns were recaptured about one hundred yards from the position originally occupied. We almost fancy Mr. Ingersol has been misled by the tale told at the Observatory, which now marks the scene of the struggle, and that the worthy sergeant who recounted the tale, recognizing the historian as a Yankee, crammed him with the version of the battle prepared for his countrymen; if so, Mr. Ingersol fared better than General Scott, who, we presume, having some appearance of respectability about him, was mistaken for an Englishman, and had the unspeakable mortification of having the spot pointed out to him, "where General Scott turned tail and ran away."

On one sentence, taken from the Quebec Gazette of the 23rd September, 1814, Mr. Ingersol bases a regular edifice of deductions, "with all our strength," wrote the Gazette, "it would be rashness to penetrate far into the United States, and might produce another Saratoga." This single sentence suffices to furnish Ingersol with material for the following extraordinary assertions:—

"Continued skirmishes, sieges, sorties, and other demonstrations, following the two pitched battles* in Canada, proved only corollaries to the problem solved by them, that the American army, like the navy, was superior to that of England. As soon as the double elements of military ascendant were well combined, and strict discipline added to stern enthusiasm, the mercenary Briton was subdued. Coarse, vulgar, English predudice, uttered by envious and odious journalism, continued their abuse of the United States as a licentious and knavish nation. But English better sense perceived, and dispassionate judgment pronounced, them also martial and formidable. Not a little of that impression came from the seemingly insignificant invasion of Canada, which, during the months of July, August, and September, 1814, not only defied, but invariably defeated the great power of Great Britain by land and water, ending, perhaps fortunately, not by the conquest of a British province, but discomfiture of British armies and fleets, wherever Americans encountered them."

It is most wonderful how Ingersol could have penned such a sentence, when the real

* Chippewa and Lundy's Lane.

state of the case is considered, and the grounds for Mr. Ingersol's boast disposed of.

If we refer to the position occupied by the Americans during one period of the year 1813, we find that nearly the whole of the western peninsula was in their possession, with the single exception of the position at Burlington heights, and if we trace the events of the war from that date we find that by the energy and strategic skill of Generals Drummond and Murray, the whole of the country thus occupied had been wrested from the invaders, that their strongest fort (Fort Niagara) had been stormed, that their whole frontier had been devastated, and that, with the solitary exception of holding Fort Erie, Mr. Ingersol had not the smallest excuse for giving to the world the statement we have quoted above.

Mr. Ingersol, however, not satisfied with the above extraordinary assertions, goes still a step further, and ascribes the success of the American troops in repelling subsequent attacks, to the prestige of General Brown's valour. "Not less," writes the veracious American, "than six thousand five hundred excellent British regular troops, without counting their hordes of Indians and Canadian militia, had been routed, mostly killed wounded, captured, all demoralized and discouraged. In defiance of the mighty efforts of the undivided strength of Britain, three or four thousand American troops held possession of that part of Canada." This mere holding of that part of Canada (Fort Erie) was, also, found by Ingersol "inestimable in its beneficial natural consequences," as it defended the Atlantic seaboard "more effectually and infinitely cheaper than a hundred thousand militia could have done. The invasion of Canada kept a very large hostile force occupied there. If Brown, instead of two or three, had been eight or ten thousand strong, they would probably have detained the British who captured Washington from venturing there."

We could cite many more instances of Mr. Ingersol's misrepresentations. It will, however, suffice to make instead a short one from General Armstrong's "Notices of the War," who, after condemning Gen. Brown for fighting the battle "by detachments,"

and pointing out how the affair should have been conducted, asks whether, "if such views had governed in the affair at Bridgewater, the trophies won on that occasion would have been lost, or would the question be yet unsettled, to which of the two armies the victory belonged?"

This admission from General Armstrong is sufficient to settle the question as to whom belonged the victory at Lundy's Lane; any admission by an American of doubt as to whether "they had whipped," being, when we consider the national character, tantamount to an acknowledgement of defeat.

Mr. Ingersol traces in these battles the origin and cause of peace. "Battles in Canada did more to make peace than all the solicitations at St. Petersburg and London, negociations and arrangements at Ghent. The treaty of Ghent without these battles would have been the shame of the United States, and the beginning of another war."

We fully concur with Ingersol that these battles had very much to do with producing peace, but we contend that it was the issue of these battles, in conjunction with the other humiliating defeats which they had experienced, that brought a vainglorious and boasting people to a sense of their real power, and that, the remembrance of their signal discomfiture in Western Canada was sufficient to outweigh the subsequent successes at New Orleans, Plattsburg and elsewhere.

The "reflections on war" of Mr. Ingersol are not less curious than his assertions as to the consequences of the battles of Lundy's Lane and Chippewa. "To the student of history," he writes, when moralizing on the effects of what he claims as victories, "the view reaches further in the doctrine of warfare, its martial, political, and territorial effects. The battles which made Cromwell the master of Great Britain and arbiter of Europe, which immortalized Turenne, and which signalized the prowess of Spain, when mistress of the world, were fought by small armies of a few thousand men."

Ingersol has here thrown new light upon some most interesting periods of history, and we learn for the first time that the battles of Naseby and Worcester in England were fought by armies of similar strength to that of General Brown. Nor is the modesty less remarkable which compares General Brown and his campaign on the Niagara frontier (one most signally condemned by General Armstrong) with the exploits of one of Louis XIV.'s most celebrated commanders, the man who, at the head of a large force, desolated the most fertile portion of Germany, and carried desolation, whilst he inspired fear, throughout the palatinate.

Our historian forgot, when enunciating the discovery that courage, strategy, and every military virtue are as well displayed on the smaller as the vaster scale, to compare the campaign, or the Canadian tournament, as he delights to call it, with Marathon or Thermopylæ. We have, however, devoted sufficient space to Mr. Ingersol and his reasons for the causes "which nerved the arms that struck so powerfully for victory at the Falls of Niagara."

The same misrepresentations which characterize Ingersol, mark the various versions given to the American people by Thompson, O'Connor, and Smith, and, according to their tales, the Americans, whose numbers they diminish by nearly one half, are represented as winning an easy victory over a force nearly double their own. For instance, Mr. Thompson makes the British force, instead of sixteen hundred and thirty-seven, only five thousand one hundred and thirty men, and, last not least, he brings to the aid of the British General *four of the fleet.* When we remember that the river is not navigable, owing to the rapidity of the current, above Queenston, which is eight miles from Lundy's Lane, this mistake of Mr. Thompson will appear the more ridiculous.

Before closing this account of the battle of

Destruction of stores and baggage. Bridgewater, or Lundy's Lane, as it is commonly termed, we will give one short extract from General Wilkinson's memoirs. The General, when noticing General Brown's orders to General Ripley to return for *the guns he had forgotten,* writes, " finding the enemy so strongly posted and in superior force, he judiciously retired ; and then a scene ensued *which has been carefully concealed from the public.* By the improvidence of General Brown (the American Turenne) the de-

ficiency of transport provided for his baggage, stores, and provisions, had not been remedied ; and a great portion of it was now necessary to the accommodation of his wounded and sick. The necessity of a retreat could be no longer concealed or delayed ; and the consequence was, that a considerable quantity of provisions, stores, and camp equipage, with a number of tents were thrown into the river, or burnt." General Wilkinson adds, "I have this fact from an officer left with the command which performed this duty."

With this declaration before him Ingersol and other Americans have the assurance to contend that a victory was gained, and that their troops retired in good order!

When claiming the action of Lundy's Lane

General Order issued by Lieutenant General Drummond. as a victory, the Americans were always compelled to qualify and explain, not so, however, General Drummond, who had the satisfaction of knowing that his troops and their gallantry, on the memorable 25th of July, were duly appreciated at head quarters, as the issuing of the following order testified :—

ADJ, GENERAL'S OFFICE,
MONTREAL, 4th Aug., 1814.

The commander of the forces has the highest satisfaction in promulgating to the troops, the District General Order, issued by Lieut. Gen. Drummond, after the action which took place on the 25th of last month, near the Falls of Niagara. His Excellency is desirous of adding to the meed of praise so deservedly bestowed by the Lieutenant General on the troops, regulars, and militia, who had the good fortune to share in this brilliant achievement, the deep sense he entertains of their services, and of the distinguished skill and energetic exertions of Lieutenant General Drummond in the measures which have terminated by repelling the invaders from his Majesty's territories.

The commander of the forces unites with Lieutenant General Drummond, in sincerely lamenting the great loss which the service has sustained by the severe wound received by Major General Riall, and his subsequent untoward capture. It will be a most pleasing part of the duty of the Commander of the Forces to bring the meritorious services of the right division of the army of the Canadas, before the gracious consideration of his Royal Highness the Prince Regent.

(Signed)   EDWARD BAINES,
Adj't. Gen. N. A.

It will be seen by this endorsation of General Drummond's general order, that the heads of departments in Canada, were saved the trouble of endeavouring to make the worse appear the better cause, a necessity which fell to the lot of Washington and Baltimorean writers. Gen. Drummond won the battle, and in his general order, which follows, he gives a manly and straightforward version of the affair. Knowing that his men were brave and disciplined, he felt that he was not called on to lavish the extravagant praise on them, for comporting themselves as soldiers, which usually marks American General orders :—

DISTRICT GENERAL ORDER.

H. Q., Falls of Niagara,
26th July, 1814.

Lieutenant General Drummond offers his sincerest and warmest thanks to the troops and militia engaged yesterday, for their exemplary steadiness, gallantry and discipline in repulsing all the efforts of a numerous and determined enemy to carry the position of Lundy's lane, near the Falls of Niagara; their exertions have been crowned with complete success, by the defeat of the enemy, and his retreat to the position of Chippewa, with the loss of two of his guns and an immense number of killed and wounded, and several hundred prisoners. When all have behaved nobly, it is unnecessary to hold up particular instances of merit in corps or individuals. The Lieutenant General cannot, however, refrain from expressing in the strongest manner his admiration of the gallantry and steadiness of the 89th regiment, under Lieutenant Colonel Morrison, and Major Clifford, who ably and gallantly supplied the Lieutenant Colonel's place after he was wounded; Light Company, 41st Regt., under Captain Glew, and detachment of the 8th or King's regiment, under Captain Campbell: and Royals acting with them; also a party of incorporated militia, by whom the brunt of the action was for a considerable time sustained, and whose loss has been very severe. To the advance under Lieutenant Colonel Pearson, consisting of the Glengarry Light Infantry, under Lieutenant Colonel Battersby; a small party of the 104th under Lieutenant Colonel Drummond; the incorporated militia under Lieutenant Colonel Robinson, and detachments from the 1st, 2nd, 4th, and 5th Lincoln militia, and 2nd York, under Lieutenant Colonel Parry, 103rd, the Lieutenant General offers his warmest thanks. They are also due to the troops which arrived under Colonel Scott, during the action, viz., the 1st or Royal Scots under Lieutenant Colonel Gordon, 8th or King's under Major Evans; 103rd regiment under Colonel Scott, Flank Company 104th with the Norfolk, Oxford, Kent and Essex Rangers, and Middlesex, under Lieutenant Colonel Hamilton.

The admirable steadiness and good conduct of the 19th Light Dragoons under Major Lisle, and of the detachment of Royal Artillery under Captain Maclachlan, are entitled to particular praise ; the latter officer having been badly wounded, the command of the Artillery devolved to Captain Maconochie, with whose gallantry and exertions Lieutenant General Drummond was highly pleased. Sergeant Austin, who directed the firing of the Congreve rockets, deserves very great credit. To the officers of the General and his personal staff, to Capt. Holland, Aid-de-camp to Major General Riall, Lieutenant General Drummond feels himself greatly indebted for the assistance they afforded him.

He has to lament being deprived (by a wound early in the action,) of the services of Major General Riall, who was most unfortunately made prisoner, while returning from the field, by a party of the enemy's cavalry, who had a momentary possession of the road, Lieutenant General Drummond has also to regret the wounds which have deprived the corps of the services of Lieut. Colonel Morrison, 89th regiment, and Lieut. Col. Robertson, of the incorporated militia. In the fall of Lieutenant Moorsom, of the

104th regiment serving as deputy assistant Adjutant General, the service has lost a gallant, * intelligent and meritorious young officer.

The Lieutenant General and President has great pleasure in dismissing to their homes the whole of the sedentary militia who have so handsomely come forward on the occasion, confident that on any future emergency, their loyalty will be again equally conspicuous.—He will perform a grateful duty in representing to his Majesty's Government, the zeal, bravery, and alacrity with which the militia have co-operated with his Majesty's troops.

(Signed)   J. HARVEY,
    Lieut. Col. and Dep. Adj. General.

The attack on Fort Erie. After the battle of Lundy's Lane, the American troops having retired to Fort Erie, there strengthened their position, enlarging the Fort and erecting new batteries, and so anxious were they to prepare for the coming storm, that, for fully a week after they sought refuge within the walls of the Old Fort, the troops were employed night and day in putting the works in such a state as might enable them to repel the attack which General Ripley felt was inevitable. These preparations were not, however, unfelt by the peaceable settlers of the country, as the buildings at Street's Mills were destroyed, on the pretext that they might afford a shelter to an attacking army. This wanton destruction of private property must not be lost sight of by the reader, as we shall ere long have to chronicle American opinions on nearly similar actions. General Drummond found it necessary, too, at this time, in order to facilitate his attack on the American position, to attack the batteries at Black Rock, and the vessels of war lying in front of Fort Erie and covering it lakeward with their broadsides.

The difficulties in accomplishing the latter of these actions were very great, and the boats necessary for the purpose had to be transported, one a distance of twenty miles, the others eight miles on the men's shoulders, These difficulties were, however, all overcome, and on the evening of the 11th of August, the boats were safely launched in

Lake Erie, and put off under the command of Captain Dobbs, with three crews of seventy-five men, to attack the American schooners. The details of this affair are so fairly given in Lieutenant Conkling's letter that it is unnecessary to do more than place it before the reader.

From Lieutenant Conklin to Captain Kennedy.

Fort-George, Upper Canada,
SIR,   August 16, 1814.

With extreme regret I have to make known to you the circumstances attending the capture of the Ohio and Somers. On the night of the 12th, between the hours of 11 and 12, the boats were seen a short distance a-head of the Somers, and were hailed from that vessel: they answered " provision-boats," which deceived the officer of the deck, as our army-boats are in the habit of passing and repassing throughout the night, and enabled them to drift athwart his hawse, and cut his cables; at the same time pouring in a heavy fire, before he discovered who they were. Instantaneously they were alongside of me, and notwithstanding my exertions, aided by Mr. M'Cally, acting sailing-master, (who was soon disabled,) I was unable to repulse them. But for a moment, I maintained the quarterdeck until my sword fell, in consequence of a shot in the shoulder, and nearly all on deck either wounded or surrounded with bayonets. As their force was an overwhelming one, I thought farther resistance vain, and gave up the vessel, with the satisfaction of having performed my duty, and defended my vessel to the last.

List of killed and wounded.

Ohio—Killed, 1 ; wounded, 6.
Somers.—Wounded, 2

The enemy's loss in killed and wounded is much more considerable ; among the killed is the commanding officer of the Netley, (lying here,) captain Ratcliffe ; he fell in attempting to come over my quarter. Notwithstanding the number of muskets and pistols which were fired, and the bustle inseparable from enterprises of the kind, neither the fort nor the Porcupine attempted to fire, as we drifted past them ; nor did we receive a shot until past Black Rock, though they might have destroyed us with ease.

We expect to be sent to Montreal, and perhaps to Quebec directly.

Edward P. Kennedy, Esq., commanding the United States Naval Force on Lake Erie.

Respectfully, your obedient servant,

A. M. CONKLING.

This was a very spirited affair, the force attacked was much superior to the attacking party, and the loss of the vessels was much felt by the Americans, although subsequent events in some measure compensated for the capture.

THE attack on this place was, perhaps, the most gallant action of the whole war, the obstinate courage of the troops was so remarkable as to elicit the praise of their enemies,—even Mr. Thomson, of Britain hating notoriety, bearing testimony on this occasion, to the gallantry exhibited by the Brito-Canadian troops.

Fort Erie.

In General Drummond's despatch, and the accompanying note, the leading particulars will be found, and the extracts from American despatches and papers will show the feeling of joy that the repulse of the British before Fort Erie inspired.

IN General Drummond's despatch a very full account is given of the repulse of the troops, under his command, before Fort Erie.

General Drummond's despatch.

From Lieutenant-General Drummond to Sir George Prevost

Camp before Fort Erie,
SIR, August 15, 1814.

Having reason to believe that a sufficient impression had been produced on the works of the enemy's Fort, by the fire of the battery which I had opened on it on the morning of the 13th, and by which the stone building was much injured, and the general outline of the parapet and embrazures very much altered, I was determined on assaulting the place; and accordingly made the necessary arrangements for attacking it, by a heavy column directed to the entrenchments on the side of Snake-hill, and by two columns to advance from the battery, and assault the fort and entrenchment on this side.

The troops destined to attack by Snake-hill, (which consisted of the King's regiment and that of De Watteville's, with the flank companies of the 89th and 100 regiments, under Lieutenant-Colonel Fischer, of the regiment of De Watteville,) marched at four o'clock yesterday afternoon, in order to gain the vicinity of the point of attack in sufficient time.

It is with the deepest regret I have to report the failure of both attacks, which were made two hours before day-light this morning. A copy of Lieutenant-Colonel Fischer's report,* herewith enclosed, will enable your Excellency to form a tolerable correct judgment of the cause of the failure of that attack; had the head of the column, which had entered the place without difficulty or opposition, been supported, the enemy must have fled from his works, (which were all taken, as was contemplated in the instructions, in reverse,) or have surrendered.

---

* *From Lieutenant-Colonel Fischer to Lieutenant-General Sir Gordon Drummond.*

SIR, Camp, August 15, 1814.

I have the honour to report to you, for the information of Lieutenant-general Drummond, that, in compliance with the instructions I received, the brigade under my command, consisting of the 8th and De Watteville's regiment, the light companies of the 89th and 100th, with a detachment of artillery, attacked this morning, at 2 o'clock, the position of the enemy on Snake-hill, and, to my great concern, failed in its attempt.

The flank companies of the brigade, who were formed under the order of major Evans of the king's regiment, for the purpose of turning the position between Snake-hill and the lake, met with a check at the abattis, which was found impenetrable, and was prevented by it to support major De Villatte, of De Watteville's and captain Powell of the quarter-master-general's department, who, actually with a few men, had turned the enemy's battery.

The column of support, consisting of the remainder of De Watteville's and the king's regiment, forming the reserve, in marching to near the lake, found themselves entangled between the rocks and the water, and, by the retreat of the flank companies, were thrown into such confusion, as to render it impossible to give them any kind of formation during the darkness of the night, at which time they were exposed to a most galling fire of the enemy's battery, and the numerous parties in the abattis; and I am perfectly convinced that the great number of missing, are men killed or severely wounded, at that time, when it was impossible to give them any assistance.

After day-break the troops formed, and retired to the camp. I enclose a return of casualties.

J. FISCHER,
Lieutenant-colonel De Watteville's regt.

The attack on the fort and entrenchments leading from it to the lake, was made at the same moment by two columns, one under Lieutenant-Colonel Drummond, 104th regiment, consisting of the flank companies 41st and 104th regiments, and a body of seamen and marines, under Captain Dobbs, of the royal navy, on the fort; the other under Colonel Scott, 103rd, consisting of the 103rd regiment, supported by two companies of the royals, was destined to attack the entrenchments. These columns advanced to the attack as soon as the firing upon Colonel Fischer's column was heard, and succeeded after a desperate resistance, in making a lodgement in the fort through the embrazures of the demi-bastion, captured the guns which they had actually turned against the enemy, who still maintained the stone building, when, most unfortunately, some ammunition, which had been placed under the platform, caught fire from the firing of the guns in the rear, and a most tremendous explosion followed, by which almost all the troops which had entered the place were dreadfully mangled. Panic was instantly communicated to the troops, who could not be persuaded that the explosion was accidental, and the enemy, at the same time, pressing forward, and commencing a heavy fire of musketry, the fort was abandoned, and our troops retreated towards the battery. I immediately pushed out the 1st battalion royals, to support and cover the retreat, a service which that valuable corps executed with great steadiness.

Our loss has been severe in killed and wounded: and I am sorry to add that almost all those returned "missing," may be considered as wounded or killed by the explosion, and left in the hands of the enemy.

The failure of these most important attacks has been occasioned by circumstances which may be considered as almost justifying the momentary panic which they produced, and which introduced a degree of confusion into the columns which, in the darkness of the night, the utmost exertions of the officers were ineffectual in removing.

The officers appear invariably to have behaved with the most perfect coolness and bravery; nor could any thing exceed the steadiness and order with which the advance of lieutenant-colonel Fischer's brigade was made, until emerging from a thick wood, it found itself suddenly stopped by an abattis, and within a heavy fire of musketry and guns from behind a formidable entrenchment. With regard to the centre and left columns, under colonel Scott and lieutenant-colonel Drummond, the persevering gallantry of both officers and men, until the unfortunate explosion, could not be surpassed. Colonel Scott, 103rd, and Lieutenant-Colonel Drummond, 104th regiments, who commanded the centre and left attacks, were unfortunately killed, and your excellency will perceive that almost every officer of those columns was either killed or wounded by the enemy's fire, or by the explosion.

My thanks are due to the under mentioned officers; viz. to Lieutenant-Colonel Fischer, who commanded the right attack; to Major Coore, aide-camp to your excellency, who accompanied that column; Major Evans, of the king's, commanding the advance; Major Villatte, De Watteville's; Captain Basden, light company 89th; Lieutenant Murray, light company 100th; I also beg to add the name of Captain Powell, of the Glengarry light infantry, employed on the staff as deputy-assistant in the quarter-master-general's department, who conducted lieutenant-colonel Fischer's column, and first entered the enemy's entrenchments, and by his coolness and gallantry particularly distinguished himself; Major Villatte, of De Watteville's regiment, who led the column of attack and entered the entrenchments; as did Lieutenant Young of the king's regiment, with about fifty men of the light companies of the king's and De Watteville's regiments: Captain Powell reports that Serjeant Powell, of the 19th Dragoons, who was perfectly acquainted with the ground, volunteered to act as guide, and preceded the leading sub-division in the most intrepid style. In the centre and left columns, the exertions of Major Smelt, 103rd regiment, who succeeded to the command of the left column, on the death of Colonel Scott; Captains Leonard and Shore, of the 104th flank companies; Captains Glew, Bullock, and O'Keefe, flank companies; 31st Captain Dobbs, Royal Navy, commanding a party of volunteer seamen and marines, are entitled to my acknowledgments (they are all wounded.) Nor can I omit mentioning, in the strongest terms of approbation, the active, zealous, and useful exertions of Captain Eliot, of the 103rd regiment, deputy assistant-quarter-master-general, who was unfortunately wounded and taken prisoner; and Captain Barney, of the 89th regiment, who had volunteered his services as a temporary assistant in the engineer department, and conducted the centre column to the attack, in which he received two dangerous wounds.

To Major Phillot, commanding the royal artillery, and Captain Sabine, who commanded the battery as well as the field-guns, and to the officers and men of that valuable branch of the service, serving under them, I have to express my entire approbation of their skill and exertions. Lieutenant Charlton, royal artillery, entered the fort with the centre column, fired several rounds upon the enemy from his own guns, and was wounded by the explosion. The ability and exertions of Lieutenant Philpot, royal engineers, and the officers and men of that department, claim my best acknowledgements.

To Lieutenant-Colonel Tucker, who commanded the reserve, and to Lieutenant-Colonel Pearson, inspecting field officer, and Lieutenant-Colonel Battersby, Glengarry light infantry, and Captain Walker, incorporated militia, I am greatly indebted for their active and unremitted attention to the security of out-posts.

To the deputy adjutant-general, and deputy quarter-master-general, Lieutenant-Colonel Harvey, and Lieutenant-Colonel Myers, and to the officers of their departments, respectively, as well as to Captain Foster, my military secretary, and the officers of my personal staff, I am under the greatest obligations for the assistance they have afforded me. My acknowledgments are due to Captain D'Alson, of the 90th regiment, Brigade-Major to the right division, and to Lieutenant-Colonel Nichol, quarter-master-general of Militia, the exertions of deputy commissioner-general Turquand, and the officers of that department, for the supply of the troops; and the care and attention of staff-surgeon O'Malley, and

the medical officers of the division, to the sick and wounded, also claim my thanks.

I have the honour to be, &c.

GORDON DRUMMOND,

Lieutenant-General.

His Excellency Sir George Provost, Bart. &c.

The result of the attack on Fort Erie was even more disastrous in its consequences to the British than had been the attack on York to the Americans. In this affair nine hundred men were either killed or wounded, and so severe was the blow, that had a less energetic commander than Drummond been in Upper Canada, or had a more able General than Brown commanded the Americans, the result of the blow at Erie might have been of the most serious character.

As it was, whether from Brown's wound, or from his incapacity, the blow was not followed up, and sufficient time was afforded to General Drummond to recover from the loss which he had experienced.

As may be imagined the victory at Fort Erie was the signal for Io Pæans all through the United States, and amongst others it appears to have particularly " gladdened the heart of Gen. Gaines that so many British and Canadians had been blown up." We subjoin his despatch and an article from a Buffalo journal on the subject:—

HEAD-QUARTERS, FORT ERIE, U. C.
Aug. 15, 7 A.M., 1814.

DEAR SIR,

My heart is gladdened with gratitude to Heaven and joy to my country, to have it in my power to inform you that the gallant army under my command has this morning beaten the enemy commanded by lieut. gen. Drummond, after a severe conflict of three hours, commencing at 2 o'clock, A.M. They attacked us on each flank—got possession of the salient bastion of the old fort Erie; which was regained at the point of the bayonet, with a dreadful slaughter. The enemy's loss in killed and prisoners is about 600; near 300 killed. Our loss is considerable, but I think not one tenth as great as that of the enemy. I will not detain the express to give you the particulars. I am preparing my force to follow up the blow.

With great respect and esteem, your obedient servant,

EDMUND P. GAINES,

Brig. Gen. Com'g.

The Hon. John Armstrong, the Sec'ry of War.

From the Buffalo Gazette, August 16.

SPLENDID DEFENCE OF FORT ERIE.

We take great pleasure in presenting our readers with the following glorious and interesting news from our gallant army at Fort Erie, received last evening from undoubted authority :—

On Sunday evening lieutenant general Drummond made his dispositions for storming Fort Erie. About half-past 2 o'clock yesterday morning the attack commenced from three coloums, one directed against the Fort, one against Towson's battery, and the third moved up the river in order to force a passage between the Fort and river. The column that approached the Fort succeeded in gaining the rampart, after having been several times repulsed ; when about 300 of them had gained the works and made a stand, an explosion from some unknown cause completely cleared the ramparts of the enemy, the most of whom were utterly destroyed. The column that moved to attack the south (or Towson's) battery made desperate charges, but were met with such firmness by our artillery and infantry, as to be compelled to fall back—they advanced a second and third time with great resolution, but being met with such distinguished gallantry, they gave way and retired. The column that marched up the river, were repulsed before they assaulted the batteries.

Shortly after the explosion, the enemy finding their efforts to gain the Fort or carry the batteries, unavailing, withdrew his forces from the whole line, and retreated to the woods. The action continued one hour and an half, during which (except the short interval that the enemy occupied the ramparts) the artillery from that fort and batteries kept up a most destructive fire, as well on the main body of the enemy as on the attacking columns. These colums were composed of the best of the British army, volunteers from every corps, the forlorn hope. The enemy's loss is estimated at rising 800.

123 rank and file passed this place this morning, for Greenbush. Colonel Drummond and six or seven officers were killed, one Dep. Q. M. Gen. (said to be captain Elliot). and two platoon officers, prisoners. Our loss, in killed does not exceed twenty, most of which we learn are of the artillery. We regret to state, that captain Williams and lieutenant M'Donough, of the artillery, are killed ; lieutenant Fontaine, missing, supposed taken prisoner.

Some of our officers were wounded, but we have not learned their names.

From the circumstance of the enemy's main body lying within grape and canister distance from the fort, their loss must be very severe, greater than what is mentioned in the above estimation. The enemy's waggons were uncommonly active yesterday morning in removing the wounded.

The prisoners are of the 8th, 100th, 103d, 104th, and De Watteville's regiments, and a few sailors.

It is impossible for us in this sketch, to say anything of the individual skill and gallantry of the officers, or the steady bravery of the men engaged in this glorious defence; we presume all did their duty. Brigadier general Gaines commanded the fort.

Our army at fort Erie continues almost daily to skirmish with the enemy, which is principally confined to the attack of pickets on both sides. There has been more or less cannonading every day during the week past, without any material advantage to either. On Wednesday a party of riflemen under captain Birdsall, attacked and drove in the enemy's picket; they lost from fifteen to twenty killed. We lost only one man.— On Friday major Morgan with a detachment from his rifle corps attacked the enemy in the skirts of the woods back of the fort; and after a brisk musketry of some time returned to the fort, with the loss of ten or twelve killed, among whom, we regret to say, was that excellent officer major Lodowick Morgan, of the 1st rifle regiment, who so gallantly repulsed the enemy at Conjockety Creek, on the morning of the 3d instant. He was interred at Buffalo, on Saturday, with all the honour due to his rank and distinguished bravery.

Our fleet on Lake Ontario, to the number of nine sail arrived off fort Niagara about eight or ten days since. The Sylph, said to be the swiftest sailer on the lake, gave chase to a British brig, which being unable to escape, was abandoned and blown up. From every appearance she was loaded with munitions of war, intended for the British forts. Commodore Chauncey commands the fleet, whose health is fast improving. Three of the enemy's small vessels lie in Niagara river, blockaded by our fleet.

We have the unpleasant task to inform the public of the loss of two United States schooners lying near Fort Erie, by capture. It appears that the enemy fitted out an expedition of nine boats, on the lake above Fort Erie, and made a simultaneous attack upon our three schooners; the Porcupine succeeded in beating them off; the Somers and Ohio were captured, and taken down the river, below the point, near Frenchman's creek. The Porcupine sailed on Sunday for Erie.

We learn that Captain Dobbs, of the British royal navy, commanded the party which captured the Somers and Ohio.

We have been correctly informed of particulars of the heroism of captain Ketchum of the 25th regiment, whose name has received the just applause of the public—though, it is regretted by his fellow-officers, that he has not been honoured with a brevet from the government. The gallant conduct of this young officer on the 5th of July, has been set forth by general Scott. The particulars which reflect on him honours equally high, are, that in the month of June previous he had marched his company from the rendezvous at Hartford—a full company of recruits, assembled by him under special authority from the commanding officer of the regiment, to form a flank company, particularly dressed and equipped, and drilled by him for light service—and all young men. The intrepid conduct of these men, so lately from the interior in opposing three times their force, when operating by themselves on that day, completely proves that the good conduct of our soldiers, however inexperienced, will depend, as in the instance of the gallant leader of this detachment upon the examples of ardor and firmness set them by their commanders.

In the action at the Falls of Niagara, Captain Ketchum is again distinguished, in being detached by Colonel Jessup to the rear of the enemy's line, supported by the Lieut. Colonel with the 5th regiment, formed at right angles, with the enemy's left flank, and keeping watch over the British regiment of dragoons, drawn up on a parallel line on his right. Thus did Ketchum under cover of the night, between two lines of the enemy, seize a party of British officers and men, among whom were Major General Riall, and an aid of Lieutenant General Drummond, (the Lieutenant General having narrowly escaped,) and bring them safely to his Colonel. Soon after Captain Ketchum had obtained from general Riall his name, and expressed to him his happiness at meeting with him—the General is said to have inquired, "where is the General?"

General Riall when at Buffalo, sent his sword with a polite note, to lieutenant Colonel Jessup—the lieutenant Colonel was there on account of his wounds.

The defeat at Fort Erie, disastrous as it was, was felt even more severely from the circumstance of a similar repulse, although not attended with such loss of life, at Conjocta Creek, near Black Rock. We admit readily that the intention of the British General to effect a diversion here and carry the batteries at Black Rock was defeated, but we cannot permit Major Morgan's statement as to numbers to pass unnoticed. The Major declares that the British numbered from twenty to fifteen hundred men, the actual number having been four hundred and sixty. It was quite unnecessary for Major Morgan to have increased the force opposed to him, in sum or ratio, as every one will readily admit the fact of his having, with little better than half the number defeated an attack which involved great results. Major Morgan's report*will be found below in our notes :—

*The Repulse at Conjocta Creek.

*REPORT OF MAJOR MORGAN.

Sir,   Fort, Erie, August 5th 1814.

Having been stationed with the 1st battalion of the 1st regiment of Riflemen at Black Rock ;

American journals were loud in their condemnation of the severities and atrocities practised by the British in the Chesapeake, but are most careful never to allow that Americans could be guilty of similar " atrocities." We find. however, on the authority of Mr. James, that an occurrence took place on Lake Erie which we believe will parallel anything, however bad, that ever occurred along the shores of the Chesapeake. We give the affair in Mr. James's words :—

Outrage at Port Talbot, on Lake Erie.

The Americans will not allow us to give an uninterrupted detail of open and honorable warfare. Among several petty outrages upon private property, one that occurred on Lake Erie is too heinous to pass unnoticed. On the 16th of August, a party of about 100 Americans and Indians landed at Port-Talbot on that lake; and robbed 50 heads of families of all their horses, and of every article of household furniture, and wearing apparel, belonging to them. The number of individuals who were thus thrown naked and destitute upon the world, amounted to 49 men, 37 women,—three of the latter, and two of the former, nearly 70 years of age, —and 148 children. A great many of the more respectable inhabitants were not only robbed, but carried off as prisoners: among them, a member of the house of assembly, Mr. Barnwell, though ill of fever and ague. An authenticated account of this most attrocious proceeding, delivered in by colonel Talbot, the owner of the settlement, stands upon the records of the "Loyal and Patriotic Society of Upper Canada ;" yet not a whisper on the subject has escaped any one American Historian.

---

on the evening of the 2d instant, I observed the British army moving up the river on the opposite shore, and suspected they might make a feint on Fort Erie, with an intention of a real attack on the Buffalo side. I immediately moved and took a position on the upper side of Conjocta Creek, and that night threw up a battery of some logs, which I found on the ground, and had the bridge torn away.

About 2 o'clock the next morning, my picquets from below gave me information of the landing of nine boats full of troops, half-a-mile below. I immediately got my men (240 in number) to their quarters, and patiently waited their approach. At a quarter past four they advanced upon us, and commenced the attack ; sending a party before to repair the bridge under the cover of their fire. When they had got at good rifle distance, I opened a heavy fire on them, which laid a number of them on the ground, and compelled them to retire. They then formed in the skirt of the wood, and kept up the fight at long shot, continually reinforcing from the Canada shore, until they had 23 boat loads, and then attempted to outflank us, by sending a large body up the creek to ford it, when I detached lieuts. Ryan, Smith and Armstrong, with about 60 men, to oppose their left wing, where they were again repulsed with considerable loss—after which they appeared disposed to give up their object, and retreated by throwing six boat loads of troops on Squaw Island, which enfiladed the creek, and prevented me from harassing their rear. Their superior numbers enabled them to take their killed and wounded off the field which we plainly saw, and observed they suffered severely. We found some of their dead thrown into the river, and covered with logs and stones, and some on the field. We also collected a number of muskets and accoutrements, with clothing that appeared to have been torn to bind their wounds. We took six prisoners, who stated the British force opposed to us, to consist of from 12 to 1500 men, commanded by lieutenant colonel Tucker, of the 41st regiment. They also state that their object was to re-capture general Riall, with other British prisoners, and destroy the public stores deposited at Buffalo. The action continued about two hours and a half. I am happy to state they were completely failed in their attempts. Our loss is trifling compared with theirs—we had two killed and eight wounded. I am sorry to inform you that captain Hamilton, lieutenants Wadsworth and M'Intosh are amongst the latter. Their gallantry in exposing themselves to encourage their men, I think entitles them to the notice of country. My whole command behaved in a manner that merited my warmest approbation ; and in justice to them, I cannot avoid mentioning the names of the officers which are as follwos :—Captain Hamilton, lieutenants Wadsworth, Ryan, Calhoun, M'Intosh, Arnold, Shortride, M'Farland, Tipton, Armstrong, Smith, Cobbs, Davidson and Austin, with ensign Page.

If, sir, you believe we have done our duty, we shall feel highly gratified.

I am, sir, respectfully, our obedient servant.

L. MORGAN.

Major 1st rifle Regiment

Major-General Brown.

RECAPITULATION OF OUR KILLED AND WOUNDED.

	Captain,	Subalterns,	Rank and file.
Wounded,	1	2	5
Killed,	0	0	2
	1	2	7
Aggregate			10

CHAPTER XXI

Little time was lost by the Americans, after General Drummond's repulse, in commencing the re-construction of the defences at Fort Erie, injured by the explosion; the completion also of the new works that were in course of erection, at the time of the assault, was pressed on so rapidly that, in a very short space of time, they were able to boast that "Fort Erie was rendered impregnable to the attacks of any other than a vastly superior force." These defences were mounted with twenty-seven heavy guns, and the garrison was reinforced by new levies of militia. It almost appeared from the strength of the reinforcements as if the Americans were resolved at all hazards to keep possession of Fort Erie as a sort of equipoise to the British holding Fort Niagara. We learn from "sketches of the war" that three hundred and twenty regulars arrived in the St. Lawrence from Lake Huron; a company of riflemen from Sandusky; and several other detachments of regulars from Batavia and Sackett's Harbour, giving in all a force of three thousand four hundred men, and besides these large numbers the Fort was protected, lakeward, by the broadsides of the St. Lawrence, Niagara, Lady Prevost, Caledonia and Porcupine.

The fortification at Fort Erie repaired.

Reduced as General Drummond was by the losses at Chippewa, Lundy's Lane, and Fort Erie, the arrival of the 6th and 82nd regiments, mustering some one thousand and forty men was insufficient to place him in a position to threaten so formidable a post, especially as he had been compelled to send six companies of the 41st to Fort George, and what was left of the 103rd to Burlington, thus leaving himself in point of numbers very little stronger than before.

The heavy and constant rains, and the low swampy grounds on which the army had been so long encamped, and the privations they had undergone, spread typhus and intermittent fevers amongst the troops, to such an extent that General Drummond, so far from being able to assume the offensive, was compelled to act most cautiously on the defensive. The position of the two armies was, at this time, as follows :—The Americans occupied Fort Erie with their rear covered by the ships. The British batteries were placed directly in front, but strange to say were guarded only by a line of piquets, the main body being about a mile and a half to the rear; we presume that this position was taken up by General Drummond on account of the ground being somewhat higher and less swampy.

From the 1st to the 17th September little occurred of consequence, except a few trifling affairs of piquets, but General Brown, who

22

had by this time entirely recovered from his wounds, having learned from stragglers the sickly condition of General Drummond's army, and that the General was meditating the removal of his forces to a healthier locality, determined to anticipate the movements, and to gain the credit of having compelled the retreat. On the afternoon of the 17th he accordingly advanced with a large force, and succeeded after a gallant resistance in carrying the whole line of batteries. The Americans were, however, not permitted sufficient time to destroy the works, indeed they were not even able to spike the guns, as detachments of the Royal Scots, the 89th, the Glengary light infantry, three companies of the 6th and seven companies of the 82nd now made their appearance, and drove the enemy, at the bayonets' point, from the batteries nearly to the glacis of Fort Erie, making several prisoners in the charge and pursuit. By five o'clock the works were again occupied and the line of piquets renewed.

As will be seen by General De Watteville's letter to General Drummond the loss of the British in this affair was very severe. The Americans acknowledge a total loss of five hundred and ten killed, wounded and prisoners.

Despatch from Major-General De Watteville,
to Lieutenant-General Drummond.
Camp before Fort-Erie,
Sept. 19, 1814.

SIR,—I have the honor to report to you, that the enemy attacked, on the 17th in the afternoon at three o'clock, our position before Fort Erie, the 2nd brigade, under colonel Fischer, composed of the 8th and de Watteville's regiments, being on duty.

Under cover of a heavy fire of his artillery from Fort Erie, and much favoured by the nature of the ground, and also by the state of the weather, the rain falling in torrents at the moment of his approach, the enemy succeeded in turning the right of our line of piquets, without being perceived, and with a very considerable force, attacked both the piquets and support, in the flank and rear: at the same time, another of the enemy's columns attacked, in front, the

piquets between No. 2 and No. 3 batteries, and, having succeeded in penetrating by No. 4 piquet, part of his force turned to his left, and thereby surrounded our right, and got almost immediate possession of No. 3 battery. The enemy then directed his attacks, with a very superior force, towards No. 2 battery; but the obstinate resistance made by the piquets, under every possible disadvantage, delayed considerably his getting possession of No. 2 battery; in which, however, he at last succeeded.

As soon as the alarm was given, the 1st brigade, being next for support, composed of the Royal Scots, the 82nd and 89th regiments, under Lieutenant-Colonel Gordon, received orders to march forward; and also the light demi-brigade under Lieutenant-Colonel Pearson: the 6th regiment remaining in reserve, under Lieutenant-Colonel Campbell. From the Concession-road, the Royal Scots, with the 89th as support, moved by the new road, and met the enemy near the block-house, on the right of No. 3 battery; whom they engaged, and, by their steady and intrepid conduct checked his further progress. The 82d regiment, and three companies of the 6th regiment, were detached to the left, in order to support Nos. 1 and 2 batteries. The enemy having, at that time, possession of No. 2 battery, and still pushing forward, seven companies of the 82d, under major Proctor, and the three companies of the 6th, under major Taylor, received directions to oppose the enemy's forces, and immediately charged them with the most intrepid bravery, driving them back across our entrenchments; and also from No. 2 battery, thereby preventing their destroying it, or damaging its guns in a considerable degree. Lieutenant-Colonel Pearson, with the Glengarry light infantry, under Lieutenant-Colonel Battersby, pushed forward by the centre-road, and attacked, and carried, with great gallantry, the new entrenchment, then in full possession of the enemy.

The enemy, being thus repulsed at every point, was forced to retire with precipitation to their works, leaving several prisoners, and a number of their wounded in our hands. By five o'clock the entrenchments were again occupied, and the line of piquets established, as it had been previous to the enemy's attack.

I have the honor to enclose a return of casualties, and the report of the officer commanding the royal artillery, respecting the damage done to ordnance and the batteries, during the time they were in the enemy's possession.

I have the honor to be, &c.

L. DE WATTEVILLE, major-gen.

Lieut-General Drummond, &c.

Return of killed and wounded, 115 killed and 494 missing and wounded.

Although we find in "sketches of the war" General Brown's boasts that a loss of five hundred and ten, exclusive of victory. of militia and volunteers, was acknowledged, and although General Brown was driven back to his stronghold, without having accomplished the objects of the sally, still· he had the modesty to term his sortie, in a letter to General Gaines, "a splendid achievement." Another American commander, General Varnum (the V should have been a B), had the effrontery to write, "our gallant little army has again signalized itself by gaining a splendid victory over a part of the enemies forces near Fort Erie. Two of the enemies batteries were carried, the guns spiked, trunnions broken off, and their magazines blown up."

The return of the officers in charge of the artillery shows that this boast of the American commander was simply a falsehood.

General Drummond now saw his little army still farther reduced by the six hundred killed and wounded, and he had the pain to find the sickness and mortality spreading as the rainy season advanced, he therefore resolved on breaking up his camp before Fort Erie. This he accordingly did, and between the 21st and 24th he removed his guns and stores and retired into comfortable quarters at Chippewa. General Drummond remained here until about the middle of October, when General Izzard with twenty-four hundred regulars joined General Brown, whose division had meanime received a reinforcement of seven hun-

dred regulars. General Izzard now assumed the chief command, and, according to the Ontario Reporter, a Buffalo paper of that day, "was to move down the Canada shore with eight thousand regular troops." Against this overwhelming force General Drummond felt that it would be madness to oppose his handful of troops, he therefore returned from Chippewa upon Fort George and Burlington Heights.

Beyond a skirmish at Lyon's Creek be-Skirmish at Lyon's tween a brigade under Creek. General Bissel, some fifteen hundred strong, and a body of six hundred and fifty men, composed of detachments from the 82nd, 100th, and Glengary regiments, under Colonel Murray, in which the British lost nineteen killed and wounded, while Mr. Thomson acknowledges a loss of sixty-seven, nothing resulted from the expedition under General Izzard, as circumstances very soon compelled him to exchange his advance for a precipitous and somewhat inglorious retreat.

As these circumstances exercised an equal influence over Commodore Chauncey's motions, it will be necessary to remind the reader that the British had been diligently endeavouring to complete their large ship the St. Lawrence, and that this vessel with her hundred guns had been launched on the 2nd of October. The launch of this vessel was the signal for Commodore Chauncey's immediate retirement from the lake to Sackett's Harbour, where he moored his ships head and stern, in anticipation of an attack from his formidable adversary. Sir James Yeo had, however, more important business on hand, so, satisfied with having frightened the American commander off the lake, he sailed on the 17th with, and landed on the 19th, five companies of the 90th regiment. The arrival of this reinforcement, although it still left the Americans as three to one, was the signal for General Izzard's retreat to Fort Erie, and the arrival of a second reinforcement, induced the American commander, although still numbering as four to three, to remove the guns and destroy the fortifications of Fort Erie, and retreat to his own side of the strait, after, according to Mr. Thomson, "a vigorous and brilliant campaign."

We cannot help imagining that had General Izzard re-taken Fort Niagara, left a strong garrison in the "impregnable" position of Fort Erie and kept Drummond in check that he would have been rather more entitled to rank his campaign of a month as a brilliant one than real facts admit of. Indeed, so far from placing it in the category of brilliant actions, we are almost tempted to stigmatize it as the act of a coward and a poltroon, and one which can only be compared with the retreat of the British commander at Plattsburg.

Lest we should be supposed to condemn General Izzard too severely, we will make one or two extracts from General Armstrong's notes and from Ingersol. Armstrong devotes six pages to the subject, and declares that when Izzard was ordered "to throw his whole force on Drummond's rear," and to leave Plattsburg to its fate, he did so with the conviction that the plans laid down by government were impracticable, and that the British would speedily be in occupation of Plattsburg.

Armstrong and Ingersol on General Izzard.

The extract from Armstrong will, however, show the opinion entertained by that officer of General Izzard's strategic skill.

"Under these and other forebodings of evil, he was careful to announce to the War Department his total disavowal of all responsibility for whatever might happen; but expressed his willingness, at the same time, to execute the orders he had received, 'as well as he knew how.'

"Beginning his movement accordingly on the 29th of August, and having in his choice two routes to Sackett's Harbor—one of which required a march of ten days, and the other a march of twenty, he made no scruple of preferring the latter; though, by doing so, he necessarily put much to hazard by giving time to Prevost to reinforce his western posts. Nor was this the only measure he adopted, having a similar tendency. "From a desire," he said, "to bring in his column fresh and ready for immediate service," he limited its daily march to fifteen miles; an indulgence altogether unnecessary,* and never granted, when there is anything urgent in the character of the service to be performed. But even this was not enough to satisfy Mr. Izzard's conservative theory; a halt of four days was made at the south end of Lake George; professedly, for the purpose of refreshing troops, not a man of whom was either sick or weary. And again: when arriving at Sackett's Harbor on the 16th, though finding that Kingston had not been reinforced, and that our fleet had a temporary ascendency on the lake,† not a single measure was taken for availing himself of these advantages, and attacking, as ordered to do, that important post. For this omission, a sympathy for Brown and his division was made the pretext. "The perils," he said, "of this heroic band are now so multiplied and menacing, as make it my first and most important duty, to leave Kingston untouched, embark my troops on board the fleet, run up to the head of the lake, land on the northern side of the Niagara, and throw myself on the rear of Drummond," This decision, though thus decidedly announced, was short-lived. A storm of wind and rain occurring, which prevented the fleet from sailing, the General now besought advice how he should proceed: whether by a land march over bad roads in wet weather, or, by waiting the cessation of the storm, avail himself of a passage by water. Strange as it may appear, he preferred the former, and in a letter of the 18th announced this intention to the government. Finding, however, that the choice he had made, was much censured by the army, and even denounced by a part of his staff,‡ as a new ruse to avoid a battle with Drummond, as he had already evaded an attack on Kingston, his resolution was shaken, his march suspended, and a correspondence opened with the naval commander on the old question, "by what

---

* *Twenty miles* formed Cæsar's justum iter dies; and if the case was urgent, considerably more.

† Such was the well-known condition of the fleet, when Izzard arrived at Sackett's Harbor.

‡ Statement of Major O'Conner, Assistant Adjutant-General of the division.

route he should move." In this attempt to obtain from that officer a sanction for his own opinion, he signally failed; no answer was vouchsafed to the question, and merely a notice given of the time and place, at which the troops would be received on board of the fleet, and 'carried to any point on Lake Ontario, he might think proper to indicate.'

"Though sensibly rebuked by the manner in which his inquiry had been treated, he felt himself in no small degree consoled by two circumstances—the latitude given him in choosing a landing-place; and the limitation put by the commodore on the number of troops the fleet could conveniently carry —when, forgetting alike the orders of the government, the promises made to Brown, and the assurances given to the quarter-master-general the evening preceding, he at once and peremptorily declared for the mouth of the Genesee! At this place, he found himself with three thousand men early in the morning of the 22d, but, as might have been readily foreseen, entirely destitute of the means of transportation. It was not, therefore, till the 24th, he resumed his movement, when, adhering to his purpose of "bringing in his corps fresh and ready for action," he directed his march, not on Buffalo, but on Batavia—where an unexpected solace for all past doubts, labors and terrors, awaited him, 'in a full assurance that, on the 17th of the month, Brown had, by a skilful and intrepid attack made upon Drummond, become his own deliverer.'

"In an interview with this officer on the 26th, though professing a willingness to discharge his remaining duty, he restricted its objects to a seige of Fort Niagara; and even hazarded an opinion, that this fort retaken, the campaign might, with propriety, terminate. To this proposition, in both its parts, Brown refused his assent—justly remarking, that, as a military post, Niagara was not worth holding by either belligerent; and that its garrison, now composed wholly of invalids and convalescents, formed no object worthy of pursuit; and again : that, as he understood the orders, under which the division of the right had marched, they pre-scribed three objects, "an attack on Kingston, which had been omitted; the relief of the division of the left, which had been accomplished; and, lastly, the *attack and capture of Drummond's army*—involving that of all the British posts on the peninsula." —"This," he added, "remains to be done, and may be accomplished, with scarcely a doubt of success, if, for the purpose, a proper direction be given to the two divisions united." It was not, however, till after the stimulus of a second conversation with Brown, that Izzard could be prevailed upon even to cross the Niagara; when, on receiving a full exposition of the proposed project of attack, and perceiving, after a short reconnoissance of Drummond's position, the probability of its success, he for a moment adopted the measure, and even detached Brown to direct some labor, preliminary to the movement; when, availing himself of information just received, that "four of the enemy's ships were now at the mouth of the river—that the navigation of the lake had been abandoned to Yeo, and that Chauncey had been driven for shelter, under the batteries of Sackett's Harbor,"—he at once relapsed into his former creed, and adopting the Hudibrastic strategy of *preserving the army for the next campaign* ordered "a retreat across the St. Lawrence, and winter quarters to be taken for the troops,"—thus literally fulfilling his own prediction, that the expedition would terminate in disappointment and disgrace.

"While Izzard was making these extraordinary displays of military skill and ardor, an expedition was organized in the west, having for its objects the security and quiet of the Michigan territory during the approaching winter, an attack on Burlington Heights, and an eventual junction with Brown's division on the Niagara. The force assigned to the service was composed of mounted yeomen, furnished by Kentucky and Ohio, one company of United States rangers, and seventy friendly Indians, making in the aggregate, seven hundred combatants. Though failing in its principal object, the movement, from the activity and judgement with which it was conducted, may not be unworthy of a short notice."

After the long and explanatory extract already given, it will be unnecessary to quote more than a few lines from Ingersol, although equally severe strictures are to be found in his pages :—

"It is difficult," says Ingersol, "if possible to justify General Izzard's prudence or affectation of prudence, a virtue, like all others, injurious by excess. Taking twenty days to get from Plattsburg, afloat on Lake Ontario, when it might have been done in ten, then causing his army to be landed, not in Canada, any where Izzard chose, as Commodore Chauncey offered his fleet to land them, but choosing the mouth of Gennesee river in New York, where they must unavoidably be detained for transportation ; not reaching the Canadian shore, at last, till the 11th October, six weeks after he left Plattsburg, and then instead of planting his standard east of Drummond, taking station west, and when united with Brown disappointing the unanimous and constant wish for an immediate attack of an enemy, who, *although entrenched, was not more than half* Izzard's number, and much dispirited."

Ingersol winds up his observations on Izzard's backwardness by remarking that "If General Izzard had by many battles established his character, such conduct would have been less objectionable. But as an officer untried, known only by a few, he was unable to make head against the military and popular current then irresistibly strong for action."

These two extracts will fully exonerate us from the charge of hasty condemnation, coming especially as one does from a writer (Ingersol) who never hesitates to distort facts, if by doing so a brighter light can be thrown upon the page of his country's history. In support of this allegation we may adduce the fact that Ingersol doubles the number of men under General Murray's command, and, not satisfied even with that, the Marquis of Tweeddale, then at Kingston suffering from the effects of his wounds, is placed at their head as a sort of foil to the praises lavished on "Daniel Bissel," an American soldier raised from the ranks, and the commander of the American brigade opposed to the noble marquis. In-

gersol's misrepresentations do not however end here, in the events which immediately followed the American retreat an equal want of candour is exhibited.

The buccaneering expedition of General MacArthur is treated by him as an expedition having for its object the destruction of depots of provisions and forage, and the cowardly miscreant's precipitate retreat before a small body dispatched to stop his predatory career is thus disposed of "a part of the 103d Regiment of the 19th Light Dragoon, and some Indian warriors, were despatched to repel and chastise MacArthur, but did not come in contact with him."

The real facts of the case were that on the 20th September a band of lawless brigands crossed over from Detroit and ravaged a whole settlement, destroying twenty-seven homesteads, and reducing the unfortunate inhabitants to the utmost misery and want. The booty carried off by these miscreants was so considerable that General McArthur was tempted under the pretext of a military expedition, to undertake precisely the same sort of thing. This he did, using the precaution however to take none but seven hundred and twenty Kentucky mounted riflemen with him.

Mr. Ingersol states that "they routed more than five hundred militia," and captured upwards of one hundred. From what source Ingersol could have learned this last fact puzzles us. No militia were at that time embodied in that section of the country, the arms had been all sent in, and so far from mustering five hundred strong, some difficulty would have been experienced in collecting fifty. Again, as to prisoners, of what did they consist? for answer we refer to Mr. James, "The one hundred and fifty prisoners consisted of peaceable inhabitants, both old and young, and drunken Indians and their squaws. The instant it was ascertained that a detachment of the 103rd regiment, numbering less than half McArthur's force, had moved from Burlington heights, the General and his gang dispersd and so rapid was their flight, that the British regulars did not get within eight miles of them."

The destruction of the mills was a most

wanton outrage on private property, and the misery entailed for the whole winter was excessive. The pretext too that, by the act, the troops were inconvenienced was altogether unfounded, inasmuch as the American Commander knew full well that the supplies for the troops were principally drawn from below, and that the destruction of the mills would be but a trifling inconvenience to the troops whilst it could not but result in the most ruinous consequences to the unoffending and peaceable inhabitants. We shall however see how American writers regard similar transactions on the Chesapeake.

We have pretty nearly disposed of the military events along the Niagara, for 1814; we have seen General Izzard and his army cross the Niagara, and retreat to winter quarters, two thousand men of his army having been dispatched to Sackett's harbour, and we have also seen General Drummond, after the expulsion of every American from British soil, retire quietly into winter quarters, the greater portion of the troops having been sent to Kingston, so completely had a sense of security been restored. We will pass then from nearly the extremity of British territory on the west, to nearly the extreme east, and take up the proceedings of Lieut. Colonel Pilkington and Sir Thomas Hardy.

Passamaquoddy bay and the events in that quarter.

The movements of these officers, and the troops under their command, will be found fully detailed in the official reports which we give at length:—

From Lieutenant-colonel Pilkington to Lieutenant-general Sir John C. Sherbrooke.

Moose Island, Passamaquoddy Bay,
Sir,   July 12, 1814.

Having sailed from Halifax on the 5th instant, accompanied by lieutenant-colonel Nicolls, of the royal engineers, and a detachment of the royal artillery, under the command of captain Dunn, I have the honour to acquaint your excellency, that we arrived at Shelburne, the place of rendezvous, on the evening of the 7th instant, where I found captain Sir Thomas Hardy, in his majesty's ship Ramillies, with two transports, having on board the 102d regiment, under the command of lieutenant-colonel Herries, which had arrived the day before. I did not fail to lay before Sir Thomas Hardy my instructions, and to consult as to the best means of carrying them into execution.

As we concurred in opinion that the success of the enterprise, with which we were entrusted, would very materially depend upon our reaching the point of attack previous to the enemy being apprised of our intentions, that officer, with his accustomed alacrity and decision, directed the ships of war and transports to get under weigh early on the following morning; and we yesterday, about 3 o'clock P.M., anchored near to the town of Eastport.

On our approach to this Island, lieutenant Oats (your excellency's aide de camp, whom you had permitted to accompany me on this service) was despatched in a boat, bearing a flag of truce, with a summons, (copy of which is transmitted,)addressed to the officer commanding, requiring that Moose Island should be surrendered to his Britannic majesty. This proposal was not accepted ; in consequence of which, the troops, which were already in the boats, pulled off under the superintendance of captain Senhouse, of the royal navy, whose arrangements were so judicious, as to ensure a successful issue. But, previous to reaching the shore, the colors of the enemy on Fort-Sullivan were hauled down : and on our landing, the capitulation was agreed to, of which the copy is enclosed.

We found in the fort a detachment of the 40th regiment of American infantry, consisting of six officers and about 80 men, under the command of Major Putnam, who surrendered themselves prisoners of war. This fort is situated on an eminence commanding the entrance to the anchorage, and within it is a block-house, and also four long 18-pounders, one 18-pound carronade, and four field-pieces. The extent of the island is about four miles in length and two in breadth and in a great state of cultivation, The militia amount to about 250, and the population is calculated at 1600.

We have also occupied Allen's and Frederick Island, so that the whole of the islands in this bay are now subject to the British flag.

It is very satisfactory to me to add, that this service has been effected, without any loss or casualty among the troops employed n it.

To captain Sir Thomas Hardy, I consider myself under the greatest obligations; having experienced every possible co-operation, with an offer to disembark, from his squadron, any proportion of seamen or marines which I considered necessary.

I beg to acknowledge my thanks to you in allowing your aide de camp, Lieutenant Oats, to accompany me on this service. He has been of great assistance to me, and will have the honor of delivering this despatch. He has also in his possession the colours and standard found in Port-Sullivan.

I have the honor to be, &c.

A. PILKINGTON, lieut.-col.
Deputy-adjutant-general.
Lieut.-gen. Sir J. C. Sherbrooke, K. B.

From captain Hardy, R. N.. and lieutenant-colonel Pilkington, to the American commander at Moose Island.

On board of his majesty's ship Ramillies, off Moose Island, July 11, 1814.

SIR,

As we are perfectly apprised of the weakness of the fort and garrison under your command, and your inability to defend Moose Island against the ships and troops of his Britannic majesty placed under our directions, we are induced, from the humane consideration of avoiding the effusion of blood, and from a regard to you and the inhabitants of the island, to prevent, if in our power, the distress and calamities which will befall them in case of resistance. We, therefore, allow you five minutes, from the time this summons is delivered, to decide upon an answer. *

———

* *From Major Putnam to Captain Hardy and Lieutenant-Colonel Pilkington.*

Fort Sullivan, July 11, 1814.

GENTLEMEN.—Conformably to your demand, I have surrendered Fort Sullivan with all the public property.†

———

† *Return of ordnance and stores found in Fort Sullivan, surrendered to his Majesty's forces, under the command of Lieutenant-Colonel Pilkington.*
Iron guns—Four 18-pounders, with standing carriages,

In the event of you not agreeing to capitulate on liberal terms, we shall deeply lament being compelled to resort to those coercive measures, which may cause destruction to the town of Eastport, but which will ultimately assure us possession of the island.

T. M HARDY, captain of H.M.S. Ramillies.
A. PILKINGTON, lieut.-col. commanding.
To the officers commanding the United States' troops on Moose Island.

Articles of Capitulation.

"Article I. The officers and troops of the United States, at present on Moose island, are to surrender themselves prisoners of war, and are to deliver up the forts, buildings, arms, ammunition, stores, and effects, with exact inventories thereof, belonging to the American government; and they are thereby transferred to his Britannic majesty, in the same manner and possession, as has been held heretofore by the American government.

Art. II. The garrison of the island shall be prisoners of war, until regularly exchanged; they will march out of the fort with the honors of war, and pile their arms at such place as will be appointed for that purpose; the officers will be permitted to proceed to the United States on their parole."

* * * * *

Ingersol is very indignant with the people of Massachusetts for what he terms their tame surrender of their freedom.

———

This I have done to stop the effusion of blood and in consideration of your superior forces.

I am, Gentlemen, &c.,
P. PUTMAN, Major commanding.

P.S.—I hope, gentlemen, every respect will be paid to the defenceless inhabitants of this island, and the private property of the officers.

side arms: two unserviceable 9-pounders, two 12-pounder carronades without carriages.
Brass guns—Two serviceable and two unserviceable light 6-pounders, with travelling carriages, side arms, &c.
Forty-two paper cartridges, filled with six pounds of powder, five flannel do., do.: 3176 unserviceable musket-ball cartridges.
Four hundred and fifty-two loose round 18-pounder shot: 55 18-pounder grape shot: 389 loose round 6-pounder: 95 6-pounder case shot.
Six barrels of horned powder, containing 100 pounds each: 100 muskets, with bayonets, belts, slings, and complete swords, with belts, scabbards, &c.
Seventy-two incomplete tents, one United States' ensign.
W. DUNN, captain royal artillery company.

We do not wonder much at this, when we remember that, on captain Hardy issuing his proclamation, calling on the people either to take the oath of allegiance, or their departure, three-fourths of the inhabitants did the former willingly.

"Without a blow struck," writes Ingersol, "part of Massachusetts passed under the British yoke, and so remained without the least resistance, till restored at the peace. It was the only part of the United States under undisputed British dominion. Two frontier fortresses Michilimacinac and Niagara, were surprised, captured, and forcibly held by the enemy during the war: and parts of Maryland and Virginia were overrun; but Massachusetts was the only State that acquiesced in such subjugation."

In writing his history, the narration of the events that occurred in this quarter must have been sadly trying to Mr. Ingersol. Having nothing to complain of on the part of the British, his only mode of accounting for the success of his Majesty's arms is by maligning the character of his own countrymen, and if his statements are worthy of credence we gather from them some curious facts as to the integrity of the great Republic in the year 1814.

"The Government of Massachusetts made no effort to prevent, if it *did not connive at, and rejoice* at its subjugation."

The same jealousy of Southern extension and opposition to the war paralyzed resistance to English invasion of Massachusetts, and part of the North East was almost peaceably and permanently reduced to English dominion, just before the Southwest defeated a much more formidable invasion there. It would take us, however, too long to follow Ingersol through all his lamentation over the falling away of the children of Massachusetts, we will, therefore, pass on to the second expedition which, under Sir John Sherbrooke, was directed against that part of Maine, lying to the eastward of the Penobscot river,—and which resulted in the temporary occupation of Castine, Belfast, and Machias, with the destruction of a large amount of shipping, including the United States frigate Adams,

of twenty-six guns, (eighteen pounds.) The proceedings will, however, be found at length in the official accounts which follow :—

From Lieutenant-General Sir J. C. Sherbrooke to Earl Bathurst.

Castine at the entrance of the Penobscot, Sept. 18, 1814.

MY LORD,—I have now the honour to inform your lordship, that after closing my despatch of the 25th ult., in which I mentioned my intention of proceeding to the Penobscot, Rear-admiral Griffiths and myself lost no time in sailing from Halifax, with such a naval force as he deemed necessary, and the troops as per margin (viz., 1st company of royal artillery, two rifle companies of the 7th battalion 60th regiment, 29th, 62nd, and 98th regiments), to accomplish the object we had in view.

Very early in the morning of the 30th, we fell in with the Rifleman sloop of war, when Captain Pearse informed us that the United States' frigate, the Adams, had got into the Penobscot, but from the apprehension of being attacked by our cruisers, if she remained at the entrance of the river, she had run up as high as Hampden, where she had landed her guns, and mounted them on shore for her protection.

On leaving Halifax, it was my original intention to have taken possession of Machias, on our way hither, but on receiving this intelligence, the admiral and myself were of opinion that no time should be lost in proceeding to our destination, and we arrived here very early on the morning of the 1st instant.

The fort of Castine, which is situated upon a peninsula of the eastern side of the Penobscot, near the entrance of that river, was summoned a little after sun-rise, but the American officer refused to surrender it, and immediately opened a fire from four 24-pounders upon a small schooner that had been sent with Lieutenant Colonel Nichols (commanding royal engineers) to reconnoitre the work.

Arrangements were immediately made for disembarking the troops, but before a landing could be effected, the enemy blew up the magazine, and escaped up the Majetaquadous river, carrying off in the boats with them two field-pieces.

As we had no means of ascertaining what force the Americans had on this peninsula, I landed a detachment of the royal artillery, with two rifle companies of the 60th and 98th regiments, under Col. Douglas, in the rear of it, with orders to secure the isthmus, and to take possession of the heights which command the town ; but I soon learned there were no regulars at Castine, except the party which had blown up the magazine and escaped, and that the militia, which were assembled there, had dispersed immediately upon our landing.

Rear-admiral Griffith and myself next turned our attention to obtaining possession of the Adams, or, if that could not be done, destroying her. The arrangement for this service having been made, the Rear-admiral entrusted the execution of it to Captain Barrie, royal navy, and as the co-operation of a land force was necessary, I directed Lieut.-Colonel John, with a detachment of artillery, the flank companies of the 29th, 62d, and 98th regiments, and one rifle company of the 60th, to accompany and co-operate with Captain Barrie on this occasion; but as Hampden is 27 miles above Castine, it appeared to me a necessary measure of precaution first to occupy a post on the western bank, which might afford support, if necessary, to the force going up the river, and at the same time prevent the armed population, which is very numerous to the southward and to the westward, from annoying the British in their operations against the Adams.

Upon inquiry, I found that Belfast, which is upon the high road leading from Hampden to Boston, and which perfectly commands the bridge, was likely to answer both these purposes, and I consequently directed Major General Gosselin to occupy that place with the 29th regiment, and maintain it till further orders.

As soon as this was accomplished, and the tide served, Rear-Admiral Griffith directed Captain Barrie to proceed to his destination, and the remainder of the troops were landed that evening at Castine.

Understanding that a strong party of the militia from the neighbouring township had assembled at about four miles from Castine, on the road leading to Bluehill, I sent out a strong patrole on the morning of the 2d, before day-break ; on arriving at the place, I was informed that the militia of the county was assembled there on the alarm guns being fired at the fort at Castine, upon our first appearance ; but that the main body had since dispersed, and gone to their respective homes. Some stragglers were, however, left, who fired upon our advanced guard, and then took to the woods ; a few of them were made prisoners. No intelligence having reached us from Captain Barrie, on Saturday night, I marched with about 700 men and two light field pieces, upon Buckstown, at 3 o'clock, on Sunday morning, the 4th instant, for the purpose of learning what progress he had made, and of affording him assistance, if required. This place is about 18 miles higher up the Penobscot than Castine, and on the eastern bank of the river. Rear-admiral Griffith accompanied me on this occasion, and as we had reason to believe that the light guns which had been taken from Castine were secreted in the neighbourhood of Buckstown, we threatened to destroy the town unless they were given up, and the two brass 6-pounders on travelling-carriages were in consequence brought to us in the course of the day, and are now in our possession.

At Buckstown, we received very satisfactory accounts of the success which had attended the force employed up the river. We learned that Captain Barrie had proceeded from Hampden up to Bangor; and the admiral sent an officer in a boat from Buckstown to communicate with him ; when, finding there was no necessity for the troops remaining longer at Buckstown, they marched back to Castine the next day.

Having ascertained that the object of the expedition up the Penobscot had been obtained, it was no longer necessary for me to occupy Belfast. I, therefore, on the evening of the 6th, directed Major-General Gosselin to embark the troops, and to join me here.

Machias being the only place now remaining where the enemy had a post between the Penobscot and Passamaquoddy bay, I ordered Lieutenant Colonel Pilkington to proceed with a detachment of royal artillery and the 29th regiment to occupy it; and as naval assistance was required, Rear-admiral Griffith directed Captain Parker, of the Tenedos, to co-operate with Lieutenant-colonel Pilkington upon this occasion.

On the morning of the 9th, Captain Barrie, with Lieutenant-colonel John, and the troops which had been employed with him up the Penobscot, returned to Castine. It seems the enemy blew up the Adams, on his strong position at Hampden being attacked; but all his artillery, two stands of colours, and a standard, with several merchant vessels, fell into our hands. This, I am happy to say, was accomplished with very little loss on our part; and your lordship will perceive, by the return sent herewith, that the only officer wounded in this affair is Captain Gall, of the 29th grenadiers.

Herewith I have the honor to transmit a copy of the report made to me by Lieut.-col. John on this occasion, in which your lordship will be pleased to observe that the Lieutenant-colonel speaks very highly of the gallantry and good conduct displayed by the troops upon this expedition, under very trying circumstances. And I beg to call your lordship's attention to the names of those officers upon whom Lieutenant-colonel John particularly bestows praise. The enterprise and intrepidity manifested by Lieutenant-colonel John, and the discipline and gallantry displayed by the troops under him, reflect great honour upon them, and demand my warmest acknowledgements; and I have to request your lordship will take a favorable opportunity of bringing the meritorious and successful services, performed by the troops employed on this occasion, under the view of his Royal Highness the Prince Regent.

As Rear-admiral Griffith will, no doubt, make a detailed report of the naval operations on this occasion, I forbear touching upon this subject, further than to solicit your lordship's attention to that part of Colonel John's report, in which he "attributes the success of this enterprise to the masterly arrangements of Captain Barrie, royal navy, who conducted it."

I have much pleasure in reporting to your lordship, that the most perfect unanimity and good understanding has prevailed between the naval and military branches of the service, during the whole progress of this expedition.

I feel it my duty to express, in the strongest terms, the great obligations I am under to Rear-admiral Griffith, for his judicious advice and ready co-operation on every occasion. And my thanks are likewise due to all the captains of the ships employed, for the assistance they have so willingly afforded the troops, and from which the happiest results have been experienced.

I have reason to be well satisfied with the gallantry and good conduct of the troops, and have to offer my thanks to Major-general Gosselin, Colonel Douglas, and the commanding officers of corps, for the alacrity shown by them, and strict discipline which has been maintained.

To the heads of departments, and to the officers of the general and of my personal staff, I am much indebted for the zealous manner in which they have discharged their respective duties.

Major Addison, my military secretary, will have the honor of delivering this despatch. He has been with me during the whole of these operations, and is well enabled to afford your lordship any information you may require.

I have entrusted the colours and standard taken from the enemy to Major Addison, who will receive your lordship's commands respecting the further disposal of them; and I take the liberty of recommending him, as a deserving officer, to your lordship's protection.—I have, &c.,

J. C. SHERBROOKE.

N.B.—The returns of killed, wounded, and missing, and of artillery, and of ordnance stores taken, are inclosed.

From Lieutenant-Colonel John to Lieutenant General Sir J. C. Sherbrooke.

BANGOR, on the Penobscot river, Sept. 3, 1814.

SIR,—In compliance with your Excellency's orders of the 1st instant, I sailed from Castine with the detachment of royal artillery, the flank companies of the 29th, 62nd, and 98th regiments, and one rifle company of the 7th battalion 60th regiment, which composed the force your Excellency did me the honour to place under my command, for the purpose of co-operating with Captain Barrie, of the Royal Navy in an expedition up this river.

On the morning of the 2d, having proceeded above the town of Frankfort, we discovered some of the enemy on their march towards Hampden, by the eastern shore, which induced me to order Brevet-major Crosdaile, with a detachment of the 98th, and some riflemen of the 60th regiment, under Lieutenant Wallace, to land and intercept them, which was accomplished; and that detachment of the enemy (as I have since learned) were prevented from joining the main body assembled at Hampden. On this occasion the enemy had one man killed, and some wounded. Major Crosdaile re-embarked without any loss. We arrived off Bald Head cove, three miles distant from Hampden, about five o'clock that evening, when Capt. Barrie agreed with me in determining to land the troops immediately. Having discovered that the enemy's piquets were advantageously posted on the north side of the cove, I directed Brevet-major Riddle, with the grenadiers of the 62nd, and Captain Ward, with the rifle company of the 60th, to dislodge them, and take up that ground, which duty was performed under Major Riddle's directions, in a most complete and satisfactory manner, by about seven o'clock; and before ten at night, the whole of the troops, including 80 marines under Captain Carter, (whom Captain Barrie had done me the honour to attach to my command,) were landed and bivouacked for the night, during which it rained incessantly. We got under arms at five o'clock this morning, the rifle-company forming the advance under Captain Ward; Brevet-major Keith, with the light company of the 62nd, bringing up the rear, and the detachment of marines, under Captain Carter, moving upon my flanks, while Captain Barrie, with the ships and gun-boats under his command, advanced at the same time up the river, on my right,

towards Hampden. In addition to the detachment of royal artillery under Lieutenant Garston, Captain Barrie had landed one 6-pounder, a 5½-inch howitzer, and a rocket apparatus, with a detachment of sailors under Lieutenant Symonds, Botely, and Slade, and Mr. Sparling, master of his Majesty's ship Bulwark.

The fog was so thick, it was impossible to form a correct idea of the features of the country, or to reconnoitre the enemy, whose number were reported to be 1,400, under the command of Brigadier-general Blake. Between seven and eight o'clock, our skirmishers in advance were so sharply engaged with the enemy, as to induce me to send forward one-half of the light company of the 29th regiment, under Captain Coaker, to their support. The column had not advanced much further, before I discovered the enemy drawn out in line, occupying a very strong and advantageous position in front of the town of Hampden, his left flanked by a high hill commanding the road and river, on which were mounted several heavy pieces of cannon; his right extending considerably beyond our left, resting upon a strong point d'appui, with an 18-pounder and some light field-pieces in advance of his centre, so pointed as completely to rake the road, and a narrow bridge at the foot of a hill, by which we were obliged to advance upon his position. As soon as he perceived our column approaching, he opened a very heavy and continued fire of grape and musketry upon us; we, however, soon crossed the bridge, deployed, and charged up the hill to get possession of his guns, one of which we found had already fallen into the hands of Captain Ward's riflemen in advance. The enemy's fire now began to slacken, and we pushed on rapidly, and succeeded in driving him at all points from his position; while Captain Coaker, with the light company of the 29th, had gained possession of the hill on the left, from whence it was discovered that the Adams frigate was on fire, and that the enemy had deserted the battery which defended her.

We were now in complete possession of the enemy's position above, and Captain

Barrie with the gun-boats had secured that below the hill. Upon this occasion 20 pieces of cannon fell into our hands, of the naval and military force, the return of which I enclose ; * after which Captain Barrie and myself determined on pursuing the enemy towards Bangor, which place we reached without opposition ; and here two brass 3-pounders, and three stands of colours, fell into our possession. Brigadier-general Blake also in this town, surrendered himself prisoner ; and, with other prisoners to the amount of 121, were admitted to their paroles. Eighty prisoners taken at Hampden are in our custody. The loss sustained by the enemy I have not had in my power correctly to ascertain ; report states it to be from 30 to 40 in killed, wounded, and missing.

Our own loss, I am happy to add, is but small; viz., 1 rank and file, killed ; 1 captain, 7 rank and file, wounded; 1 rank and file, missing. Captain Gell, of the 29th, was wounded when leading the column, which deprived me of his active and useful assistance ; but, I am happy to add, he is recovering.

I cannot close this despatch without mentioning, in the highest terms, all the troops placed under my command. They have merited my highest praise for their zeal and gallantry, which were conspicuous in the extreme. I feel most particularly indebted to Brevet-major Riddall, of the 62nd regiment, second in command; to Brevet-major Keith, of the same regiment ; Brevet-major Crosdaile and Captain M'Pherson, of the 98th ; Captains Gell and Coaker, of the 29th ; and Captain Ward, of the 7th battalion 60th regiment. The royal artillery was directed in the most judicious manner by Lieutenant Garston, from whom I derived the ablest support. I cannot speak too highly of Captain Carter and the officers and marines under his directions. He moved them in the ablest manner to the annoyance of the enemy, and so as to meet my fullest approval.

Nothing could exceed the zeal and perseverance of Lieutenants Symonds, Botely, and Slade, and Mr. Sparling, of the Royal Navy, with the detachment of seamen under their command.

From Captain Barrie I have received the ablest assistance and support; and it is to his masterly arrangement of the plan that I feel indebted for its success. Nothing could be more cordial than the co-operation of the naval and military forces on this service in every instance.

Captain Carnegie, of the Royal Navy, who most handsomely volunteered his services with this expedition, was in action with the troops at Hampden ; and I feel most particularly indebted to him for his exertions and the assistance he afforded me on this occasion. I am also greatly indebted to Lieut. Du Chatelet, of the 7th battalion, 60th regiment, who acted as major of brigade to the troops, in which capacity he rendered me very essential service.

I have the honour, &c.,
HENRY JOHN, Lt. Col.

---

* *Return of Ordnance and Stores taken.*
CASTINE, Sept. 10, 1814.

Guns—4 iron 24-pounders, 27 iron (ship) 18-pounders, 4 12-pounders, 4 brass 3-pounders.

Carriages—4 traversing 24-pounders, 8 standing 18-pounders, 2 travelling 12-pounders with limbers, 4 travelling 3-pounders with limbers.

Sponges—8 24-pounders, 20 18-pounders, 2 12-pounders, 4 3-pounders.

Ladles—2 24-pounders, 3 12-pounders, 1 3-pounder.

Wadhooks—2 24-pounder, 3 12-pounders, 1 8-pounder.

Shot—236 round 24-pounders, 500 round 18-pounders. 1 ammunition-waggon, 1 ammunition-cart, 12 common handspikes, 40 barrels of powder.

Wads—20 24-pounders, 70 18-pounders.

N.B. The Magazine in fort Castine was blown up by the enemy.

The vessel on board of which the powder was, ran on shore, and the whole destroyed.

Eleven of the 18-pounders were destroyed by order of Lieutenant-Colonel John, not having time to bring them off.

GEORGE CRAWFORD, Major,
Commanding Royal Artillery.
Lieut. Gen. Sir J. C. Sherbrooke.

*From Lieutenant-colonel Pilkington to Lieuten-
ant-general sir J. C. Sherbrooke.*

Machias, Sept. 14, 1814.

Sir,

I have the honour to acquaint your excellency, that I sailed from Penobscot bay,
with the brigade you were pleased to place
under my command, consisting of a detachment of royal artillery, with a howitzer, the
battalion companies of the 29th regiment,
and a party of the 7th battalion of the 60th
foot, on the morning of thr 9th instant; and
arrived at Buck's harbor, about 10 miles
from this place, on the following evening.

As the enemy fired several alarm guns on
our approaching the shore, it was evident
he was apprehensive of an attack: I therefore deemed it expedient to disembark the
troops with as little delay as possible; and
captain Hyde Parker, commanding the naval
force, appointed captain Stanfell to superintend this duty, and it was executed by that
officer with the utmost promptitude and
decision.

Upon reaching the shore, I ascertained
that there was only a pathway through the
woods by which we could advance and take
Fort O'Brien and the battery in reverse;
and as the guns of these works commanded
the passage of the river, upon which the
town is situated, I decided upon possessing
ourselves of them, if practicable, during the
night.

We moved forward at ten o'clock P.M. and,
after a most tedious and harrassing march,
only arrived near to the fort at break of
day, although the distance does not exceed
five miles.

The advancing guard, which consisted of
two companies of the 29th regiment, and a
detachment of riflemen of the 60th regiment,
under Major Tod, of the former crops, immediately drove in the enemy's piquets,
and upon pursuing him closely, found the
fort had been evacuated, leaving their colours, about five minutes before we entered.
Within it, and the battery, there are two 24-
pounders, three 18-pounders, several dismounted guns, and a block-house. The
party which escaped amounted to about 70
men of the 40th regiment of American infantry, and 30 of the embodied militia; the
retreat was so rapid that I was not enabled
to take any prisoners. I understand there
were a few wounded, but they secreted themselves in the wood.

Having secured the fort, we lost no time
in advancing upon Machias, which was tak-
en without any resistance; and also two
field-pieces.

The boats of the squadron, under the command of lieutenant Bouchier, of the royal
navy, and the royal marines, under lieutenant Welchmen were detached to the eastern
side of the river, and were of essential service in taking two field-pieces in that
quarter.

Notwithstanding that the militia were not
assembled to any extent in the vicinity of
the town, I was making the necessary arrangements to advance into the interior of
the country, when I received a letter from
brigadier-general Brewer, commanding the
district, wherein he engages that the milita
forces within the county of Washington shall
not bear arms, or in any way serve against
his Britannic majesty during the present
war. A similar offer having been made by
the civil officers and principal citizens of the
county, a cessation of arms was agreed upon,
and the county of Washington has passsed
under the dominion of his Britanic majesty.

I beg leave to congratulate you upon the
importance of this accession of territory
which has been wrested from the enemy;
it embraces about 100 miles of sea-coast, and
includes that intermediate tract of country
which separates the province of New Brunswick from Lower Canada.

We have taken 26 pieces of ordnance, (serviceable and unserviceable,) with a propor-
ion of arms and ammunition, returns* of

---

* *Return of Ordnance, Arms, Ammunition,
&c., taken at Machias by the troops under
the command of Lieutenant-Colonel Pilkington, 11th September, 1814.*

*Ordnance,—Fort O'Brien,—2 18-pounders,
mounted on garrison carriages, complete: 1
18-pounder carronade, mounted on garrison
carriage, complete; 1 serviceable dismounted
24-pounder; 1 dismounted serviceable 18-
pounder carronade.*

which are enclosed; and I have the pleasing satisfaction to add, that this service has been effected without the loss of a man on our part.

I cannot refrain from expressing, in the strongest manner, the admirable steadiness and good conduct of the 29th regiment, under major Hodge. The advance, under major Tod, are also entitled to my warmest thanks.

A detachment or 30 seamen from his majesty's ship Bacchante, under Mr. Bruce, master's mate, were attached to the royal artillery, under the command of lieutenant Daniel, of that corps, for the purpose of dragging the howitzer, as no other means could be procured to bring it forward; and to their unwearied exertions, and the judicious arrangement of lieutenant Daniel, I am indebted for having a 5½ inch howitzer conveyed through a country the most difficult of access I ever witnessed.

To captain Parker, of his majesty's ship Tenedos, who commanded the squadron, I feel every obligation; and I can assure you the most cordial understanding has subsisted between the two branches of the service.

I have the honour to be, &c.

A. PILKINGTON,
Lieut.-Col. Dep. Adj.-Gen.

To Lieut.-Gen. Sir J. C. Sherbrooke, K.B. &c.

From Rear-Admiral Griffith to Vice-Admiral Cochrane.

H.M.S. Endymion, off Castine, entrance of the Penobscot river, Sept. 9, 1814.

SIR,—My letter of the 23rd of August from Halifax, by the Rover, will have made you acquainted with my intention of accompanying the expedition, then about to proceed under the command of his Excellency Sir John Coape Sherbrooke, K.B., for this place.

I have now the honour to inform you, that I put to sea on the 26th ultimo, with the ships and sloop named in the margin,* and ten sail of transports, having the troops on board, and arrived off the Metinicus Islands on the morning of the 31st, where I was joined by the Bulwark, Tenedos, Rifleman, Peruvian, and Pictou. From Captain Pearse, of the Rifleman, I learned that the United States' frigate Adams had, a few days before, got into Penobscot: but not considering herself in safety there, had gone on to Hampden, a place 27 miles higher up the river, where her guns had been landed, and the position was fortifying for her protection.

Towards evening, the wind being fair and the weather favourable, the fleet made sail up the Penobscot Bay, Captain Parker in the Tenedos leading. We passed between the Metinicus and Green Islands about midnight; and steering through the channel formed by the Fox's Island and Owl's head, ran up to the eastward of Long Island, and found ourselves at day-light in the morning in sight of the fort and town of Castine. As we approached, some show of resistance was made, and a few shots were fired; but the fort was soon after abandoned and blown up. At about 8 A.M. the men of war and transports were anchored a little to the northward of the peninsula of Castine, and the smaller vessels taking a station nearer in for covering the landing, the troops were put on shore, and took possession of the town and works without opposition.

The general wishing to occupy a post at Belfast, on the western side of the bay, (through which the high road from Boston runs,) for the purpose of cutting off all communication with that side of the country,

Point Battery—2 24-pounders, mounted on garrison carriages, complete.

East Machias—2 brass 4-pounders, mounted, and harness, complete.

Machias—2 iron 4-pounders, on travelling carriages, complete; 5 24-pounders, 10 18-pounders, rendered partly unserviceable by the enemy, and completely destroyed by us.

Total—26.

Arms—164 muskets, 99 bayonets, 100 pouches. 41 belts, 2 drums.

Ammunition—20 barrels of serviceable gunpowder.
75 paper cartridges filled for 18 and 24-pounders.
2,938 musket-ball cartridges.
3 barrels of grape and case-shot.
553 round shot for 18 and 24-pounders.
6 kegs of gunpowder, 25lbs. each.
28 paper cartridges filled for 4-pounders.

J. DANIEL, Lieut. Royal Artil.

* Dragon, Endymion, Bacchante, and Sylph.

the Bacchante and Rifleman were detached with the troops destined for this service, and quiet possession was taken, and held, of that town, as long as was thought necessary.

Arrangements were immediately made for attacking the frigate at Hampden, and the General having proffered every military assistance, 600 picked men, under the command of Lieutenant-Colonel John, of the 60th regiment, were embarked the same afternoon, on board his Majesty's sloops Peruvian and Sylph, and a small transport. To this force were added the marines of the Dragon, and as many armed boats from the squadron as was thought necessary for disembarking the troops and covering their landing, and the whole placed under the command of Captain Barrie, of the Dragon; and the Lieutenant-Colonel made sail up the river at 6 o'clock that evening.

I have the honour to enclose captain Barrie's account of his proceedings; and, taking into consideration the enemy's force, and the formidable strength of his position, too much praise cannot be given him, and the officers and men under his command, for the judgment, decision, and gallantry, with which this little enterprise has been achieved.

So soon as accounts were received from Captain Barrie, that the Adams was destroyed, and the force assembled for her protection dispersed, the troops stationed at Belfast were embarked, and arrangements made for sending them to take possession of Machias, the only place occupied by the enemy's troops, between this and Passamaquoddy bay. I directed Captain Parker, of his Majesty's ship Tenedos, to receive on board Lieutenant-Colonel Pilkington, deputy adjutant general, who is appointed to command, and a small detachment of artillery and riflemen, and to take under his command the Bacchante, Rifleman, and Pictou schooner, and proceed to the attack of that place. He sailed on the 6th instant, and most likely, by this time, the troops are in possession of it. After destroying the defences, they are directed to return here.

The inhabitants of several townships east of this, have sent deputations here to tender their submission to the British authority; and such of them as could give reasonable security, that their arms would be used only for the protection of their persons and property, have been allowed to retain them. This indulgence was absolutely necessary, in order to secure the quiet and unoffending against violence and outrage from their less peaceable neighbours, and for the maintenance of the peace and tranquillity of the country. All property on shore, *bona fide* belonging to the inhabitants of the country in our possession, has been respected. All public property, and all property afloat, have been confiscated.

Sir John Sherbrooke, conceiving it to be of importance that the government should be informed without delay, of our successes here, has requested that a vessel of war may take his despatches to England.

I have, in compliance with his wishes, appropriated the Martin for that service, and Captain Senhouse will take a copy of this letter to the Secretary of the Admiralty.

I have the honour to be, &c.,

EDWARD GRIFFITH.

To Vice-admiral the Hon.

Sir Alex. Cochrane, K.B., &c.

CHAPTER XXII.

Before giving Captain Barrie's letter and the articles of capitula- New England feeling towards Great Britain. tion, which Capt. Parker found the inhabitants most ready to accede to, it will be well to adduce a few instances to prove how ready to break the connexion with the United States, were the very colonies which had set the example of rebellion in a former war, and by whose gallant and vigorous exertions the independence of a great country was secured.

A Boston Journal, the *Sentinel*, stated that "Major Putnam, Captains Fillebrown and Varnum, arrived under parole from Eastport, and speak highly of the good conduct of the British regiment there, *so abused by the Virginians for their reputed misconduct at Hampton*. The soldiers behave remarkably well there ; yet this is the corps said to have committed such outrages at Hampton."

At Dorchester from Ingersol's own testimony we learn that "when the 4th of July, 1814, was celebrated at Dorchester, where Washington commanded in 1775, one of the sentiments drunk was "our country united to Britain, and happy till the *pestilence of democracy* poisoned and blighted it."

Again it was recommended by the *Salem Gazette* that all imposts, taxes, and proceeds of captures within the state, that might go into the national treasury, be retained ; that the prisoners of war then in the state should be exchanged for such of her own citizens as were in the hands of the enemy, and, finally, that peace should be made with Great Britain, so as to leave the burden of the war on the more belligerent States, and by these means to free Massachussets from the burdens which oppressed her.

After citing these instances of loyalty, Ingersol has the inconsistency and assurance on the very next page to assert "that the hearts of the common people of New England remained American."

This was not all, however, for Timothy Pickering, Member of Congress, on the 16th March, 1814, publicly recommended that no one should give his vote "to redeem the paper money, exchequers, bills, or other loans to continue this unnecessary and iniquitous war."

The remaining incidents connected with the attacks on the American coast will be found embodied in Captain Barrie's despatch and the articles of capitulation signed.

After our expose of American feeling, we think it unnecessary to bring forward more testimony on two points. The first that, our assertion at the beginning of this history, as to the war being unpopular and forced on the country by the administration was correct ; secondly, that the evidence as to the behaviour of the troops, taken from American sources, goes far to disprove the

23

accusations made against them as regarding their conduct at Havre de Grace and Georgetown.

The despatch of Captain Barrie and the articles of capitulation are all that are necessary to place the reader in full possession of every fact of importance connected with Captain Parker's and Pilkinton's expedition.

From Captain Barrie to Rear Admiral Griffith.
H.M. sloop Sylph, off Bangor, in the Penobscot, Sept. 3, 1814.

SIR,—Having received on board the ships named in the margin,* a detachment of 20 men of the royal artillery, with one 5½-inch howitzer, commanded by Lieutenant Garsten; a party of 80 marines, commanded by Captain Carter, of the Dragon; the flank companies of the 29th, 62d, and 98th regiments, under the command of Captains Gell and Caker; Majors Riddell, Keith, and Croasdaile, and Captain Macpherson; also, a rifle company of the 7th battalion of the 60th regiment, commanded by Capt. Ward; and the whole under the orders of Lieutenant-Colonel John, of the 60th regiment; I proceeded, agreeably to your order, with the utmost despatch, up the Penobscot. Light variable winds, a most intricate channel, of which we were perfectly ignorant, and thick foggy weather, prevented my arriving off Frankfort before 2 P.M. of the 2d inst. Here Colonel John and myself thought it advisable to send a message to the inhabitants; and having received their answer, we pushed on towards Hampden, where we received intelligence that the enemy had strongly fortified himself. On our way up, several troops were observed on the east side of the river, making for Brewer; these were driven into the woods, without any loss on our side, by a party under the orders of Major Croasdaile, and the guns from the boats. The enemy had one killed and several wounded.

At 5 P.M. of the 2d inst., we arrived off Ball's-head Cove, distant three miles from Hampden. Colonel John and myself landed

* H.M.S. Peruvian and Sylph, Dragon tender, and the Harmony transport.

on the south side of the Cove to reconnoitre the ground, and obtain intelligence. Having gained the hills, we discovered the enemy's piquets advantageously posted near the highway leading to Hampden, on the north side of the cove.

We immediately determined to land 150 men, under Major Riddall, to drive in the piquets, and take up their ground. This object was obtained by 7 o'clock; and notwithstanding every difficulty, the whole of the troops were landed on the north side of the cove by ten o'clock; but it was found impossible to land the artillery at the same place. The troops bivouacked on the ground taken possession of by Major Riddall. It rained incessantly during the night. At day-break this morning, the fog cleared away for about a quarter of an hour, which enabled me to reconnoitre the enemy by water; and I found a landing-place for the artillery about two-thirds of a mile from Ball's-head. Off this place the troops halted till the artillery were mounted; and by six the whole advanced towards Hampden.

The boats under the immediate command of Lieutenant Pedler, the first of the Dragon, agreeably to a previous arrangement with Colonel John, advanced in line with the right flank of the army. The Peruvian, Sylph, Dragon's tender, and Harmony transport, were kept a little in arrear in reserve.

Our information stated the enemy's force at 1400 men, and he had chosen a most excellent position on a high hill. About a quarter of a mile to the southward of Adams' frigate, he had mounted eight 18-pounders. This fort was calculated to command both the highway, by which our troops had to advance, and the river. On a wharf close to the Adams, he had mounted fifteen 18-pounders, which completely commanded the river, which at this place, is not above three cables' lengths wide, and the land on each side is high and well wooded.

A rocket-boat, under my immediate direction, but manœuvred by Mr. Ginton, gunner, and Mr. Small, midshipman, of the Dragon, was advanced about a quarter of a mile a-head of the line of boats.

So soon as the boats got within gun-shot, the enemy opened his fire upon them from the hill and wharf, which was warmly returned. Our rockets were generally well-directed, and evidentally threw the enemy into confusion. Meantime, our troops stormed the hill with the utmost gallantry. Before the boats got within good grape-shot distance of the wharf-battery, the enemy set fire to the Adams, and he ran from his guns the moment our troops carried the hill.

I joined the army about ten minutes after this event. Colonel John and myself immediately determined to leave a sufficient force in possession of the hill, and to pursue the enemy, who was then in sight on the Bangor road, flying at full speed. The boats and ships pushed up the river, preserving their original position with the army. The enemy was too nimble for us, and most of them escaped into the woods on our left.

On approching Bangor, the inhabitants, who had opposed us at Hampden, threw off their military character; and, as magistrates, select men, &c. made an unconditional surrender of the town. Here, the pursuit stopped. About two hours afterwards, brigadier-general Blake came into the town to deliver himself as a prisoner; the general, and other prisoners, amounting to 191, were admitted to their parole.

Enclosed, I have the honor to forward you lists of the vessels we have captured or destroyed, and other necessary reports. I am happy to inform you, our loss consists only of one seaman, belonging to the Dragon, killed; captain Gell, of the 29th, and seven privates wounded; one rank and file missing.

I cannot close my report, without expressing my highest admiration of the very gallant conduct of Colonel John, and the officers and soldiers under his command; for, exclusive of the battery before-mentioned, they had difficulties to contend with on their left, which did not fall under my observation, as the enemy's field-pieces in that direction were masked. The utmost cordiality existed between the two services; and I shall ever feel obliged to colonel John for his ready co-operation in every thing that was proposed.

The officer and men bore the privations, inseparable from our confined means of accommodation, with a cheerfulness that entitles them to my warmest thanks.

Though the enemy abandoned his batteries before the ships could be brought to act against them, yet I am not less obliged to captains Kippen and Dickens, of the Peruvian and Sylph; acting-lieutenant Pearson, who commanded the Dragon's tender; lieutenant Woodin, of the Dragon; and Mr. Barnett, master of the Harmony; their zeal and indefatigable exertions in bringing up their vessels, through the most intricate navigation, were eminently conspicuous. Colonel John speaks highly in praise of Captain Carter, and the detachment of royal marines under his orders; and also of the seamen attached to the artillery, under the command of lieutenants Simmonds. Motley, L. State and Mr. Sparling, master of the Bulwark.

I have, on other occassions of service, found it a pleasing part of my duty to commend the services of lieutenant Pedler, first of the Dragon; in this instance, he com manded the boat part of the expedition most fully to my satisfaction; he was ably seconded by by lieutenants Perceval, of the Tenedos, and Ormond, of the Endymion; and Mr. Ansel, master's mate of the Dragon; this last gentleman has passed his examination nearly five years, and is an active officer well worthy of your patronage; but, in particularising him, I do not mean to detract from the other petty-officers and seamen employed in the boats; for they all most zealously performed their duty, and are equally entitled to my warmest acknowledgements. I am also most particularly indebted to the active and zealous exertions of lieutenant Carnegie, who was a volunteer on this occasion.

I can form no estimate of the enemy's absolute loss. From different stragglers I learn, that, exclusive of killed and missing, upwards of 30 lay wounded in the woods.

I have the honor to be, &c.

ROBERT BARRIE,
Capt. of H.M.S. Dragon.

ARTICLES OF CAPITULATION.

Article I. The officers and troops of the

United States, at present on Moose island, are to surrender themselves prisoners of war, and are to deliver up the forts, buildings, arms, ammunition, stores, and effects, with exact inventories thereof, belonging to the American government; and they are thereby transferred to his Britannic majesty, in the same manner and possession, as has been held heretofore by the American government.

Art. II. The garrison of the island shall be prisoners of war, until regularly exchanged; they will march out of the fort with the honors of war, and pile their arms at such place as will be appointed for that purpose; the officers will be permitted to proceed to the United States on their parole.

———

The next event of importance, in order of date, was the descent on Washington, an affair, which, although strictly a retaliation for excessive and manifold atrocities, was made the pretext for the utterance of the vilest slander by the Federalists, against not only the British army, but the entire nation. We trust, however, to bring forward such evidence, as to the conduct of the British in this affair, as will satisfy the impartial reader, both as to the falsehoods put forth by part of the American press, and the absurdities uttered in the British House of Commons, and which carried, until disproved considerable weight with a large portion of the people.

Capture of Washington, and destruction of Public Buildings.

Nor was this all; American writers have not scrupled to declare that peace was indefinitely postponed " in order that the British Government might by its military and naval instruments, deliberately commit so atrocious a violation of civilized warfare."

Says Ingersol, " The unknown caitiff who attempted to assassinate General Ross is much less detestable and unpardonable than the member of the Government, Ministry, Monarch, Regent, or whoever the miscreant may be, guilty of the infinitely greater outrage of postponing peace for several months, after the causes of war had ceased, in order to devastate the public edifices of an enemy's capital."

Without adducing one iota of proof, Ingersol makes this bold assertion, and, unsupported by evidence, he bases the whole of his reasoning on a fact so injurious to the character of the British nation. Fortunately, however, we have evidence, that the Americans had been warned of this descent being intended so far back as the 26th of June, and we know from Armstrong that even at that date preparations for the defence of the capital of the nation were commenced. That these preparations were not more complete and formidable, appears incomprehensible.

Jomini in his " summary of the art of war" when dwelling on this subject says "The English performed an enterprise which may be ranged amongst the most extraordinary ——that against the capital of the United States of America. To the great astonishment of the world, a handful of seven or eight thousand English were seen to descend in the midst of a state of ten millions of souls, penetrate a considerable distance, besiege the capital, and destroy the public establishments there; results which history may be searched in vain for another example of."

It will be well to remark that Jomini in his comments dwells not on the infraction of the recognized principles of civilized warfare, but upon the incomprehensible state in which the Americans must have been to permit a handful of men to commit such devastation in the presence of so vastly superior a force.

Before entering on the expedition, it will be as well to get rid of one charge that was made by many American journals against the commanding officers of the fleet then lying on the Chesapeake, but no proof of which has ever been attempted.

During the whole period that the English fleet were on the waters of the Chesapeake, the officers, who were sent on shore to procure provisions and water, were constantly beset by crowds of fugitive slaves, who implored to be rescued from a state of bondage. These appeals, were too piteous, always to be disregarded, and the consequence was that hundreds of them were taken on board the British vessels, from whence they were mostly transported to Halifax, a few being landed at Jamaica. This circumstance it was that afforded an excuse for the assertion of the American Government, that "the British, after receiving the negroes, shipped the wretches to the West Indies, where they were sold as slaves, for the benefit of British officers."

One of their organs the "*Norfolk Herald*" even announced that "To take cattle or other stock, would be consistent with the usages of civilized warfare; but to take negroes, who are human beings; to tear them for ever from their kindred and connexions is what we should never expect from a Christian nation, especially one that has done so much to abolish the slave trade. There are negroes in Virginia, and, we believe, in all the Southern States, who have their interests and affections as strongly engrafted in their hearts, as the whites, and who feel the sacred ties of filial, parental, and conjugal affection, equally strong, and who are warmly attached to their owners and the scenes of their nativity."

James very correctly notices this as one of the most inadvertent but happiest pieces of satire extant; and so it must appear to all. Even at the present time, no later than two days back, a New Orleans journal, the "*Creole*" contained an advertisement offering to purchase slaves from any quarter, and it is impossible to take up a Southern paper without the eye being offended and the senses disgusted with the accounts of slave sales—the attractions of a young quadroon being dwelt on and puffed with as much minuteness as the points of a horse. The revelations of the horrors of American slavery are so patent, and have excited such universal horror, that it is almost unnecessary to dwell on the unparalleled impudence which could assert that the slaves were warmly attached to their masters—slave owners selling their children, and the mother of their children: but the bare thought of these things is sickening, yet the very journals containing these advertisements were the foremost to accuse the British of having violated "the dictates of christianity and civilization."

The question, too, may be put in an-other form. It was submitted to the House of Representatives, by Mr. Fish of Vermont, and resolved, "That the committee on public lands be instructed to enquire into the expediency of giving to each deserter from the British army, during the present war, one hundred acres of the public lands, such deserter actually settling the same.

After this specimen of national honor, and considering what slavery was then in the United States, the position taken by the American press, appears the more extraordinary. The assertion that slaves were dragged away by force with the greatest cruelty is simply absurd; it was with the greatest difficulty that the British commander could victual his fleet, lying as it did on an enemy's shore, and it was not very probable that he would suffer his difficulties in that respect to be increased by the addition of loads of negroes, whom, to make profit on it, it would be necessary to feed and keep in good condition. The only marvel is that the British Commander should have allowed his feelings of humanity to overstep the strict line of duty, inasmuch as by rescuing those unhappy victims from slavery he was seriously inconveniencing the crews of the vessels under his command, and so crowding his ships as to render them almost unfit for going into action. To return, however, to the expedition.

The President of the United States, in formed officially since Preparations made by U. States Government. the 26th of June, of the approaching storm, lost no time in determining to prepare; accordingly the heads of departments and the Attorney General, were convened on the 1st July, and it was then decided, first, "that ten or twelve thousand draughts from the militia of Pennsylvania, Maryland, and Virginia, should be held in reserve in their respective States, ready to march at a moment's warning.

Secondly. That not less than two, nor more than three thousand of the afore-mentioned draughts, should be assembled for immediate service, at some central point between the Potomac and Baltimore.

Thirdly. That the militia of the District of Columbia, (we omit detail) making an aggregate of three thousand combatants, should constitute a corps at all times disposable, under the direction of the commanding General."

That these resolutions were not mere words, we have General Armstrong's testimony, who says: "Nor will it appear from the report made by the Congressional Committee of Inquiry, that any time was lost in giving effect to these measures, so far as their execution depended on the War Department. "On the 2nd July," says the Report, "the tenth military district was constituted, and the command given to General Winder. On the 4th, a requisition on the States for ninety-three thousand five hundred men was issued. On the 14th, the Governors of Pennsylvania and Virginia, acknowledged the receipt of the requisition, and promised promptitude. On the 10th, the Governor of Maryland was served with a copy of the requisition, and took measures to comply with it. On the 12th, General Winder was authorised, in case of either menaced or actual invasion, to call into service the whole of the Maryland quota (six thousand men), and on the 18th, five thousand from Pennsylvania and two thousand

from Virginia, making an aggregate (the regular infantry, cavalry, marines, flotilla men, and district militia included) of sixteen thousand six hundred men."

When we run over these great preparations, Jomini's surprise, that a handful of men should have been permitted to execute what they did, is natural, and after the admissions made by Armstrong as to their force, it is perfectly absurd in American writers to pretend that, at Bladensburg, they were conquered by superior members, or that the descents on Alexandria and Washington were not made, literally as Jomini expresses it, by a handful of men, in the face of a body outnumbering them three-fold.

Many of these reports have been drawn from Winder's despatches, but it was only to be expected that a General in Winder's position would attempt to represent matters in the most favorable light.

The two despatches which follow will give the reader a clear insight into all the plans and details of the expedition, and General Winder's despatch, which will be found in a note* will furnish a very good instance of the truth of an American bulletin.

From Brigadier-General Winder to the Secretary at War.

SIR,   Baltimore, Aug. 27, 1814.

When the enemy arrived at the mouth of the Potomac, of all the militia which I had been authorized to assemble, there were but about 1700 in the field, 13 to 1400 under General Stransbury near this place, and 250 at Bladensburg, under lieutenant-colonel Kramer; the slow progress of draft, and the imperfect organization, with the ineffectiveness of the laws to compel them to turn out, rendered it impossible to have procured more.

The militia of this state and of the contiguous parts of Virginia and Pennsylvania were called out *en masse*, but the former militia law of Pennsylvania had expired the 1st of June, or July, and the one adopted in its place is not to take effect in organizing the militia before October. No aid, therefore, had been received from that state.

After all the force that could be put at my disposal in that short time, and making such dispositions as I deemed best calculated to present the most respectable force at whatever point the enemy might strike, I was enabled (by the most active and harrassing movements of the troops) to interpose before the enemy at Bladensburg, about 5000 men, including 350 regulars and commodore Barney's command. Much the largest portion of this force arrived

on the ground when the enemy were in sight, and were disposed to support, in the best manner, the position which General Stansbury had taken. They had barely reached the ground before the action commenced, which was about one o'clock P. M. of the 24th instant, and continued about an hour. The contest was not as obstinately maintained as could have been desired, but was, by parts of the troops, sustained with great spirit and with prodigious effect; and had the whole of our force been equally firm, I am induced to believe that the enemy would have been rapulsed, notwithstanding all the disadvantages under which we fought. The artillery from Baltimore supported by major Pinkney's rifle battalion, and a part of captain Doughty's from the navy-yard, were in advance to command the pass of the bridge at Bladensburg, and played upon the enemy, as I have since learned, with very destructive effect. But the rifle troops were obliged, after some time, to retire, and of course the artillery. Superior numbers, however, rushed upon them, and made their retreat necessary, not, however, without great loss on the part of the enemy. Major Pinkney received a severe wound in his right arm after he had retired to the left flank of Stansbury's brigade. The right and centre of Stansbury's brigade, consisting of lieutenant-colonel Ragan's and Shulers regiments, generally, gave way very soon afterwards, with the

From Major-general Ross to Earl Bathurst.

Tonnant, in the Patuxent,

Aug. 30, 1814.

My Lord,

I have the honor to communicate to your lordship, that on the 24th instant, after defeating the army of the United States on that day, the troops under my command entered and took possession of the city of Washington.

It was determined between Sir Alexander Cochrane and myself, to disembark the army at the village of Benedict, on the right bank of the Patuxent, with the intention of co-operating with rear-admiral Cockburn, in an attack upon a flotilla of the enemy's gun-boats, under the command of commodore Barney. On the 20th instant, the army commenced its march, having landed the previous day without opposition; on the 21st it reached Nottingham, and on the 22d moved on to Upper Marlborough, a few miles distant from Pig point, on the Patuxent, where admiral Cockburn fell in with, and defeated the flotilla, taking and destroying the whole. Having advanced within 16 miles of Washington, and ascertained the force of the enemy to be such as might authorize an attempt at carrying his capital, I determined to make it, and accordingly put the troops in movement on the evening of the 23rd. A corps of about 1200 men appeared to oppose us, but retired after firing a few shots. On the 24th, the troops resumed their march, and reached Bladensburg, a village situate on the left bank of the eastern branch of the Potomac, about five miles from Washington.

On the opposite side of that river, the enemy was discovered strongly posted on very commanding heights, formed in two lines, his advance occupying a fortified house, which, with artillery, covered the bridge over the eastern branch, which the British had to pass. A broad and straight road leading from the bridge to Washington, ran through the enemy's position, which was carefully defended by artillery and riflemen.

exception of about 40 rallied by colonel Ragan, after having lost his horse, and the whole or a part of captain Shower's company, both of whom general Stansbury represents to have made, even thus deserted, a gallant stand. The fall which lieutenant-colonel Ragan received from his horse, together with his great efforts to maintain his position, rendered him unable to follow the retreat; we have therefore to lament that this gallant and excellent officer has been taken prisoner; he has, however, been paroled, and I met him here, recovering from the bruises occasioned by his fall. The loss of his services at this moment is serious.

The 5th Baltimore regiment, under lieutenant-colonel Sterrett, being the left of brigadier-general Stansbury's brigade, still, however, stood their ground, and except for a moment, when part of them recoiled a few steps, remained firm, and stood until ordered to retreat, with a view to prevent their being outflanked.

The reserve, under brigadier-general Smith, of the district of Columbia, with the militia of the city and Georgetown, with the regulars and some detachments of Maryland militia, flanked on their right by commodore Barney and his brave fellows, and lieutenant-colonel Beal, still were to the right on the hill, and maintained the contest for some time with great effect.

It is not with me to report the conduct of commodore Barney and his command, nor can I speak from observation, being too remote; but the concurrent testimony of all who did observe them, does them the highest justice for their brave resistance, and destructive effect they produced on the enemy. Commodore Barney, after having lost his horse, took post near one of his guns, and there unfortunately received a severe wound in the thigh, and he also fell into the hands of the enemy. Captain Miller, of the marines, was wounded in the arm fighting bravely. From the best intelligence, there remains but little doubt that the enemy lost at least 400 killed and wounded, and of these a very unusual portion killed.

Our loss cannot, I think, be estimated at more than from 30 to 40 killed, and 50 to 60 wounded they took altogether about 120 prisoners.

You will readily understand that it is impossible for me to speak minutely of the merit or demerit of particular troops so little known to me from their recent and hasty assemblage. My subsequent movements for the purpose of preserving as much of my force as possible, gaining reinforcements, protecting this place, you already know.

I am, with very great respect, sir, your obedient servant,

W. H. WINDER,

Hon. J. Armstrong, Sec. of War.   brig-gen.
10th mil. dist.

N.B. We have to lament that captain Sterrett, of the 5th Baltimore regiment, has also been wounded, but is doing well: Other officers, eno doubt, deserve notice, but I am as yet unable to particularize.

The disposition for the attack being made, it was commenced with so much impetuosity by the light brigade, consisting of the 85th light infantry, and the light infantry companies of the army under the command of colonel Thornton, that the fortified house was shortly carried, the enemy retiring to the higher grounds.

In support of the light brigade, I ordered up a brigade under the command of colonel Brooke, who, with the 44th regiment, attacked the enemy's left, the 4th regiment pressing his right with such effect, as to cause him to abandon his guns. His first line giving way, was driven on the second, which, yielding to the irresistable attack of the bayonet, and the well-directed discharge of rockets, got into confusion and fled, leaving the British masters of the field. The rapid flight of the enemy, and his knowledge of the country, precluded the posibility of many prisoners being taken, more particularly as the troops had, during the day, undergone considerable fatigue.

The enemy's army, amounting to 8 or 9000 men, with 3 or 400 cavalry, was under the command of General Winder, being formed of troops drawn from Baltimore and Pensylvania. His artillery, 10 pieces of which fell into our hands, was commanded by commodore Barney, who was wounded and taken prisoner. The artillery I directed to be destroyed.

Having halted the army for a short time, I determined to march upon Washington, and reached that city at eight o'clock that night. Judging it of consequence to complete the destruction of the public buildings with the least posible delay, so that the army might retire without loss of time, the following buildings were set fire to and consumed,— the capitol, inculding the Senate-house and House of Representaives, the Arsenal, the Dock-yard, Treasury, War-office, President's Palace, Ropewalk, and the great bridge across the Potomac; in the dock-yard a frigate nearly ready to be launched, and a sloop of war, were consumed. The two bridges leading to Washington over the eastern branch had been destroyed by the enemy, who apprehended an attack from that quar-

ter. The object of the expedition being accomplished, I determined, before any greater force of the enemy could be assembled, to withdraw the troops, and accordingly commenced retiring on the night of the 25th. On the evening of the 29th we reached Benedict, and re-embarked the following day. In the performance of the operation I have detailed, it is with the utmost satisfaction I observe to your lordship, that cheerfulness in undergoing fatigue, and anxiety for the accomplishment of the object, were conspicuous in all ranks.

To Sir A. Cochrane my thanks are due, for his ready compliance with every wish connected with the welfare of the troops and the success of the expedition. To rear-admiral Cockburn, who suggested the attack upon Washington, and who accompanied the army, I confess the greatest obligation for his cordial co-operation and advice.

Colonel Thornton, who led the attack, is entitled to every praise for the noble example he set, which was so well followed by lieutenant-colonel Wood and the 85th light infantry, and by major Jones, of the 4th foot, with the companies attached to the light brigade. I have to express my approbation of the spirited conduct of colonel Brooke, and of his brigade : the 44th regiment, which he led, distinguished itself under the command of lieutenant-colonel-Mullens ; the gallantry of the 4th foot, under the command of major France, being equally conspicuous.

The exertions of captain Mitchel, of the royal artillery, bringing the guns in to action, were unremitting ; to him, and to the detachment under his command, including captain Deacon's rocket brigade, and the marine rocket corps, I feel every obligation, Captain Lempriere, of the royal artillery, mounted a small detachment of the artillery drivers, which proved of great utility. The assistance afforded by captain Blanchard, of the royal engineers, in the duties of his department, was of great advantage. To the zealous exertions of captain Wainwright, Palmer, and Money, of the royal navy, and to those of the officers and seamen who landed with them, the service is highly indebted, the latter, captain Money, had charge of the seamen attached to marine artillery. To captain M'Dougall, of the 85th foot, who acted as my aide de camp, captain Falls, and to the officers of my staff, I feel much indebted.

I must beg leave to call your lordship's attention to the zeal and indefatigable exertions of lieutenant Evans, acting deputy quarter-master-general. The intelligence displayed by that officer, in circumstances of considerable difficulty, induces me to hope he will meet with some distinguised mark of approbation. I have reason to be satisfied with the arrangements of assistant-commissary-General Lawrence.

An attack upon an enemy so strongly posted, could not be effected without loss. I have to lament that the wounds received by colonel Thornton, and the other officers and soldiers left at Bladensburg, were such as prevented their removal. As many of the wounded as could be brought off were removed, the others being left with medical care and attendants. The arrangements made by staff surgeon Baxter for their accommodation, have been as satisfactory as circumstances would admit of. The agent for British prisoners of war very fortunately residing at Bladensburg, I have recommended the wounded officers and men to his particular attention, and trust to his being able to effect their exchange when sufficienly recovered.

* Killed 64; wounded 138.

Return of ordnance, ammunition, and ordnance-stores, taken from the enemy by the army under the command of Major-General Robert Ross, between the 19th and 25th of August, 1814.

August 19—1 24-pound carronade.
August 22.—1 6-pound field-gun, with carriage complete; 156 stand of arms, with cartouches, &c. &c.
August 24, *at Bladensburg.*—2 18-pounders, 5 12-pounders, 3 6-pounders, with field-carriages; a quantity of ammunition for the above; 220 stand of arms.
August 25, *at Washington.*—Brass: 6 18. pounders, mounted on traversing platforms; 5 12-pounders, 4 4-pounders, 1 5½ inch howitzer, 1 5½ inch mortar. Iron: 26 32-pounders, 36 24-pounders, 34 18-pounders, 27 12-pounders, 2 18-pounders, mounted on traversing platforms; 19 12-pounders, on ship-carriages; 3 13-inch mortars, 2 8-inch howitzers, 1 24-pound

Captain Smith, assistant adjutant-general to the troops, who will have the honor to deliver this despatch, I beg leave to recommend to your lordship's protection, as an officer of much merit and great promise, and capable of affording any further information that may be requistite. Sanguine in hoping for the approbation of his royal highness the prince regent, and of his majesty's government, as to the conduct of the troops under my command, I have, &c.

R. ROSS, maj-gen.

I beg leave to enclose herewith a return of the killed,* wounded, and missing in the action of the 24th instant, together with a statement of the ordnance, ammunition, and ordnance stores taken from the enemy between the 19th and 25th of August and likewise sketches of the scene of action and of the line of march.

H. M. SLOOP MANLY, OFF NOTTINGHAM,
PATUXENT, Aug. 27, 1814.
SIR,

I have the honour to inform you, that, agreeably to the intentions I notified to you in my letter of the 22d instant. I proceeded by land, on the morning of the 23d, to Upper Marlborough, to meet and confer with Major-general Ross, as to our further operations against the enemy; and we were not long in agreeing on the propriety of making an immediate attempt on the city of Washington.

gun, 5 32-pound carronades, 5 18-pound carronades, 13 12-pound guns, 2 9-pound guns, 2 6-pound guns.

Total amount of cannon taken—206; 500 barrels of powder; 100,000 rounds of musket-ball cartridges; 40 barrels of fine-grained powder; a large quantity of ammunition of different natures made up.

The navy-yard and arsenal having been set on fire by the enemy before they retired, an immense quantity of stores of every description was destroyed; of which no account could be taken. Seven or eight very heavy explosions during the night denoted that there had been large magazines of powder.

F. G. J. WILLIAMS,
lieutenant royal artillery, A. Q. M.
J. MICHELL,
captain commanding artillery.

N.B. The remains of near 2000 stand of arms were discovered which had been destroyed by the eneny.

In conformity, therefore, with the wishes of the general, I instantly sent orders for our marine and naval forces, at Pig-point, to be forthwith moved over to Mount Calvert. and for the marine-artillery, and a proportion of the seamen, to be there landed, and with the utmost possible expedition to join the army, which I at once readily agreed to accompany.

The major-general then made his dispositions, and arranged that Captain Robins, with the marines of the ships, should retain possession of Upper Marlboroguh, and that the marine-artillery and seamen should follow the army to the ground it was to occupy for the night. The army then moved on, and bivouacked before dark about five miles near Washington.

In the night, captain Palmer of the Hebrus, and captain Money of the Traave, joined us with the seamen and with the marine-artillery, under Captain Harrison. Captain Wainwright of the Tonnant, had accompanied me the day before, as had also lieutenant James Scott, acting first lieutenant of the Albion.

At daylight, on the morning of the 24th, the major-general again put the army in motion, directing his march upon Bladensburgh ; on reaching which place, with the advanced brigade, the enemy was observed drawn up in force on a rising ground beyond the town ; and by the fire he soon opened on us as we entered the place, gave us to understand he was well protected by artillery. General Ross, however, did not hesitate in immediately advancing to attack him ; although our troops were almost exhausted with the fatigue of the march they had just made, and but a small proportion of our little army had yet got up. This dashing measure was, however, I am happy to add, crowned with the success it merited ; for, in spite of the galling fire of the enemy, our troops advanced steadily on both his flanks, and in his front ; and, as soon as they arrived on even ground with him, he fled in every direction, leaving behind him 10 pieces of cannon, and a considerable number of killed and wounded ; amongst the latter Commodore Barney, and several other officers. Some other prisoners were also taken, though not many, owing to the swiftness with which the enemy went off, and the fatigue our army had previously undergone.

It would, sir, be deemed presumption in me to attempt to give you particular details respecting the nature of this battle ; I shall, therefore, only remark generally, that the enemy, 8,000 strong, on ground he had chosen as best adapted for him to defend, where he had time to erect his batteries, and concert all his measures, was dislodged, as soon reached, and a victory gained over him, by a division of the British army, not amounting to more than 1500 men, headed by our gallant general, whose brilliant achievements it is beyond my power to do justice to, and indeed no possible comment could enhance.

The seamen, with the guns, were, to their great mortification, with the rear-division, during this short, but decisive action. Those, however, attached to the rocket-brigade. were in the battle ; and I remarked, with much pleasure, the precision with which the rockets were thrown by them, under the direction of first-lieutenant Lawrence, of the marine-artillery. Mr. Jeremiah M'Daniel, master's mate of the Tonnant, a very fine young man, who was attached to this party, being severely wounded, I beg permission to recommend him to your favourable consideration. The company of marines I have on many occasions had cause to mention to you, commanded by first-lieutenant Stephens, under the temporary command of captain Reed, of the 6th West India regiment, (these companies being attached to the light brigade), and they respectively behaved with their accustomed zeal and bravery None other of the naval department were fortunate enough to arrive up in time to take their share in this battle, excepting captain Palmer, of the Hebrus, with his aid-de-camp, Mr. Arthur Wakefield, midshipmen of that ship, and lieutenant James Scott, first of the Albion, who acted as my aide-de-camp, and remained with me during the whole time.

The contest being completely ended, and the enemy having retired from the field, the general gave the army about two hours rest, when he again moved forward on Washington. It was, however, dark before we reached that city; and, on the general, myself, and some officers advancing a short way past the first houses of the town, without being accompanied by the troops, the enemy opened upon us a heavy fire of musketry, from the capitol and two other houses; these were therefore, almost immediately stormed by our people, taken possession of, and set on fire; after which the town submitted without further resistance.

The enemy himself, on our entering the town, set fire to the navy-yard, (filled with naval stores), a frigate of the largest class almost ready for launching, and a sloop of war lying off it; as he did also the fort which protected the sea-approach to Washington.

On taking possession of the city, we also set fire to the president's palace, the treasury, and the war-office; and, in the morning, captain Wainwright went with a party to see that the destruction in the navy-yard was complete; when he destroyed whatever stores and buildings had escaped the flames of the preceding night. A large quantity of ammunition and ordnance stores were likewise destroyed by us in the arsenal; as were about 200 pieces of artillery of different calibres, as well as a vast quantity of small-arms. Two rope-walks of a very extensive nature, full of tar-rope, &c., situated at a considerable distance from the yard, were likewise set fire to and consumed. In short, sir, I do not believe a vestige of public property, or a store of any kind, which could be converted to the use of the government, escaped destruction: the bridges across the Eastern Branch and the Potomac were likewise destroyed.

This general devastation being completed during the day of the 25th, we marched again, at nine that night, on our return, by Bladensburgh, to Upper Marlborough.

We arrived yesterday evening at the latter, without molestation of any sort, indeed without a single musket having been fired; and this morning we moved on to this place, where I have found his majesty's sloop Manly, the tenders, and the boats, and I have hoisted my flag, *pro tempore*, in the former. The troops will probably march tomorrow, or the next day at farthest, to Benedict for re-embarkation, and this flotilla will of course join you at the same time.

In closing, sir, my statement to you, of the arduous and highly important operations of this last week, I have a most pleasing duty to perform, in assuring you of the good conduct of the officers and men who have been serving under me. I have been particularly indebted, whilst on this service, to captain Wainwright of the Tonnant, for the assistance he has invariably afforded me; and to captain Palmer and Money, for their exertions during the march to and from Washington. To captain Nourse, who has commanded the flotilla during my absence, my acknowledgments are also most justly due, as well as to captains Sullivan, Badcock, Somerville, Ramsay, and Bruce, who have acted in it under him.

Lieutenant James Scott, now first of the Albion, has, on this occasion, rendered me essential services; and as I have had reason so often of late to mention to you the gallant and meritorious conduct of this officer, I trust you will permit me to seize this opportunity of recommending him particularly to your favorable notice and consideration.

Captain Robins, (the senior officer of marines with the fleet,) who has had, during these operations, the marines of the ships united under his orders, has executed ably and zealously the several services with which he has been entrusted, and is entitled to my best acknowledgments accordingly; as is also captain Harrison of the marine-artillery, who, with the officers and men attached to him, accompanied the army to and from Washington.

Mr. Dobie, surgeon of the Melpomene, volunteered his professional services on this occasion, and rendered much assistance to the wounded on the field of battle, as well as to many of the men taken ill on the line of march.

One colonial marine killed, 1 master's mate, 2 serjeants, and 3 colonial marines wounded, are the casualities sustained by the naval department; a general list of the killed and wounded of the whole army will, of course, accompany the report of the major-general.

I have the honour be, &c.
G. COCKBURN, rear-admiral.
Vice-admiral the hon.
Sir A. Cochrane, K. B. &c.

P.S.—Two long 6-pounders guns, intended for a battery at Nottingham, were taken off, and put on board the Brune, and one taken at Upper Marlborough was destroyed.

As usual, Messrs Thomson and Smith give *General observations on the expedition.* in their accounts the most exaggerated estimates of the attacking force, reducing, in an inverse ratio, that of their countrymen. Fortunately, they contradict each other in such a manner, and Gen. Wilkinson's testimony is so positive, that the correctness of the two British despatches is established. Mr. Thomson, in the first place, states the British force at six thousand men, just one thousand more than Mr. O'Connor, and two thousand more than Dr. Smith. In the second place, he says, speaking of the American force—"These consisted of but five thousand men, and offered battle to the English troops, but General Ross turned to his right and took the road to Marlborough."

Here is a direct insinuation that a superior body of British troops were afraid to meet an inferior force. Surely Mr. Thomson should have reflected on the consequences of making this statement, and that its absurdity must strike every one who reads even his own history. Six thousand men are afraid to fight five thousand, yet, strange to say, they persevere in their march into the heart of an enemy's country, knowing that their enemy is every moment becoming stronger. Really Mr. Thomson might have perceived the inconsistency !

General Wilkinson puts the matter in another light, and, speaking of General Ross, says—"General Ross marched from Nottingham the same morning, by the chapel road leading to Marlborough; and, on discovering the American troops, sent a detachment to his left to meet them, which advanced to the foot of the hill near Oden's house, when the American troops fell back, and the enemy resumed their march."

The real facts, independent of Wilkinson, are so notorious, that we cannot conceive how Thomson could have ventured to make his statement.

General Winder's dispatch is nearly as *General Winder's dispatch.* mendacious as Mr. Thompson's assertions. The statement as to force contained in both General Ross and Admiral Cockburn's dispatches are fully borne out by General Armstrong,[*] and Winder himself admits that his force amounted to five thousand men, yet with a superiority of more than three to one he ascribes his defeat to the disadvantages under which he laboured.

Now we ask, in what did these disadvantages consist? was it that sufficient time for preparation had not been afforded ? This could not be, as, from the 26th June, the Government had been apprised of the threatened visit. We have shown by Armstrong that it was not from inferiority of force. In what, then, did the disadvantages consist? We have no hesitation in answering—to the shameful conduct of his men, and the total want of precautions on the part of the General, in neglecting to avail himself of the military obstacles that might have been used advantageously to impede the enemy's approach. General Wilkinson writes, "Not a single bridge was broken, not a causeway destroyed, not an inundation attempted, not a tree fallen, not a rood of the road obstructed, nor a gun fired at the enemy, in a march of near forty miles, from Benedict to Upper Marlborough, by a route on which there are ten or a dozen difficult defiles; which, with a few hours' labour, six pieces of light artillery, three hundred infantry, two hundred riflemen, and sixty dragoons, might have been defended against any force that could approach them; such is the narrowness of the road, the profundity of the ravines, the steepness of the acclivities, and the sharpnets of the ridges."

We think the above extract will prove our assertion, as to Winder's capability of opposing

---

[*] Notices of the War, p. 130.

a young and dashing commander like Ross. Winder's statement as to his force is unhappily disproved by Dr. Smith, who gives a detailed list, which we subjoin:

"The army under General Winder," says doctor Smith, "consisted of:—

"United States' dragoons	140	
Maryland ditto	240	
District of Columbia ditto	50	
Virginia ditto	100	
		530
Regular infantry	500	
Seamen and marines	600	
		1100
Stansbury's brigade of militia	1353	
Sterrett's regiment, ditto	500	
Baltimore artillery, ditto	150	
Pinkney's battalion. ditto	150	
		2153
Smith's brigade, ditto	1070	
Cramer's battalion, ditto	240	
Waring's detachment, ditto	150	
Maynard's ditto, ditto	150	
		1610
Beall's and Hood's regiment of do.	800	
Volunteer corps	350	
		1150
Total at Bladensburg		6543

At hand.

Young's brigade of militia	450	
Minor's Virginia corps	600	
		1050
Grand Total		7503

General Wilkinson is very sarcastic in his account of Bladensburg. He says, "their President was in the field; every eye was turned upon the chief; every bosom throbbed with confidence, and every nerve was strung with valor. No doubts remained with the troops that in their chief magistrate they beheld their Commander-in-chief, who, like another Maurice, having, by his irresolution, exposed the country to the chances and accidents of a general engagement, had now come forward to repair the error by his activity in the field; determined to throw himself into the gap of danger, and not to survive the power of his country."

If General Wilkinson is severe on Mr. President Madison, he is equally plain spoken with respect to the troops, and bears clear testimony as to the actual numbers of the British engaged. He says, "the American force they routed by about seven hundred and fifty rank and file of the 4th and 44th regiments."

The disparity of loss between the two armies is easily accounted for, as we find twenty-four pieces of artillery marked on General Wilkinson's diagram. These completely enfiladed the bridge, and were very destructive to the advancing columns. The American loss was trifling, as they seem, in common with the President, to have acted on the principle 'He that fights and runs away,' and so forth."

By the American estimate of public property destroyed at Washington, it would appear that full satisfaction was taken for the injuries committed at Newark and elsewhere. The estimate returned to Government was as follows:—

American estimate of public property destroyed at Washington.

The committee appointed by the American congress to inquire into the circumstances attending the capture of Washington, and the destruction consequent on that event, after giving a statement of the operations in the navy-yard, report the following estimate of the public property destroyed:—

	Dollars.
The capital, including all costs,	787,163
President's house,	234,334
Public offices,	93,613
	1,115,110

But the committee remark, as the walls of the capital and president's house are good, they suppose that the sum of 460,000 dollars will be sufficient to place the buildings in the situation they were in previous to their destruction.

The losses sustained in the navy-yard are thus estimated:—

	Dollars.
In moveable property,	417,745
In buildings and fixtures	91,425
	509,170

The committee then proceed to the recapitulation of the losses in the navy-yard, with an estimate of the real losses. After deducting the value recovered from the original value of the articles, the total amount is 417,745 dollars, 51 cents.

The original value of the articles destroyed was 678,219 dollars, 71 cents, of which 260,465 dollars and 20 cents value were re covered, in anchors, musket-barrels, locks copper, timber, &c.

The most important feature in the destruction in the Navy Yard, was the destruction of the new frigate, and the Argus sloop, as it inflicted a direct blow on a naval force still in its infancy.

Both Mr. Madison, in his proclamation, and Mr. Munroe, in his letter to Admiral Cochrane, have endeavoured to show that the British, by their attack on Washington, not only outraged the rules of war, in destroying the public buildings, but by again bringing forward the Hampton and Havre de Grace affairs, they leave it to be understood that the troops behaved in the same disorderly manner imputed to them on that occasion.

The American journals of that day prove however, the contrary of this. The Columbian Centinel, of August 31st, says, "The British officers pay inviolable respect to private property, and no peaceable citizen is molested." A Baltimore writer, under date, August 27, says, "The enemy treated the inhabitants of Washington with respect,"

and Mr. Gates, the mouth-piece of the Government, whose presses and type had been destroyed, was forced to acknowledge that any mischief done, was committed by "the knavish wretches about the town, who profited by the general distress."

Even Mr. Thompson was compelled to acknowledge that "the plunder of private property was prohibited, and soldiers transgressing the order were severely punished."

One more extract which we give from a Georgetown journal of September 8, will complete our list of proofs that both Mr. Munroe and Mr. Madison have foully wronged the British soldiers by their aspersions:

"The list of plunder and destruction, copied from a vile and libellous print of that city, is a gross aud abominable fabrication, known to be such by every inhabitant. Most of the plunder was committed by rabble of the place, fostered among the citizens, and from whose villainy no place is free in times of peril and relaxation of the law. The British army, it is no more than justice to say, preserved a moderation and discipline, with respect to private persons and property, unexampled in the annals of war."

We think it unnecessary to cite further testimony in support of our assertion as to the behaviour of the British army, and now give the documents in which their character was assailed—Mr. Munroe's answer to a letter from Admiral Cochrane, and Mr. Madison's proclamation.* We also give Admiral

---

From Mr. Monroe to Sir Alexander Cochrane.

Department of State, Sept. 6, 1814.

Sir,

I had the honour to receive your letter of the 18th of August, stating that having been called on by the governor-general of the Canadas, to aid him in carrying into effect measures of retaliation against the inhabitants of the United States, for the wanton desolation committed by their army in Upper Canada, it has become your duty, conformably with the nature of the governor-general's application, to issue to the naval force under your command, an order to destroy and lay waste such towns and districts upon the coast as may be found assailable.

It is seen with the greatest surprise, that

this system of devastation which has been practiced by the British forces, so manifestly contrary to the usages of civilized warfare, is placed by you on the ground of retaliation. No sooner were the United States compelled to resort to war against Great Britain, than they resolved to wage it in a manner most consonant to the principles of humanity, and to those friendly relations which it was desirable to preserve between the two nations, after the restoration of peace. They perceived, however, with the deepest regret, that a spirit alike just and humane was neither cherished nor acted on by your government. Such an assertion would not be hazarded, if it were not supported by facts, the proof of which has perhaps already carried the same conviction to other nations that it has to the people of these states.

Cochrane's letter, as some expressions in it were laid hold of as breathing a most sanguinary and ruthless spirit:—

From vice-admiral Cochrane to Mr. Monroe.

His Majesty's ship the Tonnant, in the Patuxent river, Aug. 18, 1814.

SIR,

Having been called on by the governor-general of the Canadas to aid him in carrying into effect measures of retaliation against the inhabitants of the United States, for the wanton destruction committed by their army in Upper Canada, it has become imperiously my duty, conformably with the nature of the govenor-general's application, to issue to the naval force under my command, an order to destroy and lay waste such towns and districts upon the coast as may be found assailable.

I had hoped that this contest would have terminated, without my being obliged to resort to severities which are contrary to the usages of civilised warfare; and as it has

---

Without dwelling on the deplorable cruelties committed by the savages in the British ranks, and in British pay, on American prisoners, at the river Raisin, which to this day have never been disavowed, or atoned, I refer, as more immediately connected with the subject of your letter, to the wanton desolation that was committed at Havre-de-Grace, and at George town, early in the spring of 1813. These villages were burnt and ravaged by the naval forces of Great Britain, to the ruin of their unarmed inhabitants, who saw with astonishment they derived no protection to their property from the laws of war. During the same season, scenes of invasion and pillage, carried on under the same authority, were witnessed all along the waters of the Chesapeake, to an extent inflicting the most serious private distress, and under circumstances that justified the suspicion, that revenge and cupidity, rather than the manly motives that should dicate the hostility of a high-minded foe, led to their perpetration. The late destruction of the houses of government in this city, is another act which comes necessarily into view. In the wars of modern Europe, no examples of the kind, even among nations the most hostile to each other, can be traced. In the course of ten years past, the capitals of the principal powers of the Continent of Europe have been conquered, and occupied alternately by the victorious armies of each other, and no instance of such wanton and justifiable destruction has been seen. We must go back to distant and barbarous ages to find a parallel for the acts of which I complain. Although these acts of desolation invited, if they did not impose on the government, the necessity of retaliation, yet in no instance has it been authorized. The burning of the village of Newark, in Upper Canada, posterior to the early outrages above enumerated, was not executed on that principle. The village of Newark adjoined Fort-George, and its destruction was justified by the officer who ordered it, on the ground that it became necessary in the military operations there. The act, however, was disavowed by the government. The burning which took place at Long-point was unauthorized by the government, and the conduct of the officer subjected to the investigation of a military tribunal. For the burning of St. David's, committed by stragglers, the officer who commanded in that quarter was dismissed without a trial, for not preventing it.

I am commanded by the president distinctly to state, that it as little comports with any orders issued to the military and naval commanders of the United States, as it does with the established and known humanity of the American nation, to pursue a system which it appears you have adopted. The government owes to itself, and to the principle which it has ever held sacred, to disavow, as justly chargeable to it, any such wanton, cruel, and unjustifiable warfare.

Whatever unauthorized irregularity may have been committed by any of its troops, it would have been ready, acting on these principles of sacred and eternal obligation, to disavow, and as far as might be practicable, to repair. But in the plan of desolating warfare which your letter so explicitly makes known, and which is attempted to be excused on a plea so utterly groundless, the president perceives a spirit of deep-rooted hostility, which, without the evidence of such facts, he could not have believed existed, or would have been carried to such an extremity.

For the reparation of injuries, of whatever nature they may be, not sanctioned by the law of nations, which the naval or military forces of either power may have committed against the other, this government will always be ready to enter into reciprocal arrangements. It is presumed that your government will neither expect or propose any which are not reciprocal.

Should your government adhere to a system of desolation so contrary to the views and practice of the United States, so revolting to humanity and repugnant to the sentiments and usages of the civilized world, whilst it will be seen with the deepest regret, it must and will be met with a determination and constancy becoming a free

been with extreme reluctance and concern that I have found myself compelled to adopt this system of devastation, I shall be equally gratified if the conduct of the executive of the United States will authorise my staying such proceedings, by making reparation to the sufiering inhabitants of Upper Canada; thereby manifesting that if the destructive measures pursued by their army were ever sanctioned, they will no longer be permitted by the government.

I have the honour to be, sir, with much consideration, your most obedient humble servant.

ALEXANDER COCHRANE,

Vice-admiral and commander in chief of his Britannic majesty's ships and vessels upon the North American station.

The hon. James Monroe,
    Secretary of State, &c.
    Washington.

people, contending in a just cause for their essential rights and their dearest interests.

I have the honour to be, with great consideration, sir, your most obedient humble servant,
Vice-admiral Sir Alexander Cochrane,
    commander in chief of his Britannic
    majesty's ships and vessels.
             JAMES MUNROE.

Mr. Madison's Proclamation.

Whereas, the enemy, by sudden incursion, have succeeded in invading the capital of the nation, defended at the moment by troops less numerous than their own, and almost entirely of the militia; during their possession of which, though for a single day only, they wantonly destroyed the public edifices, having no relation in their structure to operations of war, nor used at the time for military annoyance; some of these edifices being also costly monuments of state, and of arts; and the others, depositories of the public archives, not only precious to the nation, as the memorials of its origin and its early transactions, but interesting to all nations, as contributions to the general stock of historical instruction and political science.

And, whereas, advantage has been taken of the loss of a fort, more immediately guarding the neighbouring town of Alexandria, to place the town within a range of a naval force, too long and too much in the habit of abusing its superiority, wherever it can be applied, to require, as the alternative of a general conflagration, an undisturbed plunder of private property, which has been executed in a manner peculiarly distressing to the inhabitants, who had inconsiderately cast themselves on the justice and generosity of the victor.

And, whereas, it now appears, by a direct communication from the British naval commander on the American station, to be his avowed purpose to employ the force under his direction, in destroying and laying waste such towns and districts upon the coast as may be found assailable; adding to this declaration the nsulting pretext, that it is in retaliation for a wanton destruction committed by the army of the United States in Upper Canada; when it is notorious, that no destruction has been committed, which, notwithstanding the multiplied outrages previously committed by the enemy,

was not unauthorised, and promptly shewn to be so, and that the United States have been as constant in their endeavours to reclaim the enemy from such outrages, by the contrast of their own example, as they have been ready to terminate, on reasonable condition, the war itself.

And, whereas, these proceedings and declared purposes, which exhibit a deliberate disregard of the principles of humanity, and the rules of civilized warfare, and which must give to the existing war a character of extended devastation and barbarism, at the very moment of negociation for peace, invited by the enemy himself, leave no prospect of safety to anything within the reach of his predatory and incendiary operations, but in a manly and universal determination to chastise and expel the invader.

Now, therefore, I, James Madison, President of the United States, do issue this my proclamation, exhorting all the good people, therefore, to unite their hearts and hands in giving effect to the ample means possessed for that purpose. I enjoin it on all officers, civil and military, to exert themselves in executing the duties with which they are respectively charged. And, more especially, I require the officers, commanding the respective military districts, to be vigilant and alert in providing for the defence thereof; for the more effectual accomplishment of which, they are authorised to call to the defence of exposed and threatened places, proportions of the militia, most convenient thereto, whether they be, or be not, parts of the quotas detached for the service of the United States, under requisitions of the general government.

On an occasion which appeals so forcibly to the proud feelings and patriotic devotion of the American people, none will forget what they owe to themselves; what they owe to their country; and the high destinies which await it; what to the glory acquired now, and to be maintained by their sons, with the augmented strength and resources wth which time and Heaven have blessed them. In testimony whereof, I have hereunto set my hand, and caused the seal of the United States to be affixed to these presents. Done at Washington, Sept. 1, 1814.

        By the President.
            JAMES MADISON
JAMES MUNROE, Secretary of State.

CHAPTER XXIII.

Unfortunately, Mr. Madison's proclamation given in our last chapter has been invested with an appearance of justice by the articles which appeared in the *Annual Register*, and by other passages, subsequently, in Mr. Macaulay's works. We confess we cannot regard this affair in the same light, and can only look on the proclamation as an attempt by Mr. Madison to cover his own deficiencies. In the first place, he terms an expedition, which he had been warned, two months previously, would be undertaken, a sudden incursion, and then endeavours to prove the ruthlessness of Sir George Cockburn in carrying out his plans, by the assertion that "buildings having no relation to war were destroyed."

When General Ross was fired at from the Capitol, did not that act render this building an object for legitimate attack? And, in the destruction of the houses of Representatives, and the Treasury, was a worse act committed than when Colonel Campbell, of the United States army, destroyed the dwelling-house and other buildings of a Canadian, and justified the act, as according to the usages of war, because a troop of British dragoons had just fled from them?

Ingersol has made great capital out of an article which appeared in the *Annual Regis-*ter, for 1814, and that our readers may judge of the comments for themselves, we give the extract, taking it, not from Ingersol, but the *Register* itself.

"By the capture of Washington, the American Government not only sustained a severe loss in property, but incurred much reproach from the nation, especially from the party adverse to the war, as having been the occasion of a disgrace which it had taken no effectual measures to prevent. A vulnerable part of the Republic was now exposed, and men's minds were impressed with a sense of imminent danger, where before it had been regarded only as a remote possibility. On the other hand, it cannot be concealed, that the extent of devastation practised by the victors, brought a heavy censure upon the British character, not only in America, but on the continent of Europe. *It is acknowledged, that strict discipline was observed, while the troops were in possession of Washington, and private property was anxiously protected:* but the destruction not only of every establishment connected with war, but of edifices consecrated to the purposes of civil government, and affording specimens of the advance of the fine arts among a rising people, was *thought* an indulgence of animosity more suitable to the times of barbarism, than to an age and nation in which hostility is softened by sentiments of generosity and civilised policy."

It will be seen, in this extract, that the writer distinctly says, not that the attack on Washington really was an act suited to barbarous ages, but only that it was *thought so.*

24

Mr. Ingersol, however, has not failed to quote this passage, and even so late as 1848, hints at a retaliation, to be accomplished by the burning of London, and the destruction of the capital of the nation that taught America her vulnerability, by the devastation of Washington.

A great deal too has been made of the fact that Admiral Cochrane made prizes in the Nominy River of a large quantity of tobacco, besides rescuing from slavery one hundred and thirty five slaves, and taking on board a number of cattle, to relieve his stores already overtaxed by the necessity of finding food for so many addditional mouths.

Mr. O'Connor designates all this plundered property; but Mr. O'Connor should have re-collected that he did not term the seizure of the North West Company's goods plunder, but held the capture as good prize by the maritime law of nations. We should wish, then, some American casuist to define the differences between the two cases.

Two other expeditions were undertaken almost simultaneously with the attack on Washington—one on Alexandria, the other directed against a party of militia assembled at Waltham farm.

The first of these was attended with con-
Attack on Alexandria. siderable success, as twenty one merchant vessels, laden with sixteen thousand barrels of flour, a thousand hogsheads of tobacco, besides a considerable quantity of cotton and other articles were captured. The town of Alexandria and its inhabitants, with all their property remained unmolested, as they had signified their readiness to submit without resistance to the invading party.

The second expedition ended more disas-
Sir Peter Parker's death. trously, and resulted in the death of a very gallant officer, Sir Peter Parker. This officer, while his ship was at anchor at Moor's fields, re-ceived information that two hundred Ameri-can riflemen were encamped behind a wood, about a mile from the beach, and deter-mined if possible to carry the American camp by a night attack, and, on the evening of the 29th August, he made, at the head of nearly one hundred and forty men, a most gallant attack on the American position.

The enemy were, however, very strongly posted, and after a sharp struggle the British fell back, in consequence of the death of their leader, Sir Peter Parker. It must not be omitted that the retreat of the British seamen did not commence until they had seen their opponents in full retreat before them.

On the 3rd of September the British troops, under Captain Gordon, began a retrograde march from Alexandria, and by the 9th, al-though many difficulties presented themselves by a combination of skill, diligence, and good fortune, the British Commander was enabled to withdraw and anchor his whole squadron in perfect safety.

Ingersol seems determined always to find some excuse for his countrymen, and, in the present instance, although none was required, he is prepared to assign a reason for the non-defence of Alexandria. In the first place the Captain commanding was guilty of miscon-duct and was cashiered. Secondly, the Com-mon Council were inimical to Mr. Madison's administration. Would it not have sufficed for Mr. Ingersol to state that the Sea Horse and Euryalus frigates with some other smaller vessels lay off the town, and that there could be no hesitation on the part of the defenceless inhabitants, the fighting portion of which did not exceed one hundred militia men, in chosing between security and total ruin.

American writers have exhausted the vo-cabulary of abuse in finding epithets to launch against Captain Gordon's acts, but to show how undeserved were their attacks it is but necessary to transcribe the conditions imposed on the citizens of Alexandria.

The town of Alexandria (with the exception
Gordon's terms. of public works) shall not be destroyed, unless hostilities are commenced on the part of the Americans, nor shall the inhabitants be molested in any manner whatsoever, or their dwelling houses entered, if the following articles are complied with :—

Article 1. All naval and ordnance stores must be immediately given up.

Article 2. Possession will be immediately taken of all the shipping, and their furniture must be sent on board by the owners without delay.

Article 3. Merchandise of every description must be instantly delivered up, and to prevent any irregularities that might be committed in its embarkation the merchants have it in their option to load the vessels generally employed for that purpose, when they will be towed off by us.

Article 4. Refreshments of every description to be supplied to the ships, and *paid for at the market price by bills on the British Government.*

Article 5. Officers will be appointed to see that these articles are strictly complied with, and any deviation or non-compliance on the part of the inhabitants of Alexandria will render this treaty null and void.

American historians when descanting on these terms are but too apt to dwell on Article No. 3, but we should recommend to their especial notice also No. 4, paticularly as this Article was strictly complied with, and not an article of food was taken on board the vessels without full and prompt payment. Even the Government organs at Baltimore, when indulging in every species of vituperation did not dare to deny this.

Ingersol is silent on the subject and merely contents himself with designating the prizes made as spoil, we should however like Mr. Ingersol to say what difference existed between the West Indiamen or South Sea whalers captured at sea by the Americans and merchant vessels captured in an enemy's port.

Ingersol is very bitter on both Mr. Madison and General Armstrong,

Ingersol on Madison and Armstrong.

on the one for his poltroonery, and on the latter for his contemptuous indifference of what was going on around him. He says,—

"Emerging from his hiding-place, and soon informed of the enemy's precipitate departure, the President likewise turned his steps towards deserted Washington, where his presence was the signal of universal recuperation—his own, the capital, and the country—risen like Antaeus from his fall. Such are war's vicissitudes and compensations. At Georgetown, at the tavern, in the apple orchard, and at the hovel in the woods, the commander-in-chief of the army and navy of the United States, and of the militia of the several states, when called into actual service, forces then afoot exceeding one hundred and fifty thousand men, drank the bitter lees of public disgrace, and suffered many of the pains and penalties inflicted on power degraded: encompassed by crowds of his countrymen, flying from their desolated dwellings, many of them in arms, crying aloud for his downfall, begrudging even his wife the sanctuary of a common inn: both the reviled and revilers pursued by resistless foes, bent on the indiscriminate destruction of all alike. The night following came some compensation for such punishment—the last night of Madison's exile, and eve of his restoration to almost universal favor. It was spent in the family of Quaker hosts, strangers to him, and conscientious adversaries of all war, who, with primitive hospitality, welcomed friend Madison, entertaining him and his outcast comrades in misfortune with the kindest and most touching attentions. Refreshed by sweet repose under the Quaker roof, they returned next day to Washington ; and on the way were joined by General Armstrong. After his suggestion to fortify and defend the Capitol was, with his own acquiescence, overruled by General Winder and Colonel Monroe, the Secretary of War. rode to his lodgings in the city, provided himself with a change of clothes and one of Scott's novels, with which he withdrew to a farm-house in Maryland, where he was found next morning, quietly enjoying his romance. Coldly accosted by every one of the President's party, except Mr. Madison, whose behaviour was as usual, the war secretary felt the first symptoms of that nearly universal aversion which marked his return to Washington, and protested against his continuance in the war department. Never well liked by Madison, who yielded to the political, local, and critical inducements which took General Armstrong, from commanding the garrison and important station of the city of New York, into the cabinet, his contempt for all but regular troops, and for party, if not popularity, his military and aristocratic democracy, supine and sarcastic deportment and conversation, habitual disparagement of the wilderness capital, the negligence imputed to him of its defences, and his opinion frequently expressed, that it was too insignificant to be in danger, fomenting the desire men have of a sacrifice, filled Washington with his enemies, then fevered to animosity by its destruction, and festered to rancorous hate. Men require victims, and it was natural to make them of Armstrong and Winder, as alone guilty of what all the rest were to blame for, and, which were in fact, infirmities of republican institutions. The fall of Washington endangered the removal of the seat of government from a place which both east and west began to disparage. Leading men there, Charles Carroll, of Bellevue, whose hospitable villa stood on the picturesque heights of Georgetown; John Mason, with his elegant residence on Analostan island, on the Potomac, at their feet; John Van Ness, a large landlord in the heart of the city, with many more whose property was threatened with sudden and ruinous depreciation, intimates and supporters of Madison, to personal, party, and patriotic attachments, joined solicitude for their homesteads, instinctive and irrepressible beyond all reason. The district militia swore that they would break their swords rather than wield them, directed by such a Secretary of War; and Georgetown sent a deputation to the President to tell him so, consisting of three remonstrants, one of whom was Hanson, editor of the newspaper most abusive of his administration; and another, McKenny, then contriving to promote Munroe's election as Madison's successor. Refusing to receive such envoys, too wise and just to give way to local clamor, but too mild and forbearing to spurn or rebuke it, the President compromised with what Armstrong stigmatised as a village mob, by advising him to withdraw temporarily from its vengeance, if he did not even intimate a wish that the Secretary of War would relinquish his official superintendence of the District of Columbia, promising shortly to restore him to all his faculties. General Armstrong could not remain, under such disadvantages, a member of his administration. The averted countenances of all the President's associates, when first met after the defeat, all cold, and one of them, Mr. Carroll, insulting, told the secretary that he could not stay, even though his life had not been threatened by the mili-

tary mob he defied, without forfeiting the independence he maintained. Retiring, therefore, after his interview with the President, and by his advice, to Baltimore, on the 3rd September, 1814, in the federal journal of that city, he published an indignant resignation of a place, which, throughout his incumbency, was one of continual quarrels with the generals he superintended, and of their disastrous miscarriages of the campaigns he projected. At his residence on the North River he survived till more than eighty years old. Having bravely served in the army of the Revolution, been the organ of its almost rebellious complaints by the Newberg letters which he wrote, appointed to high public trusts at home and abroad by Presidents Washington, Jefferson, and Madison, he closed his life, by military annals of the war of 1812, remarkable for accurate narrative, polished diction, and manly tone."

*   *   *   *   *   *   *   *

A few days after the Washington Expedition, it was determined that a demonstration should be made against Baltimore, and that, if there appeared to be any reasonable prospect of success, the demonstration should become a real expedition. the policy of this demonstration was apparent, when we consider that the Java frigate and several sloops and smaller vessels of war were lying there, and that an immense quantity of naval stores were deposited in the arsenal, the loss of which could not but inflict a heavy blow on the American Government.

Influenced by these considerations Sir Alexander Cochrane, Admiral Cockburn, and General Ross began to make the necessary arrangements, and from the 1st to the 11th all was a scene of busy preparation. On the 12th the troops landed at North Point, at the entrance of the River Patapsco, while the frigates, bomb vessels, and flotilla worked up the Patapsco, as well as the shoal water permitted, in order to co-operate with the army by an attack on Fort McHenry, and the other batteries about two miles from the City.

The Americans had so long sustained along the banks of the Chesapeake a series of humiliations, that it would almost appear as if, in relating the descent on Baltimore, their historians had determined to wipe away the disgrace which had been incurred, by making the most of that affair. Accordingly we find from Ingersol to Smith, not even excepting Armstrong, that the British force was magnified in the same ratio that their own was diminished. We must, however, do Armstrong the justice to observe that he was the most moderate, and only made the British as *six to three.*

We are fortunately in possession of the exact number of troops that were landed at North Point, and we will proceed to examine how much truth exists in the various American statements.

The troops which landed under the command of General Ross consisted of detachments of Royal and Marine Artillery, the remnants of the 1st battalions of the 4th, 21st, and 44th regiments, and the 85th regiment, the 1st and 2nd battalions of Marines from the ships, and a body of six hundred seamen, under Captain Edward Crofton; the whole numbering thirty-two hundred and seventy rank and file.

Here we have the official return of numbers, yet American writers, pretending to be historians, have not scrupled to swell the British numbers to eight, nine, and ten thousand. We look in vain in General Smith's dispatch for some clue as to the American numbers. We are, however, luckily, able from various admissions made by the different writers, to approximate somewhat closely to the real state of the case. For instance, we gather from Mr. Thompson that General Stricker's brigade, besides several companies of Pennsylvania militia, amounted to three thousand one hundred and eighty-five men. This was exclusive of the men stationed at the forts and batteries, who mustered one thousand strong, and when we add to these numbers the men stationed along the whole line of breastworks, estimated, by the prisoners taken, at four thousand, we find that, instead of being numerically inferior to the British, the Americans more than doubled their assailants, and considerably exceeded eight thousand men.*

* Sketches of the War, p. 340.

Having laid before the reader this statement of numbers we proceed to the expedition itself, and begin with an extract from Col. Brooke's letter, adding to it Sir Alexander Cochrane's and Admiral Cockburn's despatches, giving in our notes also an extract from General Smith's despatch* to the Secretary at War.

"About two miles beyond this point† our advance became engaged; the country was here closely wooded, and the enemy's riflemen were enabled to conceal themselves.— At this moment, the gallant General Ross received a wound in his breast which proved mortal. He only survived to recommend a young and unprovided family to the protection of his king and country.

"Thus fell, at an early age, one of the brightest ornaments of his profession; one who, whether at the head of a regiment, a brigade, or corps, had alike displayed the talents of command; who was not less beloved in his private than enthusiastically admired in his public character; and whose only fault if it may be deemed so, was an excess of gallantry, enterprise, and devotion to the service.

"If ever it were permitted to a soldier to lament those who fall in battle, we may indeed, in this instance, claim that melancholy privilege.

"Thus it is, that the honour of addressing your Lordship, and the command of this army, have devolved upon me; duties which under any other circumstances, might have been embraced as the most enviable gifts of fortune; and here I venture to solicit, through your lordship, his royal Highness the Prince Regent's consideration to the

* *Extract from Major-General Smith's Despatch.*

About the time General Stricker had taken the ground just mentioned, he was joined by Brigadier-General Winder, who had been stationed on the west side of the city, but was now ordered to march with General Douglas's brigade of Virginia militia, and the United States' Dragoons, under Captain Bird, and take post on the left of General Stricker. During these movements, the brigades of Generals Stransbury and Foreman, the seamen and marines under Commodore Rodgers, the Penn-

† Two miles from North Point.

circumstances of my succeeding, during operations of so much moment, to an officer of such high and established merit.

"Our advance continuing to press forward, the enemy's light troops were pushed to within five miles of Baltimore, where a corps of about 6000 men, six pieces of artillery, and some hundred cavalry, were discovered posted under cover of a wood, drawn up in a very dense order, and lining a strong paling, which crossed the main road nearly at right angles. The creeks and inlets of the Patapsco and Black rivers, which approach each other at this point, will in some measure account for the contracted nature of the enemy's position.

"I immediately ordered the necessary dispositions for a general attack. The light brigade under the command of Major Jones, of the 4th, consisting of the 85th light infantry, under Major Gubbins, and the light companies of the army, under Major Pringle, of the 21st, covered the whole of the front, driving the enemy's skirmishers with great loss on his main body. The 4th regiment, under Major Faunce, by a detour through some hollow ways, gained, unperceived, a lodgment close upon the enemy's left. The remainder of the light brigade, under the command of the honourable Lieutenant-Colonel Mullins, consisting of the 44th regiment under Major Johnson, the marines of the fleet under Captain Robbins, and a detachment of seamen under Captain Money of the Trave, formed a line along the enemy's front; while the left brigade, under Colonel Patterson, consisting of the 21st regiment, commanded by Major White er, the 2nd battalion of marines by Lieutenant-Colonel Malcolm, and a detachment of marines by Major Lewis, remained in columns on the road, with orders to deploy to his left, and press the enemy's right, the moment the ground became sufficiently open to admit of that movement.

"In this order, the signal being given, the whole of the troops advanced rapidly to the charge. In less than fifteen minutes, the enemy's force being utterly broken and dispersed, fled in every direction over the country, leaving on the field two pieces of cannon, with a considerable number of killed, wounded, and prisoners.

"The enemy lost, in this short but brilliant affair, from 500 to 600 in killed and wounded; while at the most moderate computation he is at least 1000 *hors de combat*. The 5th regiment of militia, in particular, has been represented as nearly annihilated.

"The day being now far advanced, and the troops (as is always the case on the first march after disembarkation) much fatigued, we halted for the night on the ground of which the enemy had been dispossessed.— Here, I received a communication from Vice-Admiral the Honourable Sir A. Cochrane, informing me that the frigates, bomb-ships, and flotilla of the fleet, would on the ensuing morning, take their stations as previously proposed.

"At day-break on the 13th, the army again advanced, and at ten o'clock I occupied a favourable position eastward of Baltimore, distant about a mile and a half, and from whence I could reconnoitre, at my leisure, the defences of that town.

"Baltimore is completely surrounded by strong but detached hills, on which the enemy had constructed a chain of palisaded redoubts, connected by a small breast-work; I have, however, reason to think, that the defence to the northward and westward of the place, were in a very unfinished state. Chinkapin hill, which lay in front of our position, completely commands the town; this was the strongest part of the line, and here the enemy seemed most apprehensive of an attack. These works were defended, according to the best information which we could obtain, by about 15,000 men, with a large train of artillery.

"Judging it perfectly feasible, with the description of forces under my command, I

---

sylvania volunteers under Colonel Cobean and Findley, the Baltimore artillery under Colonel Harris, and the marine artillery under Captain Stiles, manned the trenches and the batteries —all prepared to receive the enemy. We remained in this situation during the night.

On Tuesday, the enemy appeared in front of my entrenchments, at the distance of two miles on the Philadelphia road, from whence he had a full view of our position. He manœuvred during the morning towards our left, as if with the intention of making a circuitous march, and

made arrangements for a night-attack, during which the superiority of the enemy's artillery would not have been so much felt; and Captain McDougall, the bearer of these despatches, will have the honor to point out to your lordship, those particular points of the line which I had proposed to act on. During the evening, however, I received a communication from the commander-in-chief of the naval forces, by which I was informed that, in consequence of the entrance to the harbour being closed up by vessels sunk for that purpose by the enemy, a naval co-operation against the town and camp was found impracticable.

"Under these circumstances, and keeping in view your lordship's instructions, it was agreed between the Vice-Admiral and myself, that the capture of the town would not have been a sufficient equivalent to the loss which might probably be sustained in storming the heights.

"Having formed this resolution; after compelling the enemy to sink upwards of 20 vessels in different parts of the harbour; causing the citizens to remove almost the whole of their property to places of more security inland; obliging the government to concentrate all the military force of the surrounding states; harassing the militia, and forcing them to collect from very remote districts; causing the enemy to burn a valuable rope-walk, with other public buildings, in order to clear the glacis in front of their redoubts, besides having beaten and routed them in a general action, I retired on the 14th, three miles from the position which I had occupied, where I halted during some hours.

"This tardy movement was partly caused by an expectation that the enemy might possibly be induced to move out of his intrenchments and follow us; but he profited by the lesson which he had received on the 12th; and towards the evening I retired the troops about three miles and a half further, where I took up my ground for the night.

"Having ascertained, at a late hour on the morning of the 15th, that the enemy had no disposition to quit his intrenchments I moved down and re-embarked the army at North Point, not leaving a man behind, and carrying with me about 200 prisoners, being persons of the best families in the city, and which number might have been very considerably increased, was not the fatigue of the troops an object principally to be avoided.

"I have now to remark to your lordship, that nothing could surpass the zeal, unanimity and ardour, displayed by every description of force, whether naval, military, or marine, during the whole of these operations.

"I am highly indebted to Vice-Admiral Sir A. Cochrane, commander-in-chief of the naval forces, for the active assistance and zealous co-operation, which he was ready, upon every occasion to afford me; a disposition conspicuous in every branch of the naval service, and which cannot fail to ensure success to every combined operation of this armament.

"Captain Edward Crofton, commanding the brigade of seamen appointed to the small arms, for the animated and enthusiastic example which he held forth to his men, deserves my approbation : as do also Captains Nourse, Money, Sullivan, and Ramsay, R.N., for the steadiness and good order which they maintained in their several directions.

"I feel every obligation to Rear-Admiral Cockburn, for the counsel and assistance which he afforded me, and from which I derived the most signal benefit.

I have the honour to be, &c.,

ARTHUR BROOKE, Col. com.

Killed—39; Wounded—251.

From Sir Alexander Cochrane to Mr. Croker.

H.M.S. Tonnant Chesapeake, Sept. 1841.

"Sir,—I request that you will be pleased to inform my lords commissioners of the admi-

coming down on the Harford or York roads. Generals Winder and Stricker were ordered to adapt their movements to those of the enemy, so as to baffle this supposed intention. They executed this order with great skill and judgment, by taking an advantageous position stretching from my left across the country when the enemy was likely to approach the quarter he seemed to threaten. This movement induced the enemy to concentrate his forces (between one and two o'clock), in my front, pushing his advance to within a mile of us,

ralty, that the approaching equinoctial new moon rendering it unsafe to proceed immediately out of the Chesapeake with the combined expedition, to act upon the plans which had been concerted previous to the departure of the Iphigenia; major-general Ross and myself resolved to occupy the intermediate time to advantage, by making a demonstration upon the city of Baltimore which might be converted into a real attack, should circumstances appear to justify it; and, as our arrangements were soon made, I proceeded up this river, and anchored off the mouth of the Patapsco, on the 11th inst. where the frigates and smaller vessels entered at a convenient distance for landing the troops.

" At an early hour the next morning, the disembarkation of the army was effected without opposition, having attached to it a brigade of 600 seamen, under captain E. Crofton, (late of the Leopard), the second battalion of marines, the marines of the squadron, and the colonial black marines Rear-admiral Cockburn accompanied the general, to advise and arrange as might be deemed necessary for our combined efforts.

" So soon as the army moved forward, I hoisted my flag in the Surprise, and with the remainder of the frigates, bombs, sloops, and the rocket-ship, passed further up the river, to render what co-operation could be found practicable.

" While the bomb-vessels were working up, in order that we might open our fire upon the enemy's fort at day-break next morning, an account was brought to me, that major-general Ross, when reconnoitring the enemy had received a mortal wound by a musket-ball, which closed his glorious career before he could be brought off to the ship.

" It is a tribute due to the memory of this gallant and respected officer, to pause in my relation, while I lament the loss that his majesty's service and the army of which he was one of the brightest ornaments, have sustained by his death. The unanimity and the zeal, which he manifested on every occasion, while I had the honour of serving with him, gave life and ease to the most arduous undertakings. Too heedless of his personal security when in the field, his devotion to the care and honour of his army has caused the termination of his valuable life. The major-general has left a wife and family, for whom I am confident his grateful country will provide.

" The skirmish which had deprived the army of its brave general, was a prelude to a most decisive victory over the flower of the enemy's troops. Colonel Brooke, on whom the command devoled, having pushed forward our force to within five miles of Baltimore, where the enemy, about 6000 or 7000, had taken up an advanced position, strengthened by field-pieces, and where he had disposed himself, apparently with the intention of making a determined resistance, fell upon the enemy with such impetuosity, that he was obliged soon to give way, and fly in every direction, leaving on the field of battle a considerable number of killed and wounded, and two pieces of cannon.

" For the particulars of this brilliant affair, I beg leave to refer their lordships to rear, admiral Cockburn's despatch, transmitted herewith.

"At day-break the next morning, the bombs having taken their stations within shell-range, supported by the Surprise, with the other frigates and sloops, opened their fire upon the fort that protected the entrance of the harbour, and I had now an opportunity of observing the strength and preparations of the enemy.

"The approach to the town on the land side was defended by commanding heights, upon which was constructed a chain of redoubts, connected by a breast-work, with a ditch in front, an extensive train of artillery, and a shew of force that was reported to be from 15 to 20,000 men.

driving in our videttes, and showing an intention of attacking us that evening. I immediately drew Generals Winder and Stricker, nearer to the left of my entrenchments, and to the right of the enemy, with the intention of their falling on his right or rear, should he attack me; or, if he declined it, of attacking him in the morning. To this movement, and to the strength of my defence, which the enemy had the fairest opportunity of observing, I am induced to attribute his retreat, which was commenced at half-past one o'clock on Wednesday

" The entrance by sea, within which the town is retired nearly three miles, was entirely obstructed by a barrier of vessels sunk at the mouth of the harbour, defended inside by gun-boats, flanked on the right by a strong and regular fortification, and on the left by a battery of several heavy guns.

" These preparations rendering it impracticable to afford any essential co-operation by sea, I considered that an attack on the enemy's strong position by the army only, with such disparity of force, though confident of success, might risk a greater loss than the possession of the town would compensate for, while holding in view the ulterior operations of this force in the contemplation of his majesty's government; and therefore, as the primary object of our movement had been already fully accomplished, I communicated my observations to Colonel Brooke, who, coinciding with me in opinion, it was mutually agreed that we should withdraw.

" The following morning, the army began leisurely to retire; and so salutary was the effect produced on the enemy by the defeat he had experienced, that, notwithstanding every opportunity was offered for his repeating the conflict, with an infinite superiority, our troops re-embarked without molestation. The ships of war dropped down as the army retired.

" The result of this demonstration has been the defeat of the army of the enemy, the destruction, by themselves, of a quantity of shipping, the burning of an extensive rope-walk, and other public erections; the causing of them to remove their property from the city, and above all, the collecting and harrassing of the armed inhabitants from the surrounding country; producing a total stagnation of their commerce, and heaping upon them considerable expenses, at the same time effectually drawing off their attention and support from other important quarters.

" It has been a source of the greatest gratification to me, the continuance of that unanimity existing between the two services, which I have before noticed to their lordships; and I have reasons to assure them, that the command of the army has fallen upon a most zealous and able officer in colonel Brooke, who has followed up a system of cordiality that had been so beneficially adopted by his much-lamented chief.

" Rear-admiral Cockburn, to whom I had confided that part of the naval service which was connected with the army, evinced his usual zeal and ability, and executed his important trust to my entire satisfaction.

" Rear-admiral Malcolm, who regulated the collection, debarkation, and re-embarkation of the troops, and the supplies they required, has merited my best thanks for his indefatigable exertions; and I have to express my acknowledgements for the counsel and assistance which, in all our operations, I have received from Rear-admiral Codrington, the captain of the fleet.

" The captains of the squadron, who were employed on the various duties a-float, were all emulous to promote the service in which they were engaged, and, with the officers acting under them, are entitled to my fullest approbation.

" I beg leave to call the attention of their lordships to the report Rear-admiral Cockburn has made, of the meritorious and gallant conduct of the naval brigade; as well as to the accompanying letter from colonel Brooke, expressing his obligation to captain Edward Crofton, who commanded, and captains T. B. Sullivan, Rowland, Money, and Robert Ramsay, who had charge of divisions; and I have to recommend these officers, together with those who are particularly noticed by the Rear-admiral, to their lordship's favourable consideration.

" Captain Robyns, of the royal marines who commanded the marines of the squadron on this occasion, and in the operations

morning. In this he was so favored by the extreme darkness, and a continued rain, that we did not discover it until day-light.
I have now the pleasure of calling your attention to the brave commander of Fort M'Henry, Major Armistead, and to the operations confined to that quarter. The enemy made his approach by water at the same time that his army was advancing on the land, and commenced a discharge of bombs and rockets

against Washington, being severely wounded, I beg leave to bring him to their lordship's recollection, as having been frequently noticed for his gallant conduct during the services in the Chesapeake, and to recommend him with Lieutenant Sampson Marshall, of the Diadem, who is dangerously wounded, to their lordship's favour and protection.

"First-Lieutenant John Lawrence, of the Royal Marine Artillery, who commanded the rocket-brigade, has again rendered essential service, and is highly spoken of by Colonel Brooke.

" Captain Edward Crofton, who will have the honor of delivering this despatch, is competent to explain any further particulars; and I beg leave to recommend him to their Lordships' protection, as a most zealous and intelligent officer.

I have the honor to be, &c.,

ALEXANDER COCHRANE,

Vice-Admiral, and Commander in Chief.
To John Wilson Croker, Esq. &c.

From Rear-Admiral Cockburn to Sir Alexander Cochrane.

H. M. S. Severn, in the Patapsco.
15th Sept., 1814.

Sir,—In furtherance of the instructions I had the honor to receive from you on the 11th instant, I landed at day-light on the 12th with Major-General Ross, and the force under his command, at a place the General and myself had previously fixed upon, near to North-point, at the entrance of the Patapsco; and, in conformity with his wishes, I determined on remaining on shore, and accompanying the army, to render him every assistance within my power during the contemplated movements and operations; therefore, as soon as our landing was completed, I directed Captain Nourse, of this ship, to advance up to the Patapsco with the frigate, sloop, and bomb-ships, to bombard the fort, and threaten the water approach to Baltimore, and I moved on with the army and seamen (under Captain Edward Crofton) at-

tached to it, on the direct road leading to the above mentioned town.

"We had advanced about five miles, (without any other occurrence than taking prisoners a few light horse-men,) when the General and myself, being with the advanced guard, observed a division of the enemy posted at the turning of the road, extending into a wood on our left; a sharp fire was almost immediately opened upon us, and as quickly returned with considerable effect by our advanced guard, which pressing steadily forward, soon obliged the enemy to run off with the utmost precipitation, leaving behind him several men killed and wounded; but it is with the most heartfelt sorrow I have to add, that in this short and desultory skirmish, my gallant and highly valued friend, the Major-General, received a musket-ball through his arm into his breast, which proved fatal to him on his way to the water-side for re-embarkation.

".Our country, sir, has lost in him one of its best and bravest soldiers; and those who knew him, as I did, a friend most honored and beloved; and I trust, sir, I may be forgiven for considering it a sacred duty I owe to him to mention here, that whilst his wounds were binding up, and we were placing him on the bearer which was to carry him off the field, he assured me that the wounds he had received in the perform-ance of his duty to his country, caused him not a pang; but he felt alone anxiety for a wife and family, dearer to him than his life , whom, in the event of the fatal termination he foresaw, he recommended to the protection and notice of his Majesty's government, and the country.

" Colonel Brooke, on whom the command of the army now devolved, having come up, and the body of our troops having closed with the advance, the whole proceeded forward about two miles further, where we observed the enemy in force drawn up before us; (apparently about 6000 or 7000 strong;) on perceiving our army, he filed off into a

---

at the fort, as soon as he got within range of it. The situation of Major Armistead was peculiarly trying—the enemy having taken his position at such a distance, as to render offensive, operations on the part of the fort entirely fruit-

less, whilst their bombs and rockets were every moment falling in and about it—the officers and men, at the same time entirely exposed. The vessels, however, had the temerity to approach somewhat nearer—they were as soon compelled

large and extensive wood on his right, from which he commenced a canonade on us from his field-pieces, and drew up his men behind a thick paling, where he appeared determined to make his stand. Our field guns answered his with an evident advantage; and so soon as Colonel Brooke had made the necessary dispositions, the attack was ordered, and executed in the highest style possible. The enemy opened his musketry on us from his whole line, immediately we approached within reach of it, and kept up his fire till we reached and entered the wood, when he gave way in every direction, and was chased by us a considerable distance with great slaughter, abandoning his post at the Meeting-house, situated in this wood, and leaving all his wounded, and two of his field-guns, in our possession.

" An advance of this description, against superior numbers of an enemy so posted, could not be effected without loss. I have the honor to enclose a return of what has been suffered by those of the naval department, acting with the army on this occasion; and it is, sir, with the greatest pride and pleasure I report to you, that the brigade of seamen and small arms, commanded by Captain E. Crofton, assisted by Captain Sullivan, Money, and Ramsay, (the three senior commanders with the fleet), who commanded divisions under him, behaved with a gallantry and steadiness which would have done honor to the oldest troops, and which attracted the admiration of the army. The seamen under Mr. Jackson, master's mate of the Tonnant, attached to the rocket brigade, commanded by the first-Lieutenant Lawrence, of the marines, behaved also with equal skill and bravery. The marines, landed from the ships under the command of Captain Robyns, the senior officer of that corps, belonging to the fleet, behaved with their usual gallantry.

"Although, sir, in making to you my report of this action, I know it is right I should confine myself to mentioning only the conduct of those belonging to the naval department, yet I may be excused for venturing

further to state to you, generally, the high admiration with which I viewed the conduct of the whole army, and the ability and gallantry with which it was managed, and headed, by its brave Colonel, which insured to it the success it met with.

"The night being fast approaching, and the troops much fatigued, Colonel Brooke determined on remaining for the night on the field of battle; and, on the morning of the 13th, leaving a small guard at the Meeting-house to collect and protect the wounded, we again moved forwards towards Baltimore; on approaching which it was found to be defended by extremely strong works on every side, and immediately in front of us by an extensive hill, on which was an entrenched camp, and great quantities of artillery; and the information we collected, added to what we observed, gave us to believe that there were at least, within their works, from 15 to 20,000 men. Colonel Brooke lost no time in reconnoitring these defences; after which, he made his arrangement for storming, during the ensuing night, with his gallant little army, the entrenched camp in our front, notwithstanding all the difficulties which it presented. The subsequent communications which we opened with you, however, induced him to relinquish again the idea, and therefore yesterday morning the army retired leisurely to the Meeting-house, where it halted for some hours to make the necessary arrangements respecting the wounded and the prisoners taken on the 12th, which being completed, it made a further short movement in the evening towards the place where it had disembarked, and where it arrived this morning for re-embarkation, without suffering the slightest molestation from the enemy; who, in spite of his superiority of number, did not even venture to look at us during the slow and deliberate retreat.

"As you, sir, were in person with the advanced frigates, sloops, and bomb-vessels, and as, from the road the army took, I did not see them after quitting the beach, it would be superfluous for me to make any re-

to withdraw. During the night, whilst the enemy on the land was retreating, and whilst the bombardment was most severe, two or three rocket vessels and barges succeeded in getting up the Ferry Branch, but they were soon compelled to retire, by the forts in that quarter, commanded by Lieutenant Newcomb, of the navy, and Lieutenant Webster, of the flotilla.

port to you respecting them. I have now, therefore, only to assure you of my entire satisfaction and approbation of the conduct of every officer and man employed under me during the operations above detailed, and to express to you how particularly I consider myself indebted to Captain Edward Crofton, (acting Captain of the Royal Oak,) for the gallantry, ability, and zeal, with which he led on the brigade of seamen in the action of the 12th, and executed all the other services with which he has been entrusted since our landing ; to Captain White, (acting Captain of the Albion,) who attended me as my aide-de-camp the whole time, and rendered me every possible assistance ; to Captains Sullivan, Money, and Ramsay, who commanded divisions of the brigade of seamen ; to Lieutenant James Scott, of the Albion, whom I have had much frequent cause to mention to you on former occasions, and who in the battle of the 12th commanded a division of seamen, and behaved most gallantly, occasionally also acting as an extra aide-de-camp to myself. Captain Robyns, who commanded the marines of the fleet, and who was severely wounded during the engagement, I also beg to recommend to your favourable notice and consideration, as well as Lieutenant George C. Ormston, of the Albion, whom I placed in command of the smaller boats, to endeavour to keep up a communication between the army and navy, which he effected by great perserverance, and thereby rendered us most essential service. In short, sir, every individual seemed animated with equal anxiety to distinguish himself by good conduct on this occasion, and I trust, therefore, the whole will be deemed worthy of your approbation.

"Captain Nourse, of the Severn, was good enough to receive my flag for this service ; he rendered me great assistance in getting the ships to the different stations within the river, and when the storming of the fortified hill was contemplated, he hastened to my assistance with a reinforcement of seamen and marines ; and I should consider myself wanting in candour and justice did I not particularly point out, sir, to you, the high opinion I entertain of the enterprise and ability of this valuable officer, not only for his conduct on this occasion, but on the very many others on which I have employed him since with me in the Chesapeake.

I have the honour to be, &c.

GEO. COCKBURN, Rear Admiral.

Vice Admiral the Hon. Sir A. Cochrane, K.B.
Commander-in-chief.

Colonel Brooke to the same.

On board H. M. S. Tonnant,
September 15, 1814.

DEAR SIR,—1 beg leave to be allowed to state to you, how much much I feel indebted to Captain Crofton, commanding the brigade of sailors from His Majesty's ships under your command ; as also to Captains Sullivan, Money, and Ramsay, for their very great exertions in performing every formation made by His Majesty's troops, having seen myself those officers expose themselves to the hottest of the enemy's fire, to keep their men in the line of march with the disciplined troops. The obedient and steady conduct of the sailors, believe me, sir, excited the admiration of every individual of the army, as well as my greatest gratitude.

Believe me to be, dear sir,

ARTHUR BROOKE, Col.-com.

Vice Admiral the Hon. Sir A. Cochrane, K.B.
Commander-in-chief.

Seven killed and forty-four wounded.

The delicate manner in which General Smith disposes of the affair at North Point is not a little remarkable. To read his despatch it would be supposed that the action was only an affair of picquets. "Our videttes were driven in," says the General, without adding one syllable to the effect that he and his whole army were routed, and that such a salutary lesson was given as effectually prevented the Americans from offering the least opposition to Col. Brooke's retreat.

What says Ingersol, as to this action having been an affair of picquets : first—"during

General Smith's Despatch.

These forts also destroyed one of the barges, with all on board. The barges and battery at the Lazaretto, under the command of Lieutenant Rutter, of the flotilla, kept up a brisk, and it is believed, a successful fire, during the hottest period of the bombardment.

more than an hour the battle of North Point was well contested, * * * * * * * Secondly—" the misconduct of one regiment, Col. Ansey's, caused some confusion, and forced General Stricher to yield the field of battle." Now for General Armstrong's testimony. " The march was resumed and a battle fought of one hour and twenty minutes' continuance."

If any credit is to be attached to these statements, General Stricher must have entertained very curious ideas of a battle, if he considered North Point as a mere skirmish of videttes. Again, he says that he had an intention of "attacking him (Col. Brooke) in the morning." If such were really Colonel Stricher's intention, what was there to prevent pursuit; allowing even that Col. Brooke moved off his army unperceived, he halted within a very short distance a sufficiently long time to have allowed the American forces to overtake them, and every one is aware that a retreating army rarely fights with as much spirit as one on the advance—why, then, did not Stricher, if so anxious to fight, hang on the enemy's rear, harass his retreat and force him to give battle. We have shown that it could not have arisen from want of troops, and there is no alternative left, in spite of General Stricher's assertions to the contrary, but to ascribe it to want of inclination. We have, however, devoted quite space enough to the doughty American General.

It would be difficult to decide whether the Io Pœans of the Government Organs over the disastrous attack on Baltimore, or their denunciations of the British for the wound to their vanity, inflicted at Washington, were loudest. There is, however, very little doubt, but that it was

Opinions of the American writers on the descent on Baltimore.

to the death of General Ross alone, that the safety of Baltimore was attributable. The waters of the Patapsco were too shallow to permit the near approach of the British frigates to Fort McHenry, but it is well known that the Captains of the Severn, Euryalus, Hebrus, and Havannah frigates, offered to lighten their vessels and lay them along side of the American fort, and it would almost appear as if nothing prevented the offer being accepted, but the state of indecision into which the naval commanders were thrown by the death of General Ross. Had Sir Alexander Cochrane acted with his usual decision, the Java and other vessels of war must have been captured, Baltimore must have fallen, and instead of the annals of Great Britain recording a disaster, another victory would have been added to her long roll of triumphs.

Plattsburg.

Hitherto our task has been comparatively painless, as when we had to chronicle defeat, we have been enabled to show that to superior numbers alone was it attributable, and we have also proved by figures from American writers, that, in almost every instance where victory was achieved, it was against a superior force. It is now, however, our duty to chronicle one of the most humiliating expeditions ever sustained by a British force, and the task is the more painful as the defeat arose from no misconduct on the part of the troops, but was solely produced by the imbecility and vacillation of Sir George Provost. We will, however, permit the unfortunate commander of the British forces to tell his own tale first, and in our next chapter we will enter on a review of the whole transaction. Extracts from the the American commander, General Macomb's dispatch will be also found in our notes.*

---

* " The governor-general of the Canadas, Sir George Prevost, having collected all the disposable force in Lower Canada, with a view of conquering the country as far as Crown Point, and Ticonderoga, entered the territories of the United States on the 1st of the month, and occupied the village of Champlain: there he avowed his intentions, and issued orders and proclamations, tending to disuade the people from their allegiance, and inviting them to furnish his army with provisions. He immediately began to impress the waggons and teams in the vicinity, and loaded them with his heavy baggage and stores. From this I was persuaded he intended to attack this place. I had but just returned from the lines, where I had commanded a fine brigade, which was broken up to form the division under major-general Izard, and ordered to the westward. Being senior officer, he left me in command; and, except the four companies of the 6th regiment, I had not an organized battalion among those remaining. The garrison was composed of convalescents and recruits of the new regiments, all in the greatest confusion, as well as the ordnance and stores, and the works in no state of defence.

From Sir George Prevost to Earl Bathurst.

Head-quarters, Plattsburgh, State of N.Y.,
MY LORD, Sept. 11, 1814.

" Upon the arrival of the reinforcements from the Garonne, I lost no time in assembling three brigades on the frontier of Lower Canada, extending from the river Richelieu to the St. Lawrence, and in forming them into a division under the command of Major-General De Rottenburg, for the purpose of carrying into effect His Royal Highness the Prince Regent's commands, which had been conveyed to me by your lordship in your despatch of the 3d of June last.

"As the troops concentrated and approached the line of separation between this province and the United States, the American army abandoned its entrenched camp on the river Chazy, at Champlain ; a position I immediately seized, and occupied in force on the 3d instant. The following day, the whole of the left division advanced to the village of Chazy, without meeting the least opposition from the enemy.

"On the 5th, it halted within eight miles of this place, having surmounted the difficulties created by the obstructions in the road from the felling of trees and the removal of bridges. The next day the division moved upon Plattsburgh, in two columns, on parallel road ; the right column led by Major-General Power's brigade, supported by four companies of light infantry and a demi-brigade, under Major-General Robinson ; the left by Major-General Brisbane's brigade.

" The enemy's militia, supported by his regulars, attempted to impede the advance of the right column, but they were driven before it from all their positions, and the column entered Plattsburg. This rapid movement having reversed the strong position taken up by the enemy at Dead creek, it was precipitately abandoned by him, and his gun-boats alone left to defend the ford, and to prevent our restoring the bridges, which had been imperfectly destroyed—an inconvenience soon surmounted.

"Here I found the enemy in the occupation of an elevated ridge of land on the south branch (bank) of the Saranac, crowned with three strong redoubts and other field works, and block-houses armed with heavy ordnance, with their flotilla* at anchor out of gun-shot from the shore, consisting of a

---

To create an emulation and zeal among the officers and men in completing the works, I divided them into detachments, and placed them near the several forts ; declaring in orders, that each detachment was the garrison of its own work, and bound to defend it to the last extremity. The enemy advanced cautiously and by short marches, and our soldiers worked day and night, so that by the time he made his appearance before the place we were prepared to receive him. General Izard named the principal work Fort-Moreau ; and, to remind the troops of the actions of their brave countrymen, I called the redoubt on the right Fort-Brown, and that on the left Fort-Scott. Besides these three works, we had two blockhouses strongly fortified. Finding, on examining, the returns of the garrison, that our force did not exceed 1500 effective men for duty, and well informed that the enemy had as many thousands, I called on general Mooers, of the New York militia, and arranged with him plans for bringing forth the militia, *en masse*. The inhabitants of the village fled with their families and effects, except a few worthy citizens and some boys, who formed themselves into a party, received rifles, and were exceedingly useful. By the 4th of the month, general Mooers collected about 700 militia, and advanced seven miles on the Beckman-town road, to watch the motions of the enemy, and to skirmish with him as he advanced ; also to obstruct the roads with fallen trees, and to break up the bridges. On the lake-road at Dead creek bridge, I posted 200 men, under captain Sproul, of the 13th regiment, with orders to abattis the woods, to place obstructions in the road, and to fortify himself ; to this party I added two field pieces. In advance of that position was lieut.-col. Appling, with 110 riflemen, watching the movements of the enemy, and procuring intelligence. It was ascertained, that before day-light on the 6th, the enemy would advance in two columns on the two roads before mentioned, dividing at Sampson's a little below Chazy village. The column on the Beckman-town road proceeded most rapidly ; the militia skirmished with his advanced parties, and except a few brave men, fell back most precipitately in the greatest disorder, notwithstanding the British troops did not deign to fire on them, except by their flankers and advanced patroles. The night previous, I ordered major Wool to advance with a detachment of 250 men to support the militia, and set them an example of firmness ; also captain Leonard, of the light-artillery, was directed to proceed with two pieces to be on the ground before day ; yet he did not make his appearance until eight o'clock when the enemy had approached within

---

* The Saratoga, 26 guns ; Surprise, 20 guns ; Thunderer, 16 guns ; Preble, 7 guns ; 10 gun-boats, 14 guns.

ship, a brig, a schooner, a sloop, and ten-gun boats.

"I immediately communicated this circumstance to Captain Downie, who had been recently appointed to command the vessels * on Lake Champlain, consisting of a ship, a brig, two sloops, and 12 gun-boats; and requested his co-operation, and in the mean time batteries were constructed for the guns brought from the rear.

"On the morning of the 11th, our flotilla was seen over the isthmus which joins Cumberland-head with the main-land, steering for Plattsburgh Bay. I immediately ordered that part of the brigade under Major-General Robinson, which had been brought forward, consisting of our light infantry companies, third battalion 27th and 76th regiments, and Major-General Power's brigade, consisting of the third, fifth, and the first battalion of the 27th and 58th regiments, to force the fords of the Saranac, and advance, provided with scaling-ladders, to escalade the enemy's works upon the height; this force was placed under the command of Major-General Robinson. The batteries opened their fire the instant the ships engaged.

"It is now with deep concern I inform your lordship, that notwithstanding the intrepid valor with which Captain Downie led his flotilla into action, my most sanguine hopes of complete success were not long afterwards, blasted, by a combination, as appeared to us, of unfortunate events, to which naval warfare is peculiarly exposed. Scarcely had his majesty's troops forced a passage across the Saranac, and ascended the height on which stand the enemy's works, when I had the extreme mortification to hear the shout of victory from the enemy's works, in consequence of the British flag being lowered on board the Confiance and Linnet, and to see our gun-boats seeking their safety in flight. This unlooked for event deprived me of the co-operation of the fleet, without which the further prosecution of the service was become impracticable, I did not hesitate to arrest the course of the troops advancing to the attack, because the most complete success would have been unavailing, and the possession of the enemy's works offered no advantage to compensate for the loss we must have sustained in acquiring possession of them.

---

two miles of the village. With his conduct, therefore, I am not well pleased. Major Wool, with his party, disputed the road with great obstinacy, but the militia could not be prevailed on to stand, notwithstandimg the exertions of their general and staff-officers; although the fields were divided by strong stone walls, and they were told that the enemy could not possibly cut them off. The state dragoons of New York wear red coats; and they being on the heights to watch the enemy, gave constant alarm to the militia, who mistook them for the enemy, and feared his getting in their rear.

Finding the enemy's columns had penetrated within a mile of Plattsburg, I despatched my aide-de-camp, Lieutenant Root, to bring off the detachment at Dead creek, and to inform Lieut. Colonel Appling that I wished him to fall on the enemy's right flank. The Colonel fortunately arrived just in time to save his retreat, and to fall in with the head of a column debouching from the woods. Here he poured in a destructive fire from his riflemen at rest, and continued to annoy the enemy until he formed a junction with major Wool. The field-pieces did considerable execution among the enemy's columns.

So undaunted, however, was the enemy, that he never deployed in his whole march, always pressing on in column. Finding that every road was full of troops, crowding on us on all sides, I ordered the field-pieces to retire across the bridge, and form a battery for its protection, and to cover the retreat of the infantry, which was accordingly done, and the parties of Appling and Wool, as well as that of Sproul, retired, alternately keeping up a brisk fire until they got under cover of the works. The enemy's light troops occupied the houses near the bridge, and kept up a constant firing from the windows and balconies, and annoyed us much. I ordered them to be driven out with hot shot, which soon put the houses in flames, and obliged those sharp-shooters to retire. The whole day, until it was too late to see, the enemy's light troops endeavoured to drive our guards from the bridge, but they suffered dearly for their perseverance. An attempt was also made to cross the upper bridge, where the militia handsomely drove them back. The column which marched by the lake-road was much impeded by the obstructions, and the removal of the bridge at Dead creek; and, as it passed the creek and beach, the gallies kept up a lively and galling fire. Our troops being now all on the south side of the Saranac, I directed the planks to be taken off the bridges and piled up in the form of brest-works, to cover our par-

---

* The Confiance, 36 guns; Linnet, 18 guns; Broke, 10 guns; Shannon, 10 guns; 12 gun-oats. 16 guns.

"I have ordered the batteries to be dismantled, the guns withdrawn, and the baggage, with the wounded men who can be removed, to be sent to the rear, in order that the troops may return to Chazy to-morrow, and on the following day to Champlain, where I propose to halt until I have ascertained the use the enemy propose making of the naval ascendancy they have acquired on Lake Champlain.

"I have the honour to transmit herewith returns of the loss sustained by the left division of this army in its advance to Plattsburg, and in forcing a passage across the river Saranac. I have the honor, &c.,

GEORGE PREVOST.

Earl Bathurst, &c.

Return of killed and wounded;—2 captains, 1 ensign, 4 serjeants, 30 rank and file, 1 horse, killed, 1 general staff, 1 captain, 6 lieutenants, 7, serjeants, 135 rank and file, 2 horses, wounded; 4 lieutenants, 2 serjeants, 1 drummer, 48 rank and file, 6 horses, missing.

Missing—76th foot;—Lieutenants G Hutch, G. Ogilvie, and E. Marchington.

Canadian Chasseurs;—Lieut. E. Vigneau.

EDW. BAYNES, Adj.-Gen., N. A.

From Sir James Lucas Yeo to Mr. Croker.

H. M. S. St. Lawrence, Kingston,
Sir,   September 24, 1814.

"I have the honor to transmit, for the information of the lords commissioners of the admiralty, a copy of a letter from Captain Pring, late commander of his majesty's brig Linnet.

"It appears to me, and I have good reason to believe, that captain Downie was urged, and his ship hurried into action, before she was in a fit state to meet the enemy.

"I am also of opinion, that there was not the least necessity for our squadron giving the enemy such decided advantages, by going into their bay to engage them. Even had they been successful, it would not in the least have assisted the troops in storming the batteries; whereas, had our troops taken their batteries first, it would have obliged the enemy's squadron to quit the bay, and give ours a fair chance.

I have the honor, to be, &c.

JAMES LUCAS YEO,

Commodore and commander in chief.

J. W. Croker, Esq., &c. &c. &c.

---

ties intended for disputing the passage, which afterwards enabled us to hold the bridges against very superior numbers. **From** the 7th to the 14th, the enemy was employed in getting on his battering-train, and erecting his batteries and approaches, and constantly skirmishing at the bridges and fords. By this time the militia of New York and the volunteers of Vermont were pouring in from all quarters. I advised General Mooers to keep his force along the Saranac to prevent the enemy's crossing the river, and to send a strong body in his rear to harrass him day and night, and keep him in continual alarm. The militia behaved with great spirit after the first day, and the volunteers of Vermont were exceedingly serviceable. Our regular troops, notwithstanding the constant skirmishing, and repeated endeavours of the enemy to cross the river, kept at their work day and night, strengthening the defences, and evinced a determination to hold out to the last extremity. It was reported that the enemy only waited the arrival of his flotilla to make a general attack. About eight in the morning of the 11th, as we expected, the flotilla appeared in sight round Cumberland Head, and at nine bore down and engaged at anchor in the bay off the town. At the same instant the batteries were opened on us, and continued throwing bomb-shells, shrapnells, balls, and Congreve rockets, until sun-set when the bombardment ceased, every battery of the enemy being silenced by the superiority of our fire. The naval engagement lasted but two hours, in full view of both armies. Three efforts were made by the enemy to pass the river at the commencement of the cannonade and bombardement, with a view of assaulting the works, and they had prepared for that purpose an immense number of scaling-ladders. One attempt to cross was made at the village bridge, another at the upper bridge, and a third at a ford about three miles from the works. At the two first he was repulsed by the regulars—at the ford by the brave volunteers and militia, where he suffered severely in killed, and wounded, and prisoners: a considerable body crossed the stream, but were either killed, taken or driven back, The woods at this place were very favourable to the operations of the militia. A whole company of the 76th regiment was here destroyed, the three Lieutenants and 27 men prisoners, the Captain and the rest killed. I cannot forgo the pleasure of here stating the gallant conduct of Captain M'Glassin, of the 15th regiment, who was ordered to ford the river, and attack a party constructing a battery on the right of the enemy's line, within 500 yards of Fort-Brown, which he handsomely executed at midnight, with 50 men; drove off the working party, consisting of 150, and defeated a covering party of the same number, killing one officer and six men in the charge, and wounding many. At dusk the enemy withdrew his artillery, &c.

CHAPTER XXIV.

The unfortunate commander of the British forces, in the expedition against Plattsburg, has been almost universally made the target against which the most envenomed arrows have been directed. Peace be to his ashes, as his death was occasioned by over anxiety to hasten home in order to clear his character from the imputations cast on it, and we would that justice permitted us to pass over in silence the last act of the drama. This, however, may not be, and did not even impartiality demand a faithful narration of the unfortunate result of the most important expedition undertaken during the three years war, the loud boastings of the Americans would impose on us the necessity of showing that it was not to the men that the defeat at Plattsburg was attributable, but that to the commander alone was the disgraceful termination of the expedition due.

The attack on Plattsburg, its failure, and its consequences.

Sir James Yeo has been accused of regarding Sir George Provost with a jealous eye, we therefore make no use of his dispatch to Mr. John Wilson Croker; that however of Captain Pring contains some passages which render it very difficult to understand Sir George Provost's subsequent conduct. Captain Pring says, " in consequence of the earnest solicitation of his excellency Sir George Provost for the co-operation of the naval force on this lake (Champlain) to attack that of the enemy, who were placed for the support of their works at Plattsburg, which it was proposed should be stormed by the troops, at the same moment the naval action should commence in the bay; every possible exertion was used to accelerate the armament of the new ship, that the military movements might not be postponed at such an advanced season of the year, longer than was absolutely necessary." Sir George Provost's dispatches all tend to prove the correctness of Captain Pring's statement, that the attacks were to be simultaneous; and so confident of this was poor Captain Downie, that he addressed his men to this effect before going into action: " My lads we shall be immediately assisted by the army on shore, let us show them that our part of the duty is well done." This presumption on the part of Downie was fully warranted by Sir George's plans; and it is therefore a most extraordinary fact, that a General, who had on previous occasions proved himself a brave and energetic officer, should have on this occasion by his indecision and timidity have cast a lasting slur on himself and the army under his command. We

25

particularly mention the army as we do not consider that any discredit attached to Downie, his brother officers or men of the fleet; and when it is taken into consideration that, sixteen days before the action, the Confiance was on the stocks; had an unorganized crew, composed of different drafts of men from Quebec, many of whom only joined the day before; and were totally unknown either to the officers or to each other; was in want of gunlocks, as well as other necessary appointments not to be procured in the country, the decided advantage possessed by the enemy both in tonnage, guns and men, will be so apparent, that instead of a stain resting on the fleet the conviction will be forced on all, taking into consideration what was done, that, properly assisted by Sir G. Provost, the capture of both the American fleet and army was inevitable. Nay, so impressed with this fact was the American commander that he hesitated for some time to take possession of the British vessels that had struck their colours, as he was busily engaged in getting his own vessels out of reach of the fire which he momentarily expected would be opened on him from the captured shore batteries.

It must not be supposed that in the attempt to vindicate the conduct of the sailors, we intend to cast any reflection whatsoever on the troops. No, the men who had braved danger in many a well fought field in the Peninsula, and who had shared in the perils of Burgos, Badajoz, and St. Sebastian, were not likely to be daunted by the feeble opposition offered by fifteen hundred of the refuse of the American army, and three thousand raw militia; and had they but been properly commanded the boasting paragraphs of Messrs. Ingersol, Thompson, Smith and O'Connor would not have been forthcoming to feed the national taste for boasting.

Of all the American writers we must certainly select Ingersol as the one who has made most capital out of the defeat at Plattsburg, and although there is the most undoubted evidence to the contrary, he boldly states that Captain Downie's vessel, the Confiance, was manned with "three hundred picked seamen." Forgetful, however, of this assertion, on the next page he states that the Americans remained at anchor in "perfect quiet and order, characteristic of American naval discipline, in contrast with the clamorous defiance of British sea fights."

Now we deny Mr. Ingersol's statements as to American discipline point blank, and we confidently appeal to any one who may have had an opportunity of comparing the two services. In his anxiety to prove that nothing was wanting to complete the preparations on the part of the Americans, Ingersol treats us even to the prayer that was poured forth by McDonough on this occasion, and by way of proving that Heaven itself was auspicious, he adds, that "a cock flew upon a gun slide, clapped his wings and crowed," a signal which "Napoleon or Cæsar would have hailed with delight." As a sequitur to this auspicious omen, we are told further that on land "the renowned veterans of Wellington fled, leaving their sick and wounded," and that they were pursued by militia not one-fourth of their number. This statement hardly tallies with McComb's version. We can, however, in view of the brilliant achievements in the west, permit a thorough Yankee historian for once to indulge his desire to satisfy his fellow-countrymen with highly-coloured narratives. There is, however, one assertion put forth by Ingersol so atrocious that it must not be passed over,—it is that Sir George Provost, in order to cover his retreat "sent an officer to General Moir's house to inform his son, left in charge of it, that preliminaries of peace were signed at Ghent. This Ingersol affects to believe was a stratagem of Sir George's, but as he does not venture to adduce a single proof in support of his assertion, we can well afford to rank the statement as about equally worthy of belief with most other deductions of the same writer.

In his own anxiety to prove how perfect everything American must be, Ingersol furnishes some very conclusive evidence as to the strength of the American position. He says, "to explain the cause of this strange defeat of the British army it will be necessary to state that the Village of Plattsburg is situated on the west side of Lake Champlain; and a river called Saranac, on its way easterly, passes through this village, dividing it into two parts, and empties its waters into the bay, being a part of Lake Champlain. This stream, for the distance of four miles, or more, in consequence of its rocky shores and bottom is rendered impassable by fording, and at that time there were but two places where they crossed it on bridges. On the south side of this stream, a short distance from the lower bridge was the place selected for the forts, it being on an eminence commanding a view of the whole village. * * * * The inhabitants, together with the troops, on finding the enemy were near, threw down the upper bridge and took the plank off from the lower one, and made every other arrangement to prevent the enemy from reaching the fort.

All this shows that Provost had some difficulties to contend with, but taking them all into consideration it is yet too apparent that nothing but the military imbecility of the commander occasioned the disgrace that attached to the nation by the disastrous catastrophe of Plattsburg. It is evident that Sir George Provost did not evince on this occasion the smallest combination of plan, or sign of execution; "nor was," as Veritas observes, "any object of the expedition visible unless through its effect, that of bringing on the destruction of our fleet, without making an effort to save it, or to rescue the army from the disgrace of being tame spectators of that destruction."

Enough, however, has been said of an expedition, which we would could be blotted from the page of English history, and which must ever be a proof that, no matter what the high spirits and gallantry of troops may be, unless they are properly commanded, reverses such as that of Plattsburg must be expected, instead of the brilliant deeds of former days in the Peninsula, or the later deeds of daring at Alma, Balaclava, or Inkermann.

Passing from the north to the south, we find a task imposed on us nearly as painful as the record of British disasters at Plattsburg, viz., the attack on New Orleans.

There is little doubt that the British government originated the expedition to New Orleans under the impression that they would receive material assistance from the Spanish portion of the population, and that from the French little or no opposition might be expected. Precisely the same arguments were brought to bear on the declaration of war by the United States against Great Britain, by those who believed, or affected to believe, that Canadians desired nothing so much as to be freed from the intolerable weight of the British yoke. One conjecture proved as fallacious as the other, and the expedition against New Orleans terminated about as disastrously as any of the various invasions of Canadian territory by vapouring or gasconading militia generals.

The expedition was not, however, undertaken entirely without some probability of its paying for its expenses. For three years the cotton and sugar crops of Louisiana and Mississippi had been accumulating in the warehouses of the queen city of the South, and the promoters of the scheme anticipated that at least fifteen million of dollars must reward the invading force.

Expedition to New Orleans.

The gain to be expected from the expedition.

The first steps taken by the British commanders in this expedition were ill-advised, for without reflecting that a traitor to his country will most probably be one also to his new friends, the British commanders were most signally over-reached in their attempts to secure the assistance of Lafitte and his men (most noted pirates and the scourge of the Gulf of Mexico) both as pilots and as active agents in the proposed descent. The chief of these freebooters, however, played a most artful game with the British commanders, and while affecting to betray his country, he was in reality forwarding all their plans to the Governor of the State, and organising a vigorous defence of the important post of which he and his followers had possessed themselves. For this, (we cannot call it treachery,) good service, Lafitte, his brother and his band received full pardon from the President of the United States, fer their previous misdeeds.

Lafitte, the chief of the Banatarian pirates.

The British, deceived by Lafitte's repr sentations, directed their first attack against Fort Bowyer, situated on Mobile Point, and forming the extremity of a peninsula which is joined to the continent by a narrow isthmus, which divides Bonsecours bay from that of Perdid.

This attack on Fort Bowyer was a very

Attack on Fort Bowyer, and defeat of the British. ill-conceived, badly planned, and worse executed manœuvre, and the result of the attack was the loss of the Hermes, twenty-two gun corvette, very great injury inflicted on the Sophia, eighteen guns, and the loss in killed and wounded of seventy-two men. The Hermes grounded within musket shot of a heavy battery, and Captain Perry, her commander, finding every effort to get her off unavailing, removed his wounded and set his vessel on fire. It is needless to add that the attack on the fort was a most signal failure.

Unfortunate, however, as this affair was in loss of vessels and life, it proved equally so in the opportunity afforded to the enemy of putting forward the most outrageous assertions. One writer, Latour, in his "war in Louisiana," converts the twenty-two, and eighteen gun corvettes, the Hermes and Sophia into frigates, and states the British force at ninety-two guns and thirteen hundred and thirty men, modestly giving his own countrymen eight guns and one hundred and thirty men. Fortunately Fort Bowyer was afterwards taken and four hundred and fourteen men captured in it. The Americans acknowledge a loss of only four killed and four wounded, estimating that of the British, (ascertained from what source it is impossible to say,) at one hundred and sixty-two killed and seventy-two wounded.

After the failure of the attack on Fort

Preparations for the attack and defence of New Orleans. Bowyer the American naval commander, Commodore Patterson, turned his attention to obstructing the passage of the British flotilla, which was then preparing, with a large body of troops on board, for the attack on New Orleans, which stands on the left bank of the Mississippi, one hundred and five miles from its mouth.

For this purpose he constructed a formi-

Defence of the gun boats. dable force of gun-boats and men, but the defence made by them was about as

effective as the British attack on Fort Bowyer, and resulted in the capture or destruction of the whole flotilla, and although Lieutenant Ap Jones, whose despatch will be found below,[*] has endeavoured to make the best of the affair, there can be no doubt but that Captain Lockyier very soon convinced Lieut. Ap Jones of the difference between British and American seamen when fairly matched.

It is not only remarkable, but amusing to

Discrepancies in account of the gun-boat action. note how the American commanders and historians, in their attempts to soften down everything which might offend the national vanity have contradicted each other. Captain Jones, in his despatch, speaks of the British barges "as almost as large as the gun-boats themselves." Latour, in his anxiety to account for the bad firing of the Americans, speaks of them as "objects of so small a size, &c."

In order to test the truth of Lieut. Ap. Jones' statement, we give the size of one of the gun-boats under his command, and contrast it with that of the Hunter, styled by the Americans a British brig of war:—

	United States Boat.	Hunter.
Weight of broadside in lbs.	59	28
Crew	41	39
Tonnage	112	74

This misrepresentation was not confined to Lieutenant Jones. Commodore M'Donough, although fully aware that the smallest gun-boat was seventy-five tons, describes two

---

* From Lieutenant Jones to Com. Patterson.

New Orleans, 12th March, 1815.

SIR,

Having sufficiently recovered my strength, I do myself the honour of reporting to you the particulars of the capture of the division of United States' gun-boats late under my command.

On the 12th of December, 1814, the enemy's fleet off Ship Island increased to such a force as to render it no longer safe or prudent for me to continue on that part of the lakes with the small force which I commanded. I therefore determined to gain a station near the Malheureux islands as soon as possible, which situation would better enable me to oppose a further penetration of the enemy up the lakes, and at the same time afford me an opportunity of retreating to the Petites Coquilles if necessary.

At 10, a.m., on the 13th, I discovered a large

British vessels, some two tons smaller than this, as " sloops of war."

Do not these statements clearly convict Messrs. M'Donough and Jones of wilful misrepresentation on their face? Who ever heard of a ship's launch measuring one hundred and twelve, or even seventy-five tons, even at the present time, when the size of boats have nearly increased in the same ratio as ships? Let the reader fancy a frigate measuring one thousand and fifty tons, having to hoist up, either on deck or at the stern, boats of one hundred and twelve tons!

Again, Mr. Latour makes the British launches objects of so small a size, that it

was impossible to hit them; yet he very complacently dwells on the precision of the American fire against the larger vessels— these larger vessels being actually much smaller than the American gun-boats.

Another trifling mistake on the part of Lieut. Jones is the omission of twelve guns (four and six pounders) and two five-and-a half-inch howitzers, which were found in the captured vessels, and not included in his force, although it was evident that they had been recently used. We have, however, said enough to show how much value may be placed on the statements of either Lieut. Jones or Mr. Latour. Had we, too, not brought sufficient proofs forward, it is only necessary to add,

flotilla of barges had left the fleet, (shaping their course towards the Pas Chretien,) which I supposed to be a disembarkation of troops intended to land at that place. About 2, p.m. the enemy's flotilla having gained the Pas Chretien, and continuing their course to the westward, convinced me that an attack on the gun-boats was designed. At this time the water in the Lakes was uncommonly low, owing to the westerly wind which had prevailed for a number of days previous, and which still continued from the same quarter. Nos. 150, 162 and 163, although in the best channel, were in 12 or 18 inches less water than their draught. Every effort was made to get them afloat by throwing overboard all articles of weight that could be dispensed with. At 3. 30, the flood-tide had commenced; got under weigh, making the best of my way towards the Petites Coquilles. At 3. 45, the enemy despatched three boats to cut out the schooner Seahorse, which had been sent into the bay St. Louis that morning to assist in the removal of the public stores, which I had previously ordered. There finding a removal impracticable, I ordered preparations to be made for their destruction, least they should fall into the enemy's hands. A few discharges of grape-shot from the Seahorse compelled the three boats, which had attacked her, to retire out of reach of her guns, until they were joined by four others, when the attack was recommenced by the seven boats.— Mr. Johnson having chosen an advantageous position near the two 6-pounders mounted on the bank, maintained a sharp action for near 30 minutes, when the enemy hauled off, having one boat apparently much injured, and with the loss of several men killed and wounded. At 7. 30, an explosion at the bay, and soon after a large fire, induced me to believe the Seahorse was blown up and the public store-house set on fire, which was proved to be the fact.

About 1 a.m. on the 14th, the wind having entirely died away, and our vessels become unmanageable, came to anchor in the west-end of Malheureux island's passage. At daylight

next morning, still a perfect calm, the enemy's flotilla was about nine miles from us at anchor, but soon got in motion and rapidly advanced on us. The want of wind, and the strong ebb-tide which was setting through the pass, left me but one alternative, which was, to put myself in the most advantageous position, to give the enemy as warm a reception as possible. The commanders were all called on board and made acquainted with my intentions, and the position which each vessel was to take, the whole to form a close line abreast across the channel, anchored by the stern with springs on the cable, &c. &c., thus we remained anxiously awaiting an attack from the advancing foe, whose force I now clearly distinguished to be composed of 42 heavy launches and gun-barges, with three light gigs, manned with upwards of 1000 men and officers. About 9. 30, the Alligator (tender) which was to the southward and eastward, and endeavouring to join the division, was captured by several of the enemy's barges, when the whole flotilla came-to, with their grapnels a little out of reach of our shot, apparently making arrangements for the attack. At 10. 30, the enemy weighed, forming a line abreast in open order, and steering direct for our line, which was unfortunately in some degree broken by the force of the current, driving Nos. 156 and 163 about 100 yards in advance. As soon as the enemy came within reach of our shot, a deliberate fire from our long guns was opened upon him, but without much effect the objects being of so small a size. At 10 minutes before 11, the enemy opened a fire from the whole of his line, when the action became general and destructive on both sides. About 11. 19, the advance boats of the enemy, three in number, attempted to board No. 156, but were repulsed with the loss of nearly every officer killed or wounded, and two boats sunk. A second attempt to board was then made by four other boats, which shared almost a similar fate. At this moment I received a severe wound in my left shoulder, which compelled me to quit deck, leaving it in charge of Mr. George

that Major Latour asserts that several barges were sunk, and that " one hundred and eighty men went down in one." Of this statement we can at once declare that it was false. No boat was sunk except the Tonnant's launch, and, moreover, no barge had on board more than thirty-one men, and further, every man was saved from the Tonnant's launch.

An attempt made by Commodore Patterson afforded fine scope for renewed abuse of Britain and the acts of her commanders. This officer under pretence of ascertaining the fate of the prisoners on board the gun boats dispatched two officers, one of them a Doctor, (to make it appear we presume that the wounded would be neglected by their captors), to obtain the desired information. These officers Admiral Cochrane detained, informing them that they must not consider themselves as prisoners in the full sense of the word, but that as their visit was unseasonable, he could not permit them to return until it would be impossible for them to profit by what they had seen, and put General Jackson *au fait* as to the proposed attack on New Orleans. The attack over, they were at once released, yet this did not prevent the vilest libels being levelled against the British Commander.

Commodore Patterson's attempt to gain information by spies.

In order that the causes which led to the failure of the attack on New Orleans may be better understood we make a short extract from James' description of the natural and artificial features of the country :—

" As the country around New Orleans possesses very peculiar features, a slight digression may be necessary. The bayou Bienvenu is the creek through which all the waters of a large basin, or swamp, about 80 miles in extent, bounded on the north by the Mississippi, on the west by New Orleans, on the north-west, by bayou Sauvage, or Chefmenteur, and on the east by Lake Borgne, into which it empties. It receives the streams of several other bayous, formed by the waters of the surrounding cypress swamps and prairies, as well as of innumerable little streams from the low grounds along the river. It is navigable for vessels of 100 tons, 12 miles from its mouth. Its breadth is from 110 to 150 yards, and it has six feet water on the bar, at common tides, and nine feet at spring tides. Its principal branch is that which is called bayou Mazant, which runs towards the south-west, and receives the waters of the canals of the plantations of Villeré, Lacoste, and Laronde, upon which the British afterwards established their principal encampment. The level of the great basin, on the bank of the principal bayou, is usually 12 feet below the banks of the Mississippi. The overflowing of the waters of all those bayous and canals, occasioned by the tide of the sea, or by the winds raising the waters in the lake, forms, on all their banks, deposits of slime, which are continually raising them above the rest of the soil ; so that the interval between two bayous is below the level of their banks, and the soil is generally covered with water and mud, in which aquatic plants, or large reeds, of the height of from six to eight feet, grow in abundance. It sometimes happens that the rains, or the filtrated waters, collected in these intervals, or basins, not finding a vent, form what are called *trembling prairies ;* which are at all times impassable to men

---

Parker, master's mate, who gallantly defended the vessel until he was severely wounded, when the enemy by his superior number, succeeded in gaining possession of the deck about 10 minutes past 12 o'clock. The enemy immediately turned the guns of his prize on the other gun-boats, and fired several shot previous to striking the American colours. The action continued with unabating severity until 40 minutes past 12 o'clock, when it terminated with the surrender of No. 23, all the other vessels having previously fallen into the hands of the enemy.

In this unequal contest our loss in killed and wounded has been trifling compared to that of the enemy.

Enclosed you will receive a list of the killed and wounded, and a correct statement of the force which I had the honour to command at the commencement of the action, together with an estimate of the force I had to contend against, as acknowledged by the enemy, which will enable you to decide how far the honour of our country's flag has been supported in this conflict.

I have the honour to be, &c.

THOMAS AP CATESBY JONES.

American force, - - 25 guns—204 men.
British   do. - - 42 guns—1200 men.
British loss, - 17 killed—77 wounded.

and domestic animals. The land in Lower Louisiana slopes in the inverse direction of the soil of other countries, being most elevated on the sides of the rivers, and sinking as it recedes from them. The Mississippi, at New Orleans, periodically swells 14 or 15 feet; and is then from three to four feet above the level of its banks. To confine its waters within its bed, dikes or ramparts, called in Louisiana *levées*, have been raised on its banks, from the highlands towards its mouth, a little above the level of the highest swells; without which precaution, the lands would be entirely overflowed, from four to five months in the year. The reader will now be better able to appreciate the difficulties our troops and seamen had to encounter in transporting themselves, their baggage, provisions, and artillery, to the scene of operations on the left bank of the Mississippi."

After the capture of the gun boats the British were enabled to advance to within about six miles of the city, and here, unfortunately, in place of pressing on, the success of the enterprise was considered so certain that a halt was called to recruit the men, and allow the reinforcements to come up. Had the British despised the American soldiers less, and not made so sure of their game, the capital of the Southern Provinces with its millions must have fallen into their hands. To the halt and the advance by the bayou Bienvenu, instead of approaching by Lake Pontchartrain. so as to take the city in the rear, may be ascribed General Jackson's success and the repulse of the British.

Advance of the British.

On the halting of the British General Jackson determined to endeavour to arrest their further progress, and during those days some sharp skirmishing ensued, a good many being killed and wounded on both sides, and the Caroline, American schooner, blown up. This vessel in concert with the Louisiana sloop had effected a powerful diversion on the British flank.

Fighting on the 23rd. and 24th.

The loss of the British may be estimated on those days at two hundred and seventy-five killed and wounded, that of the Americans, according to their own account, at two hundred and thirteen.

On the evening of the 25th Sir Edward Pakenham arrived to take the command, bringing with him reinforcements which brought up the number of his troops to five thousand and forty. The Americans received also considerable reinforcements. making General Jackson's force at least fourteen thousand men.

Arrival of reinforcements.

From this date till the 8th of January a series of conflicts took place, the nature of which will be best explained by the following extract from a work written by a subaltern in the British army.

" During the 28th, 29th, 30th, 31st, strong detachments from the different corps were employed in bringing a train of heavy ordnance from the boats, with ample supply of powder and ball. The labor and difficulty of accomplishing it were beyond calculation. Nor was it the only irksome duty in which we engaged. The piquets were never mounted without suffering, sooner or latter, an attack. Sometime the enemy contented themselves with cannonading the outposts; sometimes they advanced large corps in the day, who amused themselves and us with long unprofitable skirmishes. But their more usual system was to steal forward in sections, after dark, and to harass us with a desultory and troublesome fire of musketry till morning. . . .

" As yet, neither I nor the men had ventured to light a fire. . . . But the day was piercing cold. A heavy shower fell from time to time, and the absolute discomfort of our situation proved too much for the whispers of prudence. Two fires were made to blaze up —one for the men, the other for myself and my companion. It seemed as if the American artillerymen had waited for some such object to direct their aim, for the smoke had hardly begun to ascend, when they played upon us, from a battery of five guns, as perfect a storm of grape-shot as ever whistled past the ears of men so situated, and in five minutes the fires were abandoned. But with this the enemy were not contented; under cover of the cannonade, a body of some two or three hundred infantry advanced, in extended order, from the line. . . . A most uninteresting skirmish ensued. The

Americans, it was perfectly manifest, were raw troops. They made no determined efforts; probably it was not intended they should make efforts to drive us in. But they pressed forward from time to time, creeping along the ground, and running from ditch to ditch, and retreating again as soon as they had discharged their pieces. On our side no movement whatever was made. The men lay down, as I directed, behind a row of bushes, which served at least to conceal them from their opponents, and each file regularly shifting its ground, a pace or two to the right or left, as soon as it had fired. By this means many lives were saved, for the Americans regularly returned our fire, and they never failed to direct their aim to the spots from whence our smoke ascended. The affair having lasted four or five hours, the enemy at length saw fit to withdraw, and we returned to our ditch, with trifling loss of only two wounded. . . Their cannon continued to annoy us to the last, insomuch that the very sentinels were under the necessity of hiding themselves. . . . It was now about midnight, and the darkness had become, almost without a metaphor, such as might be felt. . Worn out with fatigue, I had returned to the ditch, not to seat myself beside a comfortable blaze—for no fire had been lighted, and it would have been madness to think of lighting one—but to rest my limbs a little, and to smoke a cigar. . . The enemy, finding that their heavy artillery hardly reached our camp, had moved two field-pieces and a mortar without their lines, and, advancing them as near to the sentries as a regard for their own safety would allow, were now cannonading, not the outpost, but the main body of the British army. It was easy to perceive that the balls fell not short of their mark, Looking back towards the position, I saw that the fires were hastily covered up, and the murmur of voices which arose gave testimony that they were not thus stifled before it was necessary."

During this time the British acknowledge a loss of fifty-five killed and wounded, the Americans of fifty one.

The grand struggle which was to decide the fate of New Orleans did not, however, take place until the 8th, on the morning of which day the final attack was made by General Pakenham on General Jackson's position.

The extracts from General Lambert's despatch will enable the reader, with the assistance of the respective positions of the two armies, to understand the plan of attack and defence pretty clearly. Gen. Lambert says:

Extract of Despatch from Major General Lambert to Earl Bathurst.

"In order to give your lordship as clear a view as I can, I shall state the position of the enemy. On the left bank of the river it was simply a straight line of about a front of 1000 yards with a parapet, the right resting on the river, and the left on a wood which had been made impracticable for any body of troops to pass. This line was strengthened by flank works, and had a canal of about four feet deep generally, but not altogether of an equal width; it was supposed to narrow towards their left: about eight heavy guns were in position on this line. The Mississippi is here about 800 yards across; and they had on the right bank a heavy battery of 12 guns, which enfiladed the whole front of the position on the left bank.

" Preparations were made on our side, by very considerable labor, to clear out and widen a canal that communicated with a stream by which the boats had passed up to the place of disembarkation, to open it into the Mississippi, by which means troops could be got over to the right bank, and the cooperation of armed boats could be secured.

" The disposition of the attack was as follows:—a corps, consisting of the 85th light infantry, 200 seamen, and 400 marines, the 5th West India Regiment, and four pieces of artillery, under the command of Colonel Thornton, of the 85th, was to pass over during the night, and move along the right bank towards New Orleans, clearing its front until it reached the flanking battery of the enemy on that side, which it had orders to carry.

"The assailing of the enemy's line in front of us, was to be made by the brigade composed of the 4th, 21st, and 44th regiments, with three companies of the 95th, under Major General Gibbs, and by the 3d brigade, consisting of the 93d, two companies of the 95th, and two companies of the fusiliers and

43d, under Major General Keane: some black troops were destined to skirmish in the wood on the right; the principal attack was to be made by Major General Gibbs; the 1st brigade, consisting of the fusiliers and 43d, formed the reserve; the attacking columns were to be provided with fascines, scaling-ladders, and rafts; the whole to be at their stations before day-light. An advanced battery in our front, of six 18-pounders, was thrown up during the night, about 800 yards from the enemy's line. The attack was to be made at the earliest hour. Unlooked-for difficulties, increased by the falling of the river, occasioned considerable delay in the entrance of the armed boats, and those destined to land Colonel Thornton's corps, by which four or five hours were lost, and it was not until past five in the morning, that the 1st division, consisting of 500 men, were over. The *ensemble* of the general movement was lost, and in a point which was of the last importance to the attack on the left bank of the river, although Colonel Thornton, as your lordship will see in his report, which I enclose, ably executed in every particular his instructions, and fully justified the confidence the commander of the forces placed in his abilities. The delay attending that corps occasioned some on the left bank, and the attack did not take place until the columns were discernible from the enemy's lines at more than 200 yards distance; as they advanced, a continued and most galling fire was opened from every part of their line, and from the battery on the right bank.

"The brave commander of the forces, who never in his life could refrain from being at the post of honor, and sharing the dangers to which the troops were exposed, as soon as from his station he had made the signal for the troops to advance, galloped on to the front to animate them by his presence, and he was seen, with his hat off, encouraging them on the crest of the glacis; it was there (almost at the same time) he received two wounds, one in his knee, and another, which was almost instantly fatal, in his body; he fell in the arms of Major M'Dougall, his Aide-de-camp. The effect of this in the sight of the troops, together with Major General Gibbs and Major General Keane being both borne off wounded at the same time, with many other commanding officers, and further, the preparations to aid in crossing the ditch not being so forward as they ought to have been, from, perhaps, the men being wounded who were carrying them, caused a wavering in the column, which in such a situation became irreparable; and as I advanced with the reserve, at about 250 yards from the line, I had the mortification to observe the whole falling back upon me in the greatest confusion.

"In this situation, finding that no impression had been made, that though many men had reached the ditch, and were either drowned or obliged to surrender, and that it was impossible to restore order in the regiments where they were, I placed the reserve in position, until I could obtain such information as to determine me how to act to the best of my judgment, and whether or not I should resume the attack, and if so, I felt it could be done only by the reserve. The confidence I have in the corps composing it would have encouraged me greatly, though not without loss, which might have made the attempt of serious consequence, as I know it was the opinion of the late distinguished commander of the forces, that the carrying of the first line would not be the least arduous service. After making the best reflections I was capable of, I kept the ground the troops then held, and went to meet Vice-Admiral Sir Alexander Cochrane, and to tell him, that under all the circumstances I did not think it prudent to renew the attack that day. At about 10 o'clock, I learnt of the success of Colonel Thornton's corps on the right bank. I sent the commanding officer of the artillery, Colonel Dickson, to examine the situation of the battery, and to report if it was tenable; but informing me that he did not think it could be held with security by a smaller corps than 2000 men, I consequently ordered Lieutenant Colonel Gubbins, on whom the command had devolved, (Colonel Thornton being wounded), to retire.

"The army remained in position until night, in order to gain time to destroy the 18-pounder battery we had constructed the preceding night in advance. I then gave orders for the troops resuming the ground they occupied previous to the attack.

"Our loss has been very severe, but I trust it will not be considered, notwithstanding the failure, that this army has suffered its military character to be tarnished. I am satisfied, had I thought it right to renew the attack, that the troops would have advanced with cheerfulness. The services of both army and navy, since their landing on this coast, have been arduous beyond anything I have ever witnessed, and difficulties have been got over, with an assiduity and perseverance beyond all example, by all ranks, and the most hearty co-operation has existed between the two services.

"It is not necessary for me to expatiate to you upon the loss the army has sustained in Major General the Honorable Sir E. Pakenham, Commander-in-chief of this force, nor could I do so in adequate terms. His services and merits are so well known, that I have only, in common with the whole army, to express my sincere regret, which may be supposed at this moment to come particularly home to me

"Major General Gibbs, who died of his wounds the following day, and Major General Keane, who were both carried off the field within 20 yards of the glacis, at the head of their brigades, sufficiently speak at such a moment how they were conducting themselves. I am happy to say Major General Keane is doing well."

Major Latour makes the total British forces on the 8th amount to close on seventeen thousand men. From the official returns, however, we find that the British forces really consisted of seven thousand three hundred men, just ten thousand less than Major Latour represents. If, as we have usually found it to be, the American return of their own force was diminished in the same ratio that that of the British was increased, then the revelations contained in Mr. O'Connor's history would warrant the belief that a very large force was under General Jackson's command. According to O'Connor the total force amounted to six thousand one hundred and ninety-eight men.

Considering then the national failing it is reasonable to conclude that the American force was at least as large as that of the

Comparative strength of the Armies.

British, while it must not be lost sight of that the returns of killed and wounded show how securely entrenched they must have been. The British loss in killed and wounded amounted to two thousand and thirty-six, that of the Americans to but seventy-one. The total loss of the British in this unfortunate expedition was two thousand four hundred and ninety-two, while the American loss did not exceed three hundred and thirty-three.

On the morning after the battle General Lambert communicated with Sir A. Cochrane, and as the imprudence of making a further attack on an enemy so securely posted was obvious, it was determined that a retreat should be commenced. Accordingly on the night of the 18th instant the movement was made, and the army retired fourteen miles from their former position, and remained in bivouac until the 27th, when the whole were re-embarked.

Retreat of the British.

However unfortunate the termination of this expedition might have been, still we cannot find that discredit in any manner attaches to the troops. The fatigue they had undergone had been incessant, and the list of casualties shows that they were not chary of exposing their lives. Taking all these circumstances into consideration, and making due allowance for the damp that must have been cast on the troops at seeing three of their Generals killed and wounded, we can only ascribe the failure at New Orleans to the same cause which saved Baltimore, the premature death of a British General.

Behaviour of the troops.

After the embarkation of the troops, the departure of the fleet was delayed till the 5th of February, when they sailed, arriving on the 7th at Dauphine Island, and disembarking there.

In the following despatches will be found a full account of the investment and surrender of Fort Bowyer on the 12th :—

Extracts from Major General Lambert's Despatch to Earl Bathurst.

"It being agreed between Vice Admiral Sir Alexander Cochrane and myself that operations should be carried towards Mobile, it was decided that a force should be sent against Fort-Bowyer, situated on the eastern point of the entrance of the bay, and from every information that could be obtained, it was considered a brigade would be sufficient for this object, with a respectable force of artillery. I ordered the 2d brigade, composed of the 4th, 21st, and 44th regiments, for this service, together with such means in the engineer and artillery departments as the chief and commanding officer of the royal artillery might think expedient. The remainder of the force had orders to disembark on Isle Dauphine and encamp; and Major-General Keane, whom I am truly happy to say has returned to his duty, superintended their arrangement.

"The weather being favourable on the 7th for the landing to the eastward of Mobile point, the ships destined to move on that service sailed under the command of Captain Ricketts, of the Vengeur, but did not arrive in sufficient time that evening to do more than determine the place of disembarkation, which was about three miles from Fort-Bowyer.

"At daylight the next morning the troops got into the boats, and 600 men were landed under Lieutenant-Colonel Debbeig, of the 44th, without opposition, who immediately threw out the light companies under Lieutenant Bennett of the 4th regiment, to cover the landing of the brigade. Upon the whole being disembarked, a disposition was made to move on towards the fort, covered by the light companies. The enemy was not seen until about 1000 yards in front of their works; they gradually fell back, and no firing took place until the whole had retired into the fort, and our advance had pushed on nearly to within 300 yards.— Having reconnoitred the forts with Lieutenant-colonels Burgoyne and Dickson, we were decidedly of opinion, that the work was formidable only against an assault ; that batteries being once established, it must speedily fall. Every exertion was made by the navy to land provisions, and the necessary equipment of the battering train and engineer stores. We broke ground on the night of the 8th, and advanced a firing party to within 100 yards of the fort during the night. The position of the batteries being decided upon the next day, they were ready to receive their guns on the night of the 10th, and on the morning of the 11th the fire of a battery of four 18-pounders on the left, and two 8-inch howitzers on the right, each about 100 yards distance, two 6-pounders at about 300 yards, and eight small cohorns advantageously placed on the right, with intervals of between 100 and 200 yards, all furnished to keep up an incessant fire for two days, were prepared to open. Preparatory to commencing, I summoned the fort, allowing the commanding officer half an hour for decision upon such terms as were proposed. Finding he was inclined to consider them, I prolonged the period, at his request, and at three o'clock the fort was given up to a British guard, and British colours hoisted ; the terms being signed by Major Smith, military secretary, and Captain Ricketts, R. N., and finally approved of by the Vice-admiral and myself, I am happy to say our loss was not great ; and we are indebted for this, in a great measure, to the efficient means attached to this force. Had we been obliged to resort to any other mode of attack, the fall could not have been looked for under such favourable circumstances.

We have certain information of a force having been sent from Mobile, and disembarked about 12 miles off, in the night of the 10th, to attempt its relief; two schooners with provisions, and an intercepted letter, fell into our hands, taken by Captain Price, R.N., stationed in the bay.

Return of ordnance, ammunition, and stores, captured from the enemy in this place, on the 12th instant.

Fort-Bowyer, Feb. 14, 1815.

21 guns, 1 8-inch mortar; 1 5½-inch howitzer, and a large quantity of ammunition.

Lawrences' despatch to General Jackson, Lawrence's despatch found below in our to General Jackson. notes,* does not appear to have impressed the American commander

* Letter from Lieutenant-Colonel Lawrence to General Jackson.

Fort Bowyer, February 12, 1815.

SIR,—Imperious necessity has compelled me to enter into articles of capitulation with Major General John Lambert, commanding his Britannic Majesty's forces in front of Fort Bowyer, a

HISTORY OF THE WAR OF 1812.

with a very exalted opinion of the bravery of the defence, as he observes in a letter to the Secretary at War, of the 24th February:—

"I received the sad intelligence of Fort Bowyer; this is an event I little expected to happen, but after the most gallant resistance; that it should have taken place, without even a fire from the enemy's batteries, is as astonishing as it is mortifying."

With this expedition the war by land may be said to have terminated, as we find, leaving the British army at Mobile and Cumberland island, and passing to the Canadas, that before the reinforcements which had been sent out under General Murray, had had time afforded them to wipe away the stain left on the national honor by Plattsburg, peace sent him and them home again. Before, however, entering on the merits of the treaty or the considerations of the events we have been chronicling, we must return to the naval operations, in order to bring them down to the same date.

The concluding naval events of the war were of a very mixed aspect, and the manner in which the capture of the President was effected, not only furnished Commodore Dicatur with various apparently well-grounded causes for his capture, but, at the same time, it did not by its importance, overshadow the loss of the Cyane and Levant, both captured by the Constitution. To begin, however, with the President. We find that this vessel left New York on the 14th January for a cruise in the Bay of Bengal, and after touching the ground on a mud bank, pursued her course in company with the armed brig Macedonian. Discovered on the morning of the 15th by the fleet, then off New York; the President made every effort to escape, and would without doubt have effected that purpose, had it not been for the superior sailing

of the Endymion, Captain Hope, who succeeded in bringing his bulky adversary to action. Captain Hayes' despatch to Admiral Hotham, will, however, taken in connection with extracts from Commodore Dicatur's, afford an opportunity of judging the respective claims of the commanders:

From Captain Hayes to Rear-admiral Hotham.
Majesty, at sea, January 17, 1815.

"Sir,—I have the honour to acquaint you, that notwithstanding my utmost endeavours to keep the squadron committed to my charge close in with Sandy Hook, agreeably to your directions, for the purpose of preventing the escape of the U. S., ship President, and other vessels ready for sea at Staten Island, we were repeatedly blown off by frequent gales; but the very great attention paid to my orders and instructions by the respective captains, in situations difficult to keep company, prevented separation; and, whenever the wind did force us from the coast, I invariably, on the gale moderating, placed the squadron on that point of bearing from the Hook I judged it likely from existing circumstances, would be the enemy's track; and it is with great pleasure I have now to inform you of the success of the squadron in the capture of the U. S. ship President, Commodore Decatur, on Sunday night, after an anxious chase of 18 hours.

"On Friday the Tenedos joined me, with your order to take Captain Parker, in that ship, under my command. We were then in company with the Endymion and Ponome, off the Hook, and in sight of the enemy's ships; but that night the squadron was blown off again in a severe snow-storm. On Saturday the wind and weather became favourable for the enemy, and I had no doubt but he would attempt his escape that night. It was impossible, from the direction of the wind, to get in with the Hook;

copy of which I forward you for the purpose of effecting an immediate exchange of prisoners. Nothing but the want of provisions, and finding myself completely surrounded by thousands—batteries erected on the sand-mounds, which completely commanded the fort—and the enemy having advanced, by regular approaches, within 30 yards of the ditches, and the utter impossibility of getting any assistance or supplies, would have induced me to adopt this measure. Feeling confident, and it being the unanimous

opinion of the officers, that we could not retain the post, and that the lives of many valuable officers and soldiers would have been uselessly sacrificed, I thought it most desirable to adopt this plan. A full and correct statement will be furnished you as early as possible.

Captain Chamberlin, who bears this to E. Livingston, Esq., will relate to him every particular, which will, I hope, be satisfactory.

I am, with respect, &c.,
W. LAWRENCE, Lieut.-Col. Com.

and, as before stated, (in preference to closing the land to the southward,) we stood away to the northward and eastward, till the squadron reached the supposed track of the enemy ; and, what is a little singular, at the very instant of arriving at that point, an hour before day-light, Sandy Hook bearing W.N.W. 15 leagues, we were made happy by the sight of a ship and brig standing to the southward and eastward, and not more than two miles on the Majestic's weather-bow ; the night-signal for a general chase was made, and promptly obeyed by all the ships. *

---

* From Commodore Decatur to the American secretary of the navy.

H. B. M. ship Endymion, at sea, January 18, 1815.

SIR,—At day-light we discovered four ships in chase : one on each quarter, and two a-stern, the leading ship of the enemy a razee ; she commenced a fire upon us, but without effect. At meridian, the wind became light and baffling ; we had increased our distance from the razee, but the next ship a-stern which was also a large ship, had gained, and continued to gain upon us considerably. We immediately occupied all hands to lighten ship, by starting water, cutting away the anchors, throwing overboard provisons, cables, spare spars, boats, and every article that could be got at, keeping the sails wet, from the royals down. At 3, we had the wind quite light ; the enemy, who had now been joined by a brig, had a strong breeze, and were coming up with us rapidly.

The Endymion (mounting 50 guns, 24 pounders on the main-deck) had now approached us within gun-shot, and had commenced a fire with her bow-guns, which we returned from our stern. At five o'clock she had obtained a position on our starboard-quarter, within half point-blank shot, on which neither our stern nor quarter-guns would bear ; we were now steering E. by N. the wind N.W. I remained with her in this position for half an hour, in the hope that she would close with us on our broadside, in which case I had prepared my crew to board ; but from his continuing to yaw his ship to maintain his position, it became evident, that to close was not his intention. Every fire now cut some of our sails or rigging. To have continued our course under these circumstances, would have been placing it in his power to cripple us, without being subject to injury himself ; and to have hauled up more to the northward to bring our stern guns to bear, would have exposed us to his raking fire. It was now dusk, when I determined to alter my course south, for the purpose of bringing the enemy a-beam ; and, although their ships a-stern were drawing up fast, I felt satisfied I should be enabled to throw him out of the combat before

" In the course of the day the chase became extremely interesting, from the endeavours of the enemy to escape, and the exertions (of the British commanders) to get their respective ships alongside of him : the former, by cutting away his anchors, and throwing over-board every moveable article, with a great quantity of provisions ; and the latter, by trimming their ships in every way possible to effect their purpose. As the day advanced, the wind declined, giving the Endymion an evident advantage in sailing ; and Captain Hope's exertions enabled him to get his ship alongside of the enemy, and com-

they could come up, and was not without hopes, if the night proved dark, (of which there was every appearance,) that I might still be enabled to effect my escape. Our opponent kept off at the same instant we did, and our fire commenced at the same time. We continued engaged, steering south, and studding-sails set, two hours and a half, when we completely succeeded in dismantling her. Previously to her dropping entirely out of the action, there were intervals of minutes, when the ships were broadside, in which she did not fire a gun. At this period, (half-past 8 o'clock,) although dark, the other ships of the squadron were in sight, and almost within gun-shot. We were of course compelled to abandon her. In re-assuming our former course for the purpose of avoiding the squadron, we were compelled to present our stern to our antagonist ; but such was his state, though we were thus exposed and within range of his guns for half an hour, that he did not avail himself of this favourable opportunity of raking us. We continued this course until eleven o'clock, when two fresh ships of the enemy (the Pomone and Tenedos) had come up. The Pomone had opened her fire on the larboard bow, within musket-shot ; the other, about two cables' length a-stern, taking a raking position on our quarter ; and the rest (with the exception of the Endymion) within gun-shot. Thus situated, with about one fifth of my crew killed and wounded, my ship crippled, and a more than four-fold force opposed to me, without a chance of escape left, I deemed it my duty to surrender.

It is with emotions of pride I bear testimony to the gallantry and steadiness of every officer and man I had the honour to command on this occasion ; and I feel satisfied that the fact of their having beaten a force equal to themselves, in the presence, and almost under the guns, of so vastly a superior force, when, too, it was almost self-evident that whatever their exertions might be, they must ultimately be captured, will be taken as evidence of what they would have performed, had the force opposed to them been in any degree equal.

Of our loss in killed and wounded, I am unable, at present, to give you a correct state-

mence close action, at half an hour past 5 o'clock in the evening, which was continued with great gallantry and spirit, on both sides for two hours and a half, when the Endymion's sails being cut from the yards, the enemy got a-head: Captain Hope taking this opportunity to bend new sails, to enable him to get his ship alongside again, the action ceased; till the Pomone, getting up at half-past 11 at night, and firing a few shots, the enemy hailed to say she had already surrendered.

"The ship, on being taken possession of, proved to be the President, as above stated, commanded by Commodore Decatur.

"The vessel in company with her was the Macedonian brig, a merchant-ship, laden with provisions, which made her escape by very superior sailing.

"And now, sir, a very pleasing part of my duty is, the bearing testimony to the able and masterly manner in which the Endymion was conducted, and the gallantry with which she was fought; and when the effect produced by her well-directed fire upon the President is witnesed, it cannot be doubted but that Captain Hope would have succeeded either in capturing or sinking her, had none of the squadron been in sight.

"I have not yet been able to ascertain the loss of the President, but I believe it to be

much greater than the Endymion's, and she had six feet water in the hold when taken possession of. Both ships were very much cut in masts and rigging; and, had the present most severe gale commenced twelve hours sooner the prize would undoubtedly have sunk.

I have the honour to be, &c.
        JOHN HAYES, captain.
Rear-admiral the Hon Sir H. Hotham."

Number of persons of all descriptions on board the President, previous to the action, about 490.

Number of her guns 59.

Commodore Decatur has made the most he could of this affair, and in his attempts to make the best of a bad cause, he appears to have been ably supported by his chaplain, who seems to have been ready to swear to anything, as in the case of the chaplain of the Essex frigate. Unfortunately, however, the schoolmaster on board the President, Mr. Bowie, gave directly contrary evidence to that of the chaplain, and the circumstance of only one shot having entered the President's larboard side, the one opposed to the Pomone, affords corroborative evidence of the truth of Mr. Bowie's statement, "that no man had been hurt by the Pomone's fire," in disproof of Dicatur's assertion contained in note.* Previous to the capture of

ment; the attention of the surgeon being so entirely occupied with the wounded, that he was unable to make out a correct return when I left the President; nor shall I be able to make it until our arrival in port, we having parted company with the squadron yesterday. The enclosed list, with the exception, I fear, of its being short of the number, will be found correct.

For 24 hours after the action it was nearly calm, and the squadron were occupied in repairing the crippled ships. Such of the crew of the President as were not badly wounded, were put on board the different ships; myself and a part of my crew were put on board this ship. On the 17th we had a gale from the eastward, when this ship lost her bowsprit, fore and main-masts, and mizen-top-mast, all of which were badly wounded; and was, in consequence of her disabled condition, obliged to throw overboard all her upper-deck guns: her loss in killed and wounded must have been very great. I have not been able to ascertain the extent. Ten were buried after I came on board; (36 hours after the action;) the badly wounded, such as were obliged to keep their cots, occupy the starboard side of the gun-deck, from

the cabin-bulk-head to the main-mast. From the crippled state of the President's spars, I feel satisfied she could not have saved her masts, and I feel serious apprehensions for the safety of our wounded left on board.

It is due to Captain Hope to state, that every attention has been paid by him to myself and officers that have been placed on board his ship, that delicacy and humanity could dictate.

I have the honour to be, &c.
        STEPHEN DECATUR.
The Hon. Ben. W. Crowninshield,
        Secretary of the navy.

British squadron referred to in the letter.

Majestic razee, Endymion, Pomone, Tenedos, Despatch brig.

[*Here follow the names of 24 killed; 55 wounded.*]

* *Extract of a letter from Commodore Decatur to the American secretary of the navy.*

New York, March 6, 1815.
"In my official letter of the 18th of January, I omitted to state, that a considerable number of my killed and wounded was from the fire of the Pomone, and that the Endymion had

the President, Commodore Decatur had expressed an earnest desire to fall in with the Endymion, openly avowing his capability to capture an English line of battle ship with his frigate. Let us compare the respective sizes of the line of battle ship and the frigate:—

	Endymion.	President.
Weight of broadside, lbs.	676	916
Crew—Men	319	472
Boys	27	5
Tonnage	1277	1533

We have heard it stated by an old inhabitant of Bermuda, who saw the vessels a few days after the action, that the President, alongside of the Endymion, was "like a quart alongside of a pint bottle," and this difference in their size reflects the greater credit on Captain Hope, to whom it is a pity the opportunity was afforded of lowering, single-handed, the American mania for boasting.

Taking Commodore Dicatur's whole mystification and false stating of this affair into consideration, and comparing his statements with extracts from logs of the British evidence, the conviction is forced upon us that the American commander resorted to subterfuges and misstatements to cover his defeat, unworthy both an officer and gentleman.

The next affair that comes before us for consideration is the capture, by the Constitution, of the Cyane, mounting thirty, and the Levant eighteen guns—the one manned by one hundred and fifty-six men and twenty-six boys; the other by one hundred and fifteen men and sixteen boys. The weight of metal thrown by the Constitution's broadside equalled that of her two antagonists put together, while the British vessels only mounted carronades, and the Constitution showed on her broadside seventeen long twenty-fours. Again, the Constitution had

four hundred and seventy-two men, her antagonists two hundred and sixty-one, exclusive of boys. The particulars of the action will be found in the appendix,* and we need only remark further that the officers and crews were honourably acquitted by a Court Martial, and applauded for the gallant defence offered.

The commander of the Constitution laid claim to great credit for having captured two vessels, contending that "a divided force is better for action," the vain-glorious commander forgot, however, that, on a previous occasion, he had declared " that three large frigates, placed in the most favorable position would be compelled to yield to a seventy-four gun ship, owing to the latter being stronger in scantling and thicker in sides."

The Constitution was as strong in scantling and as thick in the sides as the President, and on the capture of that vessel it was found that she differed in no respect from the stoutest seventy-four in the British service, it is not wonderful then that her two pigmy opponents were compelled to yield to such decided superiority.

The Constitution with her two prizes arrived at Porto Praya, in the island of St. Jago on the 7th March, but on the 8th were compelled to stand out to sea to avoid capture by a British squadron. In the chase that ensued the Levant was recaptured, but strange to say the other two escaped unpursued. And we agree with James that, as this circumstance afforded the Americans grounds for asserting that the British vessels were unwilling to come to close quarters, although two of them threw a much heavier broadside than the Constitution, the suffering the larger vessels to escape reflected much discredit on the judgment of the British commanders.

an board, in addition to her own crew, one lieutenant, one master's mate, and fifty men belonging to the Saturn, and when the action ceased, was left motionless and unmanageable, until she bent new sails, rove new rigging, and fished her spars; nor did she rejoin the squadron for six hours after the action, and three hours after the surrender of the President. My sword was delivered to Captain Hayes, of the Majestic, the senior officer of the squadron, on his quarter-deck; which he, with great politeness, immediately returned. I have the honor to

enclose you my parole, by which you will perceive the British admit the President was captured by the squadron. I should have deemed it unnecessary to have drawn your attention to this document, had not the fact been stated differently in the Bermuda Gazette, on our arrival there; which statement, however, the editor was compelled to retract, through the interference of the governor, and some of the British officers of the squadron."

* See Appendix A and B.

Another nautical romance connected with this vessel was the assertion that every effort was made by Capt. Stewart to bring the British frigate La Pique to action, but that she escaped in the night after a long chase ; the best answer to this boast will be found in appendix*, and it will then be for the readers to judge on which side the disinclination to come to close quarters really existed.

The only affairs which took place after this, were the capture of the St. Lawrence, mail schooner, proceeding with tidings of peace from the Admiral at Bermuda to the United States ; of the Penguin, brig, by the U. S. ship Hornet; and that of the East India Company's armed vessel, Nautilus by the ship Peacock. A statement of the comparative force easily enables us to account for the capture of both the Penguin and Nautilus. The Penguin mounted sixteen carronades, thirty-twos, and two six-pounders ; and had a complement of one hundred and twenty two, of whom seventeen were boys ; it may also be added that out of the entire ships' crew, only twelve had been ever in action.

The Hornet carried eighteen carronades, of same weight as those of the Penguin, two long eighteens, swivels in her tops, throwing fifty shot at a discharge, and upon her quarters two similar swivels. The complement of the Hornet was one hundred and seventy-three men. The last affair between the Nautilus and Peacock was one that reflected the crowning disgrace on the American character for veracity and honour, and a glance at the annexed notes in the appendix† will prove how unworthy captain Warrington was to be considered a man. His excuses are so transparently false, and the impudent assertion that only one broadside

* See Appendix C.
† See Appendix D.

was fired, made we presume to show what execution one American broadside could do, so clearly disproved, that the only conclusion to be arrived at is that the doughty American Hero seeing how diminutive an opponent was before him determined to acquire laurels at an easy rate.

Our task is ended, and all that remains for us is to record the signing of a treaty at Ghent,* on the 24th day of December, 1814. Every one who reads the ninth article of this treaty, and reflects on the conduct of successive American Governments to the Indians, will see how false to every promise then made the nation has been. Not contented, too, with acquiring the lands of the red men, Americans do not hesitate to assert the necessity of destroying every Indian on the American continent. That by the sword and the introduction of ardent spirits they have also too well succeeded, is a subject of deep regret to those who still cherish an interest in the fate and fortunes of the aboriginal possessors of the soil.

Treaty of peace.

In what a proud position, now, did the Canadians stand at the declaration of peace, and in what a ridiculous light the American Government! Ignorant of the undying love of their country that animated every Canadian, and nerved their arms for the contest, the United States Government had boastingly announced that Canada must be conquered, as it was a rod held over their heads, a fortress which frowned haughtily on their country. What was the result of all their expeditions and proclamations, that two of their fortresses were in our possession at the time of the peace, and that, seeing a seventy-four and large frigate had been launched at Kingston, it would have been utterly impossible for them, having lost the command of the Lake, to have prevented the fall of Sackett's harbour early in 1815.

* Treaty of Peace, Appendix, &c.

APPENDIX.

A.

From Captain Stewart to the American Secretary of the Navy.

U. S. frigate Constitution, May, 1815.

SIR,—On 20th February last, the island of Maderia bearing about W.S.W. distant 60 leagues, we fell in with H. B. M. two ships of war, the Cayne and Levant, and brought them to action about 6 o'clock in the evening; both of which, after a spirited engagement of 40 minutes, surrended to the ship under my command.

Considering the advantage derived by the enemy, from a divided and more active force, as also their superiority in the weight and number of guns, I deem the speedy and decisive result of this action the strongest assurance which can be given the government, that all under my command did their duty, and gallantly supported the reputation of American seamen.

Inclosed you will receive the minutes of the action, and a list of the killed and wounded on board this ship. Also inclosed you will receive for your information, a statement of the actual force of the enemy, and the number killed and wounded on board their ships, as near as could be ascertained.

I have the honour to be, &c.

CHARLES STEWART.

Hon. B. W. Crowninshield, Secretary of the Navy, Washington.

B.

American Minutes of the Chase of the U. S. frigate Constitution, by an English squadron of three ships, from out the harbour of Port Praya, Island of St. Jago.

Commences with fresh breezes and thick foggy weather. At 5 minutes past 12, discovered a large ship through the fog, standing in Port Praya. At 8 minutes past 12, discovered two other large ships a-stern of her, also standing in for the port. From their general appearance, supposed them to be one of the enemy's squadrons; and, from the little respect hitherto paid by them to neutral waters, I deemed it most prudent to put to sea. The signal was made to the Cayne and Levant to get under weigh. At 12, after meridian, with our top-sails set, we cut our cable, and got under way, (when the Portuguese opened a fire on us from several of their batteries on shore,) the prize-ships following our motions, and stood out of the harbour of Port Praya, close under East Point, passing the enemy's squadron about gun-shot to windward of them: crossed our top-gallant yards and set foresail, mainsail, spanker, flying-gib and top-gallant sails. The enemy, seeing us under way, tacked ship, and made all sail in chase of us, As far as we could judge of their rates, from the thickness of the weather, supposed them two ships of the line, and one frigate. At half-past meridian cut away the boats towing a-stern, first cutter, and gig. At 1 P. M. found our sailing about equal with the ships on our lee-quarter, but the frigate luffing up, gaining our wake, and rather dropping a-stern of us; finding the Cayne dropping a-stern, and to-leeward, and the frigate gaining on her fast, I found it impossible to save her if she continued on the same course, without having the Constitution brought to action by their whole force. I made the signal, at 10 minutes past 1 P. M. to her to tack ship, which was complied with. This manoeuvre, I conceived would detach one of the enemy's ships in pursuit of her; while, at the same time, from her position, she would be enabled to reach the anchorage at Port Praya, before the detached ships could come up with her; but if they did not tack after her, it would afford her an opportunity to double their rear, and make her escape before the wind. They all continued in full chase of the Levant and this ship, the ship on our lee-quarter, firing, by divisions, broadsides, her shot falling short of us. At 3 P. M. by our having dropped the Levant considerably, her situation became (from the position of the enemy's frigate) similar to the Cayne. It became necessary to separate also from the Levant, or risk this ship being brought to action to cover her. I made the signal, at 5 min. past 3, for her to back which she complied with. At 12 minutes past 3 the whole of the enemy's squadron tacked in pursuit of the Levant and gave up the pursuit of this ship. This sacrifice of the Levant became necessary, for the preservation of the Constitution. Sailing-master Hixon, Midshipman Varnum, a boatswain's mate, and 12 men, were absent on duty in the fifth cutter, to bring the cartel-brig under our stern.

C

EXTRACT FROM PIQUE'S LOG-BOOK.

H.	K.	F.	Courses.	Wind.	Remarks, &c. H.M.S. Pique, Feb. 23, 1814.
1 2 &c.					At noon observed several strangers, one apparently a man-of-war in chase.

Courses.	Distance.	Latitude.	Longitude.	Bearings at noon.
N. 84 W.	142 M.	18.1 N.	67. 22	Mona Islands N. 73 W. 19 m.

H.	K.	F.	Courses.	Wind.	Remarks
1	3		N. W. ½ W.		P.M. Light airs—braced the yards by, to allow the chase to come up.—At 4, light airs,—At 4.30, observed chase take in her main-stay-sail.—At 4.50 observed her take in royal, top-gallant, lower, and top-mast, studding-sails.—Hauled to the wind on larboard tack, and made all sail to close her; hoisted an ensign. Stranger shorted sail, in 1st reef top-sails, hoisted American colours, and hauled her wind on opposite tack: appeared to be a large frigate, having 16 ports of a-side. Cleared for action; stranger S.E. by S. 3 miles.—At 5 Island of *Zachee* N. by E. 12 or 13 miles:—cloudy, lost sight of stranger:—10 in 1st reefs:—12 squally.
2	2	2		E. S. E.	
3	1	4			
4 5 6			ship's head from N.W to N.		
7	9		N. W.	E. N. E.	
8	9	6			
0	9	4	N. ½ E.		
10	9		N.		
11	10	4			
12		2	N. ½ E.		

D.

From Lieutenant Boyce to the Secretary of the East India company's marine-board.

SIR, I beg leave to acquaint you, for the information of the board, that the wounds received by me on the 30th June last, in a short but smart action with an American sloop of war, off Anjier, in the straits of Sunda, have hitherto prevented my transmitting an official report of the circumstances attending that melancholy affair.

I am happy to state, that my health is now tolerably re-established; and I think myself particularly fortunate, considering the nature of my wounds, that the honour of addressing you on this subject has been reserved for my pen, although, no doubt, public rumor has, ere this, put you in possession of most of the facts which I now do myself the honor to state, and request that you will do me the favor to submit them to the honorable board.

On the 30th June last, being off Anjier, in the straits of Sunda, on my passage to Bengal, in charge of public despatches from the Java government, about 4 P.M. a strange sail hove in sight, standing with a fair wind to the north-eastward; and, as the honorable company's cruiser Nautilus, under my command, was working to the south-westward, the two vessels approached each other rapidly; and, when the stranger was distant about three miles, I, observed that she had British colors hoisted, and knowing that universal peace had been restored to Great Britain, I dispatched a boat in charge of my master, Mr. Bartlett, to obtain intelligence, which reached the stranger nearly at the same time as the master-attendant's from the shore; and I observed, with my spying-glass, that the officers had no sooner got up to the ship's side than the crews were forcibly taken out, and both boats made fast a-stern. I prepared for action, and the stranger at once opened her tier of ports, and bore down towards us. To prevent her crossing our hawse I tacked, then shortened sail, hove to, and soon afterwards hailed the stranger, "What ship is that?" To which I received no reply, until repeated four times, and then merely "Holloo!" About this period the English blue ensign was hauled down, and American colours hoisted. I then asked "Am I to consider you in the light of a friend or an enemy?" The reply was,

"An enemy." I then informed the American captain that peace had been ratified between Great Britain and the United States of America; also, that I had the proclamation on board, and hoped that a due consideration of this would induce him to spare bloodshed. I was then commanded, in a very loud and peremptory manner, to "haul down my colours," which was immediately repeated still louder, and with the addition of "instantly;" to which I replied, "I shall do no such thing." The American then opened his fire on us, by which two men were killed at the gun near me, and I received a grape-shot, in a slanting direction, through the right cheek of my posteriors. A short but brisk action ensued, and observing some casualties, my first lieutenant, Mr. Robert Mayston, and several others, wounded, and being myself disabled by a 32-pound shot which shattered my right knee-joint, and splintered my thighbone; also considering the great disparity of force, I deemed it my duty, although I must confess that it was with no small degree of reluctance, to strike the British colours to the American. Her first lieutenant, about dusk, took possession of us. She proved to be the U. S. sloop of war Peacock, Captain Warrington, carrying twenty 32-pound carronades, and two long 18-pounders. Her crew is said to consist of 220 men.

Both vessels anchored for the night about six miles off Anjier, and in the morning I was permitted to be taken on shore, as well as the rest of the wounded in compliance with my request to that effect.

About 2 P. M. on the day following the action, the honorable company's cruiser Nautilus was restored, and Captain Warrington addressed a letter to Mr. Macgregor, master-attendant at Anjier, stating, that in consequence of the information received from him, and *the several different sources* from which he had heard that a peace had been concluded between the United States and Great Britain, he felt himself bound to desist from hostilities, and regretted that his *reasonable demand* had not been complied with by the commander of Nautilus brig the preceding afternoon.

On the 4th of July the Nautilus sailed for Batavia, where she arrived the day following, and was sent from thence to Rembang, on the coast of Java, in the temporary charge of acting lieutenant Barnes, (who was ordered on board from the honorable company's cruiser Malabar, by Captain Hepburn,) to receive such repairs as the damages she had sustained required. In the mean time I remained, on account of my wounds, on shore at Anjier, where I was most handsomely received and accommodated by the by the kindness of Colonel Yule, resident, and attended by Mr. Hervy Thompson, surgeon of the district. On the 14th of July it was deemed necessary to amputate my right leg. I submitted to the operation, and it was accordingly taken off above the knee. On the 20th following I was removed to the residence of Colonel Yule, at Ceram, and there I remained, experi-encing every mark of hospitality, and the most unlimited attention, until the return of the Nautilus from Rembang; at which period finding my health tolerably restored, I rejoined her on the 23d instant.

I beg leave to subjoin a list of the killed and wounded on board the honorable company's cruiser Nautilus, on the 30th of last June ; and, in having to lament the loss of so many, I regret that a fairer opportunity for their exertions was not afforded them, and myself, with a vessel of more equal force.

What loss the American may have sustained I am not able to say. If report is to be relied on, they had four or five men wounded, and their bow-gun dismounted.

The damage the Nautilus received in the action was considerable both to her hull and rigging. The bends on the starboard-side, (the side engaged,) were shivered from aft to the fore-chains, and the bulwark, from the chess-tree aft, much torn. The launch and cutter were both perforated with shot, the lower mast and tiller slightly wounded with grape, and the boom-main-sail shot through in many places. Two guns were disabled by the enemy's shot, and the sheet-anchor completely so, by the loss of its iron stock, ring, and fluke. Four 32-pound shot, that were found lodged, have been picked out of her : one was under the counter, very nearly level with the water. A great number of small-arms and gunner's stores were thrown overboard by the Americans on their taking possession, to clear the deck. The packets, I am happy to say, remained on board without being touched, but almost every thing below was ransacked.

It now only remains for me to do that justice to the conduct of the officers and crew of the Nautilus, on the 30th of last June, which they so well deserve, by declaring my admiration of their firmness, and thus publicly expressing my satisfaction with their conduct throughout.

The two seapoys and native servant, with amputated limbs, have, I understand, recovered, and been sent by Captain William Eatwell, of the honorable company's cruiser Benares, to Calcutta, in the honorable company's cruiser Antelope. Lieutenant Maystone's wound was once healed, but has broken out afresh ; he is however now, I am happy to say, again on the recovery.* My own cure has been greatly impeded by two unfortunate fistulas, in my stump, which have caused me to suffer much. The rest of the wounded are all well.

Evidence of Mr. Macgregor.

Question. Did you communicate to the officers of the enemy's ship, before the action between her and the honorable company's cruiser Nautilus took place, that peace had been concluded between Great Britain and the United States, and ratified by both parties? *Answer.* I did: I communicated to the first lieutenant,

* The wound subsequently mortified, and he died December 3rd, 1815.

on his informing me that I was a prisoner of war; but I scarce said it, when the captain came forward and ordered me to be taken below. I communicated the above also to the purser of the ship, in the ward-room.—Q. What time had you been on board before the commencement of the said action? A. Rather more than a quarter of an hour.—Q. Has any reply been made by any of the officers of the American sloop of war on your communication? A. Yes.—Q. By whom? A. The purser. —Q. What was the reply? A. *I do not know how we can avoid a little brush;*—and the purser ordered me to go out of the way into the side-cabin."

From Captain Warrington to the American Secretary of the Navy.

U. S. ship Peacock, Nov. 11, 1815.

" As it is probable you will hereafter see or hear some other account of a rencontre which took place between the Peacock and the East India company's brig Nautilus, on the 30th of June last, in the straits of Sunda, I take the liberty of making known to you the particulars.

In the afternoon of that day, when a-breast of Anjier, as we closed with this brig, which appeared evidently a vessel of war, and completely prepared for action, her commander hailed, and asked, if I knew there was a peace. I replied in the negative, directing him, at the same time, to haul his colours down, if it were the case, in token of it; adding that, if he did not, I should fire into her. This being refused one of the forward guns were fired at her, which was immediately returned by a broadside from the brig; our broadside was then discharged, and his colours were struck, after having six lascars killed, and seven or eight wounded. As we had not the most distant idea of peace, and this vessel was but a short distance from the fort of Anjier, I considered his assertion, coupled with his arrangement for action, a finesse on his part, to amuse us, till he could place himself under the protection of the fort. A few minutes before coming in contact with the brig, two boats, containing the master-attendant at Anjier, and an officer of the army, came on board, and as we were in momentary expectation of firing, they were, with their men, passed below. I concluded that they had been misled by the British colours, under which we had passed up the straits. No question, in consequence, were put to them; and they, very improperly, omitted mentioning that peace existed. The next day, after receiving such intelligence as they had to communicate on the subject, (part of which was official,) I gave up the vessel, first stopping her shot-holes, and putting the rigging in order.

I am aware that I may be to blame for ceasing hostilities without more authentic evidence that peace had been concluded; but, I trust, when our distance from home, with the little chance we had of receiving such evidence, are taken into consideration, I shall not be thought to have decided prematurely.

TREATY OF PEACE.

His Britannic Majesty and the United States of America, desirous of terminating the war which has so unhappily subsisted between the two countries, and of restoring, upon principles of perfect reciprocity, peace, friendship, and good understanding between them, have, for that purpose, appointed their respective plenipotentiaries, that is to say: his Britannic Majesty, on his part, has appointed the right honorable James, Lord Gambier, late admiral of the white, now admiral of the red squadron of his Majesty's fleet, Henry Goulbourn, Esq., member of the Imperial parliament, and under secretary of state, and William Adams, Esq. doctor of civil laws:—and the president of the United States, by and with the advice and consent of the senate thereof, has appointed John Quincy Adams, James A. Bayard, Henry Clay, Jonathan Russell, and Albert Gallatin, citizens of the United States, who, after a reciprocal communication of their respective full powers, have agreed upon the following articles:

Art. I.—There shall be a firm and universal peace between his Britannic Majesty and the United States, and between their respective countries, territories, cities, towns, and people, of every degree, without exception of places or persons. All hostilities, both by sea and land, shall cease as soon as this treaty has been ratified by both parties, as hereinafter mentioned. All territories, places, and possessions whatsoever, taken from either party by the other, during the war, or which may be taken after the signing of this treaty, excepting only the islands hereinafter mentioned, shall be restored without delay, and without causing any destruction, or carrying away any of the artillery or other public property originally captured in the said forts or places, and which shall remain therein, upon the exchange of the ratifications of the treaty, or any slaves, or other private property, and all archives, records, deeds, and papers, either of a public nature, or belonging to private persons, which, in the course of the war, may have fallen into the hands of the officers of either party, shall be, as far as may be practicable, forthwith restored and delivered to the proper authorities and persons to whom they respectively belong. Such of the islands in the bay of Passamaquoddy as are claimed by both parties, shall remain in the possession of the party in whose occupation they may be at the time of the exchange of the ratifications of this treaty, until the decision respecting the title to the said islands shall have been made in conformity with the fourth article of this treaty. No disposition made by this treaty, as to such possessions of the islands and territories claimed by both parties, shall, in any manner whatever, be constructed to affect the right of either.

Art. II.—Immediately after the ratification of this treaty by both parties, as hereinafter mentioned orders shall be sent to the armies, squadrons, officers, subjects, and citizens of the two powers to cease from all hostilities: and to prevent all causes of complaint which might arise on account of the prizes which may be taken at sea after the ratifications of this treaty, it is reciprocally agreed, that all vessels and effects which may be taken after the space of twelve days from the said ratifications, upon all parts of the coast of North America, from the latitude of twenty-three degrees north, to the latitude of fifty degrees north, as far eastward in the Atlantic Ocean as the thirty-sixth degree of west longitude from the meridian of Greenwich, shall be restored on each side : that the time shall be thirty days in all other parts of the Atlantic ocean, north of the equinoxial line or equator, and the same time for the British and Irish channels, for the gulf of Mexico, and all parts of the West Indies : forty days for the North Seas, for the Baltic, and for all parts of the Mediterranean. Sixty days for the Atlantic ocean south of the equator as far as the latitude of the Cape of Good Hope : ninety days for every part of the world south of the equator : and one hundred and twenty days for all other parts of the world, without exception.

Art. III.—All prisoners of war taken on either side, as well by land as sea, shall be restored as soon as practicable after the ratification of this treaty, as hereinafter mentioned, on their paying the debts which they may have contracted during their captivity. The two contracting parties respectively engage to discharge, in specie, the advances which may have been made by the other, for the sustenance and maintenance of such prisoners.

Art. IV.—Whereas it was stipulated by the second article in the treaty of peace of one thousand seven hundred and eighty three, between his Britannic Majesty and the United States of America, that the boundary of the United States should comprehend all islands within twenty leagues of any part of the shores of the United States, and lying between lines to be drawn due east from the points where the aforesaid boundries between Nova-Scotia, on the one part, and East Florida on the other, shall respectively touch the bay of Fundy, and the Atlantic ocean, excepting such islands as now are, or heretofore have been within the limits of Nova-Scotia: and whereas the several islands in the bay of Passamaquoddy, which is part of the bay of Fundy, and the island of Grand Menan, in the said bay of Fundy, are claimed by the United States as being comprehended within their aforesaid boundaries, which said islands are claimed as belonging to his Britannic majesty, as having been at the time of, and previous to, the aforesaid treaty of one thousand seven hundred and eighty-three, within the limits of the province of Nova Scotia: in order, therefore, finally to decide upon these claims, it is agreed that they shall be referred to two commissioners, to be appointed in the following manner; viz. One commissioner shall be appointed by his Britannic majesty, and one by the President of the United States, by and with the advice and consent of the senate thereof, and the said two commissioners so appointed shall be sworn impartially to ex-

amine and decide upon the said claims, according to such evidence as shall be laid before them, on the part of his Britannic Majesty and of the United States respectively. The said commissioners shall meet at St. Andrews, in the province of New Brunswick, and shall have power to adjourn to such other place or places as they shall think fit. The said commissioners shall, by a declaration or report under their hands and seals, decide to which of the two contracting parties the several islands aforesaid do respectively belong, in conformity with the true intent of the said treaty of peace of one thousand seven hundred and eighty-three. And if the said commissioners shall agree in their decision, both parties shall consider such decision as final and conclusive. It is further agreed, that in the event of two commissioners differing upon all or any of the matters so referred to them, or in the event of both or either of the said commissioners refusing or declining, or wilfully omitting, to act as such, they shall make, jointly or separately, a report or reports as well to the government of his Britannic Majesty, as to that of the United States, stating in detail the points of which they differ, and the grounds upon which their respective opinions have been formed, or the grounds upon which they, or either of them, have so refused, declined, or omitted to act. And his Britannic Majesty, and the government of the United States, hereby agree to refer the report or reports of the said commissioners, to some friendly sovereign or state, to be then named for that purpose, and who shall be requested to decide on the differences which may be stated in the said report or reports, or upon the report of one commissioner, together with the grounds upon which the other commissioner shall have refused, declined, or omitted to act, as the case may be. And if the commissioner so refusing, declining, or omitting to act, shall also wilfully omit to state the grounds upon which he has so done, in such manner that the said statement may be referred to such friendly sovereign or state, together with the report of such other commissioner, then such sovereign or state shall decide exparte upon the said report alone. And his Britannic Majesty and the government of the United States engage to consider the decision of some friendly sovereign or state to be final and conclusive, on all the matters so referred.

Art. V.—Whereas neither that point of the high lands lying due north from the source of the river St. Croix, and designated in the former treaty of peace between the two powers as the north-west angle of Nova Scotia, nor the north-westernmost head of Connecticut river, has yet been ascertained ; and whereas that part of the boundary line between the dominion of the two powers which extends from the source of the river St. Croix directly north to the above mentioned north-west angle of Nova Scotia, thence along the said high lands which divide those rivers that empty themselves into the river St. Lawrence from those which fall into the Atlantic ocean, to the north-westernmost head of Connecticut river, thence down along the middle of that river to the forty-fifth degree of north latitude: thence by a line due west on said latitude until it strikes the river Iroquois or Cataraguy, has not yet been surveyed: it is agreed, that for these several purposes, two commissioners shall be appointed, sworn, and authorized, to act exactly in the manner directed with respect to those mentioned in the next preceding article, unless otherwise specified in the present article. The said commissioners shall meet at St. Andrews, in the province of New Brunswick, and shall have power to adjourn to such other place or places as they shall think fit. The said commissioners shall have power to ascertain and determine the points above mentioned, in conformity with the provisions of the said treaty of peace of one thousand seven hundred and eighty-three, and shall cause the boundary aforesaid, from the source of the river St. Croix, to the river Iroquois or Cataraguy, to be surveyed and marked according to the said provisions. The said commissioners shall make a map of the said boundary, and annex it to a declaration under their hands and seals, certifying it to be the true map of the said boundary, and particularizing the latitude and longitude of the north-west angle of Nova Scotia, of the north-westernmost head of Connecticut river, and of such other points of the said boundary as they may deem proper. And both parties agree to consider such map and declaration as finally and conclusively fixing the said boundary. And in the event of the said two commissioners differing or both, or either of them, refusing or declining, or wilfully omitting to act, such reports, declarations, or statements, shall be made by them, or either of them, and such reference to a friendly sovereign or state, shall be made, in all respects as in the latter part of the fourth article is contained, and in as full a manner as if the same was herein repeated.

Art, VI.—Whereas by the former treaty of peace, that portion of the boundary of the United States from the point where the forty-fifth degree of north latitude strikes the river Iroquois or Cataraguy to the lake Superior, was declared to be " along the middle of said river into lake Ontario, through the middle of said lake until it strikes the communication by water between that lake and lake Erie, thence along the middle of said communication into lake Erie, through the middle of said lake until it arrives at the water communication into the lake Huron, thence through the middle of said lake to the water communication between that lake and lake Superior," And whereas doubts have arisen what was the middle of said river, lakes, and water communications, and whether certain islands lying in the same were within the dominions of his Britannic Majesty or of the United States: in order, therefore, finally to decide these doubts, they shall be referred to two commissioners, to be appointed, sworn, and authorized to act exactly in the manner directed with respect to those mentioned in the next preceding article, unless otherwise specified in

this present article. The said commissioners shall meet, in the first instance at Albany, in the state of New York, and shall have power to adjourn to such other place or places as they shall think fit. The said commissioners shall, by a report or declaration, under their hands and seals, designate the boundary through the said rivers, lakes, or water communications, and decide to which of the two contracting parties the several islands lying within the said river, lakes, and water communications, do respectively belong, in conformity with the true intent of the said treaty of one thousand seven hundred and eighty-three. And both parties agree to consider such designation and decision as final and conclusive. And in the event of the said two commissioners differing, or both, or either of them, refusing, declining, or wilfully omitting to act, such reports, declarations, or statements, shall be made by them, or either of them; and such reference to a friendly sovereign or state shall be made in all respects as in the latter part of the fourth article is contained, and in as full a manner as if the same was herein repeated.

Art. VII—It is further agreed that the said two last mentioned commissioners, after they shall have executed the duties assigned to them in the preceding article, shall be, and they are hereby authorized, upon their oaths, impartially to fix and determine, according to the true intent of the said treaty of peace of one thousand seven hundred and eighty-three, that part of the boundary between the dominions of the two powers, which extends from the water communication between lake Huron and lake Superior, to the most north-western point of the lake of the Woods, to decide to which of the two parties the several islands lying in the lakes, water communications and rivers, forming the said boundary, do respectively belong, in conformity with the true intent of the said treaty of peace of one thousand seven hundred and eighty-three; and to cause such parts of the said boundary, as require it, to be surveyed and marked. The said commissioners shall, by a report or declaration under their hands and seals, designate the boundary line aforesaid, state their decisions on the points thus referred to them, and particularize the latitude and longitude of the most north-western point of the lake of the Woods, and of such other parts of the said boundary, as they may deem proper. And both parties agree to consider such designation and decision as final and conclusive. And, in the event of the said two commissioners differing, or both, either of them, refusing, declining, or wilfully omitting to act, such reports, declarations, or statement shall be made by them, or either of them, and such reference to a friendly sovereign or state, shall be made in all respects, as in the latter part of the fourth article is contained, and in as full a manner as if the same was herein repeated.

Art. VIII.—The several boards of two commissioners mentioned in the four preceding articles, shall respectively have power to appoint a secretary, and to employ such surveyors or other persons as they shall judge necessary. Duplicates of all their respective reports, declarations, statements, and decisions, and of their accounts, and of the journal of their proceedings, shall be delivered by them to the agents of his Britannic Majesty, and to the agents of the United States, who may be respectively appointed and authorized to manage the business on behalf of their respective governments. The said commissioners shall be respectively paid in such manner as shall be agreed between the two contracting parties, such agreement being to be settled at the time of the exchange of the ratifications of this treaty ; and all other expenses attending said commissioners shall be defrayed equally by the parties. And, in case of death, sickness, resignation, or necessary absence, the place of every such commissioner respectively shall be supplied in the same manner as such commissioner was first appointed, and the new commissioner shall take the same oath or affirmation, and do the same duties. It is further agreed between the two contracting parties, that in case any of the islands mentioned in any of the preceding articles, which were in the possession of one of the parties prior to the commencement of the present war between the countries, should, by the decision of any of the boards of commissioners aforesaid, or of the sovereign or state so referred to, as in the four next preceding articles contained, fall within the dominions of the other party, all grants of lands made previous to the commencement of the war, by the party having had such possession, shall be as valid as if such island or islands had, by such decision or decisions, been adjudged to be within the dominions of the party having such possession.

Art. IX.—The United States of America engage to put an end, immediately after the ratification of the present treaty, to hostilities with all the tribes or nations of Indians, with whom they may be at war at the time of such ratification ; and forthwith to restore to such tribes or nations, respectively, all the possessions, rights, and privileges, which they may have enjoyed or been entitled to in one thousand eight hundred and eleven, previous to such hostilities : Provided always, that such tribes or nations shall agree to desist from all hostilities againt the United States of America, their citizens and subjects, upon the ratification of the present treaty being notified to such tribes or nations, and shall so desist accordingly. And his Britannic Majesty engages, on his part, to put an end immediately after the ratification of the present treaty, to hostilities with all the tribes or nations of Indians with whom he may be at war at the time of such ratification, and forthwith to restore to such tribes or nations respectively, all the possessions, rights, and privileges, which they may have enjoyed, or been entitled to, in one thousand eight hundred and eleven, previous to such hostilities : Provided always, that such tribes or nations shall agree to desist from all hostilities against his Britannic Majesty, and his subjects, upon the

ratification of the present treaty being notified to such tribes or nations, and shall so desist accordingly.

Art. X.—Whereas the traffic in slaves is irreconcilable with the principle of humanity and justice, and whereas both his Britannic Majesty and the United States are desirous of continuing their efforts to promote its entire abolition, it is hereby agreed that both the contracting parties shall use their best endeavours to accomplish so desirable an object.

Art. XI.—This treaty, when the same shall have been ratified on both sides, without alteration by either of the contracting parties and the ratifications mutually exchanged, shall be binding on both parties and the ratifications shall be exchanged at Washington, in the space of four months from this day, or sooner, if practicable.

In faith whereof, we the respective plenipotentiaries, have signed this treaty, and have thereunto affixed our seals.

Done, in triplicate, at Ghent, the twenty-fourth day of December, one thousand eight hundred and fourteen.

> GAMBIER,
> HENRY GOULBOURN,
> WILLIAM ADAMS,
> JOHN QUINCY ADAMS,
> J. A. BAYARD.
> H. CLAY,
> JONATHAN RUSSELL,
> ALBERT GALLATIN.

Now, therefore to the end of the said treaty of peace and amity may be observed with good faith, on the part of the United States, I, James Madison, President as aforesaid, have caused the premises to be made public : and I do hereby enjoin all persons bearing office, civil or military, within the United States, and all others, citizen or inhabitants thereof, or being within the same, faithfully to observe and fulfil the said treaty, and every clause and article thereof.

In testimony whereof I have caused the seal of the United States to be affixed to these presents, and signed the same with my hand.

Done at the City of Washington, this eighteenth day of February, in the year of our Lord one thousand eight hundred and fifteen, and of the sovereignty and independence of the United States the thirty-ninth,

> JAMES MADISON.

By the president,

> JAMES MONROE.

Total British and American Cruisers captured or destroyed, excluding those re-captured, during the War :—

	Vessels.	Guns.	Complements.	Tons.
British	30	530	2751	10273
American .	64	660	2994	14848

List of British and American national cruisers, captured at sea, which the opposite party succeeded in getting into port.

BRITISH.					AMERICAN.				
Ships' names.		Guns.	Comp.	Tons.	Ships' Names.		Guns.	Comp.	Tons.
Macedonian,		49	292	1081	President,		58	477	1533
Cyane,		33	171	539	Chesapeake.		49	391	1135
Alert,		20	86	393	Essex,		46	265	867
Epervier,	B.	18	117	382	Frolic,		22	171	539
Dominica,	Sc.	15	77	217	Argus,		20	125	315
Boxer,	B.	14	66	179	Wasp,		18	130*	434
St. Lawrence,	Sc.	13	51	240	Rattlesnake,	B.	16	131	305
Highflyer,	Sc.	5	39	209	Syren,	B.	16	137	350
Ballahou,	Sc.	4	20	74	Nautilus,	B.	14	106	213
					Viper,	B.	12	93	148
					Jas. Maddison,	Sc.	10	65	114
					Gun-boat,		9	45	112
					Surveyor,	Sc.	6	25	100
					Nine gun-boats,		34	267	549
No.					No				
9.	Total,	171	919	3314	22.	Total,	330	2430	6714

* Number of prisoners received.

INDEX.